Missionary Spaces
Imagining, Building, Contesting Christianities in Africa and China, 1830s-1960s

MISSIONARY SPACES
Imagining, Building, Contesting Christianities in Africa and China, 1830s-1960s

Edited by
Thomas Coomans

KADOC Artes 17

Leuven University Press

This book appears in the peer-reviewed series KADOC Artes.

Editorial board

Timothy Brittain-Catlin (University of Cambridge)
James Chappel (Duke University)
Kim Christiaens (KADOC-KU Leuven)
James Kennedy (Utrecht University)
Franziska Metzger (PH Luzern Fribourg)
Patrick Pasture (MoSa-KU Leuven)
Isabelle Saint-Martin (EPHE Paris)
Thijl Sunier (VU Amsterdam)
Nienke Roelants (Leuven University Press)
Peter Heyrman (KADOC-KU Leuven)

Cover: Christianity of Hengtang 横塘 (Wang-daong), near the town of Sijing 泗泾, section of Songjiang 松江, southwest of Shanghai 上海.
[Vanves, Compagnie de Jésus, Archives jésuites de France, Fonds iconographique]

© 2024
Leuven University Press / Presses Universitaires de Louvain / Universitaire Pers Leuven
Minderbroedersstraat 4, B-3000 Leuven

All rights reserved. Except in those cases expressly determined by law, no part of this publication may be multiplied, saved in an automated data file or made public in any way whatsoever without the express prior written consent of the publishers.

ISBN 9789462701441
D/2024/1869/20
NUR: 691

Contents

INTRODUCTION

Imagining, Building, Contesting Missionary Spaces VIII
Thomas Coomans

PART ONE – IMAGINED WORLD / ADAPTED STRATEGIES 1

1. 2
Spatial Trajectories and Missionary and Colonial Movements into Northwest Ghana since 1929: Dagara Reception of Catholic Missionary Activities
Alexis B. Tengan

2. 16
Redeeming Ukamba: Word and World, 1893-1905
Maarten Onneweer

3. 32
Islands on the Mainland: Catholic Missions and Spatial Strategies in China, 1840s-1940s
Thomas Coomans

4. 64
Co-authoring the City: Missionaries and the Colonial City of Luluaburg (Belgian Congo), 1930-1960
Bram Cleys

5. 86
The Catholic Territorialization of Taiwan: Vatican Global Strategy and Franciscan Local Parishes, 1949-1960s
Leon Bouwmeester and Thomas Coomans

PART TWO – UNIVERSAL PROJECTS / LOCALIZED ARCHITECTURES 105

6. 106
Gendered Spaces in Catholic Compounds of Late Qing China
Thomas Coomans

7. 146
Gender-Designed Catholic Churches in North China, 1830s-1920s
Thomas Coomans

8. 194
The Missionaries in the Cosmopolitan Towns of the Suez Isthmus, Egypt:
Their Role in the Formation of Identity in Architecture and Urban Planning,
1860-1937
Céline Frémaux

9. 210
Civilizing Space in West China: Re-examining the Place of the Christian
University in Chengdu, 1909-1933
Lawrence Braschi

10. 228
A Highly 'Mediated Monument' of Tropical Modernism in Central Africa:
Unpacking the Complex Agendas behind the Design and Construction of the
Collège du Saint-Esprit in Bujumbura, Burundi
Johan Lagae

Abbreviations	253
Index of Persons	254
Index of Places	257
Authors	261
Colophon	263

0.1 Mission heterotopia: the Tao Fong Shan Lutheran monastery of the Christian Mission to Buddhists in China, was designed bij Johannes Prip-Møller on a remote hill in Shatin (Hong Kong, P.R. China).
[Photo THOC, May 2014]

0.2 Spatial focus point: at the end of an avenue, the Scheut Fathers' residence marks the center of the Nioki parish (Mai-Ndombe province, Democratic Republic of Congo).
[Photo THOC, December 2008]

Introduction
Imagining, Building, Contesting Missionary Spaces

Thomas Coomans

In the nineteenth century, Christian missionaries set out to evangelize inland Africa and China, sometimes before the imperialist nations had set their sights on the same regions, sometimes after these same nations had established their authority there in one form or another (colony, semi-colony, protectorate, concession, etc.). In every case, missionaries sought to make contact with the local populations and bring them the "light of the Revealed Truth", through gospel and baptism. These were things of which the populations in questions had never heard nor really needed since they were not in "darkness" and had their own worldviews and spiritually charged cosmographies. Conversions followed from long-term social engagement through education, healthcare, technology transfer, political protection, and other actions that convinced the locals that keeping the missionaries and their foreign religion within reach, was in their interest. This "missionary encounter" required time and considerable patience from the missionaries who had to settle, erect a chapel and other buildings, adapt to the language, climate, and food, and interact with people, while remaining uncompromising on "pagan superstitions" and certain sociocultural practices.[1]

Nicolas Standaert has analyzed this complex process in several inspiring essays on the "other" in the mission, the encounter between the self and the other, interaction and in-betweenness, adaptation, accommodation, and inculturation.[2] He refutes the so-called passivity of the local communities and considers them active participants in the conversion process; Standaert also goes on to question the criteria that defined the success or failure of a Christian mission, including from a spiritual perspective.[3]

Missionary Spaces. Imagining, building, contesting christianities in Africa and China examines the multi-faceted theme of the missionary encounter[4] from the point of view of space-making, architecture, and spatial practices in cross-cultural settings from the 1830s to the 1960s. The spaces created and occupied by missionaries reveal the dynamics of the intercultural encounters within which they worked and the strategies with which they were armed to negotiate issues of race, religion, colonialism, gender, etc. How were sites chosen and purchased, the orientation of axes and buildings established, precincts defined and partitioned by walls or fences? Were plans designed by missionary-builders, colonial architects, or military engineers, based on models from their home countries or discussed with the users? Erecting buildings always involved local human and material resources: how were architectural forms and building techniques transferred and hybridized on the construction site? Why did some missionaries integrate architectural morphologies and elements from traditional architecture while others did not? Why and how were new spaces made sacred and traditional sacred places rejected or integrated?

The study of spatiality facilitates a complex understanding of the dynamics of social power and the production of knowledge, beliefs, and ideologies in colonies. The cases studied in this volume reveal that spaces and buildings were imagined, designed, located, erected, and could later be adapted to changing contexts and needs, enlarged or replaced, but could also be sources of conflict,

0.3 Walled christianity: remains of the adobe wall surrounding the Christian village of Shilawusuhao 什拉乌素壕, dominated by its church (Togtoh County, Inner Mongolia Autonomous Region, P.R. China).
[Photo THOC, May 2011]

0.4 Stone church: the very first stone church in Madagascar was erected from 1847 to 1859 by the French Catholic missionary Pierre Dalmond CSSp on Sainte-Marie Island, on a site along a lagoon and near a French fort (Ambodifotatra de Sainte-Marie, Analanjirofo Region, Republic of Madagascar).
[Photo THOC, March 2022]

1 Such as polygamy, infanticide, opium addiction, gambling, etc. [see Chapter 6, 110-112].
2 On the encounter of Matteo Ricci 利玛窦 SJ (1552-1610) and other Jesuits in seventeenth-century China: Standaert, *L'autre' dans la mission*; Standaert, "History as the art of the 'other' and the art of 'in-betweenness.'"
3 Standaert, *L'autre' dans la mission*, 112-118.
4 Bickers and Seton, eds., *Missionary Encounters. Sources and Issues*.

5 Stoler and Cooper, "Between Metropole and Colony;" Myers, *Verandas of Power. Colonialism and Space in Urban in Urban Africa*. We are grateful to Allen M. Howard for these two references.
6 Coomans, Xu, and Zhang, "Imposing and Provocative."
7 Vallgårda, "Were Christian Missionaries Colonizers? Reorienting the Debate and Exploring New Research Trajectories."
8 From 1622, Catholic missions were coordinated by the *Propaganda Fide* (Sacred Congregation for the Propagation of the Faith), whose central administration and archives were in Rome. In 1967, the name was changed to the Congregation for the Evangelization of the Peoples, which was integrated into the Dicastery for Evangelization (Roman Curia) in 2022.
9 London Missionary Society (LMS, 1795); Church Missionary Society (CMS, 1799), China Inland Mission (CIM 1865); Interdenominational Foreign Mission Association (IFMA, 1917), etc. See Friedler, *Interdenominational Faith Missions in Africa*, and Tiedemann, ed., *Handbook of Christianity in China*, vol. 1, 113-192, 532-552.

contested, and even ruined. Discussions and disagreements took place not only between the missionaries and the local populations, but also between missionaries and the colonial authorities, other missionary societies, and denominations, or between converted and non-converted locals. *Missionary Spaces* contributes to advocating the mutual accommodation between foreigners and locals, and the varied responses that may have included unintended spatial outcomes as parties struggled and compromised on where buildings should be established, what they should look like, how people should use them, and what they might mean. This approach fits within broad historiographic debates about Western imperialism and colonization in Africa and Asia, which have emphasized the contradictory nature of colonial power, the varied responses among those drawn into the colonial orbit, the mutual accommodation between colonizers and colonized, and the multi-faceted exchange of social and cultural elements.[5] Churches and other components of the built environment were highly significant sites of accommodation, as well as coercion, manipulation, contestation, and resistance. Missionaries knew that the combination of very visible buildings and of new modes of behavior in those buildings was culturally and politically "provocative."[6]

The linking of China and Africa in this volume constitutes one of its original ideas. Despite Africa and China's very different socio-cultural contexts and historical evolutions, analysis and comparison reveal patterns of challenges and conflicts, missionary methods and strategies, trials and errors. The field of architecture and spaces offers insight into the mechanisms of encounter between East and West in China, and between North and South in Africa.

Spatializing the missionary encounter

Missionary movements had a long experience of colonial evangelization, dating back to the very end of the fifteenth century and extending from the sixteenth century to the American continent, parts of Asia, and the coasts of Africa and India, before establishing themselves with varying degrees of violence and success in specific places. These missions were also meant for the colonizers themselves and the garrisons stationed in coastal forts, who needed priests, churches, and graveyards for their own religious rituals and ceremonies. In the nineteenth century, Christian missions were different in many respects.[7] First, because they were no longer dominated by the centralized Catholic Church,[8] which was instead in competition with numerous Protestant denominations who sent missionaries from Europe and the United States, some of which organized themselves into interdenominational missionary societies.[9] Nineteenth-century missions were in competition for many different reasons, which included theological arguments, the role of women, national identities, and evangelization strategies aimed at social target groups. Second, because the consequences of the Industrial Revolution, from the mid-nineteenth century in particular, gave colonizers and missionaries not only the technological tools of incontestable material conquest – with gunboats and railways as archetypes – but also of an intellectual, cultural, racial, and moral superiority, which led, in the 1880s, to the ideology of the so-called "civilizing mission" soon combined with the ideology of "Modernity." [Fig. 0.5] As argued by Edward Said in his influential 1978 book *Orientalism* and summarized by Hilde Heynen:

> Colonial discourse was intrinsic to European self-understanding: it is through their conquest and their knowledge of foreign peoples and territories (two experiences which usually were intimately

0.5 Modernity and "civilizing mission": this photo taken in Guangzhou around 1900 shows the contrast between on the one hand the paddle steamer and the sampans, on the other hand the Gothic cathedral and the wooden houses. It expresses technological and moral superiority, which, in European eyes, legitimized the Westernization of indigenous peoples (Guangdong Province, P.R. China).
[Lyon, OPM, Chine Boîte 1, Canton, BVI-102]

linked), that Europeans could position themselves as Modern, as civilized, as developed, and progressive vis-à-vis local populations that were none of that (…) The other, the non-European, was thus represented as the negation of everything that Europe imagined or desired to be.[10]

Strengthened by this moral and material superiority, missionaries gradually left the coasts and penetrated into the heart of the great continents in the footsteps of highly publicized missionary-explorers, such as Évariste Huc and Joseph Gabet across Tartary or David Livingstone in southern Africa, who influenced colonial policy and geopolitical decision-making in different ways.[11]

In what state of mind did late nineteenth-century missionaries approach their first encounter with their far-flung mission fields, especially from a spatial point of view? In addition to the numerous letters from missionaries to their families or articles by newcomers published in missionary magazines, the illustrated covers of these magazines often offered symbolic compositions that do not always boil down to radiant crosses dominating territories to be conquered [Fig. 2.1].

The 1889 cover of *Missions en Chine et au Congo* offers a fine example of visual communication aimed at a Western audience and combines different symbols with layered meanings and spatial dimensions [Fig. 0.6]. Founded in 1862, the Congregation of the Immaculate Heart of Mary (CICM), a Belgian missionary society more commonly known as the Scheut Fathers, was active in two extremely different mission fields, the Mongolian provinces, behind the Great Wall of the Chinese Empire, and the Congo Free State, privately owned by King Leopold II. In the typical Saint Luke Gothic Revival style favored by the Belgian ultramontanes,[12] the cover combines the title and five complementary visual messages intended to express the specific identity and apostolates of CICM:

- in the upper part, Christ sending the eleven apostles on mission stands for the universal Christian mission across the world's macro space;[13]
- on the left, the Immaculate Heart of Mary not only refers to CICM's Marian spirituality and name, but also to the missionary's most intimate spiritual space in the chapel or the church of his Christianity;
- in the lower left corner, the coat of arms of the Congo Free State, whose motto *Travail et Progrès* explicitly states labor as the fundament of progress, i.e. the exploitation of human and material resources as the fundament of "civilization." The Belgian missionaries considered them-

10 Heynen, "The Intertwinement of Modernism and Colonialism," 11 (based on and referring to Said, *Orientalism*). See also Heynen, "Engaging Modernism," 387-390.

11 Évariste Huc CM (1813-1860) and Joseph Gabet CM (1808-1853), two Frenchmen who explored Tartary from Manchuria and Mongolia to Tibet; David Livingstone LMS (1813-1873), a Scotsman who searched for the sources of the Nile and fought slavery in southern Africa.

12 Dujardin, "The Saint Luke School Movement and the Revival of Medieval Illumination."

13 The sentence "*Allez, enseignez toutes les nations, leur apprenant à garder tous mes commandements*" refers to Matthew 28, "[19] Go therefore and make disciples of all nations, baptizing them in the name of the Father and of the Son and of the Holy Spirit, [20] teaching them to observe all that I have commanded you (…)."

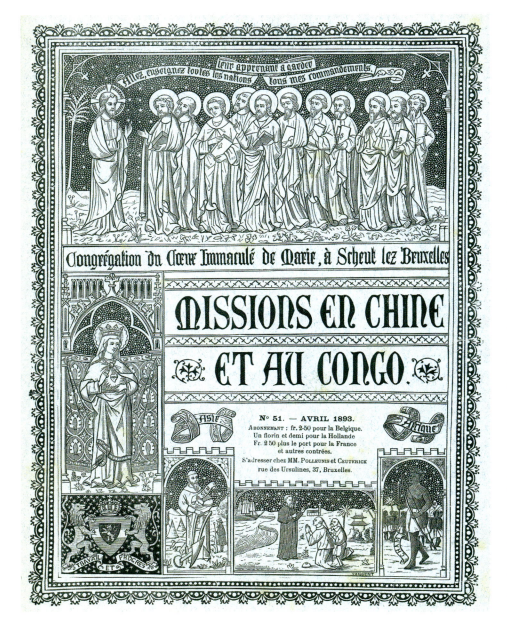

0.6 Gothic worldwide: cover of Missions en Chine et au Congo, *the journal of the Congregation of the Immaculate Heart of Mary (CICM), published in Brussels from February 1889.* [Leuven, KADOC-KU Leuven, issue 51, April 1893. Heritage Library, KYB 0026]

14   de Broux and Piret, "Le Congo était fondé dans l'intérêt de la civilisation et de la Belgique," 63-66.

selves agents of this "civilizing mission in Congo";[14]

- on the lower right, the central thumbnail shows the missionary encounter as a stereotypical image of evangelization/colonization: freshly disembarked from a Western ship, the missionary stands on the coast, holding a crucifix and blessing two welcoming, kneeling Chinese. The exotic setting with palm trees, a Western-style church, and a Chinese-roofed building localizes the space of the missionary encounter;
- at the bottom, two other crenelated thumbnails show Biblical characters from the "Table of Nations" (Genesis 10), who embody the CICM mission fields and worldview: Noah's sons Sem [Chem] for Asia (left) and Cham [Ham] for Africa (right). This Biblical creationist-mythical genealogy identifies the European missionary as a descendant of Japheth, Noah's third son, and gives a symbolic-historical dimension to space.

This cover relates to many of the topics in this volume on *Missionary Spaces in China and Africa*, notably the Christian apostolic and universal mission, Catholic missionaries' Marian spirituality, the intertwined actions of Western missionaries and national colonial powers, and the local missionary encounter with different races on different continents. All these topics include spatial aspects that range from the global missionary spatial strategies decided upon in the Vatican for Catholics or in the American and European headquarters of the Protestant missionary societies – both approved and often supported by colonial powers – to the missionary encounter at local level and the spatial arrangements of individual christianities and mission stations.

Africa and China

Historiography rarely links the missions of Africa and China, as if they were parallel worlds. Several generations of researchers working on the missions to China limited their interest to the seventeenth and eighteenth centuries. When working on the nineteenth and twentieth centuries, Africanists and Sinologists form distinct networks and do not attend the same conferences. Some Western historians familiar with the archives kept in the motherhouses of missionary societies in Europe and North America, especially when they had mission fields on both continents, understand that there were similarities and interactions not only between the spirituality and values, superiors and central services, but also between mission magazines, mission methods, and networks of procuratory houses, etc. Before being sent to their specific mission field, novices received comprehensive common training that defined their missionary identity and enabled them to adapt to different contexts. One might consider that an early twentieth-century Jesuit missionary in China had more in common with a Jesuit in Congo and in India than with a Franciscan or a Vincentian in China.

By developing a common approach to missionary spaces and architecture, *Missionary Spaces* aims to generate new multilateral perspectives and demonstrate their potential. This volume brings together ten chapters, half of which deal with African cases from Burundi, Congo, Egypt, Ghana, and Kenya, while the other half focuses on a range of cases from the China region, all of which belong to the two main continents targeted by the Christian missions in the Industrial Age.[15] However, since we have yet to meet any Chinese Africanists or African Sinologists, we hope that research on (missionary) architecture and spaces will generate new cross-overs and path of investigation, especially in the disciplines of building archaeology and heritage studies, both built and intangible.

In most African countries, missions were fully part of the 1880-1960 "phase of formal colonization",[16] while China was never formally colonized but was ruled by the Manchu Qing Dynasty (1644-1911) in ways "that are often comparable to the tactics used by other imperialists of the day".[17] The Christian missions to China from the 1860s to the 1940s were merely one of the aspects of "informal imperialism" that several foreign nations tried to exert in China.[18] The architectural and spatial consequences of this fundamental difference deserve to be investigated and compared. Some missionary societies, such as the aforementioned Scheut Fathers, were active on both continents and faced contrasting mission fields, not only in terms of geography and climate, but above all due to different socio-political and socio-cultural contexts [Chapter 4 and Chapter 8]. Of the latter, two main reasons will hold our attention here due to their direct consequences on the spatial organization of Christian communities in Africa and China, further enriching the comparative dimension of *Missionary Spaces*.

The first of these reasons is socio-cultural and concerns the level of development of African societies and Chinese society in the nineteenth century, the very place of the missionary encounter. While Mediterranean Africa and Egypt had been Christianized from the late Roman Empire and Islamized from the seventh century, and South Africa's colonization by Dutch settlers began in the mid-seventeenth century, Sub-Saharan and Central Africa, whose coasts had been lined for centuries by trading ships, were rarely explored beyond the river mouth and coastal ports, where economic transactions, especially those linked to the slave trade, took place. Explorers and missionaries who ventured into the heart of Central Africa encountered populations that in their eyes were poorly developed compared to their home country: oral cultures, animist beliefs or belief in a supreme being, primitive arts, vernacular architecture, and a myriad of small societies organized in villages grouped into numerous chiefdoms and kingdoms, some of which were past their former glory. This comparison generated a superior-inferior relationship that led to the infamous concept of the Western "civilizing mission,"[19] with all its excesses as mentioned above in reference to the motto "Labor and Progress." In terms of architecture and urbanization, the colonizers did not understand and seldom took into account existing village structures, but settled in places where the topography seemed most favorable to them [Chapter 1 and Chapter 2] and founded cities from scratch in places were resources could be exploited and transported by waterways or railways [Chapter 4 and Chapter 8]. In such colonizing contexts, Western rational urban planning introduced not only a break in

15 In the 19th and 20th centuries, Catholic and Protestant missionaries were active on all other continents, both in colonized and independent countries.
16 Tetzlaff, *Africa. An Introduction to History, Politics and Society*, 71-90.
17 Larsen, "The Qing Empire (China), Imperialism, and the Modern World," 500. See also Crossley, *A Translucent Mirror: History and Identity in Qing Imperial Ideology*.
18 Dean, "British Informal Empire: The Case of China."
19 Conklin, *A Mission to Civilize: The Republican Idea of Empire in France and West Africa*.

scale but also new forms of public spaces, with straight axes and squares dominated by public buildings, including churches, without architectural reference to traditional cultures.[20] After the Second World War, the development of modernist architecture and reinforced concrete structures found in the colonies opportunities for grand projects – including those with a missionary motivation – known as "tropical modernism" [Chapter 10, 229].

The contrast with China could not be greater. A five thousand-year-old civilization, China became a centralized empire before the Christian era and was more developed than Europe for centuries, but had remained closed to foreign influence, missed the modern turn of the Industrial Revolution, and suffered from the weakness of the late Qing Dynasty and numerous spells of social unrest. Christianity had penetrated China three times before the nineteenth century, but each time had been banned with accompanying persecutions and destruction.[21] After the Nestorians (from the mid-seventh to the mid-ninth century) and the Franciscans friars (from the mid-thirteenth to the mid-fourteenth century), the first Jesuit mission to China (1600-1721) was a fascinating intellectual and scientific encounter, but one that ended with the fiasco of the Chinese Rites controversy and the third ban on Christianity.[22] Missionaries could gradually return to China from the early 1800s, initially Protestants, followed by Catholics from 1842 in some harbor cities and, from 1860, across the whole empire.[23] These foreign missionaries encountered a rich and complex culture whose *literati* and *mandarins* were indifferent or hostile to Christianity, while the "old Christians" – the few descendants of seventeenth-century converts – had to adapt to the new reality of the Catholic Church after the French Revolution. Missionaries were not welcome in cities and were confronted with Confucian and Daoist moral values [Chapter 6, 108-111] and deeply-rooted Buddhism and Islam. Additionally, purchasing land was almost impossible for foreigners who used Chinese converts as straw men [Chapter 3, 34-35]. Consequently, until the early years of the twentieth century, Catholics and Protestants remained highly marginalized and major architectural projects were exceptional, while missionaries, Chinese Christians, and churches were often targeted by xenophobic movements, in 1870 and 1900 in particular.

The second reason is socio-political and depended on the colonial systems put in place. By the end of the nineteenth century, the whole of Africa was claimed in one way or another with the exception of Ethiopia and Liberia, as a result of what Thomas Pakenham describes in his controversial book *The Scramble for Africa*.[24] Each colonized country was ruled or "protected" by individual foreign countries and formed part of a colonial empire – British, French, Portuguese, German, Belgian, Italian – that imposed its administration, militaries, language, and economy based on private investments from international groups. Missionaries were an integral part of the colonial project among the civilizing agents of development, especially in the areas of education and healthcare, but also contributed to social peace through religion and moral values. Nineteenth-century nation-states willingly favored national missionary societies and often played off Catholic against Protestant missions according to their national religious identity or state religion. The British Empire's official support for missionary societies was limited and not exclusive, while the French lay republic favored Catholicism. The territorialization – the way territory is used to enable politics[25] – of the universal Catholic Church in colonized Africa was based on entangled collaboration between colonial nation-states, national missionary societies, and the Vatican. The major Catholic international missionary orders and societies were present in specific colonies according to their national components and with the benediction of the Propaganda Fide.[26]

China, for its part, despite the appetites of imperialist nations, was never colonized, with the exception of the three islands of

---

20 See the international bibliographical database *Villes et architecture des terrains ex-coloniaux (19ᵉ-20ᵉ siècles)*, established by Brones in 2007. Also: Bremner, ed., *Architecture and Urbanism in the British Empire*; De Meulder, *Kuvuande Mbote* [Belgian Congo].
21 Standaert, ed., *Handbook of Christianity in China*, 1, 2001.
22 Hsia, "Christianity and Empire: The Catholic Mission in Late Imperial China."
23 Tiedemann, ed., *Handbook of Christianity in China*, 2, 2010, 1-446.
24 Pakenham, *The Scramble for Africa: The White Man's Conquest of the Dark Continent from 1876 to 1912*.
25 *Constructing Territory*.
26 For instance, French Jesuits were entrusted with vicariates in the French colonies of Africa and Asia, while Belgian Jesuits held vicariates in the Belgian Congo. French Jesuits were present in China but not in the British colonies, while Belgian Jesuits were active in India and Ceylon but not in China. From 1908 to 1960, most Belgian Catholic male and female missionary orders, societies, and congregations were involved in the Belgian Congo, but the forty-four foreign Protestant denominations that sent missionaries to Belgian Congo never received the same support from the colonial authorities as the Belgian Catholics. See e.g. the nationalist publications: Piolet, *Les missions catholiques françaises*, vol. 2-5; de Moreau and Masson, *Les missionnaires Belges*.
27 Macao by Portugal (1554-1999); Hong Kong by the United Kingdom (1841-1997); Taiwan/Formosa by the Japanese Empire (1895-1945).

Hong Kong, Macao, and Taiwan.[27] Through aggressive campaigns, such as the 1839-1842 and 1856-1860 opium wars, followed by unequal treaties maintained through gunboat diplomacy, Western nations forced the late Qing Dynasty to concede portions of national territories called "foreign settlements" or "concessions." Since these concessions were administered by foreign countries for a limited time and remained under China's sovereignty, they were not full colonies but "semi-colonial" territories. There, foreign missionaries enjoyed military protection and real estate advantages they never obtained elsewhere in China [Chapter 3, 38-42]. Outside the concessions, Catholic and Protestant missionaries from different nations and denominations organized their mission fields separately and differently. Catholic missionary societies were entrusted with specific vicariates apostolic by the Propaganda Fide. This resulted in a patchwork of competing and sometimes conflicting national identities and interests, which was detrimental to the aim of the mission [Fig. 3.1]. Catholic missionaries of all nations combined could rely on the protection of diplomatic channels: the Portuguese *padrodao* was taken over by the French *protectorat* in 1885 and eventually by the Vatican in 1922, which sent a diplomat to China. Apostolic Delegate Celso Costantini 剛恆毅 was given the task of implementing the postwar Vatican missionary policy of indigenization in China and Sinicizing the Catholic Church. In his 1919 apostolic letter *Maximum Illud*, Pope Benedict XV explicitly promoted local churches and local clergy, and condemned the missionaries who did not work as "ambassadors of Christ" but as "agents of their country."[28] This new policy was aimed at the Catholic mission around the world but was, in the first instance, motivated by the situation in republican China and competition with the Protestant missions, rather than by Africa and its aforementioned colonial system. As nationalism grew in China, Egypt and elsewhere after 1945, the contestations around sacred and ostensibly secular buildings reflected a new phase that could have potentially resulted in the expulsion of missionaries and the elimination of mission spaces. The process of Sinicization of the Catholic mission in China was far from complete in 1949 when the Communists proclaimed the People's Republic of China and expelled all foreign missionaries, Catholic and Protestant, male and female, from the country.

Eventually, at the turn of the 1950s and 1960s, two considerable shifts impacted the missions in Africa. On the one hand, the decolonization process cut the ties between all the missionary societies and former colonial authorities, which were replaced by independent governments. On the other hand, the Second Vatican Council, called in 1959 and held from 1962 to 1965, eventually formalized the movements of *indigenization* and *inculturation* in Africa,[29] and accelerated the end of the Catholic missions with the elevation of the vicariates apostolic to full dioceses and their transfer from missionary vicars apostolic to indigenous bishops.

Christianities and mission heterotopias

The material and cultural embodiment of the newly established nineteenth-century parishes, their territory, and visual occupation relate to the interplay between space and religion, which has recently experienced a significant expansion in geographical and theological studies.[30] In mission fields and non-Christian countries, Christian parishes and communities, both in their social and material forms, are called *christianities*.[31] In his publication on Ming China's Christian communities, Joseph Dehergne gives two definitions of a christianity:

> The first uses the word in a more strict sense: a place that had a church (chapel) and a fixed residence, or at least a nucleus of Christians who were visited once in a while by a missionary. This definition tends to imply that the missionary

28 Benedict XV, *Maximum illud,* November 30, 1919, § 20: "We have been deeply saddened by some recent accounts of missionary life, accounts that displayed more zeal for the profit of some particular nation than for the growth of the kingdom of God. We have been astonished at the indifference of their authors to the amount of hostility these works stir up in the minds of unbelievers. This is not the way of the Catholic missionary, not if he is worthy of the name. No, the true missionary is always aware that he is not working as an agent of his country, but as an ambassador of Christ. (…)."

29 And developed since the 1960s as *acculturation, enculturation, interculturation, incarnation, Africanization, adaptation,* and *indigenization* of Christianity in Africa. See, for instance, respectively theological and anthropological approaches: Nche, Okwuosa, and Nwaoga, "Revisiting the Concept of Inculturation in a Modern Africa;" Kurgat, "The Theology of Inculturation and the African Church."

30 Brace, Bailey and Harvey, "Religion, place, and space: A framework for investigating historical geographies of religious identities and communities;" Bartoloni, Chris, MacKian and Pile, "The place of spirit: Modernity and the geographies of spirituality."

31 The term *christianity* has several meanings. Used in the singular and capitalized, *Christianity* (*Christianisme* in French), designates the Christian religion and should not be confused with *Christendom* (*la Chrétienté* in French), in the singular and capitalized, which means the Christian world as a territory. Both are not the same as the uncapitalized form, singular or plural, *christianity / christianities* (*une chrétienté / des chrétientés* in French) as used in the title of this volume and discussed here.

XV

is the center of the community. It is also closely linked with the formal establishment of a Jesuit 'residence', which did not always coincide with the creation of a Christian community. The second definition is much broader: a place with a Christian presence. This definition centers on the Christian convert. A *christianity* in this sense started already when Christian converts moved to and settled in a town without necessarily being visited by a missionary. It also occurred that missionaries passed through a place, conferred baptism and left without providing further institutional support. One has very little information on such communities.[32]

Missionary Spaces focuses on the material establishment of both types, although the missionary presence prevails over the type centered on converts due to the unequal degree of architectural information and remains, as well as available historical sources, which were essentially produced by the missionaries. The ten chapters present cases from different historical, religious, and social contexts with the aim of unraveling the strategies used by missionary societies to settle in and try to establish long-term roots in places where they were considered intruders by locals and were therefore, in most cases, initially unwelcome. Choosing a site, establishing compounds, fixing favorable orientation, creating new sacred spaces, erecting buildings for education and healthcare, segregating gender and race, were all part of missionary spatial strategies aimed at converting, building new identities, and developing long-term christianities.

Consequently, christianities were separate spaces, often segregated from the villages and towns that preexisted the missionaries' arrival. Other evolutions were possible, however. When these early missionary settlements failed, they would sometimes disappear or be abandoned and recycled [Chapter 2]. On some occasions, a successful mission, supported by the colonizing power, became the nucleus of a new city and even the seat of a vicariate apostolic [Chapter 4].

The ideal scenario involved the multiplication of christianities, both parishes and stations, like cells dividing. A first christianity with a resident missionary and parish church was at the center of a network of stations that had no church but a chapel, and were occasionally visited by a missionary [Fig. 3.5]. When the community of one of these stations reached a critical mass, a new missionary was sent to establish a parish with a church and residence. At a higher level, parishes were grouped into districts which, in turn, were grouped into sections and ultimately covered the entire territory of the vicariate apostolic [Fig. 3.4]. When specific infrastructures such as railways developed, new christianities could be established along the line and benefit from efficient connections with the center [Fig. 5.9 and Chapter 5, 96-97]. Protestant missions had a less structured and systematic method of territorial coverage and, in China, prioritized urban settlements with hospitals, schools, and universities over rural settlements.

Michel Foucault mentions the Jesuit colonies or Indian reductions of Paraguay among the six types of his seminal concept of "heterotopias". In these *reducciones,* native Guarani people remained autonomous from the Spanish colonial authority, as a "heterotopia of compensation," a space "that is other, another real space, as perfect, as meticulous, as well arranged as ours is messy, ill constructed, and jumbled":

> (…) marvelous, absolutely regulated colonies in which human perfection was effectively achieved. The Jesuits of Paraguay established colonies in which existence was regulated at every turn. The village was laid out according to a rigorous plan around a rectangular place at the foot of which was the church; on one side, there was the school; on the other, the cemetery, and then, in front of the church, an avenue set out that another crossed at right angles; each family

---

32 Standaert, "The Creation of Christian Communities," 536-537 (based on and referring to: Dehergne, "Les Chrétientés de Chine de la période Ming").

0.7 Colonial rural planning: the ordered houses and the clean horizontal space of the White Fathers' mission of Tongres-Sainte-Marie contrast with the indigenous huts. Photo around 1916-1918 (Lulinga, North Kivu, Democratic Republic of Congo).
[Leuven, KADOC-KU Leuven, Missionaries of Africa Picture Archive, KFA4779]

had its little cabin along these two axes and thus the sign of Christ was exactly reproduced. Christianity marked the space and geography of the American world with its fundamental sign. The daily life of individuals was regulated, not by the whistle, but by the bell (…).[33]

As has often been pointed out, most Europeans were particularly disturbed by what they perceived as the disorderly layout of African buildings [Fig. 0.7] and the dirty public spaces of Chinese villages and cities. With a rectilinear bias, they dictated the placement and dimensions of new structures that matched Foucault's heterotopias. Bruno De Meulder has studied the "chapel farm method" developed by the Jesuit mission of Kwango in the Congo Free State around 1900 as a network of strict organized christianities for converted natives that competed with the traditional "pagan villages."[34] At the same time, Belgian Scheut Fathers founded a series of self-contained Christian settlements in the Ordos region near the Chinese-Mongolian borderlands, which attracted Han colonizers rather than the intended Mongolians.[35]

Within a quarter of a century, the Catholic mission in Mongolia fortified 236 christianities, ranging from simple earthworks to crenellated ramparts flanked by bastions [Chapter 3, 50-51 and Chapter 6, 125-127].[36]

Tao Fong Shan 道风山 is undoubtedly the most fascinating mission heterotopia in Hong Kong, located on a remote hillside dominating Shatin, a village in the New Territories at that time. Established in 1930 by the Norwegian Lutheran missionary Karl Ludvig Reichelt 艾香德 of the Christian Mission to Buddhists in China, Tao Fong Shan was intended for converted Buddhists, including converted monks. Not only the site, but the buildings fit into the long tradition of Buddhist mountain temples. The Danish architect Johannes Prip-Møller 艾书垂, who had studied the architecture of ancient Buddhist monasteries in Jiangsu,[37] designed Tao Fong Shan as a modern, reinforced-concrete, Chinese temple-monastery in harmony with its site [Fig. 0.1].

Secluded boarding schools and university campuses could also be considered mission heterotopias. However, the two cases studied in this volume look more like utopias due to

33 Foucault, "Des espaces autres," 49 (translation Jay Miskowiec).
34 De Meulder, "Mavula: An African heterotopia in Kwango."
35 Taveirne, Han-Mongol Encounters and Missionary Endeavors.
36 Van Melckebeke, Service social de l'Église en Mongolie, 64.
37 Prip-Møller, Chinese Buddhist Monasteries.

0.8 Attractive landmark: in 1872-1874, the Scheut Fathers built their first Western-style church with a high tower in Nanhaoqian 南壕堑 in the grassland across the Great Wall, with the aim of attracting the attention of the Mongols on their way to Zhangjiakou 张家口. A christianity developed around the church, which became the starting point for the mission to Western Mongolia (Shangyi County, Hebei Province, P.R. China).
[Leuven, KADOC-KU Leuven, CICM Picture Archive: 17.4.4.4_06]

their audacious educational programs, which offered an idealized mixed-gender university education to Christian and non-Christian Chinese [Chapter 9] and an interracial high school education to the sons of Catholic white settlers and Burundians [Chapter 10]. Plans to build new Sino-Christian-style Catholic missions, seminaries, and religious houses for monastic communities in China during the Second Sino-Japanese War were also utopias.[38]

Interactions: imagining, building, contesting christianities

The title of this book refers to Henri Lefebvre's sociological trilogy "perceiving, conceiving, living spaces" from his seminal 1974 book *The Production of Space*,[39] but, on this occasion, focusses on the chrisitianities of missions in Africa and China. Missionaries worked within complex fields of social relations and power, fields in which local people, whether colonized or not, continued to struggle among themselves. Christianized spaces both provided a milieu for such interactions and were continuously re-shaped by processes of cooperation and contestation. However, missionaries went to their mission fields with pre-conceived notions about the social, political, and spiritual lives of the people they would encounter and with strategies for spreading the gospel [Chapter 1, Chapter 2 and Chapter 5]. Their sociological and psychological imaginary often bore little relation to how prospective converts actually lived. Some missionaries adapted quite well, others remained inflexibly locked into preconceived views based on their conviction that their faith and culture were superior.[40]

Legitimated by their "religious truth" and "civilizing mission," the missionaries generated new cultural practices which would be added to or replace the traditional and customary practices of the ethnic groups they encountered. Beyond religion, the multiple aspects of cultural practices included schooling, agriculture and natural resource management, education to hygiene and medical practices, everyday life practices including bodily and gendered behaviors, power relationships and conflict management, etc. These new practices all required new spaces

38 Coomans, "Une utopie missionnaire?"
39 Lefebvre, *The Production of Space*.
40 In extreme cases of failure to adapt, especially when unable to learn the local language or violent racist behavior, missionaries had to be sent back to their home countries by their superiors.

and appropriate architecture, whose spatial organization – preferably with the church or the residence in the middle of the compound – and construction techniques were also new cultural practices. With the exception of churches, which were the most symbolic and sacred buildings, the residences expressed the status and "civilized" lifestyle of the missionaries [Fig. 0.2, and Chapter 6]. Residences were often surrounded by a Western-style garden, which contrasted both with the absence of garden culture in Central Africa and the long tradition of Chinese gardens.

Missionaries never escaped the basic contradiction of being both part of and removed from local social and cultural practices. The spatial problems particular to this contradiction were physically expressed by the location of the rural and urban mission compounds, their walls, gates, and distinctive physical structures that required them to project both an inviting presence and exclusivity. Churches had to be welcoming, but not accessible to everyone without restrictions and rules of behavior. Schools and orphanages had to draw children in while protecting them, their learning, and their social interactions from intrusion by hostile forces [Chapter 6 and Chapter 10]. Higher education and university campuses were confronted with the same in-out contradiction [Chapter 9].

Missionaries recognized that buildings were located and designed to facilitate the control of bodies, minds, and if possible, also the souls of the Christians,[41] by means of gendered practices, often combined with racial practices. Missionary institutions were patriarchal in complex and contested ways, as expressed in their often ambiguous and gendered practices.[42] Not only was the segregation of sexes imposed inside most buildings (churches, schools, hospitals, etc.), but the residences of male Catholic missionaries had to be a good distance away from the enclosed houses of female missionaries – ideally with the church or a street in between – boys' schools had to be separated from girls' schools and orphanages, and seminaries had to be located in isolated and controlled locations [Chapter 6]. Even married men and women were segregated inside the mission compounds, given separate entrances and seating in the churches [Chapter 7]. Missionaries also founded residential schools that isolated young people from their communities and the traditional supervision of elders, which often raised gendered and racial suspicions and hostility [Chapter 10].

To survive and win converts, missionaries would sometimes adopt local cultural practices, such as orientating buildings according to *fengshui* in China [Chapter 3 and Chapter 7]. Churches and cathedrals, particularly their main façade and tower, designed to both express difference and exert attraction, quickly became key identity-bearing structures [Fig. 0.8]. Such projects were obviously not feasible during the initial encounter and adaptation phase because the missionaries

0.9 *Afterlife: the cemetery of St. Michael Archangel in Macao was reserved for Portuguese and Macanese Catholics; the Gothic chapel was erected in 1874-1875. [Photo THOC, September 2013]*

41 Howard, "Nodes, Networks, Landscapes, and Religions;" Howard, "Re-Making of the Past."
42 Huber and Luthekaus, eds. *Gendered Missions: Women and Men in Missionary Discourse and Practice.*

XIX

were content with vernacular-style churches and chapels that had the advantage of expressing a desire for integration with the locals. Photos showing the mission's poverty were published in missionary magazines and accompanied by captions emphasizing that "God deserves a stronger and more beautiful house" – understand, in Western style – and that "despite the poor building, faith is very fervent" [Fig. 0.14]. Parish churches, however, were generally erected by the parishioners themselves: they purchased and prepared the necessary materials, offered their labor, and contributed to the interior decoration because a church is the house of God within, by, and for the parish. The missionaries did not allow work to begin without the certainty that it would be completed, because an unfinished building would publicly reflect badly on the parish and be the object of sarcasm rather than admiration. Fundraising in Europe usually focused on church bells, whose sound would conquer the public space and punctuate the time of the christianity, as well as buildings other than churches, especially dispensaries, schools, orphanages, and leper houses.

Pilgrimages, processions, parades, funeral processions, and other well-ordered public events were ways in which Catholics mobilized and showed themselves in the public space.[43] Above all, this stimulated the feeling of belonging to a community that was not afraid to exhibit its identity, unity, or the diversity of its components, which inevitably enhanced animosity from non-Christians [Figs. 3.26, 3.28, 4.19-4.20, 8.11-8.12, 9.11]. Missionaries tried to promote pilgrimage shrines and sacred places in an effort to reshape geographic orientations and cosmographic visions of people on sites where other deities were or had been venerated in the past [Chapter 1]. Such strategies of Christianization and spatial conquest generated division between converts and non-converts of the same ethnic groups and clan families. Marian pilgrimages and devotion were proper to Catholics who distinguished themselves from Protestants. After the Marian apparitions in Lourdes in 1858, French missionaries contributed to spreading devotion to the Immaculate Conception worldwide by erecting Lourdes grottos in their parishes as far away as Inner Mongolia and the heart of Africa.

One final space deserves to be mentioned because it divided Christians and non-Christians even after their death. The Catholic cemetery, an enclosed sacred place sometimes with a chapel, was reserved for the baptized only [Fig. 0.9]. The cemeteries that contained bodies of martyrs became memorial places with mausoleums and inscriptions [Chapter 3, 51-53]. "Bush missionaries" were buried in their parish, but in more important centers the mission fathers and sisters had their specific cemeteries where they could rest in peace as communities.[44] In public cemeteries, Christian tombs were easily recognizable by their crosses, even when they were spread across the fields like in China, as were calvaries and other public crosses erected by the side of roads or on the top of hills.

Mission architectural modernity: from national styles to international Modernism

According to Ryan Dunch, "the missionary movement must be seen as one element in a globalizing modernity that has altered Western societies as well as non-Western ones in the nineteenth and twentieth centuries, and a comparative global approach to the missionary movement can help to illuminate the process of modern cultural globalization."[45] Even if nineteenth-century missionaries were conservative and often ultramontane, i.e. "anti-modern" in relation to liberal societies, they were nonetheless agents of modernity and transfer in their mission fields. In the complex process of cultural, intellectual, and technological transfer, the intermediaries, translators, and global networks played a crucial role. Samuel Moyne and Andrew Sartory have demonstrated how *mediators* are agents of circulation who establish connec-

---

43 Morelli, "L'espace du cimetière et les cortèges d'enterrements comme enjeux de pouvoir entre laïques et catholiques."

44 The famous Zhalan Cemetery 滕公栅栏, outside Fuchengmen gate 阜成门 in Beijing was established by imperial decree in 1610 and was used by Jesuits, Lazarists, and other missionaries until 1950. See: Chen, *The History on the Tombstones*.

45 Dunch, "Beyond Cultural Imperialism: Cultural Theory, Christian Missions, and Global Modernity."

tions across cultural boundaries and contribute to making intellectual cultures mutually intelligible.[46] In general, the global circulation of ideas and concepts requires large-scale *networks* of multi-directional cultural transfer. Missionaries were not only mediators and belonged to networks, but their interactions with indigenous people evolved as a function of the evolution of their networks and the general context. Consequently, we can speak of generational changes at cultural, intellectual, and technological level, all of which contributed to "modernizing modernity" – except in several extreme circumstances, such as the two world wars and civil wars that profoundly disrupted the mission networks [Chapter 5, 87-93] and affected, consciously or unconsciously, the quality of the missionaries' mediation.

In this respect, mission architecture is the material source that best expresses this generational evolution of the missions towards modernity in the public space. Each church was modern at the moment of its construction, in the sense that it brought something novel to the local Christianity and its landscape, both tangible structures, visual forms, and intangible uses. In other publications we have identified the construction sites of missionary churches as the most crucial locations for cross-cultural encounters at a local level.[47] We see the construction site as an experimental *laboratory*, a place for learning and innovative interactions between the missionary builder and local mediators, contractors, and workers – as well as the architect, if there was one. Techniques, materials, forms, and processes were transferred, implemented, and *hybridized* to a greater or lesser extent [Fig. 0.10]. Locally, this laboratory level was interconnected with global networks through Western colonialism and the Christian missions – with all their denominational and national differences – and helped disseminate aspects of Western modernity amongst indigenous peoples.

From an architectural and urbanistic point of view, nineteenth-century missionaries tended, whenever the opportunity arose,

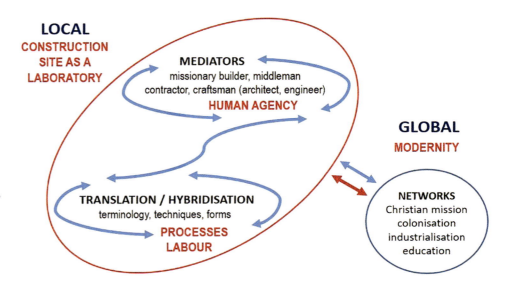

to reproduce their national architecture rather than adopting local forms and techniques. In the African colonies, these national styles marked the public space and contributed to the building of the colony's national identity in relation to its metropolis. This contrasted with the situation in China, where the diversity of religious confessions and national origins resulted in a veritable encyclopedia of styles – from Russian Orthodox in Manchuria, German Romanesque in Shandong, and English Anglican Gothic in Hong Kong, to French Catholic Gothic in Guangzhou, Italian Renaissance in Shanxi, Belgian Gothic in Inner Mongolia, etc. [Fig. 3.6] – which expressed conquering religious and national identities in the public space.[48] Missionaries erected churches with elaborate façades and high towers intended to attract Chinese people: some were indeed attracted by such strange forms, unknown construction techniques, and vast spaces, while others perceived these new forms of architecture as aggressive, disrupting to the environment's harmony, and threatening the vital energies of *fengshui* [Chapter 3, 33-34 and Chapter 6, 151-152]. The most striking case in China is undoubtedly the grand Gothic cathedral erected from 1861 to 1879 in Guangzhou after the Franco-British gunboats had destroyed the city in 1857 [Chapter 3, 42-43, 45-49]. A photo of a paddle steamer on the

0.10 The construction site as a laboratory: the most crucial place for local cross-cultural interactions with global connections (Coomans, "East Meets West on the Construction Site," 64). [THOC 2018]

46 Moyn and Sartory, *Global Intellectual History*, 9-20.
47 Coomans, "East Meets West on the Construction Site. Churches in China, 1840s-1930s," 64-65.
48 Coomans, "Church Architecture and Church Buildings: China."

XXI

0.11 Prefabricated: the CICM missionaries' wooden house stands on twelve iron pilotis and looks as if it has been "planted" at the mouth of the Congo River in Banana around 1900 (Congo Central Province, Democratic Republic of Congo).
[Leuven, KADOC-KU Leuven, CICM Picture Archive, 31.1.11_03]

49 For example, in 1930, the European (mostly Portuguese) parishioners of St Teresa in Kowloon Tong rejected the Chinese-style project supported by Apostolic Delegate Celso Costantini and opted for an early-Christian church type with a campanile reminiscent of that of St Mark's Basilica in Venice. See Coomans and Ho, "Architectural Styles and Identities in Hong Kong."
50 Koppelkamm, *Imaginary Orient Exotic Buildings*; Çelik, *Displaying the Orient*.

Pearl River around 1900 with the cathedral in the background depicts the extreme contrast of scale and technology of the vertical French Gothic stone cathedral and British steel steamboat with the vernacular buildings and frail sampans [Fig. 0.5]. The noise of the steam engine and the sound of the cathedral bells conquering the public space should complete the picture. This powerful image of colonization and modernity stages the contrast between progress and tradition, the material and moral European superiority, the unevenness in power, around which the whole discourse of the "civilizing mission" was constructed and denounced by the aforementioned Edward Said. On a smaller scale, the same scenario was repeated at thousands of sites across the late Qing Empire. In the concessions, these competing stylistic identities were juxtaposed and contributed to the cosmopolitan nature of the semi-colonial settlements.

The association of Christianity with power is demonstrated in some of the parallels between the architectural and locational strategies of colonial administrators and colonial-era missionaries, who built in historical Western styles in the center of capital cities and commissioned plans from well-known international architects [Chapter 4].

In colonial cities, when churches primarily served expatriates rather than indigenous people, architectural styles expressed national identities by referring to home-country designs. The choice of style was decided by the parishioners who financed the works rather than by the bishop.[49] The cities founded along the Suez Canal in Egypt – the new maritime route connecting Europe with Arabia, India, China, Australia, and Africa's east coast from 1869 – feature similar cosmopolitan missionary architectures, although partially controlled by the French Suez Canal Company [Chapter 8]. It is important to remember here that, throughout the nineteenth century, elements from exotic non-Western architectural styles and decorative arts – Moorish, Ottoman, Egyptian, Hindu, Japanese, Chinese, etc. – were revived in European and North American eclectic architecture, expressing, among other things, successful global trade and superiority by appropriation as promoted by the world fairs.[50] However, exotic revival styles had no, or very little, effect on Catholic and Protestant architectures.

The missions contributed to the introduction of new construction materials in deep, inland China and the heart of Africa, and trained local workers to assemble them and create modern forms, structures, and spaces. At an early stage, it happened that prefabricated buildings were shipped from Europe to Africa [Figs. 0.11 and 0.12]. In China, the shift from raw to fired brick or from blue to red brick, the use of foundation, masonry and vaulting techniques, triangulated roof trusses, iron roof sheets and bridges, to name just a few basic elements, were soon followed by the introduction of steel and later reinforced concrete, which echoed, on some occasions more rapidly than others, the successive modern architectural developments taking place in Western countries. When churches from the first generation had to be replaced by larger ones with reinforced concrete structures, their style usually continued to include elements from Western historical styles [Fig. 0.12].

After the First World War, the aforementioned apostolic letter *Maximum Illud* urged Catholic missionaries in China to abandon Gothic and other Western styles and adapt to local aesthetics in order to advance conversion and *indigenize* Christianity. The resulting Sino-Christian style was modern at that time as it translated local traditional architectural forms and elements into cement, reinforced concrete, and other industrial materials. Moreover, Sinicizing architecture was not socially and politically neutral, but was aimed at tempering growing xenophobia and competing with the Protestant missions that had a head start of more than ten years in the field [Chapter 9].[51] The Sinicization movement, which divided the missionaries into two camps, for and against, failed due to the Second World War, the Civil War, and the creation of the People's Republic of China in 1949, which interrupted almost all church construction.

In the 1920s and 1930s, no comparable indigenization movement occurred in the mission architecture of the African colonies, but modernist architects began to refer to *primitivism* in architecture as "the primary, the original, the authentic, that has to be regained" due to its aesthetic, communal, and human values.[52] Hilde Heynen has discussed the relationship between modernism and colonialism from a postmodern theoretical point of view, and admits that there is "undoubtedly, a very real kind of intertwinement between modern discourse and the discourse that justified colonialism and imperialism," but refuses to denounce modern architectural discourse "out of some sense of political correctness." She argues that modern architecture, rather than a matter of style, was first and foremost a social project – through modernist architecture the world would become a better place –, the idea of social emancipation and social progress:

> If you take Modernism seriously in this sense, it indeed is absolutely open to be appropriated by other parts of the world. The argument that the idea of a Western superiority is inherent to Modernism, should not be taken to imply that this whole ideology of liberalization and emancipation would be restricted to those people who recognize themselves as being superior.[53]

Without explicitly raising these questions, European modernist architects who worked in Africa from the late 1940s to the 1960s adapted their architecture to tropical climatic conditions by designing reinforced concrete buildings with flat roofs, often on *pilotis* (stilts), appropriately oriented, and equipped with *brise soleils* (sun breakers) and *claustra* (pierced slabs) [Fig. 0.13]. Consequently, they abandoned the colonial building type with timber, brick, or metallic verandahs, which had once been modern and offered convenient living spaces to colonialists across the world [examples of different styles: Figs. 0.2, 2.7-2.10, 4.4, 6.43, 8.14, 9.10]. This new architecture, named "tropical modernism" by Maxwell Fry and Jane Drew in 1956,[54] is represented in this book by the experimental interracial college built by the Belgian Jesuits with the support of the colonial authorities on the outskirts of Bujumbura, Burundi, from 1952 to 1961 [Chapter 10]. This modernist complex offered a range of

0.12 Scale and history: the city of Boma offers a rare example of two juxtaposed churches from different generations. The metal frame church produced in Belgium, shipped to the Congo Free State, and assembled in 1891, is the oldest church in the country (left) and was replaced in 1951 by the cathedral of Our Lady of the Assumption (right), whose reinforced concrete structure is hidden behind brick walls with references to Romanesque style (Bas Congo Province, Democratic Republic of Congo). [Leuven, KADOC-KU Leuven, CICM Picture Archive, 31-1-27_06]

51 Coomans, "The Sino-Christian Style: A Major Tool for Architectural Indigenization."
52 Heynen, "The Intertwinement of Modernism and Colonialism," 13 and 15, with references to Adolf Loos and Le Corbusier.
53 Idem, esp. 16-19 (quote p. 16). Pointing to Brasilia and Chandigarh as examples of "appropriations of the ideas of Modernity," she considers it as "part of the whole dialogue and interplay that is the result of the process of Modernization."
54 Frey and Drew, *Tropical Architecture in the Humid Zone.*

0.13 Tropical modernity: enclosed space of the Great Seminary of Theology Pope John XXIII in Ngaliema, erected in 1965 after plans by Brother Paul Dequeker CICM (Kinshasa, Democratic Republic of Congo).
[Photo THOC, December 2008]

different spaces, including courtyards and a playing field, open on a grandiose landscape between the lake and hills. Soon after the independence of Burundi – then a trust territory of the United Nations governed by Belgium – the college became the campus of the country's first university in 1964. All things considered, the Jesuits developed a project that aimed to train the elite of the future independent Burundi and gave children the finest Catholic and interracial education of the time in the best possible environment.

Structure and abstracts: ten chapters

This publication contains ten chapters, grouped into two parts, which, each at a different level, compare the missionary ideal with the reality in the field. How did the encounter with the people reshape the missionaries' universal and imagined mission, and how did it evolve during the century in question?

The first part compares the Christian worldviews of different Catholic and Protestant missionary societies with the complexity of the field, which forced them to adapt their spatial strategies in order to survive the early years, to establish themselves, and to later put down roots. The second part focuses on architectural questions in cases linked to local cultural and societal problems, such as gendered spaces in Christian compounds and churches, "civilizing" spaces in schools and on university campuses, and competing identities in shared urban spaces.

Part one – Imagined world / adapted strategies

Chapter 1 – Alexis B. Tengan analyzes the encounter of the hoe-farming Dagara people of Northwest Ghana (then Gold Coast) with the Catholic Missionaries of Africa, better known as White Fathers (MAfr), from 1929. The encounter was positively received and resulted in a rapid mass conversion that contrasted with the strong resistance put up by the Dagara to the British colonial administrators. In fact, the Dagara did not so much accommodate to Christianity as accommodate Christianity to their beliefs: the spatial trajectories developed for migrating hoe-farming entered into the dynamics of missionary church-building (social, metaphysical, and physical) and religious conversion. The missionaries moved horizontally into the Dagara cultural space centered on villages and households, as well as into their mythical and mental structures. Community members, earth priests, and missionaries negotiated the locating of parish centers and incorporated churches into the complex cosmography that linked their past to their present. Accommodation involved much more than the built environment, but spatiality was an important part of the negotiations and reveals deeper processes.

Chapter 2 – Maarten Onneweer presents the extreme case of the missionary encounter between the Evangelical Lutheran Mission of Leipzig (ELML) and the Akamba people in the land of Ukamba, now part of Kenya. Biblical interpretation or "evangelical literalism" shaped the Leipzig missionaries' view of themselves and the social and physical environment in which they found themselves from 1893 to 1905. Projecting their cosmography, the missionaries began to erect buildings that would manifest the Revealed Word of God, rather than focusing on education, technology, or commerce. Their ideal was a church on a hilltop, with a tin roof reflecting light over great distances, and a mission residence whose well-lit interior would contrast with the darkness around it. Instead, the missionaries were not only confronted with extreme droughts, pest, and famine, but the Akamba were uninterested in the European vision and no one converted.

Chapter 3 – Thomas Coomans gives a synthesis of the under-explored field of Catholic missionary spatial strategies in late-Qing and Republican China from the 1840s to the 1940s. Hostility, scale, language, climate, and collusion with the foreign imperialist powers made evangelization and land acquisition particularly difficult in China. The spatial strategy consisted of developing local christianities, which, like small islands, grew and formed archipelagos together, structured to a greater or lesser extent, and relatively autonomous networks at the level of the many Catholic missionary societies involved (SJ, CM, MEP, OFM, SVD, CICM, MM, OP, OSB, SM, etc.). This chapter is built on seven categories of "missionary islands" according to both their function and location, and relates them to several historical and geographical contexts specific to China: concession territories in the treaty ports, urban cathedral compounds, christianities in small towns and villages, Christian villages, places of memory and cemeteries, Marian pilgrimages, and monastic sites. The chapter concludes with the Vatican reformation of the mission policy aimed at Sinicizing the Catholic mission and creating a Chinese Church in the 1920s and 1930s.

Chapter 4 – Bram Cleys explores the spatial approaches deployed by Catholic missionaries from the Congregation of the Immaculate Heart of Mary (CICM, Scheut Fathers) and the Society of Saint Joseph of the Sacred Heart (SSJ, Josephite Fathers), and the Protestant missionaries from the American Presbyterian Congo Mission (APCM) to negotiate their position within the city of Luluaburg, now Kananga in the Democratic Republic of Congo. The former, benefiting from the support of the Belgian colonial authorities and railway station, obtained large plots of well-located ground to develop their cathedral and episcopal residence, a novitiate, several parishes, a college, schools, and other facilities, while the latter were barely encouraged at all. As Luluaburg grew from the 1930s and became a major city in Kasai, Catholic missionaries relocated existing churches and schools and built new facilities in order to evangelize migrants, guide the Christians in living a moral life, provide services, and assert their influence. Missionaries not only responded to changes around them, but developed a territorial strategy and actively "made space." They thus played a major role in shaping the city's physiognomy and, in effect, helped "co-author" the city. The spire and bells of Luluaburg's cathedral became a widely recognized landmark that proclaimed the presence of a bishop and a Catholic regional center.

Chapter 5 – Leon Bouwmeester and Thomas Coomans examine the relocation of Catholic missionaries after their expulsion from the People's Republic of China in 1950-1954 – a veritable disaster with complex human, spiritual, material, and geopolitical consequences – from two spatial perspectives. First, the top-down Vatican-led macrospatial strategy allocated new mission fields in Taiwan to a part of the exiled missionary societies and created seven ecclesiastical circumscriptions that would interact with the local population, the million Chinese refugees from the mainland, and the island's rulers. Benefiting from the dynamic of Vatican II, most of these new mission territories shifted to real local dioceses before the council's opening. Second, the bottom-up apostolate of a group of middle-aged Belgian Friars Minor (OFM), who were relocated from Central China to the then prefecture apostolic of Taipei in 1951, organized their local spatial strategy from a hub established near Taipei's railway station and established parishes along a railway line. Localized parish churches and residences were combined with kindergartens in response to Taiwan's specific childcare needs. The missions founded by the Belgian Franciscans were taken over by the localized Franciscan province of Taiwan and Hong Kong created in 1970.

Part two – Universal projects / localized architectures

Chapter 6 – Thomas Coomans examines how Catholic missionary architecture in China combined Western Catholic norms of gender segregation, as defined by Canon Law, and made them acceptable to Chinese Confucian norms and customs. Gender discrimination in Chinese society was a significant barrier for missionaries, as it was more radical than that practiced in nineteenth-century Western society, including by the Catholic Church. Moreover, by teaching, catechizing, and preaching to women – in particular promoting equality and condemning polygamy – missionaries contributed to the emancipation of women, but risked threatening the harmony of traditional society. This synthetic chapter explores gender-designed spaces (enclosure, circulation, and spatial organization) in various christianities in China, from rural parish compounds to cathedral complexes, schools, orphanages, and the religious houses of Western missionary nuns, Chinese consecrated Virgins, and Chinese congregations. The areas and Catholic missionary societies studied include French Jesuits (SJ) in Jiangnan and southern Hebei, Belgian Scheut Fathers (CICM) in Inner Mongolia, Dutch Franciscans (OFM) in southern Shanxi, Belgian Franciscans (OFM) in western Hubei, Daughters of Charity of St Vincent de Paul (FdlC) in Shanghai and Zhejiang, Foreign Missionnaries of Paris (MEP) in Guangdong, Guizhou and Sichuan, and, last but not least, French Jesuits (SJ) in Shanghai, especially in Xujiahui.

Chapter 7 – Building on Chapter 6, Thomas Coomans focuses on the specific issue of churches in which men and women were able to attend the same services instead of being segregated into two separate buildings. This chapter offers the first architectural historical synthesis of the origins of gender-inclusive spaces in Catholic churches in China. After introducing the meaning of the cultural differences between China's *fengshui* and the Western-Christian orientation of church buildings and gendered seating in church spaces in late Qing, the two most common gender spatial separations – longitudinal and transversal – are examined from cases across China (Hebei, Inner Mongolia, Shanxi, Hubei, Sichuan, Jiangsu, Shanghai, and Guangdong). Subsequently, the focus shifts to North China and follows the critical evaluation of gendered spaces in L-shaped, double nave, and cross-shaped churches. Invented by the French Vincentians (CM) and developed in Inner Mongolia by Belgian Scheut Fathers (CICM), the L-shaped church type (*renzitang* 人子堂) receives particular attention – its origin in North China, link with European L-shaped churches, presence in other parts of China, and the Korean L-shaped or *hanok*-church – because it offered an astonishing convergence between the gendered spatial organization of traditional local architecture and Western monastic models. The chapter concludes with the evolution of gendered spaces in the churches of Republican China.

Chapter 8 – Céline Frémaux examines the role of French missions in the formation of Catholic architectural identity and visual presence in the urban landscapes of Port-Said and Ismailia in Egypt. These two cosmopolitan towns developed from scratch along the Suez Canal, excavated from 1859 to 1869 by the Universal Company of the Maritime Canal of Suez, which also played a crucial role in more general urban planning. High-ranking company officials interacted with French missionary orders and congregations – the Franciscans (OFM), the Brothers of Christian Instruction of Ploërmel (FICP), and the Sisters of the Good Shepherd (RGS) – and helped build churches, convents, schools, etc. In 1926, Pope Pius XI created the Vicariate Apostolic of the Suez Canal (later Vicariate Apostolic of Port Said, suppressed in 1987) and entrusted it to the Franciscans. Consequently, a Romanesque-style cathedral was built after plans designed by a renowned French architect. Many other Christian communities – Uniates, Orthodox Copts, Greek Orthodox, American Protestants – and Islamic communities developed in the cosmopolitan canal towns, whose geography of places of worship indicated competing coexistence according to a strict allotment of neighborhoods. Bell-ringing, processions, and other religious events were frequent and served to underline the christianities' presence by the ephemeral occupancy of public space.

Chapter 9 – Lawrence Braschi's chapter on the West China Union University (WCUU) in the city of Chengdu (Sichuan, China) deals with the issue of contested spaces and how campus spatial development was shaped by negotiation and confrontation. Five Protestant missionary societies from the USA, Canada, and the United Kingdom – the American Methodist Episcopal Mission (AMEM), the Canadian Methodist Mission (CMM), the American Baptist Foreign Mission Society (ABFMS), the Church Missionary Society (CMS), and the Friends Foreign Mission Association (FFMA) – joined forces to found the university in 1910. To obtain land for building, missionaries had to bargain with farmers, temple owners, and families whose ancestral graves were located where college buildings were planned. In their efforts, the missionaries accepted the backing of local military officers, but this was a risky strategy given later army leaders were less forthcoming with their support. The new college buildings were early examples of "adaptive architecture" combining Western architecture and Chinese roofs. When female students were admitted to the university in 1926, several spaces had to be adapted for gender segregation and their dormitories enclosed with walls. Despite efforts at peaceful cohabitation with the local population, growing insecurity resulted in the erection of a security wall around the campus in 1930. This spatial transformation impacted the daily lives of many neighboring farmers and brick production workers accustomed to navigating the canals crossing the campus. Consequently, the missionaries were accused of creating a foreign concession by fraudulently expropriating Chinese land and the government was accused of forming a police force to protect foreigners. This chapter also shows how the architectural developments not only generated new spaces and new rules governing access to laboratories, playing fields, gardens, etc., but also how the campus gradually shifted from a primarily Christian civilizing space to a nationalist space.

Chapter 10 – Johan Lagae dedicates the last chapter of the book to another educational institution, the Collège du Saint-Esprit in Bujumbura, Burundi, erected from 1952 to 1961 by Belgian Jesuits (SJ) as an experimental interracial college for boys from the Burundese elite and European colonizers. The chapter focuses mainly on the diverse mediation of the college through images and words, drawing on a wide array of published and unpublished sources, and giving particular attention to the visual. Rather than discussing the design and construction of the college's iconic tropical modernist architecture, the author analyzes the "politics of design" that underscores the project. He demonstrates that the specific architectural language, spatial organization, and peri-urban location were powerful elements in the many ways interracial education – a "splendid experience that might set the tone for the whole Africa" – was mediated.

Visual sources, propaganda, and perception

Like no other source type, missionary photography offers a unique window into the missionary encounter with people/culture and landscapes/nature.[55] Thousands of photographs also document the work of the missionaries and their achievements, among which architecture, spaces, and built environments play a visually prime role.

55 Ho, *Developing Mission. Photography, Filmmaking and American Missionaries in Modern China*; Thompson, *Light on Darkness? Missionary Photography of Africa*; Geary, "Missionary Photography"; Vints, "Photographs of and with a Mission"; Pirotte, Sappia, and Servais, eds., *Images et diffusion du Christianisme. Expressions graphiques en contexte missionnaire.*

0.14 Humble beginnings: little church of Betsimisaraka people, "built by Father Johannes van Spreeken SJ with 300 franks" (Republic of Madagascar). Photo published in La Mission de Madagascar, Vicariat de Tananarive, 35, April 1932, 67. [Leuven, Sabbe Library of Theology, 3-053978/B]

56 Coomans and Xu, "Built Together, Heritagized Together."
57 Griffiths, "'Trained to Tell the Truth': Missionaries, Converts, and Narration," 76.
58 The *Lettres édifiantes et curieuses*, written by Jesuit missionaries (1702-1776), inspired the *Annales de la propagation de la foi* (1822-1974), *Annales de l'Oeuvre de la Sainte Enfance* (1846-1975), *Les missions catholiques* (1868-1964) and many other magazines of missionary societies. Also: Pirotte, *Périodiques missionnaires belges d'expression française, reflets de cinquante années d'évolution d'une mentalité 1889-1940*.
59 Jenkins, "On Using Historical Missionary Photographs in Modern Discussion."

Consequently, this volume on missionary spaces is abundantly illustrated with visual material that interacts with the text appropriately: not only historical photos from missionary archives and magazines, but also valuable photos taken by the authors during their fieldwork and for the heritagization of relics that are still standing.[56]

Photographs show the wide range of buildings: Christian villages and farms, chapels, churches and cathedrals, male and female missionary residences, bishops' houses and seminaries, schools and orphanages, dispensaries and hospitals, etc. Photos also show people performing in spaces, outside and inside: Christian processions in the public space, orphans playing in courtyards, groups of communicants, baptized children and married couples posing in front of churches, missionary sisters in their enclosed gardens, funerals in cemeteries, the elderly and sick on hospital wards, foundation stone ceremonies, carpenters and masons on building works, student activities on university campuses, school sports fields, etc. Photos are often the only source on early missionary buildings that were replaced as soon as possible [Fig. 0.14], on construction works for which no plans have survived, and on the many churches that were ruined during wars and revolutions. After the First World War, the numbers of photos increased considerably due to the popularization of portable cameras and 35 mm film, which helped missionaries document their daily lives. Thanks to this visual material, numerous new research questions can be raised and hypotheses formulated, about gendered spaces [Chapter 6 and Chapter 7], for instance.

The circulation of visual material between the mission fields and home countries was crucial because the congregations' propaganda needed recent photos of buildings and people showing growing christianities, evolution, construction, and modernity. From the mid-1860s to the 1960s, most missionary societies published periodical journals or magazines. Intended for their home audience, these journals described the mission's achievements with the dual aim of raising funds and stimulating missionary vocations. Despite their one-sided nature and censored narrative, mission journals played a crucial role in the perception of other people and lands by home audiences through the implicit biased lens of missionary networks.[57]

While the first missionary magazines only published selected letters sent by missionaries to their superiors, friends, and family in their home countries, illustrated magazines developed from the 1860s,[58] benefiting from the technological evolution of the illustrated press and photography as revolutionary tools for documentation and visual communication.[59] Black and white images, initially engraved after drawings or photos [Figs. 3.2 and 3.26], then photographic, often associated with geographical maps, contributed to the development of the reader's imagination and knowledge of peoples and their customs, natural landscapes, and built spaces. From about 1900 onwards, missionary societies began to print series of postcards that contributed to spreading stereotypes of successful, happy, and modern missions.

After the First World War, the Western perspective of the missionary magazines evolved notably towards greater ethnographic interest in indigenous cultures,[60] but the lens remained biased and the various Christian denominations competed more vociferously with each other. Following the evolution of the mass media, professional press agencies such as the *Agenzia Fides* (1927) circulated quality photographs and mission propaganda among a wider Western audience. From the 1960s, color offered a new perception of the mission [Fig. 10.18]. When ambitious projects to construct universities and high schools had a political dimension, professional photographers, cameramen, and journalists were sent to the colony and helped mediatize these buildings in popular magazines with much larger audiences [Chapter 10].

All things considered, this propaganda literature is an essential source of critical missiology – the interdisciplinary field focusing on missions and the cross-cultural communication of the Christian faith, using the methods of historical, theological, and other social sciences – and its most recent concerns,[61] as well as for scholars from other fields, including historical anthropology and architectural history.

Acknowledgements

The origin of this book dates back to the 2005-2008 research project "Missionary Work and Architecture in the Belgian Congo (1908-1960). Identity (re)construction between transmission of culture and dialogue", funded by the Research Foundation Flanders (FWO). Supervised by Prof. Bruno De Meulder (KU Leuven, Engineering-Architecture, OSA), the project was co-supervised by Prof. Jan De Maeyer (KU Leuven, KADOC), Prof. Johan Lagae (Ghent University, Engineering-Architecture), Prof. Nicholas Bullock (University of Cambridge, Architecture), and Dr. Sabine Cornelis (Royal Museum for Central Africa). Bram Cleys was the doctoral researcher on this project. As part of it, the international workshop "Spatializing the Missionary Encounter. The Interaction between Missionary Work and Space in Colonial settings" was held from November 21 to 24, 2007 at Arenberg Castle in Leuven by the OSA Research Group Urbanity and Architecture and KADOC-KU Leuven, Documentation and Research Centre for Religion, Culture and Society. After an opening keynote lecture by Prof. Allen M. Howard (Rutgers University) on "the Spatiality of Sacred Spaces in Africa (1800-1960)" and an introductory lecture by Prof. De Meulder on the workshop's concept, eighteen papers were presented by international scholars from Africa, Asia, Europe, and North America. *Missionary Places*, the initially planned publication, was aborted and most of the papers were published as article journals or book chapters.

Fifteen years later, in June 2022, in the context of my current research on church architecture in China, I launched the *Missionary Spaces* book project, which is based partially on the concepts of the 2007 workshop. I am grateful for the kind agreement of my colleagues Prof. Bruno De Meulder and Prof. em. Jan De Maeyer, the contributions from Bram Cleys and Prof. Johan Lagae, and the authors of the other chapters, as well as the support of Louis Coomans, Hans M. De Wolf, and Shu Changxue.

I cannot emphasize enough the role of KADOC in this new project and warmly thank director Prof. Kim Christaens, Prof. Patrick Pasture, and Dr. Peter Heyrman for welcoming the book into KADOC's Artes series. The book is greatly indebted to Luc Vints's unconditional support, Alexis Vermeylen's patient layout, and Laura Bennett's English language revisions. All my gratitude goes to the KADOC staff at the archives, picture archives, library, and image digitization, whose knowledge of the collections is instrumental to their scientific assessment. Without them, especially Patricia Quaeghebueur, Luc Vints, Carine Dujardin, and Jo Luyten, this book would not be what it has become.

60 In 1925, Pope Pius XI organized a successful Universal Missionary Exhibition in the Vatican, and in 1927 founded the Pontifical Missionary-Ethnologic Museum that presented the work of missionaries, projected films, and exhibited relics from the great religions and cultures in the world. See Cakpo, "L'exposition missionnaire de 1925"; Gangnat, Lenoble-Bart and Zorn, eds. *Mission et cinéma. Films missionnaires et Missionnaires au cinéma.*
61 Skreslet, "Thinking Missiologically about the History of Mission." Also, the four-volumes anthology edited in 2021 by Frederiks and Nagy, *Critical Readings in the History of Christian Mission.*

BIBLIOGRAPHY

Benedict XV. Apostolic letter *Maximum illud*, November 30 1919. https://www.vatican.va/content/benedict-xv/en/apost_letters/documents/hf_ben-xv_apl_19191130_maximum-illud.html

Bickers, Robert A. and Seton, Rosemary, eds. *Missionary Encounters. Sources and Issues.* Richmond: Curzon Press, 1996.

Bartoloni, Nadia; Chris, Robert; MacKian, Sara and Pile, Steve. "The Place of Spirit: Modernity and the Geographies of Spirituality." *Progress in Human Geography*, 41 (2017) 3, 338-354.

Brace, Catherine; Bailey, Adrian R. and Harvey, David C. 2006. "Religion, Place, and Space: A Framework for Investigating Historical Geographies of Religious Identities and Communities." *Progress in Human Geography*, 30 (2006) 1, 28-43.

Bremner, G. Alexander, ed. *Architecture and Urbanism in the British Empire.* Oxford: Oxford University Press, 2016.

Brones, Sophie. *Villes et architecture des terrains ex-coloniaux (19ᵉ-20ᵉ siècles). Base de données bibliographiques.* Paris: Institut national d'histoire de l'art INHA, October 2007. <https://www.inha.fr/_resources/RECHERCHE/Villes%2520et%2520terrains%2520coloniaux/bibliographie%2520Villes%2520et%2520terrains%2520coloniaux/2a-%2520Bibliographie_Architecture-TerrainsColoniaux.pdf>.

Cakpo, Érick. "L'exposition missionnaire de 1925. Une affirmation de la puissance de l'Église catholique." *Revue des Sciences Religieuses*, 87 (2013) 1: 41-59.

Çelik, Zeynep. *Displaying the Orient: Architecture of Islam at Nineteenth-Century World's Fairs.* Berkeley: University of California Press, 1992.

Chen Xinyu 陈欣雨. *Beijing Zhalan mudi lishi ji xiancun beiwen kao* 北京栅栏墓地历史及现存碑文考 [*The History on the Tombstones. Research on the History and Inscriptions of Chala Cemetery*]. Beijing: Renmin chubanshe, 2020.

Conklin, Alice L. *A Mission to Civilize: The Republican Idea of Empire in France and West Africa, 1895-1930.* Stanford: Stanford University Press, 1997.

Constructing Territory (GEOG 128, Geography of International Affairs). Penn State College of Earth and Mineral Sciences, Department of Geography. <https://www.e-education.psu.edu/geog128/node/538#:~:text=Territorialization%3A%20The%20way%20that%20territory,contest%20this%20process%20of%20territorialization> [accessed on 7 January 2024].

Coomans, Thomas. "Church Architecture and Church Buildings: China," in: Chu Yik-yi, Cindy 朱益宜 and Leung Kit-fun, Beatrice 梁潔芬, eds. *The Palgrave Handbook of the Catholic Church in East Asia*. Singapore: Springer, 2023, 80 p. <https://link.springer.com/referencework/10.1007/978-981-15-9365-9>.

Coomans, Thomas. "The Sino-Christian Style: A Major Tool for Architectural Indigenization," in: Zheng Yangwen 鄭揚文, ed. *Sinicizing Christianity* (Studies in Christian Mission 49). Leiden-Boston: Brill, 2017, 197-232.

Coomans, Thomas and Ho Puay-peng 何培斌. "Architectural Styles and Identities in Hong Kong: The Chinese and Western Designs for St Teresa's Church in Kowloon Tong, 1928-32." *Journal of the Royal Asiatic Society Hong Kong Branch* 香港皇家亞洲學會學報, 58 (2018), 81-109.

Coomans, Thomas and Xu Yitao 徐怡涛. "Built Together, Heritagized Together: Using Building Archaeology for Safeguarding Early Modern Churches in China," in: Rodrigues dos Santos, Joaquim, ed. *Preserving Transcultural Heritage: Your Way or My Way? Questions on Authenticity, Identity and Patrimonial Proceedings in the Safeguarding of Architectural Heritage Created in the Meeting of Cultures.* Lisbon: Caleidoscópio, 2017, 197-206.

Coomans, Thomas; Xu Yitao 徐怡涛 and Zhang Jianwei 张剑葳. "'Imposing and Provocative': The Design, Style, Construction and Significance of Saint Anthony's Cathedral, Xinjiang (Shanxi, China), 1936-40," in: Mascarenhas-Mateus, João and Pires, Ana Paula, eds. *History of Construction Cultures. Proceedings of the Seventh International Congress on Construction History (7ICCH), 12-16 July 2021, Lisbon*, vol. 1, London: CRC Press Balkema, 2021, 85-92.

Crossley, Pamela. *A Translucent Mirror: History and Identity in Qing Imperial Ideology.* Berkeley: University of California Press, 1999.

Dean, Britten. "British Informal Empire: The Case of China." *Journal of Commonwealth and Comparative Politics*, 14 (1976), 64-81.

de Broux, Pierre-Olivier and Piret, Bérangère. "'Le Congo était fondé dans l'intérêt de la civilisation et de la Belgique'. La notion de *civilisation* dans la Charte coloniale." *Revue interdisciplinaire d'études juridiques*, 83 (2019) 2, 51-80.

De Meulder, Bruno. *Kuvuande Mbote. Een eeuw koloniale architectuur en stedenbouw in Belgisch Kongo* [A century of colonial architecture and urbanism in Belgian Congo]. Antwerp: Houtekiet, 2000.

De Meulder, Bruno. "Mavula: An African Heterotopia in Kwango, 1895-1911." *Journal of Architectural Education*, 52 (1998), 1, 20-29.

de Moreau, Edouard (SJ) and Masson, Joseph (SJ). *Les missionnaires Belges de 1804 à nos jours*, Bruxelles: Éditions universitaires, 1944.

Dujardin, Carine. "The Saint Luke School Movement and the Revival of Medieval Illumination in Belgium (1866-1923)," in: Coomans, Thomas and De Maeyer, Jan, eds. *The Revival of medieval Illumination. Nineteenth-Century Belgium Manuscripts and Illuminations from a European Perspective.* KADOC Artes 8. Leuven: Leuven University Press, 2007, 268-293.

Dunch, Ryan. "Beyond Cultural Imperialism: Cultural Theory, Christian Missions, and Global Modernity." *History and Theory*, 41 (2002), 301-325.

Foucault, Michel. "Des espaces autres." [Lecture given on March 14, 1967.] *Architecture, Mouvement, Continuité*, 5 (October 1984), 46-49. English translation by Jay Miskowiec, "Of Other Spaces: Utopias and Heterotopias," 1984, see: <https://web.mit.edu/allanmc/www/foucault1.pdf>.

Frederiks, Martha and Nagy, Dorottya, eds. *Critical Readings in the History of Christian Mission.* 4 vol. Leiden-Boston: Brill, 2021.

Friedler, Klaus. *Interdenominational Faith Missions in Africa. History and Ecclesiology.* Malawi: Munzi Press, 2018.

Fry, Maxwell and Drew, Jane. *Tropical Architecture in the Humid Zone.* London, 1956.

Gangnat, Emilie; Lenoble-Bart, Annie and Zorn, Jean-François, eds. *Mission et cinéma. Films missionnaires et Missionnaires au cinéma.* Paris: Karthala, 2013.

Geary, Christaud M. "Missionary Photography: Private and Public Readings." *African Arts*, 24 (1991) 4, 48-59.

Griffiths, Gareth. "'Trained to Tell the Truth': Missionaries, Converts, and Narration," in: Etherington, Norman, ed. *Missions and Empire.* Oxford: Oxford University Press, 2008, 153-172.

Hervieu-Léger, Danièle. "Space and Religion: New Approaches to Religious Spatiality in Modernity." *International Journal of Urban and Regional Research*, 26 (2002) 1, 99-105.

Heynen, Hilde. "Engaging Modernism," in: Henket, Hubert-Jan and Heynen, Hilde, eds. *Back from Utopia. The Challenge of the Modern Movement.* Rotterdam: 010 Publishers, 2002, 378-398.

Heynen, Hilde. "The Intertwinment of Modernism and Colonialism: A Theoretical Perspective." *Docomomo*, 48 (2013) 1, 10-19.

Ho, Joseph W. *Developing Mission. Photography, Filmmaking and American Missionaries in Modern China.* Ithaca: Cornell University Press, 2022.

Howard, Allen M. "Nodes, Networks, Landscapes, and Religions: Reading the Social History of Tropical Africa, 1700s-1920," in: Howard, Allen M. and Shain, Richard M., eds., *The Spatial Factor in African History. The Relationship of the Social, Material, and Perceptual*. Leiden-Boston: Brill, 2005, 21-140.

Howard, Allen M. "Re-Making of the Past: Spatial Structures and Dynamics in the Sierra Leona-Guinea Plain, 1860-1920s," in: Howard, Allen M. and Shain, Richard M., eds., *The Spatial Factor in African History. The Relationship of the Social, Material, and Perceptual*. Leiden-Boston: Brill. 2005, 291-348.

Hsia Po-chia, Ronny. "Christianity and Empire: The Catholic Mission in Late Imperial China." *Studies in Church History*, 54 (June 2018), 208-224.

Huber, Mary Taylor and Luthekaus, Nancy C., eds. *Gendered Missions: Women and Men in Missionary Discourse and Practice*. Ann Arbor: University of Michigan Press, 1999.

Jenkins, Paul. "On Using Historical Missionary Photographs in Modern Discussion." *Le Fait Missionnaire*, 10 (2001) 1, 71–89.

Koppelkamm, Stefan. *Imaginary Orient Exotic Buildings of the 18th and 19th Century in Europe*. Stuttgart: Axel Menges, 2015.

Kurgat, Sussy Gumo. "The Theology of Inculturation and the African Church." *International Journal of Sociology and Anthropology*, 1 (2009) 5, 90-98.

Larsen, Kirk W. "The Qing Empire (China), Imperialism, and the Modern World." *History Compass*, 9 (2011) 6, 498-508.

Lefebvre, Henri. *The Production of Space*. Oxford: Blackwell Publishers, 1991. [Translation of *La production de l'espace*. Paris: Éditions Anthropos, 1974.]

Morelli, Anne. "L'espace du cimetière et les cortèges d'enterrements comme enjeux de pouvoir entre laïques et catholiques (Belgique, XIXe-XXe siècles)," in Dierckens, Alain and Morelli, Anne, eds. *Topographie du sacré. L'emprise religieuse sur l'espace*. Brussels: Éditions de l'Université de Bruxelles, 2008, 141-152.

Moyn, Samuel and Sartori, Andrew. "Approaches to Global Intellectual History," in: Moyn, Samuel and Sartori, Andrew, eds. *Global Intellectual History*. New York: Columbia University Press, 2015, 3-29.

Myers, Garth Andrew. *Verandas of Power. Colonialism and Space in Urban in Urban Africa (Space, Place and Society)*. Syracuse, NY: Syracuse University Press, 2003.

Nche, George C.; Okwuosa, Lawrence N. and Nwaoga Theresa C. "Revisiting the Concept of Inculturation in a Modern Africa." *HTS Teologiese Studies/Theological Studies*, 72 (2016) 1, online 6 p.

Pakenham, Thomas. *The Scramble for Africa: The White Man's Conquest of the Dark Continent from 1876 to 1912*, New York: Random House, 1991.

Piolet, Jean-Baptiste (SJ), ed. *Les missions catholiques françaises au XIXe siècle*. 6 vol. Paris: Armand Collin, 1902-1903.

Pirotte, Jean. *Périodiques missionnaires belges d'expression française, reflets de cinquante années d'évolution d'une mentalité 1889 - 1940*. Leuven: Publications Universitaires de Louvain, 1973.

Pirotte, Jean; Sappia, Caroline and Servais, Olivier, eds. *Images et diffusion du christianisme. Expressions graphiques en contexte missionnaire XVIe-XXe siècles*. Paris: Karthala, 2012.

Prip-Møller, Johannes. *Chinese Buddhist Monasteries. Their plan and its Functions as a Setting for Buddhist Monastic Life*. Copenhagen: Gads Forlag, 1937.

Said, Edward W. *Orientalism*. New York: Pantheon Books, 1978.

Skreslet, Stanley H. "Thinking Missiologically about the History of Mission." *International Bulletin of Mission Research*, 31 (2007) 2, 159-173.

Standaert, Nicolas (SJ). *L'autre' dans la mission. Leçons à partir de la Chine*. Bruxelles: Éditions Lessius, 2003.

Standaert, Nicolas (SJ). "History as the art of the 'other' and the art of 'in-betweenness'," in: Amsler, Nadine; Badea, Andreea; Heyberger, Bernard, and Windler, Christian, eds. *Catholic Missionaries in Early Modern Asia : Patterns of Localization*. London: Routledge, 2020, 207-217.

Standaert, Nicolas (SJ). "The Creation of Christian Communities," in: Standaert, Nicolas, ed. *Handbook of Christianity in China. Volume One: 635-1800*. Leiden-Boston: Brill, 2001, 534-575.

Standaert, Nicolas (SJ), ed. *Handbook of Christianity in China. Volume One: 635-1800*. Leiden-Boston: Brill, 2001.

Stoler, Ann Laura and Cooper, Frederick. "Between Metropole and Colony. Rethinking a Research Agenda," in: Cooper, Frederick and Stoler, Ann Laura, eds. *Tensions of Empire: Colonial Cultures in a Bourgeois World*. University of California Press, 1997, 1-56.

Taveirne, Patrick (CICM). *Han-Mongol Encounters and Missionary Endeavors: A History of Scheut in Ordos (Hetao), 1874-1911*. Leuven Chinese Studies 15. Leuven: Ferdinand Verbiest Institute, 2004.

Tetzlaff, Rainer. *Africa. An Introduction to History, Politics and Society*. Wiesbaden: Springer, 2022.

Thompson, T. Jack. *Light on Darkness? Missionary Photography of Africa in the Nineteenth and Early Twentieth Centuries*. Grand Rapids: William B. Eerdmans, 2012.

Tiedemann, R. Gary, ed. *Handbook of Christianity in China. Volume Two: 1800-present*. Leiden-Boston: Brill, 2010.

Vallgarda, Karen. "Were Christian Missionaries Colonizers? Reorienting the Debate and Exploring New Research Trajectories." *International Journal of Postcolonial Studies*, 18 (2016) 6, 865-886.

Van Melckebeke, Carlo (CICM). *Service social de l'Église en Mongolie*. Brussels: Éditions de Scheut, 1968.

Vints, Luc. "Photographs of and with a Mission," in: Tollebeek, Jo, *Mayombe. Ritual sculptures from the Congo*. Tielt: Lannoo, 2010, 45-51.

PART ONE
IMAGINED WORLD /
ADAPTED STRATEGIES

1
Spatial Trajectories and Missionary and Colonial Movements into Northwest Ghana since 1929

Dagara Reception of Catholic Missionary Activities

Alexis B. Tengan

The Dagara people living in the northwest corner of Ghana first came into contact with the Catholic missionary society, the Missionaries of Africa, popularly known as the White Fathers, in 1929 and since then they have witnessed dramatic changes within their physical, social and cosmic environments. The Catholic missionary encounter, unlike the colonial one which started a bit earlier, was positively received by the Dagara and has continued to be a dynamic movement that is responsible for the reshaping of Dagara cosmological and geographical notions of space and its appropriation for cultural, political and social use. Within the general cultural pattern and discourse of the Dagara peoples of Northwest Ghana, and perhaps for many African cultures, every encounter involves endless bonding relations taking place within spaces in motion which also act as agents of the encounter. There has developed a bonding relationship between Dagara society and the Catholic Church which seemed destined to last.

In the first instance, the Dagara enthusiastically accommodated Catholicism without much compulsion. The conversion of the Dagara to the new religion was a mass movement which soon led to rapid proliferation and institutionalisation of church buildings as centres for varying activities. The whole process has been a source of enigma for many internal and external observers. This is also the case mainly because the same people had demonstrated strong resistance to both French and British colonising efforts. Many scholars and rational thinking ordinary people find it difficult to accept as plausible the contexts of events described by the first missionaries in which praying for rain at particular locations and centres accounted for much of this conversion phenomenon.[1] As it turned out, the centres where particular communities gathered to pray for rain became the sites for a symptomatic movement leading to the erection of church buildings and parish institutions. This movement also led to redesigning and reshaping geographical orientations and cosmographic visions of the people in many ways. The impact of colonial rule has been far less remarkable.

Dagara notions of space and the spatial trajectories they constructed within their cosmology and geography dictated how they perceived and dealt with the movement of missionaries and colonial agents into their lives and territory.

This chapter focuses on the Dagara encounter with missionary activities, set in contrast to the encounter with colonial administrators. First, we will discuss how Dagara viewed their cosmos and how they dealt with different spatial categories and entities as they engaged in their principal social and cultural activity of hoe-farming prior to their encounter with colonialism. The space-above, figured as Rain, and the space-below, as Earth, were the globalising spatial entities within which they viewed and contextualised all encounters. Their view of the universe was captured and located in the physical and social structure of the house buildings as residential locations and of the village environment divided up into farming locations. Second, we will study how the spatial trajectories developed for migrating hoe-farming entered into the dynamics of missionary church-building (social, metaphysical and physical) and religious conversion.

1.1 Farm locations are also resident location.
a Male farmers ploughing the land.
b Female farmers planting the land.
c View on a ploughed farm: a residence of plants and trees.
[Photos: Alexis Tengan]

---

1   For a full report on these incidents, see McCoy, *Great Things Happen*, 109-124; Tengan, "Dagara Christian Conversion," 141; and Hawkins, *Writing and Colonialism in Northern Ghana*, 140-147.

Dagara spatial universe of settlements and habitats of hoe-farming[2]

As migrating hoe-farmers who have adopted a house-based model of settlement and a shifting migratory pattern of subsistence agriculture, [Fig. 1.1] the Dagara have structured their universal spatial view along two axes. The first, perceived as a vertical structure, consists of human settlements and the second, perceived as a horizontal structure, consists of farmlands and bush areas. Within this structure, each individual hoe-farmer considers himself or herself to be the focal point of the axes and as the centre of the universe. He or she views the vertical axis as spiralling concentric localities of homesteads and village stead and identifies them as kinship categories and places to visit or dwell in as part of a life cycle.

Mythical narratives and observed practices indicate that the concentric localities consist of nine spatial settlement areas, each with a descriptive name, a kinship status, and an institutional position.[3] Moreover, their cardinal positions and directions depend on the current location from within which an individual is seeking to locate his or her bearings. Hence, every individual starts human life within the first of these nine spatial categories or areas; that is, within the father's village stead (*sāā téng*) where the paternal house of Ego's father (*sāā yir*) is also situated. As Ego grows up, he/she will, through travel movements and encounters discover the other eight spatial areas and categories as house locations, starting with the mother's village stead (*ma téng*) where the paternal of Ego's mother (*ma yir*) is situated. The next area consists of the two village steads from where Ego's father and maternal uncle made their most recent long distance migrations (*sāā téng kura* and *ma téng kura*), places where ruined houses of the paternal and the maternal clans can still be located and identified [Figs. 1.2 and 1.3]. The other five areas consist of the two village steads to which Ego's paternal and maternal family ancestors made their first migration; the two village steads of

1.2 Architectural building is the first spatial encounter with nature.
a Termite hill: natural architecture.
b Human architecture: primitive structure.
c Advanced architecture: the house.
[Photos: Alexis Tengan]

1.3 Section of the house roof divided into terraces and as mapping of the significant locations.
[Photo: Alexis Tengan, 1998]

paternal and maternal mythical origins and finally the village stead of Ego's settlement as a migrating hoe-farmer.

The structural movement along the horizontal axis is also perceived as concentric cyclical overlapping extensions of six spatial categories as habitations that are identified and named according to natural elements. They consist of the Tree habitat location, the Hill habitat location, the Rock habitat location, the Wind (Vulture) habitat location, the Water (Sea) habitat location and the Desert (Hawk) habitat location. The Dagara hoe-farmer views each of these locations as residential habitats for different living elements including crops, animals, fish, minerals, birds, etc.; and considers the same as the objective means and the ends of his farming and hunting activities. The six spatial habitations, in his belief, are composed of living beings of natural elements and forces that have a well-developed house-based social system and very sophisticated kin-based social and cultural forms of interactions and practices. In other words, all knowledge and wisdom, especially on agricultural and social reproduction, come from these natural habitations and the elements within them. These are all regarded as personified sacred beings, deities and divinities and as such, they demand the religious attention of human beings. They each have kinship relations with the two globalizing spatial features of Dagara cosmology, namely, the space-above personified in Rain and the space below personified in Earth. The two, Earth and Rain, are the most significant divine beings, and the Earth Shrine (*Téngan tiɛ*) and the Rain Shrine (*Sà-dug*) remained for a long time the two most significant social and political institutions for the Dagara. As a society lacking any centralizing features such as chieftaincy and kingship, every village stead community identified the custodians of the earth cult (*Tengan sob*) and the rain cult (*Sà-dug sob*) as their head elders and chief priests capable of mobilizing the whole community beyond house-based and kin-based social and cultural ceremonies. These custodians, as first settlers of the village stead, have already mapped out the geographical borders and boundaries of the village settlement and were the first to constitute the two cults and to begin devotion to them.

The Dagara cosmographic and geographical vision of space and travel encounter was designed to understand and deal with piecemeal movements of individuals and households during peace time and within the context of hoe-farming. It was not designed

2 We have made a detailed study of Dagara hoe-farming culture (Tengan, *Hoe-farming and Social Relations among the Dagara*) and their house-based model of social structure (Id. "Space, Bonds and Social Order"). Both studies gave a detailed analysis on their notions of spaces and spatialisation within their cosmology. In this chapter, we will not repeat what has been said in these studies, but will only make a brief summary description of the spatial structure in a matter of fact manner and with the understanding that these ideas have already been justified.

3 Tengan, *Mythical narratives in Ritual*.

1.4 Colonial encounter and spaces of power. The colonial rest house still stands today but the chief's palace and power has fallen apart.
a The government rest house on "Nasaalatang" (White man's hill) in Jirapa. It was here that the first missionaries to Dagao were lodged upon their arrival on November 20, 1929.
[Photo: Michael Wood]
b Chief Ganaa's palace, front view. The only multi-storied dried-mud edifice in the Gold Coast at the time, 1929.
[Alexis Tengan Digital Collection. Cardinal Dery picture, Tamale, 2007]
c Chief Ganaa's palace, rear view: a mud-palace of a local chief promoted by the colonial rule.
[McCoy, Great Things Happen, 112-113 and Rome, Archives of the Society of Missionaries of Africa]

4 Even though slave raiding did not constitute the only source of violence, it was a major factor lasting untill the imposition of colonial rule. See Goody, *The Social Organisation of the LoWiili*, 11-16.

5 All the papers and treatises made by Furguson have been published as a complete volume. See Arhin, *The Papers of George Ekem Ferguson*. See also Tengan, *Christianity and Cultural History in Northern Ghana*; Tengan, ed., *Religion, Culture, Society and Integral Human Development*.

6 Cf. Hawkins, *Writing and Colonialism in Northern Ghana*, 39.

7 This region was, for long time, a fertile ground for slave raiding and the Dagara populations were among the hardest hit. For more details on this, see Goody, *The Social Organisation of the LoWiili*, 11-13.

to deal with violent intrusions of aliens bent on imposing strange ways of behavior and regarding them as subjects to be ruled. Yet, they knew that violence could cause the forceful dislocation of families or whole settlements. Whenever such violence occurred in the past, families had always chosen to flee from their original settlements and away from the violence. Indeed, most of Dagara families will affirm that they fled from their original homes into Northwest Ghana and Southeast Burkina Faso because of slave raiding. They describe this event as the flight of the donkeys from their hard labor (*bong zoba*).[4] The colonial and the missionary encounters were different in terms of the nature of the violence.

Missionary and colonial spatial trajectory and movement into Northwest Ghana

The historical background and the colonial trajectory

After taking control of Southern Gold Coast and Asante in 1896, the British appropriated Northern Ghana as a protectorate in 1902. The British were able, using the skills of an educated African from the coastal region, George Ekem Ferguson (1865-1897), to map out each so-called tribal area and to create paramount chieftaincies and districts for each of them.[5] They also negotiated treaties with the chiefs and other powerful men they found in the area. In Northwest Ghana, at the time, only the Wala people living in the urban centre had a chieftaincy structure. The rest of the populations were rural farmers with segmenting lineage or house-based social structures. The creation of the tribal districts and chieftaincies were the first steps toward the appropriation of the people and the land. The chiefs and the European district administrators became key figures in the proper appropriation and rule of the colonial state. According to Sean Hawkins, the British then went ahead to further appropriate the Dagara in particular in five different ways, namely, by locating them in space, by situating them in time, through the physical expropriation of their labor, by clothing their nudity and by naming them. This type of appropriation affected Dagara traditional society and culture in many ways.[6]

Paradoxically, the establishment of colonial government brought about peace in this region, allowing people to move and migrate more easily.[7] Also the establishment of cocoa plantations and mining activities in the South created new opportunities for movement and allowed the Dagara to extend their world of migration beyond Northwest Ghana and to broaden their cosmological understanding of space beyond the homestead and the village stead. Funeral and *bagr* celebrations were no longer restricted to the house and neighborhood but began to draw Dagara people from far and wide. According to reports by the first converts to Christianity, the period immediately before the coming of the Catholic missionaries in 1930 witnessed a tremendous increase in the constitution of shrines and other religious institutions and their localization in areas beyond Dagara homeland. As people began to engage in long distance trade and travel, their religious, social and cultural horizons widened. Also, the division of the whole territory into administrative districts and chiefdoms, with the intention of facilitating indirect rule, led to a new search for social and cultural identity beyond the house community. In this new search for identity, the newly appointed chiefs began to view themselves as having higher social status than other traditional institutional authorities such as the earth custodian (*Tengan-sob*) and the farm owner (*wie-sob*). In some cases, they began to consider themselves as proprietors and leaders of territorial domains. As a result there emerged fierce rivalries among chiefs and between them and other traditional authorities. The British policy of ranking chiefs in an attempt to create a hierarchical structure increased this rivalry. Hence, those who were made paramount chiefs proceeded to create sub-ethnic groups comprising different inhabitants within their territorial domains in order to try to combine their office of chief with other traditional ones, particularly the office of *Tengan-sob*. This, they felt, would give them legitimacy within the cultural system.

Colonial settlement and attempts to create new spatial domains and institutions

Colonial rule in Northwest Ghana was generally identified with the localisation of three architectural structures, namely the chief's palace found in every big village, town and settlement, the district administration found in every district capital, and lastly the government rest house also found in every big village, town and settlement. As new centres of power, each of these three had its distinctive features and aura. In the first place, the colonial administration expected the chiefs and headmen to enforce all laws passed, to help recruit labor for the mining companies and farm plantations in the South, and, later, to recruit for the army. Also, they were expected to build local roads through forced labor, collect taxes of all kinds, and take census of their populations. Because they had no traditional authority and had no place within the culture of hoe-farming, the chiefs resorted to new ways of doing things. In most cases, each chief, through the appropriate use of the powers invested in him by the colonial system, started his rule by building for himself a very large mud-castle house. He then proceeded, through polygamous marriage, to extend his family size and residential location beyond Dagara expectations and possibilities [Fig. 1.4 b-c]. In the eyes of the chief, however, this could be explained partly as an extension of the house-based social and cultural system. He also saw the use of mobilized unpaid labor for building his mud-palace as an action that the colonial system would endorse.

Indeed, he was required to use the same labor to build the administrative settlement and the rest house. As a matter of military strategy and economic convenience, colonial administrators often chose to appropriate for

their own residential locations hilly locations overlooking the village or township residence of the local population. Moreover, they often opted to build for themselves single unit round huts as their homes. The rest house also was often situated a distance away from the settlements on a hilly or bushy area [Fig. 1.4 a]. Officials often ignored the cultural and ritual processes associated with acquiring residential sites and building houses.[8] They also ignored Dagara beliefs that a single hut or a group of huts standing alone on a hilly location must be a haunted location that can only harbor anti-social beings and elements. This negative image of the colonial rest houses was reinforced when the administration decided to use force labor to build main roads linking them; and when the lifestyle of those who occupied rest houses consisted mainly in eating meat and eggs and drinking beer.

Dagara were at first ambivalent and at later negative toward colonial buildings. In one sense, they needed the images built around the chief's house and the rest house to demonstrate that they were well adjusted into the colonial state and deserved the respect and recognition accorded to the centralised and chieftaincy societies. In other words, they were quick to realize that their external image depended very much on the image the outsiders held of their chief's house and the rest house. Yet, these institutions stood as fixed locations with temporal power and represented certain practices that could not be reconciled with their cultural ideals. As long as the colonial system flourished, these institutions seemed to flourish using legitimate power.

The missionary trajectory

The Missionaries of Africa, known as the White Fathers, arrived from Upper Volta (present Burkina Faso) in Navrongo, a small town in Northeast Ghana, on Monday April 23, 1906. The first missionary fathers included two Canadians, Fathers Oscar Morin (who became vicar apostolic of Navrongo in 1934) and Léonide Barsalou, and two Frenchmen, Father Jean-Marie Chollet and Brother Eugene Gall. For their journey, they were accompanied by a contingent of about twenty Africans. They arrived in Northern Ghana at a time when a big segment of the local population, traditionally engaged in hoe-farming and living in the rural areas, was still contending with the consequences of the just outlawed raiding and still struggling to understand how colonial rule might redefine their identities and reshape their lives. Moreover, provoked by the Trans-Saharan trade in kola nuts and human beings, Islam had taken roots in the few urban centres of Northern Ghana and began to create centralized social polities that were culturally and economically outward looking. With this economic advantage they tended to marginalize and exclude a majority of the rural dwellers from their cultural life in order to feed a global system based on slave raiding and exploitative trade.

It is significant that the White Fathers arrived in Northern Ghana via the Islamic Trans-Saharan trade route and had acquired some experience of mission in the Islamic Algeria. In 1868 Cardinal Charles Lavigerie (1825-1892), French national Archbishop of Algiers and primate of Africa, founded the Missionaries of Africa.[9] The immediate objective of the foundation was to provide Christian education, religious instruction, and health security for the Arab children in Algeria orphaned by the great hunger of 1867. However, immediately after its inception, the founder redefined the objective to include the Christian conversion of the Arabs and African peoples south of the Sahara. These three objectives, health, education and Christian conversion, were linked in the travel imagination of the White Fathers as they made progress across the Sahara and into Northern Ghana. In general one would expect all travellers to construct a mental map of their journey destination based on their geographical and cosmographic understanding of the environment, and to trace a spatial trajectory that will direct their movement and reinforce their sense of purpose. The trajectory of the White Fathers' mission-

---

8   For more details on the cultural aspects of Dagara settlements, see Tengan, *Hoe-farming and Social Relations*, 127-159. On Dagara migration and settlement histories see the works of Lentz, "A Dagara Rebellion against Dagomba Rule?"; with Nugent, *Ethnicity in Ghana*; with Kuba and Werthmann, *Les Dagara et leurs voisins*.

9   See Bunson, *OSV's Encyclopedia of Catholic History*, 970-971.

ary activity started in Algiers in 1868 where they had learned to appreciate Arabic culture and Islamic religion. By the time they arrived in Northwest Ghana they had already established missions in the lake regions of Central Africa and in French Sudan, of which Northern Ghana was considered part. The missionaries who arrived in Northwest Ghana in 1929 were well equipped to understand socially and culturally the local environment.

The White Fathers asked the British colonial governor for permission to establish their first mission in Wa, an Islamic enclave in the middle of Dagara country. The colonial government refused this permission because they had already promised to reserve the area of Northwest Ghana for the Anglican missionaries. The White Fathers agreed to go to the Navrongo in the east but continued to protest by taking their complaint as far as Rome and other European capitals. Twenty years later, the governor gave in to their complaints and demands and in March 1929, the first missionaries assigned to the northwest, two Canadians, Fr. Remigius F. McCoy and Fr. Arthur Paquet and one Dutchman, Brother Basilide Koot (a construction specialist) arrived at Jirapa, the heart of Dagara country. They were accompanied by Africans employed as helpers.

The Dagara reception of the White Fathers and subsequently their message of Christianity, from all indications, appeared to have been enthusiastic and popular. To some extent it was first a movement against the strange rule of the colonial administration represented by the chiefs and their headmen, and, secondly, an occasion for the custodians of some traditional institutions to reassert their influence. The earth priests and custodians of such other ritual institutions as the Rain shrine, because of the system of indirect rule, were losing much of their power and influence. Indeed, the house location of the earth priest and the earth cult were no longer the only major centres of attention in every village stead. Real power was beginning to shift to the colonial locations, namely, the chief's house and the district administrative centre. The social, political and cultural tensions due to these shifts of locations were apparent enough and when the Catholic missionaries arrived they immediately noticed the shaky political and cultural grounds on which both Dagara society and the new colonial institutions existed. However, they also recognised the important position the institution of chieftaincy was beginning to play and understood the ambivalence and resentment the people of towards the chiefs and the colonial administration.

The arrival ceremony took on both political and cultural tones:

> The old Jirapa naa (chief), Ganaa, had been alerted by the DC and was at the foot of the hill near the rest house with his headmen and elders when Colonel Whittal and Captain Armstrong arrived followed by Monsignor Morin and his missionaries. It was a memorable reception, made all the more unforgettable by the simultaneous arrival of a swarm of locusts. Gunshots rang out; whether to welcome us or to try to scare off the locusts, I could not be sure.[10]

According to Father McCoy, the district commissioner made it clear right at this time that it was "God's idea to send these men to live and work in their midst, (…) to help them to improve their health with medical care and to improve their knowledge"; and emphasized the point "that the missionaries were not government officials or civil servants but volunteers whose only reason for coming to Jirapa was to help the people."[11]

In order to introduce themselves, the missionaries spoke directly to the people in Moré, a language akin to Dagara, while the commissioner had spoken through an interpreter. They gracefully accepted gifts and made a formal request to settle among the people. The material possessions they had and number of people following them as "family" members indicated that they were arriving as settlers and not as travellers. The chief and the elders understood this, and

10 Cf. McCoy, *Great Things Happen*, 44.
11 Ibid., 45.

1.5 The first church buildings of the White Fathers were temporary structures.
a The first Catholic church in NW Gold Coast, built in Jirapa in 1934 and dedicated to St. Joseph.
b Interior of the first church in Jirapa: sanctuary seen from the nave and Western roof structure.
[McCoy, Great Things Happen, 112-113 and Rome, Archives of the Society of Missionaries of Africa (White Fathers)]

proceeded to settle them in locations and places, that, according to Dagara cosmographic and geographic vision, were considered suitable. According to Father McCoy:

> On Sunday 1 December, the mission site was chosen with the approval of the chief, his elders, and the two *tendaana* Taabe and Moyanga. The site was one of several offered. (…). We chose the actual site for several reasons. Though they were all in the immediate area of Jirapa, this was the most central. It was about a quarter of a mile from the chief's four-storey mud compound, (…). It was a wide open space, superior to the other sites offered in that it lent itself better to eventual expansion. Last but not the least, it was clearly the choice favoured by our host, the chief.[12]

To the chief and the people, the choice of the missionaries indicated their understanding of the culture of hoe-farming and their intention to settle as local people. Every Dagara hoe-farmer would have chosen the same site for exactly the same reasons. It is also very likely that the divination ritual that had been conducted by the chief and elders before deciding which site to offer the missionaries had confirmed the chief's desire to settle the missionaries on this particular site and hence his preference.

The site was not without its own local cultural significance and problems but the point is that it fitted cosmological expectations. The land, according to the same missionary report and in their eyes, was neglected land and of no use to anyone because the soil was poor and full of brambles, stones and soft thorns. Also, according to the local belief, it was a land haunted by evil spirits. These properties, paradoxically, contrary to the missionary understanding that it was unwanted, would tend to make the site very suitable for the location of a ritual institution of social importance. Such a place would have been regarded as a collective property and a public environment. Hence, it makes sense that the chief, the elders and all the people took active part in turning this place into a settlement. Nobody can deal solely with the spirits of nature, evil or not. The report of Father McCoy also confirms this:

> When I arrived on the scene the next morning (Monday), I found the chief himself tracing out the area the huts would occupy. The ground had already been cleared and levelled, and some men were busy digging the earth to make the mud walls while women brought water. There was much well-organised activity, with the result that within ten days the five round huts forming our provisional compound

12 Ibid., 48.

were completely roofed, plastered and ready to use. On Friday, December 13, 1929, only fourteen days after our arrival, the chief and his people moved our belongings from the rest house to the new compound. In one hour, the move was completed. Two charcoal filters were set up for water and we were 'in business' [Fig.1.5].[13]

Experiencing missionary activities as spatial encounters

Unlike the colonial administration, the Catholic fathers began their work through the study of Dagara culture and language and soon came to understand the house-based kinship model, the trajectories of movements of the people as migrating hoe-farmers, and the importance that was attached to spatial locations as cultic institutions and as ritual centres. From their method of operation, they seemed to be aware that Dagara valued ritual participation over and above belief in gods or one supreme god. The Dagara were always concerned with rites to the different personified spatial categories constituting the vertical and horizontal axes of the cosmos and established cults in every location in order to effectively deal with the different spirits and deities located in them. The missionaries, therefore, saw their task of conversion, not so much as bringing religion to the people, but as introducing to them the Christian god as the one and only true god.

The missionaries' encounter with the spirits and deities of the spatial location would demonstrate to the local population how much value should be attached to their message of evangelisation. Significantly, the White Fathers began their work by inviting people to prayer and devotion under trees and in any location when there was the opportunity, instead of going to the houses of the people with the Bible in their hands or waiting in the mission houses for people to come to them. As it turned out, devotional prayer (*puoro*) soon became a very fashionable mode of religious practice, and the missionaries, together with those who went along with them, became known as those who pray (*puorbɛ*) and Christianity itself was translated as *puoro* (prayer).[14] In order to be a Christian or member of the "praying group" (*puorbɛ*), the missionaries demanded three things from the people. The response from the elders through a spokesman and after some deliberation is very illuminating:

> First you must promise to stop making sacrifices to spirits. Second, you must allow your people freedom to come to pray at the mission whenever they want to do so. And third, you must not force your daughters to marry anyone against their will. (...) The second thing God asks we all agree to that, he announced. We will not stand in the way of anyone from our village who wishes to pray with the Christians. And we can even agree to the third thing if God really insists on it, though we think He would not insist quite so much if He knew our daughters as we do. But as for the first thing He asks... He looked down and shook his head slowly. What will happen if we desert the spirits? We are afraid.[15]

The question here is what danger did Dagara believe came from these spirits and could it be taken away by prayer to the one true god instead of sacrifices to the spirits? The spirits were the spatial categories concentrically arranged in vertical and horizontal axes, within which the Dagara individually and collectively were entangled through a network of kinship relations. They ultimately belonged to either of the two spatial categories making up the cosmos, namely, the space of Rain and the space of Earth. In other words, the elders understood the request to stop sacrifices to spirits as a ban on their relationship with their ancestors and the living beings or spirits of nature (*k]nt]me*) who, as the *bagr* mythical narrations indicate, are the main sources of knowledge about hoe-farming and all other forms of production and reproduction.

13 Ibid., 49.
14 Tengan, "Dagara Christian Conversion," 134-135.
15 McCoy, *Great Things Happen*, 112.

Jack Goody has described Dagara as having a quasi-religious system consisting of institutional practices centring upon the communication between men and gods, but having neither a coherent system of beliefs nor a defined unchanging body of knowledge to unlock.[16] We would dare say that the gods Goody identified were the same spatial spirits that the missionaries encountered. Sean Hawkins on the other hand, has accused the missionaries of projecting the notion of the Christian god unto Dagara historicity much in the same way as the colonial administrators had tried to justify the institutionalisation of chieftaincy as part of a natural evolutionary process.[17] In his view, the missionaries partly invented and popularised the use of the term *Naamwin* as chief-deity within Dagara cosmology in order to see in him the Christian god that was waiting to reveal himself to the Dagara. The issues surrounding the Dagara notion of god and the process of their Christian conversions are much too complex to be fully treated here. It seems to us however, that, considering the fact that the Dagara belonged to a wider cultural area of the Mole-Dagbani group of people where the terms chiefly (*naa*) and god (*mwin*) are very well developed and often associated with each other to refer to god, the concept of god was not totally an invention. Indeed, the term *Naamwin* is very well developed in the *bagr* myths and rituals as something that is occupying the mental and imaginary space of reasoning. What was certainly an invention was the notion that god (*Naamwin*), as far as the missionaries were concerned, existed not as a Spatial Being with an identifiable location and personality but as an abstract being that is present everywhere and at all times and cannot be represented in a fetish.

It is beyond the scope of this article to delve into all the details concerning shifts in Dagara belief system in terms of Christian conversion. What is most relevant here are the spatial shifts of religious and other socio-cultural practices away from the house-based and kinship-based spatial configuration of family and kin devotion to spirits, deities, and so-called fetishes to a centralised church focus with a global outlook and vision. The Dagara viewed the missionary encounter within their social, cosmic and environmental spaces as something providential and a movement of cultural continuity that was in tune with their way of life as hoe-farmers. In an earlier work, we explained that the life of a hoe-farmer consists partly in cultivating farmlands and rearing animals within settled environments laid out as houses, homesteads and village settlements; and also partly in relating with persons and institutions within extending habitat. There seems to be no doubt that the Dagara viewed, even at very early stages, the missionaries and their settlement activity as a sort of divine providential gift that would help them enhance and enrich their hoe-farming way of life that had been under threat from centralised Islamic kingdoms and more recently, by the colonial administration. The message of ritual practice and the settlement process of establishing ritual and cultural institutions in different locations made more sense than the recruitment of force labor to build roads or to work on the chiefs' farms or cocoa plantations and gold mines in the South.

For the first time in their history, the Dagara saw themselves reorganising their whole country through the creation of parishes as centres and the building of churches, clinics and schools as new institutional centres. The creation of each parish centre always started with the selection of a particular tree easily accessible to a number of villages as a ritual centre and also as a place for catechism. The choice was always an agreement between the local community, the earth priest of the area, and the missionary fathers. The tree often established a close relationship between the new missionary phenomenon and the old rites to the earth as a traditional deity. The second stage of missionary settlement consisted of erecting chapels or small churches in the parish centres and instituting the Sunday worship, which required the participation of all Christians and all desiring to be one.[18] The cultural translation which

---

16 Goody, *The Myth of the Bagre*, 14-16.
17 Hawkins, "Disguising Chiefs and Gods as History." Local scolars reacted to this view in several ways; see Bekye, *Divine Revelation and Traditional Religion*; Der, "Missionary Enterprise in Northern Ghana."
18 Originally, the Dagara operated a six-day week with each day assigned to a village area within walking distance of five other villages as its market day (see Tengan, *Hoe-farming and Social Relations*, 116-118). They also had one day which they set aside during the farming season as a day of rest from farm labor. They called this the market day of not farming (*takodaa*). It seems that it was never commonly applied at the same time for everybody but individual communities set dates that they found convenient.

took place among the people was the recognition of Sunday not only as a day of common worship but also as an additional day of rest from farm labor and a day devoted to economic activity. As a result, large markets were soon established at a close distance to the church buildings and small townships began to develop within those areas. In terms of temporal movement, the structure of the seven-day week and the names, Monday to Sunday, as well as the structure of twelve months within the year, came to stand for activities specifically related to missionary and colonial encounters and the institutions that they established. It was always expected that the chapels and small churches roofed with grass were temporary buildings. As such, the third stage typically consisted in building very large church structures with advanced architectural designs and using foreign materials (cement, iron and steel, roof sheets etc.). These were often soon followed by the building of permanent residences for the priests, a clinic or hospital and later, the establishment of mission schools.[19]

The erection of the churches and parish buildings, often involved the participation of the whole community, men, women and children [Fig.1.6]. Even though a good amount of the money needed to erect the buildings came from outside the region, the enthusiasm and the energy with which the people made their own contributions, including financial, labor and other forms of participation, convinced them that they built the edifices through their own effort. This conviction, not only lead them to the total appropriation of the structures and their significant meanings, but above all to the conscious effort of redefining and integrating them as indigenous socio-cultural and religious entities. As such, they did not perceive missionary activity as a limited well-defined event within a specified time and space frame. On the contrary, they came to appropriate mission structures and thought patterns as part of a new cultural identity that would enable them to deal with changes taking place within real time.

The historical sketch provided by the missionaries, for example, on the establishment of Nandom parish in 1933 and its continuous growth into a deanery with many sub-parishes captures the dynamics of the bonding relationships between missionary activity and the Dagara. In this case, it is clear that the institutions of the Catholic Church, both as physical structures and as cultural symbolic objects, became the central focus and cardinal point around which Dagara social, cultural, economic and political reproductions take place today. In contrast with the colonial buildings and institutions, such as the rest houses and the chieftaincy palaces, which have continued to remain at the margins of society [Fig.1.4] and in some instances have virtually collapsed or disappeared, the bonding relations between the

1.6 Jirapa Church 1987. Missionary church buildings have become central locations replacing the chief's palace.
a Father McCoy and Joan Cameron Dewart with a group of local children in front of St. Joseph Church, Jirapa. [Photo: Dewart, January 1987]
b Interior of St. Joseph Church, Jirapa. [Photo: Dewart, 1987]
[McCoy, Great Things Happen and Rome, Archives of the Society of Missionaries of Africa]

19 The late development of mission schools was not a choice of the missionaries, but the colonial government did not allow them at the beginning. The Northern territories, especially the Northwest, according to colonial policy, was reserved as a pool for recruiting cheap labor for the cocoa plantations and mines in the South. Permission was only first given to build school in 1940.

1.7 Transformations in missionary church buildings and encounter relations: the rural church in Nandom and the urban cathedral in Tamale.
a Front view of Nandom Church, 1937.
b Front view of Our Lady of Annunciation Cathedral in Tamale, 1970s.
[Peter Cardinal Dery Album, Tamale and Alexis Tengan digital collection]

missionaries and the Dagara people through the building of churches and parishes continued to extend in all ways and in all directions. The following entry by Father Larochelle, the leader of the missionary team who constructed the church in Nandom, sums up the manner Dagara reproduced the missionary encounter:

> The people kept interest in the priest and kept coming to help in the work, bringing cowries to pay the masons and also to purchase cement and sheets. In 1935, the increase of people in Nandom market caused inflation. I called the workers and announced to them that the salaries would be increased to 300 cowries a day. The next day, the workers came in group and said: "About what you told us yesterday, we cannot accept an increase. This church is the house of OUR father, and we want to build ourselves the house of OUR father. (…). We refuse the increase.[20]

The result was that within a few years, "the stone church, which was begun in August 1935, the largest church at the time for Africa, was roofed in April 1936 and officially blessed by the Apostolic Delegate, Archbishop Antonio Riberi, on 6 January 1937."[21] [Fig.1.7] In terms of church as people: in 1934, Nandom had 165 baptised Christians; by 1940, it had 8,000, and in 1951 they numbered 19,000. The processes described for Nandom repeated themselves in 1952 in two other locations, namely, Ko and Daffiama.

In 1960 three new parishes were added. 1966 and 1971 saw single additions every year. In 1980, four parishes were created, another four in 1990 and five more in 1999. The Christian population has also increased, and the services provided by the Catholic institutions including the ritual services have become commonly accepted within Dagara society.[22]

Conclusion

As migrating hoe-farmers, the Dagara view space and movement within space as function of their hoe-farming practices. Their categorisation of space and spatial elements helped them understand their own movements and actions and that of others. One could say that the colonial movement into Dagaraland brought peace and opened up the Northwest for free movement of people including the Dagara. The manner of its implantation did not lead fully to its appropriation as a cultural practice. Colonial institutions were tolerated but not enthusiastically accepted. On the other hand, before the missionary encounter, the Dagara had already began to develop ways of expanding ritual and religious networks of institutions, both physically and mentally. They had done this firstly through the elaborate architectural and social structure of their own houses and homestead and village stead as residential spaces and, secondly, through the equally elaborate farming rituals including recitation of the myth of cultural origins, the *bagr*

20 See Gregoire, *That They May Have Life*, 38.
21 Ibid.
22 All figures have been taken from the report of the 1979 Jubilee Committee report (see Ibid.).

which allowed them to circulate between their various natural localities and habitats. This process, which began sometime before their encounter with the Catholic missionaries, is in their view being completed through the spatial configuration of parish locations and built institutions. Today, the parishes are not only religious centres but also centres for all social, cultural and economic activities. For many big villages which are now parish centres, the six-day market week has been abandoned in favor of a fixed Sunday market. Consequently, every Sunday, processions of people from the different surrounding villages of the major parishes, such as Jirapa, Nandom and Ko, will march to these centres carrying their market wares as well as wearing their Sunday dresses. They will first attend the Catholic mass service and spend the rest of the day marketing and socialising within the parish grounds.

BIBLIOGRAPHY

Arhin, K., ed. *The Papers of George Ekem Ferguson*. Leiden/Cambridge, 1984.

Bekye, Paul Kuusegme. *Divine Revelation and Traditional Religion with Particular Reference to the Dagaaba of West Africa*. Rome: Leberit Press, 1991.

Bunson, Matthew E. *OSV's Encyclopedia of Catholic History*. Huntington, Indiana: Our Sunday Visitor Pub. Division, 2004.

Dapila, Fabian N. "Catholicism and the Enculturation Process among the Dagaaba of Ghana: the Road to Progress." *Journal of Dagaare Studies* (JDS), 1 (2001) 1.

Der, Benedict G. "Missionary Enterprise in Northern Ghana 1906-1975: A Study in Impact." Ph.D Thesis, Legon: University of Ghana, 1983.

Goody, Jack. *The Social Organisation of the LoWiili*. London: Oxford University Press, 1967.

Goody, Jack. *The Myth of the Bagre*. Oxford: Claredon Press, 1972.

Hagberg, Sten and Tengan, Alexis B., eds. *Bonds and Boundaries in Northern Ghana and Southern Burkina Faso. Uppsala Studies in Cultural Anthropology*. Uppsala: Acta Universitatis Upsaliensis, 2000.

Hawkins, Sean. *Writing and Colonialism in Northern Ghana: The Encounter between the LoDagaa and "the World on Paper."* Toronto/Buffalo: University of Toronto Press, 2002.

Hawkins, Sean. "Disguising Chiefs and Gods as History: Questions on the Acephalousness of LoDagaa Politics and Religion." *Africa*, 66 (1996) 2, 202-247.

Gregoire, Victor, ed. *That They May Have Life: An Account of the Activities of the Church in North-West Ghana 1929-1979*. Wa Catholic Press, 1979.

Kuukure, Edward. *The Destiny of Man: Dagaare Beliefs in Dialogue with Christian Eschatology*. Frankfurt am Main / New York: P. Lang, 1985.

Lentz, Carola. "This is Ghanaian Territory! Land Conflicts on a West African Border." *American Ethnologist*, 30 (2003) 2, 273-289.

Lentz, Carola. "A Dagara Rebellion against Dagomba Rule?: Contested Stories of Origin in North-Western Ghana." *Journal of African History*, 35 (1994), 457-492.

Lentz, Carola and Nugent, Paul. *Ethnicity in Ghana: The Limits of Invention*. London: Macmillan, 2000.

Lentz, Carola; Kuba, Richard and Werthmann, Katja. *Les Dagara et leurs voisins. Histoire de peuplement et relations interethniques au sud-ouest du Burkina Faso*. Berichte des Sonderforschungsbereichs 268 "Westafrikanische Savanne", 15. Frankfurt, 2001.

Lobnibe, Isidore. "Writing and Colonialism in Northern Ghana: The Encounter between the LoDagaa and the 'World on Paper.'" *American Anthropologist*, 106 (2004) 2, 409-410.

McCoy, Remigius F. *Great Things Happen: A Personal Memoir of the First Christian Missionary among the Dagaabas and Sisaalas of Northern Ghana*. Montreal: Society of Missionaries of Africa, 1988.

Saaka, Yakubu, ed. *Regionalism and Public Policy in Northern Ghana*. New York: Lang, 2001.

Tengan, Alexis B. "Dagara Bagr: Ritualising Myth of Social Foundation." *Africa: Journal of the International Institute*, 69 (1999), 595-533.

Tengan, Alexis B. *Hoe-farming and Social Relations among the Dagara of Northwestern Ghana and Southwestern Burkina Faso*. Frankfurt am Main: Peter Lang, 2000.

Tengan, Alexis B. "Space, Bonds and Social Order: Dagara House-based Social System," in: Hagberg, Sten and Tengan, Alexis B., eds. *Bonds and Boundaries in Northern Ghana and Southern Burkina Faso. Uppsala Studies in Cultural Anthropology, 30*. Uppsala: Acta Universitatis Upsaliensis, 2000b, 87-103.

Tengan, Alexis B. "Social Categories and Seniority in a House-Based Society," in: Makoni, Sinfree and Stroeken, Koenraad, eds. *Ageing in Africa: Sociolinguistic and Anthropological Approaches*. London: Ashgate, 2002, 137-152.

Tengan, Alexis B. *Mythical Narratives in Ritual: Dagara black bagr*. Brussels / New York: P.I.E.-Peter Lang, 2006.

Tengan, Alexis. B. *Christianity and Cultural History in Northern Ghana: A Portrait of Cardinal Peter Poreku Dery (1918-2008)*. New York: Peter Lang, 2013.

Tengan, Alexis B., ed. *Religion, Culture, Society and Integral Human Development: Proceedings of Cardinal Poreku Deri Third Colloquium*. Legon-Accra: Sub-Saharan Publishers, 2017.

Tengan, Edward B. "The Sisala Universe: Its Composition and Structure." *Journal of Religion in Africa*, 20 (1990) 1, 2-19.

Tengan, Edward B. *The Land as Being and Cosmos: The Institution of the Earth Cult Among the Sisala of Northwestern Ghana*. Frankfurt am Main: Peter Lang, 1991.

Tengan, Edward B. *The Social Structure of the Dagara: The House and the Matriclan as Axes of Dagara Social Organization*. Tamale: St. Victor's Major Seminary, 1994.

Tengan, Edward B. "Dagara Christian Conversion in Terms of Personal Memory," in: Hagberg, Sten and Tengan, Alexis B., eds. *Bonds and Boundaries in Northern Ghana and Southern Burkina Faso. Uppsala Studies in Cultural Anthropology*. Uppsala: Acta Universitatis Upsaliensis, 2000, 133-143.

van der Geest, Kees. *"We're Managing!?" Vulnerability and Responses to Climate Variability and Change Among Rural Households in Northwest Ghana*. University of Amsterdam, 2002.

van der Geest, Kees. *"We're Managing!" Climate Change and Livelihood Vulnerability in Northwest Ghana*. Leiden: African Studies Centre, 2004.

Kleine Serie Nr. 2

Lichtstrahlen
im dunkeln Erdteile

1. bis 5. Tausend

Was Kambajungen treiben

Von

Ernst Brutzer,
Missionar

Leipzig 1904
Verlag der Ev.-luth. Mission

5 Pfennige

2
Redeeming Ukamba
Word and World, 1893-1905

Maarten Onneweer

Expectations of Light in the Dark Continent

At the turn of the nineteenth century East Africa saw the rapid expansion of several missionary societies such as the Anglican Church Missionary Society, the Methodist Church, the Scottish Industrial Mission and the lesser-known Evangelical Lutheran Mission of Leipzig. For fear of being left behind by the competition, these societies engaged in a "hurly burly race," as Oliver calls, it to set up stations and claim new mission areas farther away from the East African coast.[1] The missionary scramble for the interior enticed the Leipzig Mission to fulfil its long standing promise to the explorer and missionary Johann Ludwig Krapf (1810-1881) to set up stations among the Akamba people.

This chapter addresses the advent of their missionary encounter, the period from 1893 to 1905 in which the missionaries settled in Ukamba present Kenya and were confronted with extreme droughts, pests and famine as well as a people (the Akamba) uninterested in their mission. In this period the missionaries brought an enlightenment-critical episteme to Ukamba, one that included transformative ideas on the mission buildings and their role in the environment. Although these missionaries all studied theology and 'sincerely' believed in their dogmas, their attitudes and actions in the encounter reveals several paradoxes and uncertainties. We see how the expectations of 'Light for the Dark Continent' directed a day-to-day struggle to realize materially and visually the Word in Ukamba.

Like African reactions to many other new missions in the East African interior, the Akamba people ignored the mission completely and would not convert until after 1905.[2] Until that time the Leipzig missionaries seemed to have experienced only hardship, insecurity and disappointment. Reading their letters to Germany one is struck by the particular voicing of this hardship as a form of martyrdom. Missionary Ittameier lamented their misfortune in a newsletter called "Outcry from Ukamba:"

> To our great sorrow we are still like the preacher in the wilderness. All around us there is nothing but wilderness and bush (...) and the same goes for spiritual matters in the land of Ukamba. Wilderness, nothing but wilderness and there is no indication that any part of the Word that was spoken from the cross will fall in good ground.[3]

And so it went on for about thirteen years, the unrelenting articulation of gloomy romanticism, the missionaries failing their self-set goals but still heroically cultivating that failure in Biblical terms, equating the morality of the people with the environment. What should we make of this link between the morality of the people and the environment expressed in Biblical terms? The "evangelic literalism"[4] used by the missionaries in these accounts included particular ideas on the moral agency of the Ukamba environment that require further analyses. The accounts indicate not only how the missionaries perceived the Ukamba environment, but also what would change it: the Word. To understand the spatial configuration of the Leipzig Mission's settlement in Ukamba we need to ask the following questions: what constitutes

2.1 Ernst Brutzer, Was Kambajungen treiben, *edited by the Verlag der Evangelisch-Lutherischen Mission, Leizig, 1904. [Frankfurt am Main, Universitätsbibliothek J.C. Senckenberg: Kol Bl 53/1]*

1. Oliver, *The Missionary Factor*, 169; Fleisch, *Hundert Jahre Lutherischer Mission*, 241; Mbula, *Penetration of Christianity*, 44; Strayer, "Mission History in Africa."
2. See Pels, *A Politics of Presence*, on the importance to analyse the mission as a material presence. See Keane, "Sincerity, 'Modernity', and the Protestants." In general, the theme of this article is part of my PhD research entitled "The Social Life of Springs: Encountering Landscapes of Spirits and Development in the Kitui District Kenya," CNWS grant, Leiden University 2006-2010. Oliver, *The Missionary Factor*, 172; Kew, National Archives UK, CO/533/27; *Evangelisch Lutherisches Missionsblatt* (hereafter *ELM*) 1907, 144 and 1910, 305-309; Fleisch, *Hundert Jahre Lutherischer Mission*, 259, concluding remarks on the reasons for the conversions after 1905.
3. *ELM* 1895, 188. "Wir gleichen zu unserem großen Schmerze noch immer den Prediger in der Wüste. Denn wie er um uns herum in weitem Kreise Wüste und Wald ist (...), so ist es auch in geistlicher Beziehung um Ukamba-Lande. Wüste, bloße Wüste, ohne sichtbare Wahrnehmung, dass sich ein Teil derselben infolge des gepredigten Wortes vom Kreuze in gutes Ackerland verwandeln wollte."
4. Crapanzano, *Serving the Word*, passim.

the relation between narratives, like the one of the preacher in the wilderness, and the mission's presence in Ukamba as a physical environment? Can there be a spatial or material dimension to an imperative like 'Light for the Dark Continent' that is specific to the Leipzig Mission in Ukamba, one that emerged through or in spite of their encounter with the environment and the people? And if so, how then did these missionaries work these idioms into the material world?

The following sections show how the missionaries tried to represent Ukamba as a virgin land with a culture untouched by European influences, but still a culture containing elements of a divine original. To redeem this original from its contemporary condition became their mission (hence the title of this chapter). The efforts of the Leipzig Mission to bring a certain past into being turned history into a strategy, a practice for the present, akin to what Eric Hirsch and Charles Steward call *historicism* or *historicity*: "the manner in which persons operating under the constraints of social ideologies make sense of the past, while anticipating the future."[5] Now many, if not all, people operate under some constraint of social ideology, in this case an orthodox interpretation allowed only certain pasts to be imaginable and others appear as forgeries. The mission in Ukamba, a mission under people fallen from previous grace, required that the missionaries should seek out these elements of Akamba culture close to or reflecting a historical Biblical original, a true Ukamba. In the missionaries discourse it was called finding the "elements of truth" that still remained with the Akamba.[6]

The (evangelical) interrogation of a culture produced its own topography: the land of Ukamba. A critical topographical moment occurs when the missionaries sought to turn Ukamba into a historical fact through the attempt to ascribe a topographical historicity.

The main method the missionaries used to bring the Word to Ukamba was by itinerating and bringing the service to the heathens (*Heidenpredigt*). Another method, or perhaps technology, more particular to the Leipzig Mission and closer to the subject of this volume entailed the effort to make the Light present through the mission building. The missionaries hoped to establish a material presence in which the Word could be read and contrasted with the rest of the environment.[7] Consistent with their theology, they sought to make the Word part of the mission buildings, as translated evangelic presence.

The Leipzig Mission was part of the Evangelical Lutheran German neo-confessionalist movement that advocated a critique of enlightenment.[8] As Ernst Troeltsch summarized, the neo-confessionalists critiqued the biblicism of the Lutheran Church and wanted to "bypass the indistinctness and confessional indifference, with its subjectivism and its emphasis on a laymen religion, towards a desire for determinacy, a more objective clerical spirit, greater dogmatic precision and, thereby, a return to the confession."[9] The neo-confessionalists held that in the beginning Adam and Eve had the kernel of Lutheran Christendom as ideal religion, but lost this through the original sin. From there, two directions were taken. One direction led via enlightenment, a rationalism that negatively affected Protestantism, giving it a philosophical arrogance that made Protestants think they could surpass God through rationalism. The other direction led to Heathendom: people who lived in the twilight of humanity and aspired only Darkness in what was left of the original Truth of Christianity on earth.[10] Leipzig missionaries thus contested the Protestant idea that the interpretation of the material world was subjective, open to scientific appraisal and critical enquiry. Instead they sought a more objective Truth in the world, one that required the manifestation and materialization of the Word in the world.

---

5 Hirsch and Stewart, "Introduction," 262; also Keane, "From Fetishism to Sincerity;" Bhabha, *The Location of Culture*, 108; Pels, *A Politics of Presence*, 45.

6 See Troeltsch, *Protestantisches Christentum*, 495.

7 This relation between the material dimension of the mission-stations and the Word can easily be overlooked. As Meyer also comments: "Still more neglected have been struggles between missions and converts about the proper relationship between mind and worldly matters, between the Word and things. It seems that thereby Protestant missions' complicated stance towards material matters has eschewed closer examination." Meyer, *Translating the Devil*, 313.

8 *Aufklärungskritik*, see Nehring, *Orientalismus und Mission*; Scherer, "The Triumph of Confessionalism;" Troeltsch, *Protestantisches Christentum*.

9 Troeltsch, *Protestantisches Christentum*, 494: "Er führte über sich bei seiner Unbestimmtheit und Konfessionellen Indifferenz, bei seinem Subjektivismus uns deiner Betonung der Laienreligion hinaus zu dem Wunsche nach größerer Bestimmtheit, objektiverem Amtsgeiste, größerer dogmatische Präzision und damit wieder zurück zu den Symbolen."

10 Nehring, *Orientalismus und Mission*, 58-65; Troeltsch, *Protestantisches Christentum*, 495.

Ukamba calling, the ascribed homeland

The Hersbrucker Mission initiated three Akamba stations in East Africa before the Leipzig Mission appeared in 1893. Two of the Hersbrucker stations, Mbungu and Jimba, were near the coast, both established in 1886. The intended subject people, the Akamba, proved to be difficult since they often shifted responding to droughts, trade opportunities and threats from other groups like the Maasai. In seven years the coastal missions saw few converts of any kind, let alone Akamba, most of whom had vacated the vicinity of the missions after its settlement. With that in mind Missionaries Hoffman and Ittameier established a third station, away from the coast: the Ikutha mission, in the heartland of the Akamba. They built the station in 1893 under difficult circumstances; the route from the coast was a ten-day march through the so-called *nyika*, the infamous dry wilderness between Mombassa and the hinterland. Groups like the Wanyika, Maasai and Galla often plundered caravans and made it very difficult to get provisions or send mail.[11]

In the spirit of the scramble for Africa, encouraged by the suggestion of a railway, and possessing more funds than the Hersbrucker Mission, the Leipzig Mission took over the existing Akamba stations Mbungu, Jimba and Ikutha in 1893. The Leipzig Mission's newsletter enthusiastically though somewhat erroneously heralded the Akamba mission as 'a new mission field', calling forth new young theologians, for which "One dares to hope that among them there is no shortage of capable young men who, instead of standing idle in the market place, are prepared to follow the Lord's call for workers on the mission field."[12] The interest and hope of the mission's officials went out to the Ikutha station. They had travelled to see the three Akamba mission stations and asserted that, more than the people at the coast who were 'spoiled' by other European influences, the 'untouched heathens' around the Ikutha mission offered greater potential for a so-called native church.

The native church, or organic folk church as Mission Father Graul coined it, is particular to the Leipzig Mission and implies a strong notion of native homeland, an area in which the mission should bring back the original culture of the natives by connecting to remnant Christian elements in their original culture.[13] To understand the missionary's topographical production of Ukamba as homeland properly, that is, as a work of imagination, the historical context of the area of the mission needs to be taken into account. What the mission called the homeland of the Akamba in which the organic folk church was to emerge, was an ascribed homeland, which was called from an Edenic past from the evidence found in the present. It was ascribed in that the mission started naming and writing the history of the area. It was also ascribed because the missionaries believed it was written (in the Bible) that in the beginning, all people were nations but the heathens wondered off from the original plan.[14]

We know from earlier sources that the Akamba stronghold was a trade and caravan network that extended from settlements at the Mrima coast between Mombasa and Tanga, to Kilimanjaro and Mount Kenya and allegedly even as far as lake Nyanza (Victoria). Depending on the strength of enemy Wanyika, Galla and Maasai groups, the centre of the trade route regularly shifted, as did the Akamba settlements around it. Before 1850 the Akamba used an eastern route along the Tana River until this track became too risky due to attacks by the Galla. It led Akamba to shift the route to the west where the explorer and missionary Krapf found it on his quest to find the route to Unyamwesi, the Tana river and the source of the Nile.[15] The Leipzig missionaries followed the same route when they settled Ukamba. The route is represented on one of their maps. It is separated from the coast by a belt of wilderness, a twelve-day journey wide, and from the mountains by a six-day journey through uninhabited land [Fig. 2.2].

---

11 Fleisch, *Hundert Jahre Lutherischer Mission*, 244; *ELM* 1893; Krapf, *Reisen in Ostafrika*; Hildebrandt, "Ethnographische Notizen;" Stuart Watt, *In the Heart of Savagedom*.

12 *ELM* 1893, 5: "Man darf erwarten, dass es auch unter ihnen nicht fehlen wird an tüchtigen jungen Männern, welche, statt müßig am Markte zu stehen bereit sind, dem Rufe des Herrn nach Arbeitern auf dem Missionsfelde zu folgen." Cf. Mat 20: 1-5.

13 *ELM* 1893, 45; Nehring, *Orientalismus und Mission*; Scherer, "The Triumph of Confessionalism."

14 Hoekendijk, *Kirche und Volk*, 60. It is significant in this respect that the area of the Akamba mission later became the area of Ukamba and the mission's borders are still the same as the administrative borders today. On the role of imagining and topography, see Appadurai, *Modernity at Large*, 5; Anderson, *Imagined Communities*.

15 Krapf, *Reisen in Ostafrika*, 136; Ndolo, "The Dynamics of Social Change;" Krapf, *Travels, Researches and Missionary Labours*; Lamphear, "The Kamba and the Northern Mrima Coast."

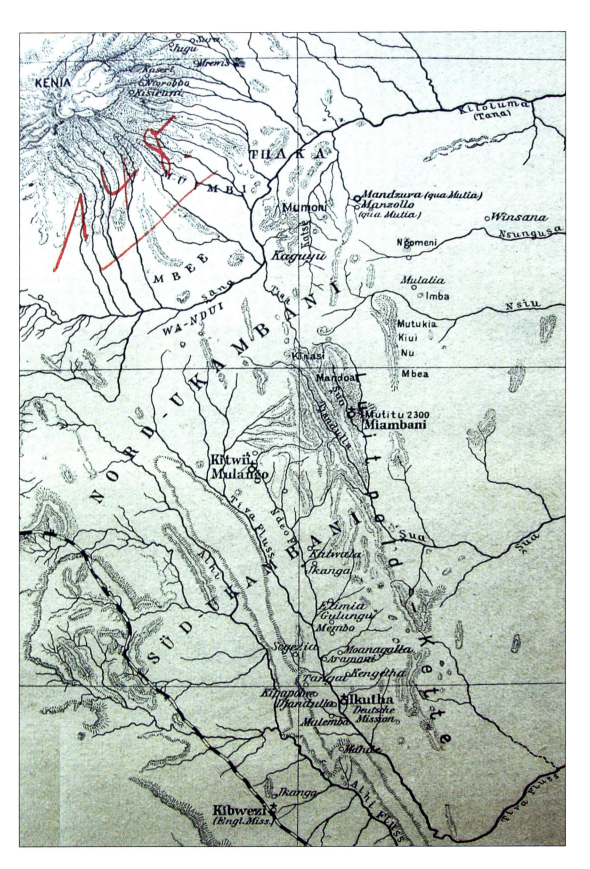

2.2 Map of Ukamba, 1896.
[Leipzig, Evangelich-Lutherisches Missionswerk, Archive]

The missionary's topographical representations of Ukamba show several peculiarities. The first is the position of the caravan route. Contrary to the impressions this map of 1896 gives, the main caravan route through Ukamba had already shifted again to the west around 1880 and went through the areas of Ulu, or Machakos as it is called now (not represented on the map). Furthermore, the map shows the mission stations in the centre of Ukamba and figures the caravan route and the *Prinz Luitpold Kette* as the backbone of the area. One of the first missionaries in Ikutha (Günther Säuberlich) and the explorer George Kolb, author of the map, introduced Ukamba as follows:

> To the north and east of the two snow-clad mountains of East Africa (Kenya and Kilimanjaro) lies a great highland. It is separated from the coast by a belt of wilderness, a twelve-day journey wide, and from the mountains by a six-day journey through uninhabited land: that is the land of Ukamba. In the west and south the river Athi, in the north and east the Tana, flows around it. From north to south a large chain of hills traverses this area, I have called it the Prins Luitpold chain since the Akamba did not have a common name for it" (...) [In Ukamba, unlike other Bantu areas] the women and children do not run away at the sight of a caravan; to the contrary, the young ladies exchange friendly greetings and the young lads (...) readily start a conversation and then volunteer to lead you to the next village.[16]

Another peculiarity in the topographic representation of Ukamba can be deduced from the above description. At the time the exploration took place there was only one station in the Ukamba region as Säuberlich described it, the Ikutha mission. Though the Jimba and Mbungu stations were not within the territory of Ukamba, they were set up as Akamba missions. Many Akamba lived along this route and, even though converts were not forthcoming, they were the only people the Leipzig Mission focussed on. Eventually, the missionaries started to call these stations *Vorstation*. This is literally, "front station" translatable as outposts for preparation of the 'real' Akamba mission.

The third and most striking peculiarity in the topographical representation is that the areas outside the reach of the Leipzig Mission are omitted. On the map as well as the above description there is no mention of the area west of Athi river, the district Ulu (today Machakos). Akamba inhabited this area and it was allotted to the Anglican Church Missionary Society. Even though the Ulu area became the commercial and political centre of Ukamba, the Leipzig missionaries did not see Ulu as the real Ukamba but named it "New Ukamba," implying that the true homeland of the Akamba lay in the area that coincided with the mission. Evidence for the novelty of the Akamba settlement in Ulu and at the coast was speculative to say the least. Most other scholars that deal with the migration and origin of the Akamba take the Ulu area as the first settlement of the Akamba when they came from areas around Kilimanjaro. Krapf on the other hand proposed that the Akamba migrated from the coast. These debates aside, the point is that the Leipzig missionaries rooted 'their' Akamba in the mission area, thereby ascribing a topographical origin of the 'tribe' in the area of the mission.[17]

The missionaries' ethnographic works in Ukamba itself can also be seen as the ascription of a topographic historicity. Most of them were keen collectors of myths, fables and folktales, but these efforts were not merely for the sake of curiosity.[18] Through the collection and representation of these narratives the missionaries tried to attach a formalized and localized oral literature to the Akamba of the area. The intention behind establishing this body of knowledge, together with their other ethnographic projects like collecting data on the religious ideas of the Akamba, was to create a standard curriculum of the Akamba located in the area of the mission. It was agreed among the mission-

16 *ELM* 1898, 175: "Im Norden und Osten der beiden schneebedeckten Bergriesen Ostafrikas (Kenia und Kilimandscharo) lieft eine große Hochebene, durch einen zwölf Tagereisen breiten Wüstengürtel von der Küste und durch sechs Tagereisen unbewohnten Gebietes vom Hochgebirge getrennt – das Land Ukamba. Im Westen und Süden wird es vom Athi umflossen, im Norden und Osten vom Tana. Von Süden nach Norden wird unser Gebiet von einem großen Gebirge durchzogen, das ich, da die Wakamba keinen Gesamtnamen dafür haben „die Prinz Leutpold Kette" genannt habe." (...) 176: "Hier laufen Frauen und Kinder nicht weg beim anblickt der Karawane; im Gegenteil, die jungen Mädchen grüssen freundlich und die jungen Burschen, besonders im Norden des Gebietes, treten aus den Weg und fangen ein Gespräch an und gewöhnlich übernimmt einer freiwillig die Führung bis zum nächsten Dorfe." cf. Kolb, *Von Mombasa durch Ukambani*; Höhnel, *Discovery of Lakes Rudolf and Stefanie*; Oliver, *The Missionary Factor*. Prinz Luitpolt (1821-1912) was the prince regent of Bavaria at the time. Missionary Säuberlich started the Akamba mission when he was still working for the Hernsbrucker Mission, which is in Bayern. The name was not taken over by the British authorities and to this day there is no common name for the chain of hills.

17 *ELM* 1898, 176. See Hobley, *Ethnology of a-Kamba*; Dundas, "The History of Kitui;" Lindblom, *The Akamba in British East Africa*; Jackson, *An Ethnohistorical Study of the Oral Traditions*; Muthiani, *Akamba from Within*; Ndeti, *Elements of Akamba Live*; Krapf, *Reisen in Ostafrika*.

18 See Lewinski, *Acht Kamba Märchen*; Kanig in *ELM* 1902.

19 *ELM* 1902, 16: "denn sie führen uns in die von alters her im Volke heimliche Vorstellungskreise ein, an die wir bei unserer Verkündigung des Evangeliums anknüpfen müssen, wen wir verstanden werden wollen."

20 Ibid., 17: "In ähnlicher Weise, wie manche alttestamentliche Geschichten die Entstehung gewisser Ortsnamen erklären – Beerseba, Eidesbrunnen, von dem Vertrage, den an diesem Brunnen Abraham mit Abimelech unter Eidschwüren schloss, oder Bethel, Gotteshaus, weil an dieser Stätte Jakob im Traum den Himmel offen sah – dienen auch einzelne Sagen der Wakamba zur Deutung von Ortsnamen."

21 Ibid., 18: "Man sieht, wie flüssig die Sagen noch sind" (author's emphasis).

aries that if they were to use ethnography to look for means to advance Christianity, it would be most useful to focus on songs and myths. Missionary Gerhard Kanig optimistically commented: "these [songs and myths] introduce us to the original realm of imagination of the people. And if we want to be understood, we have to connect to this when we preach the gospel."[19] To test the opportunities for this ethnographic connection, Kanig analysed a genre of Akamba myths explaining the origins of place names. He described two myths that deal with the origin of places Wiitu and Nzambani, both in present day Kitui district. Kanig describes how Wiitu means "the place of the girls" and that the name derived from a past event. Apparently (long ago) a group of girls fled into a cave to seek shelter from a rainstorm. One girl threw a beetle out of the cave, but then the cave closed and the girls perished. The beetle was a spirit of the cave that had punished them [Fig. 2.3].

At the other place, Nzambani, a man and woman with their daughter and a calf descended from the sky and allegedly one can still see the imprint of the man's chair on the rock. These first people were forbidden to look at the sky, but they disobeyed and then were taken back up; only the daughter and the calf remained on earth [Fig. 2.4].

Kanig had little interest in the narrative. He rejoiced in the fact that the genre could be connected to places mentioned in the Old Testament, specifically Beersheba and Bethel, which also related to past events. As he stated: "Beersheba, the well of the oath, after the treaty that Abraham made with Abimelech, or Bethel, the house of God, since at this place Jacob saw the heaven open in his dream."[20] But unlike its Biblical counterpart, Kanig found contradictory versions of the myths of both rocks, complicating the establishment of a stable and recorded history of places. The same history would be found at other rocks, while for the same rock different people would tell different stories. Kanig lamented not over the diversity of the narratives, but over the lack of fixation, the absence of a clear original: "One can see how unstable these myths *still* are."[21] The instability of the myths tied in with a more general concern of the missionaries. The indigenous myths would not connect to places of origin in a way the Old Testament descriptions did. Similarly local places of worship seemed to have no history to the missionaries, as offerings were placed and dances were held where a witchdoctor died just the year before. The problems they had with fixing Akamba culture locally and historically kept the missionaries from finding a cultural starting point for Christianity.

2.3 *The collapsed cave of Wiitu.*
[Photo: Maarten Onneweer, July 2007]

2.4 *The Nzambani rock.*
[Photo: Maarten Onneweer, June 2007]

City on a Hill: building the Light

In the period under discussion the Leipzig Mission established four new mission stations in Ukamba, and all of them closely followed the route that the explorer Krapf took in 1851 to the Tana river. In fact, all the mission stations were related to places Krapf visited. The positioning of the missions close to Krapf's route along the caravan route counts as another example of the missionaries' tendency to ascribe a historical topography to the area.[22]

In the actual construction of the mission building the missionaries seem to have gone against Krapf's advice. On the basis of his short-lived experience with a small mission station in Ukamba, Krapf had explicitly warned the missionaries against the construction of large and permanent mission buildings, since:

> He feared that by doing so the missionaries would lose their mobility, become comfortable and neglect their *Heidenpredigt* (preaching to the heathens or itinerating) in the surrounding area.[23]

Indeed, the Leipzig missionaries experienced that large permanent mission stations complicated their relation with the Akamba settlements. Though the Akamba were not complete pastoralists, they would often move when drought, trade, or enemy groups forced them to do so. The Akamba "beehive" huts had light wooden frameworks that could be carried for about one hour and reassembled [Fig. 2.6].

The stations Mbungu and Ikutha for instance were built close to several Akamba settlements, but during a long dry spell the Akamba moved further away from the mission.

The missionaries also did not build the new stations in Ukamba directly among the larger settlements of the Akamba but on the top of high rolling hills with good views over the surrounding area. When addressing the construction of the Mulango mission station,

2.5 *The Mulango mission station. [Evangelisch-Lutherisches Missionsblatt, 1901, 19]*

Missionary Säuberlich explained why he was going against Krapf's advise for makeshift mission stations and his worry for neglect of the *Heidenpredigt*:

> [we assure you] that we will avoid this danger and we will make our new mission house the point of departure for our works in the surrounding lands, making it a Light the rays of which will penetrate far into the heathenish night.[24] [Fig. 2.5]

The same was said about the mission station in Miambani, which also took more than a year to finish. As Gerholds reported:

> The building work keeps us from our actual occupation, but if one ventures to build a new mission station, a new place of Light for this dark and heathenish environment, it really has a charm of its own.[25]

It appears that the missionaries saw their mission buildings as a means to transform Ukamba. Even the architecture itself seems to suggest this, such was the emphasis on durability and visibility. They made the walls of the mission buildings half a meter thick and the cement slab extremely strong and durable (even to this day there are few cracks, see Figs. 2.7 and 2.8 for the present state of the missions). Termite resistant wood was specially brought in from the coast. The mission stations of Ikutha and Mulango have survived to this day, even though one was abandoned for more than twenty years until it was taken over by the African Inland Mis-

22 *ELM* 1909, 212-221.
23 *ELM* 1902, 463: "er Fürchtete, die Missionare könnten dadurch an Beweglichkeit verlieren, bequem werden und die Heidenpredigt draußen in der Landschaft vernachlässigen."
24 *ELM* 1902, 463: "Dass wir diese Gefahr vermeiden und unser neues Missionshaus zu einem Ausgangspunkt unserer Arbeit ringsum im Lande machen, damit er ein Licht werde, dessen Strahlen weithin dringen in die Nacht des Heidentums."
25 *ELM* 1903, 459: "Die Bauzeit hindert uns zwar an unserer eigentlichen Berufsarbeit aber wenn man eine neue Station anlegen darf, eine neue Stätte des Lichts für die finstere heidnische Umgebung, so hat das einen besonderen Reiz."

2.6 Akamba "beehive" hut. [Leipzig, Evangelich-Lutherisches Missionswerk, Archive]

26 Comaroff and Comaroff, *Of Revelation and Revolution*, chapter 6; Pels, *A Politics of Presence*; Stuart Watt, *In the Heart of Savagedom*.

27 *ELM* 1903, 112: "Das ganze Haus hat außer 3 Türen 10 Fenster, weil wir wünschen, dass sich unsere Jungen an Luft und Licht und damit auch zugleich an größere Reinlichkeit gewöhnen."

28 *ELM* 1902, 462: "Seit 23 Juli wohne ich (...) in einem neuen, schönen Hause, dessen hell glänzendes Wellblechdach und weiß getünchte Wände und Verandasäulen von den umlie-genden Höhen weither sichtbar sind. Etwas von dem alten Stationsgehöft entfernt liegt es ein wenig höher als dieses und ganz frei auf dem lang gestreckten Höhenzuge von Ikutha, über dem Bett des Tiwaflusses, fast wie, eine Stadt auf dem Berge'."

sion. When asked what he thought of the architecture, the present day pastor at Ikutha wondered why the veranda was so high and the walls so thick. He concluded that "they certainly planned to stay" [Figs. 2.7 and 2.8].

Compared with other missions in East African inland at the same stage of settlement, the amount of materials used by the Leipzig Mission was excessive. The Church Missionary Society in the neighboring Ulu district, the Catholic Holy Spirit mission in Uluguru or, further south, the non-conformist mission in Bechuanaland mostly started with simple wattle and daub construction. Small rectangular abodes with thatched roofs, often with a European interior setup, reflecting ideas of European domesticity and gendered spaces. Only later would these be replaced by more permanent structures should the mission prove successful. The non-conformist mission described by John Comaroff highlighted the importance of separation of rooms and the placement of domestic utensils within relatively simple dwellings.[26] With the mission stations of Ikutha and Mulango this was never the case.

Uncompromising in its durability, the missionaries built these stations to last and be seen. To give an idea of the magnitude of the building effort of the Mulango station, it took three porter caravans of sixty men each to transport the building material in five-day marches from the railway station Kibwezi to Mulango. Besides being built on a hill, like almost every other mission station in Africa, even the top of the hill was not enough. The missionaries raised the ground level of the building with a meter of stones and cement for no obvious reason but to gain further elevation above the rest of the land [Fig. 2.9].

The mission in Mulango looks much like the new mission in Ikutha that was built two years later in 1901. Missionary Kanig commented that they built the mission house to be lofty and light from the inside; the windows and the view should contrast with the dark and closed huts of the Akamba [Fig. 2.6].

A boy-house in Ikutha had a similar moral intention. Its architecture was to harbor the Akamba pupils in the values of hygiene implied by the production of spaces of brick and air, the quantity of openings and doorways suggesting choice and command of the light. It seemed that Kanig considered that this would rub off on the minds of the pupils:

> Besides three doors, the whole house has ten windows because we wish to provide our boys with air and light, through which they can grow accustomed to greater cleanliness.[27]

The positioning of the missions also allowed it to be seen from afar. Especially the tin iron sheets of the roof reflected the sunlight making the house visible from the surrounding areas, which exhilarated the missionaries time and again. This visibility of the mission appeared to them as a triumph of Christianity over the environment:

> Since the 23rd of July I've lived (…) in a new clean house of which the bright shining corrugated iron roof and the whitewashed walls and porch-columns can, from the surrounding heights, be seen from afar. Away from the old station compound it stands a bit higher up the hill, solitary on the long ridge of the Ikutha hill, above the floodplains of the Tiva river it is just like 'a city on the hill'.[28]

They also described the other mission buildings in verses of the sermon of the mountain, a parable that deals with the visibility of Christianity. The Light and the city on the hill relate the need for Christians to establish a visible and durable presence in their surroundings:[29]

> You are the light of the world. A city located on a hill can't be hidden. Neither do you light a lamp, and put it under a measuring basket, but on a stand; and it shines to all who are in the house.
> Even so, let your light shine before men; that they may see your good works, and glorify your Father who is in heaven.

The emphasis was not on rooms and utensils but on doors and windows, roofs and outer walls, verandas. Seldom do they mention the interior and its arrangements, mostly emphasizing the aesthetics of these parts of the construction that mediate and separate the interior from the exterior, as if the mission building also acted as a shield from the surrounding Darkness. And so we are left with the impression that the missionaries positioned the station to be seen by all as a visible source of power, built to be a place from which the power of vision emanates. A growing anticipation materializes in it, accumulating through the articulation of Biblical narratives.

2.7 The Mulango mission, 2007.
[Photo: Maarten Onneweer, July 2007]

2.8 The Ikutha mission, 2007.
[Photo: Maarten Onneweer, September 2007]

29 Matthew 5: 14-16.

2.9 The Ikutha mission, 1905. [Evangelisch-Lutherisches Missionsblatt, 1907, 187]

The Light presented itself in the material environment the missionaries manipulated and through it they turned their own presence into visual signals. These signals were not free but bound by the pretext of the mission: to bring Light through the introduction of the Word. To describe the relation as symbolism or metaphor would imply a difference between the spiritual reality and its worldly representation. But the Neo-Lutheran mission sought a return to the objective confession, not a separation of meaning and its representation in the material world. Simon Coleman's work on the Evangelical Protestants is instructive here:

> Evangelical Protestant worship is frequently characterized as involving the manipulation of language rather than objects or images. However, (...) a coherent aesthetic sensibility rooted in positive attitudes to the material world exists in evangelical practices." He continues: "discursive practices produce that which it names" and "The Word can be made to 'live' by being translated into a material indication of its efficacy, as signs of language are turned into physical signs of the presence of sacred power.[30]

Constructing the mission station seemed a controlled effort of visualising, a means to absolve the material world from its unfixed Darkness. It was to produce for the knowing viewer an image of discipline over and fixation of the environment, bound by the more encompassing narrative structure of the Word. Their effort to do so, to give the Word an entry in the material world by translating it into a presence in Ukamba, resembles a work of allegory: a narrative of metaphors or other tropes that refer to a binding pretext (the Bible) that lies outside the narrative itself. In Birgit Meyer's words:

> allegory is defined by the fact that it provides rules for the interpretation of metaphors and other tropes of which it consists. In the framework of allegory, metaphors are restricted and bound to reproduce meanings that are fixed.[31]

To understand the material dimension of the missionary encounter, we should pay attention to the integration of the Word in the world, visible or recognizable as a presence made durable in physical space.

The vision of redemption and the technology of improvement

How then did the missionaries relate (Biblical) narrative to the surroundings of the mission at large, an environment that was characterized by frequent drought, pests and famines? An engraving printed in the *Missionsblatt* will initiate this discussion. Its context and use allow an understanding of the multi-layered politics of narrative and environment envisioned by it. The engraving carries the title *Hungersnot in Ikutha* (Famine in Ikutha) and features under the section *Speisung der Hungerenden*, "To feed the hungry," the first of the Christian works of mercy[32] [Fig. 2.10].

The engraving accompanies a newsletter from Ikutha in which Missionary Kanig describes a drought that hit Ukamba, leading to a great famine that brought large crowds to the stations in search for relief. Confronted with the hungry masses Kanig commented: "God speaks gravely with our people, let us hope they understand it as such."[33] He implied that God presented the Akamba

30 Coleman "Words as Things," respectively 107, 108 and 109.
31 Meyer, *Translating the Devil*, 32.
32 *ELM* 1900, 65. See Mat 25: 42.
33 *ELM* 1900, 64: "Gott redet eine ernste sprache mit unsere Volk, möchte es dieselbe verstehen!" The drought started in 1899 and lasted until 1901. To this day it is remembered in oral history as the most severe ever. It led to a famine that Lindblom (*The Akamba in British East Africa*) estimated claimed the lives of more than half of the inhabitants of Ukamba.

2.10 "To feed the hungry in Ikutha". [Evangelisch-Lutherisches Missionsblatt, 1901, 65]

with drought and famine, a divine affliction directing the Akamba towards the mission. Through the relief food, the Akamba would participate in a scheme in which their work on the mission and the surroundings led towards their redemption. The missionaries imported large quantities of rice to the station, and even though most of the people were weak and near starvation the missionaries insisted that the stronger work for the food they received, as this would allow them to grow accustomed to regular work. Accustoming people to regular work had little to do with the preparation of an accessible workforce for the colony or a modern need to separate leisure and work by introducing paid labor. It did not matter if the hungry were productive as a workforce: "The achievements of the workers are of course small, but it is better if they work instead of receiving support for nothing."[34] Moreover, the missionaries made the people work only on the surroundings of the mission: brick making, digging wells and the like. Some had to carry earth and stone to realize the terrace of the mission building.

Three spaces can be distinguished in the engraving; we will analyse them one by one to disentangle the different narratives and show how work on the the material world is a central objective and how it is supported by the power of visibility of the mission. In the first space, the foreground, we see the mob of people being relieved of their hunger by the larger of the two tall bright white women serving relief. We can see a narrative of relief when we start reading from the left below, the black children crawling on the ground in agony; then we see the white woman, and another one, and the children she is feeding. Our view is directed that way since the whole crowd in the engraving looks at the woman, except for the three helpers of the white women standing on the right of them, sturdy and independent (but still much smaller), having regained control over their live and accepted the leadership of the mission.

There are yet more people on the engraving: on the left in the background are the men, black men working and white men instructing. All look in one direction, towards the construction. Like the three helpers of the white women their actions are purposeful and determined. They have regained control over the material world, and they are not misusing their resources but patiently following the leadership of the missionaries in its development.

34 *ELM* 1900, 64: "Die Arbeit derselben bestand in Backsteinformen, Brunnengraben usw, Andere mussten Erde und Steinen tragen zur Aufführung einer Terrasse und anderer Bauten. Die Leistungen der Arbeiter waren freilich gering, doch ist es besser dass die Leute etwas arbeiten, als dass sie umsonst unterstützt werden."

35 This reading of the engraving is inspired by Barthes's *Mythologies*. Pels (*A Politics of Presence*) also describes the use of engravings by the Holy Spirit mission in Uluguru (55-66). Contrary to the Leipzig Mission, the Holy Spirit Fathers presented icons completely detached from narratives of redemption of conversion.

What pulls these narratives together is the mission building, which fills one of the four quarters of the engraving. It also constitutes a diagonal that leads from the roof with the view from the windows, the stairs going down and the woman standing on the veranda, towards the crowd, their gazes follow the diagonal to the white woman's outreach towards the feeble and weak. It connects to the foreground in which we find a feminine narrative of relief of hunger, but also of restoration of selfhood, a repositioning of the person in the world. Then a horizontal line going from the veranda and the roof to the post and bricks carried by the two black men finally leads towards the construction.

A masculine narrative of development unfolds there, but not development as we know it now, as in the introduction and appropriation of technology. Rather, the work itself is a technology of improvement, of both the native and the surroundings.

The engraving "To feed the hungry" gives a visualization of the missionaries' intent with the Akamba. The context of the famine allows us to understand how they saw the trajectory of improvement of their situation and their environment through the attraction of the mission. In another station, Mulango, the missionaries used the same approach and wanted to illustrate this with a photo [Fig. 2.11].

However, the photo disturbs the narrative of redemption; it lacks the proper elements that signify a work of mercy. The positioning of the mission building and the people does not indicate relief or improvement. Both the famished children and the mission building stare directly at the viewer with very little opportunity for disambiguation of their relation: no narrative, just hungry children in front of a brick structure. Significantly, the mission published the engraving and not the photo. The engraving allows the gendered narrative structure of relief and improvement. In the picture it is more difficult to get all the different elements into a narrative relation that sufficiently alienates these elements from their history without distorting too much of their allegoric value in the narrative. The camera did not manipulate the eyes of the hungry, and thereby could not allegorize through vision.[35]

In a crude way the elaborate narratives in the engraving were meant to open the pockets of a German audience to finance the relief food and to reassure them that their money was well spent, a moral investment of sorts. It provides a printable public image of idealized relations and narratives set to work for a specific audience. That said, the effort to produce these relations and narratives in Ukamba differed little from the ideal in the engraving. Besides the German audience, the hungry in Ukamba found themselves coerced to enact the allegory the engraving depicted: to receive aid they worked on the mission building and its direct environment. The two largest mission buildings in Ikutha and Mulango were built in the famine years. The building work had its own role: the hungry were told that God's wrath had descended upon them through the famine and now He was showing them through the relief food to go to the mission, working to be redeemed from their sin.

The Akamba people declined to see the allegoric intentions of the missionaries. They

2.11 *"To feed the hungry in Mulango".*
[Leipzig, Evangelich-Lutherisches Missionswerk, Archive]

soon went back to their villages after the drought finished and ignored the mission as before. One of the missionaries commented on the hardship the Akamba suffered by the famine and the work they were made to do:

> We hoped that through this hard-and-fast school the Akamba people would learn to understand the sincerity of life and hard work. But yet again the people are even more self-indulgent, thievish and lazy than before.[36]

Despairingly the missionaries concluded that the satisfaction of direct needs was the only guiding principle in the Akamba engagement with the material world. They stated that the Akamba continued to use slash and burn agriculture, live in small dark huts, graze their cattle until the soil was exhausted or eroded, and take water from polluted or salty wells. The Akamba continued to live in Darkness because they were unimpressed by the European vision:

> The apathy must still be great when blacks, continually faced with the shrill contrast between the conditions of life of the missionary and their own sorry and helpless state, still proceed to do nothing and feel wealthy in alternating famines with drinking sprees.[37]

All things considered, the material capacity to produce visible contrast explains the central position of the mission building. Allegory provides a very suitable trope for this; the works of mercy aimed to improve the mission and to demonstrate to the native that the ways of the missionaries exemplified proper moral conduct.

Concluding remarks

The period discussed above closes at 1905, around the time the British district tax collectors began to show such brutality and imprudence towards the Akamba people that some were driven to the mission. The German mission provided several advantages for the Akamba, notably that the missionaries could be asked to negotiate and plead for the converts in the increasing number of tax and land disputes with the colonial administration. Consequently the situation steadily improved from 1905, reaching a peak in 1910 when numbers of converts increased and the missionaries victoriously rejoiced that: "the Akamba are coming." The acclaimed victory was of course somewhat spoiled because early colonial brutality, not Christian teaching, drove the people to the mission. The large numbers of arrivals did instigate a more pragmatic approach, and perhaps the end of imagining a Neo-Lutheran Ukamba Native Church. Furthermore, the Leipzig Mission dropped the *vorstation* mission, outside the Ukamba area. The encounter closes with the deportation of the Leipzig missionaries in 1914 as a result of the First World War. On the occasion the District Commissioner Montgomery observed, not without satisfaction, that:

> The Akamba did not appear to take much notice of the deportation of the German missionaries while in the south several, including headman Kiema wa Umo were glad and said so; apparently Mr Hoffman of Ikutha had attempted to interfere in tribal custom and the settlement of shauris (disputes) and nzama (councils) which the people resented.[38]

As Peter Pels has also shown, the "African side" of the missionary encounter needs to be taken into account and a missionary encounter should be seen in terms of the co-production of the mission.[39] In this particular occasion, the initial absenteeism followed by the pragmatism of the Akamba seems to have forced the missionaries away from their orthodox interpretation of Ukamba, but besides the non-response it remains difficult to assess the Akamba side of the encounter. The missionaries' accounts sometimes represent conversations with local inhabitants and

36 *ELM* 1901, 329: "Schon hofften wir dem Volk in dieser strengen Schule einen Begriff vom Ernst des Lebens und fleißiger Arbeit beigebracht zu haben. Aber auch jetzt ist das Volk zügelloser, diebischer und fauler denn zuvor."
37 *ELM* 1904, 532: "Der Stumpfsinn muss eben schon sehr groß sein, wenn Schwarze, denen der grelle unterschied zwischen den Lebensbedingung des Missionars und zwischen ihrem ärmlichen und hilflosen Zustand immer wieder zu Gemüte geführt wird, trotzdem fortfahren, im Nichtstun und um Wechsel von Hungern und Saufen sich reich und wohl zu fühlen."
38 Nairobi, Kenya National Archives: Kitui district annual report 1914 and 1916.
39 Pels, *A Politics of Presence*.

their ideas on the mission. They make the Akamba speak with indifference towards the message of the missionaries and depict them as more interested in trade opportunities or direct change in the environment. Missionaries present the Akamba as preoccupied with the possible (magical) influence of the Christian Gods on the rain, but some of the presented dialogues seem crafted to the extent that one resembles David Livingstone's famous conversation with a rainmaker.[40]

In present Kenya's Kitui district (the Ukamba of the missionaries), narratives of the peculiar behavior of strangers still address the first missionary encounter. One interlocutor, Emma Vatu, possibly the oldest inhabitant of the district, recounted how the people saw the Leipzig missionaries at the time. When they had just arrived in the district and knew little of the language, it appeared the missionaries memorized short sentences to proclaim at villages. One of the sentences remembered runs: "if you don't repent, God will burn Ukamba." As response, the people would jokingly say that if God would do so they would run for the river. It goes to show how these missionaries trusted the efficacy of the Word to precede its meaning.

Further enquiry revealed that the metaphysical work missionaries assigned to the mission houses left no impression whatsoever. No one mentioned the stations as worthy of specific narratives or account, besides the occasional comment that "doctor Krapf is buried there," and perhaps, as earlier discussed he was the mission's milestone. Literally, as Livingstone put it: "the end of the geographical feat was the beginning of the missionary enterprise."[41]

That is what makes the initial period of the Leipzig Mission interesting: the missionaries attempted to gear the mission stations into action to create an Ukamba fitting their conceptualization. Before the situation was taken over by pragmatism of both the missionaries and the Akamba, partly due to the increased influence of the colonial administration, this missionary encounter can be understood as a struggle to materialize certain narratives in the area. The power of vision and visibility was central in those narratives and in the spatial practices of this missionary encounter. Other mission societies included the dissemination of European technology for cultivation into their practices. Recall, for instance, Wilberforce's famed creed "Commerce and Christianity," which was later popularized by Livingstone, or that other slogan, Fowell Buxton's "Only the Bible and the plough can regenerate Africa."[42] Closer to the Leipzig Mission in Ukamba was the Scottish Industrial Mission in Kibwezi, loathed by the Leipzig missionaries since its missionaries seemed only interested in trade and cultivation.

In the initial period of the mission's settlement, the enlightenment-critical episteme of the Leipzig Mission, the orthodoxy in their understanding of the material world, and the sincerity they required from the Akamba precluded them from these forms of interaction. Their financial situation also allowed them to do so, of course, while other missions were often left to their own devices and could not afford to be orthodox. The peculiarity of the Leipzig Mission in Ukamba is not only that they refrained from commerce and technology but restricted themselves to the Word and its perceived efficacy as a technology of redemption of Ukamba.

---

40 Livingstone in Grinker and Steiner, *Perspectives on Africa*.
41 Stanley, "Commerce and Christianity." To avoid confusion, Krapf is not buried in Ukamba. The Ikutha mission has a graveyard with (at least) 9 graves of missionaries or their wives and children, most of whom died of blackwater fever.
42 Stanley, "Commerce and Christianity," passim; *ELM* 1898, 397.

BIBLIOGRAPHY

Archival sources

Evangelisch-Lutherisches Missionsblatt (*ELM*). Dresden: E. Blochmann, 1846-1941. (previous title: *Dresdener Missions Nachrichten* (Ed. Evangelisch-Lutherische Mission zu Dresden / Leipziger Mission).

Kew (Richmond, London), The National Archives of the United Kingdom.

Nairobi, Kenya National Archives.

Primary Literature

Hildebrandt, J.M. "Ethnographische Notizen über Wakamba und Ihre Nachbarn." *Zeitschrift fur Ethnologie*, (1878), 347-406.

Höhnel, Ludwig von. *Discovery of Lakes Rudolf and Stefanie: A Narrative of Count Samuel Teleki's Exploring and Hunting Expedition in Eastern Equatorial Africa in 1887 and 1888*. 1st English ed., new impression ed. Library of African studies. Travels and narratives, no. 37. London: Cass, 1968.

Kolb, George. "Von Mombasa durch Ukambani zum Kenia. Zwei Expeditionen 1894-96 von George Kolb." *Dr. A. Petermanns Geographische Mitteilungen*, (1896) 10, 221-321.

Krapf, Johann Ludwig. *Reisen in Ostafrika, Ausgeführt in den Jahren 1837-1855*. Quellen und Forschungen zur Geschichte der Geographie und der Reisen. Stuttgart: F. A. Brockhaus, Abt. Antiquarium, 1964 (1858), 2 vols.

Krapf, Johann Ludwig. *Travels, Researches and Missionary Labours during Eighteen Years Residence in East Africa. Together with Journeys to Jagga, Usambara, Ukambani, Shoa, Abessinia and Karthum, and a Coasting Voyage from Mombaz to Cape Delgado*. London: Cass, 1968.

Lindblom, Gerhard. *The Akamba in British East Africa: An Ethnological Monograph*. Archives d'études orientales, 17. Uppsala: Appelberg, 1920 (1916).

Stuart Watt, Rachel. *In the Heart of Savagedom: Reminiscences of Life and Adventure During a Quarter Century of Missionary Labours in the Wilds of East Equatorial Africa*. London/ Glasgow: Pickering & Inglis, n.d.

Troeltsch, Ernst. *Protestantisches Christentum und Kirche in der Neuzeit (1906/1909/1922)*. Eds. Christian Albrecht and Volker Drehsen. Ernst Troeltsch Kritische Gesammtausgabe, 7. Berlin / New York: Walter de Gruyter, 2004.

Secondary Literature

Anderson, Benedict. *Imagined Communities: Reflections on the Origin and Spread of Nationalism*. London: Verso, 1991.

Appadurai, Arjun. *Modernity at Large: Cultural Dimensions of Globalization*. Minnesota: University of Minnesota Press, 1996.

Barthes, Roland. *Mythologies*. Translated by Annette Lavers. New York: Hill and Wang, 1972.

Bhabha, Homi K. *The Location of Culture*. London: Routledge, 2004 (1994).

Coleman, Simon. "Words as Things: Language, Aesthetics and the Objectification of Protestant Evangelicalism." *Journal of Material Culture*, 1 (1996) 1, 107-128.

Comaroff, Jean and Comaroff, John L. *Of Revelation and Revolution*. Chicago: University of Chicago Press, 1997.

Crapanzano, Vincent. *Serving the Word: Literalism in America From the Pulpit to the Bench*. New York: New Press, 2000.

Dundas, Charles. "The History of Kitui." *The Journal of the Royal Anthropological Institute of Great Britain and Ireland*, 43 (1913), 480-549.

Fleisch, Paul. *Hundert Jahre Lutherischer Mission*. Leipzig: Verlag der Evangelisch-Lutherischen Mission, 1936.

Grinker, Roy Richard and Steiner, Christopher B. *Perspectives on Africa: A Reader in Culture, History, and Representation*. Oxford: Blackwell Publishers, 1997.

Hirsch, Eric and Stewart, Charles. "Introduction: Ethnographies of Historicity." *History and Anthropology*, 16 (2005) 3, 261-274.

Hobley, Charles William. *Ethnology of a-Kamba and Other East-African Tribes*. London: Frank Cass, 1971.

Hoekendijk, Johannes Christian. *Kirche und Volk in der Deutschen Missionswissenschaft*. Translated by E.W. Pollmann. Munich: Kaiser, 1967.

Jackson, Kernell A. *An Ethnohistorical Study of the Oral Traditions of the Akamba of Kenya*. Ph.D. diss. Los Angeles: University of California, 1972.

Keane, Webb. "From Fetishism to Sincerity: On Agency, the Speaking Subject, and Their Historicity in the Context of Religious Conversion." *Comparative Studies in Society and History*, 39 (1997) 4, 674-693.

Keane, Webb. "Sincerity, 'Modernity', and the Protestants." *Cultural Anthropology*, 17 (2002) 1, 65-72.

Lamphear, John. "The Kamba and the Northern Mrima Coast," in: Gray, Richard and Birmingham, David, eds. *Pre-Colonial African Trade: Essays on Trade in Central and Eastern Africa Before 1900*. London: Oxford University Press, 1970, 75-102.

Lewinski, Agnes von. *Acht Kamba Märchen. Erzählt von den Missionaren Pfitzinger, Kanig, Brutzer und Gerhold*. Lichtstrahlen im dunkeln Erdteile, Kleine Serie Nr. 4. Leipzig: Verlag der Evangelisch-Lutherischen Mission Leipzig, 1905.

Mbula, Judith. *Penetration of Christianity into the Akamba Traditional Family*. Unpublished Ma thesis. University of Nairobi, 1974.

Meyer, Birgit. *Translating the Devil: An African Appropriation of Pietist Protestantism: The Case of the Peki Ewe in Southeastern Ghana, 1847-1992*. PhD diss. Universiteit van Amsterdam, 1995.

Meyer, Birgit. "Christian Mind and Worldly Matters: Religion and Materiality in Nineteenth-Century Gold Coast." *Journal of Material Culture*, 2 (1997) 3, 311-37.

Muthiani, Joseph. *Akamba from Within: Egalitarianism in Social Relations*. Jericho/New York: Exposition Press, 1973.

Ndeti, Kivuto. *Elements of Akamba Live*. Nairobi: East African Publishing House, 1972.

Ndolo, Donald. *The Dynamics of Social Change in an African Society: The Akamba of Kenya*. Doctoral thesis. University of Bayreuth, 1989.

Nehring, Andreas. *Orientalismus und Mission: Die Repräsentation der Tamilischen Gesellschaft und Religion durch Leipziger Missionare 1840-1940*. Harrassowitz, 2003.

Oliver, Roland. *The Missionary Factor in East Africa*. London: Longmans, Green and Co, 1952.

Pels, Peter. *A Politics of Presence: Contacts between Missionaries and Waluguru in Late Colonial Tanganyika*. London: Harwood Academic Publishers, 1999.

Scherer, James A. "The Triumph of Confessionalism in Nineteenth-Century German Lutheran Missions." *Missio Apostolica*, (1993) 2, 71-81.

Stanley, Brian. "'Commerce and Christianity': Providence Theory, the Missionary Movement, and the Imperialism of Free Trade, 1842-1860." *The Historical Journal*, 26 (1983) 1, 71-94.

Strayer, Robert. "Mission History in Africa: New Perspectives on an Encounter." *African Studies Review*, 19 (1976) 1, 1-15.

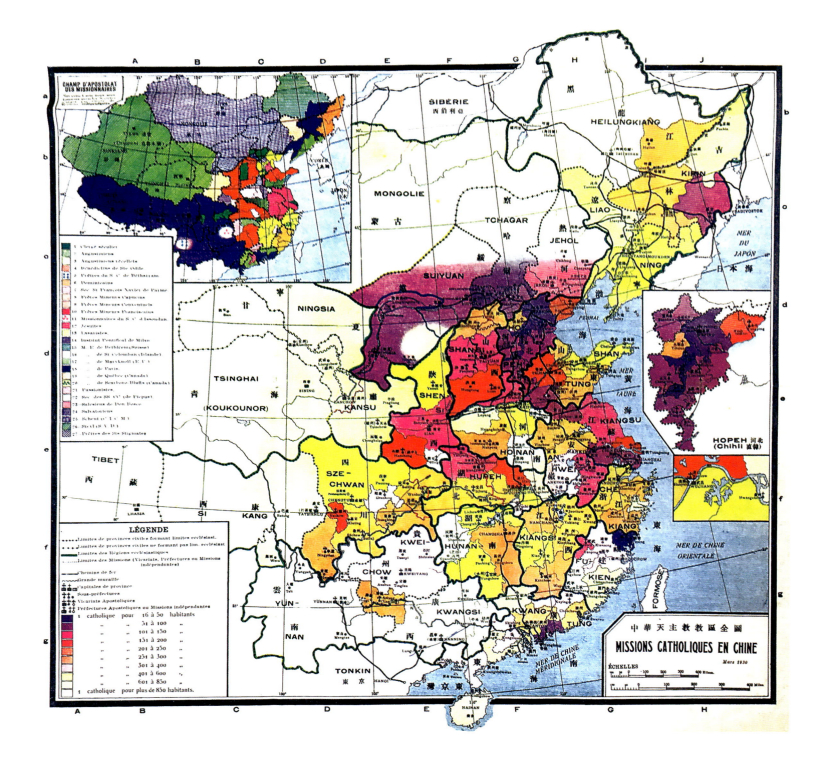

3
Islands on the Mainland
Catholic Missions and Spatial Strategies in China, 1840s-1940s

Thomas Coomans

The Christian mission to China in the nineteenth and early twentieth centuries differed fundamentally from missions to other countries. Since China had never been a colony, it was not dependent on one single Western nation which would have encouraged its own national missionaries as colonial agents. Starting in 1842, several foreign powers forced China to gradually open up to their economic, political, and moral influence. Free trade, travel, and mission were gradually obtained in all parts of China, turning some parts of the empire into semi-colonial territories. The fall of the Qing Dynasty in 1911 and the early years of the Republic of China, marked by growing nationalism, transition to modernization, and new political movements, completely changed the relationships between China and the Western countries in the 1920s. At the same time, the Holy See was redefining its missionary policy.

This chapter focuses on the less-explored field of Catholic missionary spatial strategies in China from the 1840s to the 1940s. The China missions in the previous centuries will not be discussed here since they were officially banned from 1721 to 1842.[1] The numerous Protestant and other Christian missionary societies active in China during the nineteenth and early twentieth centuries[2] will not be mentioned because their less-centralized organization and other methods of evangelization led to different territorial strategies and architectural projects, such as university campuses and hospitals.

The conditions of evangelization were particularly difficult in China and the missionaries realized that they never would succeed in turning the country into a Christian society.[3] First, the Chinese Rite controversy – the condemnations in 1715 and 1742 by Rome of Confucian traditions and worship of ancestors – excluded any possibility of converting upper-class Chinese and *literati*. Second, the collusion between missionaries and representatives of Western powers provoked anti-foreign and anti-Christian hostility, increasing the problem of land acquisition. Third, the harsh climate and the difficult language were great obstacles to the mission. The immensity of the Chinese mainland territory led to the development of many local activities and communities, which, like little islands or *heterotopias*, were individually successful. Together these islands formed archipelagos, more or less structured and rather autonomous networks at the level of the missionary societies. How did the Propaganda Fide in Rome organize the vast territory of China, efficiently divide it into ecclesiastical regions and dioceses, and entrust them to specific missionary congregations? Could missionaries purchase land and build on it?

In China, spatial organization in cities and villages is largely influenced by the rules of *fengshui* 风水, the Chinese system of geomancy that defines the appropriate locations for establishing buildings and tombs.[4] Even though missionaries considered geomancy 'pagan superstition', they could not ignore it. *Fengshui* aims at harmonizing the vital energies (*qi* 气) according to the configuration of the environment. One of its fundamental rules, which is based on the polarity of the complementary *yin* 阴 (the feminine or negative principle in nature) and *yang* 阳 (the masculine or positive principle in nature), involves the main north-south axis. Therefore the main entrance of a city, house, tomb,

3.1 Catholic Missions to China, map dated March 1930, showing the then ecclesiastical regions (bold lines) and vicariates apostolic. The colors indicate the density of Catholics – the darker, the more –, while the colors on the map in the upper left corner indicate the different missionary congregations and societies. Map published by the Jesuits of the 'Bureau sinologique de Zi-ka-wei', Xujiahui, Shanghai.
[Vanves, Compagnie de Jésus, Archives jésuites de France, Chine cartes]

1 For the best overviews, see: Standaert, *Handbook of Christianity in China, 635-1800*; Tiedemann, *Handbook of Christianity in China, 1800-present*.
2 Detailed in: Tiedemann, *Reference Guide to Christian Missionary Societies in China*.
3 Soetens, *L'Église catholique en Chine*, 11.
4 Bruun, *Fengshui in China*.

3.2 The Chinese-style church of Aupoa / Houban 後坂 (Fujian), built by a Spanish Dominican father in 1844-1849, was well integrated in the village. According to fengshui rules, it faced water and turned its back to the mountain. Engraving from Les Missions Catholiques, *9 (1877), 434.*
[Leuven, KADOC-KU Leuven, Heritage Library: KYB3962]

5   Macao was created as a diocese of the Portuguese colony in 1576. Dioceses were created in Nanjing (1660) and Beijing (1690); vicariates apostolic in Fujian (1680), Sichuan (1696), and Guizhou (1696, merged with Sichuan 1737).

6   Tiedemann, *Handbook of Christianity in China*, 344-353 and 665; lists on pages 344 (1845), 349-350 (1905), 971-976 (1924-1946); Despont, *Nouvel atlas des missions*, 20-24; Emmerich, *Atlas missionum*, 30-33; Streit, *Atlas des missions catholiques*, 11-13. See also: <www.catholic-hierarchy.org/country/dcn.html> (accessed 20 September 2022).

palace or temple, or a church as well should be turned to the south [Figs. 3.12 and 3.13]. Ideally, this axis should be combined with the energy fluxes of wind (*feng* 风) and water (*shui* 水). The main entrance, on the southern side, should be turned toward water, while the northern side should be protected by the mountain [Fig. 3.2]. Did missionaries manage to combine the Christian east-west axis and the Chinese north-south axis? How were church towers perceived by Chinese in terms of *fengshui*? [Fig. 3.3].

This chapter is built on seven categories of 'missionary islands' or *heterotopias* according to both their function and their location, and relates them to several contexts specific to China: concession territories in the treaty ports, urban cathedral compounds, Christian areas in small towns and villages, wholly Christian villages, places of memory, Marian pilgrimages, and monastic sites. The chapter concludes with the reformation of the mission policy aiming at a Chinese Church in the 1920s and 1930s. Were there patterns in the way these missionary islands generated and organized space? Were there spatial strategies of land occupation, growth, defence, orientation, building, and visibility in the public space?

Organizing the Mission's Territory and Buying Land

Territorial organization and land ownership – the basic conditions of any missionary work – were sensitive questions in China for two reasons. First, because China was such a vast territory with varied topography, in which communication was difficult if not dangerous, organizing its church administration was extremely challenging. In Rome, about 8,000 km away from China, the Congregation for the Propagation of the Faith (Propaganda Fide) coordinated the territorial organization of the Catholic mission according to its worldwide strategy based on evangelization, growth and efficiency. After the diocese of Macao 澳門 in 1576, five dioceses had been created in China in the seventeenth century.[5] From these initial five ecclesiastical circumscriptions, the number of vicariates apostolic and prefectures apostolic grew to 14 in 1850, 43 in 1905 (grouped in five regions), 118 in 1935, and 137 in 1946 when the hierarchy of the Chinese church was reorganized (20 archbishoprics, 79 dioceses, 39 prefectures apostolic) [Fig. 3.1].[6] The number of Catholics increased from about 253,000 in 1845 to 3,295,044 in 1940.

3.3 Western-style missionary compound with a church, a residence and a school built by French Lazarists in Yongjiachang 永嘉场 (Zhejiang). The vertical tower disrupts the fengshui of the site and the buildings. View from the south; photography from the 1920s.
[Paris, Archives historiques de la Congrégation de la Mission]

Second, and in contrast to these centralized statistics, the vicars apostolic and their missionaries had to rely on local converts and negotiate land with mandarins, who were not in favor of any missionary settlements. Except in Macao, Hong Kong 香港, and in the treaty ports, there was no colonial authority that would allocate land to the mission and officially entrust the mission with urbanism and planning.

Vicars apostolic exerted the jurisdiction of the pope over well-defined territories, the vicariates apostolic. Their status and function were similar to those of titular bishops of dioceses in non-missionary countries. The pope designated the vicars apostolic and the Propaganda Fide coordinated all the matters of the vicariates apostolic as well as the official relationships between the missionary societies, the Holy See, and other countries. The 1844 Treaty of Whampoa 黄埔 (Huangpu, Guangdong) authorized missionary activity in the five treaty ports that China had conceded at that time. The Treaty of Tianjin (1858) and the Convention of Peking (1860) authorized missionaries to travel through the whole Empire as well as to buy or rent buildings and land. In parallel, the Propaganda Fide reorganized the ecclesiastical territorial division in China: starting in the 1840s and with a second spurt in the 1860s, the Catholic network grew like an arborescence in which the seats of the vicariates apostolic were main hubs, almost always located in provincial capitals and important regional towns. Because local mandarins were opposed to missionary land ownership, French diplomats obtained two juridical and administrative agreements in 1865 and 1895 known as Convention Berthemy and Convention Gérard-Berthemy.[7] From 1860 to 1922, the Catholic mission to China was under the French Protectorate. Catholic missionaries of all nationalities came under the jurisdiction of the French legation in Beijing, which of course had a national agenda. From the 1880s to 1922, the lay French Third Republic succeeded in aborting any attempts at direct Sino-Vatican diplomatic relationships.[8]

Since vicars apostolic were usually missionaries from the religious society in charge of the evangelization of the vicariate, the bishop had close relationships with the provincial of the religious society in question, as well as with the other missionary societies present in the vicariate. The vicars apostolic directed all the parish priests, both missionaries and Chinese, supervised the admin-

7 Chen, "La question des propriétés immobilières."
8 There was no apostolic delegate to China until 1922 and no nuncio before 1946. Soetens, *L'Église catholique en Chine*, 16-19 and 155.

3.4 Evolution of the Jesuit mission to Jiangsu and Anhui provinces: 1. vicariate apostolic of Nanjing 南京 in 1852; 2. in 1872-1882; 3. in 1892-1902; 4. in 1912-1929; 5. creation of the vicariates of Anqing 安庆, Bengbu 蚌埠 and Wuhu 芜湖 in parts of the vicariate of Nanjing in 1921-1922; 6. subdivision of the vicariate of Nanjing and creation of the vicariates of Haimen 海门 in 1926, Xuzhou 徐州 in 1931 and Shanghai 上海 in 1933. Maps from: L. Hermand, Les étapes de la mission du Kiang-nan, Shanghai, 1933, 16-19, 52 and 58. [KU Leuven, Artes University library]

istration of all the parishes, and developed seminaries to train Chinese priests. Some bishops were real "strategists of missionary development".[9] From 1919, Rome considered the vicariates apostolic provisional. The intention was for them to grow into full-fledged dioceses with Chinese bishops, Chinese priests, and sufficient numbers of Catholics. The first six Chinese bishops were ordained by Pius XI in Rome on 28 October 1926; more followed soon.

Jesuit missionaries were always good at mapping territories and doing statistics. In 1933, Father Louis Hermand 雙國英 (1873-1939) published a series of maps and statistics showing the growth of the Jesuit mission of Kiang-nan / Jiangnan 江南 (covering Jiangsu 江苏省 and Anhui provinces 安徽省) or diocese of Nanjing 南京 (Jiangsu).[10] This case illustrates the main steps of the typical spatial missionary strategy of expansion, consolidation, and reorganization [Fig. 3.4]. In 1852, there were Catholics only in the area around Shanghai 上海 and Suzhou 苏州, and small communities in Nanjing, Zhenjiang 镇江, Yangzhou 扬州, Wuhe 五河 and Huaiyin 淮阴. In 1872-82, after the fury of the Taiping Rebellion 太平天国起义 (1850-1864), missionaries explored further upstream on the Yangtze 杨子 River in Anhui province, reaching the areas of Wuhu 芜湖 and Ningguo 宁国, as well as

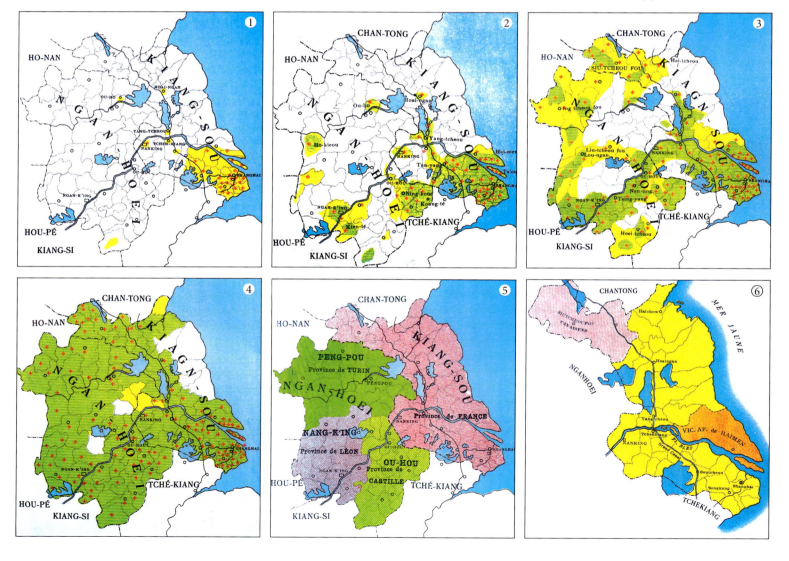

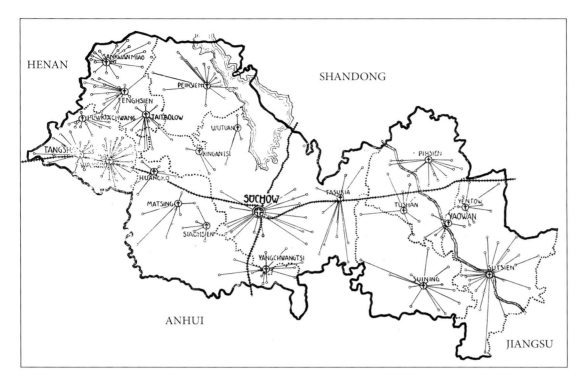

3.5 Map of the vicariate apostolic of Xuzhou / Süchow 徐州 (Jiangsu) in 1939, at the time it was managed by French Canadian Jesuits. The bishop's seat was in Xuzhou, a prefecture level city at the crossing of two railway lines. In the twenty places marked with a cross, there where permanent residences of missionaries and Chinese priests, a church, and a school. The map shows how these places were connected with 'station' villages that the missionaries visited sometimes. Map from Œuvres de la mission de Süchow 1939-1940, Xujiahui, Shanghai, 1940, 2. [Vanves, Compagnie de Jésus, Archives jésuites de France, Kiangnan]

the areas of Anqing 安庆 and Chizhou 池州. They also spread along the Grand Canal 大运河 from Changzhou 常州 to Yangzhou 扬州 and further to Huaiyin 淮阴. In 1892-1902, despite the Boxer Uprising 义和团运 (1899-1900) in the north, the density grew and families were Christianized in the north, west and south of Anhui province, and around Xuzhou 徐州 in Jiangsu province. In 1912-1922, i.e. the first decade of the Republic of China, Jesuits explored nearly the whole territory. Catholic missionaries first visited places where at least one family was Christian and founded a 'station' with an oratory [Fig. 3.5]. Such a station could grow and become a parish with a permanent missionary, while other stations receiving a missionary visit once or twice a year would use these visits to develop and expand, and eventually become parishes later. This required human resources, and the French Jesuits received help from Spanish and Italian Jesuits starting in 1914. The next step, in 1921-1929, was the division of the vicariate of Kiang-nan into four autonomous vicariates: Nanjing for the French Jesuits from Paris, Wuhu for Spanish Jesuits from Castile, Anqing for Spanish Jesuits from Léon, and Bengbu 蚌埠 for Italian Jesuits from Turin [Fig. 3.4, 5]. In 1926, a new vicariate was created in Haimen 海门 and entrusted to one of the six first Chinese bishops, the Jesuit Simon Zhu Kaimin 朱开敏 (1868-1960). In 1931, the vicariate of Xuzhou was created in the north of Jiangsu for Canadian Jesuits from Québec, and in 1933 Shanghai finally became the seat of a vicariate apostolic [Fig. 3.4, 6]. Later, in 1946, Nanjing was elevated to the rank of archdiocese, Suzhou became the seat of a diocese, and, in 1949, Haizhou 海州 became a prefecture apostolic. From 1950 onwards, no new ecclesiastical territory was created by the Propaganda Fide in China. In the following years, most foreign missionaries and vicars apostolic were expelled from the People's Republic of China.[11]

Because missionaries were often considered agents of their countries, the history of the missions in China is characterized by anti-foreign and anti-Christian sentiments.[12] Violence culminated during the Boxer Uprising, which was followed by the humiliating Boxer Protocol 辛丑条约 of 1901. Western nations and missions obtained huge compensations that encouraged them to increase

9   Lazzarotto, "A Strategist of Missionary Development in Henan." About N.G. Tacconi P.I.M.E., vicar apostolic of Kaifeng 开封 from 1916 to 1942.
10 Hermand, Les étapes de la mission du Kiang-nan. In addition: de la Servière, La nouvelle mission du Kiang-nan; Id., Histoire de la mission du Kiang-Nan; Strong, A Call to Mission, vols 1 and 2.
11 In 1950, there were 12,617 Catholic religious in China: 3,048 foreign missionary fathers and brothers belonging to 39 different missionary societies and institutes, 2,034 foreign missionary sisters, 2,557 Chinese priests, and 4,978 Chinese nuns; for 3.7 million Catholics in China (less than 1% of the Chinese population, then 552 million people).
12 Tiedemann, Handbook of Christianity in China, 338-343.

their visibility and erect rhetorical buildings. Nevertheless, it was still much easier and safer for missionary societies and institutes to buy land and build in the concession territories and in the great cities than in the mainland, where conflicts of interest constantly set missionaries and Christian Chinese against the rest of the population. Non-contested ownership was a condition for any kind of building activity. Finding appropriate places and buying enough ground to settle a mission was thus anything but easy.

**Western Islands:
The Concessions in the Treaty Ports**

The history of nineteenth- and early-twentieth-century China was deeply marked by the Unequal Treaties successively conceded from 1842 to 1901 by the Qing Dynasty after wars, revolts, and other humiliating defeats.[13] The island of Hong Kong 香港 became a British colony in 1842, and concession settlement territories were gradually gained in other cities from 1846 to 1914 by Britain, France, Japan, Russia, Germany, Austria, Italy, the United States, and Belgium.[14] If some concessions like Gulangyu 鼓浪屿 at Xiamen 厦门 (Fujian), Shamian 沙面 at Guangzhou 广州 (Guangdong), and Guangzhouwan 广州湾 (Guangdong) were real islands along the coast of China, all the other foreign concessions on the mainland were like colonial islands. As extraterritorial enclaves, they played the role of interfaces between the East and the West. Besides agents of private companies, traders, bankers, diplomats, officials, and militaries, religious from different nations and denominations also lived in the concessions. The result was a high concentration of different Western identities within the boundaries of small territories.

Churches interacted with the colonial urban setting of the concession territories and were intended to be used by the expatriates rather than by Chinese. Therefore church buildings initially adopted recognizable historical styles from specific home countries in order to express precise national and religious identities in the urban space: French Catholics in French Classic or French thirteenth-century Gothic style, British Anglicans in English Decorated Gothic style or Norman Romanesque style, Portuguese and Italian Catholics in Renaissance and Baroque styles, German Lutherans in Rhineland Romanesque, Russians in Russian-Orthodox and Byzantine styles, etc. [Fig. 3.6]. This architectural catalogue of national styles was typical of nineteenth-century national identities and could be experienced similarly to the embassies in the Legation Quarter at Beijing or the nations' streets at world exhibitions.[15]

The cosmopolitan cities of Shanghai 上海, Hong Kong, and Tianjin 天津 offered the greatest religious architectural diversity.[16] Just like in North American cities before the construction of high-rise buildings, the urban skyline was marked by church towers. In Shanghai, when there was as yet no skyscraper on the Bund, the single Gothic spire of the Anglican Holy Trinity Cathedral (1893) and the two Gothic spires of the Catholic St Ignatius Cathedral (1906-1910) competed as main landmarks. A similar visual competition existed at the foot of the Peak in Hong Kong between the Anglican St John's Cathedral (1846-1849) and the Catholic Cathedral of the Immaculate Conception (1883-1888), both in the Gothic style.

Shanghai, Hong Kong, and Tianjin, the three main international harbor cities and connections with the West, were centres of particularly intense religious activity. Besides having bishops and cathedrals, these cities hosted important schools, hospitals, and publishing houses held by several missionary societies, most of which also built a procuration house (or *procure*) in the harbor cities. These houses were directed by procurators who were responsible for the material resources, temporal interests, and logistic tasks of the congregation, had contacts with foreign banks, welcomed arriving missionaries and arranged the journeys of the returning ones, and organized transfers of all objects, goods, and materials for the mission

13 Scott, *China and the International System*; Wang, *China's Unequal Treaties*.
14 Elder, *China's Treaty Ports*; Fairbank, "The Creation of the Treaty System;" Feuerwerker, "The Foreign Presence in China," 128-141.
15 Moser and Moser, *Foreigners within the Gates*.
16 About Tianjin: Yu and Liu, *Tianjin lao jiaotang*.
17 Verhelst and Pycke, *CICM Missionaries, Past and Present*, passim. The congregation also had procuration houses in Brussels (Scheut), Antwerp, Rome, New York, New Haven, Kinshasa, Manila and Singapore.
18 Soetens, *L'Église catholique en Chine*, 35.
19 The Crédit Foncier d'Extrême Orient 義品放款銀行. See: Coomans, "China Papers."
20 Le Pichon, "Portrait of a Practical Visionary"; and <www.irfa.paris/fr/notices/notices-biographiques/robert-5> [accessed 20 February 2020].

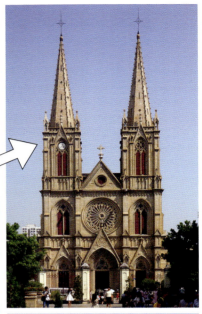

shipped from the West. The Belgian Scheut Fathers, whose missionary field was in Mongolia, had procuration houses in Shanghai, Tianjin, and Hong Kong.[17] The procurators were also involved in real-estate investments in the concession areas, speculating on the development of both the market and their activities. After the Boxer Protocol of 1901, the Lazarists, Scheut Fathers, Paris Foreign Mission Society, and Milan Foreign Mission Society invested a part of the indemnity money in land and houses within the concession areas of Shanghai and Hankow 汉口 (Wuhan 武汉, Hubei).[18] When the French secularization laws of 1902-1904 were passed in France, the religious congregations settled in the French concessions in China feared expulsion and the confiscation of their patrimony. Therefore, the French Jesuits and Lazarists converted their properties into cash by selling them to a Belgian mortgage company that had been founded at that occasion.[19] Such colonial real-estate speculations were possible in the treaty ports and were, of course, unthinkable on the mainland. Father Léon Robert 金神父 (1866-1956), the 'practical visionary' of the Paris Foreign Mission Society, undoubtedly was one of the most brilliant procurators and real-estate experts in service of the Catholic missions: assistant of the procurator in Hong Kong (1888), procurator in Shanghai (1891), *économe général* of his society for the China mission, based in Hong Kong (1903), assistant of the superior general in Paris (1921), and finally superior general of the Paris Foreign Mission Society (1935-1945).[20] Father Robert played an important role in the urban development of the French Concession in Shanghai – Père Robert Street (now Ruijin Road 瑞金路) was

3.6 Architectural styles and national identities: German Catholic cathedral in Qingdao 青岛 (Shandong), French Catholic cathedral in Guangzhou 广州 (Guangdong), English Anglican cathedral in Shanghai 上海, and Russian Orthodox cathedral in Harbin 哈尔滨 (Heilongjiang). "The Qing Empire of China, the cake of kings and emperors", cartoon by Henri Meyer, from Le Petit Journal, Paris, January 16, 1898.
[Pictures © THOC; Cartoon, Cornell University Library Digital Collections, Wikimedia Commons]

21 Soetens, *L'Église catholique en Chine*, 72-73, Yu and Liu, *Tianjin lao jiaotang*, 13-18.

22 Considered an instigator of xenophobia, Lebbe was removed to another province by his superior. Leclercq, *Vie du Père Lebbe*, 199-236. About Lebbe: Join-Lambert et al., *Vincent Lebbe et son héritage*.

23 Song and Chen, *History Remains*, 94-103, 148-159, 194-205; Mo, "The Gendered Space of the *Oriental Vatican*."

24 Coomans, "Gendered Spaces of Cahtolic Settlements in China," in this book, p. 134-139. Also Henriot and Zheng, *Atlas de Shanghai*, 25 and 85-86.

25 de la Servière, "Une université catholique en Chine."

3.7 Boundary stone of the Catholic mission, relocated near Our Lady of Lourdes' Church of Shamian Island 沙面岛 *in Guangzhou (Guangdong).* 天主堂 *tian zhu tang means 'Catholic Church'.*
[© THOC 2017]

named after him – and in Kowloon 九龙 in Hong Kong.

Extensions of colonial and concession territories gave missionary societies the opportunity to purchase new (cheap) borderlands and to speculate. Building on – and sometimes behind – borders of concessions was part of missionary spatial strategy. One of the saddest cases of collusion between missionaries and a colonial power, the 'Affair of Laoxikai', happened in Tianjin in 1917. Rome had established the vicariate apostolic of Coastal Chi-Li (later Tianjin) and entrusted it to the French Lazarists. A cathedral was soon built on the grounds of Laoxikai 老西开 outside the French concession; its design was inspired by the Cathedral of Marseille and expressed the prestige both of the French and the Catholics in the cosmopolitan harbor city. Once it was built, the French authorities, arguing their protectorate over the Catholic Church, unilaterally considered Laoxikai to be French territory and controlled it with their police.[21] Chinese citizens denounced this fait accompli as an illegal encroachment and were supported by the renowned daily paper *I Shi Bao* 益世报 (The Public Good) and its founder the Belgian Lazarist father Vincent Lebbe 雷鸣远 (1877-1940).[22] In general, the limits of mission property were marked by bilingual boundary stones [Fig. 3.7].

The most successful Catholic settlement in China was undoubtedly the quarter of the French Jesuits in Shanghai.[23] Soon after returning to Shanghai in 1842, they established a mission at a place named Xujiahui 徐家匯 (Zi-ka-wei in Shanghainese) near the tomb of the mathematician-astronomer Paul Xu Guangqi 徐光啓 (1562-1633), a convert to Catholicism who had been a friend of the Jesuit Matteo Ricci 利瑪竇 (1552-1620). Xujiahui was located west of the French concession and never would be incorporated, even after the last French extension of 1914.[24] Well situated along a canal, in an area with compounds of several wealthy Chinese families and Christian villages, Xujiahui became the major base of the Catholic Church in China [Fig. 3.8, n°5]. A chapel and a school for boys, both dedicated to St Ignatius, and a library opened their doors in 1847. They were the first Catholic school and the first modern library founded in China. The Jesuits established other educational, scientific and cultural institutions, including a minor seminary, Tushanwan 土山湾 (T'ou-Sè-Wè in Shanghainese) Orphanage and Arts & Crafts school in 1864, Tushanwan Press in 1867, a museum in 1868, an observatory in 1873, St Louis elementary school in 1884, and Hui Shi secondary school in 1920. Female institutions were located on the other side of the creek, enhancing the gender division: they included a Carmelite convent and a convent of the Helpers of the Holy Souls (*Dames Auxiliatrices du Purgatoire*), both founded in 1869, and Morning Star girls' school in 1904. All these institutions grew and transformed Xujiahui into a well-planned religious area consisting of parallel east-west oriented buildings along both sides of the creek. Successful Jesuit educational projects usually led to the foundation of a Catholic university, for example in Shanghai in 1903 with the founding of the *Université l'Aurore* or Zhendan University 震旦大學.[25] In 1908, the university moved from Xujiahui within the French concession – Dubail Avenue, now Chongqing Road, one block from the French *Hôpital Sainte-Marie*, now Ruijin Hospital

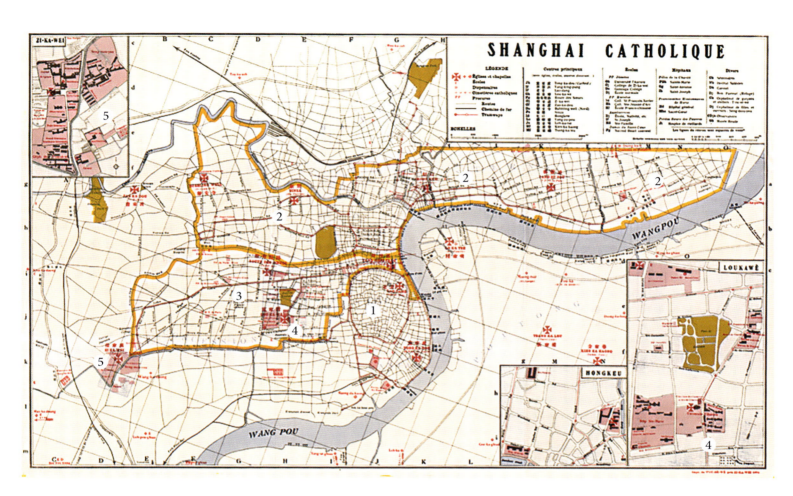

Road –, where it developed programs in humanities, engineering science and medicine until its suppression in 1952. Both sites were major centres of Catholic presence in the city, as can be seen on the map *Shanghai Catholique* from 1933 [Fig. 3.8]. One year after the university opened its doors, the cornerstone of a new church was laid in the middle of Xujiahui: the Gothic cathedral of St. Ignatius, completed in 1910, became the largest church in East Asia and the flagship of the French Jesuits in China, in the middle of their most successful mission ever.[26] The cathedral's main façade faces east and downtown Shanghai, while, as we will see later, most churches in China adopted the local tradition of turning their main façade or at least their main entrance to the south.

In 1922-1925, the Jesuits founded another university in China, the Higher Institute of Industrial and Commercial Studies in Tianjin 工商学院天津工商大学, and built a French-style campus. At the same time, in 1925, American Benedictines opened the Fu Jen Catholic University of Peking 辅仁大学, and built a Chinese-style campus for the schools of Chinese studies, philosophy, letters, and fine arts [Fig. 3.30]. In contrast to these three Catholic universities, there were thirteen universities established by the Protestants, in Beijing, Shanghai, Guangzhou, Nanjing, Chengdu 成都, Jinan 济南, Wuhan 武汉, Fuzhou 福州, Changsha 长沙, and elsewhere.[27]

Lastly, we should mention the fascinating modern colonial urban development from 1927-1935 in Kowloon Tong 九龙塘, Hong Kong, along Prince Edward Road and Waterloo Road. Catholic missionary institutions played an important role in the urbanization of this international neighborhood, which included the parish church of St Teresa's, La Salle College of the Brothers of the Christian

3.8 Catholic Shanghai, map published by the Jesuits in 1933: 1. Chinese town, 2. International concession, 3. French concession, 4. Aurora University 震旦大学 at Loukawè / Lujiawan 卢家湾 area and detail map, 5. Zikawei / Xujiahui 徐家汇 area and detail map. [Vanves, Compagnie de Jésus, Archives jésuites de France, Chine, Cartes et Plans, 2Fi, R5]

26 Haouissée, "Inauguration de l'église Saint-Ignace"; Guillen-Nuñez, "The Gothic Revival and the Architecture of the New Society of Jesus in Macao and China."
27 Bays and Widmer, *China's Christian Colleges*; Cody, "American Geometries." See also Braschi, "Civilizing Space in West China," in this book, p. 210-227.

3.9 Catholic area around Prince Edward Road at Kowloon Tong, Hong Kong, around 1940. View from the east: 1. St Teresa's Church 1931-1932, 2. La Salle College Brothers of the Christian Schools 1930-1932, 3. Maryknoll School 1936, 4. Anglican Christ Church 1936, 5. St Teresa's Hospital, Sisters of St Paul 1940, picture 1948.
[https://gwulo.com/atom/16840, courtesy Gwulo.com]

28 Coomans and Ho, "Architectural Styles and Identities in Hong Kong."
29 Coomans, "Gendered Spaces."
30 Wiest, "The Building of the Cathedral of Canton."
31 Masson, "Guangzhou shengxin dajiaotong."
32 Coomans, "Yancang yu sheng xin da jiaotang de guangmang zhihou"; Xiang, "Building."
33 USFCA, Ricci, Canton Archdiocese Archives, F2.1-052.
34 A *paifang* is often a 'chastity arch' erected to a woman who behaved righteously. The association of this traditional Chinese construction and the Virgin Mary is an interesting encounter.
35 It is not impossible that this spirit screen was a remnant of the former palace of the viceroy.
36 USFCA, Ricci, Canton Archdiocese Archives, F2.1-053: 廣州石室天主堂及屋宇地段圖, dated August 1, 1913.

Schools, a girls' school and convent of the American Maryknoll Sisters, and a hospital of the French Sisters of Charity of St Paul [Fig. 3.9]. Furthermore, the French Mission of Paris and the Pontifical Institute of Foreign Missions invested in modern housing blocks that were rented to Catholic middle-class families, mostly Portuguese and Macanese, and generated income for the mission.[28]

Cathedral Islands: For Pope and Home Country

A cathedral is the most symbolic church of a diocese and contains the seat of the bishop or the vicar apostolic. It never stands alone and is surrounded by the bishop's residence, diocesan administration offices and a seminary for the education of the priests of the diocese. In the centralized structure of the Roman Catholic Church, the bishop is the key person between the top of the hierarchy and the Catholic believers grouped in parish communities. Missionary cathedrals often include more buildings in the same compound or in the close neighborhood, such as schools and orphanages for boys and girls, and housing for the religious institutes involved in education and health care. According to gender rules, male and female institutions had to be physically separated from each other by walls or by a street.[29]

A cathedral is supposed to be the 'flagship' of the diocese and the most visible symbol of the Catholic Church in the public urban space. Building cathedrals in Western styles, with high towers and exotic Gothic forms, sometimes led to political, cultural and religious tensions, as Jean-Paul Wiest tells about the Sacred-Heart Cathedral of Guagzhou, built in 1861-1879.[30] The cathedral was erected on the site of the former palace of the Chinese viceroy, which the British and French military forces had destroyed during the Battle of Canton in December 1857. As soon as the Convention of Peking was signed in 1860, French consular authorities claimed this symbolic place as compensation for the churches that had been confiscated in the eighteenth century. Vicar apostolic Zéphirin Guillemin 明稽埒 (1814-1886) from the Paris Foreign Mission Society, built a grandiose cathedral in thirteenth-century French Gothic style and obtained funding from the French Emperor Napoleon III.[31] The verticality of the stone building completely dominated the horizontal urban landscape of Guangzhou and its single-storey wooden houses. Because of this vertical structure and the fact they were made of stone, the two Gothic spires were seen by the Chinese as disrupting the natural *fengshui* and therefore bringing bad luck. Two maps of the cathedral compound of Guangzhou shed light on the spatial organization.[32]

- The Chinese-style map is undated but goes back to the late nineteenth century [Fig. 3.10].[33] The buildings are inaccurately located and figured in the Chinese way that combines plans and elevations: the cathedral is in the middle of a walled compound that includes other clustered buildings and shops along the northern street. If one looks at the main Chinese north-south axis that runs through the cathedral, there are two other poles which must be noticed: 1) to the north, below

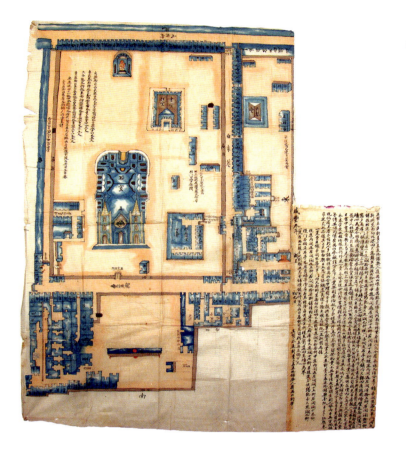
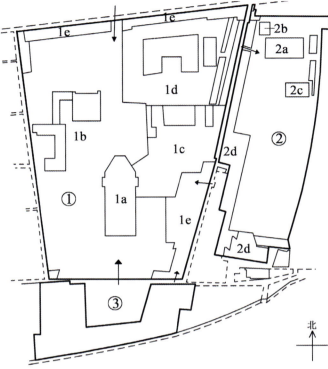

the shops along the street, is a pavilion with a statue of Mary and Jesus and the inscription 'archway of Christ' (*Yesu paifang* 耶蘇牌坊),[34] and 2) to the south, in an open area across the front street, there is a traditional spirit wall with the inscription 'screen wall' (*zhaobi* 照壁).[35] In temples, palaces and houses, such screens are placed just outside the main gate as shields that block spirits from entering through the gate. The cathedral is thus *fengshui*-oriented – Guangzhou is a remarkable example of a *fengshui*-planned city – and protected from the bad spirits like a Chinese temple.

- The second map, dated 1913, is a Western cadastral map with all the parcels, buildings and streets named in Chinese.[36] The grounds owned by the Church consisted of three blocks separated by public space [Fig. 3.11]. The main block with the cathedral includes a) the vicariate's administration (bishop's house, library, workshops) northwest of the cathedral; b) the seminary for the education of Chinese priests (Latin school, dormitory, refectory) northeast of the cathedral; c) the boys' school or Sacred Heart College, north of the seminary; d) along northern and eastern streets, forty and thirty houses respectively owned by the Church. The second block, across the eastern street, was the area for the women, nuns, and orphans. It included a flower garden, girls' school, nursery for orphaned babies, and workshops, as well as forty houses and other buildings around a small inner courtyard. The third block, south of the cathedral, consisted of a public square surrounded by about sixty houses and other buildings.

This spatial organization was thus based on specific enclosures and accesses: men and women were separated by a street; the boys' school and the seminary were separated by

3.10 Compound of the Sacred Heart Cathedral in Guangzhou 广州 (Guangdong). The accompanying text is dated 1853, but the map is obviously later: it shows the cathedral as completed around 1880.
[San Francisco, USFCA, Ricci Institute for Chinese Western Cultural History, Canton Archdiocese Archives, F2.1-052]

3.11 Compound of the Sacred Heart Cathedral in Guangzhou 广州, drawn after a cadastre map dated August 1, 1913. Part 1 comprises the cathedral (a), the bishop's centre (b), the seminary for Chinese priests (c), the Sacred Hearth College for boys (d) and rental housing along the streets. Part 2, the area for women, was separated from part 1 by a street and included a girls' school (a), a nursery for baby orphans (b), workshops (c) and rental housing (d). Part 3, a public square in front of the cathedral, included about forty houses.
[San Francisco, USFCA, Ricci Institute for Chinese Western Cultural History, Canton Archdiocese Archives, F2.1-053].

 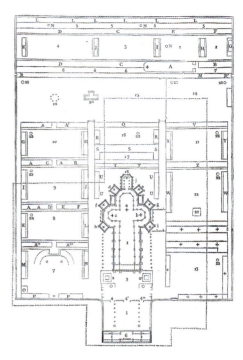

3.12 Western-style perspective drawing of Xishiku Cathedral 西什库天主堂 at Beijing 北京, dated May 1916, centre of the French Lazarists in China and symbol of the Catholic resistance against the Boxers in 1900. The general symmetrical composition refers to the spatial organisation and orientation of the Forbidden City. View from the south-east. 1. main entrance, 2. cathedral, 3. printing house, 4. residence of the vicar apostolic, 5. chapel of the community and bishop, 6. "patronage", 7. chapel of the major seminary, 8. major seminary, 9. minor seminary, 10. chapel of the minor seminary, 11. housing of the servants, 12. gardens, 13. orphanage of the Sisters of Charity, 14. chapel of the Sisters of Charity, 15. public roads.
[Paris, Archives historiques de la Congrégation de la Mission]

3.13 Plan of the Xishiku Cathedral complex in Beijing, from Favier, Péking. Histoire et description, 1902, 258-259. [KU Leuven, Maurits Sabbe Library: 3-002071/c]

enclosure walls. The most important area included the cathedral and the bishops' buildings, administration and workshops, and was accessible from two gates. For the celebrations, the cathedral was open to all baptized Catholics, but from different sides: schoolboys, seminarians, nuns and girl orphans, and Chinese parishioners all had separate entrances corresponding to the places they had to occupy inside. The cathedral was also the main parish church of Guangzhou, and therefore had a resident parish priest, and rooms for catechism and social works of the parish.

The most remarkable example of a cathedral compound is Xishiku Cathedral 西什库天主堂 in Beijing, also called North Church (北堂 Beitang).[37] At the demand of the Emperor, the North Cathedral was moved to its present location in 1887. The French Congregation of the Mission built a monumental complex about one kilometre west of the Forbidden City, whose general layout referred to that of the Forbidden City: a walled rectangular area, a main south-north axis, the centrally located cathedral expressing harmony, and a symmetrical composition of buildings regularly arranged around courtyards [Figs. 3.12 and 3.13]. The cathedral was designed in 1887-89 by Father Alphonse Favier 樊国梁 (1837-1905), who became vicar apostolic of Beijing in 1899.[38] The façade, with its two towers, three porches, and a central rose window, combines elements from Italian and French Gothic cathedrals. In front of the cathedral, two Chinese-style pavilions with imperial-yellow tile roofs protect two stone steles on which are carved the imperial decree of the removal of the church to this site.[39]

At the right or eastern side of the cathedral, the major and minor seminaries were arranged around square courtyards, while the bishop's residence and the buildings for the missionaries were symmetrically arranged at the western side. The famous printing house of the Lazarist Press was located west of the entrance alley. There were also a museum, a dispensary, stores, stables, and other ancillary buildings. At the back or northern side of Beitang, separated by a street, the female complex of the French congregation of the Daughters of Charity of Saint Vincent de Paul (Filles de la Charité) consisted of a convent, school, Holy Childhood orphanage, and workshops. One of the most dramatic episodes of the Boxer Upris-

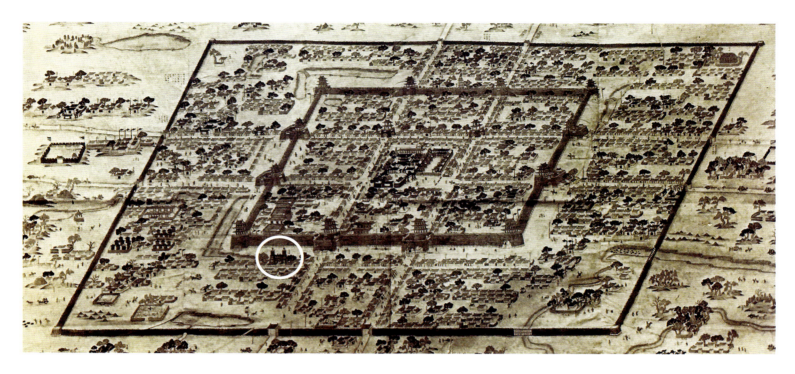

ing was the siege of *Beitang,* where about 100 Europeans and 3300 Chinese Christians had found a refuge: during the two-month siege, Vicar Apostolic Favier, 30 French marines and 14 Italian soldiers resisted heroically and saved most of the refugees.[40] From then, *Beitang* was considered a "noble Catholic acropolis."[41]

Other vicars apostolic, like Laurent Guillon 纪隆主教 (1854-1900) of the Paris Foreign Mission Society, were less lucky. On July 2, 1900, the Boxers beheaded him, and burned other missionaries and many Chinese Christians who had found a refuge in the cathedral of Shenyang 沈阳 (Liaoning), before burning the whole cathedral complex.[42] The ancient city of Shenyang (Mukden, in Manchu), the Qing capital of Manchuria, has a remarkable square plan divided in nine equal square blocks, with the palace occupying the central block.[43] Foreigners, of course, could not establish a mission within the walled city, but were allowed to build their cathedral in the area between the first and second city walls [Fig. 3.14]. In 1909-1912, a new cathedral was built on the same place with compensation money from the Chinese state. Building a shrine for the martyrs in a rhetorical Gothic style with two high spires was not only an architectural statement but a religious and political act.

Bishops encouraged Catholics to organize processions on specific occasions. Not only was the community interacting with the public space as a group, but the individual participants were also showing their identity publically. As the beginning and end of the procession, the cathedral – or the parish church at local level – acted as centre of a territory.

As will be elaborated at the end of this chapter, the 'cathedral islands' multiplied and gained importance from the mid-1920s as a consequence of the new Vatican policy of indigenization and the increasing number of new vicariates apostolic.

Parish Islands: Christian Compounds in Towns and Villages

The penetration of the mission into the deep Chinese mainland, Gansu, Mongolia and Manchuria, was anything but easy. In some provinces, like Tibet, missionaries never put down roots, but remained in the neighboring provinces of Yunnan and

3.14 Chinese-style birds eye view from the south of Shenyang 沈阳 (Liaoning), 1893. The Catholic cathedral is located outside the old city wall, close to the south-west gate.
[Paris, Institut de recherche France-Asie / Missions étrangères de Paris, photo box China 31]

37 First established by the Jesuits in 1700-1703, it was part of an exceptional 'church cross' with the South Church (南堂 *Nantang*) 1705-1711, East Church (东堂 *Dongtang*) 1721-1730, and West Church (西堂 *Xitang*) 1723. The latter three were demolished in 1900 and rebuilt later. See: Bonnet, *Les anciennes églises de Pékin;* Sweeten, *China's Old Churches,* 70-147.
38 Clark, *China Gothic,* 97-124.
39 "Consécration de la nouvelle cathédrale;" Favier, *Péking. Histoire et description,* 254-259; Tokarski, "La Mission de Pékin;" Sweeten, *China's Old Churches,* 359-367.
40 Fleming, *The Siege,* 211-221.
41 Favier, "Deux mois de siège."
42 "Mandchourie."
43 Wang and Lü, *Jindai Shenyang cheng shi xingtai yanjiu,* 65-80.

3.15 Hybrid style church in the mountain village of Xitougai 西頭岩/遲頭岩 (Guizhou), built by French fathers from the Paris Foreign Mission.
[Paris, Institut de recherche France Asie / Missions étrangères de Paris, photo box China 17]

44 Deshayes, *Tibet 1846-1952: les missionnaires de l'impossible*; Li, "Dapingzi, la première chrétienté au cœur du Yunnan."
45 Coomans, "East Meets West on the Construction Site;" Sweeten, *Christianity in Rural China*.
46 [Jung], *Le missionnaire constructeur*, 1-2 [quote translated from French]; Coomans and Xu, *Building Churches in Northern China*, 124-125.

Sichuan.[44] Most people were indifferent or hostile to the missionaries, who needed a long period of adaptation to learn the language and get used to the climate before beginning to evangelize. The first missionaries arriving in a village rented a small house or lived in caves where they fitted out a discrete oratory. As has already been said, purchasing land was allowed but subject to the agreement of the local mandarin, who by definition was suspicious. The first parish buildings were mostly modest and hybridized vernacular craftsmanship with some Western forms [Fig. 3.15].[45]

Guidelines published by Jesuits in a 1926 handbook, based on their years of experience, defined criteria for Christian missionaries settling in a northern Chinese village.

> When buying land, if possible, it is better to buy at least two or three *mu* (亩; 1 mu = 6.66 ares) at the start. Otherwise, later, when the community will have grown, the neighbors will make you 'favorable' prices, at a much higher price. As much as possible, the following locations should be avoided: (a) Do not buy outside the village. The properties are, of course, much cheaper precisely because nobody wants to settle there. There will be no neighbors, at least at one side, often on three sides. Women and girls, especially when new Christians, will not gladly make such a long journey for going to church. (b) Do not settle in the middle of a market, if it is a village with a market. The disadvantage would be the same, and even more serious for women, if they were obliged to cross these teeming crowds for going to prayer. Shouts and noise from outside will often disturb the priest during Mass and especially during the sermon. (c) If possible, preferably buy a location on the northern side of the street (if it is a street that runs from east to west). Choose a good place to the north, for the main buildings: the church, the rectory, the schools. The main gate, the stables and sometimes the kitchen, can be built to the south side. (d) Finally, more than anything else, you must avoid land that is too low and thus subject to flooding. You must thoroughly inquire about the water level in summer, especially if the location is near a river. If that is the case, the possibility remains to bank up, especially if the Christians offer to do the job.[46]

Finding the most appropriate place in a town and progressively buying up land from neighbors could cost time and money. Father Joseph Henri Guilbaud 石介臣 (1882-1962) from the French Foreign Mission reported about his parish at Dongchuan 东川, (Yunnan), in 1930 a town of 50,000 inhabitants and several hundred Christians:

3.16 Fishers town of Shenjiamen 沈家门 on Zhoushan Island 舟山岛 (Zhejiang). On a hill near the harbor, the church of Our Lady of the Rosary, the missionary's residence, and the Catholic school dominate the whole area. [Paris, Archives historiques de la Congrégation de la Mission]

there is a small chapel (...) This first installation which was only temporary, lasts for 50 years, although it is well proved that the situation of the Catholic Mission is very unfavorable to us. Having noted the serious drawbacks of our eccentric and humble location, my predecessor resolved to acquire in town, at all costs, another location better suited to our apostolic mission. For twenty years, he acquired one by one the houses included in a radius delimited in advance, he ended up making a pretty good location, right in the center of the city, on the main street. (...) the location is ready, you have to build. (...) Our installation in the city is all the more pressing with Protestant tactics and competition, so that if we do not hasten, we risk putting ourselves in an enduring state of humiliating inferiority. Placed on the main street, the Catholic Mission will attract the attention of passersby.[47]

The works usually ended with the erection of the church's tower, which dominated the town or the village [Figs. 3.16 and 3.17]. Often the confrontation with the traditional built environment was intentional and violent; it could not leave the local population indifferent. The form, style, and materials of Western-style churches could totally change the harmony of the skyline and make them a divisive subject of conversation.

Another chapter of the 1926 handbook describes how to arrange buildings within a rectangular compound to fit the orientation (e.g. main entrances facing south) and functions of buildings, as well as the climate, specific to northern China. The introduction advises: "do not use the European concessions, nor the Protestants from America, as models, but faithfully imitate the local".

The best orientation is considered that of a northern house or main house (*beiwu* 北屋, *tangwu* 堂屋) whose doors and windows face south. (…) If you want to make these houses more pleasant in the summer, you can place windows in the northern wall in order to catch the breeze. (…) The western house (*qiwu* 西屋) whose orientation faces east: in the winter it is sunny from sunrise; in the summer, from eleven o'clock on, it is out of the direct rays of the sun. The eastern house (*dongwu* 东屋), has the worst orientation because it is turned to the west. These houses are virtually uninhabitable in the summer. Therefore it must never be chosen for small chapels (doors and windows on one side, that is to say only opening to the west). One could use these western

47 Guilbaud, "Chine. Nécessité d'une église plus centrale" (quote translated from French).

3.17 The massive church built by the Belgian Franciscan missionaries protects the Christian village in the outskirts of Jingzhou 荆州 (Hubei). The church was built with thecompensation payed by the Chinese state for the murder of bishop Theotimus Verhaeghen 德希圣 (1867-1904), vicar apostolic of Yichang 宜昌. [Leuven, KADOC-KU Leuven, Picture Archive of the Flemish Franciscans: 1626]

houses in the morning for Mass. But in the summer, after midday, you could not use it for confession, or to celebrate the evening prayer. It would be better to put the chapel in the southern house (*nanwu* 南屋) whose orientation faces north. In the winter, it will not be too cold, if the community is fervent, that is to say if there are many people. The missionary's room, however, should not be put in the southern house, unless it has a good bed-stove (*kang* 炕). He should live in the northern house if possible. To keep this house dry and sound, do not forget to raise it about two feet above ground level, or at least three steps at the front door.[48]

The author of the handbook only pays attention to rational reasons related to climate, and omits to mention the special Chinese rules of spatial arrangement based on the flow of energy and the harmony with the environment (*fengshui*).

Pictures in missionary journals often show that parish settlements were isolated compounds on the outskirts of the village, where the main rules of *fengshui* seem to have been generally respected. Not only was the south-north orientation important; in mountain regions, the main buildings had to turn their backs to the hillside and face the water or river [Figs. 3.2 and 3.3]. Settlements of a certain importance would have a church, a residence for several European and Chinese priests, a Holy Childhood orphanage with an attached residence of the lay nuns working there, a boys' school, a girls' school, a house for catechumens, and a house for the elderly. All these buildings were arranged around courtyards, the facades of the main buildings as well as the main gate of the compound being turned to the south. A rectangular wall, sometimes with towers at the corners, surrounded the settlement [Fig. 3.18]. The dominating volume of the church expressed the identity of the settlement. Towers and Gothic spires in particular were Christianizing factors of space, in the way that bells were Christianizing factors of time.

Missionary literature emphasizes how miserable Chinese villages were compared to the clean and orderly mission. Pictures of well-dressed villagers welcoming their bishop on pastoral visit [Fig. 3.19] or orphans posing in front of rational school buildings contrast with the picturesque disorder of villages. One example out of many of this stereotyping is a description of a village in the

48 [Jung], *Le missionnaire constructeur*, 3-5 [quote translated from French]; Coomans and Xu, *Building Churches in Northern China*, 126-130.

3.18 The Franciscan mission of Danzishan 担子山 (Hubei) was located apart from the village and surrounded with a wall and towers. View from the south; photography around 1930.
[Leuven, KADOC-KU Leuven, Picture Archive of the Flemish Franciscans: 1626]

3.19 Pastoral visit of Mgr. André Defèbvre 戴福瑞 (1886-1967), French Lazarist vicar apostolic of Ningpo 宁波, to the village of Songpuxiang 松浦乡 (Zhejiang) in 1927.
[Paris, Archives historiques de la Congrégation de la Mission]

northwest of Hebei Province by a travelling Lazarist, from 1923:

> A Chinese village is a charming spectacle, especially in the spring when the trees are green and cover the silent group of farms with their shadows. This sight, however, should be admired from a certain distance; the more you approach, the more it turns for the worse. The adobe houses, covered with cob, are badly aligned along narrow alleys where dirty children, hungry dogs and horrible black pigs are dragging themselves along. I fear these ways and breathe deeply only when back in the fields of corn or sorghum.[49]

49 Hubrecht, "De Pékin à la Trappe de Chine," 176 (quote translated from French).

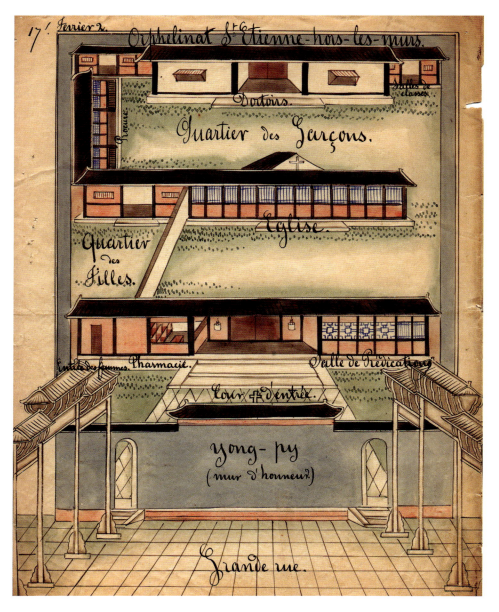

3.20 Orphanage of St Steven along the main street in Guiyang 贵阳 (Guizhou). The church is in the middle, the boys' courtyard in the back, and the girls' courtyard to the left. Drawing dated February 2.
[Paris, Institut de recherche France Asie / Missions étrangères de Paris, photo box China 19]

Rural Islands: the Christian (Fortified) Villages

Because of the difficulty of establishing parishes in existing villages, competing with the local pagodas, and developing a basic Christian settlement in a particular compound, missionaries adopted another strategy in some rural areas where hostility was particularly intense: they founded villages exclusively for Christian families. These Christian rural islands or 'reductions' were not utopias but did have to contrast with the traditional villages of the 'pagans', as the missionaries said, by displaying their moral, economic, and physical superiority. The agricultural wealth created among other things by irrigation/drainage systems and improved seed stocks resulted in a particular solidarity between Christian families. Living according to Christian mores, they refused traditional Chinese matrimonial arrangements as well as the practices of keeping concubines, foot binding, consuming opium, and abandoning baby girls. Because of this contrast, Christian villages were targeted by bandits and anti-Christian movements such as the Boxer Uprising, and therefore some were fortified with adobe walls, towers, and gates.

From the mid-1870s, the Scheut Fathers adopted this Christian colonization method in the Ordos region 鄂尔多斯 (Central Mongolia).[50] They bought large areas of remote agricultural land, improved the soil with irrigation works, and founded Christian villages.[51] The missionaries also gave seed to the farmers and so convinced people to convert and join the Christian villages. This land colonization interacted with the Chinese migration in Mongolia: the new Christian villages formed ethnically homogenous Han islands in Mongol territory that was also inhabited by Hui Muslims. This Chinese colonization method did not achieve great results before 1900, when there was massive destruction by the nomadic Mongols. From 1901, the Chinese state encouraged land clearing and exploitation, which benefited the Christian villages until 1949.

Like Christian neighborhoods in Chinese towns and villages, the Christian rural communities were called 'Christianities' by the missionaries. The newly established Christian villages needed names: some referred to Christian devotion or saints, like Meiguiyingzi 玫瑰营子 (Rosary, Inner Mongolia), or to the home towns of missionaries, like Xiaoqiaopan 小桥畔 (literally 'small bridge', Shaanxi), which the missionaries named *Klein Brugge*, Little Bruges (*brug* in Dutch means 'bridge'). After the Boxer Uprising and the destruction of many Christian villages, the compensation money from the Chinese state was used to rebuild to and acquire more land.

Besides converting people, the missionaries invested a lot of energy in educating children and orphans, who were the future of the Christian villages. The work of the Holy Childhood (*Sainte-Enfance*) was an important part of the missionaries' apostolate.[52] Orphanages for girls and to a lesser extent boys were founded in many Christian villages and towns. The largest orphanages were urban, associated with a school, and served by a community of Western missionary sisters [Fig. 3.19]. Most orphanages, however, were held by indigenous religious women called Chinese virgins.[53] The residences of the Virgins and the Holy Childhood orphanages were priority constructions in the Christian villages.

The church in the middle of the village had a bell tower that identified both the church and the village on the skyline [Fig. 3.16]. One of the most unexpected cases was the Gothic Flemish brick tower of Balagai 巴拉盖 (Inner Mongolia) that looked like the belfry of Bruges (Belgium), or the tower of a chess game on the scale of the Mongolian plain. [Fig. 3.22] This tower, built to fulfill a vow made in 1917 during a plague epidemic, was erected in thanksgiving to the Sacred Heart, and the whole village was also dedicated to the Sacred Heart.[54]

Building solid walls around the village was the most efficient way to prevent attacks from Mongols and brigands, and to protect the population.[55] The Chinese technique of building rammed walls (adobe) was commonly used, giving some villages the appearance of desert forts [Fig. 3.21]. Most Christian Chinese Han villages built by the Scheut Fathers in Ordos were fortified. In the village of Xiaoqiaopan, founded in 1878, a church, a residence and an orphanage were erected in 1884 and surrounded by an earth wall. Because of the growing danger of attack, a second wall was built in 1895 to protect the houses.[56] The village then formed a great 150 x 250m rectangle surrounded by a 6-m high earth wall with dry moat, bastions and battlements [Fig. 6.29].

Missionaries had good rifles and some of them organized the resistance of their village in 1900 against the joint attacks of Boxers and Mongols. Xiaoqiaopan heroically sustained a siege of two months. Most other Christian villages were less fortunate; they were destroyed and the population massacred.

Memory Islands: Cemeteries and Remembrance of Martyrs

Since Christian missions were associated with foreign imperialism, many missionaries were considered as acting against China's interest and identity. The Qing Emperors tried to keep Church activities under control as part of their centralized policy, but were confronted with the local governments, which

3.21 *Three Scheut Fathers posing in front of a corner tower of the fortified Christian village of Shanba* 陕霸 *(Inner Mongolia).*
[Leuven, KADOC-KU Leuven, CICM Picture Archive: 21.2.14]

3.22 *Christian village of Balagai* 巴拉盖 *(Inner Mongolia), surrounded with an earthen wall, and its brick belfry in Flemish style, erected in 1918. View from the south.*
[Leuven, Ferdinand Verbiest Institute]

50 Taveirne, *Han-Mongol Encounters and Missionary Endeavors*; Van Hecken, *Les réductions catholiques du pays des Ordos.*
51 Zhang, Sun and Zhang, "The Role of Land Management."
52 Palatre. *L'infanticide et l'œuvre de la Sainte-Enfance en Chine.*
53 See further: Coomans, "Gendered Spaces," in this book.
54 Coomans and Luo, "Mimesis, Nostalgia and Ideology," 505; Luo, *Transmission and Transformation*, 181-187; Leyssen, "Mongolie. La belle mission de Palakai," 272.
55 Van Melckebeke, *Service social de l'Église en Mongolie*, 63-77.
56 Luo, *Transmission and Transformation*, 106-119. The wall still exists today.

57 Ku, "The Shaping of the Late Qing's Policy toward Christianity."
58 Fairbank, "Patterns Behind the Tientsin Massacre;" Cohen, *China and Christianity*.
59 Sweeten, *China's Old Churches*, 182-207; Clark, *China Gothic*, 22-40 and 370-372.
60 Boxer Protocol, Beijing, September 7, 1901, Peace Agreement between the Great Powers and China, article 5. See: <www.100jia.net/china1900/ereignisse/boxerprotokoll.htm> [consulted July 2018].
61 Xiang Hongyan, "A Martyr and a Hero …"
62 Clark, *China's Saints*.
63 <http://www.vatican.va/news_services/liturgy/saints/ns_lit_doc_20001001_zhao-rong-compagni_en.html>.
64 *Les Missions Catholiques*, (1872) 161-697; (1905), 306. Masson, "Sancian: Landscape and Architecture."

3.23 *Tientsin Massacre* 天津大屠杀 *of 1870 and the fire of the French church and compound. Original printed paper fan from 1870.*
[Paris, Archives historiques de la Congrégation de la Mission, C 164 1 a 8]

generally were strongly anti-foreign and thus anti-Christian.⁵⁷ Missionaries and Chinese Christians were often massacred, churches and Christian villages burned, houses of Christians ransacked and Christian cemeteries profaned. The most violent persecutions were the Taiping Rebellion (1850-1864), the Tientsin Massacre (1870), and the Boxer Uprising (1899-1901). In the long tradition of evangelization and martyrdom, conversions increased after every massacre. Therefore, restoring the ruined cathedrals, churches, villages, and cemeteries expressed 'resurrection' and victory to a certain extent.

Both the name and the architecture of Our Lady of Victories 望海楼 (*Wang Hai Lou*) in Tianjin makes it one of the most explicitly memorial churches in China. The façade with its heavily buttressed central tower, two lateral turrets, and narrow vertical windows looks more like a medieval castle or a fort than a church. The façade was erected outside the concession area, on the most visible place of the city, in a meander of the Hai River 海河 facing the south. The church commemorates the Tientsin Massacre, a dramatic missionary incident in June 1870, that took place following rumors about Christian baptism causing death and Catholic nuns who kidnapped children for their orphanages.⁵⁸ Provocations from the French consul led to a clash that resulted in the massacre of two French diplomats, twelve French missionaries and about forty Chinese Christians, as well as the destruction of five churches [Fig. 3.23].⁵⁹ Building a memorial church was one of the reparations ordered and its façade became the most visible memorial in the public space [Fig. 3.24]. In 1900, the Boxers burned the church, but the façade was restored and a new nave built, giving the symbol a new layer.

The Boxer Protocol, signed on September 7, 1901, forced the Chinese Government to erect expiatory monuments on the places where foreigners had been killed, as well as in each of the foreign and international cemeteries where tombs had been profaned. The Protocol specifies: "It has been agreed with the Representatives of the Powers that the Legations interested shall settle the details for the erection of these monuments."⁶⁰ As already mentioned, the French legation had the exclusive protection over all the Catholic missionaries in China and therefore negotiated the indemnities. The martyr had

changed the status of the place to a 'place of memory': from then on it was sacred and the martyr had to be commemorated.[61] The monuments were big stones with inscriptions in several languages, often enhanced with a canopy and surrounded by a wall or a fence defining a sacred space [Fig. 3.24]. In some cases, a chapel and a monumental gate were built near the monument to emphasize the spatialization of the martyr [Fig. 3.25]. All these monuments, which most Chinese perceived as public and physical remnants of a humiliation, were demolished.

We have little information about the kind of commemorations the missionaries celebrated in these places and how they involved the local Christians in processions and celebrations of the martyrs' anniversaries. It probably depended on the religious institute to which the missionaries belonged, some of which encouraged a culture of martyrdom and expected the blessing of their martyrs.[62] Ultimately, Rome would decide if a martyr was to be blessed, as a function of a policy going beyond the interest of individual religious congregations, as illustrated by the canonization of 120 martyrs in China by Pope John Paul II on October 1, 2000.[63]

A memory island par excellence is Shangchuan Island 上川岛 (Guangdong), where St Francis Xavier, the Jesuit patron saint of the missions, passed away on 3 December 1552. His body was transferred to Malacca in 1553, partitioned, and relics sent to several different places. The island itself was revived as a place of remembrance in 1700 when its first monument was built. In 1869 a Gothic chapel was built on the side of the peak and a pilgrimage promoted [Fig. 3.26].[64]

Marian Islands: Pilgrimages on Hilltops

In China, mountains play a key role in the geomancy or *fengshui* (风水) that deeply roots the topographic relationships of traditional Chinese architecture with landscape and perception of space. Many mountains are sacred sites and have hilltop temples whose pagoda towers are cosmic connec-

3.24 The Gothic style Our Lady of the Victory Church, a Renaissance style triumphal gateway, and a Chinese style pavilion protecting the imperial stele commemorated the Tientsin Massacre of 1870 in the urban landscape of Tianjin. View from the south, picture from Les Missions Catholiques, 32, 1900, 541.
[Leuven, KADOC-KU Leuven, Heritage Library: KYB3962]

3.25 Cemetery of the Belgian Franciscan 'martyrs' in Yichang 宜昌 (Hubei). A Roman style triumphant arch on top of stairs, decorated with the palms of martyrs, was like a gateway to heaven. Inside the cemetery, a main axis with tombs at both sides led to a Doric style chapel.
[Leuven, KADOC-KU Leuven, Picture Archive of the Flemish Franciscans: 1626]

3.26 St Francis Xavier, the pioneering missionary in Asia, died on December 3, 1552 on Shangchuan / Sancian Island 上川岛 (Guangdong), and thus never reached mainland China. In 1869, a Gothic memorial chapel was erected on the place of the first burial of his body (left) and a church built at the edge of the village of Xindi 新地 (right). The engraving depicts a procession of villagers going from the village to the chapel on the day of its consecration.
Les Missions Catholiques, 4, 1872, 429.
[Leuven, KADOC-KU Leuven, Heritage Library: KYB3962]

tors. Missionaries, of course, knew the pilgrimage churches and abbeys on hilltops in Europe and dreamt of Christianizing sacred mountains in China. Missionary literature contains many anecdotes to this effect, such as this one reported by a Benedictine monk during a journey through the mountains of northern Hebei 河北: "[a Redemptorist father] who accompanied us from Peking, had climbed to a neighboring hill upon which stood a temple containing the usual type of idol. On seeing this symbol of false worship, he expressed the fervent hope of being someday able to replace it with a statue of the Blessed Mother."[65]

Temples on mountaintops are visible markers in landscapes, places of stability and of spiritual elevation, in Christian as well as in Buddhist culture. Building a house for a god on a mountain is a most powerful religious spatializing act, especially when a church replaces the temple of another god. It is known that pilgrimage sites on hills are places with a spiritual aura, and gates to heaven; they provide solitary quietude that naturally awakens devotion.[66]

Nineteenth-century Catholic missionaries, highly aware of the dynamic generated by major pilgrimages to the Virgin Mary, therefore launched Marian devotion and pilgrimages in China, some of which were recognized by Rome and still attract crowds of pilgrims today.[67] Moreover, the Daughters of Charity of St Vincent de Paul (*Filles de la Charité*) and the Congregation of the Mission (Lazarists or Vincentians), both important French missionary congregations in China, were directly involved in the devotion to the Miraculous Medal and the Marian pilgrimage at the Rue du Bac in Paris from 1830. French missionaries also disseminated a worldwide devotion to the Immaculate Conception of Mary, following the apparitions at Lourdes in 1858. In China, many Catholic parish churches and villages still have a grotto of Lourdes, some of which take the form of a traditional Chinese rockery, sometimes surrounded by a small garden, with a pond for goldfish and turtles, symbols of good luck and longevity.

The Marian shrine of Our Lady of Sheshan 佘山圣母 near Shanghai is an example of how Jesuits gradually conquered a Buddhist sacred mountain, first by developing local devotion, then later a regional, and finally a national pilgrimage.[68] In 1863, the French Jesuits of Shanghai bought the southern side of a hill named Sheshan 佘山 (Zô-cè in Shanghainese), on the outskirts of the city. Although the peak is only about 100 meters high, it is quite attractive because it is the highest point on the Songjiang 松江 plain. The Buddhist monastery of the 'Doctrine enlightening the world' 普照教院, built on

65 [Brandstetter], "A Journey to Hsuan Hua Fu," 35.
66 Caspers, "No places of pilgrimages without devotion(s)."
67 Burkhardt, "Ein Marientag in China."
68 Coomans, "Notre-Dame de Sheshan à Shanghai;" Id., *Sheshan jiaotang xunzong*.

3.27 Sheshan hill 佘山 near Shanghai 上海 around 1905, seen from the south. The Chinese farms in the plain contrast with the buildings of the Jesuits: the Marian pilgrimage church and the astronomical observatory on the hilltop, respectively built in 1873 and 1900, as well as the middle church from 1894, the fathers' residence and other buildings for the pilgrims.
[Vanves, Compagnie de Jésus, Archives jésuites de France, Fonds iconographique, C1]

the eastern hillside in the Song dynasty, had been demolished in the Yuan dynasty, rebuilt in the Ming dynasty, and destroyed by the Taiping in 1860. On the southern hillside, there were remains of a temple of Guanyin Pusa 观音菩萨, the Buddhist goddess of mercy. For centuries, the Chinese had buried their dead on the bamboo-planted hillsides. The Jesuits aimed to Christianize the whole 'pagan hill' and therefore paid no attention to the archaeological remains.[69] The process occurred as follows:

- First, a convalescent home for aged and tired fathers was built at the southern foot of the hill, and a small octagonal chapel with a painting of Our Lady of the Victories (a French devotion) was erected on the hilltop. In 1868, the vicar apostolic of Nanjing blessed the oratory.
- On 4 July 1870, father Agnello Della Corte 谷振聲 (1819-1896), traumatized by the Tianjin Massacre of 21 June 1870 [Fig. 3.23], climbed the hill and made a vow to build a church on it if Mary protected Shanghai. Ultimately the city was spared, and the Jesuits proclaimed it a miracle and immediately started to build a church with the help of the Chinese Christians.
- This neoclassic 'Church of the Vow', completed in 1873 and dedicated to Mary Help of Christians, became a pilgrimage site that attracted people from Shanghai in May. [Fig. 8.9] During the construction works, rumors of an impending calamity circulated among the Chinese workers.[70] Besides suspecting the missionaries of mutilating orphans and burying them under the columns of the church, the local population believed that the work on the hill and the increasing traffic on the canals leading to the hill would annoy the spirits of the earth and provoke the wrath of the dragons within the mountain, beliefs the Jesuits considered 'pagan superstitions'.[71]
- In 1894, another church, and new infrastructure for a more permanent pilgrimage and parish [Fig. 3.27], were built halfway up the southern slope.
- In 1900, the Jesuits established an astronomical observatory near the church.[72]
- From 1917, Jules Prosper Paris 姚宗李 (1846-1931), the vicar apostolic of Nanjing, wanted to replace the wooden church with a large stone-and-brick basilica. Designed by the missionary-architect Alphonse De Moerloose 和羹柏 (1858-1932) in 1920-1923, the new Western-style church was erected from 1924 to 1935 and completed by the placement of a monumental statue of Our Lady of Sheshan on top of the 35-meter-high tower.

69 Palatre, *Le pèlerinage de Notre-Dame Auxiliatrice à Zô-sè*, 7-27.
70 Chevestrier, *Notre Dame de Zô-cè*, 68-69.
71 About these gods: Kleeman, "Mountain Deities in China."
72 "L'observatoire de Zi-ka-wei."

3.28 Procession entering the Marian pilgrimage church of Donglü 东闾 (Hebei) for a pontifical mass. The terrace in front of the Gothic-style façade of the church contains a Chinese archway and steles as well as a paper mache temporary Chinese gate with a double roof. Picture from 1932, signed J.C. [Paris, Archives historiques de la Congrégation de la Mission]

In 1924, Sheshan became a national pilgrimage site when the first Synod of the Catholic Church in China, held in Shanghai, solemnly dedicated China to the Virgin Mary Queen of Chinese (*Regina Sinarum*). On 14 June 1924, Archbishop Celso Costantini 刚恆毅 (1876-1958), the delegate apostolic to China, and twenty-five members of the synod climbed on the hilltop and repeated the consecration of China to Mary. In 1943, Pope Pius XII granted Sheshan the title of minor basilica, the first one in East Asia, and in 1946 the Holy See crowned the statue of Our Lady of Sheshan. Today, the sanctuary still gives one the feeling it is a sacred island with a church, between heaven and earth.[73]

The Marian pilgrimage of Donglü 东闾 near Baoding 保定 (Hebei) finds its origin in the 'miraculous' resistance of a village to repeated attacks by the Boxers. In 1901-1903, as thanksgiving for the resistance, French missionaries of the Congregation of the Mission built a huge medieval-looking church there, which soon attracted crowds of pilgrims. During the Shanghai Synod of 1924, the image of Our Lady of Donglü was chosen to become Our Lady of China.[74] In 1932, when Pope Pius XI officially approved the pilgrimage, a great celebration was held with numerous bishops present [Fig. 3.28].

Japanese bombings destroyed the church in 1941, but the pilgrimage was revived after 1990.

Amongst other minor Marian pilgrimages,[75] the Belgian Scheut fathers promoted Our Lady of Mozishan 磨子山 in Inner Mongolia. In 1905, the Virgin appeared to a shepherd on a mountain near the Christian village of Meiguiyingzi 玫瑰营子 ('Rosary Village'). The missionaries immediately built a Gothic church on the top of the mountain, on a terrace facing south.

Monastic Islands: Deserts for Contemplation

The Propaganda Fide did not consider monastic contemplation a priority in mission countries where the goal was evangelization and pastoral works. The monastic orders, both male and female, could not compete with leading centralized missionary congregations and societies such as the Jesuits, Franciscans, Dominicans, Lazarists, and Paris Foreign Mission Society. Nevertheless, once nineteenth-century monastic revival had reached a critical mass, Trappists, Benedictines, and Carmelites began to establish abbeys in the US and Africa. The fear of anticlerical governments and prosecution,

73 The only remnant of Buddhism is a small pagoda on the eastern side of the Christianized hill.
74 Clarke, *The Virgin Mary and Catholic Identities in Chinese History*, 83-110; Sweeten, *China's Old Churches*, 333-342.
75 Amongst other Our Lady of Bliss at Zhung-Ke, Our Lady of Lourdes at Qingyang (1901). See: Anh, *Marian Shrines in China*.

especially in France, was another motivation to relocate communities as far afield as possible.⁷⁶ Contemplative communities, however, did not become aware of their original contribution to the missions until the 1920s.

The recent historical study on monastic missions to China by Father Matteo Nicolini-Zani gives a detailed overview of the difficult, promising, but ephemeral presence of Carmelite, Trappist, and Benedictine communities in China.⁷⁷ Except two French monasteries founded in 1869 and 1883, all the others were founded later, starting in the 1920s and 1930s. Most were still in the process of establishing themselves when they were affected by the Sino-Japanese war and eventually suppressed after the Chinese Civil War. These 'monastic islands' remained thus very small and had a limited influence but attracted Chinese vocations in remote places.

The first Catholic monastic community in China was the convent of French Discalced Carmelite nuns at Tushanwan 土山湾 founded in 1869, in the previously mentioned great 'French Jesuit island' of Xujiahui in Shanghai [Fig. 3.8 and Fig. 7.1].⁷⁸ The contemplative community benefited from the spiritual guidance of the Jesuits and the support of the neighboring convent and girls' school of the Helpers of the Holy Souls. Five other small communities of Carmelite nuns were established in the 1920s and 1930s.⁷⁹ Spatially, these convents were surrounded with walls to maintain their strict enclosure. The canonization of Saint Therese of Lisieux in 1925 and the promotion of her cult as patron saint of the mission after 1927 contributed to the popularity of the Carmelites and spiritual interactions between contemplative and active missionary communities.

The first men's abbey founded in East Asia was the Trappist monastery of Our Lady of Consolation 神慰院 at Yangjiaping 杨家坪 (Hebei) in 1883, populated with French monks.⁸⁰ The main motivation of the Trappists was "to give life to a new type of missiology: prayer life in the mission field".⁸¹ With its Gothic-style buildings around a large cloister, precinct walls, and a strict enclosure, located in a mountain valley about 180 km northwest of Beijing, Yangjiaping looked like a thirteenth-century Cistercian abbey. Only some secondary buildings had Chinese roofs [Fig. 3.29]. This archetypal 'monastic island' became a flourishing monastery with a community of more than a hundred monks, most of whom were Chinese. In 1928, the Trappist monastery of Our Lady of Joy 圣母神乐院 was founded near Zhengding 正定 (Hebei). In 1947, during the Chinese Civil War, Yangjiaping was destroyed and the monks dispersed, but the community of Joy fled to Hong Kong, where a monastery was built in 1951-1956 at Tai Shui Hang 大水坑 on the island of Lantau 大屿山. The community continues to lead a monastic life of contemplation on this real island in the Pearl River's delta, in the middle of the Guangdong-Hong Kong-Macao Greater Bay Area.

In 1923, the Holy See entrusted the Benedictine American Cassinese Congregation with the challenging task of establishing Fu Jen Catholic University of Peking 辅仁大学. It was inaugurated in October 1925 in a former prince's mansion close to Qianhai Lake 前海 in the heart of old Beijing. A small community of Benedictine monks and lay professors staffed the university, which developed successfully from 23 students in 1925 to 705 in 1930.⁸² Benedictine nuns founded a women's college at the Catholic University in 1930. In the wake of excessively rapid growth and financial problems due to the world's economic crisis, the Holy See replaced the Benedictines with German missionaries of the Society of the Divine Word in 1933. Although this was a failure for the Benedictines, the work they initiated continued to expand until the closure of the university in 1952. A main architectural achievement was the construction of a remarkable Chinese-style building that will be discussed later.

Other Benedictine communities came to China in the 1920s and developed different mission works, all small islands with few connexions with each other.⁸³ These Western communities welcomed Chinese novices, who were expected to gradually sinicize the

76 About the Trappists: Delpal, *Le silence des moines.*
77 Nicolini-Zani, *Christian Monks on Chinese Soil.*
78 Ibid., 58-113; Tiedemann, *Handbook of Christianity in China*, 54.
79 In Chongqing 重庆 (Sichuan) in 1920, in Jiaxing 嘉兴 (Zhejiang) in 1927, in Canton in 1933, moved to Hong Kong in 1937, in Kunming 昆明 (Yunnan) in 1936, and in Macao in 1941.
80 Nicolini-Zani, *Christian Monks on Chinese Soil*, 114-169; Jen, *The History of Our Lady of Consolation*; Limagne, *Les Trappistes en Chine.*
81 Quattrocchi, "The Trappist Monks in China," 315.
82 "From Provisional to Final Registration."
83 German and Swiss monks, who were in Korea since 1909, founded an abbey in Yanji 延吉 (Jilin) in 1928; American monks and nuns established small communities in Kaifeng 开封 (Henan) in 1934; Belgian and French monks established the Chinese priory of Xishan 西山 on a hill in the neighborhood of Chongqing 重庆 in 1929. Nicolini-Zani, *Christian Monks on Chinese Soil*, 170-259; Tiedemann, *Handbook of Christianity in China*, 3-5 and 49; Coomans, "Unexpected Connexions."

3.29 The Trappist abbey of Our-Lady of Consolation at Yangjiaping 杨家坪 (Hebei province), settled in a "valley of sorrows", like medieval Cistercian abbeys. Picture from Les Missions Catholiques, *42, 1910, 181. [Leuven, KADOC-KU Leuven, Heritage Library: KYB3962]*

84 Wiest, "Le père Lebbe et son église de style chinois".
85 Apostolic letter *Maximum illud* by Benedict XV in 1919, and encyclical *Rerum Ecclesiae* by Pius XI in 1926.
86 About these concepts: Ticozzi, "Celso Costantini's Contribution".
87 After having been the apostolic delegate to China from 1922 to 1933, Costantini was secretary of the Propaganda Fide from 1933, and was made cardinal in 1953. See: Chong, "Cardinal Celso Costantini;" Lam, "Archbishop Costantini."
88 Xu, Wu and Lai, *Zhongguo jindai jianzhushi*; Li and Wang, *The Art of Architectural Integration of Chinese and Western*.

monasteries. In 1928, Father Vincent Lebbe, who himself had been naturalized Chinese the year before, founded two fully Chinese monastic orders, in Anguo 安国 (Hebei): the Congregation of the Little Brothers of St John the Baptist 耀漢小兄弟會 and their first monastery of Beatitudes, and the Little Sisters of Therese of the Child Jesus 德來小妹妹會, similar to a Carmelite nunnery.[84]

Shifting Islands: Towards Inculturation and a Chinese Church

After the First World War, the Vatican launched a new mission policy and stressed the need for a local clergy and church.[85] In 1922, Pope Pius XI sent an apostolic delegate to China assigned to sinicize the Catholic Church. Archbishop Celso Costantini was the key person appointed to 'inculturate' or localize Catholicism in China.[86] Milestones of the process were: the first synod of bishops and superiors in Shanghai in 1924; the project to build new regional seminaries for Chinese priests; the foundation of Fu Jen Catholic University of Peking in 1925; the consecration of the six first Chinese bishops by Pope Pius XI in 1926; and the foundation of the Congregation of the Disciples of the Lord, a Chinese Catholic religious institute in 1931.[87]

In the meantime, China had decisively turned a page in its history and had entered a remarkable phase of modernization. The educational reforms of 1905, the fall of the Empire, and the birth of the Republic of China in 1911-1912, as well as new political movements – Kuomintang, 1912; May Four Movement, 1919; Communist Party, 1921 – led to instability. From 1927, the Nationalists ruled the country and steered China further on the path to modernity. Architecture and urbanism evolved on a large scale thanks to the first generation of Chinese architects, important commissions by the government, the creation of a Chinese-style modern design, the use of reinforced concrete, among other factors.[88]

Benefiting from this changing context and new policies, the different types of Catholic islands or *heterotopias* that have been

3.30 The Sino-Christian style seminary of the Chinese religious institute of the Disciples of the Lord at Xuanhua 宣化 (Hebei), viewed from the south. Picture from L'Artisan Liturgique, 10/40, 1936, 824.
[Leuven, KADOC-KU Leuven, Heritage Library: KYC372]

evoked in this chapter grew [Fig. 3.1], gained in complexity, and gradually shifted to a sinicized Christianity.[89] The Roman strategy of mission development and inculturation was based on the redistribution of the ecclesiastical circumscriptions and the creation of new vicariates apostolic, increasing the numbers of Chinese priests and bishops, schools, and hospitals. The pope wanted to change the territorial feudalism of the dioceses held by national missionary societies,[90] and affirmed that "the true missionary is always aware that he is not working as an agent of his country, but as an ambassador of Christ."[91] In 1949, there were no less than 144 ecclesiastical circumscriptions, mostly full dioceses (20 archdioceses and 85 dioceses), and 39 prefectures apostolic, the last circumscriptions in the process of emancipation from the mission.[92] Every new diocese was a subdivision of an existing larger one and so on. Several of them were assigned to Chinese bishops and diocesan clergy, while others were to new missionary societies from the United States, Canada, Ireland, Switzer-land, Poland, the Netherlands, Hungary, etc.[93]

Every new vicariate generated a new 'cathedral island'. Building seminaries, churches, cathedrals, and religious houses for new congregations, as well as schools, dispensaries, hospitals, orphanages, etc. aimed at efficiency and visibility. The number of Catholic-Chinese islands increased on the mainland, but remained marginal because the number of Chinese Catholics and catechumens never reached 1% of the total population.[94]

The most explicit and interesting spatial strategy undoubtedly dealt with the issue of architectural style. Conservative missionaries continued to build in Western styles: new cathedrals, for instance those of the Belgian Scheut Fathers in Xiwanzi 西湾子 (Hebei) and Hohhot 呼和浩特 (Inner Mongolia) in 1922-1926,[95] of the French Lazarists in Zhengding 正定 (Hebei) in 1924, of the Italian Jesuits in Bengbu 蚌埠 (Anhui) in 1925, or the German Divine Word Missionaries in Qing-dao 青岛 (Shandong) in 1931-1934, still referred to Western medieval styles with high vertical towers. In the perspective of inculturation, Archbishop Costantini condemned Gothic and Romanesque architecture and promoted a new Sino-Christian style, characterized by Chinese roofs, horizontal lines, no towers, and Chinese furniture.[96] Created

89 Zheng, Sinicizing Christianity; Soetens, L'Église catholique en Chine, 93-150.
90 In 1924, there were 24 French apostolic vicariates, 13 Italian, 6 Belgian, 5 Spanish, 5 German, 2 Dutch, 1 Portuguese, and 1 American. Planchet, Les Missions de Chine et du Japon, passim.
91 Benedict XV, Maximum Illud, 20.
92 Despont, Nouvel atlas des missions, 20-26; <www.catholic-hierarchy.org/> (accessed June 2022). In 1946 the apostolic vicariates were promoted as dioceses.
93 Tiedemann, Handbook of Christianity in China, 3-45.
94 In the years 1940-1950, there were about 3.7 million Catholics in China out of a total population of 552 million.
95 Luo, Transmission and Transformation, 209-230.
96 Costantini, "The Need of Developing a Sino-Christian Architecture;" Id., "Le problème de l'art en pays de Mission;" Id., "L'universalité de l'art Chrétien."

3.31 The Sino-Christian style main building of the Catholic University of Peking 辅仁大学, built 1929-1930, viewed from the south-west.
[Denée, Abbaye de Maredsous].

97 Gresnigt, "Chinese Architecture;" Id., "Reflections on Chinese Architecture;" Ghesquières, "Comment bâtirons-nous;" Cody, "Striking a Harmonious Chord;" Coomans, "Indigenizing Catholic Architecture in China;" Id., "Une utopie missionnaire?;" Id., "Sinicising Christian Architecture in Hong Kong."
98 Healy, "The Plans of the New University Building;" Coomans, "The 'Sino-Christian Style'," 210-222.
99 Coomans and Ho, "Architectural Styles and identities in Hong Kong."
100 Soetens, *L'Église catholique en Chine*, 139-145. Archbishop Costantini left China in 1933.
101 Bouwmeester and Coomans, "The Catholic Territorialization of Taiwan", in this book p. 87-103.

by the Dutch Benedictine father Adelbert Gresnigt 葛利斯 (1877-1956), who worked in China from 1927 to 1931, this style was adopted by the new Catholic educational buildings such as the regional seminaries of Hong Kong and Kaifeng, and the seminary of the Disciples of the Lord at Xuanhua [Fig. 3.29].[97] The construction in 1929-1930 of Fu Jen Catholic University of Peking in the new Sino-Christian style is a milestone in the history of the China mission [Fig. 3.31].[98] Behind the crenelated walls and corner towers that referred to traditional city walls and bell/drum towers, there were wings comprising a library, an auditorium, classrooms, office rooms, and dorms for 400 students, developed symmetrically around two inner courtyards. At other places, Gothic churches had 'facelifts' and received a new Chinese façade and furniture. Nevertheless, this new image and identity in the public space remained limited and sometimes failed.[99] From the early 1930s, because of the world economic crisis and the development of fascism in Europe, the China mission was no longer a priority for Rome.[100] The Japanese invasion of 1932 in the north-eastern provinces and of 1937-1938 in Beijing, Shanghai, Wuhan and Guangzhou, as well as the Communist attacks on Christian settlements, would slow down the Church's efforts and gradually reduce the number and the size of the Catholic islands on the mainland.

The Chinese Civil War and the proclamation of the People's Republic of China on October 1, 1949 led to the expulsion of all foreign missionaries and marked the end of the missions in mainland China.

After 1955, only three places remained open to Christian missions, all three being islands: Macao, Taiwan[101] and Hong Kong.

BIBLIOGRAPHY

Primary literature

Benedict XV. *Maximum illud. Apostolic Letter on the Propagation of the Faith Throughout the World*. 30 November 1919. <www.svdcuria.org/public/mission/docs/encycl/mi-en.htm>.

Bordeaux, Henry. "Une chapelle sur des tombes." *Les Missions Catholiques*, 43 (1911), 433-436.

[Brandstetter], Ildephonse. "A Journey to Hsuan Hua Fu [Xuanhua]: On Occasion of the Consecration of Bishop Peter Ch'eng." *Bulletin of the Catholic University of Peking*, 5 (October 1928), 22-36.

Burkhardt, Franz, 蒲敏道 (SJ). "Ein Marientag in China." Bethlehem, 39 (May 1934) 5, 217-220 (with map).

Chevestrier, Étienne. *Notre Dame de Zô-cè. Histoire d'un Pèlerinage à N.D. Auxiliatrice en Chine*. Shanghai, 1942. Unpublished manuscript: Vanves, French Jesuit Archives, FcH 337.

"Consécration de la nouvelle cathédrale de Pétang." *Les Missions Catholiques*, 21 (1889), 125-128.

Costantini, Celso. "The Need of Developing a Sino-Christian Architecture for our Catholic Mission." *Bulletin of the Catholic University of Peking*, 3 (September 1927), 7-15.

Costantini, Celso. "Le problème de l'art en pays de Mission." *L'Artisan liturgique*, 40 (January-March 1936), 816-819.

Costantini, Celso. "L'universalité de l'art chrétien." *Dossiers de la Commission Synodale / Digest of the Synodal Commission*, 5 (May 1932), 410-417.

de la Servière, Joseph. *La nouvelle mission du Kiang-nan (1840-1922)*. Shanghai-Xujiahui, 1925.

de la Servière, Joseph. "Une université catholique en Chine. L'Aurore à Shanghai." *Relations de Chine*, 23 (1925) 2, 65-86.

Deshayes, Laurent. *Tibet 1846-1952: les missionnaires de l'impossible*. Paris, 1900.

Favier, Alphonse. *Péking. Histoire et description*. Paris-Lille, 1902.

Favier, Pierre-Marie-Alphonse. "Deux mois de siège. Journal." *Les Missions Catholiques*, 32 (1900), 541-546 and 553-561.

"From Provisional to Final Registration. A Record of events intervening between the University's first and fifth year." *Bulletin of the Catholic University of Peking*, 7 (December 1930), 103-130.

Ghesquières, Albert. "Comment bâtirons-nous dispensaires, écoles, mission catholique, chapelles, séminaires et communautés religieuses en Chine?." *Collectanea Commissionis Synodalis*, 14 (1941), 1-80.

Gresnigt, Adelbert. "Chinese Architecture." *Bulletin of the Catholic University of Peking*, 4 (1928), 33-45.

Gresnigt, Adelbert. "Reflections on Chinese Architecture." *Bulletin of the Catholic University of Peking*, 8 (1931), 3-26.

Guilbaud, Joseph Henri. "Chine. Nécessité d'une église plus centrale." *Les Missions Catholiques*, 62 (1930), 550-551.

Haouissée, Auguste. "Inauguration de l'église Saint-Ignace à Zi-Ka-Wei." *Relations de Chine*, 9 (1911) 1, 15-22.

Healy, Sylvester. "The Plans of the New University Building." *Bulletin of the Catholic University of Peking*, 6 (1929), 3-12.

Hermand, Louis. *Les étapes de la mission du Kiang-nan 1842-1922 et de la mission de Nanking 1922-1932, Chine. Jésuites, Province de France*. Shanghai-Xujiahui, 1933.

Hubrecht, Alphonse. "De Pékin à la Trappe de Chine." *Les Missions Catholiques*, 55 (1923), 154-156, 176-177, 190-191, 200-201, 210-213.

[Jung, Paul]. *Le missionnaire constructeur. Conseils-plans*. Xianxian, 1926.

Lécroart, Henri. "Sien-hsien (Tchély-Sud-Est)." *Les Missions Catholiques*, 57 (1925), 366-367.

Leyssen, Jaak. "Mongolie. La belle mission de Palakai." *Les Missions Catholiques*, 56 (1924), 258-259, 271-272, 284-285, 296-297, 309-310.

Limagne, Auguste. *Les Trappistes en Chine*. Paris, 1911.

"L'observatoire de Zi-ka-wei (L'action scientifique de nos missionnaires)." *Les Missions Catholiques*, 62 (1930), 530-531.

"Mandchourie." *Les Missions Catholiques*, 32 (1900), 395-403 and 33 (1901), 253.

Palatre, Gabriel. *Le pèlerinage de Notre-Dame Auxiliatrice à Zô-Sè, dans le vicariat apostolique de Nan-kin*. Shanghai, 1875.

Palatre, Gabriel. *L'infanticide et l'œuvre de la Sainte-Enfance en Chine*. Shanghai, 1878.

Planchet, Jean-Marie. *Les Missions de Chine et du Japon*. Beijing, 1925.

Rondelez, Valère. *La chrétienté de Siwantze. Un centre d'activité missionnaire en Mongolie*. S.l., 1938.

Streit, Charles. *Atlas des missions catholiques contenant tous les territoires des missions de toute la terre*. Steyl, 1906.

Tokarski, M. "La Mission de Pékin." *Les Missions Catholiques*, 48 (1916), 301-302.

Secondary literature

Anh Thu Tran. *Marian Shrines in China*. Vancouver, 2009.

Bays, Daniel H. and Widmer, Ellen, eds. *China's Christian Colleges: Cross-Cultural Connections, 1900-1950*. Stanford, 2009.

Bonnet, Paul. *Les anciennes églises de Pékin. Notes d'Histoire*. S.l., 1945.

Bouwmeester, Leon and Coomans, Thomas. "The Catholic Territorialization of Taiwan. Vatican Global Strategy and Franciscan Local Parishes, 1949-1960s," in: Coomans, Thomas, ed. *Missionary Spaces. Imagining, Building, Contesting Christianities in Africa and China, 1830s-1960s*. Leuven, 2024, 86-103.

Braschi, Lawrence. "Civilizing Space in West China. Re-examining the Place of the Christian University in Chengdu, 1909-1933," in: Coomans, Thomas, ed. *Missionary Spaces. Imagining, Building, Contesting Christianities in Africa and China, 1830-1960*. Leuven, 2024, 211-227.

Bruun, Ole. *Fengshui in China: Geomantic Divination between State Orthodoxy and Popular Religion*. Honolulu, 2003.

Caspers, Charles M.A. "No places of pilgrimages without devotion(s)," in: Coomans, Thomas; De Dijn, Herman; De Maeyer Jan; Heynickx, Rajesh and Verschaffel, Bart, eds. *Loci Sacri. Understanding Sacred Places*. KADOC Studies on Religion, Culture and Society 9. Leuven, 2012, 125-137.

Chen Tsung-ming Alexandre 陳聰銘. "La question des propriétés immobilières et foncières des missions catholiques en Chine (1860-1949)," in: Chen Tsung-ming Alexandre, ed. *Le Christianisme en Chine aux XIXe et XXe siècles. Figures, événements et missions-œuvres*. Leuven Chinese Studies 31. Leuven, 2015, 13-44.

Chong, Francis. "Cardinal Celso Costantini and the Chinese Catholic Church." *Tripod*, 28 (2008) 148. <www.hsstudyc.org.hk/en/tripod_en/en_tripod_148_05.html>.

Clark, Anthony E. *China's Saints: Catholic Martyrdom During the Qing (1644-1911)*. Studies in Christianity in China. Bethlehem, 2011.

Clark, Anthony E. *China Gothic: The Bishop of Beijing and His Cathedral*. Washington, 2020.

Clarke, Jeremy. *The Virgin Mary and Catholic Identities in Chinese History*. Hong Kong, 2013.

Cody, Jeffrey W. "American Geometries and the Architecture of Christian Campuses in China," in: Bays, Daniel H. and Widmer, Ellen, eds. *China's Christian Colleges: Cross-Cultural Connections, 1900-1950*. Stanford, 2009, 27-56.

Cody, Jeffrey W. "Striking a Harmonious Chord: Foreign Missionaries and Chinese-style Buildings, 1911-1949." *Architronic. The Electronic Journal of Architecture*, 5 (1996) 3, 1-30. <http://corbu2.caed.kent.edu/architronic/>.

Cohen, Paul A. *China and Christianity: The Missionary Movement and the Growth of Chinese Anti-Foreignism, 1860-1870*. Cambridge MA, 1963.

Coomans, Thomas. "La création d'un style architectural sino-chrétien. L'œuvre d'Adelbert Gresnigt, moine-artiste bénédictin en Chine (1927-1932)." *Revue bénédictine*, 123 (2013), 128-170.

Coomans, Thomas. "China Papers: The architecture archives of the building company Crédit Foncier d'Extrême-Orient (1907-59)." *ABE Journal. European architecture beyond Europe*, 5 (2014) 689. <http://dev.abejournal.eu/index.php?id=689>.

Coomans, Thomas. "Indigenizing Catholic Architecture in China: From Western-Gothic to Sino-Christian Design, 1900-1940," in: Yik-yi Chu, Cindy, ed. *Catholicism in China, 1900-Present. The Development of the Chinese Church*. New York, 2014, 125-144.

Coomans, Thomas. "Une utopie missionnaire? Construire des églises, des séminaires et des écoles catholiques dans la Chine en pleine tourmente (1941)," in: Tsung-ming Alexandre Chen 陳聰銘, ed. *Le Christianisme en Chine aux XIXᵉ et XXᵉ siècles. Figures, événements et missions-œuvres*. Leuven Chinese Studies 31. Leuven, 2015, 45-79.

Coomans, Thomas. "Sinicising Christian Architecture in Hong Kong: Father Gresnigt, Catholic Indigenisation, and the South China Regional Seminary, 1927-31." *Journal of the Royal Asiatic Society Hong Kong Branch*, 56 (2016), 133-160.

Coomans, Thomas. "The 'Sino-Christian Style': A Major Tool for Architectural Indigenization" in: Yangwen Zheng 鄭揚文, ed. *Sinicizing Christianity*. Studies in Christian Mission 49. Leiden-Boston, 2017, 197-232.

Coomans, Thomas. "East Meets West on the Construction Site. Churches in China, 1840s-1930s." *Construction History*, 33 (2018) 2, 63-84.

Coomans, Thomas. "Notre-Dame de Sheshan à Shanghai, basilique des Jésuites français en Chine, 1867-1936." *Bulletin monumental*, 176 (2018), 129-156.

Coomans, Thomas 高曼士. "Yancang yu sheng xin da jiaotang de guangmang zhihou: Ta cha ji ren zhi wan Qing Guangzhou qita jidujiao jianzhu 掩藏于圣心大教堂的光芒之后：踏查及认知晚清广州其它基督教建筑" [Overshadowed by the Cathedral: Towards Mapping and Understanding the Other Christian Buildings in Late Qing Canton]. *Xīxue dong jian yanjiu 西学东渐研究* [*Research on Eastern Trend of Western Learning*], 7 (2019), 162-193.

Coomans, Thomas. "Unexpected Connections. The Benedictine Abbey of Maredsous and Christian Architecture in China, 1900-1930s." *Revue bénédictine*, 131 (2021) 1, 264-299.

B. Coomans, Thomas 高曼士. *Sheshan jiaotang xun cong: chaosheng jianzhu he lishitujing 佘山教堂寻踪：朝圣建筑和历史图景* [*Tracing the Sheshan Church: Pilgrimage Architecture and Landscape*] (开放的上海城市建筑史丛书 / Open Shanghai Urban Architecture History Series, 3). Shanghai: Tongji University Press, 2023, 303 p.

Coomans, Thomas. "Church Architecture and Church Buildings: China," in: Chu Yik-yi, Cindy 朱益宜 and Leung Kit-fun, Beatrice 梁潔芬, eds. *The Palgrave Handbook of the Catholic Church in East Asia*, Singapore: Springer, 2023, 80 p.

Coomans, Thomas. "Gendered Spaces in Catholic Compounds in Late Qing China," in: Coomans, Thomas, ed. *Missionary Spaces. Imagining, Building, Contesting Christianities in Africa and China, 1830s-1960s*. Leuven, 2024, 106-145.

Coomans, Thomas. "Gender-Designed Catholic Churches in North China, 1830s-1920s," in: Coomans, Thomas, ed. *Missionary Spaces. Imagining, Building, Contesting Christianities in Africa and China, 1830s-1960s*. Leuven, 2024, 146-193.

Coomans, Thomas and Ho Puey-peng 何培斌. "Architectural Styles and Identities in Hong Kong: The Chinese and Western Designs for St Teresa's Church in Kowloon Tong, 1928-32." *Journal of the Royal Asiatic Society Hong Kong*, 58 (2018), 81-109.

Coomans, Thomas and Luo Wei 罗微. "Mimesis, Nostalgia and Ideology: The Scheut Fathers and Home-Country-Based Church Design in China," in: *History of the Catholic Church in China. From its Beginning to the Scheut Fathers and 20th Century. Unveiling some Less Known Sources, Sounds and Pictures*. Leuven Chinese Studies 29. Leuven, 2015, 495-522.

Coomans, Thomas 高曼士 and Xu Yitao 徐怡涛. *Bolai yu bentu. —1926 nian Faguo chuanjiao shi suo zhuan zhongguo beifang jiaotang yingzao zhi yanjiu 徐怡涛，舶来与本土——1926年法国传教士所撰中国北方教堂营造之研究* [*Building Churches in Northern China. A 1926 Handbook in Context*]. Beijing, 2016.

Delpal, Bernard. *Le silence des moines. Les Trappistes au XIXᵉ siècle: France, Algérie, Syrie. L'histoire dans l'actualité*. Paris, 1998.

de la Servière, Joseph. *Histoire de la mission du Kiang-Nan. Jésuites de la province de France (Paris)*. 2 vol. Shanghai, 1914.

Despont, J. *Nouvel atlas des missions*. Paris-Lyon, 1951.

Elder, Chris. *China's Treaty Ports: Half Love and Half Hate*. Oxford, 1999.

Emmerich, Henricus. *Atlas missionum, a sacra Congregatione de Propaganda Fide dependitum*. Vatican City, 1958.

Fairbank, John K. "Patterns Behind the Tientsin Massacre." *Harvard Journal of Asiatic Studies*, 20 (1957) 3-4, 480-511.

Fairbank, John K. "The Creation of the Treaty System," in: Twitchett, Denis and Fairbank, John K., eds. *The Cambridge History of China*, vol. 10. Cambridge, 1978, 213–263.

Feuerwerker, Albert. "The Foreign Presence in China," in: Twitchett, Denis and Fairbank, John K., eds. *The Cambridge History of China*, vol. 12. Cambridge, 1983, 128-207.

Fleming, Peter. *The Siege at Peking*. Oxford, 1984.

Guillen-Nuñez, César. "The Gothic Revival and the Architecture of the New Society of Jesus in Macao and China," in: Maryks, Robert A. and Wright, Jonathan, eds. *Jesuit Survival and Restoration. A Global History 1773-1900*. Leiden-Boston, 2015, 280-300.

Henriot, Christian and Zheng, Zu'an. *Atlas de Shanghai. Espaces et représentations de 1849 à nos jours*. Collection Asie Orientale. Paris, 1999.

Jen, Stanislaus. *The History of Our Lady of Consolation Yang kia ping*. Hong Kong, 1978.

Join-Lambert, Arnaud; Servais, Paul; Shen Chung Hen and De Payen, Éric, eds. *Vincent Lebbe et son héritage*. Louvain-la-Neuve, 2017.

Kleeman, Terry F. "Mountain Deities in China: The Domestication of the Mountain God and the Subjugation of the Margins." *The Journal of the American Oriental Society*, 114 (1994), 226-238.

Ku Wei-ying 古偉瀛. "The Shaping of the Late Qing's Policy toward Christianity," in: Heyndrickx, Jeroom, ed. *Historiography of the Chinese Catholic Church. Nineteenth and Twentieth Centuries*. Leuven Chinese Studies 1. Leuven, 1994, 105-124.

Lam, Anthony. "Archbishop Costantini and the First Plenary Council of Shanghai (1924)." *Tripod 鼎*, 28 (2008) 148. <www.hsstudyc.org.hk/en/tripod_en/en_tripod_148_04.html>.

Lazzarotto, Angelo S. "A Strategist of Missionary Development in Henan: Bishop Joseph Noé Tacconi (1873-1942)," in: De Ridder, Koen, ed. *Footsteps in Deserted Villages: Missionary Cases, Strategies, and Practice in Qing China*. Leuven Chinese Studies 8. Leuven, 2000, 55-83.

Leclercq, Jacques. *Vie du Père Lebbe*. Tournai-Paris, 1955.

Le Pichon, Alain. "Portrait of a Practical Visionary: Father Léon Robert MEP and the Sisters of St Paul de Chartres in Hong Kong 1914-19." *Journal of the Royal Asiatic Society Hong Kong Branch*, 52 (2012), 225-266.

Li Guoqiang. "Dapingzi, la première chrétienté au coeur du Yunnan (1835-1925)." *Bulletin de l'École Française d'Extrême-Orient*, 106 (2020), 276-320.

Li Haiqing 李海清 and Wang Xiaoqian 汪晓茜. *The Art of Architectural Integration of Chinese and Western*. Beijing, 2015.

Luo Wei 罗微. *Transmission and Transformation of European Church Types in China: The Churches of the Scheut Mission beyond the Great Wall, 1865-1955*. PhD dissertation in Engineering: Architecture. KU Leuven, 2013.

Masson, Matthieu 馬崇義. "Guangzhou shengxin dajiaotong de sheji he jianzao" 广州圣心大教堂的设计和建造 [The design and construction of the Sacred Heart Cathedral of Canton]. *Xixue dong jian yanjiu* 西学东渐研究 [Research on Eastern Trend of Western Learning], 7 (2019).

Masson, Matthieu. "Sancian, Landscape and Architecture of the Burial Place of St. Francis Xavier." *Hong Kong Journal of Catholic Studies*, 10 (2019), 173-222.

Mo Wei 莫为. "The Gendered Space of the 'Oriental Vatican' – Zi-ka-wei, the French Jesuits and the Evolution of Papal Diplomacy." *Religions*, 9/9, 2018, 278. https://doi.org/10.3390/rel9090278.

Moser, Michael J. and Moser, Yeone Wei-Chi. *Foreigners within the Gates. The Legations at Peking*. Oxford, 1993.

Nicolini-Zani, Matteo. *Christian Monks on Chinese Soil: A History of Monastic Missions to China*. Collegeville, 2016.

Quattrocchi, Paoli Beltrame. "The Trappist Monks in China," in: Heyndrickx, Jeroom, ed. *Historiography of the Chinese Catholic Church. Nineteenth and Twentieth Centuries*. Leuven Chinese Studies 1. Leuven, 1994, 315-317.

Scott, David. *China and the International System, 1840-1949: Power, Presence, and Perception in a Century of Humiliation*. New York, 2008.

Soetens, Claude. *L'Église catholique en Chine au XXᵉ siècle*. Paris, 1997.

Song Haojie 宋浩杰 and Chen Xiangyan 陈翔燕, eds. *Tushanwan jiyi* 土山湾记忆 [Memory of T'ou-sè-wè]. Shanghai, 2010.

Standaert, Nicolas, ed. *Handbook of Christianity in China. Volume One: 635-1800*. Handbook of Oriental Studies 15/1. Leiden-Boston, 2000.

Strong, David. *A Call to Mission: A History of the Jesuits in China 1842-1954*. Volume One: *The French Romance*. Adelaide, 2018.

Strong, David. *A Call to Mission: A History of the Jesuits in China 1842-1954*. Volume Two: *The Wider European and American Adventure*. Adelaide, 2018.

Sweeten, Alan Richard. *Christianity in Rural China. Conflict and Accommodation in Jianxi Province, 1860-1900*. Ann Arbor, 2001.

Sweeten, Alan Richard. *China's Old Churches: The History, Architecture, and Legacy of Catholic Sacred Structures in Beijing, Tianjin, and Hebei Province*. Studies in the History of Christianity in East Asia. Leiden, 2019.

Taveirne, Patrick. *Han-Mongol Encounters and Missionary Endeavors: A History of Scheut in Ordos (Hetao), 1874-1911*. Leuven Chinese Studies 15. Leuven, 2004.

The Catholic Historical Review, 104 (2019) 4, 636-658. https://doi.org/10.1353/cat.2019.0014

Ticozzi, Sergio. "Celso Costantini's Contribution to the Localization and Inculturation of the Church in China." *Tripod* 鼎, 28 (2008) 148. <http://www.hsstudyc.org.hk/en/tripod_en/en_tripod_148_03.html>.

Tiedemann, R. Gary. *Reference Guide to Christian Missionary Societies in China from the Sixtieth to the Twentieth Century*. Armonk-London, 2009.

Tiedemann, R. Gary, ed. *Handbook of Christianity in China. Volume Two: 1800 to the Present*. Handbook of Oriental Studies 15/2. Leiden-Boston, 2010.

Van Hecken, Joseph. *Les réductions catholiques du pays des Ordos. Une méthode d'apostolat des missionnaires de Scheut*. Cahiers de la Nouvelle revue de science missionnaire / Schriftenreihe der neuen Zeitschrift für Missionswissenschaft 15. Schöneck Beckenried, 1957.

Van Melckebeke, Carlo. *Service social de l'Église en Mongolie*. Brussels, 1969.

Verhelst, Daniël and Pycke, Nestor, eds. *CICM Missionaries, Past and Present 1862-1987. History of the Congregation of the Immaculate Heart of Mary (Scheut/Missionhurst)*. Leuven, 1995.

Wang Dong 王栋. *China's Unequal Treaties: Narrating National History*. Langham MD, 2005.

Wang He 王鹤 and Lü Haiping 吕海平. *Jindai Shenyang cheng shi xingtai yanjiu* 近代沈阳成师形态研究 [A research on urban morphological transformation of Shenyang in modern times]. Beijing, 2015.

Wiest, Jean-Paul. "The Building of the Cathedral of Canton: Political, Cultural and Religious Clashes," in: *Religion and Culture: Past Approaches, Present Globalisation, Futures Challenges (International Symposium on Religion and Culture, 2002: Macau)*. Macau, 2004, 231-252.

Wiest, Jean-Paul. "Le père Lebbe et son église de style chinois," in: Join-Lambert, Arnaud; Servais, Paul; Shen Chung Hen and De Payen, Éric, eds. *Vincent Lebbe et son heritage*. Louvain-la-Neuve, 2017, 85-106.

Xiang Hongyan. "Building an Ecclesiastical Real Estate Empire in Late Imperial China." *The Catholic Historical Review*, 104 (2019) 4, 636-658.

Xiang Hongyan. "A Martyr and a Hero: Political Ideologies and Religious Experiences in Modern China," in: Chen Tsung-ming, Alexandre, ed., *Catholicism's Encounters with China*. Leuven, 2018, 255-274.

Xu Subin 徐苏斌, Wu Jiang 伍江 and Lai Delin 赖德霖, eds. *Zhongguo jindai jianzhushi* 中国近代建筑史 [Modern architecture history in China]. 5 vols. Beijing, 2016.

Yu Xueyun 于学蕴 and Liu Lin 刘琳. *Tianjin lao jiaotang* 天津老教堂 [Tianjin's Old Churches]. Tianjin, 2005.

Zhang Xiaohong 张晓虹, Sun Tao 孙涛 and Zhang Jingshu. "The Role of Land Management in Shaping Arid/Semi-Arid Landscapes: The Case of the Catholic Church (CICM) in Western Inner Mongolia from the 1870s (Late Qing Dynasty) to the 1940s (Republic of China)." *Geographical Research*, 47 (2009) 1, 24-33.

Zheng Yangwen 鄭揚文, ed. *Sinicizing Christianity*. Studies in Christian Mission 49. Leiden-Boston, 2017.

< www.catholic-hierarchy.org/> (31 July 2018)

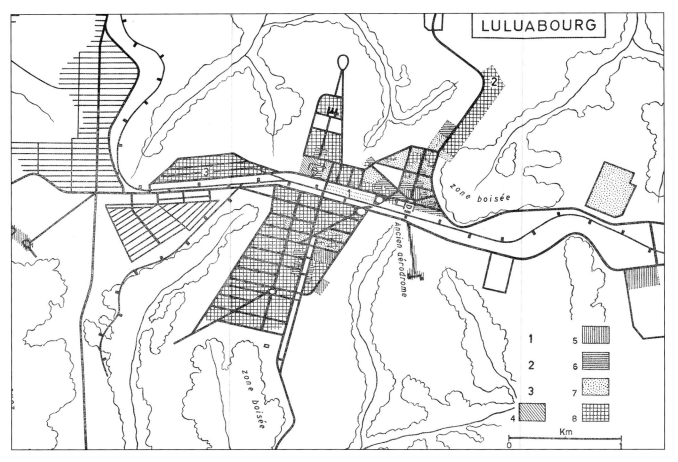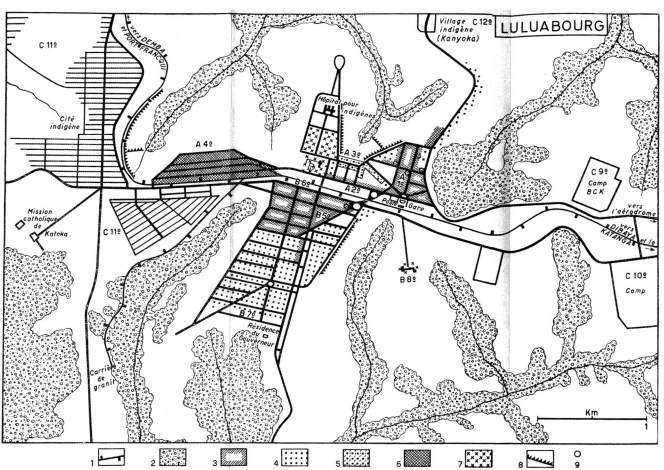

4
Co-authoring the City
Missionaries and the Colonial City of Luluaburg (Belgian Congo), 1930-1960

Bram Cleys

While both the urban history of colonial Africa and the history of colonial urbanism – two interrelated but distinct fields of study – have developed significantly over the past decades, many questions remain unanswered and many approaches of investigation relatively unexplored. One of these questions is the place of religion, more specifically missionary work, in histories of colonial urbanism and urbanity. Although a number of studies have been published on the varying degrees of success with which Muslim cities were redefined by European colonizers and more broadly on the history of urban Muslim communities in colonial settings,[1] the place of Catholic or Protestant missionaries as producers of colonial urbanity remains understudied. Even as the nature of the relationship between missionaries and colonizers remains a topic of much scholarly debate, it is obvious that missionaries and their institutions were important co-producers of the colonial city.[2] In the same way, they have contributed to a distinctly Christian urban identity.

In this chapter the encounter between Catholic and Protestant missionary work and the city will be detailed by exploring five spatial approaches deployed by Catholic and Protestant missionaries to negotiate their position within the city of Luluaburg (today, Kananga, Democratic Republic of the Congo). In an effort to respond to the city's expansion, both Catholic and Protestant missionaries engaged with urban life through these diverse processes for creating space. With varying levels of success, they attempted to spatially co-produce colonial Luluaburg, while simultaneously forging Christian urban subjects.

Luluaburg offers a particularly interesting case study of the position of missionaries in the colonial city as its emergence on the colonial scene was relatively late, coming at a time when both Protestant and Catholic missionaries had been working in the area for over forty years. As the city developed at a rather steady pace for at least the first fifteen years, missionaries succeeded in defining their position towards it and claiming effective co-authorship over it. Although the greater Luluaburg area had played an important role since the early nineteenth century if not before, predominantly in economic terms, the foundation of Luluaburg on that particular site was undoubtedly a colonial phenomenon. From a hub for the pre-colonial long distance Luso-African commerce, it became one of the most important railway stations on the colonial BCK-railway (Compagnie du Chemin de fer du Bas-Congo au Katanga) connecting the mineral mines of Katanga with the Kasai River and the Atlantic Ocean beyond.

Founded by traders in the first half of the 1920s, some years before the completion of the railway line, it witnessed a slow growth in the early 1930s after the local territorial administrator Benoît Moritz moved his seat from the west bank of the river to the new station, previously known as Luluagare in 1931.[3] In 1885, the German explorer Herman von Wissmann (1853-1905) had founded the station on a slope overlooking the west bank of the river and named it Luluaburg. After this transfer, the old Luluaburg settlement lost its function and gradually the new settlement came to be known as Luluaburg rather than Luluagare [Fig. 4.3].[4] The population grew in the 1930s, increased significantly

4.1 Phases of expansion of Luluaburg.
[Nicolaï and Jacques, La transformation des paysages congolais par le chemin de fer, fig. 28]

4.2 Map of Luluaburg (1954) with the Katoka mission on the left.
[Nicolaï and Jacques, La transformation des paysages congolais par le chemin de fer, fig. 27]

1 Çelik, *The Remaking of Istanbul*; Id., *Urban Forms and Colonial Confrontations*.
2 See amongst others: Prudhomme, *Missions chrétiennes et colonisation*; Porter, "'Cultural Imperialism' and Protestant Missionary Enterprise;" Id., *Religion versus Empire?*
3 One year later this transfer was officialized by the governor of the Kasai Province. Nicolaï and Jacques, *La transformation des paysages congolais*, 167; Van Keerberghen, *Brève histoire des paroisses de la ville de Kananga*, 8.
4 Consequently, the original station was referred by its indigenous name Malandji. The Scheut Fathers named their mission Luluaburg Saint-Joseph, founded in 1891 about 15 kilometers further.

4.3 The larger Luluaburg region with the three Luluaburgs: the old State station Luluaburg/Malandji, the new city Luluagare/Luluaburg and the mission station of Luluaburg Saint-Joseph, also called Mikalayi Saint-Joseph.
[Nicolaï, La transformation des paysages congolais par le chemin de fer, 165]

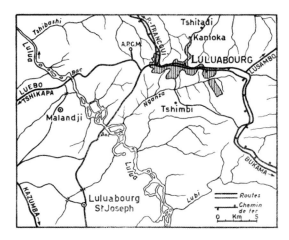

5   Nicolaï and Jacques, *La transformation des paysages congolais*, 134-135, 182-190. Cleys, "Catholic Missionaries and the Production of Kasai as a Colonial Landscape." Luluaburg and Lusambo were among the oldest colonial settlements in Kasai and played a crucial military role in the so-called Arab War. Wandja and Ndjusuku wa Lutula, "Le rôle historique du poste de Lusambo."

6   RMCA, 82.58 Papers Georges Verriest: Comité de Direction de l'Office des Cités Africaines, "La crise du logement au Congo belge et l'Office des Cités Africaines," Oct. 14, 1959. For a general overview of Luluaburg's early history, see Nicolaï and Jacques, *La transformation des paysages congolais*, 164-170; de Saint-Moulin and Kayemba, "Origine et évolution de la ville de Kananga." For an extensive discussion of Luluaburg's demographic evolution at the end of the colonial era, see Lux, "Migrations, accroissement et urbanisation de la population congolaise de Luluabourg."

7   Scheut Fathers from the Congregation of the Immaculate Heart of Mary, a Belgian male missionary religious institute founded in 1862 in Scheut near Brussels. See Verhelst and Pycke, *C.I.C.M. Missionaries Past and Present*.

8   GAS, 3936: *Stichting der missie van Kananga. Luluaburg St-Clement*, s.d. (c. 1940).

during the Second World War and expanded in the 1950s, after the city became the administrative center of the Kasai Province.[5] This move sanctioned the drastic geographical transformation of the Kasai landscape brought about by the construction of the railroad. While Luluaburg and the settlements along the railway line attracted all the development, the former capital Lusambo and locations situated at a distance from the railroad lost their importance. From a humble center in its early days Luluaburg thus developed into the fourth largest city in the Congo by the end of the colonial era in 1960.[6]

The first missionaries who began working at what was then nothing more than an inconspicuous railway stop were the Scheut Fathers from the Congregation of the Immaculate Heart of Mary (CICM).[7] In 1928, Catechist Nsanka Joseph took up residence in Luluagare. He was trained, appointed, and supervised by the Scheut Fathers of Luluaburg Saint-Joseph, the Kasai's oldest Catholic mission station (1891), situated about 30 kilometers from Luluagare on the other side of the Lulua River. Two years later, the favourable position of this new settlement – accessible from large parts of the province thanks to the railway line – was exploited when Vicar Apostolic Auguste De Clercq CICM (1870/1918-1938/1939) asked the Josephite Fathers to open a secondary school there.

From 1930 to the end of the colonial era in 1960, both Catholic and Protestant missionaries developed a broad range of pastoral initiatives to evangelize Luluaburg's booming population and guide Christians in leading moral lives. By 1960, Catholic missionaries were operating seven parishes and several schools, while Protestants worshipped in five churches and had schools on at least four sites.

In this chapter we will analyze the spatial strategies behind the spread of these apostolic activities, which to a lesser or greater extent, helped shape the city.

A church for a city still to come

With the relocation of the territorial administrator's office from old Luluaburg on the left bank of the Lulua River to Luluagare in 1931, the settlement made an initial leap in its evolution. As it gradually developed from one of several railway stations along the BCK line into a regional commercial center, the need to establish a fully equipped mission station in Luluagare was felt increasingly urgently by the CICM missionaries. In 1935, fathers Aimé Lippens (1887-1958) and Gustave Mercenier (1904-1982) settled within the limits of the *circonscription urbaine* (urban settlement) and took over the activities that had been carried out by the catechist Nsanka Joseph. Evangelization of the population in and around Luluagare had previously been the responsibility of the mission station of Mikalayi Saint-Joseph since 1928. The newly founded mission station – christened Saint-Clément – was seperated from Mikalayi and took over the territory on the right bank of the Lulua River [Fig. 4.3]. The humble beginnings of this first urban mission station were described in typically heroic missionary prose:

> The mission station of Mikalayi donated us a dozen chairs, a table, some windows, cutlery and a mass vestment, while the two apostles bravely undertook the first beginning. There was a dilapidated hangar that served as a church

and some similarly dilapidated school buildings with about 300 pupils.[8]

In the early years, school buildings were erected to house the increasing number of students coming from the growing *cité* for the indigenous population and the surrounding villages. A double-floored brick residence for the missionaries was completed in 1938 [Fig. 4.4] replacing the temporary construction erected for the peregrinating missionary Paul Van Merris (1885-1943). A cross-shaped brick church was built between 1936 and 1942 as a substitute for the adobe chapel used by the catechists.[9]

At the time of its foundation, the plot that had been secured for the Saint-Clément station lay on the outskirts of the urban settlement [Fig. 4.1], between the European settlement and the *cité*. However, as Luluaburg expanded over the next fifteen years, this site would become one of the hearts of the city. The new administrative quarter was laid out on the other side of the railway line, perpendicular to the mission station; this district included not only the new city hall, but also the provincial administration and palace of the provincial governor. Consequently, completed in 1942, the new church, was positioned along one of the city's most important avenues and was visible from many points. Designed by the brother-architect Lambert Lantin CICM (1906-1969), this new church demonstrated a number of features that performed its representative function [Fig. 4.5].[10] In addition to its dimensions, which were necessary to welcome a growing number of faithful, the new church was positioned on an open site to maximize visibility. Most striking however is Saint-Clément's campanile. This detached tower type with its early Christian references was rediscovered by Catholic reformers of church architecture in Europe at the beginning of the century and applied in several churches in Congo. Saint-Clément's spire has become one of the most recognizable landmarks in the city.[11]

At the time of its foundation, Saint-Clément was the only Catholic parish church in the city, serving both its Congolese and European population, and as such, the church building had a strong representative function. Through its positioning and architectural vocabulary it not only offered an expressive image of Catholic faith, but also claimed a dominant place for Catholicism in the (re)presentation of the city. It created a focal point in the expanding urban fabric. During the early years of its existence, the church dominated its, then still humble, surroundings. By 1950, when the city had expanded drastically, the providence of the Catholic missionaries had been proven right. It was a church built for a city still to come or, as one contemporary observed:

> Sign of permanence, the big tower of Saint-Clément Cathedral, has demanded itself what it has come to do there… In ten years' time, it has had the time to come back from this impression.[12]

It is striking to note that the representative function conferred on this religious building betrays a contemporary vernacular. The campanile, interior layout, and architectural vocabulary were all clearly inspired by interwar discussions about liturgical architecture.

4.4 The residence of the CICM missionaries in Saint-Clément, erected in 1938, later the Procuratory office.
[Leuven, KADOC-KU Leuven, CICM Picture Archive: 27.5.17]

9   GAS, 3936: *Stichting der missie van Kananga Luluaburg St. Clément*, 3807: Letter to the vicar-general, June 22, 1935, *Parva relatio de statu spirituali et materiali*, July 3, 1935; Letter to the vicar-general, July 7, 1935. Van Keerberghen, *Brève histoire*, 8-9.

10 Brother Lambert Lantin studied architecture at the St. Luke School of Art before joining the CICM in 1932. In the Kasai Province, he erected many buildings. In the early 1950s he was appointed head of the vicariate's central 'drawing room', an architectural office. GAS, 5159: Letter of Mgr Bernard Mels, Mikalayi, Feb. 21, 1959.

11 On architectural strategies of churches in the Belgian Congo, see Cleys and De Meulder, "La construction des églises."

12 Mondele, "Croquis Luluabourgeois."

4.5 Built as a church, Saint-Clément soon became a cathedral.
[Leuven, KADOC-KU Leuven, CICM Picture Archive: 27.5.16]

13 Van Keerberghen, *Brève histoire*, 9-11.

The large nave with adjoining *ambulatoria* and short sanctuary is an obvious example of the desire of Christocentric church design to make the sanctuary visible to as many participants as possible. In the majority of other mission stations established by Scheut Fathers in rural contexts, churches are still designed in an archetypical Gothic Revival idiom. The explicit choice of a more contemporary architectural vocabulary is an indication of the attention paid to Luluaburg's first church.

In the years that followed its foundation, the Saint-Clément settlement developed to house the growing number of services carried out by the missionaries to serve both the European and Congolese populations [Fig. 4.6]. At the same time, it also accommodated some of the central works of the CICM mission. In 1950, most of their provincial administration services were moved to Luluaburg. Since 1912, the Scheut provincial house had been located in the rural mission station of Hemptinne Saint-Benoît (today Bunkonde). Increasing administrative regulations and the convenience of nearby transport facilities made the transfer of the CICM provincial administration to Luluaburg inevitable, however, especially after the Provincial Governor Firmin Peigneux (1904-1968) relocated his administration from Lusambo to Luluaburg. The CICM provincial house was located in Katoka (see below), but the procuratory house, which was responsible for the financial and logistical support of the Scheut province of Kasai, was established in Saint-Clément. Since its foundation in 1935, a missionary had been appointed adjunct-procurator, responsible for distributing goods arriving at the railway station to the many mission stations across Kasai. From 1950 onwards, all procurator services were housed in the former missionary residence of Saint-Clément [Fig. 4.4], which was also set up as *maison de passage* for newly arrived missionaries before their appointment to a mission station. A new residence for the priest was then built behind the church.[13]

In addition to its role as a space for liturgy and civic representation, Saint-Clément functioned primarily as a site of education for Luluaburg's population. Until the establishment of the Notre-Dame parish in 1948, Saint-Clément was the only Catholic settlement and thus responsible for reaching the entire population. Most schools were later relocated to Katoka [Fig. 4.2], where they were not only closer to the new *cité indigène*, but also found more space to welcome the growing number of students. In addition to a smaller primary school for Congolese children that remained in the city center, a new school

4.6 *The complex of Saint-Clément, aerial view from the southeast c. 1945. [Ghent, General Archive of the Sisters of Charity of Jesus and Mary, Image & Sound: DC4-CON-Luluabourg-K1769]*

operated by the Sisters of Charity of Ghent opened for European girls in 1941. Territorial Administrator Moritz had succeeded in attracting nuns to teach the children of Luluaburg's growing European communities and the other centers along the railway line. As a consequence of the Second World War, they could no longer be sent to Europe as usually for their education. Supervised by Brother Lantin, a modern school complex with boarding school was built just behind the church in 1942 [Figs. 4.6 and 4.7]. In 1950, the Saint-Louis boy's secondary school also opened in temporary constructions on this site.

The Catholic institutions and their students were not isolated from the urban trajectory, but integrated into the urban fabric. While a clear hierarchical layout can be understood from the spatial organization of the plot – with the church at the entrance to the concession and the schools and convents set back from the street – the entire complex was bordered by public streets [Fig. 4.6]. Moreover, by slightly setting back the church from the street, a public plaza was created in front of its south façade. Erected on private ground obtained in full concession by the missionaries, the church surroundings were designed in such a way as to be part and parcel of the city.

This architectural gesture made by the Saint-Clément mission towards the city was sanctioned by the colonial government's decision to locate the state-run *Hôpital des Indigènes* (native hospital) in the same quarter. This new construction, "remarkable in modernism and cleanliness" as one observer put it,[14] consisted of a central building with four connecting wings and was erected on a plot behind the Sisters of Charity's convent. From its opening in 1951, the sisters were employed as nurses by the state and were responsible for the daily care of the patients under the supervision of a state doctor. General management was carried out by the colonial medical service.[15]

Grouping mission schools and state hospitals in the same district was in keeping with the functional zoning that had inspired Luluaburg's urban plan. Partly because of Luluaburg's topography, consisting of a series of hills crisscrossed by deep valleys, the colony's chief urbanist Maurice C. Heymans (1909-1991) had designed a plan for Luluaburg that led the city out as a cluster of interlinked functional units each assigned to a hill top.[16] This geography dominated by hills also left

14 GASC, 9.2.9: Unidentified newspaper clipping "Luluabourg compte un des plus beaux Hôpitaux Indigènes de la Colonie," 1951.

15 GASC, 9.2.9: Kananga: Letter of unidentified sister to Sister Jenna, Luluaburg, Aug. 13, 1945; 9.2.9: Mikalayi: *Memoriaal Mikalayi. 1894-1950*, 1950; Vints and Etambala, *100 jaar Zusters van Liefde J.M.*, 149, 163-164; Kapinga wa Nkaya, *Les Sœurs de la Charité de Jésus et de Marie*, 125-129.

16 On M.C. Heymans and colonial urbanism in Belgian Congo, see De Meulder, *Kuvuande Mbote*.

4.7 Janua Coeli School for European children.
[Ghent, General Archive of the Sisters of Charity of Jesus and Mary, Image & Sound: A66-CON-Kananga-07c]

17   Saint-Louis College was the only exception to this racial segregation (see below).
18   On colonial educational policy, see Depaepe and Van Rompaey, *In het teken van de bevoogding*.
19   PAS, Concessions Anciennes: Convention N° D.3 between Colonie du Congo Belge (Province de Lusambo) and Pères Joséphites, Jan. 9, 1934. This section on the Josephite school is primarily based on Scheitler, *Histoire de l'Église catholique au Kasayi*, 261-265; Van Keerberghen, *Histoire de l'enseignement catholique*, 195-200; Id., *Brève histoire*, 38.
20   No precise population data exist for the period before WWII: de Saint Moulin and Kayemba, "Origine et évolution de la ville de Kananga," 514-515, refer to one source that estimates the population of Luluagare and its surroundings in 1931 to 15,000 inhabitants. They establish the total population increase from 51,885 in 1950 to 61,641 in 1955 and 121,049 in 1959. André Lux ("Migrations, accroissement et urbanisation," 696) shows the population increase through an index with the year 1950 as base 100 (1951: 86.5; 1952: 115.6; 1953: 165.7; 1954: 212.7; 1955: 265.8; 1956: 323.4; 1957: 362). The native population of the *cité* increased from 11,205 in 1948 to 53,281 in 1958 (RMCA, 82.58 Papers G. Verriest: Comité de Direction de l'Office des Cités Africaines, hand written note, 1958).
21   People from the surroundings rarely attended mass in this church, except in 1951-1952 during the construction of Notre-Dame Church. See Van Keerberghen, *Brève histoire*, 30-31, 38.

the distinction between a European city and an indigenous town less clearly differentiated than in older colonial cities. While the residential quarters for both groups were still located a considerable distance from one other, other city zones were not racially segregated.

This was undoubtedly true of the area around Saint-Clément with its mix of, on the one hand, European housing and schooling and, on the other, schooling and medical care for the Congolese population. Throughout the colonial period educational and healthcare institutions remained separated along racial lines, but the planned division between the European city and the Congolese *cités* was actually a perforated boundary.[17] At night the boundary was strictly guarded, but during the day this neighborhood was a stage on which the everyday lives of a broad range of people played out across racial divides.

The campus as enclave

As early as four years before the establishment of the Saint-Clément mission station, a secondary school for the education of clerks – the highest position a Congolese could obtain in the colonial administration – had been opened across the then limits of the urban settlement of Luluagare. It replaced a similar school that had been operated by the CICM missionaries in Mikalayi since 1924, but opened up to the best students from all the mission stations in the Kasai vicariate. Its location near the Luluagare railway station made it easier for these pupils to get to school. In accordance with contemporary educational regulations, a significant part of school time was dedicated to manual labour, most often put into practice by cultivating school fields.[18] In order to have sufficient space for these fields, the missionaries applied for an extensive piece of land. As it was located outside the limits of the *circonscription urbaine* and at a distance from surrounding villages, a convention signed in 1934 between the Josephite Fathers and the colonial State granted a large piece of land of 100 ha to the missionaries to be used for erecting a chapel, schools and housing for the fathers [Fig. 4.8]. Throughout the colonial period – and to a large extent until today – this area maintained an ambivalent position towards the city. On the one hand, it remained isolated from the urban agglomeration, constituting an autonomous zone within the city; on the other hand, it depended on its proximity for its population and functions.[19]

A school campus in the 1930s and the 1940s, this settlement in the Katoka quarter – as this concession was known – became a focal point for Luluaburg's Catholic social life after the Second World War. The city's sudden boom – estimates for the ten-year period between 1950 and 1960 range from a twofold to a fivefold increase – encouraged the missionaries to expand their activities for the urban population.[20] While the Saint-Clément station offered significant visibility in the civic centre of the city, it was not large enough to expand the schools and other institutions. Once the Katoka concession was integrated into the city limits, its eccentric position became an advantage. This was especially true in the wake of the establishment of a new quarter nearby for the city's Congolese population [Fig. 4.2]. More than merely an institution for secondary education for the greater Kasai area, Katoka became the operational base for Catholic missionaries to reach Luluaburg's Congolese inhabitants. The first step in this spatial conversion took place in 1948 when the Scheut Fathers established a new parish along the *avenue Roi Baudouin* that bordered the Josephite concession. As the new parish was located closer to what was then the city's largest indigenous neighborhood, they relocated their schools for Congolese children to this new and open space. The church building constructed by the Josephite Fathers in 1936-1937 was intended only to serve students attending their schools [Fig. 4.9].[21]

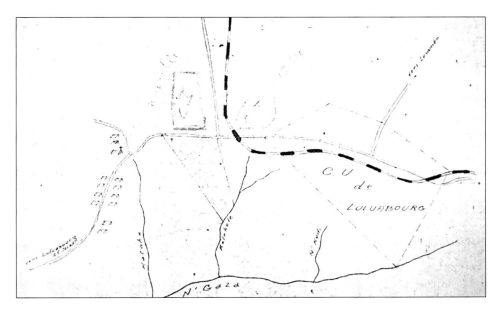

4.8 Katoka concession.
[Kananga, Provincial Archive of Scheut: Convention N° D.3, 9/1/1934]

When the first church turned out to be too small, a new church was dedicated to Notre-Dame in 1953 [Fig. 4.10]. After the foundation of the Notre-Dame parish, the missionaries also made Katoka the seat of several of their apostolic works aimed at Luluaburg's urban population. In keeping with the Catholic Action – which dominated the social thinking of the Catholic Church during that period – a broad array of social works was set up, each focused on a specific group. These included Boy Scout and Girl Scout groups for children and young people, a *cercle* for *évolués*, the Eucharist Crusade,

4.9 Former church of the Josephite School, built in 1936-1937, since 1964 Sainte-Famille parish church.
[Leuven, KADOC-KU Leuven, CICM Picture Archive: 27.5.17]

4.10 Former church of Notre-Dame, built in 1951-1952. [Photo: Bram Cleys]

22 Vellut, "Introduction," 12-14. In 1955, Georges Kettel CICM (1897-1972), vicar apostolic of Kabinda (eastern Kasai) wrote: "If we want to avoid our missionary action from being deficient, we must add social action. (…) It is necessary that our apostolic zeal prolongs our influence beyond the school in the household and the families." GASC, 3.5.4.2./1: Mgr Kettel, Circular letter, July 1955.

23 Van Keerberghen, *Brève histoire*, 31, 38; GASC, 9.2.9: Letter of Sr. Clementine to Sr. M. Irmine, Janua Coeli, Feb. 15, 1954; V., "Cinéma pour indigènes." On the history of cinema in Kananga and the Belgian Congo more broadly, see: Ramirez and Rolot, *Histoire du cinéma colonial,* and Convents, *Image & Démocratie*.

the Legion of Mary, etc. Since the mid-1920s, Catholic missionaries had begun establishing these social movements in urban settings as part of their effort to forge new social identities for the inhabitants of the so-called *centre extra-coutumiers* (extra-customary centers). For the missionaries, these social movements were essential to extend their influence beyond schooling and liturgy into the daily life of families and households. At the same time, for the Congolese believers, these movements offered environments of belonging – which many had lost by migrating to the city – while also creating possibilities for emancipation. Although under strict surveillance by male and female missionaries, the Catholic Action movements provided ample room for laymen to take up responsibility. The same arguments were later used to plead for a social apostolate in the rural areas.[22]

In Luluaburg, most of these movements met in buildings around the Katoka church or on the (former) Josephite concession. One of the most remarkable initiatives, which would also attract significant attention from the contemporary press, was the building of the Luluafilm complex in around 1952. This multi-use movie theater was constructed on the initiative of Father Albert Van Haelst CICM (1903-1976), the instigator and driving force behind Luluafilm which produced and distributed movies for Catholic audiences. Both his own movies – among which the *Matamata and Pilipili* comedy series were the most famous – and selected foreign films were screened in this hall [Fig. 4.11]. His movies were initially shown in other locations across the city, but the considerable success of his performances required a specific building. As trips to movie theaters became increasingly popular, the Catholic missionaries tried to control which movies their followers could see, differentiating between the locals and the *évolués*, a colonial category developed to refer to a top tier of Congolese society that aspired to integrate into the European community.[23]

Parallel to the development of this urban apostolate by the CICM missionaries, the Sisters of Charity expanded their activities towards the urban female population and households. This female religious institute had collaborated with the Scheut Fathers on several mission stations and had been working near Saint-Clément in Luluaburg since 1941. They took over part of the buildings evacuated by the Josephite Fathers in 1950 (see below). Like the Scheut Fathers, they transferred their schools for Congolese children from the city center to Katoka. In 1954, Scheut donated 12 hectares within their concession to the Sisters to allow them to further develop their own works.[24]

The central position of Katoka in Catholic missionary work in Luluaburg was further consolidated in 1950 when the Scheut Fathers took over the school concession from the Josephite Fathers and converted it into their provincial headquarters. This was made possible after the Josephite Fathers exchanged this plot for a new concession in the Mushenge-Mweka-area to the north of Kasai and relocated their secondary school there.[25] In addition to the offices of their provincial administration, the CICM clustered several other key congregation services – such as the slaughterhouse for their cattle farms and a printing office – on their newly acquired concession. The Katoka complex was developed in two parts: a public space for education, liturgy and urban apostolate, and a private space for internal services and sacred seclusion. Unlike at the Saint-Clément settlement, this division between internal and external services was reflected spatially by a foreground versus background setting. The buildings used for the internal services of the CICM congregation were sited to the northwest of the concession, while those with a more public function were located on the southeast along the access roads.

In 1954, the CICM further strengthened the importance of Katoka as a key nucleus in their own internal network with the foundation of a noviciate for Congolese men wanting to enter their congregation. In 1932, a major seminary had been established at Kabwe, 70 kilometers south of Luluaburg, for the education of diocesan priests. Whereas an indigenous brother congregation had been founded by Vicar Apostolic Auguste De Clercq in 1928, entrance to the CICM had been closed for Congolese believers. As for many buildings belonging to the Catholic missions in Luluaburg, the noviciate

of Katoka was designed by brother-architect Lambert Lantin. It was located behind the provincial house and focused away from the public gaze [Fig. 4.12]. As the housing needs of Luluaburg's expanding population increasingly encroached on areas of the Katoka concession the noviciate made up the wings of the concession isolated from all other buildings.[26]

The diversification of mission activities attracted ever larger crowds of Christians to Katoka – schoolchildren, parishioners, members of the various social movements, novices, etc. However, thanks to the internal organizations of the site, it remained an enclave in the city, simultaneously inside and outside the burgeoning urban fabric. With the exception of the church of Notre-Dame, the primary school for boys and a state-owned technical school which were situated along the *avenue Roi Baudouin*, all other buildings were set back at a considerable distance from the avenue. They could only be reached along an access road bordering the concession of the Sisters of Charity. As the Catholic missionaries had obtained property rights for sizable plots on both sides of this avenue, they could control a large social

4.11 Luluafilm hall.
[Leuven, KADOC-KU Leuven, CICM Picture Archive: 27.3.7]

24 PAS: *Acte de Cession* between the CICM and the Sisters of Charity of Ghent in Kasai March 9, 1954. In 1953, CICM had already handed over 30 ha to the State, which built a school for technical education run by CICM (PAS: *Procès-verbal d'arpentage et de bornage n° 600*, Dec. 21, 1953).
25 PAS: Letter of Martin Miserez, representative of the Josephites, to the governor of Luluaburg Province, Mweka, Jan. 12, 1950; Letter of the *Conservateur des Titres Fonciers* L. Guissart to Martin Miserez, Luluaburg, April 13, 1950.
26 Scheitler, *Histoire de l'Église catholique au Kasayi*, 234-235, 280-285; Verhelst and Pycke, *C.I.C.M. Missionaries*, 314-316.

4.12 Scheut Noviciate at Katoka. [Leuven, KADOC-KU Leuven, CICM Picture Archive: 27.5.18]

space in an important part of the city. With the expansion of the urban population and surface area, Katoka became part and parcel of Luluaburg's urban center. Through the internal organization of their concession, the Catholic missionaries succeeded in isolating themselves and their followers from the hustle and bustle.

This same spatial logic inspired the establishment of the new CICM secondary school for European boys, Saint-Louis College.[27] It opened its doors in 1950 at the request of the growing European community. However, its preliminary school buildings near the cathedral of Saint-Clément soon became too small and a new location was to be found. A concession was obtained in 1953 at the outer limit of a new European residential quarter, again on the edge of the then urbanized area, to the east side of the city. The school principal Father Désiré Rombouts CICM (1915-1986) envisioned an enclosed college setting that would isolate Saint-Louis' students from urban life.[28] At the outset, only European children were accepted to the college. Eventually, some years later, Congolese children who had passed a strict state test were also admitted.

One major difference between this and the Katoka complex lay in the architectural language of the buildings. The cloister and chapel unit for the missionaries-teachers and the student dormitories, erected between 1957 and 1960, are particularly striking for their architectural quality [Fig. 4.13]. Both building units were oriented towards the street and constituted the face of the boarding school. Despite its marginal location, the autonomous Catholic space exerted an appeal due to the high architectural quality of this front façade. As the design of Saint-

4.13 Saint-Louis College aerial view from the northeast, c. 1960. [Leuven, KADOC-KU Leuven, CICM Picture Archive]

4.14 Chapel of the Saint-Louis College from northwest.
[Photo: Bram Cleys]

Clément Cathedral had been in the early 1940s, it was a clear gesture towards the city and its inhabitants. With their contemporary tropical modernist style, the buildings of the European school intended to attract parents and students to this Catholic college [Fig. 4.14].

The choice of this architectural modernity was immediately aimed at countering the state school for European children that had opened its doors in 1950. From 1950 to 1959, Belgian politics was dominated by the Second School War between clerical and non-clerical parties over the place of religion in education. This conflict was also played out in the colony in what Isidore Ndaywel è Nziem has called "the tropicalization of Belgian dissents."[29] Until the Second World War, education in the colony – both for European and Congolese children – had been virtually dominated by Catholic and Protestant missionaries, but this monopoly was challenged from 1948 onwards as a consequence of this colonial 'school war'. The *athénées*, state-run schools, were founded in the major cities of the colony, first for European children and soon followed by separate schools for Congolese children. Catholic missionaries opposed this evolution vehemently and sought ways to hold their advantageous position firmly and for as long as possible. The modern building commissioned for Saint-Louis College was part of a strategic competition with the brand new and fully equipped buildings of the *athénée*.

Protestant urban apostolate: working from the margins

The encounter of the Protestant missionaries with the city followed a completely different trajectory. The Protestants who carried out activities in Luluaburg in the colonial period were all members of the American Presbyterian Congo Mission (APCM). This American congregation had settled in Luebo, in the northern part of the Kasai Province, in 1891. Although the first Catholic missionary, Eméry Cambier CICM (1865-1943), was appointed to the state post of Luluaburg in December of the same year, the APCM was never able to develop missionary work at the same pace as the Scheut Fathers. The main reason for this was the complete difference in the colonial state's policy towards Protestant missionaries. From the time of Leopold II's Congo Free State until the end of the colonial period, Protestant missions were hampered in their development while Catholic mission congregations were fully supported by the colonial administration. As Belgium was a predominantly Catholic country, all Protestant mission congregations had foreign

27 The same settlement strategy was applied by the Catholic Church of Kasai in the post-colonial period for the new buildings for the seminary (1970) and the Université Notre-Dame du Kasayi (early 1990s).
28 The Jesuits applied the same strategy on advanced education settlements at the fringe of urban agglomerations in Lovanium University, Léopoldville (Mantels, *Geleerd in de tropen*) and the interracial Collège du Saint-Esprit, Bujumbura, Burundi (Lagae, "A Highly 'Mediated Monument' of Tropical Modernism" in this book, p. 229-251).
29 Ndaywel è Nziem, *Histoire du Zaïre*, 496. See also Briffaerts, "De schoolstrijd in Belgisch Congo."

30 AAPCM, 23-2: Letter of APCM-missionary to the vice-governor-general, Dec. 28, 1922; 70-12: Letter of the APCM's legal representative to the district commissar, Luebo, Jan. 4, 1923.

31 AAPCM, 9-22: Letter of Charles L. Crane to Mission Secretary Allen M. Craig, Montreat, Aug. 13, 1940.

32 AAPCM, 9-27: Letter of H.M. Washburn to the Women's Work Committee, Feb. 25, 1943. Reviewing the APCM's realizations in the 1950s, Vernon A. Anderson (*Still Led in Triumph*, 25) mentioned: "Luluabourg is a Roman Catholic stronghold with more than a hundred priests and nuns working in the city. There are also eleven Protestant missionaries, five Protestant churches and a number of preaching outposts which are served by three Congolese pastors and their assistants."

33 AAPCM, 70-17: Letter of Dr Stixrud to the governor of Kasai, Luebo, Feb. 10, 1942; N'Kashama, *Formation et édification d'une église autochtone*, 25.

34 A short article in a local journal mentions the visit of Pandit Nehru, who was welcomed and housed by the local Muslim community (*Kasaï. Bi-hebdomadaire indépendant*, 3). An underground Greek-orthodox community for Greek merchants and their families developed a Greek-orthodox school from the mid-1980s (conversation with Kabwe Pierre, Kananga, July 20, 2007). The document GAS, 3936: *Stichting der missie van Kananga Luluaburg St-Clement* mentions several Jewish traders in the city, but no trace of their religious practice was found. A broad range of charismatic religio-political movements called 'sects', were considered subver-sive and closely monitored. For reports on their activity in Luluaburg, see RMCA, 66.20 Papers Auguste Gilliaert:

roots. Moreover, the Ministry of Colonies was dominated by members of the Catholic party. This meant that Catholic mission officials had close links to representatives of the colonial administration. One of the most noticeable consequences on the ground was the differential treatment of applications for concessions. While the Catholic missionaries were able to obtain large concessions relatively quickly, Protestant missionaries were confronted with constant maneuvers to delay the application process, with regular rejections and ultimately comparatively smaller plots.

The American Presbyterian Congo Mission was faced with the same difficulties. In 1922, they had applied for a concession near the (old) Luluaburg state station, which they subsequently withdrew after the territorial administrator declared his opposition.[30] In the new Luluaburg, they failed to obtain a concession within the urban limits, despite repeated attempts. Unlike the Catholic missionaries, they were forced to wait until the Second World War to take advantage of Luluaburg's central position in Kasai. In 1927, they received the permission to erect a *gîte d'étappe* on the outskirts of the city, but it would not be until 1940 that they could begin to think about establishing a full mission station in the growing city. In that year, APCM missionary Charles Crane pointed out the need to have a mission station in Luluaburg for the first time. In a letter to the mission secretary general of the Presbyterian Church of the USA he wrote:

> We should by all means get an equipment at Luluabourg that will help us hold our own there, or we shall lose out completely. We have lost literally hundreds of our former adherents because of our poor and inadequate equipment.[31]

Several arguments were cited to justify the opening of this new station. The first was the city's central position in the APCM's mission field, which made it the ideal location for their business administration. The state's plans at that time to move its provincial administration to Luluaburg only highlighted this course of action. However, as important as this organizational argument was, Catholic missionaries had already gained a strong ecucational foothold. While the Protestants only had two village schools with chapels led by Congolese evangelists, the Catholics were running two fully equipped schools and a large mission station. In previous decades, this competition between the two denominations had already provided significant motivation for the expansion of missionary networks on both sides. Writing about their plan to open full primary schools on the new mission station, H.M. Washburn, an APCM-missionary, wrote that this choice was:

> not to compete with the Catholics, but to train and educate the children of our protestant Christians. Whenever these are compelled by circumstances to attend the Catholic School, they are subjected to a strong influence and propaganda to convert them to the church of Rome.[32]

In 1941, a concession request was filed with the state, but was not granted until 1944. Two years later building works were finished and the mission station fully occupied. Ndesha mission, named after a local river, was built on a hill just outside the boundaries of the city of Luluaburg [Fig. 4.15]. Opposition from the state administration had again forced them to apply for a concession outside the *circonscription urbaine*.[33] The Protestant missionaries were spatially marginalized and forced to carry out their urban work from the city's periphery. Unlike the Catholic missionaries, they were unable to spatially mark their presence in the city. During the 1950s they succeeded in obtaining small plots in three of the new neighborhoods that housed the immigrant population of Luluaburg – Kamilabi, Katoka and Tshimbi – but were never able to claim the same visibility and representative power as the Saint-Clément complex or even the Catholic Katoka complex. Despite the dissent on religious-ideological themes that dominated Belgian metropolitan and colonial debate, Catholicism was allowed to make a clear mark on Luluaburg. Other religions were either confined to the border zones of the city or to an underground life, as was the case for Islam, Judaism, the Greek-Orthodox Church, and the so-called 'sects'. Tracking down information on the activities of these religious communities is extremely challenging.[34]

The Ndesha station was used as operational base for the APCM's work among the urban and rural population. While the Catholics had several mission stations in the immediate rural area around Luluaburg – Mikalayi Saint-Joseph on the left bank of the Lulua River, Ntambue Saint-Bernard just east of the city, and Demba to the north – the closest mission station of the APCM, Mutoto, was more than 50 kilometers from the city. Missionaries and pastors stationed at Ndesha made regular tours of the Protestant communities in a wide circle around Luluaburg. Children from these villages could come to the city to follow the full cycle of primary education, which was not offered in the village schools. Beside this central school and a church, the mission station housed the offices of the APCM legal representative and a small dispensary. While medical evangelism had always been a cornerstone of Protestant work elsewhere, the APCM missionaries would never operate a full medical service in Luluaburg during the colonial period. Only in the late 1960s a fully equipped hospital was established in Tshikaji, on the outskirts of Luluaburg.

While forced by the colonial state authorities to operate from the periphery of the Luluaburg agglomeration, the evangelic strategies followed by the Presbyterian missionaries were not dissimilar from those deployed by the Catholics. Much like them, they advanced a broad range of initiatives which aimed to support their believers in all aspects of daily life. A 1952 study of the challenges of the urban environment proposed "a Christ-centered and Church-centered program." In addition to the supervision of dignified and inspiring worship, this program was intended to consist of "an adequate seven-day-a-week, all-round program for the whole life of the Christian Community."[35] Similar to the Catholics who had initiated several social movements, each directed towards a specific age, gender or social group, the APCM proposed as part of this program not only education and evangelization in a strict sense, but also separate gatherings for men, women, adolescents, and children.[36] This social apostolate was not exclusive to Luluaburg and was launched in mission stations in smaller centers and rural areas at roughly the same time. However, as was the case for the Catholic missionaries, it was executed more intensively and consistently in Luluaburg. Despite rivalry and dissent, both groups of missionaries shared the same assessment of the situation in the colonial urban settings and developed the same approach. Having left their villages to settle in the city, the migrant population of Luluaburg was disconnected from its customary leaders and traditions. The integral apostolate of both the Catholic and Protestant missionaries – "accompanying their believers from the cradle to the grave," according to a popular

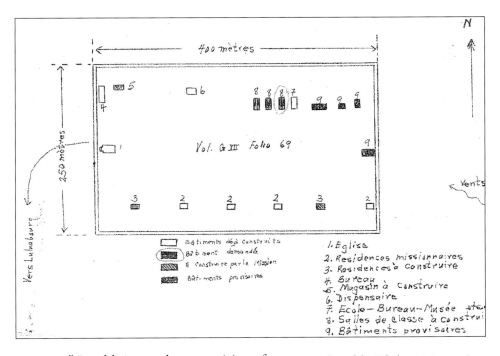

4.15 Plan of the Ndesha mission station on a ground of 10 hectares, 1949. [Philadelphia, Presbyterian Historical Socety, AAPCM: 43-7]

Maintien et rétablissement de l'ordre public, 1954. In 1971, Haldor E. Heimer completed a study on the then independent Kimbanguist Church and Bapostolo in Luluaburg (*The Kimbanguists and the Bapostolo*).

35 AAPCM, 23-6: Suggestions for panel discussion on challenges in urban centres. Mission Meeting, 1952, 1952.

36 AAPCM, 72-3: Women's and Children's Work in the Centres at Luluabourg, 1954-1955; 23-10: Note on APCM's youth work, s.d.

4.16 Church of Saint-Jean de la Croix in Katoka II.
[Leuven, KADOC-KU Leuven, CICM Picture Archive: 27.5.18]

Catholic aphorism – not only enabled them to fight back against the perceived disadvantages of this migration for Luluaburg's 'detribalized' population, but would, in the long run, also create a new identity, based on religion instead of ethnic background. That this strategy had failed, was proven from 1958 onwards, when the Bena Lulua and the Baluba, two ethnic groups that had lived in the Luluaburg area before the colonization, clashed with increasing violence, resulting in the evacuation of all Baluba to the Bakwanga area about 150 kilometers east of Luluaburg.[37]

Tackling urban migration

The economic boom of the post-war period sparked a strong growth in Luluaburg's population. Until around 1950, both Protestant and Catholic pastoral strategies had been based on isolating their urban Christians on their settlements – Saint-Clément for the Catholics, Ndesha for the Protestants – to educate them and celebrate the liturgy. With the burgeoning population and the migrant quarters springing up around the city, this was no longer adequate after the war. As the city grew at an ever-increasing rate, the building of new churches and schools became necessary. The establishment of Notre-Dame near the new Congolese residential neighborhood in 1948 had been an initial response to this need. However, in the years that followed, increasing numbers of people migrated to the city and settled in new quarters that sprouted up around the center. As the surface area of Luluaburg expanded through the emergence of residential settlements with varying degrees of spontaneity, new missionary foundations in these satellite communities became inevitable. In the 1950s, Catholic missionaries founded four new parishes in Luluaburg and one in its rural periphery, while APCM missionaries were operating three by the end of this period. The Catholic rural parish, Ntambue Saint-Bernard, was founded in 1950 with the explicit aim of serving the rural population and prevent migration to Luluaburg.

While these structures sought to maximize visibility through a conscious choice of location, at the same time they had to fit into a larger urban fabric that was already in existence by the time the missionaries settled. In this respect, the new apostolic strategy also reflects a new spatial logic. On the one hand, the Catholic secondary stations in particular were designed in such a way as to function as civic centers for the various satellite cities. On the other hand, they had to be inserted into an existing urban infrastructure and in no way had the same urban structuring effect as the Katoka complex or Saint-Clément quarter.

The four peripheral stations established by Catholic missionaries again combined liturgy, education, and social work. In general these new parishes originated in primary schools that had been founded some years before for the children of new arrivals. This decentralized apostolic work was given a high priority. When rumors spread that one of the leading missionaries of this work in the *cités* was to be transferred to another vicariate, one of his colleagues wrote to the CICM general superior: "You know that we

37 Etambala, *De teloorgang van een modelkolonie*, 279-322.

will slowly lose the *cité* if we do not work on it intensively."[38] Offering schooling and social activities in the residential neighborhoods around the city was not only a means of increasing the socio-economic standing of the population of those quarters, but was considered a necessity by the missionaries as it was the only way to access the daily lives of the Christian population.[39]

While built on considerably smaller pieces of land than the two large CICM complexes in the city center, both the implementation of the plots in the surrounding street fabric of the residential neighborhoods and their internal layout were designed to maximize the structures' visibility. The Saint-Jean de la Croix church in Katoka II (1957) was positioned perpendicular to the main thoroughfare, thus marking its end point [Fig. 4.16]. The Sainte-Thérèse Church at Nganza stood at the side of a large open area that functioned as soccer field for young people and a public space for the neighborhood. In a way that can be compared to the CICM's design for the Saint-Clément complex, through the conscious positioning of the churches on the plots they had secured, public spaces were created to serve the entire neighborhood.

Also similar to Saint-Clément, the buildings in these new parishes were all constructed following modern building techniques and models. However, this time the choice to build modern was not motivated by representation, but by necessity. The growth rate of Luluaburg's population and the dire need in the suburbs urged the missionaries to intervene quickly. In an initial phase, they fashioned temporary constructions [Fig. 4.17], out of twigs and pisé. As soon as possible, these were replaced by decent but low-budget buildings. Only prefab construction methods and reinforced concrete-framed churches allowed this type of construction.

Much like the Catholics, from 1950 onwards the Protestant missionaries reacted to the growing urban population in an expanding Luluaburg by opening decentralized secondary schools in the *centres extra-coutumiers* of Kamilabi, Katoka and Tshimbi.

4.17 Temporary school for girls, Tshimbi, 1957.
[Ghent, General Archive of the Sisters of Charity of Jesus and Mary, Image & Sound: F1-CON-Kananga-005]

Schooling was considered the best way to integrate these young migrant residents. The rapid expansion of their urban work was made possible by new government regulations introduced in 1948 that allowed Protestant mission congregations to apply for state subsidies for their schools. Subsidies had previously been the preserve of Catholic missions. The 1948 financial agreement made it possible for the APCM to expand their work more freely and to fully compete with the Catholic mission schools. Moreover, unlike in the larger cities of Léopoldville / Kinshasa, Elisabethville / Lubumbashi or even Coquilhatville / Mbandaka, the new financial support was issued before the Catholic missionaries were able to monopolize primary education in Luluaburg.[40]

In the first half of the 1950s in particular, the APCM was able to keep up with the Catholic mission schools in terms of student numbers.[41] The relative success of the APCM missionaries in Luluaburg in this period was primarily the result of the early establishment of schools in the residential neighborhoods. In Kamilabi, the Protestant school complex was established in 1950, while the Catholics did not construct a temporary school there until several years later, and a separate station, Sacré Cœur, would not open until early 1956. In Tshimbi, Catholic and Protestant missionaries both began secondary stations around 1954. Due to the lack of financial and human resources to sustain

38 GAS, 3817: Letter of Father Sanderman to the superior general, May 10, 1958.
39 On the living conditions in the different quarters of Luluaburg, see Lux, "Le niveau de vie des chômeurs de Luluabourg."
40 Depaepe and Van Rompaey, *In het teken van de bevoogding*, 132-139; Ndaywel è Nziem, *Histoire du Zaïre*, 497.
41 In 1954 they indicated that their schools counted 1,200 pupils, while the Catholic schools had an estimated attendance of around 2,000. This was in obvious contrast to the ratio registered in the older colonial cities Léopoldville (6,200 over 21,000) and Elisabethville (2,300 over 16,000). AAPCM, 63-16: William Rule, *Should the A.P.C.M. enter the urban fields of Leopoldville and Elisabethville?*, April 1954.

4.18 Church of Luluaburg's Centre Extra-Coutumier, today Ndesha cité. [Photo: Bram Cleys]

42 Anderson, *Still Led in Triumph*, 32.
43 AAPCM, 23-8: Letter of Earl S. King to the chief administrator of the territory of Luluaburg, Kasha-Luputa, March 3, 1954; 43-7: Letter of Earl S. King to the governor-general, Luluaburg, Feb. 19, 1954; 63-6: William Rule, *Findings of the Committee on Urban Centres*, Sept. 23, 1953. Van Keerberghen, *Brève histoire*, 3, 42-44; N'Kashama, *Formation et édification d'une église autochtone*, 26.

such expansion, this trend was subsequently broken. While the CICM had a stronger presence in the rural fringe around Luluaburg and established two new secondary stations in Katoka II (Saint-Jean de la Croix, 1956) and Kanyuka (Saint-Thomas, 1958), the APCM did not open any new complexes before 1960. This also implied a relative decline of the student numbers compared to the Catholic schools.

Moreover, while the Scheut Fathers established churches in all these settlements, the first Protestant parish within the city limits was not founded until 1957 in Ndesha *cité* [Fig. 4.18]. Despite repeated calls to make provisions for housing APCM missionaries within Luluaburg, this did not happen until 1960. According to the Mission Meeting, religious leadership in the city had to be taken on by Congolese pastors and evangelists. However, it was long felt that they were insufficiently trained to take responsibility for the higher educated urban Christians. The Protestant missionaries judged that the evangelization of an urban population demanded quite different approaches to the rural work they were used to. In 1959, in a review of the work done by the APCM in the past decade, APCM legal representative Vernon A. Anderson (1896-1999) reported that: "the familiar methods of small village or isolated station work did not fit into the patterns of city life. 'Urban work' demanded fresh approaches and different procedures."[42] Consequently, better trained pastoral workers were not given responsibility for an urban parish until the late 1950s.[43]

Public demonstrations as territorial strategy

Not all the spatial strategies deployed by missionaries to negotiate their position within the city involved buildings or settlement planning. In line with the guidelines of the Catholic Action, mass demonstrations of believers were considered one of the most powerful evangelical tools. On different occasions and increasingly during the 1950s, students, members of the various social movements, and ordinary Christians were rallied by clergy members to claim visibility for a prosperous Catholic Church in the city [Fig. 4.19]. In this way it was not only a fruitful apostolic method, but also a powerful territorial strategy, especially since Protestants organized demonstrations in public places much less systematically.

When King Baudouin of Belgium visited Luluaburg on his extensive and highly publicized tour through the colony in 1955, the Sisters of Charity knitted flags and erected triumphal arches along the road between their Katoka School and the city center. On the day of the royal visit, they marched down this road with their students in school uniform towards the center to greet the king, and did not go unnoticed.

> We saw the doors of almost every house open… and the people came out and engaged in discussions… It would have been a wonderful advertisement for our school… But it does not need advertisement, several class groups have neither classrooms nor desks and Mother Marie-Daniel has had to refuse many students already.
> In the center of the city, they were arranged on both sides of a broad avenue…

and we waited… the Catholic schools… us with the girls and the Fathers with the boys towered clearly above the secular and Protestant schools. Will we be able to continue the battle? The secular schools will again receive a large number of new school buildings… and we stay poor.[44]

In October 1958, a large parade in which every Catholic school in the city participated, was organized on the occasion of the fiftieth anniversary of the annexation of the Congo by Belgium. In the words of Provincial Superior Karel De Wilde CICM (1908-1994): "the more than 10,000 pupils of our second grade have made an exceptional impression on the population, as much for their spirit, order and cleanliness as for their discipline."[45] Catholic ambition was intertwined with a Belgian nationalist and pro-colonial agenda. This was an opportunity for the Catholic mission to demonstrate its support for the colonial state and reclaim the privileged position threatened by the growing tensions around schooling in the mid-1950s.

That the Catholic Church still held a central position in the communal life of the city had already been proven in June 1958. On the occasion of the twenty-fifth jubilee of the ordination of Mgr Bernard Mels CICM (1908-1992), a public celebration was organized in front of Saint-Clément's Cathedral. After a thanksgiving mass – in line with the important place held by Marian devotion in the spirituality of the Scheut Fathers – a spectacular drama was performed by European and Congolese actors based on the life of Bernadette Soubirous, the French girl who reported apparitions of the Virgin Mary in Lourdes in 1858 [Fig. 4.20].[46] Between 30,000 and 50,000 people from Luluaburg and beyond attended this event. A collection, to fund the construction of a new church, was organized to which anyone could contribute. While this was clearly a celebration of religious inspiration no doubt for many in attendance it went far beyond that. It was a city-wide festivity, held in a central location and thus transcended the Catholic community. In this public performance a bridge was built between the Catholic Church and the people of the colonial city of Luluaburg as a whole.[47] Further proof of the central role held by the veneration of Mary in the Scheut Fathers' Catholicism was given in 1959 when they established a Marian pilgrimage in the park around their provincial house and opened it to the public as a secluded place for meditation.

With these processions and public events, the Catholic missionaries actively tried to appropriate the city as a Catholic space. Writing about similar Catholic processions in Ouagadougou (Burkina Faso), Laurent Fourchard interpreted them as part of the territorial strategy deployed by Catholic missionaries to deal with the city.[48] The same goes for Luluaburg. Through the secondary stations erected in the satellite districts the Catholic missionaries multiplied their presence in all parts of the city and the street parades bear witness to their success. Moreover, while in Katoka, for example, Congolese Christians were isolated from urban life in a parallel spatial constellation, they were temporarily put on display during demonstrations and processions. Rooted in the social thinking of the Catholic Action, these mass events were

4.19 Procession in Katoka, 1954. [Ghent, General Archive of the Sisters of Charity of Jesus and Mary, Image & Sound: A245-CON-Katoka-22d]

44 GASC, 9.2.9: Katoka 1. Werking: Sister Marie-Godelieve, Missienieuws Katoka, June 1955.
45 GAS, 3817: Letter of De Wilde to the general superior, Oct. 19, 1958.
46 GAS, 3817: Letter of Provincial Superior De Wilde to Father Rooyakker, April 24, 1959.
47 GAS, 3817: Letter of Father Sanderman to the provincial superior, May 10, 1958; Letter of Father De Wilde to Father Degryse, June 27, 1958. Van Keerbergen, *Brève histoire*, 12.
48 Fourchard, "Naissance du baroque colonial," 155.

4.20 Scenic play Bernadette, 1958. [Kananga, Provincial Archive of Scheut]

based on disciplined lay people under the guidance of the clergy. As such, they did not create opportunities for the expression of free individual Catholic believers, but were carefully orchestrated mass events that projected an image of the Catholic Church as a unified body.

The festivities to mark bishop Mels' anniversary would be one of the last instances in which the Church had the opportunity to present itself as the natural leader of the population of Luluaburg. The only comparable mass event overseen by the Catholics was the ordination on July 1, 1959 of Joseph Nkongolo (1916-1999) as bishop of Luebo – the first Congolese to be ordained as a bishop, – a celebration that brought about 20,000 proud Kasaians to the provincial capital. By then, however, tensions between Bena Lulua and Baluba, the city's two largest ethnic communities, had begun to escalate and would result in heavy fighting months later, burning and looting, not only in Luluaburg, but throughout Kasai. Many people on both sides would die; many houses would be destroyed and the conflict would lead to the large-scale evacuation of the Baluba to eastern Kasai, their supposed place of origin. Although the Catholic missionaries and their institutions, as well as the Protestants, were not targeted during this conflict, they inevitably got caught up in it. Both parties were blamed for supporting the other. In the months preceding independence, on June 30 1960, this inter-ethnic conflict mingled with a Congolese nationalist agenda. As students, teachers, nurses, Congolese priests, and nuns participated in the hostilities or fled them, the Church as an institution was forced into a secondary position on Luluaburg's socio-political scene. The underlying idea on which these mass manifestations of Catholic Action had been built – that the predominantly 'white' and Belgian clergy were the natural leaders of a homogenous Catholic mass – turned out to be an illusion. While the conflict between the Baluba and the Lulua caused great uproar in its time, it is now a forgotten episode in the history of the decolonization of the Democratic Republic of the Congo (DRC).[49]

Presbyterian missionaries, who did not share a similar view of social issues, hardly ever played this spatial logic of organizing rallies in the public domain. If the relative success of their schools allowed them to partly compensate for their inability to claim a central place in the city, their non-participation in similar public demonstrations reveals a different approach to urban work in particular and evangelization in general. They took a much lower profile than the Belgian Catholic missionaries. While the Catholics left their mark on the city as a physical and social space and claimed co-authority over it, the Protestant missionaries focused their efforts entirely on the conversion and guidance of the urban population as an aggregate of individual believers. These two divergent spatial models were inspired by divergent spiritualities and situated in the specific features of the Belgian colonial project.

49 See Chomé, *Le drame de Luluabourg*; Nicolaï, "Conflits entre groups africains et decolonisation au Kasaï;" Kalanda, *Baluba et Lulua*; Gérard-Libois and Verhaegen, *Congo 1960*; Rae, "Note d'histoire;" Etambala, *De teloorgang van een modelkolonie*, 279-322.

Conclusion: co-authoring the city

The precise implications of the bloody civil war between Bena Lulua and Luba – and the role played by both Catholics and Protestants – in an assessment of the success of missionary work in Luluaburg is hard to judge based on the current state of academic understanding and falls to a large extent outside the remit of this contribution. It is clear that it forced the white missionaries to re-evaluate their position with regard to Congolese laics and clergy members; it also nuances their ability to educate urban Christians, whose new Christian identity may have been capable of erasing their former 'customary' or 'tribal' identification. From an urbanistic point of view, however, this event barely influenced the strong impact missionaries and their institutions had on Luluaburg's urban form.

In the period between 1928 and 1960, both Catholic and Protestant missionaries devised various spatial strategies to negotiate their position within the developing colonial city of Luluaburg. While the APCM was forced by the colonial state to operate from the city margins, the CICM and the other Catholic missionaries succeeded in co-authoring the layout of Luluaburg. During the first two decades, when Luluaburg was nothing more than a commercial center along the railway line, the Josephite school was among the largest structures in the settlement's vicinity. Long outside the boundaries of the urban settlement, even after the city expanded and the new indigenous district was laid out next to it, the Katoka concession would mark the western frontier. Throughout the colonial period, it remained a parallel urban constituent, both inside and outside the urban network.

Largely as a consequence of the specific topography of Luluaburg, the city was composed of different clearly separated neighborhoods plugged into a central artery. If the Katoka complex was situated at the end of this artery, Saint-Clément Cathedral dominated the center. Although the early settlement had developed around the railway station, the establishment of the new administrative district created a new center. Situated somewhat eccentrically on the other side of the railway line, thanks to its clever position and design, the cathedral was visible from many parts of the city and was one of the first landmarks seen by new arrivals. While from the outset, the concession on which Saint-Clément Cathedral was founded also housed schools and later a hospital for the Congolese population of the booming city, spatially its primary function lay in the representation of the Catholic Church as a vital power in Luluaburg's social life. In this respect, the cathedral acted as an emblem for the ongoing dialogue between the colonial state and the Catholic Church about their respective position in colonial Congo.

If in their encounter with the city the missionaries succeeded in co-authoring its urban fabric and architectural image, they were themselves shaped and transformed by this meeting. In the 1950s in particular, to cope with the fast-growing migrant population and the associated expanding urban surface area, new initiatives were developed with the intention of safeguarding the missionaries' control over their believers. Many of these initiatives had already been tested by Catholic and Protestant missionaries in the larger cities of the Belgian Congo (most prominently in Léopoldville and Elisabethville). Advanced schooling, sports facilities, youth movements, women's groups or *cercles,* were all designed to create social environments in which Luluaburg's urban inhabitants could be encouraged to be good Christians, whether Catholic or Protestant. Both groups of missionaries to a large extent followed a similar approach: the emphasis was not on the conversion of the greatest number of people, but on the guidance of Christian subjects prepared to face the corruptions of the colonial city. Conversely, for urban Christians, these pastoral initiatives offered opportunities for emancipation and the formation of new social identities. As this approach implied the presence of missionaries in every residential neighborhood across the booming city, both Catholic and Protestant establishments were multiplied throughout Luluaburg.

Mass manifestations and public processions were a vital component of interwar European Catholicism but should also be interpreted as a defensive strategy from the Catholic missionaries to secure their position within post-war Luluaburg. In their appropriation of public spaces such as streets and squares they were reacting to threats against their position, most specifically manifested in the breaching of the religious monopoly on education by the erection of state-run lay *athénées*. It was at the same time a way for the Catholics to showcase their success by their ability to rally and direct large sections of Luluaburg's urban population.

ACKNOWLEDGEMENTS

This chapter was prepared within the framework of my PhD-research at KU Leuven "Spatializing Missionary Work. Architecture, missionary work and space in Kasai, Belgian Congo, ca. 1890-1960," supervised by prof. Jan De Maeyer and prof. Bruno De Meulder. It was part of a research project financed by FWO-Research Foundation Flanders. Additional research in Philadelphia (Presbyterian Historical Society) and the Democratic Republic of the Congo was financed by FWO and the Academische Stichting Leuven. The author is grateful to Catherine Coquery-Vidrovitch, Johan Lagae, Elisabeth Cameron and the editors for feedback on previous versions of this chapter.

BIBLIOGRAPHY

Sources and primary Literature

Ghent (Belgium), General Archive of the Sisters of Charity of Jesus and Mary (GASC)

Kananga (DRC), Provincial Archive of Scheut – Kasai Province (PAS)

Leuven (Belgium), KADOC-KU Leuven General Archive of Scheut (Congregation of the Immaculate Heart of Mary) (GAS) Picture Archive of Scheut

Philadelphia (USA): Presbyterian Historical Society, Archive of the American Presbyterian Congo Mission (AAPCM)

Tervuren (Belgium), Royal Museum for Central Africa, Department of History (RMCA) Papers Auguste Gilliaert (56.60/66.20) Papers Georges Verriest (82.58)

Anderson, Vernon A. *Still Led in Triumph*. Nashville: Board of World Missions. Presbyterian Church USA, 1959.

Heyse, Théodore. *Cessions et concessions foncières du Congo belge. Première Série. Extraits de Congo, novembre 1927 à décembre 1928*. Brussels: Goemaere, 1928.

Kasaï. Bi-hebdomadaire indépendant, 3 (April 1, 1950) 74, 1.

Mondele, "Croquis Luluabourgeois. Une ville qui naît", *Kasaï. Bi-hebdomadaire indépendant*, 3 (Nov. 18, 1950) 106, 1, 16.

Nicolaï, Henri and Jacques, Jules. *La transformation des paysages congolais par le chemin de fer; l'exemple du BCK*. Koninklijk Belgisch Koloniaal Instituut. Sectie voor Natuur- en Geneeskundige Wetenschappen. Verhandelingen. Verzameling in-8°. Brussels: Koninklijk Belgisch Koloniaal Instituut, 1954.

V., "Cinéma pour indigènes," *Kasai. Bi-hebdomadaire independent*, 2 (Nov. 19, 1949) 54, 1.

"Une bonne nouvelle pour les sportifs," *Kasai. Bi-hebdomadaire independent*, 4 (Feb. 3, 1951) 117, 12

Secondary Literature

Briffaerts, Jan. "De schoolstrijd in Belgisch Congo (1930-1958)" in: Witte, Els; De Groof, Jan and Tyssens, Jeffrey, eds. *Het schoolpact van 1958. Ontstaan, grondlijnen en toepassing van een Belgisch compromis*. Brussels: VUB Press, 1999, 331-358.

Briffaerts, Jan. *'Als Kongo op de schoolbank wil'. De onderwijspraktijk in het lager onderwijs in Belgisch Congo (1925-1960)*. Leuven: Acco, 2007.

Briffaerts, Jan and Dhondt, Pieter. "The Dangers of Urban Development: Missionary Discourse on Education and Urban Growth, Belgian Congo (1920-1960)." *Neue Zeitschrift für Missionswissenschaft*, 59 (2003) 2, 81-102.

Çelik, Zeynep. *The Remaking of Istanbul: Portrait of an Ottoman City in the Nineteenth Century*. Seattle/London: University of Washington Press, 1986.

Çelik, Zeynep. *Urban Forms and Colonial Confrontations: Algiers under French Rule*. Berkeley/Los Angeles/London: University of California Press, 1997.

Chomé, Jules. *Le Drame de Luluabourg*. Études Congolaises 1. Brussels: Editions de Remarques Congolaises, 1960.

Cleys, Bram. "Catholic Missionaries and the Production of Kasai as a Colonial Landscape," in: Viaene, Vincent; Cleys Bram and De Maeyer, Jan, eds. *Religion, Colonization and Decolonization in Congo, 1885-1960* (KADOC Studies, 22). Leuven: Leuven University Press, 2020, 116-139.

Cleys, Bram and De Meulder, Bruno. "La construction des églises dans les missions périphériques du Congo belge (1890-1960). Une pratique 'bricolée' et ambitieuse," in: Dierkens, Alain and Morelli, Anne, eds. *Topographie du sacré. L'emprise religieuse sur l'espace*. Brussels: Éditions de l'Université de Bruxelles, 2008, 165-175.

Convents, Guido. *Images & Démocratie. Les Congolais face au cinéma et à l'audiovisuel. Une histoire politico-culturelle du Congo des Belges jusqu'à la République démocratique du Congo (1896-2006)*. Kessel-Lo: Afrika Filmfestival, 2006.

De Meulder, Bruno. *Kuvuande Mbote. Een eeuw koloniale architectuur en stedenbouw in Kongo*. Antwerp: Houtekiet, De Singel, 2000.

Depaepe, Marc, Lefebvre, René and Etambala, Zana Aziza. *'Tot glorie van God en tot zaligheid der zielen'. Brieven van Moeder Marie Adonia Depaepe over haar leven en werk als Zuster van Liefde van Jezus en Maria in Belgisch Kongo (1909-1961)*. Antwerp: Standaard Uitgeverij, 1992.

Depaepe, Marc and Van Rompaey, Lies. *In het teken van de bevoogding. De educatieve actie in Belgisch-Kongo (1908-1960)*. Leuven/Apeldoorn: Garant, 1995.

de Saint Moulin, Léon and Kayemba, M. T. "Origine et évolution de la ville de Kananga," in: Madiya, Faik-Nzuji and Sulzman, E., eds. *Mélanges de culture et de linguistique africaines publiés à la mémoire de Leo Stappers*. Berlin: Reiner Verlag, 1983, 505-524.

Etambala, Zana Aziza. *De teloorgang van een modelkolonie. Belgisch Congo, 1958-1960*. Leuven: Acco, 2008.

Fourchard, Laurent. "Naissance du baroque colonial. Les cérémonies catholiques à Ouagadougou. 1900-1945," in: Goerg, Odile, ed. *Fêtes urbaines en Afrique. Espaces, identités et pouvoirs*. Paris: Karthala, 1999, 149-165.

Gerard-Libois, Jules and Verhaegen, Benoit. *Congo 1960*. Brussels: Éditions du CRISP, 1961.

Goh, Robbie B.H. "Deus ex Machina: Evangelical Sites, Urbanism, and the Construction of Social Identities," in: Bishop, Ryan; Philips, John and Wei Wei Yeo, eds. *Postcolonial Urbanism. Southeast Asian Cities and Global Processes*. New York/London: Routledge, 2003, 305-321.

Heimer, Haldor Eugène. *The Kimbanguists and the Bapostolo: A study of two African independent churches in Luluabourg, Congo in relation to similar churches and in the context of Lulua traditional culture and religion*. Thesis (PhD). Hebron: Hartford Seminary Foundation, 1972.

Kabamba, Kabata. "Dynamique territoriale du Kasayi (Congo-Kinshasa). Incidences des changements socio-politiques et économiques sur la recomposition spatiale." *Bulletin de la Société géographique de Liège*, 39 (2000) 2, 101-114.

Kalanda, Mabika. *Baluba et Lulua. Une ethnie à la recherche d'un nouvel équilibre*. Études Congolaises 2. Brussels: Éditions Remarques congolaises, 1959.

Kapinga wa Nkaya, Marguerite-Astrid. *Les Sœurs de la Charité de Jésus et de Marie. Un siècle de présence au Zaïre 1892-1992*. Kinshasa: Sœurs de la Charité de J.M., 1992.

Lagae, Johan. "A Highly 'Mediated Monument' of Tropical Modernism in Central Africa. Unpacking the complex agendas behind the design and construction of the Collège du Saint-Esprit in Bujumbura, Burundi," in: Coomans, Thomas, ed. *Missionary Spaces. Imagining, Building, Contesting Christianities in Africa and China, 1830s-1960s*. Leuven: Leuven University Press, 2024, 229-251.

Lagae, Johan. *Kongo zoals het is. Drie architectuurverhalen uit de Belgische kolonisatiegeschiedenis (1920-1960)*. Thesis (PhD) University of Ghent, 2002.

Lux, André. "Migrations, accroissement et urbanisation de la population congolaise de Luluabourg." *Zaire*, 12 (1958) 7, 675-724.

Lux, André. "Migrations, accroissement et urbanisation de la population congolaise de Luluabourg (seconde partie)." *Zaire*, 12 (1958) 8, 819-877.

Lux, André. "Le niveau de vie des chômeurs de Luluabourg." *Zaire*, 14 (1960), 3-34.

Mantels, Ruben. *Geleerd in de tropen. Leuven, Congo & de wetenschap, 1885-1960*. Leuven: Universitaire Pers Leuven, 2007.

Mutshipayi Petumpenyi Bakajika, Étienne. *Le Presbytérianisme en République Démocratique du Congo (1891-1991). Une étude analytico-critique du support de l'A.P.C.M., de la C.P.C par la base et les nouvelles perspectives au troisième millénaire*. Thesis (PhD). Yaoundé, 2001.

Ndaywel è Nziem, Isidore. *Histoire du Zaire: De l'héritage ancien à l'âge contemporain*. Louvain-la-Neuve: Duculot, 1997.

Nicolaï, H. "Conflits entre groupes africains et décolonisation au Kasai." *Revue de l'Université de Bruxelles*, 12 (1960) 1-2, 131-144.

N'Kashama Batubenge Mbau, Simon. *Formation et édification d'une église autochtone. Le cas de la Communauté Presbytérienne au Congo (1919-1970)*. Thesis (Lic.). Kinshasa, 2003.

Porter, Andrew. "'Cultural Imperialism' and Protestant Missionary Enterprise, 1780-1914." *The Journal of Imperial and Commonwealth History*. 25 (1997) 3, 367-391.

Porter, Andrew. *Religion versus Empire? British Protestant missionaries and overseas expansion 1700-1914*. Manchester: Manchester University Press, 2004.

Prudhomme, Claude. *Missions chrétiennes et colonisation. XVI-XXe siècle*. Paris: Cerf, 2005.

Rae, Marcellin. "Note d'histoire et de droit coutumier sur le litige Lulua-Baluba avant le 30 juin 1960." *Bulletin des Séances. Académie Royale des Sciences d'Outre-Mer*, (1961), 366-376.

Ramirez, Francis and Rolot, Christian. *Histoire du cinéma colonial au Zaïre, au Rwanda et au Burundi*. Annales-série in-8°, Sciences historiques, 7. Tervuren: Royal Museum for Central Africa, 1985.

Scheitler, Marcel. *Histoire de l'Église catholique au Kasayi, 1891-1938*. Kananga: Imprimerie Katoka, 1991².

Van Keerberghen, Joseph. *Histoire de l'enseignement catholique dans le vicariat de Luluabourg, 1891-1947*. Kananga: Éd. de l'Archidiocèse, 1985.

Van Keerberghen, Joseph. *Histoire de l'enseignement catholique dans le vicariat de Luluabourg, 1948-1960*. Kananga: Éd. de l'Archidiocèse, 1990.

Van Keerberghen, Joseph. *Brève histoire des paroisses de la ville de Kananga*. Unpublished document, 1995.

Vellut, Jean-Luc. "Introduction," in: Vellut, Jean-Luc, ed. *Itinéraires croisés de la modernité. Congo belge (1920-1950)*. Afrika-Studies/Cahiers africains 43-44. Brussels: CEDAF, 2000, 7-24.

Verhelst, Daniël and Daniëls, Hyacint, eds. *Scheut vroeger en nu, 1862-1987*. Ancorae 10. Leuven: Universitaire Pers Leuven, 1991. [English edition: Verhelst, Daniël and Pycke, Nestor. *C.I.C.M. Missionaries Past and Present 1862-1987*. Leuven University Press, 1995.]

Vints, Luc and Etambala, Zana Aziza. *100 jaar Zusters van Liefde J.M. in Zaïre, 1891-1991*. Brussels: Congregatie van de Zusters van Liefde van Jezus en Maria / Leuven: KADOC, 1992.

Wandja, Afumba and Ndjusuku wa Lutula, Omatete. "Le rôle historique du poste de Lusambo dans la conquête coloniale." *Zaïre-Afrique*, 31(1991) 253-254, 185-201.

5
The Catholic Territorialization of Taiwan

Vatican Global Strategy and Franciscan Local Parishes, 1949-1960s

Leon Bouwmeester and Thomas Coomans

The concept of territorialization is defined as "the way that territory is used to enable politics."[1] The withdrawal of the government of the Republic of China (ROC), with more than a million people, to Taiwan Island in the wake of defeat in the Chinese Civil War and the establishment of the People's Republic of China (PRC) on October 1, 1949 implied a complete societal and territorial reorganization of Taiwan. This came only four years after the Japanese decolonization of Formosa following the end of the Second World War.

This chapter describes, contextualizes, and discusses spatial aspects of the relocation from the China Catholic mission to Taiwan. In 1950, the PRC founded a State Administration for Religious Affairs and expelled all foreign Catholic and Protestant missionaries from Mainland China between 1950 and 1955. Moreover, all the missionaries' immovable assets were confiscated, including churches, schools, universities, hospitals, orphanages, and all their contents. Most Chinese bishops, priests, and members of religious orders, both male and female, remained in the PRC. This "reluctant exodus" immediately generated a "debacle debate," with the laying of political, cultural, social, and economic charges regarding the extent of the failure of the Catholic mission in China.[2] The expelled missionaries were welcomed in Hong Kong, from where they returned to their home countries or were assigned to other mission fields in Hong Kong, Macao, and Taiwan, in particular.

We will begin by analyzing how the Holy See organized the Catholic territorialization of Taiwan during the fourteen-year spell from 1949 to 1963. How were seven dioceses defined and why were these new ecclesiastical circumscriptions allocated to specific missionary societies? This top-down Vatican-led macrospatial strategy entrusted experienced missionaries a new mission field with the goal of establishing a localized diocesan organization within the Catholic Church, which would also interact appropriately with the new territorialization of Taiwan by the Kuomintang (KMT). This chapter then goes on to focus on the case of the Belgian Franciscan missionaries who were relocated from the diocese of Yichang 宜昌 (Hubei) in China to the archdiocese of Taipei 台北 in Taiwan. In which district of the capital city did they establish their headquarters and develop their bottom-up apostolate? How did they go about spatially organizing their stations in the countryside?

From one prefecture apostolic to seven dioceses

The establishment of ecclesiastical circumscriptions by the Holy See is one of the Catholic Church's highest-level macrospatial governance tasks. A diocese is a circumscription that covers a specific geographical area and is entrusted to a bishop.[3] Vicariates apostolic and prefectures apostolic are not mature enough as circumscriptions to be elevated to the level of diocese and are instead entrusted to a vicar apostolic or prefect apostolic.[4] Most mission territories are vicariates or prefectures that come under the authority of the Congregation for the Evangelization of Peoples (Propaganda Fide). The latter "direct[s] and coordinate[s] throughout the world" and "deals with everything pertaining

5.1 Map from 1958 showing Taiwan, then divided in five ecclesiastical circumscriptions: the archdiocese of Taipei and the prefectures apostolic of Kiayi, Taichung, Kaohsiung, and Hwalien. The dioceses of Taichung and Hsinchu do not yet exist. Detail of a map published in Emmerich, *Atlas missionum*, 1958, 32-33.
[Leuven, KADOC-KU Leuven, Heritage Library: KE15]

1 *Constructing Territory*.
2 Ling, "Demise of the Missionary Enterprise."
3 Code of Canon Law, canon 369.
4 *Ibid.*, canon 371§1.

5   *Ibid.*, articles 85 and 89.
6   The Taiwanese Catholic Church had a population of 300,000 at its peak in the 1960s, calculated for 1969-1970 from the website *Catholic Hierarchy*.
7   Catholic Hierarchy, www.catholic-hierarchy.org/
8   Sanroman, *Formosa, campo de Dios*, 57-67. An article published in *Les Missions Catholiques* (1877), mentions three mission stations on the island.
9   Chinese Regional Bishop's Conference, *Catholic Church Directory Taiwan*, 45.
10 The Treaty of Shimonoseki 馬關條約, ending the First Sino-Japanese War, was signed on April 17, 1895.
11 Prefect apostolic Clemente Fernández 林茂才 OP (1879-1952) in 1913, and his successor Thomas de la Hoz 楊多默 OP (1879-1949), see Chiang, *Tianzhujiao zai Taiwan*, 126; Yang, *From Europe to Taiwan*, 184. In 1961, a Taiwanese Dominican, Joseph Cheng Tien-siang 鄭天祥 OP (1922-1990) became bishop of Kaohsiung.
12 Leung, "Actors. The Missionaries," 797.

to the establishment and change of ecclesiastical circumscriptions and to the provision of these Churches."[5]

Dioceses, however, carry functions that transcend mere regional work. Why did the Propaganda Fide directly elevate the Taiwanese prefectures apostolic to full dioceses, skipping the intermediate status of vicariate apostolic? In the case of Taiwan, the erection of prefectures apostolic and dioceses took into account not only the size of the territories and numbers of faithful,[6] but the Holy See promoted its mission work through spatial governance at a higher level in the global mission fields. As we will see, an acceleration of the emancipation of missionary territories occurred in the process that led to the Second Vatican Council. The precise dates, names, and statistics of the dioceses, as well as the names and dates of the bishops, have been retrieved from the official website *Catholic Hierarchy*.[7]

The Taiwanese Church before 1949

In the seventeenth century, the first missionary to set foot on Formosa—the "beautiful isle," as Taiwan was known at the time—was a Spanish Dominican.[8] Formosa originally belonged to the vicariate apostolic of Fujian 福建 (Fukien), which was divided into the vicariates apostolic of Fuzhou 福州 (Fuchow) and Xiamen 廈門 (Amoy) in 1883.[9] Formosa was part of the vicariates apostolic of Xiamen [Fig. 5.2] until the Qing dynasty ceded the island to the Empire of Japan in 1895.[10] In 1913, Formosa became a prefecture apostolic entrusted by the Propaganda Fide to the Spanish Dominicans, who played a rather marginal role on the island until 1961.[11]

In Taiwan, during the Japanese occupation (1895-1945), the presence of the Catholic Church was not noticeable. Spanish Dominicans, the pioneers of the Taiwan mission, never numbered more than 15 priests. There were three local clergy to assist the Dominicans in the pastoral care to a few thousand Catholics. (…) In 1930, there were less than 100 [Protestant] missionaries in Taiwan, with 107 churches and 9,000 church-goers. In 1949 there were 70,000 Protestants and 350 churches.[12]

Although Japan officially colonized Formosa for half a century, the island was never dependent on the Japanese Catholic Church. In August 1945, Japan was defeated in the

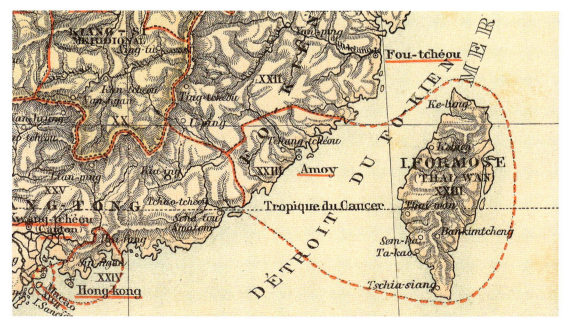

5.2 Prior to the Japanese colonization of Formosa, the island was part of the vicariate apostolic of Amoy (Xiamen). Further to the south-west are the diocese of Macao and the vicariates apostolic of Canton (Guangzhou) and Hong Kong. Detail of a map published in Werner, Atlas des missions catholiques, 1886, 12.
[Leuven, KADOC-KU Leuven, Heritage Library: KLZ]

5.3 "China's back door:" most missionaries expelled from the People's Republic of China had to cross on foot over the bridge across the Sham Chun River, which marked the boundary with Hong Kong's New Territories. Undated photo, between 1950 and 1955, showing Dutch Franciscan nuns.
[Utrecht, Het Utrechts Archief, 1224: Dutch Franciscans, China mission, 306]

Second World War and gave up the sovereignty of Taiwan. Consequently, the ROC entered Taiwan and still rules it today.[13]

The year 1949, crucial to the history of China and Taiwan, had considerable consequences on the Catholic Church and the Christian Church. In 1949, the Republic of China (ROC) lost the Chinese Civil War to the Communist Party of China (CPC) and transferred a large number of soldiers, civil servants, and refugees to Taiwan.[14] Once the Communist Party had established the PRC, all foreign missionaries were expelled from Mainland China between 1950 and 1955. According to 1948 statistics, the Catholic mission in China included 2,676 foreign priests, 632 brothers, and 5,112 foreign sisters,[15] i.e. more than 8,400 members of religious orders belonging to 48 male missionary societies and 59 female missionary societies from Europe and North America.[16] Psychologically traumatized and often in poor physical condition, the expelled missionaries exited the PRC at the land border with Hong Kong and were welcomed into the British colony by the local Catholic diocese and missionary society procurators [Fig. 5.3]. Many of them returned to their home countries, while others remained in Hong Kong and Macao to serve their apostolate among the refugees, or were sent to Taiwan and other countries where overseas Chinese communities were based.

Missionary congregations from Europe and America came to Taiwan with numerous senior missionaries, including several former bishops who had lost their dioceses in China. For the sake of the war and their Chinese dream, these exiled bishops, priests, brothers, and nuns relocated to Taiwan.

> In 1956, Taiwan had more than 300 Catholic foreign missionaries and 95 Chinese clergy, not to mention numerous religious women. Like the missions in Hong Kong and Macau, with the inflow of manpower as well as financial assistance from abroad, the Catholic Church in Taiwan became much more active than at any time before.[17]

The number of missionaries rose in the years that followed. In 1960, eighteen male religious institutes worked on Taiwan Island, with the addition of a further four before 1970.[18] The number of female congregations was even larger: 53 female religious institutes with 919 members in 1969.[19]

13 The Administrative Region of Taiwan was reset by the ROC government in 1950. The counties and cities mentioned in this chapter are indicated according to the 1950 setting. A same-name city is always either located in or surrounded by the same-name county; therefore, when a place is mentioned without noting whether it is a city or county, both the city and county are implied.

14 A total of about 1.1 million Chinese soldiers, their families, and other refugees. This number was established in 2018 by: Yap, "Waishengren de renshu, laiyuan yu fenbu," 16.

15 Leung, "Actors. The Missionaries," 794-795.

16 Tiedemann, *Reference Guide*, 1-86.

17 Leung, "Actors. The Missionaries," 797. In 1965, Protestants numbered 278,700 and churches had increased to 1,796.

18 Tiedemann ed., *Handbook of Christianity in China*, 805.

19 *Taiwan Catholic Directory*.

The initial design of three prefectures in the north, center, and south (1949-1951)

In 1949, the Propaganda Fide unveiled its plans to establish the ecclesiastical province of Taiwan. This began on December 30, 1949, when the prefecture apostolic of Formosa was renamed the prefecture apostolic of Kaohsiung 高雄, losing the northern part of its territory, where the new prefecture apostolic of Taipei 台北 was erected. Father Joseph Arregui y Yparaguirre 陳若瑟 OP (1903-1979), who had been appointed prefect of Formosa in March 1948, became prefect of Kaohsiung, while Father Joseph Kuo Joshih 郭若石 CDD (1906-1995) was appointed prefect of Taipei in June 1950.

On August 10 1950, the territories of Taichung 台中, Changhua 彰化, and Nantou 南投 were hived off from the prefecture of Kaohsiung to erect the prefecture apostolic of Taichung, which was entrusted to the Catholic Foreign Mission Society of America, known as the Maryknoll Fathers and Brothers. The first prefect was William F. Kupfer 蔡文興 MM (1909-1998) - before being posted to Taiwan in 1951, he had served his apostolate in Guangxi 廣西 (China) for fifteen years and worked as the local superior and procurator of Maryknoll House in Stanley Bay 赤柱 (Hong Kong) for three years.[20] The erection of the prefecture of Taichung had a unique significance in domestic and international politics - the Taiwanese provincial government was moved to the center of Taiwan in the 1950s, giving the area more importance,[21] and the new American prefect apostolic supported close cooperation between the Republic of China and the United States. In the 1950s, the United States officially provided economic and defense support to strengthen Taiwan Island against communist expansion.[22] Humanitarian assistance was provided through the Agricultural Trade Development and Assistance Act of 1954, known as Public Law 480. The National Catholic Welfare Committee 天主教福利會, originating in the United States, was one of two Church organizations jointly designated by the ROC and American governments to assume the majority of social assistance work and take responsibility for the coordination and distribution of US aid until the arrival of the last batch of supplies in Taiwan in 1968.[23] In summary, the American prefect, who was extremely familiar with China, led dozens of American missionaries across the Taiwan Strait to the center of "Free China" to face "Red China." On April 16 1962, the same area was elevated to the diocese of Taichung and apostolic prefect Kupfer was appointed its first bishop.

A necessary division: Hwalien and Kiayi (1952)

On August 7 1952, the Holy See announced four orders: firstly, Taiwan would become the twenty-first ecclesiastical province of China; secondly, the prefecture of Taipei would be elevated to the archdiocese of Taipei due to its position as the "temporary capital of the Republic of China"; thirdly and fourthly, the prefectures apostolic of Hwalien 花蓮 and Kiayi 嘉義 would be erected on territories that the prefecture of Kaohsiung had lost [Fig. 5.1]. The very different contexts of the latter two of these deserve to be discussed.[24]

A long mountain range spans the center of Taiwan from north to south, separating the east and west coasts of the island. The territory of Hwalien covered a vast area on the eastern part of the island, where the population was low and composed mainly of minority groups of indigenous people.[25] Because these minority groups converted in greater numbers than others, the Catholic population ratio of the territory of Hwalien was three times higher than the national average.[26] Consequently, there were good reasons for making the area of Hwalien an autonomous prefecture apostolic [Fig. 5.4]. The Propaganda Fide entrusted it to missionaries from the French Foreign Mission, and André Vérineux 費聲遠 MEP (1897-1983), who had previously been bishop of Yingkou 營口 (Liaoning, China), served as apostolic administrator of Hwalien until July 1973.[27]

---

20 See: Bishop William F. Kupfer MM.
21 The Taiwanese provincial government was first established in Wufeng 霧峰 (Taichung) before moving to Zhongxing New Village 中興新村 (Nantou). See Chen, "Away from Taipei," 138.
22 *The Mutual Security Act* was in effect from October 10 1951 to June 30, 1965.
23 Chao, *Meiyuan yu Taiwan de shehui jiuzhu*, 2. The other was a Protestant organization: Taiwan Christian Service 基督教福利會.
24 Chinese Regional Bishop's Conference. *Catholic Church Directory Taiwan (2017)*, (25).
25 According the Taiwan Census, the population ratio of indigenous people was 2.42% (221,774) in 1956 and 1.9% (266,728) in 1966.
26 The Apostolic Prefecture of Hwalien had more than 46,000 Catholics in 1963, accounting for 16.4% of the total population. In the meantime, the Catholic population was 5% of the total population of Taiwan. Moal and Liao, *Les ecclésiastiques français de la côte est de Taïwan*, 45
27 https://irfa.paris/en/missionnaire/3233-verineux-andre/

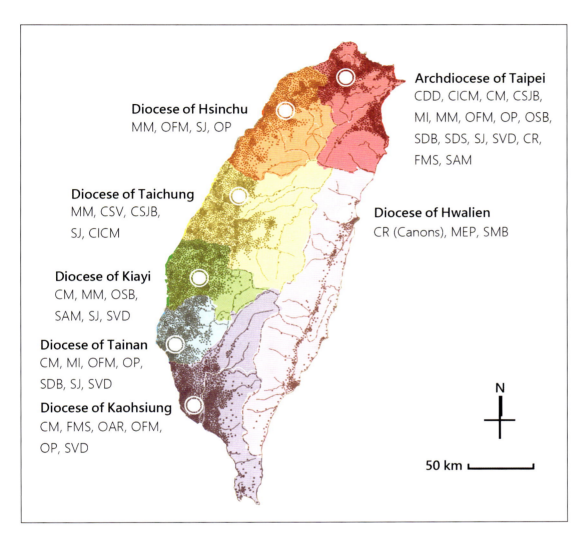

5.4. Map of the final stage of the territorialization of the Catholic Church in Taiwan in 1963. Reference is made to the spread of missionary congregations across the dioceses.
CDD: Congregation of the Disciples of the Lord; CICM: Scheut; CM: Lazarist; CR (Canons): Canons Regular; CR: Resurrectionist; CSJB: Congregation of Saint John the Baptist; CSV: Viatorian; FMS: Marist Brothers; MEP: French Foreign Mission; MI: Camillian; MM: Maryknoll; OAR: Augustinian Recollects; OFM: Franciscan; OP: Dominican; OSB: Benedictine; SAM: Auxiliaries of the Mission; SDB: Salesian; SDS: Salvatorian; SJ: Jesuit; SMB: Swiss Bethlehem Fathers; SVD: Divine Word Missionaries.
[Leon Bouwmeester, 2023]

Compared with Hwalien, the prefecture apostolic of Kiayi covered a humbler area on the southwestern part of Taiwan Island, which numbered fewer Catholics and also lacked the support of a large mission congregation. However, the elevation of the prefecture of Kiayi solved two missionary problems at once. Firstly, the Jesuits, who had been expelled from several dioceses in China, wanted to enter Hsinchu to begin a new mission led by the American Eugene Fahy 費濟時 SJ (1911-1996), exiled bishop of Yangzhou 揚州 (Jiangsu, China). This course of action appeared delicate because Thomas Niu Huiching 牛會卿 (1895-1973), the exiled bishop of Yanggu 陽穀 (Shandong, China), was already developing missionary work in Hsinchu. Secondly, Niu was a Chinese bishop who had not yet retired and would have been able to play a more active role as a bishop than when working on his own as a guest in a diocese. Eventually, the Propaganda Fide decided to appoint Bishop Niu Huiching as apostolic administrator of Kiayi from August 1952 to August 1969, leaving room for the Jesuits to develop in the area of Hsinchu.[28]

More Chinese bishops for Taiwan: Hsinchu and Tainan (1961)

On March 21, 1961, the Holy See erected two more ecclesiastical circumscriptions in Taiwan: the dioceses of Hsinchu 新竹 and Tainan 台南. Although these dioceses were the last two ecclesial circumscriptions to be

28 Mateo, *China Jesuits in East-Asia starting from zero 1949-1957*, 275.

erected, they immediately became full dioceses instead of transitioning through the stages of prefecture apostolic or vicariate apostolic. Neither of the new bishops belonged to a missionary congregation or were Taiwanese, but were instead Chinese diocesan priests with high profiles. Father Peter Tou Paozin 杜寶晉 (1911-1986), bishop of Hsinchu, was very familiar with the administrative management of the Church. After having studied in Rome at the Pontifical Urban University, he had served as secretary-general of the university.[29] Father Stanislaus Lo Kuang 羅光 (1911-2004), bishop of Tainan, was an academic who had taught Chinese philosophy and literature at the Pontifical Urban University for twenty-five years.[30]

The diocese of Hsinchu had a diverse nature in terms of both Church and society, which required the administrative wisdom of the bishop. The diocese included three major international congregations - Italian Franciscans, American Maryknolls, and American Jesuits - each with a bishop in exile. Society, meanwhile, included not only Taiwanese and post-war immigrants, but also the main Hakka 客家 people settlements in Taiwan and several indigenous tribes in the mountain areas.

The diocese of Tainan was a completely different case, limited to the Tainan area and Penghu Island. Moreover, the very small number of Catholics - about 20,000 in 1965 - represented only half of the Catholic population of the diocese of Hsinchu during the same period. As Taiwan's most historical city, Tainan had played a special role in the island's history as capital city of the Kingdom of Tungning 東寧王國 (1661-1683). Tainan was a wealthy and populated harbor and trading city with a long history and rich culture.[31] Accordingly, the Holy See deliberately selected a Chinese priest, a scholar devoted to Chinese culture and philosophy, as bishop.

Since 1961, the ecclesiastical circumscriptions in Taiwan have remained unchanged.[32] The most senior prefecture apostolic of Kaohsiung was elevated to a diocese in March 1961, the prefectures of Taichung and Kiayi in April 1962, and the prefecture of Hwalien in March 1963. It took fourteen years to complete the Taiwanese Church's transition from one prefecture apostolic to seven dioceses, which is quite remarkable and unique [Fig. 5.5].

Vatican territorial strategy for Taiwan

This territorialization required adaptation to both the island's specific physical geography and its human geography; the balance of indigenous peoples, ethnic groups, and the descendants of those who had migrated centuries earlier had been deeply impacted by the 1945 expulsion of the Japanese and the 1949 migration of mostly Han Chinese from different regions of the mainland. The Holy See had significant but somewhat atypical human resources at its disposal, consisting of middle-aged missionaries, including exiled bishops, from different countries and cultures who had little in common except the Catholic faith, obedience to papal supremacy, and vivid memories of the traumatic failed mission in China.

In the 1950s and 1960s, Chiang Kaishek 蔣中正 (1887-1975), the KMT, and most missionaries dreamt of reconquering Mainland China.[33] Consequently, they considered their presence on the island temporary. By elevating Taiwan to the twenty-first ecclesiastical province of China in 1952, the Holy See affirmed that Communist China was not a lost territory. The Holy See also pursued its policy of Sinicization,[34] which had been implemented in the Republic of China from 1922 and had led to the multiplication of vicariates apostolic in the 1920s and 1930s, and the consecration of Chinese vicars apostolic from 1926. On April 11, 1946, Pope Pius XII established the Chinese Catholic hierarchy by elevating 99 vicariates apostolic in 20 Chinese archdioceses and 79 dioceses; 34 prefectures apostolic kept their status. However, the number of Chinese – three archbishops and seventeen bishops – was much too low and more were appointed between 1946 and 1949. This was an important step in the process of Sinicization, but it came too late and

---

29 Diocese of Hsinchu, *Tiaoyue wushi hsinchu jiaoqu aihuo xinchuan jishi*, 52.

30 Lo kuang, *Mu lu wenji*, vol. 7, 146.

31 Tainan counts the largest number (22) of Taiwan's 109 national monuments. See National Heritage List of Taiwan.

32 With the exception of the erection of the "Apostolic Administration of Kinmen or Quemoy Islands and Matzu" in 1968. See *Catholic Hierarchy*: www.catholic-hierarchy.org/diocese/dkinm.html.

33 Archbishop Paul Yu Pin 于斌 (1901-1978), elevated to the cardinalate in 1969, was "a keen supporter of president Chiang Kai-shek, a member of the National Assembly, and strongly endorsed KMT rule." Wong, "Christian Protesters for Democracy in Taiwan," 290.

34 Zheng, "Introductions. Christianity: Towards a theory of Sinicization."

5.5 The China bishops conference during the Second Vatican Council in Rome included the exiled bishops as well as bishops from Taiwan, Hong Kong, and Macao, November 1963.
[Utrecht, Het Utrechts Archief, 1224: Dutch Franciscans, China mission, 293/9]

was often too hastily prepared because of the context of the Chinese Civil War.[35] After 1949, many mainland dioceses remained without or with exiled bishops.

The previously discussed gradual erection of one archdiocese and six dioceses in Taiwan was a rapid shift from a mission territory to a real local Church, which undoubtedly benefited both from the 1946-1949 movement in China and the momentum of preparation for the Second Vatican Council from mid-1959 onwards. When the Council opened in October 1962, the recently elevated archbishop of Taipei and the bishops of Hsinchu, Kaohsiung, Kiayi, Taichung, and Tainan were council fathers in their own right,[36] and could fully participate in the council's work. The bishops in exile also participated in the council [Fig. 5.6], including those whom the Propaganda Fide had posted to other territories, such as the aforementioned André Vérineux MEP, Eugene Fahy SJ, and Thomas Niu Huiching.[37] At that time, five of the seven bishops of Taiwanese dioceses were Chinese. The re-establishment of Fu Jen Catholic University 天主教輔仁大學 by the Jesuits, SVD missionaries, and Chinese clergy at the request of Pope John XXIII in Taipei in 1961 benefited from the same momentum.[38] The Holy See had effectively territorialized Taiwan by methodically organizing ecclesiastical circumscriptions, promoting leaders, and distributing available human resources.

Every stage in the spatial organization was developed around a single concern: how to properly manage the various issues in order to build a true local Church. Examining the development of upper-level missionary spaces is not only a question of observing the historical growth trajectory of a local Church, but also about paying attention to the missionary significance and the policy and governance aspects of the Church to allow the spaces to become part of the Catholic Church's strategic practice, rather than merely a backdrop for historical events.

35 Soetens, *L'Église catholique en Chine au XXᵉ siècle*, 156-157; Strong, *A Call to Mission*, vol.1, 360-363.
36 Chen, *Yubin shuji zhuan*, 152-154.
37 *Patres Conciliares Ecclesiae Sinensis Roma Praesentes*. Most exiled bishops of Chinese dioceses attended the Council, but the Chinese bishops who remained in China were unable to.
38 Lin and Leung, "Taiwan Catholic Higher Education," 164.

5.6 The modern church of Queen of the Peace in Yiwan 宜灣天使之后天主堂 *– erected by the Dutch Franciscan Jorrit de Boer OFM on a rock along the east coast of Taiwan in the then prefecture of Hwalien – contrasts with the traditional housing and indigenous people. The photo is dated 1962 and a comment on the back reads: "The three women in the foreground are from the mountains. The elderly among them are all still tattooed. The one in the center draws quietly on her pipe".*
[Utrecht, Het Utrechts Archief, 1224: Dutch Franciscans, China mission, 306]

39 Dujardin, *Missionering en Moderniteit*. On settlements and compounds of Belgian OFM missionaries in China, see Coomans, "Islands on the Mainland" and Coomans, "Gendered Spaces of Catholic Settlements in Late Qing China," in this book.
40 Bouwmeester,"Relocating the China Mission."
41 Leuven, KADOC-KU Leuven, PAFF: 2181-2186, 2548 (Manuscripts by Father Hugelier, 1956, 1956, [1960], 1963-64, 1962-63, 1961-62, 1969).

Belgian Franciscans in the archdiocese of Taipei

Contrary to the top-down global decision-making of the Holy See and Propaganda Fide, the missionaries who were relocated to Taiwan had to fit into the territorialization process and start from scratch. How did these middle-aged missionaries organize their new mission field, in which the people, language, landscape, and climate were often different from what they had experienced in Mainland China? How did they organize their new mission spaces both when living in their urban community in Taipei and when assigned to particular rural missionary stations with the aim of rooting a Catholic parish?

To answer these questions, we have combined archival research and fieldwork to study the case of twelve Belgian Franciscans relocated to Taiwan from 1951, to the then prefecture apostolic of Taipei. These missionaries belonged to the Franciscan Flemish Province of Saint Joseph, which had run the vicariate apostolic of Yichang 宜昌 (Hupei, China) from 1870 to 1953.[39] This section does not address issues of architecture, style, construction, or heritage, which we have developed in another publication.[40] Instead, we will investigate the strategies behind the location of their parishes and the specific spatial settlement and arrangements of their churches and compounds.

A series of scrapbooks made by Father Gentiel Hugelier 恩特里 OFM (1896-1975) provide a lively illustrated chronological record of the missionaries' works, including construction.[41] Additional visual and written sources, such as letters, photographs, design plans, and other records, were retrieved from Franciscan archives in Taiwan and Leuven (KADOC), and are complemented by interviews with friars and priests gathered during fieldwork in 2019, 2020, and 2022.

From relocated Franciscan missionaries to a localized Franciscan province

The presence of Franciscan missionaries in China has a long and complex history that dates back to the late thirteenth century, before being interrupted and then resumed on several occasions. The first Franciscans were Italian friars who reached China along the Silk Road in 1294, at the time of the Mongol-led Yuan dynasty. They established an archdiocese in Beijing before spreading across the empire, but were suppressed as soon as the Ming dynasty came to power in 1368. The second Franciscan mission was initially staffed with Spanish friars from Mexico and the Philippines in 1633, but ended in 1801 with the last clandestine missionary's death in Shandong. The third and most successful Franciscan mission from 1839 to 1955 stretched across twenty-six ecclesiastical circumscriptions in Shandong, Shaanxi, Shanxi, Hubei, and Hunan.[42] Friars Minor, Franciscans Conventuals, and Capuchins came from Italy, Spain, Germany, France, Belgium, the Netherlands, Austria, Hungary, Ireland, and the United States.[43] Various branches of Franciscan nuns, including the Franciscan Missionaries of Mary, were active in schools, orphanages, hospitals, dispensaries, etc.[44] Both male and female Franciscan communities included Chinese friars, nuns, and bishops.[45]

From 1951, only forty or forty-one German, Italian, Belgian, Dutch, and Chinese Franciscans reached Taiwan,[46] a small number of the total number of Franciscans expelled from Mainland China. The Propaganda Fide assigned the Germans to the prefecture of Tainan, the Italians to Hsinchu, and the Belgians to Taipei.[47] At the same time, the Franciscan minister general in Rome appointed the Belgian Franciscan Dunstanus Put 童達德 OFM (1893-1974) as East Asia Regional Superior (*delegatus generalis*) to head and manage the apostolic work of all Franciscans in the East Asia region, which included Hong Kong, Taiwan, Macao, and Malacca.[48]

In this first phase, developing a local Church and stimulating an indigenous diocesan priesthood in Taiwan prevailed over the interests of building a Franciscan province in Taiwan. This dilemma had existed since Pope Benedict XV's apostolic letter *Maximum illud* (1919) and launched a missiological shift that proposed a change in focus from "the salvation of the individuals" to "the localization of the Church" (*inplantatio ecclesiae*), emphasizing the need to set down roots for local churches and develop local clergies, rather than promoting national or other interests [Fig. 5.5].[49] Discussions around localizing the Church *vs* "localizing the Order" (*inplantatio ordinis*), i.e., spreading the Franciscan order and spirit to different cultures, were typical for the friars at that time. Moreover, although the friars worked as parish priests, they aspired to a better balance with community life in accordance with their monastic vocation and identity.[50] However, seen within the previously discussed Holy See strategy, which aimed at establishing a local Church in Taiwan as quickly as possible, the foreign Franciscans were at the service of local bishops and managed by their regional general delegate. Last but not least, the cultural policy of the nationalist governments in Taiwan also influenced the Catholics and Protestants towards Sinicization.[51]

After the Second Vatican Council, 1962-1965, and the consolidation of the Catholic Church in Taiwan, the time came to create a Taiwanese Franciscan province. The foreign Franciscans were ageing and a new generation of Taiwanese and Chinese Franciscans had to take over, enculturate the charisma of Francis and Clare of Assisi, and stimulate local Franciscan vocations. The Our Lady Queen of China Province, of the Order of Friars Minor in Taiwan and Hong Kong, was eventually created in 1970.[52]

The hub of the Belgian Franciscans in Taipei

Father Methodius Van Steenwinckel 孟照琨 OFM (1891-1969) was the first of twelve Belgian Franciscans to reach Taipei in

---

42 Tiedemann, *Reference Guide*, 26-32.

43 Camps and McCloskey, *The Friars Minor in China*.

44 Tiedemann, *Reference Guide*, 56-60.

45 The first batch of six Chinese bishops consecrated in Rome by Pope Pius XI on October 28 1926 included two Franciscans: Odoric Simon Cheng Hede 成和德 OFM (1873-1928), prefect of Puqi 蒲圻 (Hebei), and Aloysius Chen Guodi 陳國砥 OFM (1875-1930), prefect of Fenyang 汾阳 (Shanxi).

46 According to the *Necrologium* of Our Lady Queen of China Province and the group pictures from Hong Kong (Taishan, OLQC-OFM). Han, *Fang ji xiao xiongdi hui zai Zhongguo wangzhe lu*, no page number.

47 Tiedemann, *Reference Guide*, 26-32.

48 Father Put served as *delegatus generalis* from 1949 to 1959. He was succeeded by the American Ralphus Reilly 雷益勵 OFM (1900-1970) from 1959 to 1969. Interview with Father Thomas Chen OFM, by the author, Daxi (Taiwan), July 27 2019.

49 Taveirne, "Re-reading the Apostolic Letter *Maximum illud*."

50 Brocanelli, "La missione cuore della vita francescana," 24-25. The friars had been confronted with this dilemma since the 1920s, see Dujardin, *Missionering en Moderniteit*, 149-160. About architectural indigenization, see Coomans, "Church Architecture and Church Buildings: China," 2023.

51 Chen, "The Orientation of the Taiwanese Catholic Church during Chiang Kai-shek's Government."

52 Han and Lai, *Zhonghua fangjihui sheng jianshi*, 10.

5.7 The Ximen friary and chapel in Taipei after its completion in 1959.
[Leuven, KADOC-KU Leuven, Picture Archive of the Flemish Franciscans: 2545]

5.8 The Belgian Franciscans at a community gathering at Ximen Friary in 1962.
[Leuven, KADOC-KU Leuven, Picture Archive of the Flemish Franciscans: 2185]

53 Han and Lai, *Zhonghua fangjihui sheng jianshi*, 9.
54 Taishan, OLQC-OFM: Han Cheng-liang, "Qingzhu bilishi dixiong laitai," 12-13.
55 Father Claudio Pogoraro OFM, interviewed by the author, Taishan (Taiwan), August 12, 2019.
56 Taishan, OLQC-OFM: Lapolla, *Storia della Provincia Francescana regina della Cina (1950-2000)*; Taishan, OLQC-OFM: Han Cheng-liang, "Qingzhu bilishi dixiong laitai," 13.
57 Xinbeishi ruifang qugongsuo, "Jiaotongpian," 2. <https://www.ruifang.ntpc.gov.tw/content/?parent_id=10036> [accessed July 27, 2020].

1951.[53] On their arrival in Taipei, the Belgian Franciscans installed their friary and chapel in a residential house in Ximenting 西門町, a strategic location in the city center where many other congregations and religious institutes were also based. Moreover, Ximenting, the district of the west gate of the old Taipei city walls 臺北府城, was close to Taipei's main train station 台北火車站. Father Gaspar Han Chengliang 韓承良 OFM (1928-2004) remembered that:

> (…) in front of the church there was (…) a red-light district brothel that was (…) usually lit with a red light. Every time the elderly Father Methodius Van Steenwinckel would pass the red light, he would always pay respect [daqian 打千] to it and make the sign of the cross because he thought it was the lamp of a sanctuary.[54]

From the description of the immediate environment and the Ximen church's unusual neighbors, it was clearly located in a poor area, where rent and land prices were relatively cheap. However, the friary became the Franciscan hub for visiting other parishes by train and interacting with missionaries from other congregations in the city. Originally of Japanese construction, the Ximen friary and church were rebuilt in a Western modern style in 1964 [Fig. 5.7].

In the course of the 1950's, the Flemish friars spread to the parishes which they had founded outside the city. Although each friar had his own mission station, they would come together once a month at their hub at the Ximen Friary [Fig. 5.8] to share experiences and strengthen their brotherhood.[55] Coming from the Hubei province, where they had worked before, the friars had to adapt to the Taiwanese lifestyle, which included the Hokkien language, different eating habits, clothing styles, climate, etc.

Missionary stations along a railway line

From Ximen friary, the Belgian Franciscans were sent out across the area east of Taipei, to the border of Yilan County 宜蘭縣. The archbishop of Taipei, Joseph Kuo Joshih CDD, initially assigned four places to the friars to found their new missions along a railway line connecting with Ximen station: Nansongshan 南松山 in 1953, Ruifang 瑞芳 in 1956, Nangang 南港 in 1960, and Xizhi 汐止 in 1963.[56] From these locations, the missionaries founded eight more parishes in Chenggong village 成功新村, Sijiaoting 四腳亭, Neihu 內湖, Shuinandong 水湳洞, Jinguashi 金瓜石, Lianhe village 聯合新村, Zhonglun 中崙, and Yongchun 永春.

The location of these mission stations reveals that most of the first-generation churches were built along the railway line

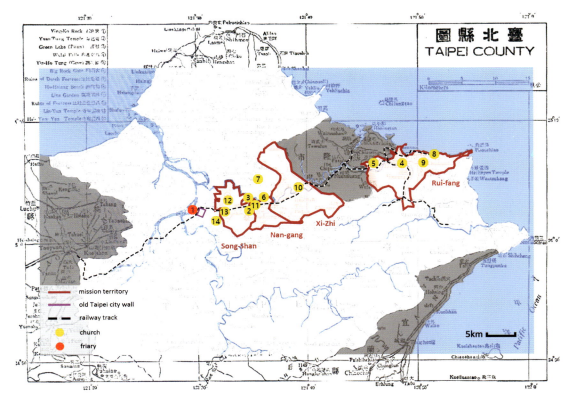

5.9 Map of Taipei County in 1960 with the Franciscan mission stations. The names and years of completion of the churches are: 1. Ximen 西門 in Taipei (1959), 2. Chenggong village 成功新村 (1951), 3. Nansongshan 南松山 (1953), 4. Ruifang 瑞芳 (1956), 5. Sijiaoting 四腳亭 (1957), 6. Nangang village 南港村 (1960), 7. Neihu 內湖 (1961), 8. Shuinandong 水湳洞 (1961), 9. Jinguashi 金瓜石 (1961), 10. Xizhi 汐止 (1963), 11. Nangang 南港 (1964), 12. Lianhe village 聯合新村 (1967), 13. Zhonglun 中崙 (1968), 14. Yongchun 永春 (unknown).
[Leon Bouwmeester, 2023]

that ran east-west through the diocese of Taipei, connecting the aforementioned Ximen station to the northeast coast 東北角海岸 [Fig. 5.9]. The Japanese government had laid the first section of the line in 1902 and extended it to the northeast coast in 1931, reaching a total length of 125.4 kilometers.[57] It crossed the Taipei-Keelung metropolitan area 台北都會區, today the most crowded area in Taiwan. The 1931 extension included four sections: the northern section of the main line 縱貫線北段, the Yilan line 宜蘭線 in the direction of Yilan on the east coast, the Shen'ao line 深澳線 in the direction of the coal-mining area of Shen'ao, and the Jinguashi line 金瓜石線, to the Jinguashi gold mine. The main line and the Yilan line allowed people to travel from the west of Taiwan to the east. Most of the churches could be reached by this line. From Badu 八堵 station, the Yilan line, with a length of 96.3 kilometers, passes Ruifang church and Sijiaoting church. The other two lines ran through the area of Shuinandong church and Jinguashi church.

The first church was built in Nansongshan in 1953, near the railroad. From there, the missionaries extended their network east- and westwards along the railway, which eventually became the backbone of the mission's spatial development. Friars could visit further neighboring areas by motorbike or bicycle [Fig. 5.10].

5.10 Meeting of friars in Nangang parish, September 9, 1960.
[Leuven, KADOC-KU Leuven, Picture Archive of the Flemish Franciscans: 2183]

5.11 Bird eye's view of the project of Nangang church, unknown architect, 1960.
[© Leuven, KADOC-KU Leuven, Picture Archive of the Flemish Franciscans: 2183]

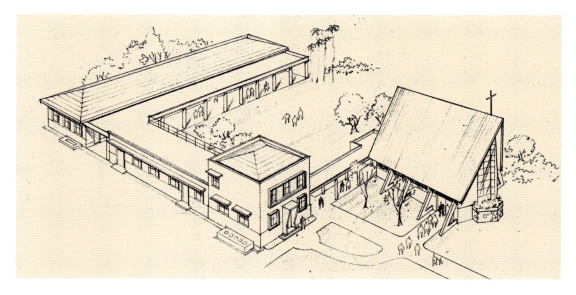

A three-staged development

When assigned to a particular mission field, the Franciscan missionaries would begin by visiting Catholic families and exploring opportunities for purchasing or renting a suitable place or house in which to live. Such houses in the Taiwanese or Japanese vernacular styles had to be adapted to their new use as a mission station, which included a chapel, a day room where the missionary could eat and welcome visitors, a private room for the missionary, where he could carry out his intellectual work and sleep, and a kitchen.[58] Missionaries would sometimes rent a condominium in a three or four-story building.[59] Only when the local community grew bigger and had regular parishioners would land be purchased and permanent buildings erected with the help of the parishioners.

Missionaries were also expected to raise funds for the brand-new parish, find affordable land, and work on feasible building plans. The choice of appropriate land was not obvious as only around 26% of Taiwan's geography is flat, while around 27% is sloped and nearly 47% mountainous. As a result, missionaries were often faced with uneven sites, especially when building churches in rural areas. Father Hugelier mentions the difficulty in purchasing suitable land for a missionary station. He did eventually purchase a plot, not because the location was suitable - it was located "too far away from the main road" - but because it was within the limits of his budget.[60] Once, such a location turned in his favor, when, in 1969, the Zhongxiaodong Road, part of the new Neihu and Nangang Master-plan specifications for the Taipei City Government,[61] was laid in front of the Nangang church.

The second stage saw the development of a cluster of parish buildings, which usually consisted of a two-story structure with a liturgical space and other rooms for the parish, plus some additional bungalows that could be used as a kindergarten. Some of these buildings were laid out around a courtyard, which served as a playground for the children. Not every parish was able to achieve such a complex from the start, however. The first-generation buildings from the 1950s and 1960s were modest, functional, and lacking in localized architectural forms. These gave a modern or Western-looking face to the Catholic religion.

The two-stage building process of Nangang church is as a good example. The entire design, including the new church, kindergarten, and parish spaces was part of the original plan [Fig. 5.11], but Father Hugelier chose to realize it in two phases. The first phase, in 1957, consisted of a two-story concrete cube-shaped building containing

---

58 As was the case for Ximen church, Zhonglun Church, Jinguashi, and Shuinandong church.
59 For example, Youngchun church.
60 Leuven, KADOC-KU Leuven, PAFF: 2183: Manuscript by Father Hugelier, p. 5b, 1956.
61 Public Works Department, Taipei City Government, Niding Nangang Neuhu liangdiqu zhuyao jihuaan (jihuabianhao: 058025). Taipei: Taipei City Government, 1969.

the activity spaces on the ground floor and a temporary chapel, which was combined with the parish space, on the upper floor. An educational L-shaped single-story building was connected with the parish space, while the playground was enclosed by buildings and gardens [Fig. 5.12].⁶² Six years on, in 1963, Father Hugelier initiated the second phase of the construction, which included a formal church decorated with colorful glass windows and a bell tower with curved lines. The church had a different design than in the 1957 plan [Fig. 5.11]: it was larger, had a capacity of 300 seats, and its tower was much more visible in the landscape [Fig. 5.13].⁶³ When the new church was completed, the temporary chapel in the two-story building was transferred and the space reused for the pastor's housing. The two-phased construction was not only financially motivated, but was undoubtedly linked to the small number of parishioners in the early years. The difference in size between the 1957 project and the 1963 church suggests that the parish developed well during these six years, notably thanks to the kindergarten strategy discussed below.

Both the Xizhi church and the Sijiaoting church were built on a slope, from which they derived their unique architectural form. The former had three levels and an entrance at each: the upper entrance was the main entrance to the church, while the side entrance provided access to the kindergarten on the lower level [Fig. 5.15]. The latter was located along a slope and the missionaries used multiple stairs to link the church building, priest's house, parish office, and garden, all at different heights [Fig. 5.14]. We were unable to find any evidence of the influence of *fengshui* 风水 or geomancy on the design or orientation of the churches. The missionaries established their churches directly facing the road rather than along the specific south-north axis, as was common in traditional Mainland Chinese architecture.⁶⁴

A third step developed from the 1970s, when the parishes began replacing first-generation churches with larger, more elaborate and attractive buildings that echoed the new liturgical prescriptions of the Second Vatican Council.⁶⁵ Consequently, eight of the fourteen parish churches built by the Belgian Franciscans were demolished and replaced with new structures.⁶⁶

Kindergartens

Preschool education in Taiwan began under Japanese rule in 1897, but mainly served the colonial policy. By 1951, there were 203 kindergartens on the island, of which only 26 were private and had high tuition fees.⁶⁷ The increasing employment rate of women in Taiwan in the late 1950s resulted in a dire need for childcare. In 1965, 50% of the women aged from 20 to 24 and 30% of the women aged 25-29 contributed to the female la-

5.12 Father Hugelier posing in front of his residence (left) and kindergarten (back right) of Nangang Parish, c. 1961-1962. The residence served as a temporary church until the permanent church was built.
[Leuven, KADOC-KU Leuven, Picture Archive of the Flemish Franciscans: 2183]

5.13 Nangang, the final church and tower as completed in 1963.
[Nangang, collection of a parishioner]

62 Leuven, KADOC-KU Leuven, PAFF: 2181: Hugelier, 1956, 3b.
63 Leuven, KADOC-KU Leuven, PAFF: 2184: Hugelier, 1964-1965.
64 *Feng shui* is a geomantic practice in Chinese architecture in which a structure or site is chosen or configured so as to harmonize with the spiritual forces that inhabit it. See Coomans, "Islands on the Mainland," in this book, p. 33-34, 48, 53.
65 This third step is beyond the scope of this chapter.
66 The churches of Chenggong village, Nansongshan, Ruifang, Ximen, Nangang Village, Shuinandong, Xizhi, Nangang.
67 Wong, "The Development of Early Childhood Education in Taiwan: A Historical Perspective," 2012, 13.

5.14 *The Sijiaoting parish combines a church (right) and a residence (rear) on the slope of a hill reachable with stairs. [Leuven, KADOC-KU Leuven, Picture Archive of the Flemish Franciscans: 2548]*

68 Li and Yang, *Transitional Patterns of Female Labor Force Participation in Taiwan*, 2004, 114.
69 Fertility indicators in data query, population projections for the ROC (Taiwan), National Development Council, https://pop-proj.ndc.gov.tw/dataSearch2.aspx?r=2&uid=2104&pid=59 [accessed July 28, 2020]
70 Chinese Regional Bishops' Conference, *Taiwan Catholic Church statistics*, 1982, 164.
71 High school in Neihu, 1961. Kindergartens in Nansongshan, 1953; Ruifang, 1956; Sijiaoting, 1957; Nangang Village, 1960; Shuinandong, 1961; Jinguashi, 1961; Xizhi, 1963; Nangang, 1964; Zhonglun, 1968.
72 Taishan, OLQC-OFM: Lapolla, *Storia della Provincia Francescana regina della Cina*.
73 The legislative history of "Act Governing the Appointment of Educators," Online sorting system of legislation, Legislative Yuan, <https://lis.ly.gov.tw/lglawc/lawsingle?00184EBB53C6000000000000000000A000000002FFFFFD^04630074041900^00000000000> [accessed January 20, 2023].
74 Interview with Father Chen by the author, Daxi 大溪 (Taiwan), July 27, 2019.
75 Interview with Monsignor Joseph Ti-Kang, archbishop emeritus of Taipei, by the author, Bali 八里 (Taiwan), July 17, 2019.

bor force,[68] while the total fertility rate in the same year was 4.83 children per woman.[69] In a situation where 30% to 50% of Taiwanese women were in employment but at the same time giving birth to almost five children, the need for kindergartens grew exponentially.

Catholic missionaries were aware of this social issue and understood that kindergartens were an opportunity to connect with and evangelize local people, young mothers, and female teachers. Women, who played crucial roles in rural areas, traditional villages, and Taiwanese families, formed a special social circle that benefited missionary works [Fig. 5.15]. Establishing kindergartens became a common phenomenon in Taiwan's parishes in the 1950s and 1960s.

In Taipei, the earliest statistics available (1980) mention no fewer than 76 kindergartens in the 96 parishes of the archdiocese.[70] Nine of the fourteen parishes founded by the Flemish Franciscans between 1951 and 1968 included a kindergarten and only one parish a junior high school.[71] On May 22 1958, Archbishop Kuo Joshih of Taipei concluded an agreement with the Minister General of the Order of Friars Minor, Agostino Sépinski OFM (1900-1978), allowing the Franciscans to freely establish kindergartens without further request.[72] This proved the archbishop's confidence in the friars' educational and pastoral mission, as well as his support towards the parishes' financial autonomy. Moreover, it was easier to start a kindergarten than to operate educational institutes at higher levels. Because mandatory education in Taiwan did not include early childhood education, the requirements for school presidents, teachers, and the buildings of kindergartens were much lower than those for primary schools and other educational institutes. For example, the Belgian Franciscans founded Saint Francis High School 方濟中學 in Taipei in 1964, but were unable to find a school president because no friar fulfilled the qualifications required by the government.[73] Eventually, Father Thomas Chen Peiqian 申培謙 OFM (1927-2022), a high school teacher in Hong Kong and PhD graduate in Sociology, was brought over and appointed the first president of Saint Francis High School in 1965.[74]

Kindergartens were not only a tool for rooting the Catholic Church at a local level, they also helped develop a missionary station into a mature and autonomous parish by increasing the size of the community and generating extra funds for other missionary works.[75] There were also real-estate aspects:

since the chapel or church and educational building were designed as independent structures, the latter could be sold separately if necessary. For instance, Saint Francis kindergarten, a subsidiary component of Zhonglun church, was sold to obtain the necessary funds for the building of the abovementioned Saint Francis High School.

From an architectural point of view, kindergartens were near but separated from the church and priest's residence, which were sometimes linked by a covered corridor. Kindergarten buildings had their own independent yard. In the original design for Nangang church, the kindergarten, corridor, and chapel defined an inward U-shaped private space; the main entrance of the church faced the inner courtyard [Fig. 5.11]. Eventually, a different church was built, the main entrance of which was turned outwards and not linked to the other buildings through a gallery [Fig. 5.13], distinguishing the church's activity space from that of the kindergarten. A similar design also appeared at Xizhi, where the church's main entrance was on the front and gave access to the liturgical space. The kindergarten, located on the left, had its own entrance and playground [Fig. 5.16].

Opportunity-based spatial strategies

The Belgian Franciscans developed Christianities based on local needs and their previous personal missionary experiences in Mainland China. Organizing Christianized space at station or parish level was one of the most elementary actions for a missionary, who knew the powers of attraction of contrasting architecture on eminent sites [Fig. 5.6]. Another obvious spatial strategy was the combination of parish churches and kindergartens in response to childcare needs in Taiwan in the 1950s–1960s. Both are indicative of concerted opportunity-based efforts to root parishes locally.

Regionally, having lived in southwestern Hupei, the missionaries knew the difficulties of traveling through mountainous regions and the time wasted on bad roads, even to nearby locations. Being assigned to an area served by a railway line considerably changed the time and spatial organization of the missionaries, helping them gather believers and reach people. They set up their hub in the neighborhood of Taipei Ximen station and let the trains carry them to their mission stations, which they had established based on the opportunities offered by the Japanese-built line. This considerable improvement

5.15 Kindergarten of Nangang parish with teachers and Father Hugelier, 1961.
[Leuven, KADOC-KU Leuven, Picture Archive of the Flemish Franciscans: 2182]

5.16. Xizhi parish building combining the Saint Francis Church, a school, and other rooms for the parish in a four-story building, 1969.
[Leuven, KADOC-KU Leuven, Picture Archive of the Flemish Franciscans: 2548]

was modern and efficient because the regular train schedule allowed them to organize their time and travel, to visit other friars in their stations, or to meet regularly all together at their headquarters in Taipei. Goods and supplies, including modern building materials, could be easily transported to their parishes, which were never remote. They also benefited from the gradual urbanization generated by the railway line.

There were few opportunities to speak of after the debacle of the China mission in 1949. The relocation of thousands of traumatized missionaries by equally traumatized Church leaders could have been even more dramatic. Taiwan's territorialization, however, offered the Holy See unprecedented opportunities: the evangelization of an island with hundreds of experienced missionaries, not to mention the support of the governments of the ROC and US. The most unexpected opportunity was undoubtedly the momentum created by Pope John XXIII's convocation of the Second Vatican Council on January 25 1959, which accelerated the process of localizing the Taiwanese Church by elevating the prefectures apostolic to dioceses in 1961-1962. The same dynamic localized the Catholic Churches of South-Korea in 1962, Vietnam in 1960, and Indonesia in 1961, as well as the Churches of African countries, such as the (then Belgian) Congo in 1959.

BIBLIOGRAPHY

Primary sources / archives

Taishan (Taiwan), Archives of Our Lady Queen of China OFM Province (OLQC-OFM):
- Padre Tobias Lapolla OFM, *Storia della Provincia Francescana regina della Cina* (1950-2000) (Fr. Pogoraro OFM oral translated), date unknown, no page number.
- Han Chengliang 韓承良, "Qingzhu bilishi dixiong laitai chuanjiao wushi zhounian" 慶祝比利時弟兄來台傳教五十周年" [Celebrating the 50th Anniversary of Belgian Brothers Missioning to Taiwan], in *Bilishi fang ji hui zai Nangang, Xizhi, Ruifang kaijiao jin qing* 比利時方濟會在南港、汐止、瑞芳開教金慶 [*Belgian Franciscans teach Jinqing in Nangang, Xizhi, and Ruifang*], [2003], unpublished.

Leuven (Belgium), KADOC-KU Leuven, Picture Archive of the Flemish Franciscans (PAFF):
- 2181-2186, 2548: Scrap books, Fr. Gentiel Hugelier, 1956, 1956, [1960], 1963-64, 1962-63, 1961-62, 1969.

Taipei (Taiwan), Taipei City Government, Public Works Department:
- *Niding Nangang Neuhu liangdiqu zhuyao jihuaan (jihuabianhao: 058025)* 擬訂南港內湖兩地區主要計畫案 (計畫編號; 058025) [Draft of major plans for the two areas of Nangang Neihu (case no. 058025)], 1969.

Secondary literature

Bouwmeester, Leon 朱柏寧. "From Mainland to Island.The Architectural Legacy of Belgian Franciscan Missionaries, in Early Postwar Taipei," in: Van Mulder, Jonas; Coomans, Thomas and Vanysacker, Dries, eds. *Cross-Cultural Impacts. Critical Approaches to Missionary Heritage*. Leuven: Leuven University Press, 2024.

Brocanelli, Vincenzo. "La missione cuore della vita francescana." *Vita minorum*, 80 (2), 2009, 1-153.

Camps, Arnulf and McCloskey, Pat. *The Friars Minor in China (1294-1955), especially the years 1925-55, based on the research of Friars Bernward Willeke and Domenico Gandolfi OFM*. New York-Rome: St. Bonaventure University & General Curia OFM, 1995.

Chao, Chenyang 趙振揚. *Meiyuan yu Taiwan de shehui jiuzhu-yi 480 gongfa weizhu de taolun* 美援與臺灣的社會救助—以480公法為主的討論 [*American Aid and Taiwan's Social Assistance: Discussion Focusing on Public Law 480*]. Unpublished Master's thesis, National Taiwan Normal University, Taipei, 2015.

Chen, Fangcung 陳方中. *Yubin shuji zhuan* 于斌樞機傳 [*Biography of Cardinal Yü Pin*]. Taipei: The Commercial Press, 2001.

Chen, Tsungming, Alexandre 陳聰銘. "The Orientation of the Taiwanese Catholic Church during Chiang Kai-shek's Government: Sinicization in the Pursuit of Identity," *Ching Feng*, n.s., 9 (2008-2009) 1-2, 3-21.

Chen, Yinhung 陳胤宏. "Away from Taipei: The Evacuation of Taiwan Provincial Government (1945-1960)" / 從中央到地方：臺灣省政府之疏遷, *Historical Journal of Chu Nan*, 14 (2012), 121-154.

Chiang, Chuante 江傳德. *Tianzhujiao zai Taiwan* 天主教在台灣 [*Catholicism in Taiwan*]. Tainan: Catholic Window Press, 1992.

Chinese Regional Bishop's Conference. *Catholic Church Directory Taiwan (2017)*. Taipei: Secretaries of Chinese Regional Bishop's Conference, 2017.

Constructing Territory (GEOG 128, Geography of International Affairs). Penn State College of Earth and Mineral Sciences, Department of Geography. https://www.e-education.psu.edu/geog128/node/538#:~:text=Territorialization%3A%20The%20way%20that%20territory,contest%20this%20process%20of%20territorialization. [accessed on January 10, 2023].

Coomans, Thomas. "Islands on the Mainland. Catholic Missions and Spatial Strategies in Late Qing and Republican China," in: Coomans, Thomas, ed. *Missionary Spaces. Imagining, Building, Contesting Christianities in Africa and China, 1830s-1960s*. Leuven, 2024, 32-63.

Coomans, Thomas. "Gendered Spaces in Catholic Compounds of Late Qing China," in Coomans, Thomas, ed. *Missionary Spaces. Imagining, Building, Contesting Christianities in Africa and China, 1830s-1960s*. Leuven, 2024, 106-145.

Coomans, Thomas. "Church Architecture and Church Buildings: China," in: Chu, Cindy Yik-yi 朱益宜 and Leung Kit-fun, Beatrice 梁潔芬, eds. *The Palgrave Handbook of the Catholic Church in East Asia*, Springer, 2020-2023. <https://link.springer.com/referencework/10.1007/978-981-15-9365-9>.

Diocese of Hsinchu. *Tiaoyue wushi hsinchu jiaoqu aihuo xinchuan jishi (1961-2011)* 跳躍五十新竹教區愛火薪傳紀實 (1961-2011) [50th Anniversary Album of Diocese of Hsinchu (1961-2011)]. Hsinchu: Catholic Diocese of Hsinchu, 2012.

Dujardin, Carine. *Missionering en Moderniteit. De Belgische Minderbroeders in China, 1872-1940* (KADOC-Studies 19). Leuven: Leuven University Press, 1996.

Emmerich, Henricus SVD, ed. *Atlas missionum a sacra Congregatione de Propagande Fide dependentium*. Vatican City, 1958.

Han Chengliang 韓承良. *Fang ji xiao xiongdi hui zai Zhongguo wangzhe lu* 方濟小兄弟會在中國亡者錄, 2004, no page number.

Han Chengliang 韓承良, Lai Lihua 賴利華, *Zhonghua fangjihui sheng jianshi* 中華方濟會省簡史 [A brief history of the Franciscan province in China]. Taipei: Si gao shengjing xuehui chubanshi, 1992.

Lardinois, Olivier 丁立偉 SJ, Chan Changhui 詹嬪慧, Sun Tachuan 孫大川. *Church Alive: the Catholic Church among the Aboriginal People of Taiwan. Past, Present and Future / Huoli jiaohui: Tianzhujiao zai Taiwan yuan zhumin shijie de guoqu xianzai weilai* 活力教會：天主教在台灣原住民世界的過去現在未來. Taipei: Kuangchi Cultural, 2005.

Les Missions Catholiques, 9 (1877), 373-375, 386-388, 411-412.

Leung Kit-fun, Beatrice 梁潔芬. "Actors. The Missionaries", in: Tiedemann, R. Gary. ed. *Handbook of Christianity in China. Volume Two: 1800 to the Present*. Leiden-Boston, 2010, 793-809.

Lin Yaotang, Peter 林耀堂 and Leung Kit Fun, Beatrice 梁潔芬. "Taiwan Catholic Higher Education: Its Contribution to the Greater China Region", in: So H.K., Francis; Leung Kit Fun, Beatrice and Mylod, Ellen Mary, eds. *The Catholic Church in Taiwan: Birth, Growth and Development*. London: Palgrave Macmillan, 2017, 153-178.

Ling Oi Ki 凌愛基. "Demise of the Missionary Enterprise", in: Tiedemann, R. Gary. ed. *Handbook of Christianity in China. Volume Two: 1800 to the Present*. Leiden-Boston, 2010, 766-781.

Lo Kuang, Stanislaus 羅光. *Mu lu wenji* 牧盧文集 [Autobiography]. New Taipei: Prophet, 1972.

Mateo, Fernando SJ. *China Jesuits in East-Asia starting from zero 1949-1957*. Unpublished Jesuit internal book, 1994.

Moal, Yves 劉一峰 and Liao, Zu-Chun 廖紫均. *Les ecclésiastiques français de la côte est de Taïwan / Taiwan dong haiʾan de Faguo mu zhe* 台灣東海岸的法國牧者. Taichung: National Museum of Natural Science, 2010.

Patres Conciliares Ecclesiae Sinensis Roma Praesentes, *Concilium Oecumenicum Vaticanum* II, 11 October 1962.

Présence des Missions Étrangères à Taiwan, 1950-1975. Repères historiques. Paris: IRFA, 2021. https://irfa.paris/wp-content/uploads/2021/12/Tai%CC%88wan-IRFA.pdf

Sanroman, Miguel Angel OP. *Formosa, campo de Dios 1626-1642 / Meili dao zhu de zuangtian* 美麗島主的莊田. Tainan: Catholic Window Press, 2013.

Soetens, Claude. *L'Église catholique en Chine au XXᵉ siècle*. Paris: Beauchesne, 1997.

Strong, *A Call to Mission*, vol. 1, 360-363.

Taveirne, Patrick 譚永亮 CICM. "Re-reading the Apostolic Letter *Maximum illud*," in: Ku Weiying 古偉瀛 and Zhao Xiaoyang 赵晓阳 eds. *Jidu zongjiao yu jindai Zhongguo* 基督宗教与近代中國 [Multi-aspect Studies on Christianity in modern China]. Beijing: Social Sciences Academic Press, 2014, 64-87.

Tiedemann, R. Gary, ed. *Handbook of Christianity in China. Volume Two: 1800 to the Present*. Leiden-Boston: Brill, 2010.

Tiedemann, R. Gary. *Reference Guide to Christian Missionary Societies in China from the Sixteenth to the Twentieth Century*. Armonk-London: Sharpe, 2009.

Werner, Oscar SJ. *Atlas des missions catholiques. Vingt cartes teintées, avec texte explicative*. Freiburg im Breisgau: B. Herder, 1886.

Wong, Bibiana. "Christian Protesters for Democracy in Taiwan: A Study of Two American Missionaries under Taiwanese Martial Law." *International Journal for the Study of the Christian Church*, 16 (2016) 4, 288-304.

Xinbeishi ruifang qugongsuo 新北市瑞芳區公所 [New Taipei City Ruifang District Office], "Jiaotongpian" 交通篇 [traffic], *Ruifang zhenzhi* 瑞芳鎮誌 [The history of Ruifang], publication of Ruifang District Office, 2002. <https://www.ruifang.ntpc.gov.tw/content/?parent_id=10036> [accessed on 27 July 2020].

Yang Chiachin 楊嘉欽. *From Europe to Taiwan: The Holy Rosary Province of Dominicans' Mission in Taiwan / Cong Ouzhou dao Taiwan: Daoming hui meigui sheng Taiwan chuanjiao yanjiu* 從歐洲到台灣：道明會玫瑰省台灣傳教研究. New Taipei: Hua Mu Lan Publisher, 2013.

Yap, Kohua 葉高華. "Waishengren de renshu, laiyuan yu fenbu 外省人的人數、來源與分布" [population, origin and distribution of mainlanders]. *Taiwan xue tongxun* 臺灣學通訊 [*Taiwan Studies Newsletter*], 103 (2018), 15-17.

Zheng Yangwen 鄭揚文. "Introduction. Christianity: Towards a Theory of Sinicization," in: Zheng Yangwen ed. *Sinicizing Christianity*. Leiden-Boston: Brill, 2017, 1-30.

Online Resources

Bigmorr, 2012, Catholic dioceses of Taiwan, digital image, https://commons.wikimedia.org/wiki/File:Catholic_dioceses_of_Taiwan.svg [accessed on December 10, 2022].

Bishop William F. Kupfer MM, website of Maryknoll mission archives, <https://maryknollmissionarchives.org/deceased-fathers-bro/bishop-william-f-kupfer-mm/> [accessed on April 12, 2021].

Catholic Hierarchy, <https://www.catholic-hierarchy.org/>.

Code of Canon Law (English), <https://www.vatican.va/archive/cod-iuris-canonici/cic_index_en.html> [accessed on January 10, 2023].

National Heritage List of Taiwan, <https://nchdb.boch.gov.tw/assets/advanceSearch?limit=12&offset=0&query=%7B%22assetsClassifyType%22:null,%22govInstitutionCode%22:null,%22belongCity%22:null,%22belongCityId%22:null,%22classifyCode%22:%5B%221.1%22%5D,%22assetsClassifyCode%22:%5B%221.1.1%22%5D,%22buildingYearCode%22:%5B%5D,%22assetsTypeCode%22:%5B%5D%7D&sort=id&order=desc&classifyCode=1.1> [accessed on December 10, 2022].

Treaty of Shimonoseki 馬關條約. The website of the Ministry of Foreign Affairs of the Republic of China (Taiwan), <https://www.mofa.gov.tw/cp.aspx?n=198> [accessed on January 10, 2023].

Zhongguo dili yanjiusuo 中國地理研究所 [Institute of Geography of China]. *Taiwan jianming ditu* 台灣簡明地圖 [*Concise Map of Taiwan*]. Taipei: Zhongguo lvxing guanguang fuwu she 中國旅行觀光服務社 [China Travel Service], 1960.

PART TWO
UNIVERSAL PROJECTS /
LOCALIZED ARCHITECTURES

6 Gendered Spaces in Catholic Compounds of Late Qing China

Thomas Coomans

Introduction

Gendered space refers to the myriad ways in which space in all its forms – material, discursive, metaphorical, emotional, and the like – is produced by and productive of gender norms and relations. Like other social relations, gender is a sociospatial phenomenon that becomes material through enactments which reinforce and/or challenge dominant norms and relations.

Because the meaning of gender changes over time and space, understanding the spatial manifestations of gender provides a powerful window into how categories of gender are defined, embodied, and imbued with specific characteristics and significance. The gendering of space has specific, material consequences for people's daily lives, their mobility, and their sense of identity.[1]

This definition of gendered spaces by Tiffany Muller Myrdhal fully applies in the particular context of the encounter between European Catholic missionaries and Late Qing China. From the years 1840-1860, missionaries returned to the Middle Kingdom to resume their apostolate, which had been interrupted in the mid-eighteenth century. Late Qing society, locked into its traditional system and faced with internal revolts and the imperialist appetites of Western nations, was slow to open up to modernity. Conservative Confucian values did not help call this immobility into question and fueled hostility towards foreigners.

Missionaries who came into contact with other societies and cultures with different gender relations had to adapt enough to be accepted, but could not deviate from the canonical distinctions in force in the Catholic Church. As the nineteenth- and early twentieth-century Catholic Church was strongly clericalized, Western-born and -educated male and female members of Catholic religious orders, institutes, and societies were the product of a clearly segregated society and church. Before the Second Vatican Council and the evolution of Western society in the 1960s, gender segregation in the Catholic Church was strict.[2] Male and female religious institutes were completely separate and subject to different kinds of spatial and psychological enclosures, which were particularly strict in the case of female contemplative monastic orders. There were no mixed primary or secondary Catholic educational institutions, and the youth and Catholic action movements were clearly segregated, as were parishioners within the churches. The only exception was the need for the indispensable presence of male chaplains in female communities and institutions to celebrate the Eucharist, receive confession, and deliver the other sacraments with which only priests were entrusted.

Gender segregation in Chinese society was a significant barrier for foreigners, as it was more radical than that practiced in nineteenth-century Western society, including by the Catholic Church and other Christian denominations. Catholic missionaries who applied their segregation standards in churches, schools, orphanages, etc. were often accused of immorality because they dared to address women and allowed them to access churches at the same time as men. Moreover, by teaching, catechizing, and preaching to women – in particular promoting equality

6.1 The gender segregation of the Catholic French Mission of Xujiahui, Shanghai, was defined by the Zhaojiabang canal: two bridges were the only connections between the female compounds on the east bank and the Jesuit settlement on the west bank. The Tushanwan bridge connected the boys' orphanage and the convent of the Discalced Carmelites. Photo by Father Joseph de Reviers de Mauny SJ (1892-1974), dated 1932.
[Vanves, Compagnie de Jésus, Archives jésuites de France, Fonds iconographique]

1. Muller Myrdahl, "Gendered Space," abstract.
2. Köhler, "Gendered Segregation in the Church."

3   Mo, "The Gendered Space of the 'Oriental Vatican' – Zi-ka-wei;" Xiang, "Building and Ecclesiastical Real Estate Empire;" Coomans, "Yancang yu sheng xin da jiaotang de guangmang zhihou."

4   See contributions in handbooks: Zhang, "Women in the Chinese Catholic Church: Local and Foreign Sisters and Gender Relations;" Tiedemann, "Catholic religious communities of women (foreigners);" Tiedemann, "Catholic religious communities of Chinese women."

5   Visual sources from missionary archives in Belgium, France, and the Netherlands. See bibliography.

6   French Jesuits (SJ) in Jiangnan (Jiangsu, Anhui, and Shanghai), and southeast Hebei; Belgian Scheut Fathers (CICM) in northwest Hebei and Inner Mongolia; Dutch Franciscans (OFM) in south Shanxi; Belgian Franciscans (OFM) in southwest Hubei; and French Foreign Mission (MEP) in Guizhou.

7   Coomans, "Islands on the Mainland. Catholic Missions and Spatial Strategies in Late Qing and Republican China," in this book, p. 33-63. Id., "Gender-Designed Catholic Churches in North China 1830s-1920s," in this book, p. 147-193.

8   Wiest, "Bringing Christ to the Nations: Shifting Models of Mission among Jesuits in China."

9   Camps, "Actors: Catholic Missionaries."

and condemning polygamy – missionaries contributed to the emancipation of women and threatened the harmony of traditional society.

This chapter examines how Catholic missionaries dealt with the issue of gender segregation and designed gendered spaces in their various establishments in China, from rural parish compounds to cathedral complexes. How did missionary architecture in China combine Western Catholic norms of gender segregation, as defined by Canon Law, and make them acceptable to Chinese Confucian norms and customs? With the exception of specific studies on gendered spaces in Shanghai and the spatial analysis of the cathedral compound in Guangzhou,[3] the subject has yet to be explored. In the literature on female religious communities in China – Western missionary nuns, Chinese consecrated Virgins, and Chinese congregations – the spatial issues of enclosure, circulation, and spatial organization have not been addressed as such.[4]

Given the destruction and conversion of most missionary buildings after the expulsion of the missionaries from China in 1949-1954, as well as the recent modernization of the surviving hospitals and schools founded by them, our research is based primarily on visual sources, in particular several rare plans of architectural complexes with explanatory captions, usefully supplemented by old photographs (for example Figs. 6.11-6.12, 6.16, 6.32-6.33 and 6.38-6.39).[5] Some of the latter provide information on the back as to the identification of the buildings shown, a date, or even comments added by the missionaries (for example Figs. 6.18, 6.22, 6.24 and 6.26). In missionary journals and propaganda literature from the 1840s to 1940s, gender considerations are omnipresent, but the question of gendered spaces and architecture must be deciphered from between the lines. We should not forget that most authors were missionary single men – with all their certainties and prejudices – who were addressing a conservative Western Catholic readership convinced of its cultural superiority.

After introducing the status of women in traditional Chinese Confucian society, the problems faced by Catholic missionaries, and the different kinds of female religious communities in China, we will see how missionaries designed and organized their compounds based on gender segregation. How did missionaries adapt existing buildings? How were walls used to segregate and protect Christian communities? How could men and women be segregated by public space? How could the central location of the church contribute to both segregation and encounter? Different spatial configurations will be defined and analyzed on the basis of various examples chosen from across China.[6] In every case, local topography and community growth were determining factors.

This chapter is part of a trilogy published in this book, which includes one chapter on the spatial strategies of the Catholic missions in China and another on gendered spaces in churches in northern China.[7]

Agents of Catholicism in a Confucian society

The missionaries who arrived in China in the nineteenth century had different worldviews compared to those of the seventeenth- and eighteenth-century Jesuit missions.[8] They belonged to the generation of the "Catholic Revival" that followed the great upheavals of the French Revolution in Europe. These male and female missionaries, most of whom originated from rural areas that had not, or barely, been impacted by the Industrial Revolution, felt called to contribute to the Catholic Church's universal missionary project, as coordinated from the Vatican by the Sacred Congregation of the Propagation of the Faith (*Propaganda Fide*). Convinced of the superiority of their civilization, religion, and race, nineteenth-century missionaries had a conservative and ultramontane worldview, based on the concept of a hierarchized and patriarchal Catholic Church, ruled with authority by the pope.[9] Only the successful development of devotion to the Virgin Mary[10] contributed to the "feminization" of the Catholic faith worldwide.[11] The proliferation of new female religious institutes, including female missionary societies, is another characteristic of the nineteenth-century Catholic church.[12] In China, Marian devotions and pilgrimages became a driving force behind the Catholic mission.[13]

In the years 1840-1860, missionaries were gradually able to officially return to China after a long period of prohibition from 1723. Chinese Christians had survived persecution thanks to the lay agency of male leaders and male and female catechists. Due to the extremely limited number of Chinese priests and clandestine foreign missionaries, Christian communities had learned to function on their own, receiving annual visits from itinerant priests.[14] After 1840-1860, the relationships between these "old Christians" and "new missionaries" often provoked misunderstandings that arose because the latter were keen to reassert their control, notably with regard to leadership, finances, and the role of women in the liturgy.[15] However, in Chinese society governed by Confucian rules, foreign missionaries were unable to work without Chinese priests, laymen or laywomen. After providing an introduction to gender inequality in traditional Chinese society, this section presents the various agents of the Catholic apostolate in late Qing China – foreign missionaries, Chinese Virgins, foreign nuns, and Chinese sisters – whose daily life had to be regulated by gendered spaces.

Gender discrimination in Chinese Confucian society

In his writings on kinship and religion in China, the British anthropologist Maurice Freedman (1929-1975) argued that being a woman in the traditional male-dominated Confucian society was a disadvantage. "Every aspect of her society and its values left the Chinese woman in no doubt on that score. In the family into which she was born she might indeed be well affectionately treated, but this favorable treatment rested on the paradox that she was merely a temporary member of it."[16] Once married, a woman was cut off from her birth family and physically "transported" to another space, the house of her husband's family; she legally passed under the control of her husband, who had claims on her labor and sexual services.[17] Her main task was to give birth to a boy to continue the husband's lineage.[18] Moreover, there was always a patriarch imbued with the customary law and Confucian values of propriety and order, who controlled their kinsmen and wives.[19]

Gender discrimination was a common social phenomenon in pre-modern China. Gender patterns and female virtues defined by Confucius 孔子 (551-479 BC) and his disciples were deeply ingrained in people's minds. According to the philosopher Mencius 孟子 (c. 372-289 BC), "man and woman should not touch hands when they give or receive things" (男女授受不亲 *nannü shoushou bu qin*). A reputable woman should not be touched by any man except her own husband, and young women should not be seen by adult male strangers. In her dissertation on *Christianity and Gender in South-East China*, Cai Xiang-yu summarizes:

> The ideal female virtues according to Confucian values were spelled out in such traditional texts as the *Family Regulations of Zhu Zi* (朱子治家格言 *Zhuzi zhi jia geyan*, 1617-1689), well known in all the Confucian households, or two elementary primers for boys and girls, *Tree Character Classic* (三字经 *Sanzi Jing*, thirteenth century) and *The Thousand Character Classic* (千字文 *Qianziwen*, AD 502-549). These books helped to shape the Confucian gender ideal in the mind of the common people.

Throughout her whole life, a Chinese woman was never independent. According to the "three obediences" (三从 *sancong*), she should obey her father and brothers before marriage (未嫁从父 *wei jia congfu*), her husband when

---

10 Boosted by the Marian apparition at the rue du Bac in Paris (1830), the proclamation of the Dogma of the Immaculate Conception (1854), and the Marian apparitions in Lourdes (1858).

11 Mínguez-Blasco, "Between Virgins and Priests: The Feminisation of Catholicism and Priestly Masculinity."

12 Langlois, *Le catholicisme au féminin*.

13 Clarke, *The Virgin Mary and Catholic Identities in Chinese History*, 51-82; Coomans, *Sheshan jiaotang xun cong*.

14 In 1810, there were about 210,000 Catholics in China, 7 bishops, 80 Chinese priests, and 23 foreign missionaries. See Camps, "Actors: Catholic Missionaries," 115-132; Charbonnier, "Chinese Catholics in the Early Nineteenth Century."

15 Standaert, "The Chinese Mission without Jesuits," 84-88 and 90-95.

16 Freedman, "The Family in China, Past and Present," 245. Also: Watson, "Afterword. Marriage and Gender Inequality."

17 Gao, "Women for Men: Confucianism and Social Injustice against Women in China."

18 Freedman, "Rites and Duties, or Chinese Marriage."

19 Gallagher, "Women and Gender."

married (既嫁从夫 *ji jia cong fu*), and her sons in widowhood (夫死从子 *fu si congzi*). Furthermore, the "four virtues" (四德 *side*) required of a woman by the Confucian values were morality (妇德 *fu de*), proper speech (妇言 *fu yan*), a modest manner (妇容 *fu rong*), and diligent work (妇功 *fu gong*). The "three obediences and four virtues" (三从四德 *sancong-side*) served as the criteria for Chinese family life; men used them as a yardstick to measure their wives' conduct and women tried to ensure that their behavior conformed to these rules.

The proper work for a woman was managing the household, but she should not be involved in the decision making about its important affairs. To acquire knowledge for the sake of gaining intelligence was not a female priority according to the old saying that "ignorance is woman's virtue" (女子无才便是德 *nüzi wu cai bian shi de*). If a woman was intelligent, she should assist her husband, complementing his shortcomings. The ideal relationship of a couple in a Confucian family was "the woman should admire the virtue of chastity, the man should model himself to those who have ability and wisdom; the husband guides, his wife follows". And "to treat each other with respect as a host treats his guest" (相敬如宾 *xiangjing rubin*) was a norm of behavior to achieve the harmony of a couple.[20]

The difficulties of missionary integration

A Catholic parish priest is not only the leader of the spiritual and material matters of the parish, above all he is "constituted as sacred minister by the sacrament of holy order".[21] "Through a special gift of the Holy Spirit, this sacrament enables the ordained to exercise a *sacred power* in the name and with the authority of Christ for the service of the People of God".[22] In the Catholic Church, this sacrament is exclusively reserved for men and gives priests an unparalleled status.

Nineteenth-century missionaries were exponents of the Western Catholic culture of the Catholic Revival, romantics drawn to adventure and martyrdom, anti-modern ultramontane militants obedient to the pope, imbued with a cultural superiority and national identity.[23] However, despite their special training, missionaries were not the "supermen" often depicted in propaganda literature. Loneliness was the most significant human problem encountered by parish priests in China [Figs. 6.3 and 6.4]. "Bushmen" (*broussards*), as the French Jesuits would call them, had very limited contact with other missionaries and foreigners and lived in remote places with local communities whose language and culture they did not share. They tended to criticize Chinese priests and were confronted with slow progress in their apostolate. Priests celebrated daily mass and did spiritual exercises, which varied from one missionary congregation to another. According to their letters, many were homesick, depressed, and anxious because of the insecurity. Internal reports reveal that several lacked obedience to their superiors, suffered from alcoholism, or behaved inappropriately with women, which led to a loss of authority and prestige.[24] The vicars apostolic and superiors tried by all kinds of means – correspondence, annual retreats, visits, etc. – to support the spiritual life of their missionaries, but were confronted with insufficient human resources and remoteness resulting from the great distances between Christianities.

Last but not least, the Catholic missionaries who came back to China from the 1840s onwards had to obey the ban on the Confucian ritual practice of venerating ancestors. This ban had been decided and confirmed by several popes during the first half of the eighteenth century and caused the Chinese Rites Controversy and all its fatal consequences for Christianity in China.[25] Accordingly, nineteenth-century missionaries asked Chinese Catholic converts to refrain from worshiping their ancestors in familial temples, cemeteries, or at home. This developed restrictions about lineage benefits and could lead to conflicts between Catholics and non-Catholics within their kin group because moral standards applied to every-

---

20 Cai, *Christianity and Gender in South-East China*, 5-7.
21 *Code of Canon Law. Book IV-1. The Sacraments*, VI, canon 1008.
22 *Compendium of the Catechism of the Catholic Church*, 323 (the sacrament of Holy Orders).
23 Dujardin, *Missionering en moderniteit*, 160-180.
24 Ibidem, 143-149.
25 Mungello, *The Chinese Rites Controversy*.
26 Examples from rural Jiangxi: Sweeten, *Christianity in Rural China*, 72-97.
27 Zurndorfer, "Polygamy and Masculinity in China."

one, especially in local society.[26] Confucian literati for whom filial piety was extremely important could only condemn Christianity in general and missionaries in particular. The Chinese Rites Controversy as implemented by missionaries was a segregating factor between Catholics and non-Catholics, regardless of gender.

Foreign missionaries confronted with gender segregation in China

While Catholic and Protestant missionaries had no choice but to accommodate Confucian family values and traditions, there were other social aspects of late Qing China that they could not accept in Christian families and excluded from their membership. First, missionaries condemned polygamy and strictly prohibited Christian men from taking concubines, which was the Chinese way of giving legal status to mistress(es) within established families and increasing the chance of having male offspring [Fig. 6.2].[27] The missionaries also objected to a baptized girl marrying a non-Catholic or, even worse, becoming a concubine or having to share her husband with a concubine. These situations were not uncommon in Christianized families for whom marriage remained a transaction. The missionaries also challenged the practice of foot-binding, which was not unrelated to polygamy, but was not systematically imposed to all women.[28] Second, opium addiction, most widespread among men, had disastrous consequences for families, leading to impoverishment and death. As the missionaries considered it a plague from the devil, they excluded opium smokers from Christian communities.[29] Cultivating opium was forbidden by the Holy See and missionaries had to withhold baptism from peasants who cultivated opium. Gambling, another plague in China, was also condemned by the Catholic Church. Third, the infanticide of new-born children, especially girls, who were commonly abandoned by poor families, deeply shocked the missionaries.[30] With the help of the Chinese Virgins, they tried to

save babies, or at least baptize them and give them a decent burial. This often provoked negative reactions from locals, who believed that missionaries were kidnapping the babies and that baptism caused death. Orphanages of the Holy Childhood were established in the district centers of the mission[31] to save abandoned babies and educate them as Catholics.[32] Through effective written and visual propaganda, often directed specifically at Western children, funds were raised throughout Europe [Fig. 6.5].[33]

From the seventeenth century onwards, Catholic missionaries faced considerable problems caused by the strict gender discrimination of traditional Chinese society, which prohibited them from approaching or talking to women, visiting families in their homes, or taking care of orphan girls [Fig. 6.4]. Preaching to and catechizing women was a form of education and stimulated individual thought, which was highly suspect. The sacrament of communion, which involved the priest placing the host in the communicant's mouth, was considered an unacceptable gesture of intimacy. The sacrament of confession, by definition a personal and secret dialogue with a priest in an isolated space, was misunderstood. As for the sacra-

6.2 Chinese scholar (literatus) and his family, including his wife, concubines, and two children. Jiangnan, late Qing. [Vanves, Compagnie de Jésus, Archives jésuites de France, FI, J3]

28 McMahon, "Polygyny, Bound Feet, and Perversion."
29 Lodwick, "Missionaries and Opium."
30 The first study on infanticide was published in 1878 by Father Gabriel Palatre 柏立德 SJ (1830-1878): L'infanticide et l'œuvre de la Sainte-Enfance en Chine.
31 For example: Borao Mateo, "Catholic Orphanages in Fujian."
32 Orphanages were sponsored by the Œuvre de la Sainte-Enfance, an international Catholic association founded in France in 1843 to save Chinese children. Its activity developed in all the Catholic mission fields and it became the Pontifical Association of the Holy Childhood in 1922.
33 Among others, Les petits Chinois ou la Sainte Enfance au Vicariat de Nankin, by the Father Gustave Gibert 壽瑞徵 SJ (1862-1936). Also: Harrison, "A Penny for the Little Chinese."

6.3 Father Pierre de Prunelé 晋都禄 SJ (1881-1969) and his catechist leaving a parish in the Pudong area to tour the mission stations, 1920s.
[Lyon, Oeuvres pontificales missionnaires, Iconographic collection, Shanghai]

6.4 New Year's greetings and benediction in the village of Gaojiazhuang 高家庄 (Kaokiatchoang, Shanxi), in front of the residence of a Dutch Franciscan missionary, undated. Notice the rope attached to the two trees, which marks the spatial segregation line between the men in front of the priest and the women to the left.
[Utrecht, Het Utrechts Archief, 1224: Dutch Franciscans, China mission, 294/56]

34 For example: Dannic, "Variété. Fiançailles à la vieille mode chinoise."
35 De Sica, *De Ratione agendi cum Sinensis*, for instance, includes chapters on "the benefit of private conversation with pagans and Christians" (2) and the "discretion and prudence necessary in entering the houses of the heathen" (6).
36 X, *Monita ad missionarios provinciae nankinensis*; Zi, *Parva rerum Sinensium adumbratio…*, and *Supplementum*, 1872.

ment of marriage, missionaries were confronted with all sorts of delicate situations, the details of which can be found in the letters they sent to their vicar apostolic for advice.[34] In the 1870s, the Jesuit missionaries of Jiangnan published several manuals in Latin for internal use on how to behave with the Chinese,[35] warnings to missionaries,[36] and how to resolve cases of consciousness,[37] all of which included gender considerations. The French vicar apostolic Adrien Languillat 郎懷仁 SJ (1808-1878) published a treaty on marriage in Chinese.[38] The missionaries understood that social pressure was much stronger on Christians who lived in "pagan" towns and villages alongside non-Christian families than in fully Christianized villages, where morality and solidarity developed more easily, no opium was cultivated or consumed, polygamy and gambling were prohibited, and children were not abandoned.

Consequently, the missionaries needed the help of "auxiliary" women, both Chinese Virgins for the evangelization of Chinese women and the apostolate in rural China, and Western missionary nuns for developing modern healthcare and education in urban hospitals, girls' schools, and Holy Childhood orphanages. Some missionary societies also had foreign and Chinese male auxiliaries, such as Jesuit coadjutor brothers,[39] or Franciscan brothers and tertiaries, who were often "controversial partners."[40] They took care of material tasks in the infirmary, gatehouse, laundry room, garden, etc. Others had technical talents and ran the mission printing presses or construction sites. The brothers had specific vocations; as they did not know Latin, they were excluded from the priesthood, preaching, or teaching, but their responsibilities in China gave them a level of autonomy they could never have achieved in Europe and which sometimes led to abuses. Foreign brothers from Europe were swiftly joined by Chinese brothers who knew the region and local dialects well. Historical sources and literature on the coadjutor brothers are much more limited than those on the Jesuit fathers.[41]

Chinese Virgins, foreign nuns, and Chinese sisters

Three different kinds of Catholic female religious communities developed over time in China: consecrated Chinese Virgins, foreign nuns belonging to female missionary institutes, and Chinese sisters belonging to both female missionary institutes and newly created indigenous female religious communities. Chinese women could also become nuns in the convents of foreign missionary societies, both active and contemplative. In a recent handbook chapter on "Women in the Chinese Catholic Church: local and foreign sisters and gender relations," Yu Zhang discusses the gaps and challenges in this area of research:

Regrettably, despite women's significant role in Catholicism, they have long been marginalized and neglected in research on this topic. We know very little about the lives of devout Chinese Catholic women before the twentieth century. The minimal materials published on these women raise more questions than they answer. Most studies have focused on prominent missionaries and elite male Chinese converts, ignoring the women involved in the missions. It is time to examine who Catholic women in China are, their roles in building Chinese Catholic communities, and their past and present lifestyles, aspirations, challenges, and struggles. These topics have been part of a broader enquiry into how Chinese Christians internalized a religion originating outside China and how they translated and appropriated the Church's institutionalization efforts. (…) Chinese Catholic women have since the seventeenth century walked a fine line between the enclosed lifestyle required by Confucian teachings and Western religious life in an increasingly globalized world.[42]

The Chinese Virgins were "Christian laywomen who consecrated their lives to the service of God and the mission; bound by a private vow of chastity, they continued to live with their families, where they instructed the women and children."[43] Their unusual religious vocation in Confucian society dated back to the seventeenth-century Jesuit mission. In the eighteenth century, French missionaries from Yunnan and Sichuan set down rules defining the specific apostolate of the Virgins, which consisted of external catechism and the care of abandoned girls. In 1832, the Holy See recognized the value of their apostolate, approved the rules for Virgins, and made them applicable to the whole of China.[44] In accordance with Confucian social rules, they lived with their families and operated as the main catechists of women and girls in local communities. Their role in the transmission of the Christian faith during the time of prohibition was crucial. However, their religious training and spiritual guidance remained basic and, according to Canon Law, they were unable to administer the sacraments. When the missionaries returned to China, the Virgins proved to be valuable as native female auxiliaries in the organization of specific liturgies and prayers for women, collecting abandoned babies, and baptizing them in secret. In an attempt to increase control over the Virgins and improve

37 X, *Appendices ad casus conscientiae resolutos*; De Sica, *Ad casus conscientiae resolutos*.
38 Languillat, *Sheng pei gui an*, 1865.
39 Moore, "Coadjutor Brothers on the Foreign Missions."
40 Dujardin, *Missionering en Moderniteit*, 140-143.
41 Coomans, "East Meets West on the Construction Site."
42 Zhang, "Women in the Chinese Catholic Church."
43 Most of this paragraph is based on the pioneering work of Tiedemann, "Controlling the Virgins: Female Propagators of the Faith and the Catholic Hierarchy in China" (quote p. 503). See also: Menegon, *Ancestors, Virgins, and Friars: Christianity as a Local Religion in Late Imperial China*.
44 From then on, Virgins would appear in the public space and were known by various names, such as *guniang* 姑娘, *chuanjiao guniang* 传教姑娘, *tongzhen guniang* 童贞姑娘, *zhennü* 贞女, and *gugu* 姑姑.

6.5 Six Chinese Virgins and forty-eight orphans in front of the Holy Childhood orphanage in Shanhou 山後 (Inner Mongolia), undated.
[Leuven, KADOC-KU Leuven, CICM Picture Archive: 18.2.1.5_11]

6.6 Group of fifteen Chinese Virgins working with Scheut Fathers in Inner Mongolia, undated.
[Leuven, KADOC-KU Leuven, CICM Picture Archive: 17.4.4.4_15]

6.7 Vernacular courtyard house used as the first convent of the Belgian sisters Franciscan Missionaries of Mary, established in Xiwanzi (Hebei) in 1898. Photo from Missions en Chine et au Congo, *13 (1901), 137.*
[Leuven, KADOC-KU Leuven, Heritage Library, KYB27]

45 Tiedemann, "Catholic religious communities of women (foreigners)."
46 Li, "Chinese Christian Virgins and Catholic communities of women."
47 Tiedemann, "Catholic religious communities of Chinese women," 589-590.
48 For example, at the Hôpital Sainte-Marie in Shanghai and the Sacred-Heart Hospital in Hangzhou, the convent and school of the Sisters of the Sacred Heart of Jesus in Shanghai. In Hong Kong, the built heritage of foreign missionary societies is better preserved because it has been used without interruption until today, despite undergoing transformations.

their identity, the French Jesuits of Jiangnan founded an indigenous congregation called *Vierges Présentandines* (later the Association of the Presentation of the Blessed Virgin) in 1855. Similar sisterhoods dependent on diocesan bishops provided Virgins with better religious education and disciplinary rules. In urban parishes with permanent priests, they lived in communities and worked as catechists, teachers, and caregivers in orphanages, homes for the elderly, and hospitals [Fig. 6.5]. Once they had made their permanent vow of chastity, Virgins were sent to remote rural mission stations that received priest visits only once or twice a year. There were usually two of them, living in a small house near the local chapel; they would have responsibility for the Catholic families in the village and their indispensable support for the mission and evangelism contributed greatly to the Church and Chinese society [Fig. 6.6].

From the 1860s onwards, French, Italian, Belgian, and other European nuns belonging to female missionary institutes began to arrive in China and were assigned to schools, hospitals, and orphanages [Fig. 6.7].[45] They lived a regular religious life in enclosed convents that included a chapel, living quarters, and a garden. Virgins came into contact with these convents and many were attracted to life in a communal environment, while others rejected the model [Fig. 6.8].[46]

There were in fact two ways in which Chinese women could enter religious communities. European congregations accepted indigenous candidates into their institutes, offering them moral and material security as well as a proven Rule. The foundation of indigenous congregations, especially for women, with their own Rules was another possibility. The creation of Chinese sisterhoods would not only advance work amongst women, especially in the countryside where foreign sisters could not go, but also accelerate the process of establishing an indigenous Chinese Catholic Church. This is, of course, an idea that had been promoted by the Vatican since at least the mid-nineteenth century.[47]

Needless to say, questions relating to the material living environment of these Chinese sisters and foreign nuns have not yet been posed in architectural or spatial terms – except in the case of Xujiahui in Shanghai, which will be discussed later. There is no doubt that few of their buildings have survived into the twenty-first century. During our fieldwork, however, we have seen some heritagized remains integrated into large urban complexes,[48] but also in unexpected places.[49] These huge gaps for the architectural historian are partially compensated by the missionary institutes' illustrated propaganda magazines, which contain valuable visual sources [Figs. 6.7, 6.8 and 6.9].

Accommodating urban compounds

The extremely complex and controversial question of land and real estate properties owned by Catholic missions in China in the years 1860-1949 will not be discussed here.[50] In short, after the Second Opium War, treaties authorized missionaries to acquire land and buildings, directly or through intermediaries, not only in the treaty ports but all over China. The same treaties ensured them the restitution of church property confiscated in the eighteenth century or, when not possible, compensation for these lost properties. In the case of both the acquisition and restitution of real estate, the missionary societies and local congregations became the owners of well-located buildings within cities. They had to adapt these to their needs, gradually enlarge them as they grew, increase them through active real estate strategies, and eventually often demolish and replace them with Western-style buildings, including churches. This process happened with varying degrees of speed depending on the success and location of the mission, but by the 1930s many traditional-style Chinese urban wooden buildings purchased in the nineteenth century had been replaced by modern multi-story masonry buildings. Old plans and photos, when they exist, are the main sources for studying this process.

Traditional Chinese urban architecture develops around inner courtyards whose layout is dictated by orientation and hierarchy of function [Fig. 6.10].[51] This spatial organization and the regular bay-structured buildings suited the rational mind of Western missionaries, who could distribute their residence, the boys' and girls' schools, orphanage, rooms for elderly, pharmacy, and ancillary functions around different courtyards, according to a clear segregation of sexes. We will see that determining the location of the church was most crucial, as it had to be at the intersection of several courtyards and large enough to accommodate both genders under the same roof while maintaining separate spaces and accesses.

Gradual transformations

An exceptional article published in 1908 describes and accurately identifies each room in the mission compound in the prefecture city of Anshun 安顺市 (Ganchouen, Guizhou), and specifies that it will make the reader "acquainted with the residence of Anshun and also with the broad outline of the organization of other important missionary residences", i.e., their general orientation and gendered spatial layout.[52] It also includes a Chinese-style plan from 1869 and a Western-style ground plan from 1906, a comparison

6.8 Western-dressed Chinese Daughter of Charity of Saint Vincent de Paul doing the laundry with orphans in a convent in Zhejiang, undated.
[Paris, Archives historiques de la Congrégation de la Mission, Iconographic collection]

6.9. A feminine place for Marian spiritual resourcing: the convent chapel of the Daughters of Charity of Saint Vincent de Paul at the Sainte-Marie Hospital in Shanghai, late 1910s.
[Paris, Archives historiques de la Congrégation de la Mission, Iconographic collection]

49 For example: the dispensary of the Sisters of Saint Joseph in Xuanhua.
50 Chen, "La question des propriétés immobilières et foncières."
51 Liu, *La Maison chinoise*, 110-171.
52 Faguet, "La résidence de Ganchouen," 33. In all likelihood, the name of the author is misspelled and should be Father Jules Faguais 樊儒略 MEP (1847-1902), a missionary to Sichuan who passed away six years before the article was published, however. On MEP in Guizhou, see Launay, *Histoire des missions de Chine. Mission du Kouy-Tcheou*, 3.

6.10 Panorama of the city of Anshun (Guizhou) showing the main street and dense network of courtyard houses, around 1900.
[Paris, Institut de recherche France-Asie / Missions étrangères de Paris, photo box China 17]

53 Faguet, "La résidence de Gan-Chouen," 33. Father Lamy was the parish priest of Anshun for forty-three years and is to be credited with all the work.
54 Coomans, "Gender-Designed Catholic Churches in North China."
55 Faguet, "La résidence de Gan-Chouen," 38 (translated from the French).
56 This orphanage could accommodate up to two hundred children, but turned out to be too small. Father Lamy obtained other buildings to establish a second orphanage in Anshun.
57 The premises for the elderly were located near the women's main gate and at the corner of the courtyard between the church and the vegetable garden.

of which shows the different ways of representing space, as well as the evolution of the buildings, gendered spaces, and circulation. The complex was the former residence of the local governor (*daotai* 道台) of Anshun and had been donated to the Paris Foreign Mission Society by the governor-general of Yunnan and Guizhou in 1865 [Fig. 6.11]. Father Eugène Lamy 納密 MEP (1841-1909) "transformed it into a missionary residence, church, orphanage, convent, and school; little by little this transformation became clearer, increased to reach the near perfection to which it is today".[53]

The 1869 plan shows the initial conversion of the governor's residence and identifies its main components [Fig. 6.11]. To the south, the outer courtyard is a space at the intersection of the main street, marked by two gateways and a screen wall. Only open to men, the gatehouse provides access to the courtyard of the boys' orphanage. To the north, a wooden gallery from the former residence is marked as the "location of the future church". Further to the north, the walled courtyard, governor's formal hall, and garden serve as the missionaries' residence and a temporary chapel. To the west, an elongated plot enclosed by a wall includes a building for the orphaned girls and the Chinese Virgins. Between the men's and women's compounds, a narrow passage for women connects the main street to the temporary chapel and the location of the future church. This passage also serves as a buffer zone between the orphanages for boys and girls.

The 1906 plan shows how the complex develops additional courtyards, two-story buildings, and more elaborate segregated circulation [Fig. 6.12]. The outer courtyard has disappeared and the men's gatehouse remains the only access to the boys' orphanage, church, and residence. The women's compound is completely reorganized around four courtyards run by the Virgins: a small courtyard with a parlor from which one could either access the girls' orphanage to the west or to a service courtyard to the north. Serving as a buffer zone between both orphanages, the service courtyard is bordered by a gallery connecting the women's main gate and church, in a similar way to the women's passage to the temporary chapel in the 1869 plan. The nave of the church is divided into segregated parts for men and women, each connected with their respective orphanages and main gates.[54] East of the church, the missionaries' courtyard is connected to the boys' orphanage, sacristy and a room where female parishioners and Virgins could be confessed by a priest. The article mentions a small window and a bell near the sacristy: "when women want to speak to the missionary, they ring the bell, and it is through this window that the father sees them and chats with them."[55]

If the spaces allocated to men and women are strictly segregated from the street entrances to the church, a comparison of the spaces shows that the boys' courtyard and classrooms are larger than those of the girls, which also include the rooms of the Virgins and a school for external girls.[56] The female spaces are obviously more cramped and more populated, but the girls had the opportunity to work in the vegetable garden. Each courtyard has its own sanitary facilities. Elderly men and women contributed to maintaining good order in the complex by monitoring the comings and goings.[57]

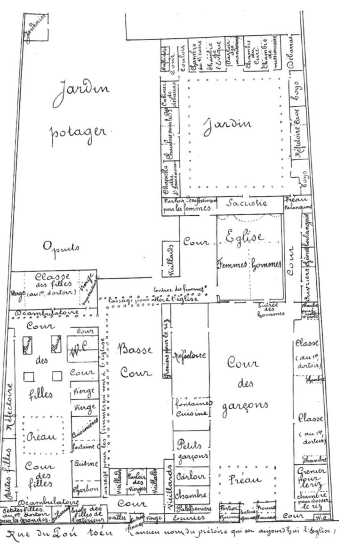

6.11 Former governor's residence in Anshun, converted into a mission, Chinese-style plan dated 1869: 1. main street, 2. outer courtyard, public space, 3. main gate with pharmacy (left) and parlor (right), 4. boys' orphanage with dormitories on both sides, 5. axial paved path through the playgrounds, 6. location of the future church, 7. temporary chapel, 8. missionaries' residence, 9. procuratory of the mission, 10. garden, 11. passageway or women's access to the chapel and future church, 12. girls' orphanage, 13. vegetable garden. Reproduced in Faguet, "La résidence de Gan-Chouen" and in Launay, Mission du Kouy-Tcheou, 3, Pl. III. [Original colour plan: Paris, Institut de recherche France-Asie / Missions étrangères de Paris, 2772]

6.12 Western-style plan of the mission of Anshun in 1906, reproduced in Faguet, "La résidence de Gan-Chouen" and in Launay, Mission du Kouy-Tcheou, 3, Pl. IV. [KU Leuven, Sabbe Library of Theology: B266.51]

Arranged around an enclosed garden, the missionaries resided in the complex's finest buildings, conducive to rest and meditation, which were located farthest from street noise, the orphans, and the Virgins.

Re-claiming late Ming missionary property

To some extent, the rational Western spatial organization around inner and outer courtyards adapted well to the traditional Chinese courtyard system. We might say that in China, Catholic gender segregation was accommodated to the spatial organization of Confucian-based courtyard houses. The main problem, however, was the location of the church, which, as the most important building, had to be on the northern side of the main courtyard and accessible to everybody. As long as the missionaries were in a phase of integration and adaptation, they could be satisfied with a reused Chinese building, but as soon the community grew, large Western-style churches with bell towers that dominated the urban skyline were erected. Towers affirmed the identity of a new religion from abroad and aroused the pride of the Christians, while sparking the curiosity or animosity of "pagans".

The case of the historical county of Xinjiang 新绛县, formerly Jiangzhou 绛州 (Kiangchow, Shanxi), offers a good example of spatio-temporal stratification over four centuries of Christian presence. In 1620, Jesuits reached Xinjiang, managed to settle in the viceroy's residence – which legitimized the mission and gave it great prestige – and began to evangelize Shanxi.[58] After their expulsion in 1724, the buildings were reassigned to higher education and hosted the Dong Yong Academy 东雍书院. In the 1860s, Italian Franciscans recovered the buildings, which were taken over by Dutch Franciscans from the vicariate apostolic of Lu'an 潞安 in 1890.[59] From then on, the complex was developed into three walled compounds of several courtyards each: the parish compound, including an old Ming hall used as a church and the missionaries' residence, the women's compound for the Little Sisters of Saint Joseph from Heerlen (The Netherlands),[60] and the compound for the boys' school [Fig. 6.13]. Old photos show the remarkable location of these buildings on the upper loess terrace within the walled city, whose skyline was dominated by the single pagoda of Longxing Temple 龙兴寺, dating from the Tang dynasty [Fig. 6.14]. The main gate of each compound opened onto a street along the southern edge of the terrace. When women went to the church, they had to leave their compound to access the parish compound from the street.

In 1936, Xinjiang became the seat of a new prefecture apostolic led by the Dutch prefect Quintinus Pessers 孔昭明 OFM (1896-1995). It took him four years to erect a Gothic cathedral, on the easternmost side of the old parish buildings, the most favorable location as far as the cityscape was concerned. The Japanese invasion interrupted the work, which was completed in 1940.[61] The pre-existing gender division with the Dutch sisters and schools required some adaptation in order to fit a cathedral compound with an episcopal residence. From then on, the cathedral's façade with two Gothic spears became a second landmark on the urban skyline in competition with the old pagoda [Fig. 6.15].

Growing across the main street

The two aforementioned cases in which previous structures were accommodated have demonstrated the challenges faced by the missionaries when it came to segregating gender, especially in differentiating movement between the street and church. Despite inner walls and buffer zones, promiscuity became a problem as soon as communities began to grow. It then became necessary to purchase land in the neighborhood to relocate the women's activities. The church remained the only space where the whole community gathered on certain occasions and according to specific rules.[62]

One scenario involved purchasing land across a side or back street on which to develop the women's compound, which included the girls' school, orphanage, and Virgins' convent. As in Guangzhou, where the women's compound was east of the cathedral compound, separated by a narrow street [Figs. 3.10 and 3.11], and in the North Cathedral of Beijing, where a street separated the women from the rear side (north) of the cathedral compound [Figs. 3.12 and 3.13]. According to Chinese geomancy, a church should be established on the north side of an east-west street, so that its main façade faces south.[63] The case of the prefecture city of Puyang 濮阳市 (Kaizhou, southeast Zhili, now northeast Henan) shows a radically different spatial layout developed on either side of the main street.[64] In a letter from 1892, Father Émile Japiot 畢如春 SJ (1849-1902) describes the compound's early spatial organization and his strategy for interacting with the Chinese through a hall for receiving mandarins, a pharmacy-dispensary offering Chinese and Western medicine, and a boys' school.[65] A catechumenate was also erected for preparing converts for baptism. The letter mentions neither women and Virgins, nor girls and orphans. The Boxers razed the mission of Kaizhou in 1900, but a sketched plan from around 1910 shows how new mission compounds were organized on either side of the main east-west street, benefiting from governmental compensation [Fig. 6.16]:

> The development of Catholic works in the town of *K'aitcheou* (south of our Mission): church, college, two schools for pagans, hospice, orphanage, school for Virgins.
> The works of men are all south of the street; the works of women are all north of the street, except for the hospice for elderly women. This is only the main parish; there is another parish (the *Sikie*) in the western quarter. Twenty years ago, there was nothing in *K'aitcheou*.[66]

The large Gothic church with its axial tower facing north, chancel turned to the south, and wide transept still exists and confirms the unusual orientation mentioned on the plan. Located in the middle of the main compound, the church is preceded on the street side by

6.13 Mission of Xinjiang (Shanxi) on the highest terrace within the city wall, seen from the south. On the back of the photos a missionary has identified the three compounds from right to left as "residence of the parish priest / sisters / school, my house".
[Utrecht, Het Utrechts Archief, 1224: Dutch Franciscans, China mission, 290/8]

6.14 Mission of Xinjiang (Shanxi) on the highest terrace within the city wall, seen from the west.
[Utrecht, Het Utrechts Archief, 1224: Dutch Franciscans, China mission,288/40]

6.15 Mission of Xinjiang (Shanxi) with the cathedral completed in 1940, seen from the south-west.
[Utrecht, Het Utrechts Archief, 1224: Dutch Franciscans, China mission, 290/8-291/43]

58 The famous scholar Father Alfonso Vagnone 高一志 SJ (1568-1640) died in Xinjiang in 1640.
59 Kramer, *De Nederlandse Minderbroeders.*
60 The Dutch Sisters of Xinjiang ran dispensaries, a hospital, kindergarten, orphanage, home for the elderly, school, and an "ouvroir."
61 Coomans, Xu, and Zhang, "Imposing and Provocative."
62 Coomans, "Gender Designed Catholic Church Architecture in Northern China."
63 Jung, *Le missionnaire constructeur…*, 2; Coomans and Xu, *Building Churches in Northern China*, 125.
64 Established in 1890 by the French Jesuits, the mission was taken over by Hungarian Jesuits in 1935. See Strong, *A Call to Mission*, vol. 1, 379-425, and vol. 2, 195-235.
65 Japiot, "Lettre…," 35-38.
66 Legend of the undated [c. 1910] plan: AFSI, Fonds iconographique, series F1, S2, no. 2 (translated from the French).

6.16 Sketched plan of the mission in Puyang, c. 1910: 1. main east (left) – west (right) street of Puyang, 2. street to the south, 3. compound main gate, 4. church, 5. Jesuit residence, 6. parlor, 7. school for "little pagans boys", 8. college, 9. chicken yard (buffer), 10. elderly women, 11. school for "little pagan girls", 12. ancillary buildings and worksite, 13. orphanage, 14. chapel, 15. Virgins' school, 16. Virgins' garden. [Vanves, Compagnie de Jésus, Archives jésuites de France, cartes et plans serie F1, S2, no. 2]

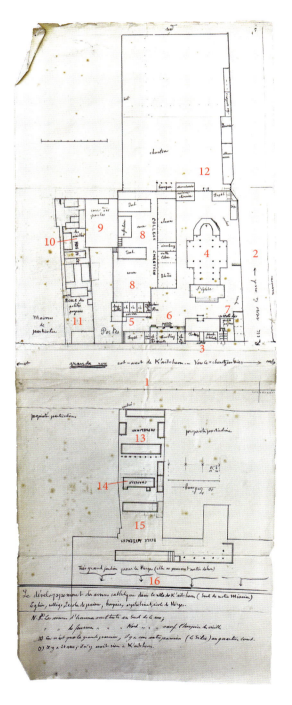

67 Rome, ARSI, China plans, no number: *Delineatio construendae residentiae cum scholis in Missionae Taming Provinciae Hungariae in oppido Puyanghsien (Hopeh)*, approved by Father Nicolas Szarvas 查宗夏 SJ (1890-1965), superior of the mission.

the gatehouse, "school for little pagan boys," parlor (*keting*), where the vicar apostolic could welcome the local authorities, and the father's residence. East of the church, the Catholic college's compound included classrooms, dormitories, a refectory, and a Chinese kitchen. East of the college and separated from it by a buffer courtyard, two female compounds included a hospice for elderly women and a "school for little pagan girls." North of the church, a large unbuilt piece of land surrounded by ancillary buildings could be used for further development, but was obviously not assigned to women. In the second half of the 1930s, the French Jesuits were replaces by Hungarian Jesuits who developed projects for the construction of a new residence and boys' school.[67]

The Virgins' compound was on the northern side of the street. The first courtyard was an orphanage, followed by several courtyards with a chapel and the school for the Virgins. North of that school building, the plan mentions "a very large garden for the Virgins (they can't go outside)." This secluded area for educating the Virgins was located in the heart of the block. Having their own chapel, these women had no reason to cross the street or to go to the main church. The segregation was nearly total, although they were able to see the church tower and hear its bells.

Gendered topography in rural Christianities

The location of women in the parish compound could not give rise to any kind of gossip or scandal. It was therefore vital to maintain as much distance as possible between the priest's residence and the boys' school on the one hand, and the dwelling of the Virgins, the girls' orphanage and school, on the other. Women, of course, had access to the church at specific times, but their presence in other areas had to be regulated and enclosed by walls and gates. Although the general principle of segregation was clear, its application varied depending on local factors, such as the rural or urban context, the type of Christianity – a Christian village or a community in a mixed village –, the topography, or the size of the mission jurisdiction.

Missionary archives preserve many photos of rural missions established across northern and southern China, which show that the layout of rural Catholic parishes was not left to chance but resulted from systematic planning around identical components. In addition to a favorable topography and orientation compatible with geomancy,[68] the enclosure, its defense, gendered subdivision, and the prominent position of the church were determining factors. The Chinese south-north orientation or the traditional east-west Christian orientation of the church determined the layout of the courtyards and areas devolved to men and women. The church was usually the last building to be erected, and a chapel or provisional church served for worship until the community had reached a critical mass and the permanent presence of a priest was ensured. Further developments, such as the establishment of an orphanage and women's convent, continued the construction on the basis of the initial gendered layout.

The male core of Christianity

The basic type of established rural parish consisted of a chapel or church with an adjacent residence for the priest, both into an enclosed space delimited by a wall broken by a gate. For practical reasons related to his ministry, the priest was required to live near the church in a "residence" suitable to his status and prestige.[69] Some residences were vernacular houses, but as soon as missionaries had the means, they would build Western- or hybrid-style residences, and stimulated the parishioners to erect a foreign-style church. This would trigger the curiosity of the locals, who had never seen this type of architecture in their rural areas, as well as their admiration of the missionary's garden, the rockery of the Lourdes' grotto, etc. [Fig. 6.17].

Residences included a room in which the missionary would sleep and work, as well as a living room, where he could eat and welcome guests. On the plains of northern China and Inner Mongolia, rooms were equipped with heatable brick beds (kang 炕); in the Loess Plateau, cave houses were often used as residences. The kitchen and toilet were either integrated into the residence or annexed. More important parishes were served by two priests–one foreign and the other Chinese, or an older and younger father–and larger residences could have an upper floor with additional rooms to accommodate visiting missionaries.

One or several servants called "boys" (pédissèques in French) lived in the kitchen or another annex and took care of the kitchen, heating and water, garden, vegetable garden, and stable. The priest could also count on the presence of a Chinese catechist for social and spiritual matters regarding the local Catholics. The catechist visited families in every village or hamlet inhabited by Catholics who belonged to the parish. If necessary, the parish could provide one or several men to monitor the missionary's safety around the clock, as the residences often attracted brigands in search of money. These trusted men oversaw comings and goings, served as armed bodyguards, kept the priest informed about what was going on in the parish, and helped him in his practical tasks, including dealing with the local authorities and supervising construction works. The catechists and, if necessary, a bodyguard would accompany the missionary on his long journeys to visit other Christianities [Fig. 6.3].

A boys' school and playground were often included in the enclosed area. Boys from the village would attend daily to receive basic instruction from a teacher paid by the mission who lived close to the parish compound

6.17 Mission of the Scheut Fathers in Halagou 哈拉沟 (northwestern Hebei), Gothic church designed by Father Alphonse De Moerloose around 1916 and Western-style residence. Photo by Father Jacques de Vigneron CICM, c. 1925. [Leuven, KADOC-KU Leuven, CICM Picture Archive: 17.4.4.3_03]

68 See chapter 3: Coomans, "Islands on the Mainland."
69 "Résidence" in French. Catholic missionary sources never use the words "rectory" or "presbytery," "cure" or "presbytère" (French), "pastorij" (Dutch), etc., which are used in Europe to designate the house of a parish priest.

6.18 Mission of Weiyuankou 韦源口 *village (Hubei), around 1920. Writing on the back of the photo reads: "This represents one of the final stages in the developments of a mission, for we now have here grounds and a complete combination of church, school, and mission-home, with a Chinese house outside the wall for the teacher and his family."*
[Utrecht, Het Utrechts Archief, 1224: Dutch Franciscans, China mission, 8-23-2]

6.19 Mission of the Scheut Fathers in Laohugou 老虎沟 *village (formerly Jehol, now Hebei), around 1900. The L-shaped vernacular-style church stands in the middle; the missionary's residence is in the prolongation of the men's nave (right) and the girls' orphanage and Virgins building to the side of the women's nave (left).*
[Leuven, KADOC-KU Leuven, CICM Picture Archive: Album Joseph Segers, 18.3.4_02]

6.20 Mission of Qianjia 钱家 *(Ziéka, Pudong, Shanghai), around 1910.*
[Vanves, Compagnie de Jésus, Archives jésuites de France, FCh 362]

6.21 Mission of the Franciscans in Yaojiazhuang 姚嫁莊 *village (Shanxi), around 1910. The church and residence are on a terrace, while the schools for boys and girls (left) are partially carved into the Loess.*
[Utrecht, Het Utrechts Archief, 1224: Dutch Franciscans, China mission, 289/52]

6.22 Mission of Zhangpingzi 長坪子 *(Tchangpintze, Sichuan). On the back of the photo, Father Lucien Boiteux* 何维光 *MEP (1902-1944) wrote: "In the center, the church. To the right of the church (left in the photo), my dwellings, from where I draw these lines for you. Behind (we can't see it), the boys' school. To the left of the church (right of the photo), the girls' school. June 21, 1928."*
[Lyon, Oeuvres pontificales missionnaires, Fonds iconograhique]

[Fig. 6.18]. To make the school more attractive, the boys would receive rice at lunchtime, which was prepared in a kitchen shared with the residence. The priest taught catechism to the boys, preferably in the church. After school, the classroom could be used to teach male catechumens preparing for baptism. There was usually a stable near the residence or in a separate ancillary courtyard – the missionary had need of a horse or a donkey to visit the Christianities in his parish.

The spatial arrangement of all these components depended on the topography and land available. On the dry plains of northern China and Mongolia, vast areas could be purchased and laid out according to the strict south-north orientation dictated by the climate [Fig. 6.17 and Fig. 6.19]. The churches tended to be low-rise and both the residences and schools had only one floor. In the water and paddy field landscape of the Songjiang area and Yangtze River delta, the white volumes of churches and residences contrasted with the vernacular houses of the Christianities [Fig. 6.20]. In the regions of the Loess Plateau (Shanxi, Shaanxi, and Gansu) many residences, schools, and chapels were housed in cave dwellings (*yaodong* 窑洞), while the churches were erected on available terraces and oriented depending on the topography [Fig. 6.21]. In the mountain regions of south and southwest China, parish compounds were erected on terraces, making them visible from a great distance. The diversity of building types and styles included colorful hybrid churches in Guizhou and Sichuan provinces [Figs. 3.15 and 6.22] and U-shape Western-style compounds of southwest Hubei [Figs. 6.23 and 6.26]. This overview is incomplete as the Chinese landscape varies infinitely, but it suffices to illustrate the preponderant influence of topographic and geomantic rules on the spatial arrangement of parish compounds.

Women in less prominent locations

An analysis of the spatial arrangements of female buildings and compounds presents greater challenges as photographs tend to focus on churches and residences. Groups of orphan girls accompanied by Chinese Virgins or nuns are depicted rather than buildings because photos were used to communicate with Western readers about the work of the Holy Childhood for fundraising purposes. When depicted, female buildings in rural areas seem of poorer architectural quality and smaller, despite the fact that more people lived in them than in the male compounds [Figs. 6.5 and 6.6].

In villages, the girls' school, orphanage, and Virgins' dwelling were strictly segregated from the male compound and included their own kitchen and sanitary facilities. Orphan girls took care of the vegetable garden and laundry, and were involved in a range of

manual work such as spinning, weaving, sewing, basketry, etc., which ensured a financial return for their sustenance. Arrangements between male and female courtyards and compounds varied according to the local social customs and topography:

- Female buildings could be on a different site, but close enough for them to attend church easily. In mountain regions such as western Hubei, they were less prominently located than the church and residence [Figs. 6.23-6.26].
- Female buildings could also be in a proper precinct adjacent to that of the men, or separated from it by a buffer space.
- Female buildings within the same compound as the male buildings were separated from them by the church. The church was in the middle, with boys' and girls' schools on either side, which, when they were of a certain size, had their own enclosure. The priest's residence was always on the opposite side to the girls' school and the teachers did not live in the compound [Fig. 6.22].

A rural parish not yet supplied with its definitive church can be seen in rare photographs; the site reserved for the church forms a void in the middle of the compound's gendered layout. A panoramic view of the village of Zhuizishan 锥子山 (formerly Jehol, today Hebei) shows the empty space set aside for the future church, while a part of the residence was used as a temporary church [Fig. 6.27]. We do not know if the church was eventually built or how it was oriented, but the general layout suggests it was east-west planned, with its main entrance facing the main gate and valley.

6.23 The Franciscan mission in Hualiling 花梨岭 (Enshi Autonomous Prefecture, Hubei) c.1905: the fortified buildings for men -church, residence, boys' school- are on top of a small hill while the buildings for women -convent, chapel, orphanage- on the other side of the valley are not fortified and differently oriented.
[Leuven, KADOC-KU Leuven, Picture Archive of the Flemish Franciscans: 1626]

6.24 Franciscan parish of Shazidi 沙子地 (Chatseti, Hubei), with a comment on the back of the photo: "view of the church, residence (behind the church) and the girls' orphanage (at the bottom of the mound)," c. 1905.
[Leuven, KADOC-KU Leuven, Picture Archive of the Flemish Franciscans: 1626]

6.25 Compared to Fig. 6.23, the old buildings of the former Hualiling mission and their gendered settlement on both sides of the valley are well preserved. Photo taken by Yu Lina in May 2023.
[Peking University, School of Archaeology and Museology]

6.26 Franciscan parish of Xishahe 细沙河 (Sichaho, Badong county, Hubei), at an altitude of 1,400 meters in the mountains, with a comment on the back of the photo: "left, the church and the residence, and the boys' school; right the girls' school."
[Leuven, KADOC-KU Leuven, Picture Archive of the Flemish Franciscans: 1626]

6.27. Gendered compound of the mission of Zhuizishan 锥子山 (Hebei) seen from the south-east. The main gate opens onto the central square and a slightly raised plot is earmarked for the future church. Comments on the back of the photo identify the kitchen, the missionary's residence, the boys' school on the north side (right), the cemetery, and the vegetable garden further north. South of the square were the Virgins and the girls' school.
[Leuven, KADOC-KU Leuven, CICM Picture Archive: 18.3.3_23]

Together behind fortified walls

The permanent insecurity during the late Qing Empire made Christian villages easy targets for brigands and rebels. Because these rural communities could not count on the intervention of the imperial army and were too far away from the treaty ports to ask for Western military protection, they organized themselves by erecting fortified walls, buying rifles, and training guards. When the village was besieged, the women, children, and elderly took refuge in the church and prayed for the community's salvation, while the missionaries and men fought around the walls. However, this failed to prevent Christians from being massacred in their churches without distinction of gender or age. When the Boxers reached Beijing, about 100 foreigners and 3,300 Chinese Christians, including some 2,700 women and children, found refuge within the precinct of Beitang Cathedral. During the siege from June 14 to August 16 1900, more than 400 were killed or died of disease and starvation. Most of the women and children who gathered within the cathedral were saved, but the French Daughters of Charity and the Holy Childhood orphans who were in the women's compound, separated by a street from the cathedral complex [see Fig. 3.12], suffered the greatest harm. The gender segregation that was meant to protect women and orphans made them easier targets.[70] Two cases of fortified rural Christian villages from East China and North China are discussed in this section, based on rare bird's-eye views that give a good overall sense of how women and men remained segregated, even when included within the larger walled mission complexes.

Houjiazhuang 侯家庄 (Howkiachwan, Jiangsu), founded in 1890 by French Jesuits,[71] became a Christian village in the prefecture city of Xuzhou 徐州 (Süchow, Jiangsu).[72] Due to its location on the border of Jiangsu, Shandong, Henan, and Anhui provinces, the region was very unstable and controlled by clans, secret societies, and gangs of brigands. The Big Swords Society 大刀会 followed by the Boxers 义和拳 pillaged the region, targeting foreigners and Christians. The mission of Houjiazhuang was razed in 1896, soon rebuilt, and resisted attacks in 1897 and 1900.[73] A perspective drawing from the south-east shows a rational system of outer and inner walls and fortified gates [Fig. 6.28], which insured a physical defense against brigands and strict gender segregation.[74] The outer wall depicted in the foreground includes two distinctly enclosed compounds for men and women. The former is dominated by the church, its two crenellated towers, and the two-story

70 Clark, *China Gothic*, 117-124.
71 By Father Leopold Gain 艾赉沃 SJ (1852-1930), See X, *Le père L. Gain*, 23-78.
72 In 1931, the district of Xuzhou was detached from the vicariate apostolic of Nanjing and entrusted to Canadian Jesuits from Québec. In 1935, Xuzhou became a vicariate apostolic and in 1946 a diocese. See Coomans, "Islands on the Mainland," Figs. 3.4, 6 and 3.5.
73 X, *Le père L. Gain*, 69; Renaud, *Süchow, diocèse de Chine*, 222, 232.
74 Renaud, *Süchow, diocèse de Chine*, 98-123, Fig. between p. 158-159.

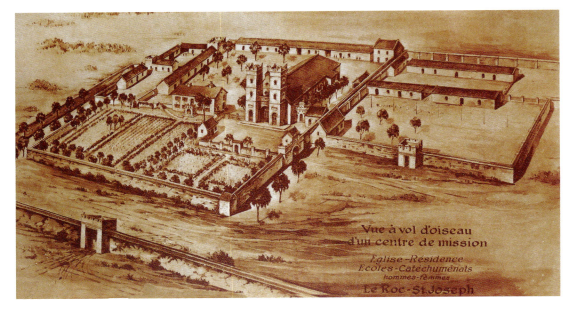

6.28 The mission of the Jesuits in Houjiazhuang 侯家庄 (Jiangsu) juxtaposed a large walled compound for men, including the church, with a smaller, walled compound for women, both enclosed by an outer wall. Drawing from: Renaud, Süchow, diocèse de Chine, 158-159. [Leuven, KU Leuven, Sabbe Library of Theology: B266.51]

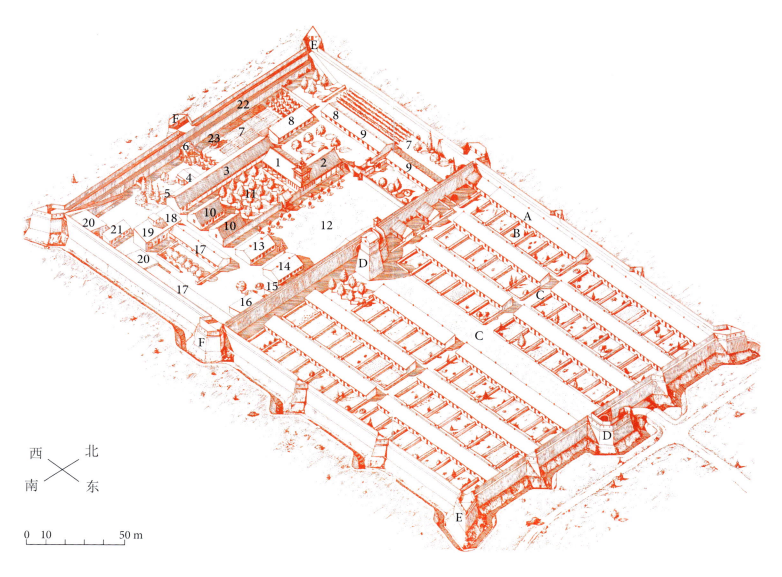

6.29 Fortified village of Xiaoqiaopan 小桥畔 (Shaanxi province), drawing by W. J. Capers, around 1970, after documents collected by father Carlo Van Melckebeke and father Jozef Van Hecken. Axonometric view from the south-east. Published in Carlo Van Melckebeke, Service social de l'Église en Mongolie, 1968, 68-69.
[Leuven, KADOC-KU Leuven, Heritage Library: KB9322]

A. houses of Christians
B. courtyard in front of individual houses
C. street
D. large bastions in front of the gates
E. corner bastion
F. small bastion

1. church of the men
2. church of the women
3. house of the missionaries
4. kitchen
5. annex to the room of the priest
6. grotto of Our Lady of Lourdes
7. vegetable garden and vines
8. Holy Childhood and Chinese Virgins
9. girls' school
10. missionaries' bedrooms
11. inner courtyard of the residence
12. outer courtyard
13. servants' room
14. managers' office
15. little storage
16. stable
17. boys' school
18. barn
19. mill
20. barn for straw
21. workshops and storages
22. first earthen wall
23. well

residence, to the north-west of which are the courtyards for the boys' orphanage and school, and ancillary buildings. The latter includes the Virgins' building, girls' orphanage, and school. It is worth noticing that the section where the compounds are contiguous is separated by a narrow buffer zone between two parallel walls. Because both compounds had no direct communication, the women going to church had to leave their enclosure through a gate and enter the men's enclosure through another gate to reach the church's enclosed forecourt.

The Christianity of Xiaoqiaopan 小桥畔 (Shaanxi), the most famous among the numerous fortified Christian villages in the then provinces of Mongolia, Gansu, and Jehol, was founded in 1878 by Belgian Scheut Fathers for Han converts and fortified against Muslim attacks from Gansu. It was therefore surrounded by a solid earth wall.[75] This remarkable rationally designed village formed a rectangle of 150 by 250 meters; a transversal wall divided its inner area of 3.75 hectares into two halves [Fig. 6.29]. The eastern part, a perfect square measuring 150 x 150 meters, contained about sixty row houses, all south-oriented with individual front courtyards, symmetrically ordered on either side of a central street connecting the village's main entrance to the mission compound. The western half or mission compound, 150 x 100 meters, was gender divided into several parts. Across the main square stood the church and missionary residence enclosure, arranged around an inner garden. East of the square, the Holy Childhood orphanage, a house of Chinese diocesan sisters of the Congregation of Mary 圣母院, and a girls' school were arranged around two smaller courtyards. The boys' school and farm buildings were on the opposite side. The areas between the earth wall, residence, and women's buildings were used for growing vegetables and fruit, while the area between the earth wall and the boys' school included ancillary buildings. The centrally located church of Xiaoqiaopan had an unusual L-shape and formed the intersection between the two gendered areas.[76]

Women at the edge of the cathedral compound

The seats of their ecclesiastical circumscriptions were established by bishops in provincial capitals or other significant cities, where they developed built complexes with elaborate architectural programs around a prominent cathedral church. Cathedral compounds were a predominantly male world and included the bishop's residence and administration, the diocesan seminary, central services (guesthouse, infirmary, pharmacy, printing house), and ancillary buildings (carpentry, other workshops, etc.). The cathedral was usually located in the center of the complex and was accessible from all sides, which avoided complicated circulation systems and unwanted encounters, including with laymen and women. The female compound was at the edge of the cathedral complex or was detached but close to it, and could include several different female communities. The cathedral's central position often constituted a barrier to the promiscuity of women with the bishop's compound and the seminary, in particular.

The two most remarkable cathedral complexes erected in late Qing China are the Sacred Heart Cathedral in Guangzhou and the North Cathedral in Beijing.[77] In both cases, the main cathedral compound and women's compound were separated by a buffer street: east of the cathedral in Guangzhou [Figs. 3.10 and 3.11] and at the back or north side in Beijing [Figs. 3.12 and 3.13].

Three additional and lesser-known cases showing different configurations are examined here, based on plans with detailed identification. Unlike the French Foreign Mission Society in Guangzhou and the Lazarists in Beijing, the Jesuits in Xianxian and the Franciscans in Lu'an established their cathedral compounds on the outskirts of small cities.[78] In Daming, the third case, the Jesuits did not design a cathedral complex, but the cathedral built subsequently resulted in an unusual spatial setting and adaptations.

75 The six-meter-high earth wall, six-meters-wide at its base, with a dry moat, bastions, parapet walks, and battlements was completed in 1884, extended in 1895, and resisted a long siege by the Boxers in 1900. Additional work was carried out in 1917 to resist brigands. Van Melckebeke, *Service social de l'Église en Mongolie*, 65-66.

76 Discussed in next chapter: Coomans, "Gender Designed Catholic Churches in North China."

77 Discussed in chapter 3: Coomans, "Islands on the Mainland."

78 Most buildings were demolished during the second half of the twentieth century. Two postmodern Gothic cathedrals have recently been erected on both sites. On this phenomenon, see Coomans, "Western, Modern, and Postmodern Gothic Churches in Twentieth-Century China," 196-201.

The cathedral in the middle

The cathedral in Lu'an 潞安 (today Changzhi 长治, Shanxi) featured an unusual orientation and layout due to the location of the bishop's residence and courtyard at the back of the cathedral. Moreover, a network of inner walls and a street on either side of the cathedral ensured a rational circulation system and gender segregation. The following section is based on a general plan and several old photographs found in the archives of the Dutch Franciscans.[79] The cathedral discussed here was demolished in 1978; the new Changzhi diocese cathedral was built on another site in 2005.

In 1890 the prefecture-level city Lu'an (*Luanfu*) became the seat of the vicariate apostolic of South Shanxi, run by Dutch Franciscans. In 1900, the Boxers ravaged Shanxi and razed the old cathedral and the other Catholic buildings of Lu'an to the ground.[80] Soon after, in 1901, the vicar apostolic Odoricus Timmer 翟守仁 OFM (1859-1943) oversaw the construction of the new cathedral compound of Lu'an with government compensation. He also restored the ruined mission and new churches across the vicariate for the increasing number of Catholics. In 1922, the first batch of Little Sisters of Saint Joseph (Franciscan sisters from Heerlen) from the Netherlands reached Lu'an. In 1929, a diocesan congregation was founded for Chinese sisters, the Franciscan Sisters of Saint Elizabeth,[81] who contributed to Lu'an's heyday in the early 1930s.

An undated map shows the cathedral complex of Lu'an at the time of its heyday [Fig. 6.30]. Since the Boxers had razed all the old buildings to the ground and the townspeople had stolen the building materials,[82] the new complex was rebuilt from scratch. A Gothic single-nave memorial cathedral dominated the complex, with its slender façade facing north–instead of the south or west–in the direction of the city center; the entire spatial organization followed this unusual orientation. The almost rectangular walled compound was aligned to the north along a street and divided into four long plots extending to the south, each further subdivided into courtyards that interacted through appropriate connections. Large unbuilt spaces to the south and east were used for growing vegetables and remained available for future extensions. The cathedral stood in the middle of a main square, accessible from the street through an axial gateway. South of the cathedral, the bishop's residence, rationally organized around a square courtyard, was prohibited to women.

An internal street ran along the eastern side of the cathedral and the residence, leading on to the minor seminary; it was reserved for men and was accessible from the main street through a controlled gateway. West of this internal street, the part of the complex reserved for women had its own gateway and was subdivided into ten small courtyards surrounding the north-south oriented double-storied convent building that included the sisters' chapel and cells. With the exception of three courtyards reserved for the sisters, the others were assigned to specific groups requiring appropriate care– the orphans of the Holy Childhood, disabled children, elderly women, elderly men (the latter being sited furthest away from the former), the sisters' farm, and a small inner hospital. On the other side of the main street, the mission's outer hospital was divided into two gendered courtyards. Separated from the women's courtyards by the bishop's ancillary buildings and stables, the minor seminary occupied two large courtyards in the southern part of the complex, which were strictly reserved for priests and seminarians.[83] As usual, it was surrounded by open buffer spaces (vegetable gardens) and was located furthest from the noise of the schools and main street. In the northeast section of the complex, the schools developed around three courtyards, including a prep school to the minor seminary, a girls' school, and a boys' school.[84]

---

79 Utrecht, Het Utrechts Archief: 1224: Dutch Franciscans, China mission.

80 Timmer, *Het apostolisch-vicariaat van Zuid-Shansi*, 25-57.

81 Founded by Bishop Fortunatus Spruit 苗其秀 OFM (1880-1943). See Camps and McCloskey, *The Friars Minor in China*, 132-161.

82 Timmer, *Het apostolisch-vicariaat van Zuid-Shansi*, 44-45.

83 The vicariate apostolic of Southern Shanxi had no major seminary. Trainee priests completed their education in the Regional Seminary of Datong 大同 (Northern Shanxi).

84 Although this location was a Franciscan reference to the cathedral of Siena and other Italian bell towers, the Dutch Franciscans opted for the Gothic style, which better expressed their national identity than the Italianate style of the cathedrals of Taiyuan and Datong, built by Italian Franciscans. Gothic was also used at the Franciscan cathedrals of Xinjiang, Jinan 济南 (Shandong), and Kaifeng 开封 (Henan), the latter of which had a free-standing campanile located at the rear.

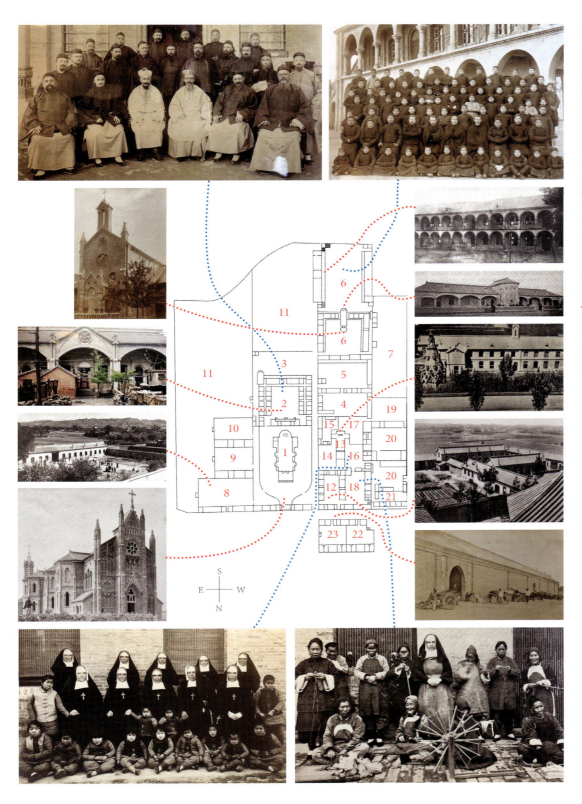

6.30. Cathedral complex of Lu'an, early 1930s: 1. cathedral, 2. bishop's and Dutch Franciscans' residence, including a chapel, reception hall, refectory, and library, 3. English garden, 4. staff of the residence, kitchen, and workshops, including a Chinese printing press, 5. stables, 6. minor seminary and chapel, 7. seminary vegetable garden, 8. prep school to the minor seminary, 9. girls' school, 10. boys' school, 11. vegetable garden, 12. sisters' first courtyard, 13. convent and chapel of the Little Sisters of St. Joseph, 14. sisters' vegetable garden, 15. sisters' workshops, 16. Holy Childhood orphanage, 17. disabled children, 18. elderly women, 19. elderly men, 20. sisters' farm, 21. inner hospital, 22-23. outer hospital divided in separate parts for women and men.
[© Utrecht, Het Utrechts Archief, 1224: Dutch Franciscans, China Mission, 289/5 (plan), 287/30, 287/31, 287/32, 288/28, 288/29, 289/1, 298/1 (photos). Plan redrawn by Luo Yuansheng, 2023]

85 The old Diocese of Beijing was divided into the three vicariates of Northern Zhili (including Beijing), Southwestern Zhili, and Southeastern Zhili. The latter's first vicar apostolic was the French bishop Adrien Languillat 郎懷仁 SJ (1808-1878).

86 Becker, "Le Village de Tchang-kia-tchoang," 272-273.

87 Strong, *A Call to Mission*, 1, 379-425; Sweeten, *China's Old Churches*, 269-273. The Holy Heart of Jesus could contain 2,000 people; it belonged to the first generation of large Catholic Gothic churches in China, with the cathedral of Guangzhou (1861-1879) and the second North Church in Beijing (1865-1867, demolished 1887).

88 A new cathedral in the Gothic style was built in 2000-2003 on the same site, but 50 meters further east than the old cathedral and reoriented by 180 degrees; its façade is thus west-facing. A dozen secondary buildings from the old complex are still standing, including the old novitiate chapel.

89 Leroy, *En Chine au Tché-Li S.-E*, 58-61. Other description from 1899 in X, "Tchang-kia-tchoang."

90 Strong, *A Call to Mission*, 1, 400 and 407.

6.31 Bird's eye view of the cathedral complex of Zhangjiazhuang from the northeast in the mid-1890s: A. cathedral, B. Virgins' courtyard and girls' orphanage, C. diocesan seminary, D. boys' college and orphanage, E. farm, F. bishop's residence and Jesuit community "enclosure", G. "new building" for the fathers, H. stables, I. rampart. Drawing published in Leroy, En Chine au Tché-Li S.-E, 1900. [Leuven, KU Leuven, Sabbe Library of Theology, 266-51 LERO]

A fortified rural cathedral complex

In 1856, the Propaganda Fide created the vicariate apostolic of Southeastern Zhili in today's Hebei province and entrusted it to the French Jesuits.[85] Four years later, after the end of the Second Opium War, the new bishop established his seat in the old Christian village of Zhangjiazhuang 张家庄 (Hebei) which was located only a few kilometers from the county-level town of Xianxian 献县.[86] A cathedral complex in a village was rather uncommon because it was unable to benefit from either urban facilities, a city wall, or a prestige location. The Jesuits soon developed a rational building complex with segregated areas for men and women around a large cathedral erected from 1863 to 1866.[87] East-west oriented – with its main entrance and 32-meter-high tower turned, unusually, to the east – this Gothic cathedral survived the Boxer Upraising, but was demolished in 1974.[88] Today, Zhangjiazhuang has completely lost its rural aspect and is an urbanized neighborhood of Xianxian city.

Three documents help us understand how the cathedral compound of Zhangjiazhuang was arranged in late Qing, before and after its partial destruction by the Boxers. They reveal the location, size, and evolution of the women's courtyards in the south-east corner of the male-dominated fortified rural complex. A description and bird's eye view [Fig. 6.31] depict Zhangjiazhuang before 1900:

> From a distance the appearance is singular; it looks like an island emerging, not from the ocean, but from a vast plain; the approaches are fortified and defended by three cannons shining on their carriages. (…) As a whole, it gives the idea of a mediaeval construction that comes from the fortress, the monastery, the city, and the university. Here, reality and appearances do not contradict each other. Tchang-kia-tchouang is a little like that that. The bishop has his cathedral there; the apostolic vicariate, its seminary; the mission, its schools or colleges; the Society of Jesus, its family home.[89]

According to a detailed plan from 1879 [Fig. 6.32], the women's courtyard, which included a girls' orphanage, school, and the dwelling of the Virgins, was located in the south-east corner of the complex and was clearly a reused pre-existing structure.

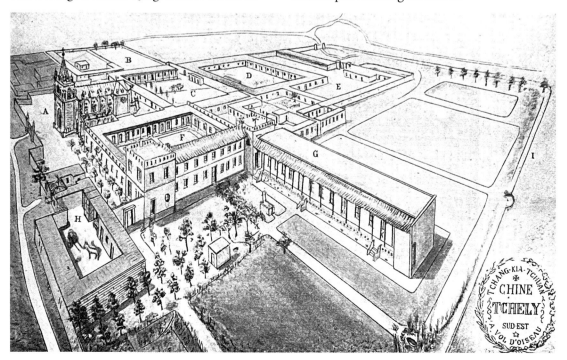

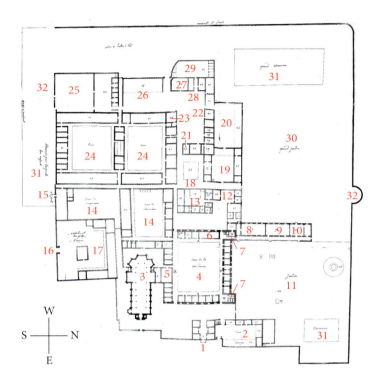
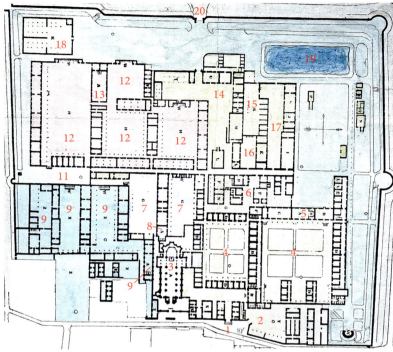

It was not aligned with the general grid of the Jesuit complex generated by the cathedral, and its entrance gate was correctly turned to the south, while the rest of the complex followed the cathedral's unusual east-west orientation. The northern side of the women's courtyard was separated from the cathedral by an east-west alley leading to the seminary, whose second courtyard was adjacent to the women's western wall. Such contiguity was definitely not optimal and would be improved during future waves of development. Further west, a long rectilinear transversal internal street divided the precinct from south to north and structured the space and circulation.

From July 1900 until the arrival of French troops in October 1900, the Boxers ravaged Xianxian County, killing many Christians and two Jesuits, demolishing the residence of Zhangjiazhuang, but not the cathedral.[90] After peace was restored in 1903, famine and droughts kept the region precarious. A plan of the mission compound shows the state of the restored complex in 1910, after it had benefited from government compensations [Fig. 6.33]. A comparison with the 1879 plan

6.32 Cathedral complex of the Jesuits in Zhangjiazhuang in 1879: 1. main or east entrance, 2. stables, 3. cathedral, 4. residence courtyard, 5. mandarins reception hall, 6. library, 7. tower, 8. refectory, 9. chapel, 10. recreation room, 11. fathers' garden, 12. (European) kitchen and cellars, 13. brothers' workshops (printing press, images, photography, book binding), 14. seminary, 15. secondary or south gate, 16. entrance gate to the women's courtyard, 17. girls' orphanage and Chinese Virgins, 18. south-north transversal internal street, 19. brothers' painting and joinery workshops, 20. woodwork shed, 21. servants' refectory, 22. storage and grain cellar, 23. Chinese kitchen, 24. boys' school and orphanage, 25. teachers' housing, 26. fuel, 27. carpentry, 28. cow stables, 29. pig stables, 30. vegetable garden, 31. pond, 32. defensive wall and ditch.
[Vanves, Compagnie de Jésus, Archives jésuites de France, maps and plan, F1, S2, no. 2]

6.33 Cathedral complex of the Jesuits in Zhangjiazhuang in 1910, colored printed plan: 1. main or west gate, 2. stables, 3. cathedral, 4. residence, 5. fathers' chapel, 6. kitchen complex, 7. seminary, 8. chapel seminary, 9. women's compound, 10. women's chapel, 11. buffer between the women's compound and the boys' school, at the southern end of the transversal internal street, 12. boys' high school (collège), 13. school chapel, 14. storage and servants, 15. joinery, 16. infirmary and library on the upper floor, 17. printing press, 18. carpentry, 19. pond, 20. back or east gate.
[Vanves, Compagnie de Jésus, Archives jésuites de France, maps and plans series F1, S2, no. 2]

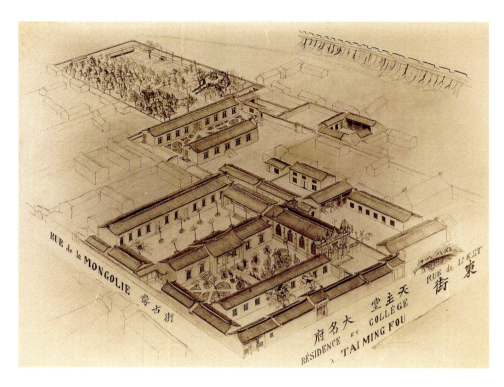

6.34 Bird's-eye view of the French Jesuit mission in Daming (Hebei) seen from the south-west, before its destruction in 1900.
[Vanves, Compagnie de Jésus, Archives jésuites de France, GMCI]

91 Strong, *A Call to Mission*, 1, 389, 442.
92 As in the other Jesuit vicariates in China, there were also Chinese Virgins of Presentation, who lived in association without common life or vows other than celibacy.
93 Respectively, the French nuns of the Society of the Helpers of the Holy Souls (*Auxiliatrices du Purgatoire*), the American Sisters Adorers of the Precious Blood (*Adoratrices du Précieux Sang*), and the Chinese Sisters of Our Lady of Purgatory. See Tiedemann, *Reference Guide to Christian Missionary Societies in China*, 60, 77, 95, 100.
94 Coomans and Xu, *Building Churches in Northern China*, 284-305; Sweeten, *China's Old Churches*, 274-281.

shows an increase in buildings around better structured courtyards, but the general organization of the functions remained unchanged. The residence, kitchen area, workshop areas, boys' high school, and women's enclosure had expanded in a centrifugal manner around newly created courtyards.

The most important changes occurred on the southern side of the complex, where ground had been purchased and the precinct expanded to the south, allowing the doubling of the surface area of the boys' school and the complete reorganization of the women's compound. The college, which was part of the Jesuit educational curriculum in preparation for seminary and university, developed around four spacious courtyards. The former, misaligned women's courtyard had been replaced by well-planned courtyards for school girls, orphans, and Virgins. The size difference between the spacious boys' courtyards and narrow courtyards for girls – of whom there were undoubtedly more – was typical of the belief that boys needed more space for recreation and physical exercise. The plan shows the women's compound as incomplete or under construction, and was clearly intended to close

off the cathedral complex's southwest corner [Fig. 6.33]. The women's gate was now on the east side, near the chapel of the Virgins, separated from the cathedral by an alley leading to the seminary. The location of the seminary adjacent to the women's enclosure was still not optimal, especially since the seminary could not expand in any direction. The western wall of the women's compound was separated from the college by a buffer zone in the prolongation of the transversal internal street.

Unlike the Jesuits of Shanghai, those of Xianxian had long failed to attract French female missionary congregations, nor had they succeeded in establishing a diocesan congregation for Chinese sisters.[91] This was probably due to the fact that Chinese Virgins had long been established in south-east Hebei, where there were many long-standing Christians.[92] The first French nuns arrived in Zhangjiazhuang in 1922, followed, in 1924, by American sisters, and eventually a diocesan congregation for Chinese women in 1932.[93] These nuns gradually replaced the Virgins and spread throughout the vicariate apostolic.

A cathedral on the women's side

About 450 kilometers south of Xianxian, the mission of Daming 大名 (today the southernmost part of Hebei) had a different destiny.[94] In 1861, the Jesuits returned to a region in which they had had a presence in the seventeenth century and managed to re-establish themselves in the town in 1867. They purchased land within the city walls, on the northern side of the main street near the East Gate. A bird's eye drawing shows the complex before 1900; it consisted of a north-south oriented chapel and several courtyards, including a residence with garden and a boys' school west of the chapel, stables, and ancillary buildings east of the chapel. Further to the north-east were the Virgins' section, a girls' orphanage and school, and a large garden with rockeries [Fig. 6.34]. In August 1900, the Boxers demolished the entire complex, which was rebuilt on a larger scale thanks to government compensation. The men's compound subsequently occupied

6.35 Catholic compounds on the north side of the main street of Daming (Hebei) seen from the East Gate in July 1913.
[Vanves, Compagnie de Jésus, Archives jésuites de France, GMC]

6.36 Catholic compounds on both sides of the main street of Daming (Hebei) seen from the East Gate in the early 1920s, after the completion of the great Gothic church.
[Vanves, Compagnie de Jésus, Archives jésuites de France, GMC]

the whole northern side of the street and saw the development of a school complex, which included a larger residence for the fathers, a church, two elementary schools for Catholic and non-Catholic boys, and a famous French College (*fawen* 法文) and boarding school, which provided preparation for university [Fig. 6.35]. The Virgins, girls' school, and the hospice for elderly women were relegated to the southern side of the street. As they had their own chapel, they had no reason to cross the street to attend mass in the men's church.[95]

In 1917, the large plot of a former government office (*yamen* 衙门) was purchased on the southern side of the street, on which a great Gothic church was erected from 1918 to 1921 [Fig. 6.36]. The new church disrupted the gender organization on both sides of the street; not only were its façade and tower unusually turned to the north, facing the street and the men's compound, the church was also on the women's side of the street and disconnected from the fathers' residence. From then on, the men and schoolboys had no choice but to cross the street. In 1935, the Holy See established the prefecture apostolic of Daming, which became a full diocese in 1947. Consequently, the great Gothic church became a cathedral and a residence for the bishop was erected near the cathedral and women's compound.[96]

95 A situation similar to that of the Jesuit mission of Puyang, in the same area, as discussed above.
96 Rome, Archivum Societats Iesu, China plans, no number: The Gothic church and several buildings in the men's complex are still standing. See: Coomans and Xu, *Building Churches in Northern China*, 284-367.

Gender-segregated by a canal: Xujiahui in Shanghai

The Jesuit settlement of Xujiahui 徐家汇 (Zi-ka-wei) is a fascinating French-Chinese story; it grew from a village west of Shanghai to the most important Catholic mission in China, dominated by a cathedral that is said to be the largest in East Asia. The Jesuit settlement developed from 1847 thanks to support from foreign and Chinese Catholic families from Shanghai and resources from France, but never was part of the French Concession. Benefiting from the Shanghai boom, Xujiahui reached its apogee in the first half of the twentieth century, when it hosted the 1924 Plenary Council of the Catholic Church in China and became the seat of the vicariate apostolic of Shanghai in 1933 [Fig. 3.4, no. 6], which was elevated to a diocese in 1946. Today, Xujiahui is a core district of the Shanghai megacity. For our purposes, the most important topographical transformation was the replacement of the Zhaojiabang 肇嘉浜 (Tschao Kia Pang) canal with an urban highway. This canal was not only the historical backbone of Xujiahui, but had segregated the male Catholic compounds on the west bank from the female Catholic compounds on the east bank.

Several studies have been written about Xujiahui,[97] focusing on the cathedral, library, observatory, and the famous arts and crafts workshops of the Tushanwan 土山湾 (T'ou-sè-wè) boys' orphanage in particular,[98] but a comprehensive architectural history of the entire settlement and its evolution is still lacking due to Xujiahui's missing archives.[99] Moreover, scholars have primarily discussed Xujiahui's development in the 1920s and 1930s, and the most important buildings which are still standing and are well documented by photos and city maps.[100]

The following section investigates the early phases of development of the built complex, from 1847 to the 1910s, during which the four main compounds were established, gendered spaces were gradually shaped on both sides of the Zhaojiabang canal, and were interconnected by two bridges located at strategic points. Our main sources are three unpublished maps with detailed legends showing Xujiahui in 1847, 1882, and 1908, as well as two perspective drawing from 1861 and c.1880, all five reproduced here [Figs. 6.37-6.41], and descriptions from books by Father Augustin Colombel SJ 高龍鞶 (1833-1905) on the Jesuit Jiangnan mission written before 1900.[101]

Reconnecting with ancient roots

Christianity was brought to Shanghai in around 1608 by Xu Guangqi 徐光启 (1562-1633), a friend of Matteo Ricci SJ 利玛窦 (1552-1610). Whenever his political career in Beijing allowed, Xu would stay in Shanghai, at the time a modest county capital city. Xu Guangqi died in 1633 and was buried in a tomb that still can be seen in Xujiahui [Fig. 6.38, F]. Despite the Jesuits' departure in 1724, the links between Shanghai, Pudong, and Songjiang Catholics and the Jesuits were still alive in 1842. Welcomed and helped by the "old Christians," the missionaries were nevertheless forced to reform, reorganize, and re-catechize these communities which had been long neglected.[102] They also managed to recover some of their former properties, including their cemetery in 1846 and former church 老堂 (Laotang) in 1861. In the meantime, the Jesuits had built Saint Francis Xavier's Church in the Dongjiadu 董家渡 suburb in 1847-1848 and a seminary in 1853.

Also in 1847, the Jesuits purchased a small plot of land of about 30 x 70 meters in Xujiahui, east of the Christian village of the Xu family and an old chapel near the north-south oriented Zhaojiabang canal. The nearby tomb of Xu Guangqi was a landmark and precious relic for both the Jesuits and Chinese Catholics. A map of Xujiahui in 1847 shows how the missionaries took advantage of the local geography which, as in much of Shanghai's outskirts, consisted of marshy land drained by countless small and larger canals forming an irregular grid [Fig. 6.38].

---

97 Among others: Fink, *Si-ka-wei und seine Umgebung*; King, "The Xujiahui Library of Shanghai;" Li, *Lishi shang de Xujiahui*; Li, "Xujiahui – Tushanwan;" Song, *Lishi shang de Xujiahui*.

98 T'ou-sè-wè Museum 土山湾博物馆, in the orphanage's only remaining building. See Ma, *Pedagogy, Display, and Sympathy*.

99 Despite its attractive title "The Gendered Space of the 'Oriental Vatican'. Zi-ka-wei, the French Jesuits and the Evolution of Papal Diplomacy" Mo Wei's article (2018) remains general about Xujiahui's layout and spatial evolution, and focuses on the French protectorate of the China mission.

100 Notably the 1933 Catholic Shanghai map. See Fig. 3.8, no. 5.

101 Colombel, *Histoire de la mission du Kiang-nan*, vol. 3/1, 235-243, 578-583, 832-834; vol. 3/2, 237-261; vol. 3/3, 398-498. Also: de La Servière *Histoire de la mission du Kiang-Nan*.

102 Mariani, "The Phoenix Raises from its Ashes."

103 Colombel, *Histoire de la mission du Kiang-nan*, 3/1, between 832-833.

104 Following the defeat of the Taiping in 1864, the Jesuits consolidated their Shanghai mission in the suburb of Dongjiadu, founded the new Saint Joseph's Parish at Yangjingban 洋泾浜 in the French Concession, and developed their compound in Xujiahui. In 1863, they purchased land in Sheshan and built a sanatorium for fathers; from 1873, it would become a Marian shrine. See Coomans, *Sheshan jiaotang xun cong*.

Trails and wooden bridges connected these sites, but transportation was mainly by boat. The main or Zhaojiabang canal connected the water network of the Songjiang 松江 plain with Shanghai and the Huangpu 黄浦 river. The land was used for growing rice, but was also home to small farming villages, temples, and burials.

The Jesuits began by building a residence where missionaries could perform their annual retreat, the elderly could rest, and the sick recover. In 1851, they replaced the old chapel with a church dedicated to Saint Ignace. During the ten years that followed, the complex developed around several courtyards, including a high school (*collège*), servants' quarters, ancillary buildings, and a garden. A bird's-eye view of the compound [Fig. 6.37] shows this first, exclusively male, settlement in 1863.[103] In 1860-1864, between the end of the Second Opium War and the final defeat of the Taiping, French soldiers established barracks and an observation tower north of the Jesuits' garden to control the canal and protect the mission. The development of a road between Xujiahui and Shanghai was one of the consequences of the military presence on the site.

As the unequal treaties of 1860 and 1861 soon allowed missionaries to settle throughout China, the Jesuits began transforming Xujiahui into their main base in Shanghai and Jiangnan.[104] At that time, the seat of the vicariate apostolic was in Nanjing, and Xujiahui was not a cathedral complex, but a Jesuit bridgehead with a residence and school, a place where more ambitious projects would soon develop.

Shifting the canal, relocating establishments from Shanghai, and attracting French nuns

Because the expansion of their compound was blocked to the west and south by Chinese homes, to the north by barracks, and to the east by the canal, the Jesuits decided to reshape the landscape by shifting the canal more than 150 meters to the east.[105] Land was purchased and the work was carried out in 1863 thanks to the support of local Christians and Chinese and French families in Shanghai whose children attended the Xujiahui boarding school.[106] A map of Xujiahui in 1882 shows the new course of the canal, which now had four bends, and the remaining sections of the old bend [Fig. 6.39]. To the north of the gained land, the fathers erected a large multistoried building surrounded by gardens that included their new residence, infirmary, and study library. The old residence was reassigned to the seminary of the Society of Jesus, which was relocated from Dongjiadu to Xujiahui. The school of Saint Ignace was demolished and a new multistoried school building erected in 1879 [Fig. 6.40].

Further to the south, at Tushanwan, where the canal made a turn to the west around an earth mound, the Jesuits relocated the boys' orphanage from Dongjiadu and established the new compound for the Tushanwan orphanage arts and crafts school in 1864, a chapel in 1866, and additional workshops. In 1867, the T'ou-Sè-Wè Press was established and equipped with modern machinery for printing religious and scientific publications in various languages.[107]

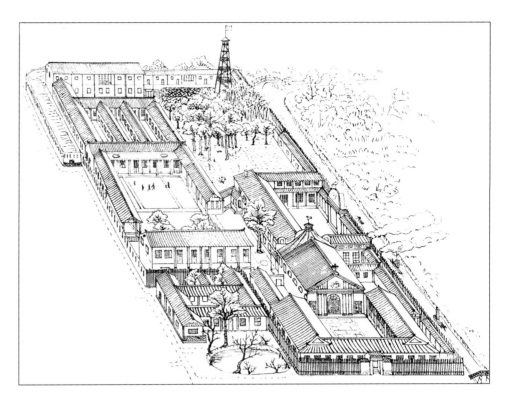

6.37. Bird's-eye view of Xujiahui (Shanghai) in 1863 seen from the south. The western side of the complex (right) is delimited by the original Zhaojiabang canal. Drawing published in: Colombel, Histoire de la mission du Kiang-nan, 3/1, between 832-833.
[Vanves, Compagnie de Jésus, Archives jésuites de France]

105 Colombel, *Histoire de la mission du Kiang-nan*, vol. 3/1, 238 and 833.
106 Li, *Lishi shang de Xujiahui*.
107 Tushanwan was run by Jesuit brothers specialized in different arts and crafts, including painting, sculpture, goldsmithery, metal and bell casting, printing, photography, and woodwork (joinery and carpentry). See: de La Servière, *L'orphelinat de T'ou-Sè-Wè*; Ma, *Pedagogy, Display, and Sympathy*.

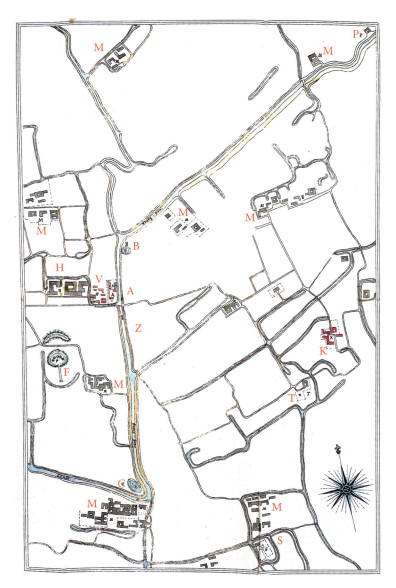
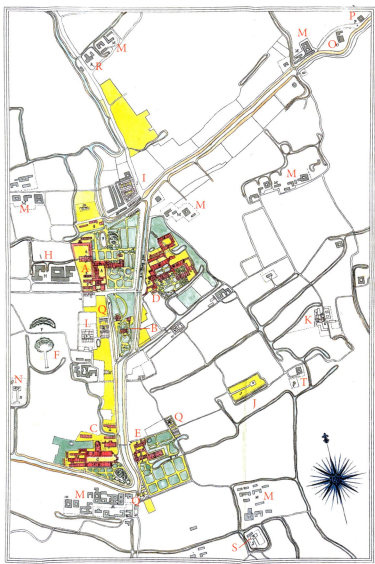

6.38 Printed map of Xujiahui in 1847 showing the networks of canals, the villages and main tombs: A. residence of the missionaries, 1. old chapel of the Christianity of Xujiahui, 2. residence built in 1847 by the Jesuits; B. earth mound; C. earth mound named Tushanwan; F. tomb of Xu Guangqi; H. pagan village of the Xu (Siu) family; K. Wangjiatang Christianity and church; M. pagan villages; P. Zen Kin Miao pagoda; S. tomb of the pagan family Lu (Lo); T. tomb of the pagan family Mo; U. Christian village of the Xu (Siu) family; Z. Zhaojiabang canal. The map makes a distinction between "pagan" villages in grey and Christianities in red, and mentions cemeteries which predated the missionaries' arrival.
[Vanves, Compagnie de Jésus, Archives jésuites de France, series F1, R5]

6.39 Map of Xujiahui in 1882 showing the development of five poles A-B-C-D-E on both sides of the shifted Zhaojiabang canal: A. residence of the missionaries, 1. church (1851), 2. old residence (1847), 3. old rooms (1855), 4. major seminary / old residence (1863), 5. new residence and scholastics (1867), 6. college (1879), 7. housing of the catechists, 8. servants and ancillary buildings, 9. sections of the old canal relocated in 1863; B. observatory, 1. meteorological observatory (1873), 2. magnetograph (1876), 3. old gas holder (1879); C. boys' orphanage of Tushanwan, 1. church (1866), 2. workshops and dormitories (1864), 3. new workshops and dormitories (1870, 1875), 4. infirmary, 5. ancillary buildings, housing of masters and workers; D. Shengmuyuan establishment of the Helpers of the Holy Soul, 1. church (1868), 2-3. sisters (1868), 4. boarding school (1868), 5. orphanage (1868), 6. outer school and pharmacy (1868), 7. laundry (1873), 8. catechumens (1876); E. Carmel of Saint Joseph (1874), 1. church, 2. nuns' choir, 3. nuns' cells, surrounded by a ditch, 4. cells of the postulants, 5. parlors and gatehouse; F. tomb of Xu Guangqi; G. houses of the Christian Xu family; H. pagan village of the Xu family; I. village of Xujiahui (established in 1861); J. Christian cemetery; K. Christianity and church of Wangjiatang; L. houses of two wealthy Christians; M. pagan villages; N. cemetery of the pagan family Xu; O. silk factory; P. Zen Kin Liao pagoda; Q. Christian villages, R. European pub and restaurant; S. tomb of the pagan family Lu; T. tomb of the pagan family Mo.
[Vanves, Compagnie de Jésus, Archives jésuites de France, F1, R5]

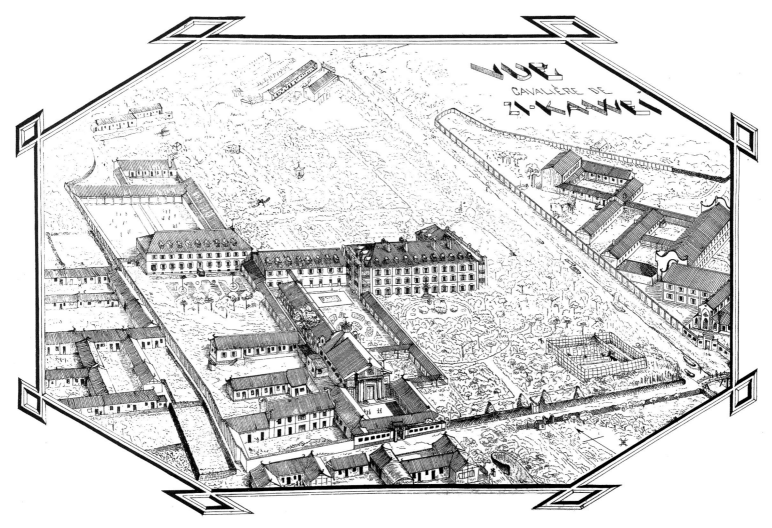

The Jesuits attracted nuns from two French religious institutes – one active, the other contemplative – and settled them on the east bank of the new course of the canal.[108] These foreign nuns belonged to the first generation of female Catholic missionaries in China. The Helpers of the Holy Souls (*Auxiliatrices du Purgatoire*) arrived in Shanghai in 1867 and, in 1869, were installed in a large compound east of Xujiahui, named Shengmuyuan 聖母院 (Holy Mother Garden), which not only included their convent and chapel, but also buildings for a community of Chinese Virgins of Presentation (*Présentandines*), a boarding school for girls from Shanghai, a girls' orphanage funded by the French work of the Holy Childhood, and a pharmacy [Fig. 6.40].[109] By establishing French and Chinese communities near each other, the Jesuits aimed to stimulate monastic life among the Virgins. Also in 1869, five Discalced Carmelites arrived in Shanghai and settled in the Carmel of Saint Joseph in 1874, on the east bank of the canal, opposite Tushanwan orphanage [Fig. 6.1]. This first contemplative nunnery in China hoped to become a centre of ascetic and mystic life for Chinese Catholic women.[110] The strict enclosure obeyed the same spatial regulations as any Western Carmel.

It is striking to note that the orientation of the male and female buildings was not identical and that their alignments differed by approximately twenty degrees [Figs. 6.39 and 6.40]. Xujiahui and Tushanwan faced about ten degrees southwest while Shengmuyuan

6.40 *Bird's eye view of Xujiahui from the south in around 1890. From left to right: the college for boys, seminary, old Saint Ignatius church, fathers' residence, and library, separated by the relocated Zhaojiabang canal from the Shengmuyuan sisters' convent and girls' school. Drawing by a Tushanwan orphan.*
[Vanves, Compagnie de Jésus, Archives jésuites de France, maps and plans]

108 Mo, "The Gendered Space of the 'Oriental Vatican.'"
109 X, "Le Sen-mou-yeu."
110 In 1874, the community included seven French and nine Chinese nuns. See Nicolini-Zani, *Christian Monks on Chinese Soil*, 63-79.

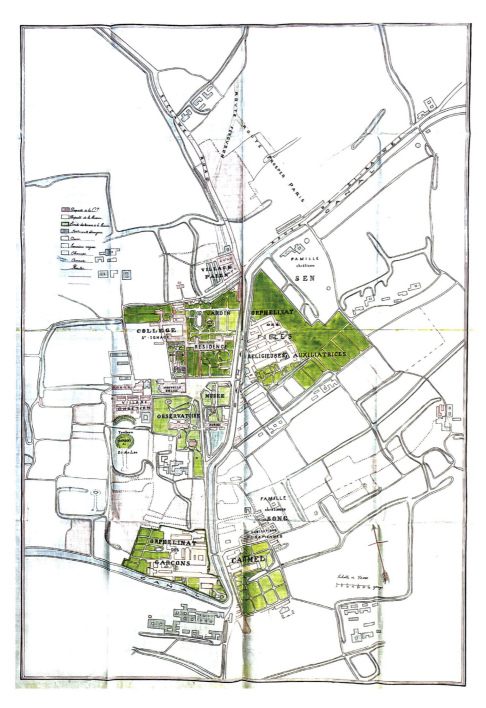

6.41 Map of Xujiahui (Shanghai) in 1908. The buildings belonging to the Society of Jesus are coloured pink, while those belonging to the mission - Tushanwan orphanage, Shengmuyuan orphanage, and the Carmelite convent - are colored yellow. Land belonging to the mission is coloured green. [Vanves, Compagnie de Jésus, Archives jésuites de France, F1, R5]

and the Carmel faced about ten degrees southeast. In all likelihood, this was due to the network of plots and canals, but the orientation of the female buildings should be considered better.[111] The canal was thus not only the main waterway to Shanghai, but also a barrier that ensured effective gender segregation in addition to the precinct walls of the compounds. Only two bridges crossed the canal, one connecting Xujiahui and Shengmuyuan, the other Tushanwan and the Carmelite monastery [Fig. 6.1]. From Xujiahui, it was an easy walk for the fathers to the two convents to celebrate daily mass for the sisters or to the chapels of Saint Ignace's high school and Tushanwan orphanage.

After establishing the four compounds of Xujiahui, Shengmuyuan, Tushanwan, and the Carmel on the recomposed landscape in the 1860s, the Jesuits launched their ambitious Kiang-Nan Scientific Plan in 1872.[112] The land on the west bank of the shifted canal between Xujiahui and Tushanwan became a campus for scientific research in the pure Jesuit tradition. The Natural History Museum was relocated from Nanjing to Xujiahui in 1873, and the first meteorological observatory and a magnetograph were established in 1876.[113] A comparison of the 1847 and 1882 maps gives the measure of the ambitious project the Jesuits achieved in thirty-five years [Figs. 6.38 and 6.39]. Once located on either side of the canal, the compounds continued to grow.

Growth, moves, and the consolidation of the gendered landscape

During the first decade of the twentieth century, the Jesuits progressed on all fronts and confirmed Shanghai's central position in China's Catholic mission. Urbanization gradually reached Xujiahui and traffic increased thanks to a road and tramway to Shanghai. A third map shows the development of Xujiahui in 1908: almost all the first-generation buildings were replaced with larger concrete structures [Fig. 6.41]. The metamorphosis began in 1899-1901 with the erection of a new observatory, followed by the construction of a new Saint Ignatius Church – the future cathedral – from 1903 to 1910. Built on an east-west axis, the main entrance of this church unusually faced east, i.e., to the canal, the bridge, and the women's compound of Shengmuyuan. In 1903, the Jesuits launched a challenging project for Aurora University

震旦大学 in Xujiahui, before moving it quickly, in 1908, to Luojiawan 罗家湾 in the French Concession, near the Sainte-Marie hospital. It became one of Shanghai's main universities, but women were not admitted until the late 1930s.[114]

Tushanwan and Shengmuyuan continued to develop their project to bring orphaned boys and girls up as Catholics and provide them with a vocational education. The orphans spent around fifteen years in their respective single-sex environments, which were their only "family". The dearest wish of the Jesuits and Helpers of the Soul was that they would go on to have their own Catholic families. Consequently, marriages were arranged, with the future couple's first meeting usually taking place on the bridge. Hybrid Western-Chinese wedding ceremonies were held in Xulun 叙伦 Hall, a dedicated facility that included a bridal room and kitchen. The missionaries financed a part of these ceremonies, which were celebratory but frugal.[115] West of Xujiahui, the Jesuits founded a Christian village where these new families were welcome. Other orphans decided to take religious vows to become brother Jesuits, sister Helpers of the Soul, or Virgins of the Presentation. To become a priest, men had to know Latin, which only boys were able to learn at high schools such Saint Ignatius in Xujiahui. These were the main sources for the vocational recruitment of Chinese Jesuits and diocesan priests. The road to the priesthood was long and included the major seminary for diocesan priests and the novitiate for Jesuits, which were rebuilt on a large scale in Xujiahui in 1928.

The 1908 map distinguishes the properties of the Society of Jesus from those of the apostolic vicariate. The compounds of the Shengmuyuan and Carmelite nuns, as well as the boys' and girls' orphanages and their respective chapels, belonged to the vicariate, while Saint Ignatius Church, the residence, high school, and the scientific establishments belonged to the Society of Jesus. The lack of an archive prevents a detailed investigation of this complex real estate distribution and its later consequences.[116] Xujiahui's prominent position on China's Catholic landscape was reinforced in 1924 when it hosted the plenary council of the Catholic Church in China, and was confirmed in 1933 with the erection of the apostolic vicariate of Shanghai and the elevation of Saint Ignatius Church to the rank of cathedral. From then on, the bishop of Shanghai lived in a newly built residence in Xujiahui.

Despite all these developments, the gender division set up in the 1860s remained unchanged and the four compounds were gradually consolidated, proving that shifting a section of the canal had been a visionary decision [Fig. 6.41]. Soon after the establishment of the People's Republic of China in 1949, the foreign missionaries were expelled, the orphanages closed, and the buildings reallocated.

Today, Xujiahui is a bustling urban district at the heart of Shanghai, with a subway station where three lines intersect and skyscrapers much higher than the cathedral. The Zhaojiabang canal has disappeared to be replaced by an urban highway, on either side of which the Xujiahui Cathedral and the Shengmuyen Chapel still face each other [Fig. 6.42].

111 "If you really want to aim at perfection, you should turn about ten degrees to the southeast. So you will have the winter sun very early in the morning and in the summer you will be spared its direct rays earlier in the afternoon. The direction to the southwest would naturally create the opposite effect." Jung, *Le missionnaire-constructeur*, 3. Also Coomans and Xu, *Building Churches*, 126-127 and 374.
112 Mo, "Assessing Jesuit Intellectual Apostolate in Modern Shanghai."
113 Founded in Nanjing in 1868, the museum developed botanical and zoological research and collections. See Belval, "Le Musée d'Histoire Naturelle de Zi-ka-wei."
114 de La Servière, "Une université catholique en Chine. L'Aurore."
115 Zhu, "Xulun Hall of T'ou-Sè-Wè and Marriage Ceremony."
116 According to the map, the Jesuits had purchased land for the Christian villages they helped develop.

6.42 The footprint of Xujiahui's gendered spaces is still tangible today: the North Caoxi Road is established exactly on the axis of the Zhaojiabang canal as it was moved in 1863. View from the north with remains of the Sengmuyuan on the left and Xujiahui on the right.
[Photo THOC, May 2023]

Catholic gendered spaces in the Republican era

The cases presented in this chapter have shown how the sense of Catholic community – often separate from local Chinese society – and the need for gender segregation were accommodated according to local human and topographical contexts. Given the inequality of the position of men and women in late Qing Chinese society and in the nineteenth-century Catholic Church, we might wonder whether it would not be more appropriate to view this gender segregation as gender discrimination.[117] Gender segregation separates men and women on the basis of gender, but considers them as equal, while gender discrimination treats men and women differently primarily on the basis of gender. Having developed an architectural and spatial approach based mainly on plans and visual sources, and lacking precise historical or anthropological information about most specific cases, we have consistently used the notion of segregation, which highlights the Catholic Church's desire for equality between men and women, despite their specific vocations, rather than the notion of discrimination, which would suggest gender-based prejudicial behavior and action. In this regard, the Catholic Church in China can be considered less discriminating against women than late Qing Chinese society, steeped in the Confucian principles.[118]

The progressive and modern Western ideals promoted in China by the New Culture Movement (新文化运动 *Xin Wenhua Yundong*) in the 1910s and 1920s questioned the Confucian principles that ordered family and society, especially the traditional patriarchal family and the status of women.[119] The Catholic mission had contributed to the emancipation of women by advocating monogamy, marital affection, and, to a certain extent, gender equality. However, the Catholic missionaries never questioned the specific vocation of women for marriage and motherhood, or for a consecrated life as nuns serving in orphanages, schools, hospitals, or other forms of social care. This fitted with the world view of the centralized and male-dominated hierarchy of the Catholic Church. Consequently, until 1949, Catholic architecture and spatial organization in China were based on the same principles of gender segregation as in Europe, America, and the other mission fields in Africa and Asia.[120] Unlike Catholics, the Protestant missions, which preferably evangelized middle-class Chinese and were more active in urban contexts, developed higher education for girls and promoted women's leadership in society and the Church, as Bible women for instance.[121]

After the First World War, the Catholic mission in China faced two key issues. Firstly, Rome had come to understand that the nineteenth-century Eurocentric model of the "civilizing mission" and the French protectorate had become counterproductive, especially in Republican China. Pope Benedict XV's apostolic letter *Maximum Illud*, November 30, 1919, launched the worldwide movement of indigenization that asked missionaries to serve the universal Church and the local people rather than their own home country, and promoted local priests and bishops.[122] In China's transitional society of the 1920s and 1930s, the Catholic Church had to adapt to growing competition with Protestants and confrontation with Nationalists and Communists. The second issue was the need to increase Catholic human resources in China, both by sending more missionaries and educating more Chinese priests and nuns. According to the *Propaganda Fide* policy, the latter would eventually take over from the foreign missionaries and run an autonomous Church.

The number of religious institutes for women increased considerably after the First World War and Catholic sisters contributed to the modernization of Chinese society.[123] On the one hand, the diocesan bishops established Chinese sisterhoods – local associations of diocesan right – in most vicariates apostolic of China. In 1940, there were 76 Chinese Catholic sisterhoods of women and

---

117 The author is grateful to Prof. Hilde Heynen for drawing his attention to this important difference.
118 See also the next chapter: Coomans, "Gender Designed Catholic Churches in North China."
119 Glosser, "The 'Truth I Have Learned';" Stevens, "Figuring Modernity."
120 See other contributions in this book.
121 Kwok, *Chinese Women and Christianity*, 80-86, 173-178; *Christian Women and Modern China*.
122 Taveirne, "Re-reading the Apostolic Letter *Maximum Illud*."
123 Tiedemann, *Reference Guide to Christian Missionary Societies in China*, 49-107; Clark, "Saving the Children."

a total of 4,472 sisters. On the other hand, the number of foreign Catholic female missionary institutes increased and their diverse origins included more European and North American countries. This development was parallel to that of missionary institutes for men and responded to the same need for human resources following the increase in the number of Catholics and the multiplication of dioceses in China. In 1940, there were 2,457 foreign nuns in China, belonging to 81 Catholic missionary institutes for women.[124]

The ambitious and urgent paradigm shift initiated by *Maximum illud* required appropriate architecture, not so much in the rural parishes of deep China as in cities, where the modernization of society was underway. Sinicizing architecture was one of the answers provided by Catholic progressives.[125] The aforementioned multiplication of vicariates apostolic from the 1920s implied the creation of new cathedral compounds, seminaries, and administrative centers, as discussed in the cases of Xinjiang, Xianxian, and Daming. The arrival in China of a new generation of male and female missionaries from other countries, especially the United States, brought another approach to missions and generated a wave of construction of new parochial buildings, schools, hospitals, etc. Thanks to the development of the railways, the spread of industrial construction materials made it possible to erect modern buildings with concrete structures, designed by professional architects rather than brother carpenters. The latter, however, continued to be active in the rural areas of deep China, far from the railroads and modernity.[126]

When a mission grew and found itself unable to purchase adjacent land within the same area, such as in Xianxian, or on the other side of the street, as in Puyang and Daming, the women were usually relocated to allow the men to develop further, moving the priest's residence away from the church was unthinkable. The result of this growth process was not only a change of scale, but it also generated large, modern, single-sex establishments in cities and concession territories.

Urban hospitals, often founded in late Qing, developed considerably during the Republic thanks to the erection of concrete buildings, equipment modernization, and by attracting a new generation of Chinese doctors educated abroad or at universities in China. Religious congregations of women continued to play a major role in nursing, from local dispensaries to large hospitals [Fig. 6.43]. Numerous new Catholic female missionary congregations came to China and developed in the field of social work, which included the basic education of girls, orphanages, homes for the elderly, hospitals, and dispensaries.[127]

6.43 In Ningbo 宁波 (Zhejiang), the French Daughters of Charity of Saint Vincent de Paul ran the women's house of the Holy Childhood founded downtown in 1852 and the men's Saint Joseph Hospital founded on the outskirts in 1861. Both included a chapel, hospital, dispensary, home for the elderly, a section for disabled adults, and an orphanage. In 1935, the former was managed by three French and eleven Chinese sisters, and the latter by nine French and six Chinese sisters. The photo depicts the Saint Joseph Hospital in the 1920s. [Paris, Archives historiques de la Congrégation de la Mission]

124 Tiedemann, *Handbook of Christianity in China*, 977-986.
125 About the Sinicization of Christian architecture, see Coomans, "The 'Sino-Christian Style.'"
126 Coomans and Luo, "Missionary-Builders."
127 Tiedemann, *Reference Guide to Christian Missionary Societies in China*, 49-86.

6.44. Inauguration of the modern building of the Saint Mary department 聖母院 for women of Aurora University in Yangzhou (Jiangsu), April 1936. [Vanves, Compagnie de Jésus, Archives jésuites de France, Fonds iconographique]

128 Dujardin, "The Three Wise Men Came from the East."
129 Such as the American Marianists (Society of Mary), from 1933.
130 On the HK regional seminary, see Coomans, "Sinicising Christian Architecture in Hong Kong."
131 Tiedemann, "The Chinese Clergy."
132 A third Catholic university, Fujen Catholic University of Peking 輔仁大學, was founded by the Propaganda Fide and American Benedictines in Beijing in 1925 [Fig. 3.31], see Liu, "Two Universities," 415.
133 Le Pichon, "Portrait of a Practical Visionary."
134 On studies about women in China during the twentieth century, see: Herstatter, "State of the field."
135 Among the abundant literature on this subject: Hooper, "Women in China: Mao v. Confucius;" Diamant, Revolutionizing the Family.
136 Yang and Yan, "The Annihilation of Femininity in Mao's China."

New male institutions, however, were primarily educational, including high schools, seminaries, and universities, with the aim of developing a Chinese Catholic elite, stimulating priestly vocations, and educating university students. High schools (collèges) for boys, sometimes named "minor seminaries", were founded in many large Chinese cities and were also accessible to non-Catholic children, who were taught sciences, Western culture, and languages, including Latin.[128] In addition to the Jesuits, other congregations specializing in education came to China and built large single-sex complexes.[129] A dozen inter-diocesan or "regional seminaries" were created to accommodate large numbers of seminarians, advanced-level teachers in theology and philosophy, and libraries.[130] The first Chinese male religious congregations were created in the 1920s, and required a motherhouse and training center.[131]

Despite this, Catholics lagged behind Protestants in higher and university education. Unlike Protestant universities and colleges, the Catholic universities in Shanghai, Tianjin, and Beijing were single-sex male and did not accept female students until the very late 1930s.[132] As girls were excluded from the priesthood and had almost no access to university, Catholics did not prioritize higher education for girls except in Shanghai and regions with a scholarly tradition, where they competed with Protestant higher education and modern architecture [Fig. 6.41].

Hong Kong, the hub of Catholic missions to China, built many large single-sex complexes for boys and girls, and offers the best examples of continuity today. The South China Regional Seminary (now the Holy Spirit Seminary) in Aberdeen, the hospital complexes of the Sisters of Saint Paul of Chartres at Causeway Bay 銅鑼灣 and the Sisters of the Precious Blood at Sham Shui Po 深水埗, the girls' schools of the Canossian Sisters and the Maryknoll Sisters in Kowloon, the boys' schools of the Jesuits, Salesians, etc. and many houses for male and female religious communities are examples of modern architecture from the 1920s and 1930s.[133]

The contrast with rural China, where late Qing Christianities and Confucian-based gender relations remained nearly unchanged, was extreme.[134] The establishment of the Communist PCR in 1949 would revolutionize gender relations, marriage, and eradicate Confucianism (the Four Olds 四旧, 1966).[135]

However, Mao Zhedong's political slogan "The times have changed, men and women are the same 时代不同了,男女都一样" resulted in other forms of gender inequality during the Cultural Revolution.[136]

BIBLIOGRAPHY

Visual sources

Original plans and photos were traced in the following missionary archives:
- French Jesuits (AFSI): Vanves, Archives jésuites de France
- Jesuits / Society of Jesus (ARSI): Rome, Archivum Romanum Societatis Iesu
- Congregation of the Immaculate Heart of Mary (CICM): Leuven, KADOC-KU Leuven, Archief Scheutisten Generalaat
- Flemish Franciscans (OFM): Leuven, KADOC-KU Leuven, Archief Vlaamse Minderbroeders
- Dutch Franciscans (OFM): Utrecht, Het Utrechts Archief 1224
- French Paris Mission (MEP): Paris, IRFA Institut de Recherche France-Asie, Missions étrangères de Paris
- Pontifical Missionary Works (OPM): Lyon, Oeuvres Pontificales Missionnaires
- Lazarists / Vincentians (CM): Paris, Archives historiques de la Congrégation de la Mission

Primary literature

Becker, Émile (SJ). "Le village de Tchang-kia-tchoang. Lettre du R.P. Becker au R.P. Provincial de Champagne (24 mai 1893)." *Lettres de Jersey*, 12 (November 1893) 2, 272-281.

Belval, Henri (SJ). "Le Musée d'Histoire Naturelle de Zi-ka-wei et le nouveau Musée Heude." *Relations de Chine*, 31 (1933) 2, 428-437

Code of Canon Law. Book IV-1. The Sacraments, title VI, canon 1008. <https://www.vatican.va/archive/cod-iuris-canonici/eng/documents/cic_lib4-cann998-1165_en.html#TITLE_VI>.

Colombel, Augustin (SJ). *Histoire de la mission du Kiang-nan* 江南. 3/1. *Du P. Claude Gotteland 1840, à l'épiscopat de Mgr Languillat 1865*. Shanghai-Xujiahui: T'ou-sè-wè, [1899-1900].

Colombel, Augustin (SJ). *Histoire de la mission du Kiang-nan* 江南. 3/2. *L'épiscopat de Mgr Languillat 1865-1878*. Shanghai-Xujiahui: T'ou-sè-wè, [1899-1900].

Colombel, Augustin (SJ). *Histoire de la mission du Kiang-nan* 江南. 3/3. *L'épiscopat de Mgr Garnier 1879-1898. Mgr. Simon 1899*. Shanghai-Xujiahui: T'ou-sè-wè, [1900].

Compendium of the Catechism of the Catholic Church, 323 (the sacrament of Holly Orders). <https://www.vatican.va/archive/compendium_ccc/documents/archive_2005_compendium-ccc_en.html>.

Dannic Joseph (SJ). "Variété. Fiançailles à la vieille mode chinoise. / Le mariage, nouveau style." *Relations de Chine. Kiang-Nan*, January-April 1918, 48-55.

de La Servière, Joseph (SJ). *Histoire de la mission du Kiang-Nan. Jésuites de la province de France (Paris)*. 2 vol.. Shanghai, [1914].

de La Servière, Joseph (SJ). *L'orphelinat de T'ou-Sè-Wè. Son histoire. Son état présent*. Shanghai, 1914.

de La Servière, Joseph (SJ). "Une université catholique en Chine. L'Aurore à Shanghai." *Relations de Chine*, 23 (1925) 2, 65-86.

De Sica, Louis Marie (SJ). *De Ratione agendi cum Sinensibus, ad Sodalem* [The Ways of Dealing with the Chinese], to the Member. Zikawei, 1877, 54 p. [AFSI, FCh 408]

De Sica, Louis Marie (SJ). *Ad casus conscientiae resolutos Appendic Secunda in missione Nankinensi*. Changhai, Mission Catholique, T'ou-sè-wè, 1884, 98 p. [AFSI, FCh 408]

Faguet, M. [Faguais, Jules 樊儒略] (MEP). "La résidence de Gan-Chouen, Kouy-Tcheou." *Annales de la Société des Missions-étrangères et de l'œuvre des partants*, 11 (1908) 61, 33-38.

Fink, C. *Si-ka-wei und seine Umgebung*. Shanghai-Qingdao, [ca 1900].

Gibert, Gustave (SJ) 壽瑞徵. *Les petits Chinois ou la Sainte Enfance au Vicariat de Nankin. Histoires vraies avec des illustrations*. 2 vol. Paris, 1926.

Japiot, Emil (SJ) 畢如春. "Lettre du P. Japiot à Mgr Bulté, 24 août 1892." *Lettres de Jersey*, 12 (April 1893) 1, 34-39.

[Jung, Paul (SJ)]. *Le missionnaire-constructeur. Conseils-plans*. Xianxian: Sien-hsien press, 1926.

Kramer, Constans 康济民 (OFM). *De Nederlandse Minderbroeders in de Apostolische Prefectuur van Kiangchow 1936-1954* [translated as *The Kiangchow Story. The Dutch Franciscans in South-West Shansi (1936-1954)*]. Katwijk: Twentieth-century Franciscan mission in China project (unpublished manuscript, Het Utrechts Archief, 1224 Franciscanen Nederland, missie, collectie China, no. 4.306).

Languillat, Adrien 郎怀仁 (SJ). *Sheng pei gui an* 圣配规案 [Rules of the holy marriage]. S.l. 1865. [AFSI FCH 405]

Launay, Adrien (MEP). *Histoire des missions de Chine. Mission du Kouy-Tcheou*, 3. Paris, 1908.

Leroy, Henri-Joseph (SJ). *En Chine au Tché-Li S.-E. Une mission d'après les missionnaires*. Lille-Tournai: Société Saint-Augustin - Desclée, De Brouwer, 1900.

Palatre, Gabriel (SJ). *L'infanticide et l'œuvre de la Sainte-Enfance en Chine*. Shanghai: T'ou-sè-wè, 1878.

Timmer, Odoricus (OFM). *Het apostolisch-vicariaat van Zuid-Shansi in de eerste vijf-en-twintig Jaren (1890-1915)*. Leiden: Théonville, 1915.

Van Melckebeke, Carlo (CICM). *Service social de l'Église en Mongolie*. Brussels: Scheut, 1968.

Zi, Stephanus (SJ). *Parva rerum Sinensium adumbratio scholasticis ad sinas recens appulsis accomodata* [Chinese affairs arranged for scholars recently landed in China]. Shanghai, Tou-chan-wan, 1879, 68 p. [AFSI, FCh 408]

X. *Appendices ad casus conscientiae resolutos in missione nankinensi* [Appendices to the cases of consciousness resolved in the Nanking mission], Shanghai: Mission Catholique, T'ou-sè-wè, 1879, 103 p. [AFSI, FCh 408].

X,. *Le père L. Gain, S.J. (1852-1930) apôtre du Siu-tcheou fou, Vicariat de Nan-king*. Shanghai: Imprimerie T'ou-sè-wè, 1931.

X. "Le Sen-mou-yeu. Quelques notes de la supérieure de l'établissement." *Relations de Chine. Kiang-Nan*, 1 (October 1903) 2, 120-127.

X. *Monita ad missionarios provinciae nankinensis* [Warning to the missionaries of the province of Nanking]. Shanghai: A.H. De Carvalho, 1871, 120 p. [AFSI, FCh 408]

X. *Monita ad missionarios provinciae nankinensis. Supplementum* [Warning to the missionaries of the province of Nanking, supplement]. Paris: A. Le Clere, 1872. 29 p. [AFSI, FCh 408]

X. "Tchang-kia-tchoang." *Chine et Ceylan. Lettres de missionnaires de la Compagnie de Jésus (Province de Champagne)*, 3 (October 1899), 188-191.

Secondary literature

Borao Mateo, Eugenio, José. "Catholic Orphanages in Fujian during the 19th and 20th Centuries." *Hanxue yanjiu* 漢學研究 [*Sinology Research*], 39 (2021) 3, 187-229.

Cai Xiang-yu. *Christianity and Gender in South-East China: The Chaozhou Missions (1849-1949)*. PhD dissertation, Leiden University, Faculty of Humanities, Institute of History, 2012. <https://scholarlypublications.universiteitleiden.nl/handle/1887/18940>.

Camps, Arnulf. "Actors: Catholic Missionaries (1800-1860)," in: Tiedeman, R. Gary, ed. *Handbook of Christianity in China. Volume Two: 1800-present*. Leiden-Boston: Brill, 2010, 115-132.

Camps, Arnulf and McCloskey, Pat. *The Friars Minor in China (1294-1955), especially the years 1925-55, based on the research of Friars Bernward Willeke and Domenico Gandolfi, OFM*. New York: St. Bonaventure Institute; Rome: General Curia OFM, 1995.

Charbonnier, Jean (MEP). "Chinese Catholics in the Early Nineteenth Century," in: Tiedeman, R. Gary, ed. *Handbook of Christianity in China. Volume Two: 1800-present*. Leiden-Boston: Brill, 2010, 115-132

Chen Tsung-ming, Alexandre 陳聰銘. "La question des propriétés immobilières et foncières des missions catholiques en Chine (1860-1949)," in: Chen Tsung-ming, Alexandre, ed. *Le Christianisme en Chine aux XIXᵉ et XXᵉ siècles. Figures, événements et missions-œuvres*. Leuven, 2015, 13-44.

Clark, Anthony E. "'Saving the Children': Catholic Sisters and Social Reform in Republican China," in: Washington, Garrett L., ed. *Christianity and the Modern Woman in East Asia*. Boston-Leiden, 2018, 62-82.

Clark, Anthony E. *China Gothic. The Bishop of Beijing and His Cathedral*. Seattle: University of Washington Press, 2019.

Clarke, Jeremy (SJ). *The Virgin Mary and Catholic Identities in Chinese History*. Hong Kong: Hong Kong University Press, 2013.

Coomans, Thomas. "Sinicising Christian Architecture in Hong Kong: Father Gresnigt, Catholic Indigenisation, and the South China Regional Seminary, 1927-31." *Journal of the Royal Asiatic Society Hong Kong Branch*, 56 (2016), 133-160.

Coomans, Thomas. "The 'Sino-Christian Style': A Major Tool for Architectural Indigenization," in: Zheng Yangwen, ed. *Sinicizing Christianity*. Leiden-Boston: Brill, 2017, 197-232.

Coomans, Thomas [高曼士]. "Yancang yu sheng xin da jiaotang de guangmang zhihou: Ta cha ji ren zhi wan qing Guangzhou qita jidujiao jianzhu" 掩藏于圣心大教堂的光芒之后：踏查及认知晚清广州其它基督教建筑 [Overshadowed by the Cathedral: Towards Mapping and Understanding the Other Christian Buildings in Late Qing Canton], in: *Xixue dong jian yanjiu* 西学东渐研究 [Research on Eastern Trend of Western Learning] 7. Beijing: The Commercial Press, 2019,162-193.

Coomans, Thomas. "Western, Modern, and Postmodern Gothic Churches in Twentieth Century China: Styles, Identities and Memories," in: Borngässer, Barbara and Klein, Bruno, eds. *Global Gothic. Gothic Church Building in the 20th and 21st centuries*. Leuven: Leuven University Press, 2022, 179-201.

Coomans, Thomas 高曼士. *Sheshan jiaotang xun cong: chaosheng jianzhu he lishitujing* 佘山教堂寻踪：朝圣建筑和历史图景 [Tracing the Sheshan Church: Pilgrimage Architecture and Landscape]. Shanghai: Tongji Press, 2023.

Coomans, Thomas. "Islands on the Mainland. Catholic Missions and Spatial Strategies in China, 1840s-1940s," in: Coomans, Thomas, ed. *Missionary Spaces. Imagining, Building, Contesting Christianities in Africa and China, 1830s-1960s*. Leuven, 2024, 32-63.

Coomans, Thomas. "Gender-Designed Catholic Churches in North China, 1830s-1920s," in: Coomans, Thomas, ed. *Missionary Spaces. Imagining, Building, Contesting Christianities in Africa and China, 1830s-1960s*. Leuven, 2024, 146-193.

Coomans, Thomas and Luo Wei 罗薇. "Missionary-Builders: Scheut Fathers as Church Designers and Constructors in Northern China," in: Chen, Tsung-ming, Alexandre 陳聰銘, ed. *Catholicism's Encounters with China. 17th to 20th Century* (Leuven Chinese Studies 39). Leuven: Ferdinand Verbiest Institute, 2018, 333-364.

Coomans, Thomas [高曼士] and Xu Yitao 徐怡涛. *Building Churches in Northern China. A 1926 Handbook in Context* / 来与本土——1926年法国传教士所撰中国北方教堂营造之研究. Beijing: Intellectual Property Rights Publishing House, 2016.

Coomans, Thomas, Xu Yitao 徐怡涛, and Zhang Jianwei 张剑葳, "*Imposing and Provocative*: The Design, Style, Construction and Significance of Saint Anthony's Cathedral, Xinjiang (Shanxi, China), 1936-40," in: Mascarenhas-Mateus, João and Pires, Ana Paula, eds. *History of Construction Cultures. Proceedings of the Seventh International Congress on Construction History (7ICCH), 12-16 July 2021, Lisbon*. Vol. 1. London-New York: Taylor & Francis, 2021, 85-92.

Diamant, Neil J. *Revolutionizing the Family: Politics, Love, and Divorce in Urban and Rural China, 1949-1968*. Berkeley: University of California Press, 2000.

Dujardin, Carine. *Missionering en moderniteit. De Belgische minderbroeders in China 1872-1940* (KADOC-Studies 19). Leuven: Leuven University Press, 1996.

Dujardin, Carine. "The Three Wise Men Came from the East. Interaction between Missiology and Missionary Practice in Asia, 1890-1940," in: Dujardin, Carine and Prudhomme, Claude, eds., *Mission and Science. Missiology Revisited Missiologie revisitée, 1850-1940*. Leuven: Leuven University Press, 2015, 287-310.

Freedman, Maurice. "Rites and Duties, or Chinese Marriage," in: Skinner, William, ed. *The Study of Chinese Society. Essays by Maurice Freedman*. Stanford University Press, 1979, 255-272.

Freedman, Maurice. "The Family in China, Past and Present," in: Skinner, William, ed. *The Study of Chinese Society. Essays by Maurice Freedman*. Stanford University Press, 1979, 240-254.

Gao Xiongya. "Women Existing for Men: Confucianism and Social Injustice against Women in China." *Race, Gender & Class*, 10 (2003) 3, 114-125.

Gallagher, Mary. "Women and Gender," in: Giskin, Howard and Walsh, Bettye S., eds. *An Introduction to Chinese Culture through the Family*. Albany: State University of New York Press, 2001, 89-105.

Glosser, Susan E. "'The Truth I Have Learned': Nationalism, Family Reform, and Male Identity in China's New Culture Movement, 1915-1923," in: Brownell, Susan and Wasserstrom, Jeffrey, eds. *Chinese Feminities / Chinese Masculinities. A Reader*. Berkeley-Los Angeles: University of California Press, 2002, 120-144.

Harrison, Henrietta. "*A Penny for the Little Chinese*: The French Holy Childhood Association in China, 1843-1951." *The American Historical Review*, 113 (2008) 1, 72-92. <https://doi.org/10.1086/ahr.113.1.72>.

Hershatter, Gail. "State of the Field: Women in China's long Twentieth Century." *The Journal of Asian Studies*, 63 (2004) 4, 991-1065.

Hooper, Beverley. "Women in China: Mao v. Confucius." *Labour History*, 29 (1975), 132-145.

Köhler, Wiebke. "Gender Segregation in the Church," in: Betz, Hans Dieter; Browning, Don S.; Bernd Janowski, and Eberhard Jüngel, eds. *Religion Past & Present. Encyclopedia of Theology and Religion*, vol. 5. Leiden-Boston: Brill, 2009, 329-330.

King, Gail. "The Xujiahui Library of Shanghai." *Libraries and Culture*, 32 (1997) 4, 456-469.

Kwok, Pui-lan. *Chinese Women and Christianity 1860-1927*. Atlanta: Scholars Press, 1992.

Langlois, Claude. *Le catholicisme au féminin. Les congrégations françaises à supérieure générale au XIXe siècle*. Paris: Cerf, 1984.

Le Pichon, Alain. "Portrait of a Practical Visionary: Father Léon Robert MEP and the Sisters of St Paul de Chartres in Hong Kong 1914-19." *Journal of the Royal Asiatic Society Hong Kong Branch*, 52 (2012), 225-266.

Li Ji 李紀. "Chinese Christian Virgins and Catholic Communities of Women in Northeast China." *The Chinese Historical Review*, 20 (2013) 1, 16-32.

Li Mingyi 李明毅, ed. *Lishi shang de Xujiahui* 历史上的徐家汇 [Xujiahui in history]. Shanghai: Shanghai Culture Publishing House, 2015.

Li Tiangang 李天綱. "Xujiahui – Tushanwan. Parmi les sources de la culture shanghaienne moderne," in: Espagne, Michel; Gary, Julie and Guangyao Jin, eds. *Conférences Chinoises de la rue d'Ulm*. Paris: Dermopolis, 2017, 461-482.

Liu Dunzhen 刘敦桢. *La maison chinoise* (translated by Georges Métailié, Marie-Hélène Métailié, Sophie Clément-Charpentier, and Pierre Clément). Paris: Berger-Levrault, 1980.

Liu Xian 刘贤. "Two Universities and two Eras of Catholicism in China: Fu Jen University and Aurora University, 1903-1937." *Christian Higher Education*, 8 (2009) 5, 405-421.

Lodwick, Kathleen L. "Missionaries and Opium!," in: Tiedeman, R. Gary, ed. *Handbook of Christianity in China. Volume Two: 1800-present*. Leiden-Boston: Brill, 2010, 354-360.

Ma Li. *Christian Women and Modern China. Recovering a Women's History of Chinese Protestantism*. Lexington Books/Fortress, 2021.

Ma Hsingyo, William. *Pedagogy, Display, and Sympathy at the French Jesuit Orphanage Workshops of Tushanwan in Early-twentieth Century Shanghai*. Unpublished PhD dissertation, Berkeley: University of California, History of Art, 2016.

Mariani, Paul (SJ). "The Phoenix Rises from its Ashes. The Restoration of the Jesuit Shanghai Mission," in: Maryks, Robert Aleksander and Wright, Jonathan, eds. *Jesuit Survival and Restoration. A Global History, 1773-1900*. Leiden-Boston, 2014, 299-314.

McMahon, Keith. "Polygyny, Bound Feet, and Perversion." *Extrême-Orient Extrême-Occident*, special issue, 2012, 159-188. <https://doi.org/10.4000/extremeorient.215>.

Menegon, Eugenio. *Ancestors, Virgins, and Friars: Christianity as a Local Religion in Late Imperial China* (Harvard-Yenching Institute Monograph Series, 69). Harvard University Press, 2009.

Mínguez-Blasco, Raúl. "Between Virgins and Priests: The Feminisation of Catholicism and Priestly Masculinity in Nineteenth-Century Spain." *Gender & History*, 33 (2021) 1, 94-110.

Mo Wei 莫为. "The Gendered Space of the 'Oriental Vatican'. Zi-ka-wei, the French Jesuits and the Evolution of Papal Diplomacy." *Religions*, 9 (2018) 9, article 278, 13 p. <https://doi.org/10.3390/rel9090278>.

Mo Wei 莫为. "Assessing Jesuit Intellectual Apostolate in Modern Shanghai (1847-1949)." *Religions*, 12 (2021) 3, article 159. <https://doi.org/10.3390/rel12030159>.

Moore, P.L. "Coadjutor Brothers on the Foreign Missions." *The Woodstock Letters*, 74 (1945), 5-20, 111-124.

Muller Myrdahl, Tiffany. "Gendered Space," in: Orum, Anthony M., ed. *The Wiley Blackwell Encyclopedia of Urban and Regional Studies*, 2019. <doi/abs/10.1002/9781118568446.eurs0116>.

Mungello, David E., ed. *The Chinese Rites Controversy: Its History and Meaning* (Monumenta Serica Monograph Series, 33). Nettetal: Steyler Verlag, 1994.

Nicolini-Zani, Matteo. *Christian Monks on Chinese Soil. A History of Monastic Missions to China*. Collegeville MN: Liturgical Press, 2016.

Renaud, Rosario. *Süchow, diocèse de Chine, 1882-1931*. Montreal: Éditions Bellarmin, 1955.

Song Haojie 宋浩杰, ed. *Lishi shang de Xujiahui* 历史上的徐家汇 [*Zikawei History*]. Shanghai: Shanghai Culture Publishing House, 2005.

Standaert, Nicolas (SJ). "The Chinese Mission without Jesuits: The Suppression ad Restauration of the Society of Jesus in China." *Ching Feng*, 16 (2017) 1-2, 79-96.

Stevens, Sarah E. "Figuring Modernity: The New Woman and the Modern Girl in Republican China." *National Women's Studies Association Journal*, 15 (2003) 3, 82-103.

Strong, David (SJ). *A Call to Mission. A History of the Jesuits in China 1842-1954*. Volume 1: *The French Romance*. Adelaide: ATF Press, 2018.

Strong, David (SJ). *A Call to Mission. A History of the Jesuits in China 1842-1954*. Volume 2: *The Wider European and American Adventure*. Adelaide: ATF Press, 2018.

Sweeten, Alan Richard. *China's Old Churches. The History, Architecture, and Legacy of Catholic Sacred Structures in Beijing, Tianjin, and Hebei Province*. Leiden-Boston: Brill, 2020.

Sweeten, Alan Richard. *Christianity in Rural China. Conflict and Accommodation in Jiangxi Province, 1860-1900*. Ann Arbor: University of Michigan Press, 2001.

Taveirne, Patrick 譚永亮 (CICM). "Re-reading the Apostolic Letter *Maximum Illud*," in: Ku Weiying 古伟瀛 and Zhao Xiaoyang 赵晓阳, eds. *Jidu zongjiao yu jindai Zhongguo* 基督宗教与近代中国 [*Multi-aspect Studies on Christianity in modern China*]. Beijing: Social Sciences Academic Press, 2014, 64-87.

Tiedemann, R. Gary. "Controlling the Virgins: Female Propagators of the Faith and the Catholic Hierarchy in China." *Women's History Review*, 17 (2008) 4, 501-520.

Tiedemann, R. Gary. *Reference Guide to Christian Missionary Societies in China from the sixteenth to the twentieth century*. Armonk-London: Sharpe, 2009.

Tiedemann, R. Gary, ed. *Handbook of Christianity in China: Volume Two: 1800-Present*. Leiden-Boston: Brill, 2010.

Tiedemann, R. Gary. "Catholic religious communities of women (foreigners)," in: Tiedeman, R. Gary, ed. *Handbook of Christianity in China: Volume Two: 1800-Present*. Leiden-Boston: Brill, 2010, 526-531.

Tiedemann, R. Gary. "Catholic religious communities of Chinese women," in: Tiedeman, R. Gary, ed. *Handbook of Christianity in China: Volume Two: 1800-Present*. Leiden-Boston: Brill, 2010, 587-599.

Tiedemann, R. Gary. "The Chinese Clergy," in: Tiedeman, R. Gary, ed. *Handbook of Christianity in China: Volume Two: 1800-Present*. Leiden-Boston: Brill, 2010, 571-586.

Watson, Rubie S. "Afterword. Marriage and Gender Inequality," in: Watson, Rubie S. and Buckley Ebrey, Patricia, eds. *Marriage and Inequality in Chinese Society*. Berkeley: University of California Press, 1991, 347-368. <http://ark.cdlib.org/ark:/13030/ft6p3007p1/>.

Wiest, Jean-Paul. "Bringing Christ to the Nations: Shifting Models of Mission among Jesuits in China." *The Catholic Historical Review*, 83 (1997) 4, 654-681.

Xiang Hongyan. "Building and Ecclesiastical Real Estate Empire in Late Imperial China." *Catholic Historical Review*, 104 (2019) 4, 636-658.

Yang Wenqi and Yan Fei. "The Annihilation of Femininity in Mao's China: Gender Inequality of Sent-down Youth during the Cultural Revolution." *China Information*, 31 (2017) 1, 63-80.

Zhang Yu. "Women in the Chinese Catholic Church: Local and Foreign Sisters and Gender Relations," in: Chu Yik-yi, Cindy and Leung Kit-fun, Beatrice, eds. *The Palgrave Handbook of the Catholic Church in East Asia / Vol. on China*. Singapore: Palgrave Macmillan, 2021. <https://doi.org/10.1007/978-981-15-9365-9_7-1>.

Zhu Chunfeng 朱春峰. "Xulun Hall of T'ou-Sè-Wè and the Marriage Ceremony of Orphans / Tushanwan xuluntang yu gu'ermen de hunqu yishi 土山湾叙伦堂与孤儿们的婚娶意识," in: Song Haojie 宋浩杰, ed. *Memory of T'ou-Sè-Wè / Tushanwan jiyi* 土山湾记忆. Shanghai: 学林出版社 Xuelin Press, 2010, 133-138.

Zurndorfer, Harriet. "Polygamy and Masculinity in China. Past and Present," in: Kam, Louise, ed. *Changing Chinese Masculinities: From Imperial Pillars of State to Global Real Men*. Hong Kong: Hong Kong University Press, 2016, 13-33. <https://doi.org/10.5790/hongkong/9789888208562.003.0002>.

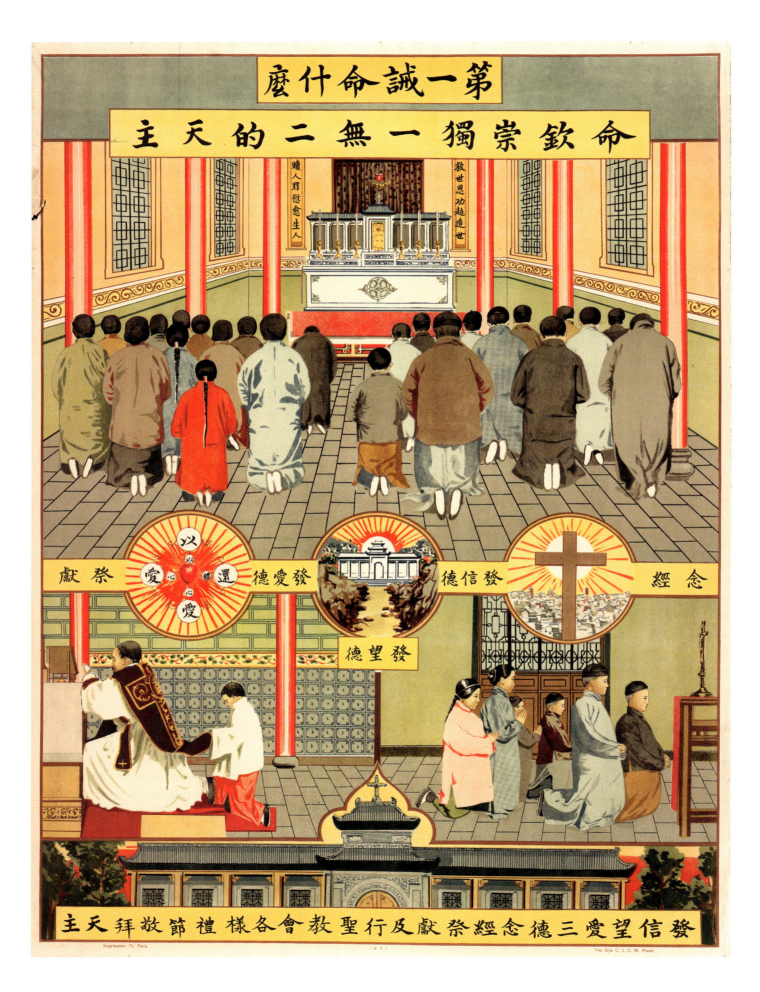

7
Gender-Designed Catholic Churches in North China, 1830s-1920s

Thomas Coomans

Governed by Confucian morality, the strict gender segregation of imperial Chinese society forced Catholic missionaries to adapt the ways in which they evangelized Chinese men and women, which included catechism, sacred liturgy, and sacred spaces. Prior to the nineteenth century, missionaries did not dare to build churches in which men and women could worship together.

When and how were early gender-inclusive churches designed and their interiors organized so as to reconcile the Catholic parish community with the Chinese sociocultural setting, or to attract women to the church and give them a feeling of safety? To what extent were European church types transferable to China?

Gender segregation in the church space was not simply a matter of view and seating, orientation and flow, but also depended on agreement from the bishop and, even more importantly, on the parishioners' degree of openness to change. The combination of all these parameters could create dilemmas, as we will discuss based on a rare letter from 1904, in which a missionary-architect explains the pros and cons of different church types.

This chapter offers the first architectural historical synthesis of gendered spaces in churches and is part of a larger project on gender-segregated spaces in Catholic compounds in China.[1] Besides the traditional missionary sources, our method analyses visual sources, especially interior church photographs that show liturgical arrangements and furnishing before their adaptation during the Republican era, when gender segregation was relaxed, or destruction in the 1950s-1960s [Fig. 7.1].[2]

Systematic investigations into the photographic archives of most Catholic missionary congregations active in late Qing China[3] have revealed that similar gender segregation practices were applied throughout China. It seems, however, that some regions were stricter than others, especially the rural areas of North China, Mongolia, and Manchuria, and the neighboring late Joseon Dynasty in Korea.

In the absence of anthropological comparative studies on the subject, we are unable to specify the extent to which the patriarchal norms were only Confucian or also ethnic in these areas. Evidence of innovative gender-related architectural types, especially the L-shaped church from the 1860s, has been found in the CICM archives and magazines, and completed by fieldwork in Inner Mongolia and northern Hebei.[4]

After introducing the meaning of the cultural differences between the Chinese and Western-Christian orientations of church buildings and gendered seating in church spaces in late Qing, we will examine the two most common gender spatial separations: longitudinal and transversal. Subsequently, the focus will shift to North China and follow the critical evaluation of gendered spaces in L-shaped, double-nave, and cross-shaped churches.[5] L-shaped churches in particular will hold our attention as they offer an astonishing convergence between the gendered spatial organization of traditional local architecture and Western monastic models [Fig. 7.2].

7.1 The plate of the First Commandment from the Catholic catechism Wenda Xiangjie *depicts gendered behavior in the church and domestic space. Sino-Christian illustration by Father Leo Van Dijk CICM, 1928.*
[KADOC-KU Leuven, CICM Generalate Archive, 6563]

1   Coomans, "Gendered Spaces," in this book.
2   Despite two mentions of photographic archives (p. 114 and 514), Tiedemann's *Handbook of Christianity in China* omits the value of iconographic sources, although they do contain unique information, as this chapter proves.
3   See bibliography.
4   Fieldwork was carried out in May 2011 together with Luo Wei in the context of her PhD research at KU Leuven: Luo, *Transmission and Transformation* (2013). Other aspects of CICM churches have been developed in Coomans and Luo, "Exporting Flemish Gothic Architecture;" Luo, "Renzitang;" Coomans and Luo, "Mimesis, Nostalgia and Ideology;" Coomans and Luo, "Missionary-builders;" Luo, "Saibei Shengmu xin hui jiaotang jianzhu yanjiu;" Coomans, "Pugin Worldwide." Important complements on L-shaped churches were found in Sweeten, *China's Old Churches*, 104-106, 239-244.
5   A letter from Father Alphonse De Moerloose CICM (1904) and a short article by Father Jozef Nuyts CICM "En tournée à travers le Vicariat" (1938).

7.2 Catholics from Laohugou village (Hebei) pose south of their L-shaped parish church: the men in front of their right nave and the women in front of their left nave and door above which can be read "women's hall" (女[堂]). Symmetrically, above the men's door, pictured on Fig. 7.28, "men's hall" (男堂) was written. Photo dated 1907. [Leuven, Ferdinand Verbiest Institute, Picture Archive CH-0382]

7.3 CICM father preaching in an unidentified church in Inner Mongolia: he stands on the central axis, the men sit in the left part of the nave and the left aisle, while the women are relegated to the right aisle and their view is obstructed by columns. Photo before 1911, from Missions de Scheut, 30 (1922), 160. [Leuven, KADOC-KU Leuven, Heritage Library, KYB27]

Men and women under the same roof: the shift to gender-inclusive churches

From the beginning, access to women met with difficulties because of their confinement to the home and the separate spheres between women and men known as *nei* 内 and *wai* 外, which prohibited (physical) contact between men and women. As a result, priests often had only indirect access to women (…). In order to avoid suspicion, missionaries soon organized not only separate liturgies but also separate meeting places for men and women. As time progressed, and churches were constructed, there were also special churches for women.[6]

Seventeenth- and eighteenth-century Jesuits accommodated themselves to the masculinity of the Confucian *literati* elites, their moral virtue, and lifestyle, including "views on and behavior toward women [which] were determined by a set of assumptions about gender propriety and space."[7] Their perception of Chinese society was biased and defined by their acquaintance with the upper class, whose women lived secluded lives in domestic spaces. Since missionaries could only access elite women with the consent and in the presence of men, with controlled communication through curtains and screens, they rapidly understood that intermediaries, especially women catechists, were indispensable agents for evangelizing women. While converted men worshipped in churches, women were initially only baptized and worshipped in domestic oratories, and later, from the 1630s onward, could visit small women's churches called "Holy Mother's churches" (*Shengmu tang* 圣母堂), which implied that they were allowed to leave their homes, occasionally attend mass at major church festivals, and meet missionaries to receive sacraments.[8] However, the Jesuit way of adapting the performance of the sacrament to Chinese gender sensitivities was declared illegitimate by the Roman authori-

---

6 Standaert, *Handbook of Christianity in China*, 393-398 (quote p. 395).
7 Amsler, *Jesuits and Matriarchs*, chapters 1 and 2 (quote p. 32).
8 Amsler, *Jesuits and Matriarchs*, 47-66 (especially 54-59: "from oratories to women's churches, 1600-1640").

ties and became an important point of the Chinese Rites Controversy. Chinese Catholic women's congregations were headed by senior sedentary female leaders and helped by itinerant female catechists who had considerable agency and religious autonomy. Nadine Amsler concludes her seminal study *Jesuits and Matriarchs. Domestic Worship in Early Modern China*:

> If we look at Chinese Catholicism from a gender perspective, it becomes evident that the bustling religious life of Catholic churches principally reflects the male aspect of Chinese Catholic communal religiosity. Rather than being oriented toward churches, women's communal religiosity was predominantly domestic, with the house oratory as its center of gravity.[9]

During the period of the prohibition of Christianity in the eighteenth and early nineteenth centuries, the role of female catechists, also known as "Chinese Virgins", was crucial to the transmission of the faith, both because of the lack of priests and their exclusive access to women in domestic spaces. When missionaries returned to China from the 1840s, they relied on the Chinese Virgins as female propagators of the faith. After the Second Opium War, the 1860 Peking Convention recognized the full civil rights of Christians, including the right to evangelize across the whole country, own land property, and erect churches, which contributed to the development of Christianity. At that time, however, "Catholicism in China was an insignificant, marginalized religion burdened by the legacy of the Rites Controversy; strong pockets remained only in remote rural areas."[10] As children of the French Revolution and the Industrial Revolution, nineteenth-century European missionaries looked at Chinese society through a lens that differed from that of their predecessors. Having learned from the Chinese Rites Controversy, they were keen to no longer make the same adaptation "mistakes" – which had led to the Kangxi Emperor's ban on Christianity in 1721 – and wanted to express their foreign identity to some extent. They also made efforts to "control the Chinese Virgins" and gradually introduced European female missionary congregations into China.[11]

Building new churches from the 1860s onwards gave missionaries the opportunity to question traditional Confucian gender segregation and bring men and women under the same roof, in semi-public spaces, to attend religious services, share the Eucharist, and listen to preaching [Figs. 7.3 and 7.4]. "This violated social norms and led some people to see the church as an immoral and filthy place; and other things Catholics did were considered improper."[12] The benefits of this policy far outweighed the risks, however. On the one hand, gender-inclusive churches showed that the Catholic religion proclaimed the equality of all believers in Christ and

7.4 Group of Catholics posing in front of the main altar of the small Marian church of The Admirable Mother on Chongming Island (崇明岛, Shanghai): the women stand on the left and the men on the right. The contrast between the decorated chancel and the rudimentary pews in the nave is striking. [Vanves, Compagnie de Jésus, Archives jésuites de France, FI]

9   Amsler, *Jesuits and Matriarchs*, 111.
10 Wiest, "Specific Catholic Groups, 1860-1900," 238.
11 Tiedemann, "Controlling the Virgins;" also developed in Coomans, "Gendered Spaces," in this book.
12 Sweeten, *Christianity in Rural China*, 48-49 (quote p. 49).

enhanced the feeling of community. On the other hand, it broke the monopoly of the Chinese Virgins regarding access to women, who could then begin to appreciate the spiritual, moral, and liturgical authority of the (foreign) priest. The shift from single-sex to mixed churches – along with the missionaries' condemnation of polygamy, infanticide, foot binding, opium production and addiction, etc.[13] – contributed to elevating the status of women in late Qing society.

From the 1860s, the Protestant missionaries experienced similar social and local problems as Catholics regarding relations between male and female members of congregations, but our research does not include Protestant missions, except for some comparisons. The answers, however, may differ due to the less centralized and more flexible organization of the Protestants, the presence of female missionaries and Bible women, and a different sense of participation, which gave women more leadership opportunities within Protestant communities.[14] Moreover, several Protestant denominations transferred other Western architectural types to China, such as auditorium churches and urban multi-story churches, whose interiors and flow differ greatly.

Church orientation and gendered seating

Once the decision had been made to bring men and women together in one building, the question immediately arose as to which parts of the church would be allocated to women and men respectively. This was not self-evident because the symbolic values of both the gendered seating locations – right/left or front/rear – and the orientations of the buildings – east-west or south-north – are not the same in Chinese and Western/Christian cultures. What were these different symbolic significations and how did they impact the gender division of church interiors across China? To what extent could missionaries be flexible about orientation and gendered seating in churches and the practice of Latin rites? What Western spatial aspects could Chinese geomancy and Confucian principles not accept?

Western-Catholic tradition versus Chinese geomantic and Confucian principles

Since the early ninth century, the east-west orientation of Christian churches, with the chancel and high altar to the liturgical east and the main portal of the nave to the liturgical west, was based on the principle that the priest, when celebrating, and the worshippers, when praying, should face toward the east (*ad orientem*).[15] This symbolism is cosmic and linked to the daily cycle of the sun, from sunrise to sunset: the return of light/life after the darkness of the night/death was a metaphor for Christ's resurrection. Prayers, rituals, and processions are explicitly linked to the two hierarchized poles of the sacramental space of the altar/chancel to the east and the rhetorical space of the pulpit/nave to the west. The liturgical reform resulting from the Council of Trent (1545-1563) required that the longitudinal axis of a church, from the main portal to the high altar, be free of any obstacle to the sight of the tabernacle; this was subsequently placed in the center of the high altar as a staged spatial focal point expressing the Real Presence of Christ in the Catholic Church – according to the doctrine of transubstantiation – and the sacred dimension of the church as God's house. In a nineteenth-century urban context, the east-west orientation of new churches was less strict than in the Middle Ages, but ultramontane Catholics continued to strictly apply the practice of orientation as advocated by Augustus W.N. Pugin (1812-1852):

> Now this beautiful passage of light from sunrise to sunset, with all its striking and sublime effects, is utterly lost in a church placed in any other than the ancient position. In short, there are both mystical and natural reasons for adhering to antiquity in this practice, a depar-

13 Questioning gender segregation and promoting Christianities also motivated the missionaries to reject other social aspects of late Qing society such as polygamy, foot-binding, opium addiction, gambling, and infanticide. See Coomans, "Gendered Spaces," in this book, p. 111-112.

14 Kwok, *Chinese Women and Christianity 1860-1927*; Li Ma, *Christian Women and Modern China. Recovering a Women's History of Chinese Protestantism*, 3-73.

15 As theorized by William Durand (c.1237-1296) in *The Rationale divinorum officium*, book 1, 8: "A church should also be built as follows: that its head properly look towards the east (…) namely, towards the rising point of the equinoctial sun, thus signifying that the Church, while battling in this world, should display moderation and equanimity, in both prosperity and adversity; it should not therefore face the rising point of the midsummer sun, as some do." Also: McCluskey, "Orientation of Christian Churches."

7.5. Group photo of Catholic families posing on the south slope of the church of Xishahe (细沙河, Longpi 龙坯, Hubei). Closer inspection reveals that the men and women are strictly separated and the generations hierarchized. [Leuven, KADOC-KU Leuven, Picture Archive of the Flemish Franciscans: KFH2001]

ture from which can only be justified under the most urgent necessity.[16]

Gender segregation has been common practice in the places of worship of most religions throughout the ages. Until the liturgical reforms of the 1960s, gender segregation was inscribed in the Canon Law of the Catholic Church.[17] The most usual gendered traditional seating in churches, when looking to the main altar/east, placed the men to the right of the main axis and the women to the left.[18] According to the above discussed orientation, women sat on the northern side of the nave (the Gospel side) and men on the southern side (the Epistle side), which was warmer and better lit [Fig. 7.5].[19] Another traditional gendered seating plan located the men in the fore part of the nave and the women in the rear: "the men are in the front part and the women in the inner part since man is the head of the woman and therefore her leader."[20]

In Confucian societies, gender segregation had been established for several thousand years and traditional books helped shape the Confucian gender ideal in the minds of the elite and common people alike.[21] "Male left, female right" (做男友女 zuonan younü) is an established principle in Chinese culture and is related to the ancient *Yin* 阴 and *Yang* 阳 opposing principles in nature, which define left as *Yin*/female/negative and right as *Yang*/male/positive. The *Yang* orientations of south, east, and left were considered superior to the *Yin* orientations of north, west, and right. Moreover, in accordance with the rules of Chinese geomancy (风水 *fengshui*), buildings and tombs had, among other things, to face south in order to harmonize vital energies (气 *qi*) with the configuration of the environment, as has been discussed in a previous chapter.[22] The principle of the main entrance of buildings opening to the south was more strictly respected on the plains of northern China than in the rugged landscapes of southern China, no doubt also because of climatic differences and protection against the freezing north winds.

16 Pugin, *The Present State of Ecclesiastical Architecture*, 15.
17 *1917 Codex Iuris Canonicis*. Canon 1262 § 1: "It is desirable that, in accordance with the ancient discipline, the women in the church should be separated from the men." This practice has been relaxed since the Second Vatican Council (1962-1965) but is still in use in some places.
18 From the priest's point of view, facing the nave, women on the right and men on the left.
19 Durand, *The Rationale divinorum officium*, book 1, 46: "The men remain in the southern part, the women in the northern or northeast part in order to show that the stronger saints ought to stand against the greater temptations of this world, the weaker ones against the lesser temptations; or the stronger or firmer sex ought to be situated in a more open place (…)."
20 Durand, *The Rationale divinorum officium*, book 1, 46.
21 Zhu Yongchun, *Family Regulations* (朱子治家格言 *Zhuzi zhi jia geyan*, 1617-1689), *Tree Character Classic* (三字经 *Sanzi Jing*, thirteenth century), *The Thousand Character Classic* (千字文 *Qianziwen*, AD 502-549). See Coomans, "Gendered Spaces," in this book, p. 33-34.
22 Coomans, "Islands on the Mainland," in this book, p. 109-110.

7.6. Laying of the cornerstone of a small church in Shanxi (unspecified location) by Father Epiphanius Frericks OFM (+1940): the priests wear the Chinese-Catholic sacrificial hat (祭巾 jijin) and stand together with the men inside the raising walls under construction, while the women stand outside.
[Utrecht, Het Utrechts Archief, 1224: Dutch Franciscans, China mission, postcard]

---

23 The prohibition was eventually abolished by Pope Pius XII on December 8, 1939 and Chinese customs were no longer considered superstitious. See Soetens, *L'Église catholique en Chine,* 145-150.
24 Doré, *Recherches sur les superstitions en Chine,* 1/1, 280-289 (quote p. 288, author's translation).
25 Sweeten, *China's Old Churches,* 63-65 (quote p. 63).
26 Hermand, "Monsieur le doyen bâtit," 94 (author's translation).

Many nineteenth-century missionaries in China were ultramontane and unwilling to compromise on their Catholic liturgical rules, especially as Rome maintained its prohibition of Chinese rites.[23] Consequently, they considered geomancy, Yin-Yang principles, etc. as mere "superstitions." The rare references to *fengshui* in nineteenth-century Jesuit sources are extremely negative, such as this excerpt from Father Henri Doré's 禄是遒 SJ (1859-1931) encyclopaedic *Research on Superstitions in China*: "The theory of *Fong-choei* is not only false, but it creates a disturbance among the people and opens the door to a plethora of vexations; in a word, it is pernicious."[24] The missionaries, however, quickly realized that they had to adapt to these fundamental principles of Chinese culture if they were to have any chance of successful evangelization [Fig. 7.6]. Alan Richard Sweeten summarizes their dilemma:

> Geomancy was in fact a double-edge sword: concessions to it or incorporation of it into plot plans implied abidance with an unacceptable practice, though ignoring fengshui might cause unintended complications. Lay Catholics had trouble discerning exactly how fengshui conflicted with their religious beliefs but knew that in a community setting their non-Christian neighbors would blame a misplaced church, and them, for any deleterious natural occurrence. If people saw a building as improperly located, they might attribute to this everything from bad weather to inadequate harvests.[25]

Towards a cultural acculturation compromise

Missionary builders could not ignore the importance of Chinese orientation and gendered practices, which were inevitably discussed on any church construction site. Without naming *fengshui* in their writing, they did consider it in the design of their churches and the spatial organisation of their architectural complexes. Reading between the lines, there is evidence that the question of orientation was a much-discussed issue even before the work began. One rare example from 1923, the case of the church of Tushan (土山, Pixian 邳县, Jiangsu), is reported by Father Louis Hermand 双国英 SJ (1873-1939):

> The orientation is a disaster: sun in the morning and evening, no air in the summer. Moreover, for lack of space, I cannot give my church an east-west orientation. The challenge consists in finding a form that will reconcile the layout of the plot and the best orientation. Why not a Greek cross? Transepts as long as the nave; the chancel should be a little shorter.[26]

It is above all fieldwork combined with the analysis of old photos that leads us to believe that the south-north orientation was commonly adopted and even sometimes combined in a creative way with east-west orientation. Church naves, whether aisled

7.7 Morphologies of gender-designed churches in late Qing North China: A. single-sex churches, B1. longitudinally divided church, B2. transversally divided church, B3. transversally divided church with eastwards-oriented chancel, B4. church with chancel between the men's and women's naves, C1. double-nave church, C2. longitudinally divided church with transept, C3. transversally divided church with transept, C4. L-shaped church. Colours: chancel (yellow), women's nave (green), men's nave (pink).
[THOC 2023]

or not, could be gender divided in different ways, sometimes longitudinally, sometimes transversely [Fig. 7.7]. This had consequences on access to the gendered spaces in the nave because the doorways reserved for men and women had to be separate, whereas both should ideally have faced south.[27] Accordingly, we would like to theorize six rules for the design of churches experienced in one way or another in Late Qing China.

- *South-north orientation*. The missionaries abandoned their norm of east-west orientation because they realized that only south-north orientation was acceptable to the Chinese. They clearly chose not to run the risk of building ominous churches in which parishioners would feel uncomfortable or, worse, refuse to enter. Since the parishioners funded the construction of their church, the final decision was up to them. In urban contexts, parishes were often first established in existing residences which were traditionally designed around oriented courtyards and inserted into the general structure of secular urban fabrics.[28] When churches were rebuilt on a larger scale, their style and morphology generally became more explicitly Western, but their orientation remained Chinese. Only in treaty port concession areas where churches were funded with Western money did orientation matter less than visibility in the Western urban setting.

  When visiting south-north oriented churches in China for the first time, I was surprised to see warm evening sunlight entering from the left [Fig. 7.22], usually the cold northern side of churches in Europe. As a photographer, I was perturbed to miss the rising sunlight on the axis of the apse and the deep light of sunset penetrating from the west, and understood Pugin's aforementioned remark better.

- *In transversally divided churches, men are always in front*. There was little discussion on this point because the Catholic

27 Orientation and *fengshui* have been discussed in Coomans, "Islands on the Mainland," in this book, p. 33-34.
28 Coomans, "Gendered Spaces," in this book, p. 115-120 and 132-133.

7.8 Main south façade of the transversally gender-divided church of "Moung-Ko-Tchenn" (?, Inner Mongolia): the men pose in front of the main door, which gives access to their section of the church, while the women are standing near their rear door. In the foremost left bay is the priest's door to the sacristy and the chancel.
[Leuven, KADOC-KU Leuven, CICM Picture Archive: 18.3.3/01]

7.9 Nave of the village church of Haolaishan (壕赖山, Inner Mongolia), from the priest's viewpoint in the chancel: the south/left wall includes the windows and door, while the north/right wall is blind. The original fore-rear gendered seating has been replaced by left-right seating; no old furnishings remain.
[Photo THOC, May 2011]

29 In some places Confucianism was taken literally and "male left, female right" was not questioned, as can be seen in a pre-1900 interior photo of Beitang cathedral in Beijing.

30 Otto, "Mongolie Centrale…," 9: "The extreme susceptibility of public morality in China has obliged the missionaries to give no hold to the criticism of the pagans. This is why the two sexes are always strictly separated in churches and chapels (…), each sex having a special entrance."

and Confucian traditions agreed on the precedence of men. This division was perpetuated in rural churches until 1949, but later abandoned [Fig. 7.22]. The discussion focused more on whether the space should be longitudinally or transversely gender-divided.

- *In longitudinally divided churches, women are generally on the left/north side.* This observation is mainly based on the location of the side altars which, in China, are usually dedicated to the Virgin Mary (women's side) and Saint Joseph (men's side). The former is usually on the left/north side and the latter on the right/south side. Western-Catholic gendered seating thus prevails over the Chinese, but, due to the south-north orientation, the eastern male side fits with the positive *Yang* orientation. Old photos showing the congregation in the space confirm the

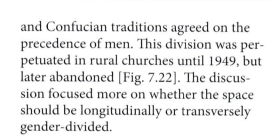

"men right, women left" seating [Figs. 7.4 and 7.13], which is often still perpetuated today in China. Despite this, some old photos do also show cases of "men left, women right" [Fig. 7.3].[29]

- *Men and women had separate entrances, usually south facing.* As men and women were not allowed to touch each other and jostling had to be avoided, Chinese churches had strict gendered circulatory systems and more doors than in Europe.[30] Both the men and women's main gates had to be to the south. Aisled churches and cathedrals often also have lateral doors at the east and west sides. However, when a church has a transept, the doors are at the southern side of the arms and not on the transversal axis as in Europe [Fig. 7.7 C1 and C2].

- *Combination of Chinese and European orientations.* Perhaps the most original type is the transversal church, the main façade of which, like the north building of a courtyard house (*siheyuan* 四合院), is the long south side with its main door in the central bay, and whose interior space is stretched transversely east-west with the main altar located east [Fig. 7.7 B3]. This type reconciles the Western-Christian orientation and the Chinese orientation, has its entrances to the south and, when looking toward the altar, lo-

cates the men at the front and the women at the back. For several reasons, churches of this type were popular in North China: not only did they have the size and orientation of a house, but their north façade was blind – or dug into the loess – to protect the space from the winter wind, and the altar faced east [Figs. 7.8 and 7.9].

- *In all cases, the chancel is prohibited to women and laymen.* As in all Catholic churches at the time, only the clergymen, altar boys, and sacristan had access to the chancel, which was the most sacred space in the church because it included the high altar and the tabernacle, as well as to the side altars when they existed [Fig. 7.10]. Towards the nave, the chancel was clearly delimited by one or more steps and the communion rail. The chancel communicates with the sacristy located at the back or on either side of the apse, and provided with an exterior door. We only know what the altars, liturgical furniture, and decorations with statues, paintings, printed images, banners, carpets, etc. looked like from old photographs.[31]

These design rules developed in the 1860s as answers to the then new architectural program of gender-inclusive churches, and constituted a considerable evolution compared with earlier single-sex churches. All things considered, this shows that the missionaries were flexible enough to adapt to the scale of the communities and to local social gendered relations, which varied in time and space. From then on, men and women could form a community together by being physically in the same space and mentally in communion through prayer, songs, and sacraments. In any case, families were gender separated: men and boys on one side, women, girls and little children on the other. As it was inappropriate for women to look at men, they were veiled when going to church, attending mass, or addressing a missionary.[32]

Separated by partitions, screens, fences, and communion rails

The easiest way to separate men and women was to divide the nave longitudinally or transversally with a screen, fence, or railing (*lankan* or *lanjian* 阑槛).[33] Their location, height, and style varied and were chosen on a case-by-case basis. Old photos prove that partitions, screens, and fences were used in late Qing churches across China. Partitions and screens could be roughly two meters high and blocked the congregation's view, while fences and railings were lower and only intended for gender control as their rail and supports did not block the view.

7.10 The south-north oriented church of Dongjiadu (董家, Shanghai), view from the choir loft to the tripartite space. In the left photo, c.1880, the church is empty, the communion rail separates the chancel from the nave, and a screen divides the nave longitudinally. The right photo, c.1910, shows a solemn mass with abundant decoration, clerics and choir boys in the chancel, men on the right, and women on the left in the nave, but no longer a screen.
[Vanves, Compagnie de Jésus, Archives jésuites de France, FI]

31 Most were systematically destroyed during the Mao era.
32 Rondelez, *La Chrétienté de Siwantze*, 71 (quote from a source dated 1866).
33 X, "À propos de l'église à angle droit."

7.11 This unidentified small single-nave church in Korea is gender-divided with a curtain. The viewpoint is that of the priest: the veiled women face the altar from the right, while the men stand in the opposite part of the nave, closer to the door. Engraving from Les missions catholiques, *31 (August 1899), 361.*
[Leuven, KADOC-KU Leuven, Heritage Library, KYB3962]

7.12. High mass in the cathedral of Taiyuan in the early 1920s: view from the choir loft showing the tripartite space with clergymen in the chancel, the men in the right part of the nave, and the women in the left part.
[Utrecht, Het Utrechts Archief, 1224: Dutch Franciscans, China mission, 289/71]

34 Bret, "Dans la Corée septentrionale," 361.
35 By staying on the door side, the men protected the women. So, "The Origin of Korean Church Architecture," 225-226. Regarding the issue of gender division in Korea, see the section on L-shaped churches.
36 Masson, "L'invention d'une architecture sino-chrétienne," 159. This small church (10 meters by 17 meters) was replaced in 1874-1876 by a larger hybrid-style cathedral that still stands today.

Longitudinal division – right and left spaces

In house chapels and small sacred spaces for worship, a curtain hung from the ridge beam or on a timber structure could separate women and men as shown by a Korean illustration.³⁴ Taken from the altar, this photo-based engraving confirms the priest's dominant position and excellent view of the two groups who were side by side under the same roof [Fig. 7.11]. The women, with their heads veiled, are facing the altar from the right, while the outer door is on the men's side.³⁵ As it was not possible to hang such curtains in larger spaces because the roof frames were higher and air flows stronger, wooden partitions and screens were used for dividing the space longitudinally. An early documented example is the Chinese-style church of Saint Joseph in Guiyang 贵阳 (Guizhou), built in 1849-1850 by Father Étienne Albrand 白斯德望 MEP (1805-1853),³⁶ who describes the partition as "a man's-height wooden screen, from the holy table to the double entrance gate, separates the men from the women, who can all see the altar and pray together without seeing each other."³⁷

A photo of the cathedral of Taiyuan 太原 (Shanxi) taken during a pontifical mass clearly shows how the divided space was occupied by three groups: the bishop and the clergy are in the chancel marked out by a communion rail with balusters, while, in the nave, the men on the right and the women on the left are separated by a high screen set down the long axis [Fig. 7.12]. It is no coincidence that the photographer climbed on the choir loft to avoid the screen and placed his camera in the corner of the men's section of the nave rather than on the main axis. A closer look reveals that there is more space between the screen and the men's seats to allow the bishop and clergymen to process along the men's nave from the main portal to the chancel. Such processions were part of the common episcopal liturgy in cathedrals and could not take place on the women's side of the screen.

In large aisled churches and cathedrals in which the men's and women's areas included proper side altars, parallel longitudinal circulation systems from the doors located on either side of the main portal were required [Fig. 7.13]. This configuration presented a significant problem, however, as the screen

7.13 The Regina Martyrum Church in Suifu (叙州府, now Yibin 宜宾市, Sichuan). The main façade has a central portal and two gendered lateral portals, which open onto the gender-divided nave through a central partition.
[Lyon, Oeuvres Pontificales Missionnaires, fonds iconographique, FXX5]

7.14. Parish church of Gaojiazhuang (高家庄, Lucheng 路程, Shanxi) built in 1883: the screen with Chinese paintings is shifted to the women's side. There are no pews in the nave, only cushions in the women's nave.
[Utrecht, Het Utrechts Archief, 1224: Dutch Franciscans, China mission, 289/24]

running from the main portal to the high altar was an obstacle to procession rituals. In small churches, where the chancel was closer to the congregation and processions were limited to the priest and altar boys, the view towards the altar was better and a low longitudinal screen was not an obstacle. Since the partition screen was a piece of furniture, it was not always exactly along the axis and could be easily moved, depending on circumstances, toward the women's side to allow processions along the axis [Fig. 7.14]. In all these cases, however, the longitudinal screen remained a physical and visual obstacle and was also a waste of space.

The most appropriate solution to the processional liturgy was to clear the main axis of the nave and contain the men and women by means of two parallel railings or fences. Therefore, not only could the processions proceed unhindered, but the whole congregation could enjoy an equal view of the processions and the high altar [Figs. 7.15 and 7.16]. Discussions around the choice of screens or railings would undoubtedly have given rise to disputes between conservative

37 Letter from Étienne Albrand to his brother François, Guiyang, May 1, 1850 (Paris, IRFA, AMEP, vol. 544, 86), quoted by Masson, "L'invention d'une architecture sino-chrétienne," 159-160 (with an old plan).

7.15. Romanesque-style church of Xinzhuang (新庄, Shanxi): elaborate railings define the axial processional lane to the main altar; the pulpit is on the left side.
[Utrecht, Het Utrechts Archief, 1224: Dutch Franciscans, China mission, 289/13-14]

7.16 Local pilgrimage to Our Lady of Lourdes in the Trinity Church of Chongming Island (崇明岛, Shanghai): the space is longitudinally divided with railings. Photo dated 1902.
[Vanves, Compagnie de Jésus, Archives jésuites de France, Fonds iconographque, Q3, Album 1913]

38 Coomans, *Sheshan jiaotang xunzong*, 80-87.
39 Ibidem, 115-126.
40 Nuyts, "En tournée dans le vicariat," 217; on the vicariate of Central Mongolia (author's translation).

and progressive parishioners. As the railings were generally movable, some flexibility about their height, location, and "transparency" was possible without impacting the building itself or questioning the principle of gender segregation. It should be noted that men and women did not always attend church at the same time, especially during prayers and masses celebrated at the side altars. Even then, women and men were expected to remain in their assigned part of the church and enter through their own door.

In busy pilgrimage churches and shrines, gender control railings were used to prevent jostling and manage the flow of pilgrims along different one-way routes that led the men and women to their intended sections of the church. At the Marian shrine of Sheshan 佘山圣母 (Jiangsu, now Shanghai), the first pilgrimage church erected on the hill from 1871 to 1873 was designed on a central Greek cross plan: the main portal opened to the south and was reserved for processions of bishops and priests, while women had to enter the church through the south-west door and the west transept door, and men by doors located symmetrically on the east side.[38] Inside the church, railings defined an axial processional space and separated boxes for men and women, including at the side of the communion rail [Fig. 7.17]. Corresponding with the division inside the church, the gendered outside space was symmetrically organized around two esplanades, the western for women and the eastern for men. As early as 1873, there was a single-sex hall or large room on each of these esplanades in which female and male pilgrims could rest and wait their turn before entering the church. When the church was full, these halls could occasionally be used to say mass. At the end of each esplanade a small octagonal chapel was dedicated to Saint Joseph, on the men's side, and to the holy angels on the women's side. The zigzag path on the southern slope of the hill was a Way of the Cross and was used for the processional ascent of well-defined groups, while the two side paths allowed men and women to descend separately with more freedom.[39]

Transversal division – fore and rear spaces

[Another separation] is to give the women's church a special entrance at the back, separated quite simply from the men, who are at the front, by a communion rail to which the priest comes to distribute the Eucharist. Men enter through one or two side doors. If the church has the shape of a cross (…), the back of the main nave is reserved for women, while the front and the transept are left to men.[40]

In North China, the façades of small east-west oriented single-nave churches, which included the doors and windows, faced south, while the north façade was blind to protect the interior from freezing winter winds. Such churches were transversally divided into three parts by two communion rails that defined the chancel, the male and female areas, preventing women and men from mixing while allowing them to congregate, pray, and sing in the same room. Each section had its own doorway: the chancel in the eastern bay was only accessible from the sacristy to the priest, sacristan, and altar boys; the main entrance of the church, in the central bay of the south façade, gave access to the men's section of the church and was also used as a main entrance by the priest and for processions; the western bays were for women, who entered from another, usually smaller door in the south side [Figs. 7.7 B3, 7.8 and 7.18]. Placing the men toward the front obliged them to focus on the altar and priest in the chancel, or on the pulpit when the priest was preaching [Fig. 7.19].

Not only was the space for men better located, but it was often also more spacious. According to photographs and the location of the men's door, the number of bays reserved for women was fewer and their door was smaller and sometimes relegated to the back/west side of the church. In the small Marian church of Dabaogou 大保沟

7.17 Pilgrimage church of Sheshan hill: southern slope with zigzag ascending Way of the Cross and gender-segregated descending path, from Les missions catholiques, *9 (July 13, 1877), 423; and interior divided by fences, seen from the rear of the men's side, photo c.1900. [Leuven, KADOC-KU Leuven, Heritage Library, KYB3962, and Vanves, Archives jésuites de France, FI, Q3, Album 1913]*

7.18 South façade of the transversal church of Tumenzishan (土门子山, Jehol): the men's bays, door, and traceried windows are larger and more adorned than those of the women. [Leuven, KADOC-KU Leuven, CICM Picture Archive: 13.3.2/01]

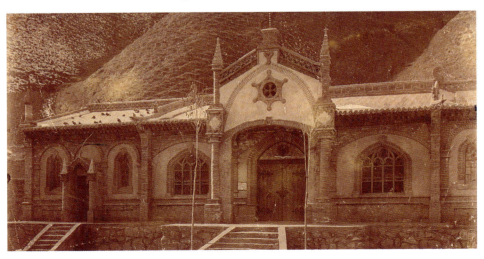

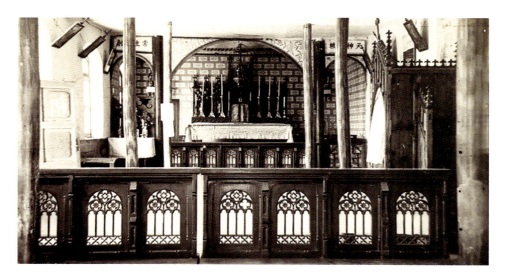

7.19 Village church of Wusungtulu (?, Jehol): view from the women's rear section to the main altar; the men's fore section is marked out by two communion rails with Gothic tracery decoration. [Leuven, KADOC-KU Leuven, CICM Picture Archive: 20.2.15/01]

7.20 The small Chinese-style church of Dabaogou (Shanxi), built 1901, looks like the main building of a traditional *siheyuan* courtyard house, facing south and set on a raised platform. Inside, the men's nave seen from the priest's viewpoint: the main/south door is on the left while the screen in the back marks the women's section. The church has been enlarged to the right/north. [Photo THOC, June 2019]

(Shanxi), built in 1901 and enlarged in 1985, we noted that the area reserved for men included three bays, while the women had only the two rear bays, which were poorly lit and adapted from a half floor – probably meant for children – and accessible by a steep staircase.[41] A transversal partition with glass doors separated these two rear bays for women and children from the men's nave [Fig. 7.20].

Larger, aisled churches could also be divided transversally from one side wall to the other by communion rails, with an opening in the middle to allow processions along the longitudinal axis [Fig. 7.21]. The priest first gave communion to the men at the front communion rail, then moved to the back communion rail to give communion to the women. A short description of the parish church of Qilaowengeqi 其老文個氣 (Inner Mongolia) explains:

> Like in Italy, most churches in China do not have chairs. People kneel on the ground: many of the faithful bring a small carpet [cushion] each time they come to church. The communion rail near the altar is for men; the other is for the women who stand behind the men during services. The missionaries follow in this the Chinese customs which prescribe the separation of the sexes. Men and women do not enter the church by the same door.[42]

In other churches with three naves, there was no central processional axis, but the communion rails and pews occupied the full width of the central nave. Processions had to take the aisles, which were free of pews and communion rails. Such was the case of the village church of Shebiya 舍必崖 (Shabernoor, Inner Mongolia), a Western-style building erected in 1904-1905 after the plans of Father De Moerloose CICM.[43] The longitudinal axis of this church is north-south: the south or rear entrance is for women, while men entered through two side doors located

in the central bay on the east and west sides [Fig. 7.7 B2]. The aisles are narrow and were mainly intended initially for movement inside the building. Today, the furniture has been rearranged and spatial organization and flow have radically changed: the longitudinal axis is free, the communion rails have disappeared, and gender segregation is still practiced but differently: men on the right and women on the left [Fig. 7.22]. In addition, the large window behind the altar has been bricked up to protect the chancel and nave from northerly winds. This is a good illustration of how the combination of fieldwork and an old photograph allows us to understand the evolution of spatial arrangements and liturgical furnishings.

7.21 The church of Manhui (蛮会, Inner Mongolia) faces south, but the chancel is to the west and the bell tower to the east. The entrances are: the sacristy (west), the men's portal (center), and the women's door behind the north-east corner. Inside the communion railings are open on the central axis but continue through the aisles. Photos after 1900.
[Leuven, KADOC-KU Leuven, CICM Picture Archive: 21.2.7/01-02]

7.22 Original and current use of space in the church of Shebiya (Inner Mongolia): built in 1904, the nave was transversally divided, with communion rails separating the men and the women, while today the space is longitudinally divided.
[Leuven, KADOC-KU Leuven, CICM Picture Archive: 20.2.13/02, and Photo THOC, May 2011]

41 The interior of the seven-bay rectangular church (20.85 m long; 5.80 m width) is divided from east to west into: one-bay sacristy, one-bay chancel, three bays for the men, including the central door, and two bays with gallery for the women. The 1985 extension of the church is on the north side and longitudinal. Fieldwork notes, June 15 2019. With thanks to Father Andrew Zhang Dongliang 张东亮 and Father Peter Wu Yanbin 武岩斌.
42 X, "Intérieur de l'église de Ts'i-lao-wen-ke-ts'i."
43 Coomans and Luo, "Exporting Flemish Gothic," 229-337.

The missionary-architect's dilemma in North China

In North China, the task of the church builder was concerned less with the location of railings, screens, and furniture – which depended on priests and parishioners – and more with the design and construction of solid and inexpensive churches that would resist the harsh climate, respond to the requirements of sacred liturgy, and ensure gender segregation. As discussed above, such inclusive congregations risked being accused by non-Catholics of not respecting Confucian principles and holding immoral mixed assemblies. The presence of Muslim communities in the regions of North China where the Belgian missionaries of the Congregation of the Immaculate Heart of Mary (henceforth CICM) were active, particularly in Gansu, Ningxia, and Inner Mongolia, contributed to making the issue even more sensitive. It is precisely in these vicariates apostolic behind the Great Wall[44] that experiments were carried out with innovative gender designed architectural church types.

Father Alphonse De Moerloose 和羹柏 CICM (1858-1932), a missionary-architect trained at the Saint Luke Art School in Ghent (Belgium), was sent to North China in 1885 and was involved in numerous church building projects from around 1900 until his retirement in 1929.[45] He first spent fourteen years in the vicariate apostolic of Gansu, not as an architect but as a parish priest. His artistic activity seems to have been limited to the design of Gothic-style church furnishing and decoration. In 1899, Bishop Jerome Van Aertselaer 方济众 CICM (1845-1924) relocated De Moerloose to the apostolic vicariate of Central Mongolia and commissioned him to design a seminary with a chapel in Xiwanzi (西弯子, Chongli 崇礼, Hebei). Shortly after his arrival, the 1900 Boxer Uprising destroyed many churches in the CICM vicariates and killed thousands of Christians and dozens of missionaries.[46] The construction of parish churches was usually financed by the parishioners, which, in the early mission stage, often resulted in poor architecture or endless building work. The situation changed after the Boxer Uprising due to indemnity money from the State for demolished churches. These circumstances were De Moerloose's chance of a lifetime: from being an average missionary in Gansu, he became the most important church builder of his generation in North China. His reputation exceeded the CICM and other French-speaking missionary societies also called on his services.[47] In December 1909, he left CICM and became a diocesan priest in the vicariate of Beijing, which facilitated his architectural work.

In a letter to Vicar apostolic Van Aertselaer, dated February 18 1904, Father De Moerloose mentions his architectural and liturgical dilemma about church types and gendered spaces. This exceptional source plunges us into the heart of the architectural debate and confirms the role of the vicar apostolic as guardian of liturgical prescriptions and final decision-maker in church design, in accordance with the prescriptions of Canon Law.[48] Seeking to make himself understood by his superior, Father De Moerloose adds small sketches in the margins of his letter and concludes with a personal proposal [Fig. 7.23].

> I am currently busy with the church of Tsi-sou-mou [Qisumu]; these drawings will be completed in two or three days. I was obliged to follow the existing foundations which, with the women's church, form *jenn tze t'ang* [*renzitang*] or a right angle [Fig. 7.24]. If I were free, I would certainly not have chosen this form and am happy to learn that Your Excellency is not in favor of it at all. I liked the V-shape even less, which we tried out earlier in Sa-perh [Shabo'er?]. I remember very well that regarding the program for the house of Si-wantze [Xiwanzi], Your Excellency expressed the desire to have a chapel with two naves. Among the old churches of Flanders there are

---

44 Erected in 1840, the vicariate apostolic of Mongolia was divided into three vicariates in 1883: Eastern Mongolia (Jehol), Southwestern Mongolia (Suiyuan / Hohot), and Central Mongolia (Xiwanzi); in 1922, a section of the latter became the prefecture apostolic of Outer Mongolia (Ulaanbaatar). See Verhelst and Pycke, *CICM Missionaries*, passim, Luo, *Transmission and Transformation*, and <https://www.catholic-hierarchy.org/>.

45 Coomans, "Pugin Worldwide", 167-171; Coomans, *Sheshan jiaotang* xunzong, 169-212; Coomans, "Unexpected Connections," 275-281; Coomans, "Sint-Lucasneogotiek in Noord-China;" Coomans and Luo, "Mimesis, Nostalgia and Ideology," 499-502; Coomans and Luo, "Exporting Flemish Gothic;" Coomans and Luo, "Missionary-Builders," 335-337; Van Hecken, "Alphonse Frédéric De Moerloose."

46 *Missions en Chine et au Congo* (1901, 1902, 1903): passim.

47 He designed churches for Lazarists in Hebei, Trappists in Hebei, and Jesuits in Hebei and in Shanghai.

48 *1917 Codex Iuris Canonicis.* Canon 1162 to Canon 1171.

49 Letter from A. De Moerloose to J. Van Aertselaer, Gaojiayingzi 高家营子 ([northwest] Hebei), February 18, 1904 (author's translation from French). Leuven, KADOC-KU Leuven, CICM Generalate Archive, 4562.

some of this kind, but this form has been abandoned for two main reasons, the first of which is that the main altar does not face the center of the building, only half of it is seen; the second is that a double nave requires a double roof whose interior slopes meet in a central cornice, which causes great inconvenience. I pointed out to Your Excellency that in these countries the snow would rush between these two roofs and a zinc water pipe would be impractical, we experienced this in Siwan [Xiwanzi]. The best way to counter this would be to make this water pipe out of carved stone. The obstacle is therefore more practical than aesthetic. This is a question to be studied.

In San tao ho [Sandaohe], where the church has this shape, we wanted to circumvent the difficulty by making an almost flat roof across the whole building, but everyone agrees that the effect produced is disastrous; it is like a huge brick kiln.

If a church plan for Siwan [Xiwanzi] had been requested, I had intended to try the full cross form. The men would occupy the front part, the women the two transepts, while the choir would be reserved for the clergy and seminarians. In the center, a stone altar without an altarpiece, in full view of every part of the church.[49]

First, Father De Moerloose mentions "L-shaped churches" and "V-shaped churches," two types he and his bishop agree on rejecting. Even so, he admits that he is currently drawing up plans for an L-shaped church and has to reuse existing foundations. No doubt the parishioners at that particular site were keen on this church type and the architect did not succeed in convincing them to change their minds. Second, Father De Moerloose evokes the "double-nave church," which the bishop had been keen to build in Xiwanzi at some stage. Being against this church type himself, the architect tries to convince his superior using liturgical, constructive, and aesthetic arguments. Third, he concludes with a proposal for a "cross-

7.23 In his letter to Vicar apostolic Jerome Van Aertselaer CICM, February 18, 1904, Father Alphonse De Moerloose CICM, adding sketches to the words, gives his opinion about L-shaped churches, double-nave churches, and cross-shaped churches.
[Leuven, KADOC-KU Leuven, CICM Generalate Archive, 4562]

7.24 The Gothic-style church of Meiguiyingzi (Inner Mongolia) was designed by Father De Moerloose CICM in 1904 despite the fact that he was against L-shaped churches, but was unable to oppose the will of the local congregation. Photo from the south-east by Father Frantz Van Dorpe CICM, 1912.
[Knokke, family archives Cécile Masureel-Van Dorpe]

50   Aubin, "Christian Art and Architecture," 736.
51   Luo, *Transmission and Transformation*, 97-104 (Xiwanzi), 105-119 (Xiaoqiaopan), 149-160 (Meiguiyingzi); Luo, "Saibei Shengmu xin hui jiaotang jianzhu yanjiu," 392-394; Luo, "Renzitang;" Coomans and Luo, "Mimesis, Nostalgia and Ideology," 498-499, 515.
52   Van Koot, "Aperçu sur le vicariat," 195. It is unclear if he V-shaped church of *Sa-perh* mentioned in Father De Moerloos's 1904 letter is the same or a post-Boxer reconstruction.

7.25 *The ideal type L-shaped church of Shabo'er (Inner Mongolia), designed as a perfect symmetrical composition by Father Edmond Rubbens CICM in 1888. Engraving from* Missions en Chine et au Congo, *13 (February 1890), 201. [Leuven, KADOC-KU Leuven, Heritage Library, KYB27]*

shaped church," where the altar would be at the crossing, the clergy in the choir, the men in the nave, and the women in the transept arms. We will discuss these three church types from cases in North China in the following sections.

L-shaped churches or renzitang

In North China, the design of small churches was usually in the shape of the letter 'L', called renzitang 人子堂 by the Christians, or, according to the missionaries, "pants church," after the manner of winter trousers that stand upright by themselves when filled with wool and padding. Thus, a church consists of two identical buildings, each with its own entrance, communion rails, confessional, stations of the cross, one building for men and another for women, joined at right angles. On the inside, the junction of the two naves is indicated by a high altar and a little bell tower on the outside.[50]

These L-shaped churches have been viewed as a curiosity by historians, who demonstrated their amusement by using the Dutch nickname "pants churches" (*broekkerk*), as given by the Flemish CICM Fathers. Architectural analysis, however, remains limited to two or three cases and general considerations.[51] This section will define the specific architectural type of the L-shaped church – and its variant, the V-shaped church – in North China and contextualize Father De Moerloose's letter. Furthermore, four questions related to the L-shaped church type will be discussed: its origin in North China, its links with European L-shaped churches, its presence in other parts of China, and the Korean L-shaped or *hanok*-church. The most salient point is that these churches were all gender-designed in order to keep men and women in separate spaces from which they could see the main altar without seeing each other. We will look more closely at the chronology of the earliest cases and note that the 1860s, following the Second Opium War, were crucial years. The then adaptation of a European monastic type to missionary parish churches in late Qing North China in order to accommodate Confucian social gender segregation is a fascinating transfer of spatial design.

Defining an architectural type

Two engravings published in the 1889 and 1890 issues of *Missions en Chine at au Congo* briefly introduce Chinese *renzitang* churches to the European reader. One shows the ideal type, while the other describes the archetype, one of the earliest and best-documented completed projects; their combination allows us to define the architectural type, which will be compared with seven other identified cases – detailed in Appendix 1 – to introduce nuances about size, orientation, style, and furniture.

First, the compound of Shabo'er 沙钵儿 (Inner Mongolia, Appendix 1.2) is depicted as an ideal layout imagined by a nineteenth-century Western rational mind imbued with symmetry and gender segregation [Fig. 7.25]. The project was commissioned in 1888 to Father Rubbens.[52] In a *fengshui* landscape,

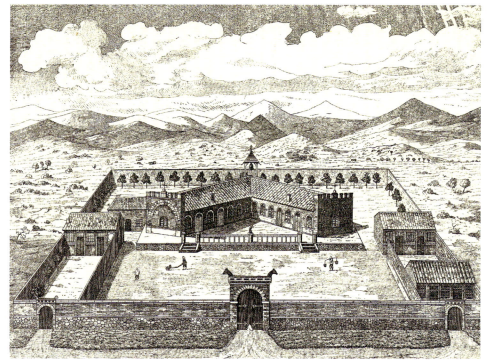

the compound faces south and has three entrances: the central gate opens onto a square and the church, while the left doorway gives access to the boys' school and the missionary's residence, and the right doorway to the girls' school and the Chinese Virgins' house, according to the gendered spatial arrangements of a parish compound.⁵³ The L-shaped church is symmetrically sited on a terrace with two wings, each at 45 degrees to the main axis. Both wings have the same number of windows and doors, all of which face south.

The second engraving shows the L-shaped church of Xiwanzi 西弯子 (Hebei, Appendix1) before 1889, seen from the courtyard [Fig. 7.26], and is accompanied by a description:

> At first glance, this does not look like a church. (…) The church is made of two wings meeting at a right angle, and the altar is at the intersection, under a kind of tower in the shape of a lantern. A *lang-dze* [*langzi* 廊子] or peristyle, runs along the inner facades. The [other] two wings, which complete the square, form the missionary's house.⁵⁴

The architecture was fully Chinese, from the terrace, the timber bay structure, and the curved roof to the lantern tower at the crossing. This church, named the "Double Love Hall" (*shuang ai tang* 双爱堂), was erected by French Lazarists in 1862 and handed over to the Belgian CICM in December 1865. The L-shaped type showed close links with northern Chinese domestic architecture that reflected Confucian principles and gender differentiation, especially the traditional courtyard house (*siheyuan* 四合院).⁵⁵ The width of the naves (about eight meters) and the lantern above the main altar gave the church a monumental character that exceeded the function of the courtyard house. The axis of the men's nave was southwest-northeast oriented and its northwestern wall was parallel with the street [Fig. 7.31]. A Chinese gate, located west of the men's nave,

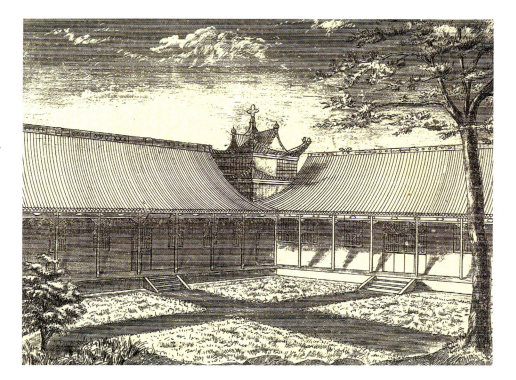

opened onto a front courtyard with a screen wall, which was connected to the western corner of the main courtyard [Fig. 7.46]. An interior view taken from the men's nave towards the high altar shows the thin timber columns supporting the Chinese roof structure partially hidden by a velum, while four much larger columns support the lantern tower [Fig. 7.27]. To the right of the chancel, three semicircular arches open onto the women's nave. The unusual location of the pulpit inside the chancel made the preacher visible from both the men's and women's naves. In 1883, the *Propagande fide* reorganized the mission to Mongolia and created several vicariates apostolic. Xiwanze became the seat of the vicariate apostolic of Central Mongolia, inciting the CICM to improve the architecture of their cathedral. In 1888, they suppressed the Chinese lantern tower and erected a brick bell tower and sacristy in the Gothic style on the main axis behind the chancel [Fig. 7.31]. This change of style and size made the L-shaped church more visible on the skyline and contributed to enhancing its status as a cathedral. The Double Love Hall, with the exception of the Gothic tower,

7.26 The Double Love Hall in Xiwanzi (Hebei), erected in 1862, seen from the southern corner of the courtyard. The men's nave is on the left, the women's nave on the right, each with their own doorway to the south, and a Chinese lantern tower marks the crossing. Engraving from Missions en Chine et au Congo, *1 (February 1889), 8. [Leuven, KADOC-KU Leuven, Heritage Library, KYB27]*

53 Coomans, "Gendered-Segregated Spaces," in this book, p. 120-127.
54 Otto, "Mongolie Centrale," 9 (author's translation).
55 Liu, *La Maison chinoise*, 110-171.

7.27 Interior view of the men's nave and chancel of the Double Love Hall in Xiwanzi: on the right side, the arches that open onto the women's side are visible, while the pulpit stands in the chancel. [Leuven, KADOC-KU Leuven, CICM Picture Archive: 17.4.5/07]

56 Romanesque cathedral-type church with two towers, a high nave with aisles, large transept, choir with ambulatory and radiating chapels, and a capacity of 2,000 people. Dieu, "La nouvelle cathédrale de Si-wan-tze;" X, "La nouvelle église de Si-wan-tez;" Rondelez, *La chrétienté de Siwantze*, 106-109; Luo, *Transmission and Transformation*, 209-220, 432-440.

57 When facing the altar: men left and women right in Xiwanzi, Dafagong, Tongjiayingzi, and Shabo'er; women left and men right in Xiaoqiaopan, Laohugou, Majiazi, and Meiguiyingzi.

was demolished in 1930 after the inauguration of a grand, fully Western-style cathedral in 1926.[56] A photo taken during the demolition work shows a section of the women's nave, which was large, long, and low [Fig. 7.47]. The total capacity of the cathedral was about 1,000 people.

Seven other *renzitang* churches dating from the 1860s to the 1900s have been identified in the CICM picture archive and magazines. These cases allow us to discuss variants of the above defined L-shaped church type according to orientation, size, and style. Additional details and illustrations can be found in Appendix 3-9. More *renzitang* churches undoubtedly existed in the vicariates of Central Mongolia, Eastern Mongolia, and Southwestern Mongolia but, as far we know, they were not photographed and gradually disappeared.

In the identified cases, men and women were not systematically in the left or right nave.[57] The main criterion seems to have been that the main entrance for men should be to the south. However, the ideal church of Shabo'er is offset by 45 degrees in order to allow the two doors to open onto the triangular terrace to the south, while the cathedral of Xiwanzi formed two sides of a square courtyard, which was also offset 45 degrees from the cardinal points.

Due to the topography, *fengshui* rules, and other buildings in the compound, the men's nave could be transversally or longitudinally oriented south-north. In the first case, the main entrance is on the long south façade like a Chinese house, allowing the main altar to be positioned to the east of the men's nave [Fig. 7.7 C4]; in the second case, the main entrance is on the short façade like a Western church, but on the Chinese south-north axis.[58] This not only proves the preeminence of men, but also of the priest because the main altar always faced the men's nave. Women had to content themselves with a side view of the high altar. Furthermore, photos show that the women's nave was often shorter than the men's,[59] while the women were more assiduous churchgoers and kept their young children close by. Above the two doors of Laohugou's (老虎沟 Hebei, Appendix 3) church the inscriptions 男人堂 (*nanren tang*) and 女人堂 (*nüren tang*) identified the doorways to the men's and women's naves respectively [Figs. 7.2 and 7.28]. In certain circumstances, the missionaries were perplexed by the lack of flexibility for separate entrances:

> And the day of the wedding, you say? Oh! Very simple and above all very Chinese. Once the ceremony has concluded beneath the altar, sir goes out through one door, and madam retires through the other.[60]

There is no information about architectural discussions with the Chinese parishioners. Although the L-shaped church is a well-defined type, photographs reveal a variety of sizes and styles. Some styles were Chinese, others Gothic, and others still hybrid. The small church of Laohugou looked like an average north Chinese house, while the more elaborate church of Xiaoqiaopan 小桥畔 (Shaanxi, Appendix 4) combined two

7.28 CICM missionaries posing in front of the men's nave (left) and the priest's residence (center) in Laohugou village (Hebei). Above the men's door is written "men's hall" (男堂). Photo from Father Jozef Segers's memorial photo album, 1918, no. 5.
[Leuven, KADOC-KU Leuven, CICM Picture Archive: 18.3.3/04 – KFH 1776]

naves with *langzi* outer galeries and a masonry crossing surmounted with a remarkable Chinese lantern tower that provided zenithal light for the Gothic-style main altar [Figs. 7.29 and 7.50]. Hybrid forms could differ greatly, as in Dafagong 大法公 (Inner Mongolia, Appendix 6) and Tongjiayingzi 佟家营子 (Inner Mongolia, Appendix 7), in their way of combining Gothic elements with different vernacular architectures [Figs. 7.55 and 7.56]. In 1904, Father De Moerloose designed the monumental L-shaped church of Meiguiyingzi 玫瑰营子 (Inner Mongolia, Appendix 9) in the pure Saint Luke Gothic style, which failed to match the climate of Inner Mongolia and was quickly criticized [Figs. 7.24 and 7.55].[61]

Last but not least, the V-shaped church of Tousumu 头苏木 (Inner Mongolia, Appendix 8) is depicted twice in the CICM magazine [Figs. 7.30 and 7.54].[62] From the photos, the angle between the two naves is acute, in all likelihood 60 degrees. In his 1904 letter, Father De Moerloose mentions the V-shaped church of Sa-perh (Shabo'er) and adds that he disliked it more than the L-shape. It is easy to understand why, since articulating the masonry and the roof frames of two buildings at 60 degrees is more difficult than at 90 degrees. The main advantage of the V-shape church was the view from and of the main altar, which was positioned at the intersection of the axes of both naves. This reduced the visual discomfort of the celebrant priest when looking at both naves, but did not improve the disastrous acoustics.

We can conclude this section with a comment by Father Jozeph Nuyts 饶启迪 CICM (1898-1986) who, in 1938, at a time when gender relations were being relaxed in Chinese society, reflected on the L-shaped church type:

[In the] L-shaped church [église d'équerre], (…) the altar faced the men's nave, but was shown in profile to the women's nave. This arrangement took full account of the separation of the sexes as required by ancient Chinese customs, since the men and women could not even see each other, but it brought with it serious inconveniences. First, this triangle with a door at each end gave rise to formidable drafts dur-

58 Main entrance on the short south side in Meiguiyingzi, Tousumu, and Dafagong. Main entrance on the long south side in Xiaoqiaopan, Laohugou, Tongjiayingzi, Shabo'er, and Majiazi. The men's and women's entrances are on the long side of their respective naves in Xiwanzi, Laohugou, Shabo'er, and Majiazi.
59 Shorter women's naves in Laohugou, Tongjiayingzi, and Majiazi; equal length in Xiwanzi, Xiaoqiaopan, Meiguiyingzi, Shabo'er, Dafagong, and Tousumu. In Xiwanzi, the women's opening to the nave consisted of three arches supported by two columns [Fig. 7.27].
60 X, "À propos de l'église à angle droit."
61 Nuyts, "En tournée à travers le Vicariat," 218-219.
62 X, "À propos de l'église à angle droit;" X. "Chine. L'église de T'eou-sou-mou."

7.29 Father Jan-Baptist Steenackers CICM built the remarkable L-shaped church of Xiaoqiaopan (Shaanxi) in 1884: view from the south-east with the men's nave on the left, the women's nave on the right, and the Chinese lantern tower at the crossing; interior view of the chancel from the men's nave, with a Gothic-style high altar designed by Father De Moerloose CICM in 1890.
[Leuven, KADOC-KU Leuven, CICM Picture Archive: 21.2.4/01-02]

7.30 The V-Shaped church of Tousumu (Inner Mongolia) was symmetrically designed with an equal men's nave (right) and women's nave (left). Photo from Missions en Chine et au Congo, *23 (1911), 15.*
[Leuven, KADOC-KU Leuven, Heritage Library, KYB27]

ing the icy months of our Mongolian winters. Preaching required an expenditure of voice and breath that obtained little result, since one preached from the altar, turned towards the men and the sounds were lost in their nave. Another disadvantage: the cacophony necessarily resulting from the separation of the two groups of faithful. Our Chinese have still kept the wonderful habit of praying in choir during mass, of singing their morning and evening prayers, litanies, stations of the cross, etc. together (...) In the L-shaped churches, as one could not hear from one wing to the other, it was absolutely incoherent, and this prayer was nothing but a hubbub of absolutely unbearable vociferations... even for Chinese people.[63]

"Conciliating Chinese customs with Christian habits": the origin of L-shaped churches in North China

The L-shaped Double Love Hall of Xiwanzi was built in 1862 by French Lazarist missionaries before the arrival of the first CICM Fathers in 1865. It replaced an older church built on another site in Xiwanzi in 1835-1836 by the French Joseph-Martial Mouly 孟振生 CM (1807-1868), the first vicar apostolic of Mongolia in 1840, who used the then newly built church of Xiwanzi as his cathedral.[64] Considered the first church in North China to bring men and women together under the same roof, this church is only known from a long and remarkable description by Father Mouly, written in a 1836 letter to his superior in Paris and published in the *Annales de la Propagation de la Foi* in 1838.[65] The letter begins with an architectural description of the single-nave building:

> This church is, I have no doubt, the largest in China. It is seventy Chinese feet long and thirty-five wide [a double square is about 22.4 x 11.2 meters]; it is built according to the rules of local architecture. The foundations, at the height of half a foot above ground, are of stone; the wall outside is in beautiful gray brick; inside, except for a three-foot brick plinth, everything is adobe covered with whitewash. The roof

is covered with fluted tiles; the pavement is in square bricks. Behind the high altar is a building thirty feet long by twenty wide [about 9.6 x 6.4 meters], intended for women. The church is in a courtyard; two high walls block the view from the street side. One enters by a large gateway, similar to that of the houses of wealthy Chinese. A brick pathway, lined with stones, leads to the church's various doors. The high altar is in painted wood, raised on a brick step. (…) The church is not vaulted; one can see the whole frame of the roof, but the view is not disagreeable, because the beams are, like the windows and the doors, varnished with a kind of oil that gives the wood a beautiful luster. The chancel takes twenty feet from the length of the church and keeps the width of thirty-five feet, so that all ceremonies can be performed there with ease; it is separated from the nave by a wooden rood screen [*portail*]. Since pews and chairs are not in use in China [Figs. 7.3, 7.14 and 7.21], we have none in the nave: small felt carpets, laid out in order, are used by the Christians to kneel during prayer, and to sit during preaching.[66]

The most important point for the issue that concerns us is how Father Mouly brought men and women together under one roof and kept them apart "in order to conciliate Chinese customs with Christian habits" (*afin de concilier les usages chinois avec les habitudes chrétiennes*). This innovation was bold because Confucian morality had previously required men and women to worship in different places. Father Mouly's letter continues:

It would be completely contrary to Chinese customs for women to attend Church services with men: they never entered our church in Peking; they had their own chapels and oratories. We wanted to establish things here [in Xiwanzi] on the same footing; we feared above all, by doing otherwise, that we would scandalize the infidels. In order to conciliate Chinese customs with Christian habits, I erected the building behind the altar: it is exclusively intended for women, who have a different door to the men, without ever being able to meet with them. A light bamboo louver similar to those the Chinese have at their doors separates the women from the chancel and prevents them from being seen, without preventing them from seeing what is being done at the altar. By this means I have spared Chinese delicacy, preserved the practice of the Church, and facilitated general instruction for the missionaries.[67]

Both quotes fail to mention an L-shaped plan, but locate the women's building "behind the altar" (*derrière l'autel*), or rather in the prolongation of the chancel but hidden by a bamboo louver partition (*claire-voie en bambou*) [Fig. 7.7 B4]. Father Mouly specifies that he erected the women's building behind the altar (*j'ai construit le bâtiment qui se trouve derrière l'autel*) – which suggests that the church for men already existed – from which women could hear and see without being seen.[68] In his book on Xiwanzi published in 1938, Father Valère Rondelez 隆德理 CICM (1904-1983) confuses the 1836 church with that built in 1862 and erroneously asserts that the former had a right-angled wing for women like the latter.[69] This mistake has been repeated by other authors.[70] At this stage, we could conclude that the church of 1836 was not a *renzitang*, but the first step towards an L-shaped church, as it was the first church in North China to bring men and women under the same roof. According to Alan Richard Sweeten,

[this practice] constituted an upgrade in [women's] treatment, even though the social taboo against the mixed seating of men and women remained in place (…). The [church] Mouly built at Xiwanzi is significant because it represents the permanent establishment of Catholicism in a rural community through a variety of socio-religious and architectural adjustments.[71]

In 1846, Father Mouly moved from Xiwanzi to Beijing where he was appointed apostolic ad-

63 Nuyts, "En tournée dans le vicariat," 215-216.
64 In 1862, this church was converted into an orphanage of the Holy Childhood.
65 Mouly, "Lettre (November 6, 1836)", 44-50. It was recently translated into English by Sweeten, *China's Old Churches*, 239-244. Since this translation is not perfect, we have provided another that is closer to the French text and its choppy style.
66 Mouly, "Lettre (November 6, 1836)," 44-45 (author's translation).
67 Ibidem.
68 Sweeten, *China's Old Churches*, 105, 243-244. Regarding the bamboo screen, the author adds "Mouly aligned his [screen] on a north-south axis, and, following custom, had women sit on the west side (if placing the pews, the right side), which Chinese consider inferior to the east". However, we do not know if the church was east-west or south-north oriented.
69 Rondelez, *La Chrétienté de Siwantze*, 48, 70-71.
70 Dieu, "La nouvelle cathédrale de Si-wan-tze," 1923, page, believes that the Double Love Hall was built in 1836 and attributes it to Father Mouly; Luo, *Transmission and Transformation*, 101-102, takes over from Rondelez and Dieu.
71 Sweeten, *China's Old Churches*, 244.

7.31 Double Love Hall of Xiwanzi from the south-west street showing the gate to the front courtyard, men's nave, and tower added in 1883 when the church was elevated to a cathedral.
[Leuven, KADOC-KU Leuven, CICM Picture Archive: 17.4.5]

72 Camps, "Actors," 128-130.
73 Bishop Florent Daguin 孔 (1815-1859), Mouly's successor as coadjutor (1847) and vicar apostolic (1857) of Mongolia, passed away in Kulitu 苦立图 and was buried there in 1859.
74 In 1869, he became vicar apostolic of Southwest Zhili; in 1884, vicar apostolic of North Zhili and Beijing. Van den Brandt, *Les Lazaristes en Chine*, 59 (no 155).
75 Sweeten, *China's Old Churches*, 104-106.
76 Commissioned by Bishop Mouly's successor, Vicar apostolic Louis Gabriel Delaplace 田嘉璧 CM (1820-1884), it was designed by Father Alphonse Favier 樊國樑 CM (1837-1905) in 1879, and completed by 1884. On this church and its rebuilding after the 1900 Boxers Uprising, see Sweeten, *China's Old Churches*, 104-106, and Clark, *China Gothic*, 61-65.
77 We only know the exceptional Renaissance-style church of the Benedictine nunnery of San Maurizio al Monastero Maggiore in Milan, 1503-1518. Its large single nave is divided by a high transverse dividing wall towards which both the nuns' choir and the secular part of the church face. The chancel and the main altar are at the laity's side; an opening with an iron grid is inserted between the retable and altar table (similar as the schema on Fig. 7.7 B4).
78 As, for example, at San Giorgio Maggiore in Venice, by Andrea Palladio, 1566-1576.

ministrator and became vicar apostolic of Beijing and northern Zhili in 1856 until his death in 1868.⁷² After the Second Opium War, the 1860 Peking Convention authorized missionary activity across the whole country including the construction of churches. Benefitting from this favorable context, the Double Love Hall was erected in Xiwanzi in 1862 as main church of the vicariate apostolic of Mongolia [Figs. 7.26 and 7.31]. From 1859 to 1866, however, the seat of the vicariate apostolic of Mongolia remained vacant.⁷³ Consequently, the provicar Father François-Ferdinand Tagliabue 戴济世 CM (1822-1890), who oversaw the vicariate apostolic of Mongolia until the arrival of the CICM, may be considered the builder of the Double Love Hall.⁷⁴

The Double Love Hall of 1862 was the first *renzitang* built in Xiwanzi, but not the first in North China. In his study of Beijing's old churches, Sweeten describes the fourth East Church – Saint Joseph's – as an L-shaped building commissioned by Father Mouly, then vicar apostolic of Beijing.⁷⁵ Its erection was authorized a couple of months after the appalling destruction of the Old Summer Palace by the British and French troops on October 18-21 1860. Designed as a temporary building, this L-shaped church left few memories as it was soon replaced by a monumental, stylistically eclectic, and expensive new East Church (*Dongtang*), at Wangfujing Street.⁷⁶

Several hypotheses can be formulated as to why the 1836 church type, in which men and women were on the same axis on either side of the chancel [Fig. 7.7 B4], was abandoned in favor of the L-shaped plan. From a symbolic point of view, placing women on the main axis of the church behind the altar and tabernacle was highly unusual in the Catholic tradition and certainly posed a problem.⁷⁷ The spaces behind the main altar connected with the chancel are "backstage" locations, such as sacristies, or most sacred spaces, such as radiating chapels along an ambulatory, sacramental chapels, or depositories. There are also "retro-choirs," with chapels and sepultures, which appeared from the Middle Ages in major churches and cathedrals in Europe. From the Counter Reformation to the twentieth century, some male monastic churches developed a small choir – sometimes named *chorino* – for the night offices behind the main altar, which is double faced.⁷⁸ From a practical point of view, stretching the church on its longitudinal axis could pose a problem because traditional architecture in North China consists of transversal buildings arranged around courtyards. By breaking the longitudinal axis, the L-shaped church was able to fit with two sides of a courtyard, but also solved the symbolic issue by placing women on a transversal axis, allowing better visual communication with the high altar through a larger opening without louvers.

L-shaped chapels of nunneries

Among the many architectural types of Catholic churches in Europe, the L-shaped church is never used for parish churches but is specific to monastic communities of strictly cloistered nuns. It had a certain

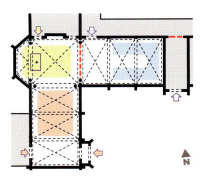

7.32 Gothic style L-shaped chapel of the Fichermont nunnery of Dominican Missionaries in Waterloo (Belgium), built in 1927: outer view from the southeast (the portal marks the left wing of the laymen); inner view of the laymen's wing to the crossing; inner view of the sisters wing to the crossing separated with a metal fence, and the apse containing the main altar; plan: chancel (yellow), nuns' choir (blue), laymen (pink).
[Postcards Nels, c. 1930, private collection; plan THOC]

success from the early nineteenth-century Catholic revival to the Second Vatican Council, which relaxed the rules of monastic enclosure.[79] Contemplative female orders such as the Carmelites, Poor Clares, Dominicans, Benedictines, Ursulines, Visitandines, etc. adopted L-shaped plans, which does not mean that all the churches of these orders were L-shaped.[80] In these cases, one nave is reserved for the nuns and forms their monastic choir, while the other nave is for the laity from both sexes [Fig. 7.32]. The chancel and altar are positioned at the intersection of the two naves, facing the nuns' choir, but separated from it by iron bars. Unlike in a parish church, where most celebrations draw worshipers of both sexes, monastic churches only allowed laity to attend certain liturgies and therefore functioned mostly as a choir in a single-nave chapel. Father Mouly does not refer to L-shaped models from Europe in his aforementioned letters. However, Father Rondelez does mention that "Mouly built [his church] after the model of convent churches of cloistered nuns, where two wings intersecting at right angle allow two categories of faithful to see the altar located at the top of the angle without seeing each other."[81]

All things considered, both the Fourth East Church in Beijing at the turn of 1860 and 1861, and the 1862 Double Love Hall of Xiwanzi were contemporary *renzitang* that served as models for rural parish churches. As an innovative building type, the L-shaped church was a successful early form of acculturated church building in North China and can be attributed to the Lazarists of Beijing and Xiwanzi, especially to Vicar apostolic Joseph-Martial Mouly, whose 1836 letter expressed the will to "spare Chinese delicacy, preserve the practice of the Church, and facilitate general instruction for the missionaries" (*Par ce moyen j'ai ménagé la délicatesse chinoise, conservé la pratique de l'Église, et facilité aux missionnaires l'instruction générale*) by bringing men and women under the same roof while keeping them firmly segregated. When the 1860 Peking Convention allowed for the building of churches, the monastic L-shaped church type proved to be acceptable to Catholic communities with Confucian roots and spread in a rural context.

79 Coomans, *Life inside the Cloister*, 98-99.
80 Cases in Belgium include the Gothic revival Benedictine abbey church of Maredret, by architect August Van Assche, 1902-1904, the Fichermont nunnery of Dominican Missionaries in Waterloo, 1927, and the church of the monastery of the Visitation in Kraainem, by architect Dom Paul Bellot OSB, 1929-1930.
81 Rondelez, *La Chrétienté de Siwantze*, 48.

7.33 At Saint Louis Church, in Tianjin's French Concession, the Sisters of Charity had their own choir attached to the side of the chancel. The exterior view shows the differing heights of the chancel and the sacristy (left) and the nuns' choir (right), both with a door to a back courtyard. Inside, a large round arched opening connects the nuns' choir and the chancel, providing a side view of the high altar.
[Photo THOC, June 2023]

82 Nicolini-Zani, *Christian Monks on Chinese Soil*, 63-79, 111.
83 Coomans, "Gender-Segregated Spaces," in this book, p. 106 and 135-138.
84 Clark, *China Gothic*, 59-61.
85 Ten Daughters of Charity were raped and killed by the mob during the massacre.
86 Sweeten, *China's Old Churches*, 105, note 105, refers to: "In the Country of Blessed Clet," *Annales de la Propagation de la Foi*, 76 (1913), 146-147.
87 Men's nave, south-north oriented with main gate to the south and windows on the east and west sides: 3.25 m width by 8.15 m long (26.45 m²); women's nave, east-west oriented with door and windows only on the south side: c.4.25 m width by c.7 m long (c.30 m²); chancel at the crossing: c.4.25 m by

L-shaped churches in China and Korea

Were L-shaped churches erected in other parts of China from the 1860s to the early twentieth century or was this architectural type limited to the vicariates of Mongolia? In the literature, missionary magazines, and photographic archives consulted, little evidence was found of *renzitang* churches comparable to those of the CICMs. Lazarist sources in particular caught our attention, but in vain. This section brings together snippets of information that hint at four paths for further investigation into churches with an L-shaped design related to gender segregation: churches in nunneries and convents, parish churches in other parts of China, Protestant churches, and parish churches in Korea.

There were few convents for cloistered contemplative sisters in China, as missionary sisters were mostly active in orphanages, hospitals, girls' schools, etc. However, the Discalced Carmelites took part in the missionary effort in China by offering the way of contemplative life to Chinese women.[82] French Carmelite nuns arrived in Shanghai in 1869 and moved into Saint Joseph's Carmel, which was built for them in 1873-1874 in Xujiahui along the Zhaojiabang canal facing the orphanage of Tushanwan. The carmel included two courtyards, one of which was flanked on two sides by an L-shaped church [Figs. 6.1 and 6.39, 2].[83] Active nuns also needed chapels in which to hold community prayers, individual devotion–including adoration of the Blessed Sacrament–and attend mass. Depending on the size of the community, such chapels could be part of their residence, independent buildings [Fig. 6.9], or attached to a parish church. At exactly the same time as the Carmelites in Shanghai, the Lazarists erected the church of Saint Louis in the French Concession of Tianjin in 1871-1872, after plans by Father Favier CM.[84] This parish church for Catholic expats was located near a hospital and orphanage run by the French Daughters of Charity (*Filles de la Charité*), who also attended the church. They had their own choir located perpendicularly to the chancel, with a good lateral view of the main altar through a large round arched opening [Fig. 7.33]. Saint Louis is not an L-shaped church – it is a large three-nave hall church in which laymen and laywomen sat on both sides of the main axis – but the L-shaped spatial arrangement of the sisters' chapel allowed them to see without being seen and access their choir from an outer door linked to a back courtyard, on the opposite side of the street and the main façade. This must have given the sisters a feeling of enclosure and safety within the church and the French Concession, which they needed after the traumatic Tianjin massacre in 1870 [Fig. 3.23].[85]

There were undoubtedly L-shaped churches in other regions of China besides those in the CICM vicariates apostolic, beginning with the vicariates held by the Lazarists. The aforementioned Fourth East Church in Beijing existed from 1861 to the early 1880s and was certainly not an isolated case. Very little is known about the first generation of churches built after the 1860 Beijing Convention that were soon replaced and not photographed. Alan Richard Sweeten mentions two cases of L-shaped churches in Jiangxi:

> The bishop of the Vicariate of Jiangxi North writes of (…) a chapel at the village of Lingjia 凌家村 that had two sections, one for the men directly in front of the chancel, the other for women "who occupy another nave or, rather, another chapel to the right of the altar [that is, if facing the congregation]." An earlier prelate, Géraud Bray, having served in North China and Mongolia, brought the style to Jiangxi, but it was not popular among locals, nor among the next generation of missionaries.[86]

This unsuccessful attempt by Father Bray 白振铎 CM (1825-1905), a Lazarist who had served in Mongolia and Hebei in the 1850s and 1860s, to transfer the L-shaped church type to Jiangxi, where he became vicar apostolic in 1870, is interesting in that it reveals resistance to the *renzitang* in South China from both locals and foreign missionaries.

During fieldwork in Shanxi in 2019, I saw and recorded a ruined L-shaped church on the site of the former village of Tanlicun 滩里村 (Taiyuan city) in the loess landscape, in all likelihood erected by Italian Franciscans at an unknown date. The remains show that the original church had whitewashed mud brick walls and was covered with a barrel vault like cave dwellings in the area. A fired brick skin was later added to the outside of the mud brick walls, including a main façade with a portal, pilasters, and a stepped gable [Fig. 7.34]. Facing south, this small church had an inner surface area of approximately 70 m² and offered a nearly equal amount space to men and women.[87]

Contrasting in size and context, the church of the Scottish United Presbyterian Mission in Shenyang 沈阳 (Liaoning), the Manchu capital, is a large L-shaped building erected in 1907 and still standing despite major transformations and extensions in the 1990s.[88] A large south-north oriented men's nave is flanked by a smaller west nave and a square tower, while the women's nave extends perpendicularly to the west. The building is in the Western style and the naves are covered with wooden ceilings. Other cases of Catholic and Protestant L-shaped churches are mentioned in Northeast China.[89]

Shenyang is not far from Korea and religious exchanges were common. It is notable that the Scottish missionary John Ross 罗约翰 (1841-1915), the founder of the Scottish Presbyterian mission in Shenyang, directed the first Korean translation of the New Testament (1887), had it printed in Shenyang, and distributed to Korea from 1882.

After the persecutions of Christians ended in Korea in 1873, the Joseon dynasty gradually opened its doors to foreigners from 1876-1886, including to Catholic and Protestant missionaries. The first chapels and churches were established in traditional Korean houses (*hanok* 한옥, 韓屋).

7.34 Ruined L-shaped church of Tanlicun (Shanxi): view from the location of the main altar in the direction of the men's nave and portal, while the women's nave is on the left.
[Photo THOC, June 2019]

3.25 m (c.13.80 m²); total interior surface area: c.70 m². There is no information about the dating of this church. Fieldwork notes, June 15 2019. With thanks to Father Andrew Zhang Dongliang 张东亮, who brought me to this remote site. In 2020-2021, the complex was rebuilt and integrates the old façade of the church.

88 In the early 1990s, a vast new square hall was erected on the site of the courtyard and linked to the two old L-shaped naves by the replacement of their south and west walls by concrete columns. Fieldwork notes March 15, 2019. With thanks to Prof. Lü Haiping 吕海平, who introduced me to this church.

89 Oak, "Spatial Characteristics," 275; Hong and Yee, 127 (both mentioned by So, "The Origin of Korean Church Architecture," 222).

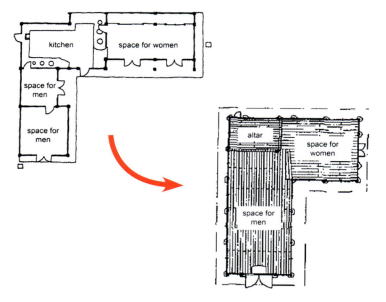
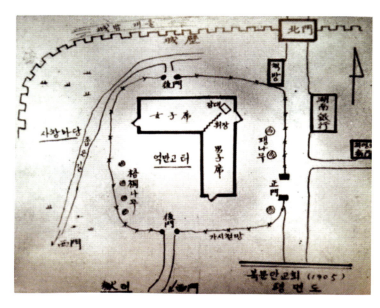

7.35 Comparison of the plans for a Korean L-shaped hanok house from Yongin Korean Folk Village and an early L-shaped church established by the American Southern Presbyterian Mission in 1905.
[From So John, "The Origin of Korean Church Architecture," 227, 4a-4b]

7.36 The Korean L-shaped Gwangju Bungmunan Church (광주 북문안 교회, 光州 北門內敎會, currently Gwangju First Presbyterian Church): the men are in the south-north nave (right), the women in the west-east nave (left), and the pulpit is placed diagonally in the northeast corner in front of a diagonal curtain. Plan of the church in its compound, dated 1905, published in X. Gwangjujeilgyohoegusimnyeonsa, 45.
[National Library of Korea (Kang Youngji)]

90 Lee and Yoon, "The changes of the plan type of Protestant church architecture in Korea, with focus on gender segregation."
91 Hong and Yee, "The L-shaped church in Korean Protestant churches;" Chung, "Birth and development phases of L-shaped church architecture in Korea." The author is grateful to Kang Youngji for her help in understanding these Korean articles.

Deeply influenced by Confucian morality and characterized by a strict gender segregation, *hanok* timber houses often have an L-shaped plan: one wing is for men and the other for women, with the kitchen and common space at the intersection. The transfer of this spatial domestic arrangement to a religious use by Catholics and Protestants was obvious. Men and women remained separated and had their own gates, the altar or pulpit was placed in the common internal corner, and a screen was added in front of the altar in order to prevent men and women from gazing [Figs. 7.35 and 7.36]. As communities grew, this indigenous L-shaped type could be enlarged or a Western church type preferred. From the 1920s, L-shaped churches only remained in some rural locations.[90]

Several authors have published on the relationship between early Korean L-shaped churches and *hanok* houses.[91] While some see influences from Manchuria and even China, John So argues over the different gender-based spatial distributions in Chinese and Korean cultures – especially between the *siheyuan* house and the *hanok* house – and concludes in favor of the specific Korean-Confucian origin of the Korean L-shaped church.[92] For chronological and geographical reasons, Chinese L-shaped churches could not have been influenced by early Korean churches because the Chinese *renzitang* had existed since the early 1860s, before the lifting of the ban on Christianity in Korea, and its link with European female monastic L-shaped churches has been established. Moreover, the first Catholic missionaries came to Korea from Beijing and North China to Korea.[93] For there to have been any influence, it must have gone from North and Northeast China to Korea, but it is more likely that both types emerged concurrently under circumstances of persecution. In any case, both the gender-segregated spaces of the Korean *hanok*-churches and Chinese *renzitang*-churches were rooted in the Confucian tradition and are remarkable cases of indigenized church architecture.

Double-nave churches

We may wonder why, in his 1904 letter, Father De Moerloose argues insistently against double-nave churches. This unusual church type is a monumental evolution of the earlier discussed singe nave church longitudinally divided with a partition. If the latter met with some success in Southwestern Mongolia before and after the Boxers ravaged the area in 1900, the former remained exceptional. De Moerloose also mentions Bishop Van

Aertselaer's wish to erect a double-nave chapel in Xiwanzi and obviously tried to dissuade him from such a project. His argument is based on experience from his homecountry and refers to the hall churches with two or three parallel naves of the same height and width erected in the County of Flanders in the fourteenth and fifteenth centuries,[94] which were abandoned mainly for two reasons. The first was liturgical and concerned the asymmetrical position of the chancel and main altar, which could not be placed on the axis of the row of columns between the two naves, but had to be at the eastern end of one nave to the detriment of the other. Since the Council of Trent, the view of the main altar and tabernacle as the focal point of the whole church space was an important liturgical requirement and led to the suppression of double-nave churches. The second reason was difficulties with the flow of rainwater and snow: "a double nave requires a double roof with interior slopes that meet in a central cornice, which causes great inconvenience," such as water infiltration damage to the roofs and wooden columns that support the junction of the roofs. This practical problem could be solved by covering the two naves with one large and almost flat saddle roof, as father De Moerloose had experienced at the church of Sandaohe (三道河, Inner Mongolia). However, this had an aesthetic impact on the appearance of the church exterior: "everyone agrees that the effect produced is disastrous; it is like a huge brick kiln."[95] The first large double-nave church in Southwestern Mongolia was erected in 1893 in Sanshenggong (三盛公, Inner Mongolia) by Vicar apostolic Ferdinand Hamer 韓默理 CICM (1840-1900). Until 1900, this fortified village was the center of the vicariate and the church served briefly as a cathedral surrounded by the bishop's residence, a seminary, school, convent, etc.[96] The cathedral is a large rectangular brick box with buttresses, narrow lancet windows, and an almost flat roof hidden by a balustrade crowning the walls. From a distance it looked more like a Saharan mosque than a Catholic church [Fig. 7.37]. The vast interior space is south-north oriented and consists of two equal naves of seven bays, separated by a row of high timber columns on the axis of the chancel. Between the columns, a high wooden partition separated the women's nave to the west and the men's nave to the east. An additional, narrow nave enlarges the men's side to the east and was separated from it by a second row of columns without a partition screen, giving the whole building an unusual asymmetry [Figs. 7.37]. The cathedral's processional portal was located in the central bay of the eastern façade and opened onto a square on the other side of which stood the bishop's residence and the main building of the mission, topped by a bell tower. Both naves were covered with a lowered arch-shaped barrel vault, which hid the timber structure and

92 So, "The Origin of Korean Church Architecture," 222-225.
93 By sea across the Bohai Sea and Korea Bay, and by land from Jehol, Manchuria and the northern Korean boundary (Yalu River). The Catholic missionary Pierre Maubant MEP (1803-1839) was the first to reach Korea in 1836, while the American Presbyterians entered Korea in 1884.
94 These medieval brick churches were well known to the architects of the Saint Luke schools who studied, drew, and restored them. Coomans, "Pugin Worldwide."
95 Letter from A. De Moerloose to J. Van Aertselaer, February 18 1904 (Leuven, KADOC-KU Leuven, CICM Generalate Archive, 4562).
96 The church and a school building are still standing. Heyndrickx, "The Great Leap Forward," 60-66 (100 Years Sanshenggong).

Fig. 7.37 The cathedral of Sanshenggong (Inner Mongolia) is asymmetrically designed. The interior view shows the double men's nave separated from the single women's nave by a partition established between the columns of the axial row. The exterior view of the blind northern wall of the chancel and the western wall of the women's nave was taken by Maynard Owen Williams during a stage of the Citroën Yellow Cruise in January 1932.
[Leuven, KADOC-KU Leuven, CICM Picture Archive: 21-2-13/01 and 13/04]

7.38 Chancel of the double-nave church of Dukou 渡口 (Inner Mongolia) seen from the men's nave: the men's space is defined by the partition and first column of the central row (left) and the communion rail, while the Gothic-style decorated chancel includes the high altar and the men's side altar dedicated to Saint Joseph (right).
[Leuven, KADOC-KU Leuven, CICM Picture Archive: 21.2.17/01]

7.39 Double-nave cathedral of Ershisiqingdi (Inner Mongolia) with central partition, row of columns, and visible roof structure; interior view from the southwest corner.
[Leuven, KADOC-KU Leuven, CICM Picture Archive: 20.2.2/04]

97 De Moerloose was not involved in the design of the cathedral, but only in the decoration of the chancel, consisting of painted imitation of stone masonry with regular joints, a colored frieze underlining the pointed arch above the main altar, and several round medallions with symbols, saints, and other stenciled motifs. Verhelst and Pycke, *CICM Missionaries Past and Present*, 99-109.

contributed to good acoustics. The pulpit was established above the partition of the first bay and a Gothic-style communion rail separated the two main naves from the chancel, which included the high altar, one altar on the women's side, and two altars on the men's side. The chancel walls were painted with a Gothic polychrome decoration by Father De Moerloose in the typical style of the Belgian Saint Luke Schools.[97]

A close-up photo of the chancel of the smaller double-aisled parish church in the neighboring county of Dukou 渡口 (Inner Mongolia) shows an identical Saint Luke-style wall decoration with medallions and a Latin inscription, clearly made after Father De Moerloose's indications [Fig. 7.38]. The photo also shows how the wooden partition was inserted into the first column located near the first step of the chancel and is aligned with the communion rail and the men's altar dedicated to Saint Joseph. The partition was high enough to prevent men and women from seeing each other, but was also an obstacle to the priest's ideal view of the congregation.

In March 1900, Vicar apostolic Hamer moved the center of the mission from Sanshenggong to Ershisiqingdi (二十四顷地, Inner Mongolia), which was better located for the apostolate but not fortified. Four months later, on July 25 1900, he and many Christians were massacred and the church ruined. When the time came to rebuild the mission with state indemnity, Father Willem Lemmens 兰广济 CICM (1860-1943), the procurator of Southwest Mongolia and then parish priest of Ershisiqingdi, asked Father De Moerloose to draw up plans for a new church, but he was too busy and declined.[98] Consequently, Father Lemmens had no choice but to design and erect a large double-nave church with a single tower himself in 1904-1905,[99] which served as a cathedral until the seat of the vicariate apostolic was relocated to Suiyuan (绥远, now Hohhot 呼和浩特, Inner Mongolia).

The former cathedral of Ershisiqingdi is still standing today.[100] Its plan, about 50 meters long and north-south oriented, was undoubtedly inspired by that of the cathedral of Sanshenggong, with the exception of the fact that it is perfectly symmetrical, had one tower, two naves, a pseudo-transept, and a chancel with five altars. A row of eight columns divides the space into two naves [Fig. 7.39], whose entrances are symmetrically placed on the two lateral sides, in the first southern bay and in the reduced transept arms. Partitions, which are no longer in place today, were located between the columns. While Sanshenggong was covered with two lowered barrel vaults, Ershisiqingdi has a visible Western-style timber roof structure, with a slight slope of 20 degrees and trusses with a span of 24.50 meters supported in the middle by a wooden column. This is what Father De Moerloose considered a "disastrous effect" and unaesthetic for a church. It reminded him of industrial buildings, in particular a brick kiln – he must have been referring to the roof structure of a Hoffmann kiln.[101] His criticism seems to have been heeded because when we consulted the photo archives, they failed to reveal any other churches of this type in Inner Mongolia.

Father Jozef Nuyts 饒所迪 CICM (1898-1986) summarizes the advantages and disadvantages of double-nave churches and aligns his opinion with that of Father De Moerloose:

> A second attempt was in vogue for some years. We were building a vast church, very wide, which was easy with columns to support the top of the roof. A wooden partition, six, seven feet high, joined these ridge columns from the entrance doors at the back of the church to the communion rails that stood in front of the chancel on either side of the partition. Therefore, it was, in fact, two churches juxtaposed under the same roof. Again, Chinese customs were intact, the acoustics were good, but this time visibility was at stake. The altar in the choir was not visible either to those standing at the back of the church, or to those kneeling too close to the median partition, and, moreover, this row of columns and wooden partition were dismal in appearance. It looked like a hangar, had nothing of a temple about it, and the Chinese themselves realized that.[102]

Cross-shaped churches

The transept, or transversal space that gives a church the shape of a cross, has taken many different forms over the centuries according to its various uses.[103] Besides the cosmic symbolism of the Christian cross, a transept enlarges the volume and gives more majesty to the space between the nave and the chancel. Its construction, however, brings with it significant additional costs, the technical complications of articulating walls and roof structures, and possible stability problems, especially when the crossing is vaulted with stone or surmounted with a lantern tower or dome. Consequently, such architectural developments were very rare in China's late Qing churches and limited to the most prestigious cathedrals and churches in cities where Western architects and engineers, as well as specialized workers, were available.[104]

Father De Moerloose ends his 1904 letter to Vicar apostolic Van Aertselaer with a sketch of a typical cathedral plan composed of an aisled nave, a large aisled transept, and a chancel with an apse and ambulatory. On reaching the end of his letter, the architect digresses slightly from the issue of gendered spaces in average parish churches to the bishop's new Xiwanzi Cathedral project (*si l'on avait demandé un plan d'église pour Si-wan, j'avais l'intention d'essayer la forme de croix complète…*).[105] In this "full cross" space, he attributes the nave to the men, the transept arms to the women, and the apse to the clergy and seminarians [Fig. 7.28]. His idea of placing the altar at the crossing was too far ahead of his time and would not become the norm until the liturgical reforms of the Second Vatican Council. From a gender perspective, De Moerloose's idea is as polarizing as L-shaped churches because it gives males – clergymen and laymen – exclusive use of the auspicious south-north space. In addition, women are spread over two spaces, i.e., divided and relegated to lateral areas.

As the main altar was never located at the crossing – with such notable exceptions as Saint Peter's Basilica in Rome – but in the middle of the chancel, it was common practice to locate men in the transept and crossing, as recalled by Father Nuyts in 1938:

> If the church has the shape of a cross (…), the back of the main nave is reserved for women, while the front and the transept are left to men. The choir is not very deep, but very wide and, since there are no columns anywhere, everything can be seen from all corners of the church.[106]

98 Letters W. Lemmens to J. Van Aertselaer, December 17, 1903 and June 2, 1904 (Leuven, KADOC-KU Leuven, CICM Generalate Archive, 4544) and a letter from A. De Moerloose to J. Van Aertselaer, October 6, 1903 (Leuven, KADOC-KU Leuven, CICM Generalate Archive, 4562).

99 This Dutch CICM had a certain amount of architectural experience as he had built the aforementioned church of Sandaohe (*c.*1895) and the former church of Ershisiqingdi (1897). Van Hecken, *Documentatie*, vol. X, 148-150.

100 Luo, *Transmission and Transformation*, 196-209, 424-431.

101 For a photo of this type of timber roof, see <https://www.lowtechmagazine.com/2009/10/hoffmann-kilns-brick-and-tile-production.html> (accessed July 20, 2023).

102 Nuyts, "En tournée dans le vicariat," 216-217.

103 Lheure, *La transept de la Rome antique à Vatican II*.

104 Notable real transepts and crossings as high as the nave and choir of late Qing churches still standing include: the cathedrals of Hong Kong, Guangzhou, Shanghai, Beitang in Beijing, Jinan, Ningbo, Kaifeng, Wuhu, Xuanhua, etc.; the parish churches of Dongjiadu, Saint Joseph, Tangmuqiao in Shanghai. As far we know only Xikai cathedral in Tianjin has a dome at the crossing, though uncompleted.

105 See aforementioned full text and translation. Letter from A. De Moerloose to J. Van Aertselaer, February 18, 1904. Leuven, KADOC-KU Leuven, CICM Generalate Archive: 4562.

106 Nuyts, "En tournée dans le vicariat", 217, with the church of Gonghui 公会 (Inner Mongolia) as an example.

7.40 The parish church of Gonghui (公会, Central Mongolia), erected in the 1920s, has unusual transept arms ending each with a polygonal apse. [Leuven, KADOC-KU Leuven, CICM Picture Archive: 17.4.7.7/017]

107 Of his buildings, the churches of Xuanhua 宣化 (Hebei), Halagou 哈拉沟 (Inner Mongolia), Lulong 庐龙, Yongpingfu 永平府 (Hebei), and Sheshan 佘山 (Shanghai) have a real transept, while those of Liangcheng 凉城 (Inner Mongolia) and Shuangshuzi 双树子 (Hebei) have reduced transepts. On Xuanhua, see Coomans and Luo, "Exporting Flemish Gothic Architecture to China," 237-245.

108 In Europe, cathedrals and large churches have portals in the middle of the two facades of the transept. In China, transepts do not have portals facing each other, but only doorways on the southern side of both arms.

109 Luo, *Transmission and Transformation*, 131-140, 363-373. Author's fieldnotes.

110 Two letters from A. De Moerloose to J. Van Aertselaer, October 6, 1903 and May 22, 1904 (Leuven, KADOC-KU Leuven, CICM Generalate Archive, 4562). Also: two pictures in *Missions en Chine et au Congo*, 1907, between p. 176-177 (Siang-hoa-ti).

111 From the 1920s, however, due to both the growing numbers of Catholics and new structural possibilities, transepts appeared in more churches. The enlargement of Liangcheng's church is not dated, but reinforced cement was used for the large arches of the new crossing and the chancel. These arches made it possible to avoid two columns and a better view from the transept arms to the chancel was guaranteed.

After the Boxer Upraising, governmental indemnities made it possible to design more elaborate churches and include full or reduced transepts. A Catholic architect from the Saint Luke's Schools, which promoted cross-shaped churches, Father De Moerloose was in favor of the transept, whether real or reduced [Fig. 6.17].¹⁰⁷ The latter is not as high as the nave and there is consequently no crossing, but it does give the church's exterior the shape of a cross and offers the option to add side doorways [Fig. 7.7 C1 and C2].¹⁰⁸ On rare occasions, transept arms end with an apse, making the design compatible with doors that faced south was [Fig. 7.40].

We will look more closely at the parish church of Liangcheng 凉城 (formerly Xianghuodi, Inner Mongolia) as it offers a rare case of a shift from a reduced transept to a real transept,¹⁰⁹ with the redevelopment of the gendered spaces as consequence. First, in 1903-1904, Father De Moerloose built a south-north oriented brick church composed of an aisled nave with a south-east tower, a short transept lower than the nave, a crossing, and a chancel with side chapels [Fig. 7.41].¹¹⁰ The church's three doorways faced south: the main portal in the façade and two smaller doors in the southeast and southwest corners of the transept. In all likelihood, men occupied the fore space of the transept and the crossing, while women were in the nave. Second, in the 1920s,¹¹¹ the chancel of De Moerloose's church was demolished and a large transept and deep polygonal chancel flanked by two side chapels were erected north of the earlier, small transept. As this new transept alone forms three transverse naves with rows of pillars and round arches, this enlargement more than doubled the capacity of the church. From then on, the church had two transepts: the women occupied the nave and transept of the earlier church and the men the entirety of the new transept, which was accessible through two additional doorways in each arm. Today the separation of men at the front and women at the back no longer applies.

Father de Moerloose's suggestion of placing the chancel under the crossing was not entirely unfounded, however, but applicable in very specific cases, such as chapels in medical institutions that were required to segregate several groups of people for pro-

7.41 The church of Liangcheng (Inner Mongolia), built in 1903 by Father De Moerloose CICM, included a reduced transept, but was enlarged in the 1920s with a higher and much longer transept. Inside, the priest's point of view in the chancel offered an axial perspective of the nave of the original church used by the women, and two diagonal perspectives to the added transept arms and crossing used by the men. Colors on the plan: chancel (yellow), transept for the men (pink), nave for the women (green). The gender segregation no longer exists today.
[Leuven, KADOC-KU Leuven, CICM Picture Archive: 17.4.4/05, Plans THOC, 2023 after LW & THOC 2011 in Luo, *Transmission and Transformation*, 2013, Fig.36, and Photos THOC, May 2011]

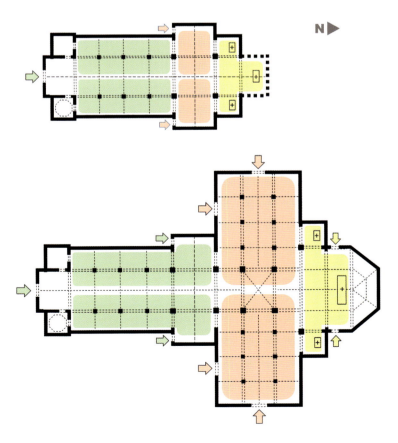

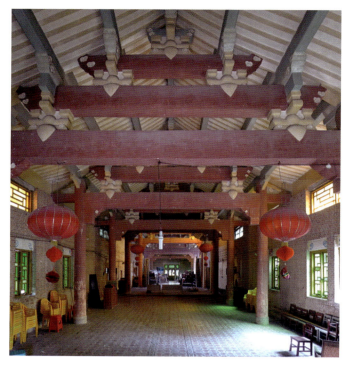
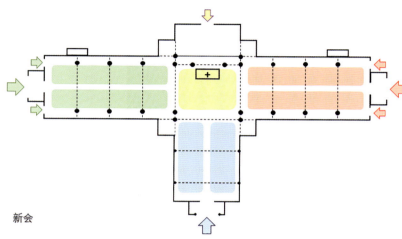

7.42 Cross-shaped church of Xin Hui Lepers' village (Guangdong), designed in 1938 by Brother Albert Staubli MM: view from the men's transept arm in the direction of the chancel and the women's transept arm. The opening to the nave in the middle left has been walled up. Plan: chancel (yellow), sic women (green), sic men (pink), healthy churchgoers (blue). [Plan and photo THOC, September 2013]

112 Since the Renaissance, hospital design had placed chapels where different sick wards crossed. Nineteenth-century cross-shaped prisons adopted a similar pattern with a central chapel.
113 Fieldwork notes, September 9 2013. With thanks to Bishop Paul Liang Jiansen 梁建森 and Sister Ann Reusch MM, who introduced me to this place.
114 Hershatter, *Women in China's Long Twentieth Century*, 80-81.
115 Zhu, "Emancipation in Everyday Life," 51.
116 Stevens, "Figuring Modernity: The New Woman and the Modern Girl in Republican China."

phylaxis reasons.[112] In the leper colony of Xinhui 新会 (Guangdong), a cross-shaped church still stands in which the male and female lepers were each in one of the long arms of the transept, while healthy members of the congregation were in a short nave, with the head of the church serving as the sacristy. This remarkable church was designed by the Swiss Maryknoll brother-architect Albert Staubli MM 斯托利 (1895-1967) in 1938 in modern Chinese style, including a reinforced cement structure and numerous small windows ensuring appropriate ventilation [Fig. 7.42].[113] As the short head of the cross-plan was behind the main altar and its Chinese-style canopy, the liturgical space could be described as T-shaped (丁字 *tingzi*), with the chancel at the crossing. We can imagine that this layout had the same visual and acoustic disadvantages as L-shaped churches, but allowed the various components of the leper colony to worship together and strengthened their sense of community.

Evolution in Modern Republican Society

Catholic and Protestant missionaries contributed to the early stages of women's emancipation in late Qing China,[114] which was also promoted by small groups of reformist intellectuals. While the latter "considered China's Confucian tradition to be patriarchal and uncivilized, women's emancipation served as the measuring stick of modernization and the degree to which it was becoming civilized."[115] With the New Culture Movement (新文化运动 *Xin Wenhua Yundong*), the May Fourth Movement (五四运动 *Wusi Yundong*), growing numbers of male and female Chinese students studying abroad, and the struggle for free choice marriage and women's suffrage, the emancipation of women made great progress, but not to the same degree in different parts of China. The urban "new woman" and "modern girl" had the opportunity to benefit from educational improvements and the nation's focus on modernity,[116] but this barely reached rural women before the 1950s.

We have already established how, from the 1860s, gender-inclusive churches in which men and women worshipped together under the same roof had been a major architectural shift in China. We have also seen how this contributed to the development of the sense of community and, to a certain extent, of gender equality in late Qing Catholic parishes. In the changing and contrasting Republican context, the Catholic Church in China maintained the same positions on women, marriage, and family as in Europe and other parts of the world. They continued to establish rural parishes, rescue and bring up orphaned boys and girls, and promote basic education, but prioritized higher education for boys. The Catholic mission to China's major shift from the mid-1920s was the adaptation of unchanged religious content – Catholic dogmas, doctrine, sacramental rituals, etc. – to Chinese culture by Sinicizing architecture and art.[117] Consequently, the architectural style of several new churches [Fig. 7.52], furniture, liturgical ornaments, and imagery was Sinicized. In the meantime, the partitions, screens, and fences discussed above had been removed from church interiors and gendered spaces limited to separate seating as in Europe. L-shaped churches gradually disappeared in favor of larger brick churches in which men and women sat in the same nave on either side of the central aisle.

In 1928, the Belgian missionary-artist Leo Van Dijk 狄化淳 CICM (1878-1951) published the first Sinicized illustrated catechism.[118] Catechetical materials for children and adults are tools of evangelization and the images they contain express ideas and behavior as much as the words. Several of the forty chromolithographs promote prayer and church attendance. They depict church interiors with women on the left and men on the right, chancels occupied only by the priest and choir boys, and family devotional scenes in which men stand in front of the domestic altar with the women behind them [Fig. 7.1]. As another missionary from the vicariate of Central Mongolia noted in 1926, L-shaped churches were no longer necessary because "mores have currently changed in this respect."[119]

Late Qing Catholic churches with galleries above the aisles are extremely uncommon and the use of these galleries remains unclear. The French Jesuit brother-carpenter Léon Mariot 马历耀 SJ (1830-1902) designed and built two of these churches in 1867-1870 for the parish of Lujiabang (菉葭浜, Jiangsu) – which needed extra space for welcoming gatherings of Catholic fishermen – and for the French Sisters Auxiliatrices at the Shengmuyuan (圣母院, Xujiahui 徐家汇, Shanghai) [Fig. 7.43].[120] From the 1920s, when reinforced concrete became available, growing urban communities solved the

117 Coomans, "The Sino-Christian Style: A Major Tool for Architectural Indigenization."
118 Van Dijk, *Wenda Xiangjie*. Original drawings at KADOC-KU Leuven, CICM Archive, 6563.
119 X, "L'église de T'eou-sou-mou": "actuellement les mœurs ont changé à cet égard."
120 X, "Nécrologie. Le frère Léon Mariot," 1903, 142.

7.43 Two timber churches with galleries above the aisles designed and built by the brother-carpenter Léon Mariot SJ in 1867-1870 for the parish of Lujiabang (Jiangsu) and for the French Sisters Auxiliatrices at the Shengmuyuan (Xujiahui, Shanghai).
[Vanves, Compagnie de Jésus, Archives jésuites de France, FIMC, Q3, Album 1913]

7.44 To provide more seats in Saint Joseph's Church in Shanghai, galleries were set up in the triforium of the nave and lofts in the transept arms; view from the northern triforium to the southern side.
[Photo THOC, June 2011]

7.45 Solemn mass in the church of the Sacred Heart Hospital in Shanghai, 1935: clergymen in the chancel, men in the nave, women and children in the aisles and galleries.
[Louvain-la-Neuve, ARCA, Archives SAM, Album 13]

121 For example, Saint Teresa's Church in Shanghai, by French Jesuits (1930-1931), or the cathedral of Yichang (宜昌 Hubei) by Belgian Franciscans (1933-1934).
122 For example, in the two first bays of the naves of the cathedrals of Taiyuan (Shanxi) and Hohhot (Inner Mongolia).
123 Fieldwork notes during renovation work in the church, June 9 2011.
124 Photo taken during the first national congress of the Catholic Action in Shanghai in 1935. SAM Archives, Album 13. <https://digitalcommons.whitworth.edu/album13/75>.
125 Diamant, "Re-examining the Impact of the 1950 Marriage Law."

problem of lack of space by building concrete churches with galleries,[121] or galleries were inserted into existing churches using a reinforced concrete structure and adding concrete staircases.[122] In Saint-Joseph's Church in Shanghai's French concession, built 1860-1861, a whole upper floor was later inserted by adding transept lofts, erecting staircases, and opening the blind arches of the nave's triforium to create a gallery between the roof and vault of the aisles [Fig. 7.44].[123] It is unclear who was expected to go to these places – children, women, lower class people? – which were uncomfortable, difficult to reach, and conducive to distraction due to the bird's eye view of the chancel and assembled congregation. An interior photo of the chapel of the Heart Hospital in Shanghai, built 1931, taken during high mass, clearly shows a fourfold gender-hierarchical seating plan: first, the clergy and choir boys are in the chancel, which is well defined by the communion rail; second, the men are seated in the nave while the central axis to the chancel is kept free for the procession of clergy; third, the women are in the aisles, including nuns in the right aisle; fourth, nurses and children are in the galleries [Fig. 7.45]. The pictured ceremony was an exception and may not reflect the daily use of the chapel,[124] but does illustrate the spatial hierarchy of a male-dominated Catholic institution in China's most advanced city of the time.

The New Marriage Law 新婚姻法 (May 1, 1950), passed under the People's Republic of China, definitively abolished feudal marriage and marriage by purchase, imposed officially registered marriages, and established the free choice of partners (and divorce), monogamy, equal rights for both sexes, and the protection of the lawful interests of women and children as fundamental principles.[125]

Appendix
L-shaped parish churches in Inner Mongolia

A systematic examination of the photographic archive of the Congregation of the Immaculate Heart of Mary (CICM) at KADOC-KU Leuven enabled us to identify eight L-shaped churches and one V-shaped church. They are presented here in chronological order, with basic information about their context, builders, and dates.

1. Xiwanzi 西弯子 (now Chongli 崇礼, Hebei)

The history of Xiwanzi, a mountain village north of Beijing that became the seat of a diocese and the center of the Belgian CICM mission to Mongolia, has been studied by several historians who have established the chronology of the successive churches and cathedrals.[126] The area was evangelized in the early eighteenth century by the French Jesuit Dominique Parrenin 巴多明 SJ (1665-1741) and an oratory was erected in Xiwanzi; this was converted into a Buddhist temple in 1768.[127] In 1829, a group of French Lazarists expelled from Beijing settled in Xiwanzi, and in 1835-1836, Father Joseph-Martial Mouly 孟振生 CM (1807-1868) built a innovative church, considered the first in North China to bring men and women under the same church roof. This church was not L-shaped and has been earlier analyzed.[128] In 1840, Pope Gregory XVI erected the vicariate of Mongolia and appointed Father Mouly as its first vicar apostolic until 1846, when he was promoted vicar apostolic of Beijing. In 1862, the Lazarists built a new church in Xiwanzi, on a different site to Mouly's church, which was converted into an orphanage of the Holy Childhood.

The L-shaped church of 1862, named the "Double Love Hall" (*shuang ai tang* 双爱堂), is a key building for our research into gender designed churches because it belongs to a generation of new churches that benefitted from the freedoms guaranteed by the 1860 Peking Convention. In all likelihood, it was built and consecrated by Father François-Ferdinand Tagliabue 戴济世 CM (1822-1890), the provicar who oversaw the vicariate apostolic of Mongolia until the arrival of the CICM in December 1865. The Belgian Fathers described the Double Love Hall as follows:

> The new church, which is 20.8 meters long and 7.9 meters wide, is built according to the rules of local architecture. In the nave, seven or eight Chinese lanterns with their ornaments and Chinese inscriptions on silks are suspended. The walls are adorned with several pictures painted by a Chinese artist and a quantity of flowers and inscriptions. A gallery has been set up for the musicians of the village to occupy on feast days. The roof structure, supported by fourteen wooden columns that divide the church into three naves, is masked with canvas. The roof is covered with fluted tiles and the floor is covered with square bricks. Like the church of 1835 [sic], this one has on the side of the epistle [the right side when facing the altar] a vast building exclusively intended for women.[129]

The February 1889 issue of *Missions en Chine at au Congo* includes a full-page engraving [Fig. 7.26] and a short description of the Double Love Hall.[130] The vernacular-style church was composed of two naves and *langzi* 廊子 corridors meeting at a right angle and forming the northwestern and northeastern sides of a courtyard. Each wing has a south-facing doorway to the courtyard. A Chinese lantern tower marks the crossing of the southwest-northeast oriented men's nave and the northwest-southeast oriented women's nave. Only the cross at the top of the lantern tower indicates the building's identity. The northwestern wall of the men's nave was parallel with the street and separated from it by a blind wall which, like a traditional house, was only pierced by a Chinese gate [Fig. 7.31]. Located west of the men's nave, this gate opened into a front courtyard with a screen wall and a small passageway to the western corner of the main courtyard [Fig. 7.46].

126 Dieu, "La nouvelle cathédrale de Si-wan-tze," 98-103. Luo, *Transmission and Transformation*, 101-104. See above, note 69.
127 Patrick Taveirne, *Han-Mongol Encounters and Missionary Endeavors: A History of Scheut in Ordos (Hetao), 1874-1911*, 2004, p. 200-201.
128 See: "The origin of L-shaped churches in North China." Rondelez, *La Chrétienté de Siwantze*, 71, confuses the churches from 1835 and 1860, considering them as one and the same. This error has been repeated by Luo and other authors.
129 Description from 1866 quoted by Rondelez, *La Chrétienté de Siwantze*, 70-71 (author's translation).
130 Otto, "Mongolie Centrale," 8.

7.46 On entering the front courtyard of the cathedral of Xiwanzi, you were greeted by a traditional screen and accessed the main courtyard though the small doorway in the corner. On the left, the back wall of the men's nave did not have a door to the front courtyard. [Leuven, KADOC-KU Leuven, CICM Picture Archive: 17.4.5/05]

7.47 The cathedral area of Xiwanzi in 1930: south of the brand-new Romanesque cathedral, significant remains of the Double Love Hall are still standing: the men's nave has already been demolished, leaving the 1883 Gothic tower free-standing and showing a section of the women's nave (arrow). [Leuven, KADOC-KU Leuven, CICM Picture Archive: 17.4.5/05]

131 X, "La nouvelle église de Si-wanzi," 147-148; Verhelst and Pycke, *CICM Missionaries*, 58 and Fig 14.

132 Explicit allusions to this project in the letter from A. De Moerloose to J. Van Aertselaer, Gaojiayingzi, February 18, 1904. Leuven, KADOC-KU Leuven, CICM Generalate Archive, 4562 [Fig. 7.23].

133 Dieu, "La nouvelle cathédrale de Si-wan-zi;" X, "La nouvelle église de Si-wan-zi."

The two halls were large and the church is said to have had a capacity of 1,000 people. An interior view taken from the men's nave towards the high altar shows the thin timber columns supporting the Chinese roof structure partially hidden by a low velum, while four much larger columns support the lantern tower above a Gothic-style altar and tabernacle [Fig. 7.27]. Two steps, a communion rail, and a timber triumphant ellipse-shaped arch with painted spandrels and tympanum separate the nave from the chancel. On the right (southeast) side of the chancel, another triumphant arch made of three round arches marks the limit of the women's nave, which was long and aisled, as can be seen on a photo taken during its demolition in the early 1930s [Fig. 7.47]. On the opposite side, the unusual location of the pulpit inside the chancel made the preacher visible from both the men's and women's naves. However, although the men's nave was facing the main altar, it had a side view of the pulpit, while the women's nave was facing the pulpit and had a side view of the main altar. Two secondary altars are located in the left (northwest) aisle facing the women's nave, one under a canopy in the first bay of the nave, the other in the first bay of the chancel.

The engraving shows the Double Love Hall before its transformation in 1888, shortly after Xiwanzi became the seat of the vicariate apostolic of Central Mongolia (1883) and Father Jacques Bax 巴耆贤 CICM (1824-1895) was appointed vicar apostolic. He gave his cathedral a Western appearance by demolishing the Chinese style lantern tower and erecting a Gothic-style bell tower and sacristy at the northeastern end of the men's nave [Fig. 7.31]. The new brick tower was designed by Father Petrus Dierickx 孔模范 CICM (1862-1946) in 1887 and its construction was supervised by the parish priest Petrus Chao 兆.[131] In 1900, Xiwanzi resisted the Boxers but the vicariate was ruined. Consequently, Vicar apostolic Jerome Van Aertselaer 方剂众 CICM (1845-1924) gave priority to parish churches and postponed his project to erect a Gothic cathedral in Xiwanzi after plans by Father De Moerloose.[132] Eventually, in 1923, he commissioned Father Leo De Smedt 石德懋 CICM (1881-1951), then director of the seminary and later vicar apostolic of Xiwanzi, to draw up the plans for the new cathedral, which was erected from 1924 to 1926 on a different site to that of the old cathedral.[133] In 1930, the old cathedral was demolished, with the exception of its bell tower, which was integrated in a new school building erected on the site.

All things considered, the remarkable Double Love Hall of Xiwanzi existed for 68 years (1862-1930) and served as the cathedral of the vicariate apostolic of Central

Mongolia for 43 years (1883-1926). The successive towers expressed the scale of the evolution of Catholic church architecture in North China: from acculturated and barely distinguishable from vernacular domestic architecture so as not to attract attention to an initial statement in the public space, with a Western-style tower and its chiming bells, and finally to the construction of a new grand Western-style cathedral. From the point of view of gendered spaces, the L-shaped type forming two sides of a courtyard reflected traditional domestic architecture, but its use for a church building was innovative in the early 1860s. It survived until the 1920s, which is remarkable if all the disadvantages of this type are considered, especially for a cathedral, in addition to the evolution of society in the early twentieth century. No doubt the community was attached to this form of gender segregation and the missionaries did not have the means to make a more modern cathedral a reality before the 1920s. The contrast between the old and new cathedral, built in 1926, could not have been sharper [Fig. 7.50].

2. Shabo'er 沙钵儿 (Cha-pa-eul, Inner Mongolia)

The February 1890 issue of *Missions en Chine at au Congo* includes a full-page engraving [Fig. 7.25] and a short note about the "résidence de Cha-pa-eul."[134] Designed by Father Edmond Rubbens 刘拯灵 CICM (1859-1929), the then parish priest of Shabo'er (1888-1892) who became the CICM provincial superior of Central Mongolia during the post-Boxer reconstruction (1903-1913), at the time of Bishop Van Aertselaer and Father De Moerloose.[135] In his letter of 1904, the latter mentions a V-shaped church in Shabo'er, but there is insufficient information to make comparisons with the engraving and draw conclusions.

The engraving of Shabo'er is a remarkable source because it offers the design of an L-shaped church in the middle of a parish compound, which is depicted as an ideally oriented and symmetrically gendered composition. In a *fengshui* landscape with mountains in the background, the compound faces south and has three entrances: the main gate on the central axis opens onto a square and the church, while the two side doorways give access to the boys' and girls' schools. The L-shaped church is sited symmetrically on a terrace with two wings at 45 degrees to the main axis. Two distinct staircases lead to the triangular terrace, and the building whose equal number of round arched windows and doors and crenellated gables seem Western in style. A roof turret with a visible bell marks the junction of the wings above the chancel. To the left, a small building attached to the church only could be the missionary's residence and the sacristy, suggesting that the west is the men's side. Accordingly, this would make the left courtyard the boys' school and the right courtyard the girls' school and orphanage, with a room for Chinese Virgins. The latter and the missionary's residence were thus diametrically opposite each other. In this design, the women would occupy the east wing (right) of the church and the men the west wing (left).

3. Laohugou 老虎沟 ("Old tiger valley", Hebei)

This vernacular-style parish church is well documented as the burial place of Father Theophile Verbist 南懷義 CICM (1823-1868), the founder of the CICM and leader of the first batch of Scheut Fathers in Mongolia.[136] On February 23 1868 he passed away in the Christian village of Laohugou and was buried in the local *renzitang*, which was renovated in 1878. The founder's body was buried in the chancel, first in front of the main altar and later in a vault along the northern wall, before being repatriated to Belgium in 1931.[137] In 1891 and 1900, the remains of two martyrs – the Chinese priest Petrus Lin Daoyuan 林道原 (1837-1891), massacred with other Christians in the neighboring village of Sanshijiazi 三十家子, and the parish priest Father Jozef Segers 司化隆 CICM

134 Van Koot, "Aperçu," 193-195, 201.
135 Van Overmeire, Gui and Pan, *Elenchus CICM*, 426; Verhelst and Pycke, *CICM Missionnaries*, 88, 158, 164.
136 Father Verbist died from typhus twenty-seven months arriving in China. Verhelst and Pycke, *CICM Missionaries Past and Present*, 52-54.
137 Nols, "Vicariat de Jehol. L'exhumation des restes." On Father Verbist's mausoleum in the motherhouse of Scheut in Brussels, see Coomans and Luo "Mimesis, Nostalgia and Ideology," 513-514.

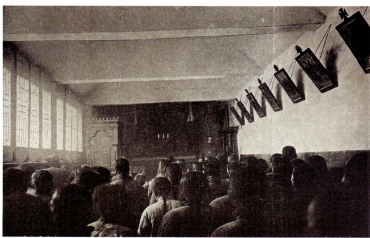

7.48 The chancel of the church of Laohugou seen from the women's nave: side view of the main altar and front view of the tripartite memorial monument. [Leuven, Ferdinand Verbiest Institute, Picture Archive, CH-0382]

7.49 CICM father catechizing in the men's nave of the church of Laohugou: only the southern side has windows, while the stations of the Way of the Cross hang on the blind northern wall. Photo before 1911, published by Arthur Segers in Martyre du Révérend Père Joseph Segers, *5. [Leuven, KADOC-KU Leuven, Heritage Library, KB8984]*

138 Van Koot, "Aperçu sur le vicariat de la Mongolie Centrale" and Idem,"Les livres sybillins de la Chine" (with engraving). Segers, *Martyre du révérend père Joseph Segers*; Father Segers memorial photo album, KADOC-KU Leuven, CICM Picture Archive: 18.3.3.4 – KFH 1776.
139 X. "Dans la petite église de la Vallée des Tigres" (author's translation).
140 Heyndrickx, *Verbist Study Notes*, 22-23.
141 With the above mentioned Presbyterian Church in Shenyang.

(1868-1900), killed during the Boxer Uprising – were buried in the chancel, and a tripartite memorial, including Father Verbiest, was erected near the altar.

Old photographs and engravings reveal that the Chinese *renzitang* church in the middle of the parish compound looked like a vernacular four-bay house, south facing with a perpendicular wing of three bays, the former being the men's nave and the latter the women's [Fig. 6.19].¹³⁸ Doors and windows were only on the south wall of the men's nave and the east wall of the women's nave, both facing the courtyard. Above the doors, the inscriptions *nanren tang* 男人堂 and *nüren tang* 女人堂 identified the entrances to the men's and women's naves respectively [Figs. 7.2 and 7.28]. Several interior photos of the church show the chancel and memorial [Fig. 7.49]. A caption accompanying a photo of the women's nave [Fig. 7.48] specifies:

Men see the altar from the front; women see it from the side. The priest preaches from the altar. Here, we have in the foreground the women's communion rail. The harmonium is placed in the women's church because, in this small village, due to the lack of well-trained men, the orphans and the Virgins of the Holy Childhood sing the Latin songs. The harmonium is useless for ordinary songs in Chinese. Chinese lanterns hang from the ceiling. On the side of the choir against the wall we can see the monument built to the founder and two martyrs.¹³⁹

The church and its contents were demolished in the Mao era, but the villagers rebuilt the church in the 1980s: "out of respect for the history of their village and their old church, they built the new church exactly on the same spot as the old church and in the same style as the old one."¹⁴⁰ The new church of Laohugou is one of the rare L-shaped type to still be in use in China today.¹⁴¹

4. Xiaoqiaopan 小桥畔 (Shaanxi)

The Sacred Heart *renzitang* church of the fortified Christianity of Xiaoqiaopan was erected in 1884 by Father Jan-Baptist Steenackers 司福音 CICM (1848-1912) with local craftsmen.¹⁴² Xiaoqiaopan means "little bridge" but was translated as "Klein Brugge" ("Little Bruges") by the missionaries (in Flemish, "brug" means bridge). The church stood in the middle of the mission compound, with the main façade of its men's nave facing south towards the residence and the boys' school, and its women's nave facing the girls' school, orphanage, and building for the Chinese Virgins [Fig. 6.29]. The L-shape contributed to defining two courtyards, both connected to the compound's main square via separate doorways. There are no photos showing the northern and western sides of the L-shaped church.

The most remarkable part of the church was its timber lantern tower erected at the crossing of the two naves, which took the form of a Chinese pavilion and was the highest building in the mission compound [Figs. 7.29 and 7.50]. Seen from the flat surrounding landscape, the top of the pavilion and its cross soared higher than the wall of the village and marked the skyline. An interior view to the chancel from the men's nave shows the four solid wooden columns that support the lantern tower and a circular opening in the ceiling through which zenithal light shines on the high altar. The Gothic-style altar – designed by Father De Moerloose and carved by master carpenter Wang 王 in 1890 – and its Latin inscriptions contrast with the Chinese structure and inscriptions on silks [Fig. 7.29]. Like the main altar, two side altars are turned in the direction of the men's nave, which was vaulted with planks to protect it from the cold. This church has been demolished.

5. Majiazi 馬架子 (Inner Mongolia)

Father Heliodoor Devos 德玉亮 CICM (1847-1887) "built the church and residence and the Holy childhood in Majiazi. He had already proved his skill and competence as an architect and craftsman by restoring the church of Laohugou in 1878. He built in Majiazi a stone [sic, for brick] church with a tiled roof and a double, perpendicularly joined nave."[143] An undated photo shows the church from the southeast: on the right, the men's wing has six bays, while the women's wing on the left has only four bays [Fig. 7.51].[144] It is worth noting that the men's door opens onto a large terrace that runs parallel with the men's wing, while the women obviously had no access to the terrace since their door opened directly onto the square. The brick masonry and metal roofing are Western.

6. Dafagong 大法公 (Mongol: Ulān Bōrük, Inner Mongolia)

This modest *renzitang* church was built by Father Karel Verellen 袁萬福 CICM (1859-1925) around 1890.[145] A photo shows a small Gothic brick chapel with a pitched saddle roof flanked with two low, flat-roofed naves [Fig. 7.52]. The main façade of the chapel faces south and is decorated with a blind pointed arch and ends with a Gothic wooden roof turret; the ridge of the roof is adorned with *fleur-de-lys* and the sloping gables with Gothic crockets. Two staircases lead to the two doors facing south: one in the axis of the chapel towards the men's nave; the other (hidden in the photo by the side wall of the verandah), towards the women's nave.

7. Tongjiayingzi 佟家營子 (Inner Mongolia)

In this Christian village founded in 1890 and sponsored by a lady from Wijnegem (Belgium), a *renzitang* church was soon built and dedicated to Saint Anthony. A photo taken from the courtyard shows the main south facade with the main entrance and a

7.50 The L-shaped church of Xiaoqiaopan from the southeast.
[Leuven, KADOC-KU Leuven, CICM Picture Archive: 21.2.4/05]

142 Coomans, "Gender-Segregated Spaces," in this book, p. 126-127; Luo, *Transmission and Transformation*, 112-119; Van Melckebeke, *Service social de l'Église en Mongolie*, 63-77.
143 Verhelst and Pycke, *CICM Missionaries Past and Present*, 61.
144 Other photo, from the east, "Après la messe à Ma kia tzeu," in *Missions en Chine et au Congo*, 25 (1913), 156.
145 Father Verellen was the parish priest of Dafadong from 1888 to 1891. Van Overmeire, Gui and Pan, *Elenchus CICM*, 631.

7.51 *The L-shaped church of Majiazi seen from the courtyard with a group of men posing on the terrace in front of the men's door.*
[Leuven, KADOC-KU Leuven, CICM Picture Archive: 18.3.3/019]

7.52 *Father Karel Verellen CICM posing in front of his hybrid style L-shaped church of Dafagong, around 1890.*
[Leuven, KADOC-KU Leuven, CICM Picture Archive: 19.32/02]

shorter wing to the right [Fig. 7.53]. There is no lantern tower at the crossing. A sketch on the back of the photo identifies the different parts: the main wing is that of the men, the short wing of the women, the appendix at the intersection of the two wings is the sacristy, and the building to the right is the missionaries' residence. This hybrid-style brick church had Gothic looking double lancet windows, imported metal roof sheets, and Chinese geometric decorative patterns on the south gable.

8. Tousumu 头蘇木 *(Inner Mongolia)*

This parish church is known to us only by two photos published in the CICM magazine, both with an explanatory caption [Figs. 7.30 and 7.54]. In Western style, the *renzitang* is perfectly symmetrical and shows a similar rational design to the project for the church of Shabo'er. The same number of bays, lancet windows, buttresses, and two portals identically located on the axis of each nave contrast with the asymmetry of most other aforementioned *renzitang* churches. If we look closely at the two photos, there is evidence that the two naves are not at 90 degrees but rather at 60 degrees. There is a small window in the angle at the intersec-

7.53 *The L-shaped church of Tongjia-yingzi (Inner Mongolia), seen from the courtyard. Identification of the gendered spaces sketched on the back of the photo.*
[Leuven, KADOC-KU Leuven, CICM Picture Archive: 18.3.3/01]

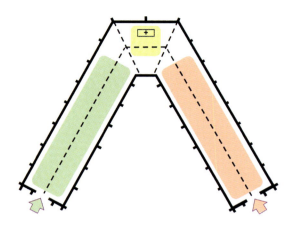

tion, and the ridges of the two roofs do not meet at a right angle. The altar was not on the axis of either wing but against an oblique wall forming the back of the chancel and equally visible from both naves. We do not know if the north-south axis was at an equal distance from both naves, nor which was for the men or for the women. The caption of a photo published in 1926 explicitly mentions the acute angle and the reasons why the Western style was chosen:

> This church is double: one wing is for men; another is for women. (…) At the top of the acute angle formed by the two wings of this church is the altar. It is from the altar that the priest must preach to the two groups of faithful. The acoustics are defective in churches of this type. The roof is covered with sheets. An elegantly curved Chinese roof would obviously look much nicer, but it would be horribly expensive and would soon be in ruins. Chinese buildings are beautiful but not very durable and very impractical. In today's China, almost all official buildings are in the European or American style.[146]

9. Meiguiyingzi 玫瑰营子 ("the Rosary Village") in the Qisumu district 七蘇木 (Inner Mongolia)

This *renzitang* contrasts sharply with all the preceding ones [Figs. 7.24, 7.55 and 7.56]. It was designed in 1904 by Father Alphonse De Moerloose for a village with a large Catholic parish. As discussed earlier, the missionary-architect was against L-shaped churches, but the local congregation probably gave him no choice. Benefiting from state indemnity made it possible to build the church in the Saint Luke Gothic style, which was more expensive because it included carved stones, large windows, and elaborate Western carpentry. Seven letters from Father De Moerloose to Bishop Van Aertselaer from August 1902 to June 1904 mention the church.[147] After visiting the site twice in 1902, the architect completed the plans by February 1904 and visited the site again in June to organize the work into two phases. The men's nave was built first, followed by the women's nave.

> In Tsi-sou-mu, the old church which will be used for women will hardly last more than a few years. There are wide slits. I have examined it and found that the walls are earthen with half a brick outer facing. I have arranged the new main building so that I can later add the same wing for the women that is now being built for the men.[148]

The work was directed by a trusted Chinese foreman whom De Moerloose had trained in Gothic architecture. The date of completion is not known as correspondence with the bishop stopped as soon construction began. Several photos taken by Father Frantz Van Dorpe 陶维新 CICM (1878-1944), the parish priest of Meiguiyingzi at the time of the

7.54 The V-Shaped church of Tousumu (Inner Mongolia). Plan, reconstruction hypothesis (THOC 2024): chancel (yellow), women's nave (green), and men's nave (pink). Photo from Missions de Scheut, 34 (1926) 5, 101.
[Leuven, KADOC-KU Leuven, Heritage Library, KYB27]

146 X. "L'église de T'eou-sou-mou."
147 KADOC, CICM Archives, 1.2.5.1.5.14. The letters name the church Qisumu (name of the district) instead of Meiguiyingzi (name of the village). Luo, *Transmission and Transformation*, 154-156.
148 Letter from A. De Moerloose to J. Van Aertselaer, February 18, 1904. Leuven, KADOC-KU Leuven, CICM Generelate Archive: 4562.

7.55 The church of Meiguiyingzi: exterior view from the southwest showing the two equal Gothic style-naves. Photo Father Frantz Van Dorpe CICM, 1912. [Knokke, family archives Cécile Masureel-Van Dorpe]

7.56 Main façade of the men's nave with Gothic-style portal, side doors, lancet windows, and an oculus. The date MCMIV is written on the top of the gable. [Leuven, KADOC-KU Leuven, CICM Picture Archive: 17.4.4.11/05]

construction, show the completed church.[149] The men's nave was north-south oriented and the women's nave east-west, with the main entrances on the longitudinal axis of both naves. The church was vast – each nave was 24 meters long and 9 meters wide – had no aisles and was covered with a 9 meter-high wooden barrel vault [Fig. 7.57]. Each bay was lit by Gothic double lancet windows and an oculus,[150] which contributed to the grand interior but was totally inappropriate for the climate and criticized by the users:

He [De Moerloose] did not pay attention to the particular features of our region and its excessive climate. These high chapels, with thin walls, many windows, and thin wooden ceilings have pleasant forms, but the priest and churchgoers are to be pitied when they are obliged to gather to pray in minus 30-35 degrees [C] or oppressive heat. You are either freezing or suffocating; standing with your arms spread during the canon of the mass is torture, as is giving communion to crowds. Priests and Christians have experienced this pity; however, the vogue for this style, so beautiful but so unpractical, was slow to disappear.[151]

Today only the women's nave remains and serves as the church of the Catholic parish of Meiguiyingzi.[152] Not only was the men's nave demolished and a new façade erected at the junction of the women's nave, but the latter was lowered by almost half of its interior height (the new ceiling is between the tip of the lancets and the bottom of the oculus). This was how the building's users solved the problem of too much space, freezing in the winter and suffocating in the summer.

149 In 1907-09, Father Van Dorpe built the Marian pilgrimage church of Mozishan 磨子山 on the top of a hill dominating the Qisumu plain. According to its style, it could also have been designed by Father De Moerloose. See Van Dorpe, "Notre Dame de Lourdes en Mongolie Centrale."
150 Typical thirteen-century Gothic-style, like, for example, the windows of the refectory of the abbey of Villers (Belgium), the ruins of which De Moerloose visited during his architectural studies.
151 Nuyts, "En tournée à travers le vicariat," 218-219.
152 Luo, *Transmission and Transformation*, 158-159, 389-391 (Luo Wei visited Meiguiyingzi in March 2010).

7.57. The church of Meiguiyingzi: interior view of the chancel from the men's nave; the Gothic altars face the men's nave. Photo Father Franz Van Dorpe CICM, 1912.
[Knokke, family archives Cécile Masureel-Van Dorpe]

BIBLIOGRAPHY

Archives and Photo Archive

Knokke, Family archive Cécile Masureel-Van Dorpe.
Leuven, KADOC-KU Leuven, Archives of the Generalate of the Congregation of the Immaculate Heart of Mary (CICM):
- P.I.a.1.2.5.1.5.14: letters from Father Alphonse De Moerloose to Vicar apostolic Jerôme Van Aertselaer.
- 6563: catechetic plates by Father Leo Van Dijk.
- Picture archive.

Leuven, Ferdinand Verbiest Institute: photographic archive
Louvain-la-Neuve, ARCA, Archives de la Société des Auxiliaires des Missions
Lyon, Oeuvres Pontificales Missionnaires, fonds iconographique
Utrecht, Het Utrechts Archief, 1224: Dutch Franciscans, China mission
Vanves, Compagnie de Jésus, Archives jésuites de France, fonds iconographique des missions de Chine (FIMC)

Primary literature

1917 Codex Iuris Canonicis. Libreria Editrice Vaticana <https://www.jgray.org/codes/cic17lat.html>.
Bret, Eusèbe 白 (MEP). "Dans la Corée septentrionale." *Les Missions catholiques*, 1574-1581 (14 April–22 September 1899), passim 169-454.
De Vigneron, Jacques 陶开化 (CICM), "Mei-koei-ing-zi (Village du Rosaire)." *Missions de Scheut*, 34 (1926) 8, 176-182.
Dieu, Léon 梁天专 (CICM). "La nouvelle cathédrale de Si-wan-zi. Bénédiction de la première pierre." *Missions de Scheut*, 31 (1923), 98-103.
Doré, Henri 禄是逎 (SJ). *Recherches sur les superstitions en Chine. Première partie: les pratiques superstitieuses*, vol. 1/1 (Variétés sinologiques 32). Shanghai-Xujiahui: T'ou-sé-wé Presses, 1911.
Durand, Guillaume / William (OP). *The Rationale divinorum officium of William Durand of Mende: A New Translation of the Prologue and Book One*, by Timothy M. Thibodeau. New York: Columbia University Press, 2007.
Hermand, Louis 双国英 (SJ). "Monsieur le doyen bâtit." *Relations de Chine*, 5 (July 1913), 92-97.
Missions de Scheut. 1889-1890

Mouly, Joseph-Martial 孟振生 (CM). "Lettre de M. Mouly, missionnaire lazariste en Chine, supérieur de la mission de Pékin, à M. Nozo, supérieur général de la Congrégation de St-Lazare (6 novembre 1836)." *Annales de la Propagation de la Foi. Recueil périodique des lettres des évêques et des missionnaires des missions des deux mondes…*, 61 (November 1838), 35-55.
Nols, Joseph 欧化民 (CICM). "Vicariat de Jehol. L'exhumation des restes mortels de notre fondateur, le T.R.P. Verbist." *Missions de Scheut* 39 (April 1931) 4, 78-83.
Nuyts, Jozef 饶所迪 (CICM). "En tournée à travers le Vicariat." *Missions de Scheut*, 46 (1938), 213-219.
Otto, Hubert 陶福音 (CICM). "Mongolie Centrale. Comment se donnent les missions aux Chrétiens chinois." *Missions en Chine et au Congo*, 1 (February 1889), 5-9.
Pugin, Augustus Welby Northmore. *The Present State of Ecclesiastical Architecture in England*. London: Charles Dolman, 1843 <https://archive.org/details/presentstateofec00pugi/page/n5/mode/2up>.
Rondelez, Valère 隆德理 (CICM). *La Chrétienté de Siwantze. Un centre d'activité missionnaire en Mongolie*. Xiwanzi, 1938.

Segers, Arthur 司化兴 (CICM). *Martyre du révérend père Joseph Segers, missionnaire de Scheut à Lao-Hou-Keou (Mongolie orientale)*. Antwerp, 1920.

Van den Brandt, Joseph 方立中 (CM). *Les Lazaristes en Chine 1687-1935. Notes biographiques*, Beijing: Imprimerie des Lazaristes, 1936.

Van Dijk, Leo 狄化淳 (CICM). *Wenda Xiangjie* 问答像解 [*Illustrated Catechism*]. Shanghai: Pu Ai Tang, 1928.

Van Dorpe, Frantz 陶维新 (CICM). "Notre Dame de Lourdes en Mongolie Centrale." *Missions en Chine, au Congo et aux Philippines*, 20 (August 1908) 8, 169-171.

Van Hecken, Joseph Leonard 贺歌南 (CICM). *Monseigneur Alphonse Bermyn: dokumenten over het missieleven van een voortrekker in Mongolië, 1878-1915*. Wijnegem: Hertoghs, 1947.

Van Hecken, Joseph Leonard 贺歌南 (CICM). *Documentatie betreffende de missiegeschiedenis van het apostolisch vicariaat Zuidwest-Mongolië, Ordos*. Schilde: CICM, 1980-1981.

Van Koot, Daniel-Bernard 高達道 (CICM). "Aperçu sur le vicariat de la Mongolie Centrale." *Missions en Chine et au Congo*, 13 (February 1890), 193-195 and 201.

Van Koot, Daniel-Bernard 高達道 (CICM). "Les livres sybillins de la Chine", in *Missions en Chine et au Congo*, (January 1891), 369-372.

Van Melckebeke, Carlo 王守礼 (CICM). "Trois églises." *Missions de Scheut*, 40 (1932) 4, 84-85.

Van Melckebeke, Carlo 王守礼 (CICM). *Service social de l'Église en Mongolie*. Brussels, 1969.

X, "À propos de l'église à angle droit." *Missions de Scheut*, 23 (December 1911) 12, 15.

X. "Dans la petite église de la Vallée des Tigres où est enterré le corps du T.R.P. Verbist, notre fondateur." *Missions de Scheut*, 36 (1928), 77.

X, "Intérieur de l'église de Ts'i-lao-wen-ke-ts'i." *Missions de Scheut*, 34 (September 1926) 9, 213.

X. "L'église de T'eou-sou-mou." *Missions de Scheut*, 34 (May 1926) 5, 101.

X, "La nouvelle église de Si-wan-tze." *Missions de Scheut*, 34 (July 1926) 7, 145-152.

X, "Nécrologie. Le frère Léon Mariot." *Relations de Chine. Kiang-Nan*, 1 (XX 1903), 141-142.

Secondary literature

Amsler, Nadine. *Jesuits and Matriarchs. Domestic Worship in Early Modern China*. Seattle: University of Washington Press, 2018. Online publication: <https://uw.manifoldapp.org/read/jesuits-and-matriarchs/section/5d914065-094c-4cb2-b181-132d18f252a6#tit>.

Aubin, Françoise. "Christian Art and Architecture," in Tiedeman, R. Gary, ed. *Handbook of Christianity in China*. Volume Two: *1800-present*. Leiden-Boston: Brill, 2010, 733-741.

Camps, Arnulf. "Actors. Catholic Missionaries (1800-1860)," in: Tiedeman, R. Gary, ed. *Handbook of Christianity in China*. Volume Two: *1800-present*. Leiden-Boston, 2010, 115-132.

Chung, Chang-Won 정창원. "Giyeokjahyeong gyohoegeonchugui tansaenggiwongwa jeongaeyangsange gwanhan yeoksajeok yeongu" ㄱ자형 교회건축의 탄생기원과 전개양상에 관한 역사적 연구 [A Historical Study on the Birth and Development Phase of L-shaped Church Architecture in Korea]. *Daehangeonchukakoenonmunjip Gyeheokgye* 大韓建築學會論文集 劃系 [*Journal of the Architectural Institute of Korea, Planning & Design*], 20 (November 2004) 11, 175-182.

Clark, Anthony E. *China Gothic. The Bishop of Beijing and His Cathedral*. Seattle: University of Washigton Press, 2019.

Coomans, Thomas. "Islands on the Mainland. Catholic Missions and Spatial Strategies in China, 1840s-1940s," in: Coomans, Thomas, ed. *Missionary Spaces. Imagining, Building, Contesting Christianities in Africa and China, 1840-1960*. Leuven, 2023, 33-63.

Coomans, Thomas. "Gendered Spaces in Catholic Compounds in Late Qing China," in: Coomans, Thomas, ed. *Missionary Spaces. Imagining, Building, Contesting Christianities in Africa and China, 1840- 1960*. Leuven, 2023, 107-145.

Coomans, Thomas. "Unexpected Connections: The Benedictine Abbey of Maredsous and Christian Architecture in China, 1900-1930s." *Revue Bénédictine*, 131 (2021) 1, 264-299.

Coomans Thomas 高曼士, *Sheshan jiaotang xunzong: jianzhu, chaosheng, lishi tujing (Kaifang de Shanghai chengshi jianzhu shi congshu*, 3) 佘山教堂寻踪：朝圣建筑和历史途径（开放的上海城市建筑史丛书, 3) [The Basilica of Sheshan: pilgrimage architecture and historical landscape], Shanghai: Tongji University Press, 2023.

Coomans, Thomas. *Life inside the Cloister. Understanding Monastic Architecture: Tradition, Reformations, Adaptive Reuse*. Leuven, 2018.

Coomans, Thomas. "The Sino-Christian Style: A Major Tool for Architectural Indigenization," in: Zheng Yangwen 鄭揚文, ed. *Sinicizing Christianity* (Studies in Christian Mission 49). Leiden-Boston: Brill, 2017, 197-232.

Coomans, Thomas. "Pugin Worldwide. From *Les Vrais Principes* and the Belgian St Luke Schools to Northern China and Inner Mongolia," in: Brittain-Catlin, Timothy; De Maeyer, Jan, and Bressani, Martin, eds. *Gothic Revival Worldwide. A.W.N. Pugin's Global Influence*. Leuven, 2016, 156-171.

Coomans, Thomas. "Sint-Lucasneogotiek in Noord-China. Alphonse De Moerloose, missionaris en architect." *M&L. Monumenten, Landschappen en Archeologie*, 32 (2013) 5, 6-33.

Coomans, Thomas and Luo Wei 罗薇. "Exporting Flemish Gothic Architecture to China: Meaning and context of the churches of Shebiya (Inner Mongolia) and Xuanhua (Hebei) built by missionary-architect Alphonse De Moerloose in 1903-1906." *Relicta. Heritage Research in Flanders*, 9 (2012), 219-262.

Coomans, Thomas, and Luo Wei 罗薇. "Mimesis, Nostalgia and Ideology: The Scheut Fathers and Home-country-based Church Design in China," in: *History of the Catholic Church in China: From its Beginning to the Scheut Fathers and 20th Century. Unveiling some less known Sources, Sounds and Pictures*. Leuven, 2015, 495-522.

Coomans, Thomas, and Luo Wei 罗薇. "Missionary-builders: Scheut Fathers as Church Designers and Constructors in Northern China," in: Chen Tsung-ming, Alexandre 陳聰銘, ed. *Catholicism's Encounters with China, 17th to 20th Century*. Leuven, 2018, 334-364.

Diamant, Neil J. "Re-examining the Impact of the 1950 Marriage Law: State Improvisation, Local Initiative and Rural Family Change." *The China Quarterly* 161 (March 2000), 171-198.

Garan, Frédéric. *Itinéraires photographiques, de la Chine aux "Missions Catholiques" (1880-1940). Perception de la Chine à travers les archives photographiques des O.P.M. et la revue des Missions Catholiques*. Unpublished PhD, Lyon: Université Lumière–Lyon 2, 1999.

Hershatter, Gail. *Women in China's Long Twentieth Century*. Berkeley-Los Angeles-London: University of California Press, 2007.

Heyndrickx, Jeroom 韩德力 (CICM). "The Great Leap Forward! A Visit to China, April 1993." *Verbist Study Notes*, 12 (July 1993), 49-67.

Heyndrickx, Jeroom 韩德力 (CICM). "Information on former CICM Dioceses in N. China." *Verbist Study Notes*, 13 (December 1995), 19-43.

Hong, Seung Jai 홍승재, and Yee, Myoung Kwan 이명관. "'Giyeok' jahyeong gyohoe geonchuge gwanhan yeongu" ㄱ'자형 교회 건축에 관한 연구 [A Study on the L-shaped Church in Korean Protestant churches]. *Geonchugyeoksayeongu* 建築歷史研究 [*Journal of Architectural History*], 7 (December 1998) 4, 113-130.

Kwok, Pui-lan. *Chinese Women and Christianity 1860-1927* (Academy Series 75). Atlanta: Scholars Press, 1992.

Lee, Hee-Jun 이희준, and Yoon, In-Suk 윤인석. "Hanguk Gaesingyo gyohoegeonchugui pyeongmyeonhyeongtae byeoncheon yeongu: 'Namnyeoyubyeol' gwannyeomgwa hoejungseogui namnyeo wichireul jungsimeuro" 한국 개신교 교회건축의 평면형태 변천 연구: '남녀유별' 관념과 회중석의 남녀 위치를 중심으로 [The Changes of Plan Type of Protestant Church Architecture in Korea, with Focus on gender segregation (男女有別) and the location of gendered seats]. *Geonchugyeoksayeongu* 建築歷史研究 [*Journal of Architectural History*], 14 (September 2005) 3, 129-148.

Lheure, Michel. *Le transept de la Rome antique à Vatican II*. Paris: Picard, 2007.

Li Ma, *Christian Women and Modern China. Recovering a Women's History of Chinese Protestantism*. Lanham, MD: Lexington Books, 2021.

Liu Dunzhen 刘敦桢. *La maison chinoise* (translated by Georges Métailié, Marie-Hélène Métailié, Sophie Clément-Charpentier, and Pierre Clément). Paris: Bibliothèque Berger-Levrault, 1980.

Luo Wei 罗薇. *Transmission and Transformation of European Church Types in China. The Churches of the Scheut Missions beyond the Great Wall, 1865-1955*. PhD dissertation. KU Leuven: Faculty of Engineering Science, Department of Architecture, 2013.

Luo Wei 罗薇. "'Renzitang'—Wei zunzhong Zhongguo chuantong er jianzao de jiaotang" 人字堂–为尊重中国传统而建造的教堂 [L-shaped Churches–Conforming to Chinese Tradition]. *Zhongguo jianzhu shi lun hui kan* 中国建筑史论汇刊 [*Transactions on the History of Chinese Architecture*], 9. Beijing: Tsinghua University Press, 2014, 361-385.

Luo Wei 罗薇. "Saibei Shengmu xin hui jiaotang jianzhu yanjiu 塞北圣母心会教堂建筑研究" [Research on CICM Church Architecture North of the Great Wall]" in Lai Delin 赖德霖, Wu Jiang 伍江 and Xu Subin 徐苏斌, eds. *Zhongguo jindai jianzho shi* 中国近代建筑史 [History of Modern Chinese Architecture], vol. 1. Beijing: China Architecture and Building Press, 2016, 387-402.

Masson, Matthieu (MEP). "L'invention d'une architecture sino-chrétienne: l'église Saint-Joseph de Guiyang (1850)." *La Maison-Dieu*, 295 (2019) 1, 141-169.

McCluskey, Stephen C. "Orientation of Christian Churches," in: Ruggles, C.L.N. ed. *Handbook of Archaeoastronomy and Ethnoastronomy*. New York: Spinger Science and Business Media News, 2015, chapter 154, 1703-1710. Doi 10.1007/978-1-4614-6141-8_173

Nicolini-Zani, Matteo. *Christian Monks on Chinese Soil. A History of Monastic Missions to China*, Collegeville: Liturgical Press, 2016.

Oak, Sung-Deuk. "Spatial Characteristics of the Early Protestant Churches in Korea: Christian Modernity and Indigenization, 1895–1912." *Journal of Eastern Studies* 141 (2008), 267-321.

Perrin, Joël, and Vasco Rocca, Sandra, eds. *Thesaurus of Religious Objects, Furniture, Objects, Linen, Clothing and Musical Instruments of the Roman Catholic Faith / Thesaurus des objets religieux, meubles, objets linges, vêtements et instruments de musique du culte catholique romain*. Paris: CNMS - Éditions du Patrimoine, 1999.

So, John. "The Origin of Korean Church Architecture. Arrangement, Space, and Daylight in the Korean *Hanok*." *Religion and the Arts* 23 (2019), 217-239.

Soetens, Claude. *L'Église catholique en Chine au XXe siècle*. Paris: Beauchesne, 1997.

Stevens, Sarah E. "Figuring Modernity: The New Woman and the Modern Girl in Republican China." *National Women's Studies Association Journal* (*NWSA Journal*) 15 (2003) 3, 82-103.

Sweeten, Alan Richard. *China's Old Churches. The History, Architecture, and Legacy of Catholic Sacred Structures in Beijing, Tianjin, and Hebei Province*. Leiden-Boston: Brill, 2020.

Tiedemann, R. Gary, ed. *Handbook of Christianity in China*. Volume Two: *1800 to the Present*, Leiden-Boston: Brill, 2010.

Van Hecken, Joseph Leonard 贺歌南 (CICM). "Alphonse Frédéric De Moerloose CICM (1858-1931) et son œuvre d'architecte en Chine." *Neue Zeitschrift für Missionswissenschaft / Nouvelle Revue de Science missionnaire* 24 (1968) 3, 161-178.

Van Overmeire, Dirk, Gu Weiying 古偉瀛, and Pan Yuling 潘玉玲. *Zai hua shengmu shengxin hui shi minglu* 在華聖母聖心會士名錄 [*Elenchus of CICM in China*]. Taipei, 2008.

Verhelst, Daniël (CICM), and Pycke, Nestor (CICM). *C.I.C.M. Missionaries Past and Present 1862-1987. History of the Congregation of the Immaculate Heart of Mary (Scheut/Missionhurst)*. Leuven: Leuven University Press, 1995.

Wiest, Jean-Paul. "Specific Catholic Groups, 1860-1900," in: Tiedeman, R. Gary, ed. *Handbook of Christianity in China. Volume Two: 1800-present*. Leiden-Boston: Brill, 2010, 238-246.

X. *Gwangjujeilgyohoegusimnyeonsa: 1904–1994* / 대한예수교장로회 광주제일교회 / 光州第一教會九十年史: 1904–1994 [The ninety-year history of Gwangju First Presbyterian Church: 1904-1994]. Gwangju: Gwangju First Presbyterian Church of the Presbyterian Church of Korea, 1994, 45 and 274-277.

Zhu Qian. "Emancipation in Everyday Life: Women's Singleness and Feminism in 1920s China." *International Journal of Gender and Women's Studies* 7 (2019) 2, 47-57.

Zhuang Hongzhong, and Loopmans, Maarten. "The Spread and the Distribution of Catholicism beyond the Great Wall (1860s–1940s): Based on Analysis of GIS," in: Chen Tsung-ming, Alexandre 陳聰銘, ed. *Catholicism's Encounters with China, 17th to 20th Century*. Leuven: Ferdinand Verbiest Institute, 2018, 309-331.

Websites

<https://www.catholic-hierarchy.org/>

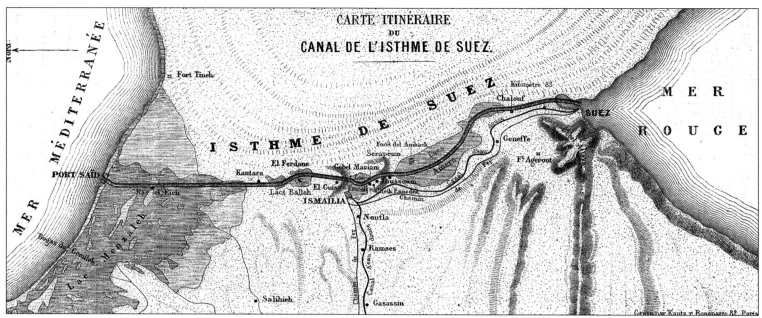

8
The Missionaries in the Cosmopolitan Towns of the Suez Isthmus, Egypt

Their Role in the Formation of Identity in Architecture and Urban Planning, 1860-1937

Céline Frémaux

While the provisional chapels hastily set up in the encampments at the Suez Canal drill site (1859–1869) resembled those of the missions' home countries, the permanent churches in the towns of the isthmus were influenced by traditional French religious architecture. In 1930, the Catholic vicar apostolic of the Suez Canal zone stated that he had opened in Ismailia "a French church, a church of France which lends a French personality to Ismailia."[1] [Fig. 8.2] The choice of a Neo-Romanesque style for this church and the cathedral of Port Said in 1937 went against Catholic clerical ideas that church architecture in mission countries should not merely transpose European styles.[2] What were the reasons behind this stylistic divergence? Was it due to specific factors on the ground? Did the missionaries play a role in the formation of the canal towns and the construction of their churches?

Answers to these questions can be found in an analysis of the missionary presence and Catholic churches built on the Suez isthmus, from the first temporary chapel erected at the building site encampment by the Mediterranean in 1860, to the blessing of Port Said cathedral in 1937, which marked almost eighty years of Catholic presence in the isthmus. This study is based on private archives, namely those of the Suez Maritime Canal Universal Company and the religious orders, which were easier to access. The latter included the archives of the Franciscans, title holders of the vicariate apostolic of the canal area, the Brothers of Christian Instruction of Ploërmel, the Sisters of the Good Shepherd (Sœurs du Bon Pasteur), responsible for teaching in the canal towns, and finally, the Vatican, which provide information about the relationships between the religious missions settled on the isthmus.

The first step is to assess the influence of the frameworks of towns as cosmopolitan as those of the Suez isthmus on the missionaries' use of space and religious architectural design. Spatial strategies and the methods of presence of the Catholic missions will then be considered. Finally, the role of the Suez Canal Company in planning a specific urban landscape and the interaction between company members and the religious orders in the design of these Catholic churches will be analyzed.

Spatial constructions of identity

Port Said on the Mediterranean, Ismailia in the center of the isthmus, and Suez/Port Tawfiq on the Red Sea were created and developed on concessionary ground initially to host the European workers building and managing the canal [Fig. 8.1].[3] The land granted by the viceroy of Egypt to Ferdinand de Lesseps (1805–1894) in 1854[4] included that on which ports and warehouses were established, as well as the parcels of land on which houses and services for the personnel, including churches, were built.

The Suez Canal towns were similar, in their population structure, to cosmopolitan Mediterranean towns. Egyptians, Greeks, Italians, French, and Levantines, all attracted by the opportunities for work, lived in juxtaposed neighborhoods. Like most Mediterranean ports during the Ottoman rule and colonization, these towns were melting pots

8.1 Suez isthmus plan, 1869.
[Fontane and Riou. Le canal maritime de Suez illustré, 4]

8.2 The Catholic church of Saint Francis de Sales in Ismailia.
[Photo: author's collection]

1 Extract from the speech pronounced by Mgr Ange-Marie Hiral at the church of Ismailia on February 9, 1930. *Le Rayon*, March 1930.
2 Dubois, *Le répertoire africain*, 89.
3 Cf. the presentation of the research project financed by the Agence nationale de la recherche: Frémaux and Volait, "Inventing Space in the Age of Empire."
4 On November 30, 1854, the viceroy of Egypt, Mohamed Said Pasha, signed a decree conceding to Ferdinand de Lesseps the rights "to dig into the Suez isthmus, exploit a passage suitable for navigation, create or appropriate two sufficient entrances, one for the Mediterranean, the other for the Red Sea."

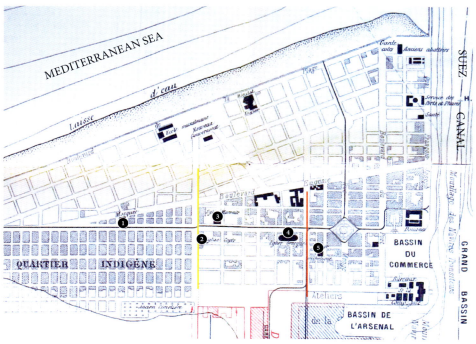

8.3 Urbanism and places of worship in Port Said. Plan of 1905.
1. Mosque
2. Coptic Orthodox church
3. Maronite church
4. Greek Orthodox church
5. Roman Catholic church
[ANMT, 1995060 0056]

8.4 A cathedral for the Suez canal vicariate. Plan of Port Said in 1930.
1. New cathedral
2. Old church
[ANMT, 1995060 0056]

distinguished by a specific urban framework that tells us a great deal about the coexistence of the populations, as Robert Ilbert has shown in his thesis on Alexandria.[5] While the features of the cohabitation of the various communities in cosmopolitan towns have been widely studied in the social sciences,[6] the places of worship of the different concessions and their uses of space remain an underexplored area of study.[7] In the towns of Port Said and Ismailia in particular, places of worship were an important part of the ways in which the community meshed together in urban spaces.

Community meshing in space

Since the onset of urbanization in the isthmus towns, missions of every origin occupied space in the towns. This is made clear by maps of Port Said and Ismailia. In Port Said, either because of their social status or numbers, the most significant communities had places of worship from the early days of urban development. The Catholic church was built near De Lesseps Square, at the center of the company employee neighborhood, home to the villas of company employees. Other places of worship were spread out along the main road, De Lesseps Street, perpendicular to the canal. The Orthodox church was situated in the Greek quarter adjacent to the villa area; beyond it were the Maronite and Coptic churches; and finally, in the indigenous quarter, farthest from the canal, was Port Said's first mosque. [Fig. 8.3] When the canal area became a vicariate apostolic, the cathedral of Mary Queen of the World was built in the new town center on land stretching along the beach, allowing it to receive boats from all over the world as they entered the canal [Fig. 8.4].

In Ismailia, a town built from scratch in 1862,[8] the places of worship were established according to a similar logic. The company's principal buildings were located in the central area around Champollion Square: Ferdinand de Lesseps' chalet, the offices, and the main employee villas. The church of

8.5 View of Empress Avenue, the main street of Ismailia, from the square in front of the railway station, c.1930. [Post card, private collection]

St Francis of Sales was built on a raised plot of ground near the square, on a major road, Empress Avenue, leading from the railway station to the harbor. Delegations visiting the isthmus by train from Cairo all passed along this axis. The Catholic church was therefore not only located in the heart of the European quarter, but was also in view of passing visitors. When a new church was built on the same grounds in the 1920s, the company management committee was careful to alter its orientation so that it faced Empress Avenue [Fig. 8.5].[9] The Greek Orthodox church dominated the Greek quarter, a commercial district in which the most significant community of immigrants was concentrated. Finally, in the Arab quarter, the town's first mosque was sited along Muhammad Ali Quay on Lake Timsah [Fig. 8.6].

The geography of places of worship in the towns indicates the coexistence of the communities according to a strict allotment of the neighborhoods. Although places of worship contributed to creating a sense of identity in each neighborhood and became focal points, they were also built on strategic sites in terms of visibility, with the aim of competing with each other in a very real rivalry. Studies of the influence of the Jesuits in Cairo have shown that throughout Egypt, Catholic missions were developed from 1880 onwards with the aim of drawing Orthodox Copts to the "true fold, which is that of St. Peter,"[10] while competing with the American Protestant missions and absorbing Catholics from other churches, the Uniates in particular. In the canal towns, where communities of every origin rubbed shoulders, the role of the Catholic missionaries was also to compete with the representatives of other religions. Thus, the erection of the vicariate apostolic of the canal in 1926 was justified in Article 4 of the Creation Act: its purpose was to give moral and spiritual support during the development of the zone – which had a population of 132,000 inhabitants, 11,000 of whom were Catholic – but also to prevent a Greek Orthodox or Protestant bishopric from being implanted (a request was made to the company by the Greek Orthodox community).[11]

5 Ilbert, *Alexandrie, 1830-1930*; Ilbert and Yannakakis, *Alexandrie 1860-1960*.
6 See the contributions of historians, sociologists and anthropologists collected in Décobert, *Valeurs et distance*.
7 On this subject, see Anastassiadou-Dumont, "Identités confessionnelles et espace urbain en terres d'islam," and the contributions of Ciranna, "Italian Architects and Holy Space in Egypt" and "Italian Architects: The Builders of Churches in the Capitals of the Mediterranean."
8 Frémaux, "Histoires, architectures."
9 Roubaix, Archives nationales du monde du travail (National Archives of the World of Work), Collection of the Association du Souvenir de Ferdinand de Lesseps et du canal de Suez (hereafter ANMT), 1995060 1001: Minutes of the meeting of the management committee, 26 June 1924.
10 Mayeur, "Un collège jésuite face à la société multiconfessionnelle égyptienne," 265.
11 Vatican City, Archive of the Congregrazione della Affari Ecclesiastici Straordinari (Congregation for Extraordinary Ecclesiastical Affairs) (hereafter AES): Africa Egitto 1925-1947; Pos 18 Fas 6: Sacra Congregazione de Propaganda Fide. Anno 1926, n° 17, Luglio. The vicariate apostolic of the Suez Canal was created on July 12, 1926 through an act by Pope Pius XI.

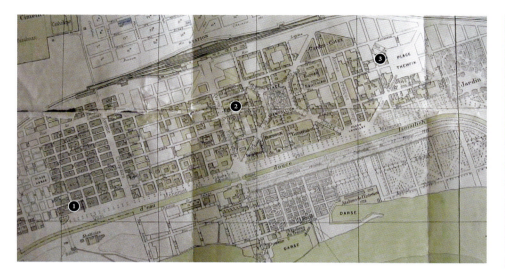

8.6 Urbanism and places of worship in Ismailia. Plan of 1912.
1. Mosque
2. Roman Catholic church
3. Greek Othodox church
[ANMT, 1995060 3564]

8.7 Italian church in Port Said. Emilio Scarpa architect, 1932.
[Photo: Arnaud Duboistesselin, 2005]

Religious architecture as an expression of identity

The appropriation of space as an expression of identity is a recurring phenomenon in non-European towns with cosmopolitan populations. Religious architecture is one of its most evident manifestations. Each community develops its own cultural references. In the cosmopolitan towns of Egypt, especially in the first thirty years of the twentieth century, Italian architects used forms and designs characteristic of European historical religious architecture. The stylistic choices made by the project backers and architects were, according to Simonetta Ciranna, the expression of a desire to assert the religious autonomy and ethnic identity of the religious communities and the national community.[12] The inspiration that guided the Italian architect Emilio Scarpa in designing the church of Sainte-Marie-Auxiliatrice in Port Said in 1932 came from Gothic religious architecture.[13] This church, along with the Italian schools and consulate, forms an Italian-style islet in the isthmus's main town. While the Neo-Romanesque style was generally used for churches built by Italian architects in Egypt,[14] the Gothic style may have been developed in Port Said to distinguish the Italian church from the French community's nearby Neo-Romanesque church [Fig. 8.7].

Meanwhile, the Greeks took their reference from Neo-Classical architecture. Vassilis Colonas notes that, in cosmopolitan towns such as Alexandria, community establishments, with churches and monasteries at the forefront, were the first to be built. The style used contributed to underlining the presence of the Greek community in the town. The Alexandrian Greeks constructed a huge number of monuments influenced by Neo-Classical architecture, the vocabulary of which established artistic and ideological links between the community and the city, but also distinguished it from the town's public architecture and from styles used by other communities.[15] In order to build Port Said's Greek church as a replacement for the primitive chapel, a variety of plans were studied, from simple quadrilateral structures to Byzantine-style monuments. Finally, it was a young engineer, Raymond Antonius, who designed the blueprints, inspired by "the superb Greek churches, especially the 'Little Metropolis,' near the cathedral of Athens."[16] He designed a building with lines that recalled the "beautiful Greek style," a cruciform shape dominated by a dome supported by pendentives. It was inaugurated in 1940.

The architecture of the Catholic churches showed the influence of historical Italian and French styles. In Port Said, the church of St Eugenia resembled an Italian Renaissance church, with its porch surrounded by

12   Ciranna, "Italian Architects and Holy Space in Egypt," 49.
13   Godoli and Giacomelli, *Architetti e Ingegneri dal Levante al Magreb*, 317.
14   Ciranna, "Italian Architects and Holy Space in Egypt," 49.
15   Colonas, "Présence grecque et héritage architectural à Alexandrie," 79.
16   Hakim, "A Port-Saïd," 4.

columns with Doric capitals, its triangular pediments, and its volutes. [Fig. 8.8] Built by Minorite monks, it combined references to the two "guardian" powers: its Italian Neo-Renaissance style referred to the Franciscans' country of origin and its dedication to St Eugenia was a reminder of France's predominance in the region. The architecture of the Catholic churches on the isthmus, financed by the company and serviced by Franciscans from the provinces of France, adopted the vocabulary of the Romanesque style, a primordial reference for religious architecture in France. The example of the construction of the Neo-Romanesque church of Ismailia will be detailed below.

The presence of the Catholic missions in the Suez Canal towns

In these urban spaces punctuated by the places of worship of the various religions, what spatial strategies were established by the Catholic congregations? The Catholic missionary presence made itself felt progressively in the Suez Canal towns, initially through buildings, from the first provisional places of worship to the erection of the cathedral of the vicariate apostolic in Port Said, followed by the temporary occupation of public spaces, an immaterial expression of the missionary presence in the canal towns.

Buildings: a material expression of the missionary presence

The first places of worship on the Suez isthmus, like the majority of other dwellings or industrial buildings from the time that the canal was being dug, no longer exist. The first chapels were provisional constructions in towns that were building sites and were replaced in the 1900s by permanent buildings. Nevertheless, the mission archives contain valuable information as to these early stages. As was customary in colonized countries, the first chapels were provisional constructions made from local materials or were set up in

8.8 Sainte-Eugénie church in Port Said. [Photo: Hyppolite Arnoux, ca 1890. ANMT, 1995060 1491]

buildings which had originally served a different purpose.

Whether in Port Said or Ismailia in the 1860s, or later in the new town of Port Fouad established on the Asian shore of the canal opposite Port Said, the missionaries established a religious presence in the towns with whatever was at their disposal. The first chapel in Ismailia was built in 1862 by Father Gibbon, Ferdinand de Lesseps' former philosophy teacher, when he was called upon by the canal's creator to guarantee a Catholic presence in the town that was home to the company's administration.[17] The rudimentary building was made of matting, a traditional construction method in rural Egypt. In 1864, the company's management committee in Paris approved a request to build a church and hospice in Ismailia and decided to finance the construction costs.[18] The support of the company was greatly appreciated by the clergy. In fact, the bishop of Alexandria returned to Ismailia on September 8, 1864, not even three months after laying the first stone, to bless the church of St Francis of Sales, "wanting, with this double visit in such

17 Paris/Caïro, Archives of the Franciscans (hereafter AF): P. Bernard de Milan, "Chronique de la paroisse latine d'Ismaïlia" (original version in Italian), 1862-1871. The town of Ismailia was established in April 1862 and Father Gibbon arrived in October of the same year.

18 Ibid.: Letter from Voisin, agent, to Father Erasme, April 28, 1865.

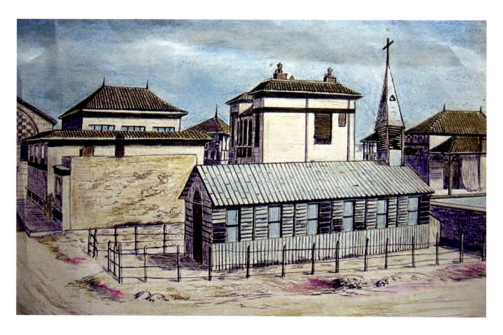

8.9 Port Fouad first chapel, an example of temporary places of Catholic worship in the Suez isthmus. [ABCI]

19 Ibid.: Letter from Brother Bernard d'Orléans to Ferdinand de Lesseps, September 8, 1864.
20 Piquet, "Port-Fouad."
21 Photographs of board constructions used as chapels in some Parisian suburbs were published in the journal run by the Dominicans Couturier et Régamey, *L'Art sacré*, March-April 1958.
22 Rome, Archives of the Brothers of Christian Instruction of Ploërmel (hereafter ABCI), 404/2: Work of the Mission. 8th session: March 1-July 31, 1933 by Brother Roland-Marie.
23 Frémaux, *Construire des églises en France*, 189.
24 ABCI, 404/1.1.001: Egyptian Mission.
25 AF: Libro delle memorie dell' ospizio di Porto-Saïdo, no date.
26 AF: Note on the settlement of the Franciscan fathers, no date.

a short time, to demonstrate to the company the estimation and profound admiration it had created for its many good actions."[19]

After the First World War,[20] conscious of the impact of a nearby church on the congregation of the new town of Port Fouad, the Brothers of Ploërmel took charge of building a school and chapel. This would allow the parish priest, who had previously been living in Port Said, to move to his own jurisdiction. The chapel was a simple construction of planks topped with a small square bell tower [Fig. 8.9] and can be compared to the chapels built by missionaries in the majority of colonies and underprivileged Paris suburbs in the aftermath of the Second World War.[21] Its aim was to ensure the Church's presence despite the absence of resources. In this case, for the monks, who were teachers, it was less about conversion than about ensuring Catholicism had the opportunity to put down roots: "It is to be hoped that the young students will soon appreciate the devotion of the Brothers, for these forty or so small children, although they are baptized, tend to imitate their parents (Europeans, foremen, and laborers in the company workshops), who like the Brothers, but do not feel the urgency of attending to their Christian duties."[22] The same findings were made in France in the interwar period by early studies in religious sociology. New parishes were established in the Paris area, with the aim of reaching a parish ratio of one church for every 10,000 inhabitants. This aim was set by Cardinal Jean Verdier (1864–1940) in 1931, the date of the creation of the Chantiers du Cardinal[23], the charity set up by Cardinal Verdier in the new Paris parishes in 1931 to meet the need for religious facilities in the Île-de-France region. On the isthmus, the presence of the congregations did indeed have an impact. While, on the face of it, the establishment of the Port Fouad school did not lead to conversions, it did have a noteworthy effect. One Ploërmel brother reported that "the most tangible result obtained by the school was attendance at Sunday mass."[24]

In other cases, missionaries lodged in premises provided for them by the company. The first religious institute to settle on the isthmus was that of the Minorites. On December 1, 1860, only a few months after work had begun, Father Erasme received orders in Alexandria to go to Damietta to provide spiritual assistance to the company's French employees.[25] The company's agent in Egypt, François-Philippe Voisin, gave him one of the company buildings, the ground floor of which was used as a chapel. The parish of St Eugenia in Port Said was built on May 30, 1863.[26] Its church was built by the Minorites in 1890.

Beyond the religious framework, missionaries from both male and female institutes were called to the isthmus by the company for their expertise in medical care and teaching. The company made lodgings and the necessary premises available to them, but these were often in pre-existing buildings, which did not always include facilities to cater for their spiritual needs. When the Sisters of the Good Shepherd, who were asked by Ferdinand de Lesseps to teach and maintain a small hospital, arrived in Port Said in April 1863, they were installed in a company property on the Mediterranean coast. The housing had originally been built for company employees and its layout was not always suitable for the nuns' needs. The Sisters soon lamented that: "It is quite comfortable, except that, as the stairs are outside, we are seen on all sides when we are obliged to go upstairs, which is very unpleasant."[27] They also missed having a chapel: "We need a chapel, especially in winter, because, as the wind is very cold and the water fills Port Said, we will not be able to get to the church."[28] They finally managed to adapt the premises to their needs by closing the outdoor stairs and setting up an oratory in two rooms the following year. They did not move into appropriate lodgings until about twenty years later. An establishment known as the "Couvreux Refuge," which included a nursery school and a convent for the Sisters of the Good Shepherd, was financed by the widow of one of Ferdinand de Lesseps' most active associates.[29] The work was entrusted to Edouard Cepeck, the parish architect. Similarly, when the Brothers of Christian Instruction arrived in Ismailia in 1923 to take over the teaching that had been run until then by the lay mission, they were installed in a house in the central square of the European quarter, a former employee villa that had been set up as a school [Fig. 8.10]. They had to wait until the 1940s, when the number of students had increased, to take possession of a proper school, equipped with a chapel and financed by the company.

From when drilling for the Suez Canal first began, the missionary presence left its mark through temporary buildings which were soon replaced by those that were more ambitious. The first constructions, churches and schools built for the European workers, reveal the involvement of the various participants who determined the characteristics of the missionary presence in the Suez Canal towns from the outset. The religious orders were agents for the Catholic presence in the canal area and they responded to the precise needs for which the company was responsible in order to maintain its employees on the isthmus. The company expressed its assumption of this responsibility through imposing buildings.

Ephemeral occupancy of space

Processions and other religious events in the Suez Canal towns were frequent and served to underline the missionary presence in another way. Were these ways of occupying public space simply a reaction to the modes of expression of the missionary presence, or do they, like the buildings, reveal the religious and supra-religious issues at stake?

Processions as a way of occupying space assumed an apostolic character. To use not only church squares but also the neighboring streets and to organize processions along a precise route is an offensive strategy for claiming one's place in an urban space [Figs. 8.11 and 8.12]. This was indeed the objective of the religious orders, showing that the presence of the missionaries concealed a true apostolic ambition. The speech made by Mgr Vincic upon the laying of the first stone of St Eugenia's Church in Port Said in 1890 is a testament to that. Without mentioning the religious duties of the Christian communities, he asserted that the real aim of penetration on the isthmus was the propagation of religion[30] and that the religious education of the missionary students was intended to produce a leveraging effect. It was with this aim that the Eucharistic Crusade was

8.10 Brothers of Ploërmel's first school in Ismailia, c. 1925.
[ABCI, 804.2]

27 Extract from the correspondence of S.M. de Sainte Elisabeth, April 1863, cited by Cassis, *Pages d'histoire*, 118.
28 Ibid., 127.
29 Cf. Montel, *Le chantier du canal de Suez*, 260. Alphonse Couvreux was one of the businessmen responsible for digging the canal from 1863 onward.
30 AF: P. Bernard de Milan, "Chronique de la paroisse latine d'Ismaïlia" (original version in Italian), 1862-1871.

8.11 Saint Sacrament Procession in Ismailia, s.d.
[ABCI, 804.2]

8.12 Saint Sacrament procession in Ismailia from the hospital to the town centre, s.d.
[ABCI, 804.2]

31 AF: Photograph of the patrons of the bells of the church of St Francis of Ismailia [Fig. 8.13]: Marquis Louis de Voguë, president, and Edgar Bonnet, vice-president, February 8, 1930.
32 *Le Réveil*, October 30, 1929.
33 *Journal du Caire*, August 6, 1929.
34 Frémaux, "Ismaïlia."

founded in Ismailia by a parish priest in 1932. As the name suggests, these Crusaders led apostolic actions. One of their most striking operations was the organization of religious processions under the auspices of group meetings across Egypt. In 1936, the town of Ismailia received students from every Catholic school in Egypt on the occasion of the assembly of the Eucharistic Crusade. Groups marched through the town, holding the Catholic Church's colors aloft, ensuring the visibility of missionary work well beyond the French quarter through the ceremony's pomp.

The inauguration of buildings was also an opportunity for events that went beyond what was usual in a place of worship. Dedication ceremonies involved walking around the new church and bringing together the various participants in the building process. It was an occasion for reasserting links between the company and the Church. This was evident when the bells were hung in Ismailia's new church in 1930; their patrons, proud to pose on the porch of the church of St Francis, were none other than the company president and vice-president [Fig. 8.13].[31] The establishment of the bishop in the wake of the creation of the Suez Canal vicariate apostolic was an event which highlighted not only the missionary presence, but also the relationship between the company and the Catholic Church. In 1929, the new bishop arrived at the company's Port Said offices, an edifice symbolic of company power on the isthmus [Fig. 8.14]. His arrival was facilitated by the company's provision of a ship, the *Aigrette*.[32] In addition, Mgr Hiral was invited the day after his arrival to lunch with Baron Louis de Benoist, the company's agent.[33]

While through processions, the congregations were able to appropriate the town and carry out apostolic works, they also provided an opportunity for the company to make itself known in the presence of the religious authorities.

The company's role in town planning and sacred architecture

The Suez Canal Company had the greatest influence on the organization of its granted land; being French-administered, it implemented the elements of a genuine French-style urban landscape.[34] Its control over the establishment and architecture of the places of worship of various religions allowed it to

shape the canal towns into something not unlike the seaside towns of the Normandy coast.[35] The architecture of the Catholic churches was the product of a collaboration between the company's representatives and the clergy and was an important vector in the affirmation of French culture.

A French-style landscape in a Muslim country

Population diversity in the Suez isthmus towns resulted in numerous different religious communities, to all of whom the company made it its duty to extend support. As well as taking into account the needs of the personnel, regardless of their origins, this line of conduct also facilitated control and even allowed the company to influence the construction of places of worship. Each request for funding was the object of a dossier backed up with precise figures and accompanied by blueprints. Requests were received favorably where the need was proven and the aesthetics of the building approved by the competent services.

With regard to the dossiers that were accepted, this system of financing places of worship for all religions appears to have been a way for the company to ensure its control of the spatial organization and of the town-planning and architectural quality of the canal towns. In Ismailia in particular, situated in the center of the isthmus, where company visitors were lodged, several mosques were financed with the objective of eradicating the informal places of worship that were disfiguring the town. With regard to the mosques near the water plant or on Muhammad Ali Quay, the question was one of the town's cleanliness and beauty. The company agent considered giving up land for the former because "along the southern banks of the Ismailia canal, very close to the water plant, there are some 'places of worship', compounds that have been thrown together, made of clay, whose presence leads the poor to invade the water's edge, which may contribute to the pollution of the water."[36] The company also promised to pay a substantial allocation on condition that the outer surface of the mosque was subject to its services and that its construction included the necessary sanitary facilities. For the latter, situated on Muhammad Ali Quay, along the canal, the arguments used were similar:

8.13 *Godfathers of the bells of Ismailia's church, 1930.*
[ABCI]

8.14 *Reception of Mgr Hiral in front of the Company's offices in Port Said, 1929.*
[ANMT, 1995060 1004]

35 Henri Baillère describes Ismailia and its "comfortable, elegant houses which, with their picturesque decoration and their original physiognomy, could make [the visitor] believe that he finds himself on the coast of France, in Trouville or Etretat." Baillère, *En Égypte*, 128.
36 ANMT, 1995060 1001: Letter from de Benoist, agent, to the general manager of the Company, January 18, 1937.

8.15 Watercolour of a French church, s.d.
[ANMT, 1995060 3222]

On the banks of the freshwater canal, at the level of the provisions trading post, there is a place of worship. It used to be a bamboo cabin and has been replaced by a corrugated iron shed. This building spoils the banks of the canal and ruins the view of the lawns and gardens. The best solution to evacuate it is to propose another place of worship in a more discreet place. The construction should be shaped like a mosque of small dimensions, particularly with regard to the height of the minaret.[37]

A significant grant was made to cover construction costs. The company's desire to impose the image of a French town on Muslim land is evident in its precision of sensitive criteria, such as limiting the height of the minaret.

A national style for the isthmus churches

This objective is clearly visible in the architecture of the Catholic churches. However, did the missionaries intervene in their design?

Most of the Catholic churches on the isthmus were a product of collaboration between the company and the Catholic Church, following the example of those financed by manufacturers in French industrial towns.[38] They were prestigious buildings which ensured the company's reputation as well as the beautification of the canal towns. The Marquis Louis de Voguë (1868–1948), president of the company in 1930, highlighted this matter when he reported to the management committee about his impressions during a trip to Egypt, which was distinguished by the inauguration of the Defense Monument at the Djebel Mariam and the consecration of the Ismailia church: "The monument and the church have a beautiful effect and are an honor to the company."[39]

The churches financed by the company clearly displayed a French style. For Port Tawfiq, which was entirely divided by the company into plots containing housing, administrative buildings, and workshops, a Norman church model was used. The origins of the project are still a mystery at this stage of research, but the reference has been documented. The company archives retain patchy correspondence, a watercolor showing a French village over which stands a small church with a square bell tower and covered porch, and blueprints for the new church at

---

37 ANMT, 1995060 1001: Letter from the director to the general manager of the Company, October 20, 1948.
38 For example: Bergeron, *Le Creusot*; Frémaux, "La chapelle d'Hem."
39 ANMT, 1995060 1001: Minutes of the meeting of the management committee, March 3, 1930.

Port Tawfiq [Figs. 8.15 and 8.16]. This representation is used here as the archetype of the French village organized around a Catholic place of worship and corresponds aptly to the company's desire to recreate familiar urban landscapes in the desert for employees coming from France. The church of St Francis of Sales in Ismailia and the cathedral of Mary Queen of the World in Port Said were the most important places of worship on the isthmus [Fig. 8.17]. They are highly visible due to their privileged locations at the center of the European quarters, their dimensions, and their style.

An analysis of sources for the construction of the Ismailia church reveals the parts played by the various stakeholders in its design. Preliminary studies of the building's functional aspects were carried out by the monks and specifications were scrupulously prepared by the Franciscans in tandem with one of the company engineers. They describe an edifice with three naves measuring 800 square meters, with a significant internal elevation in order to provide good ventilation during the hot summers and comprising an internal gallery and a system to protect the façade from the sun.[40] At the same time, the Franciscans ordered a convent adjacent to the church and shaped their design in such a way as to harmonize with it. The Franciscan Father Alexis Bogey assured his superior that: "The new building will be a good, beautiful, and solid hospice which will perfectly correspond with the Suez Canal Company's desire that it and the church be aesthetic."[41] The company then imposed its stylistic choices. As far as the company administrators were concerned, the aesthetic aspect was most important when building a church in Ismailia. The management committee, which was invited to decide on the project, was made aware of the fact that the existing chapel dated back to 1864, had become insufficient, and, above all, was "devoid of artistic character."[42] Aside from ensuring that the finished building's proportions would cater for future needs, the company management wanted it to have "a sufficiently monumental character" and checked its aesthetic qualities in the blueprints. The company chose a chief architect of historical monuments, Louis-Jean Hulot (1871–1959), who was completing the Sacré-Cœur basilica in Montmartre at that time and whose reputation was guaranteed: "First prize of Rome, architect for the French government, for the archdiocese of Paris, and for the Sacré-Cœur basilica in Montmartre."[43] He was asked for rough blueprints in order to allow the company management "to make a decision concerning the type of construction, its establishment, and its general shape."[44] The project was approved on October 25, 1923 [Fig. 8.2].

The church was shaped and organized like a traditional church, initially planned like a basilica with three naves. This choice confirms Simonetta Ciranna's remark that the architecture of churches for European populations on non-European land took its references from traditional styles rather than the liturgical evolutions of the time.[45] This layout was very successful in church-building in France during that same period,

40 ANMT, 1995060 1001: Letter from Paul Solente, engineer, to the director, February 8, 1923.
41 AF: Letter from Father Alexis Bogey to the Very Reverend Father, June 21, 1926.
42 ANMT, 1995060 1001: Minutes of the meeting of the management committee, June 26, 1924.
43 ANMT, 1995060 1004: RP Sylvestre Chauleur, *La cathédrale Marie reine du monde, Port-Saïd (Egypte)*, Alexandria: Printing press of the brothers' professional school, 1947.
44 ANMT, 1995060 1001: Letter from Bahon, assistant director to Hulot, architect, March 24, 1923.
45 Ciranna, "Italian Architects and Holy Space in Egypt," 49.

8.16 Port Tawfiq's church and girl's school project, Pereq architect, 1885. [ANMT, 1995060 3222]

8.17 Port Said's cathedral, Louis-Jean Hulot architect, 1937.
[© Sean Sprague / Alamy Stock Photo: BEPFYE]

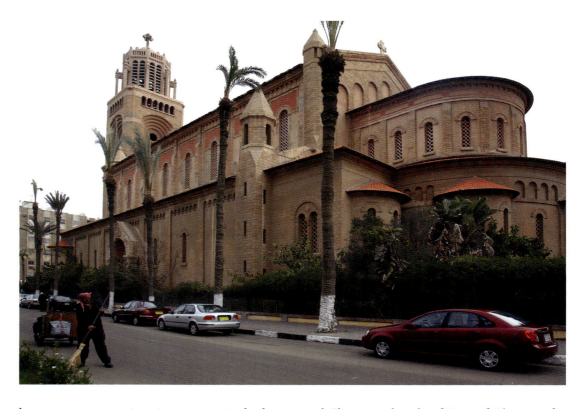

46 Le Bas, *Des sanctuaires hors les murs*, 161.
47 Duval, "La nouvelle église d'Ismaïlia," 373.
48 See for example Frémaux, *La Reconstruction dans l'Est de la Somme*.

but most constructions in major cities had a single interior space. This was made possible by the technical qualities of new materials such as concrete and responded to developments brought about by the Liturgical Movement, which called for a better view of the altar from the congregation seating. At the same period in Paris, the majority of new churches adopted a basilica layout with a single nave.[46] When Louis-Jean Hulot (1871-1959) designed the parish church of Saint-Maurice-de-la-Boissière in Montreuil for the Chantiers du Cardinal in 1931–1932, he chose the traditional shape used for the church in Ismailia: a Latin cross layout and a nave separated by columns from the aisles. The Neo-Romanesque style of the church of Ismailia differed greatly from the innovative experiments of an architect such as Paul Tournon (1881–1964), who used concrete structures in the Saint-Esprit church in Paris (1928) and the cathedral in Casablanca (1930). The church of Ismailia has three semi-domed apses and a lantern tower above the crossing of the transept and the nave; its cradle-shaped bays are reminiscent of medieval Christian churches [Fig. 8.2]. The use of materials such as stone, brick, and Roman tiles reinforced the traditional appearance of the church. Although the rough-stone was local and some stone had been mined in quarries in Fayed and Cairo, the church did not look like an Egyptian building. The only concession to the specificity of the location was with regard to climactic considerations. The architect included an insulation space to offer protection from the heat between the surface paneling and the roofing. He designed a more visible frieze with holes in it, which ran along the base of the roof space to ensure constant ventilation. For the same purpose, he added thick clay screens glazed on the inside surface to the bays, a procedure which "gave the building something unexpected, the color of terracotta in the general harmony"[47] [Fig. 8.18]. The sculpted decor of the building was relatively traditional, far-removed from the innovative experiments of some Reconstruction building sites in France.[48] The Parisian sculptor Pierre Seguin (1872–1958) created a decor with patterns of palms and interlacing, similar to that which

8.18 Project of Ismailia's new church, Louis-Jean Hulot architect, 1923. [ANMT, 1995060 319]

he had designed, under Hulot's direction, for the Sacré-Cœur basilica.[49] While scarabs appear at the base of the porch's triangular pediment, these were less a reference to the iconographic repertoire of Ancient Egyptian art than a homage to the Suez Canal Company, which had appropriated the symbol [Fig. 8.19].

Several years later, in 1930, Louis-Jean Hulot was made responsible for the design of the Port Said cathedral. He again adopted a Neo-Romanesque style, an affirmation of the French presence at the junction of the shores of the Mediterranean and the canal.

A number of parties – the missionaries for the functional choices and the Suez Canal Company for the stylistic choices – participated in designing the church in Ismailia and the cathedral of Port Said. The layouts and styles chosen for the two buildings were the mark of a national architecture, as Romanesque art was perceived in the interwar as the original style of French religious architecture and the first expression of the national genius.[50] Dominique Jarrassé also notes that, in the context of the establishment of the French protectorate in Tunisia, the architect Victor Tondu pushed Francization to its limits by having recourse to the purest Romano-Byzantine style to produce a combination of the most famous French synagogues.[51] The criteria for "French" architecture in the Catholic churches of the isthmus towns was above all a reflection of the company's desire to associate the Catholic Church with its actions in the isthmus and to export an image of France.

The events of 1956 sounded the death knell of the Catholic religious missions' activities on the Suez isthmus at the same time as they signaled the end of the French and European presence there.[52] The Catholic churches were converted into Coptic places of worship a few years later. They are evidence, nevertheless, through their place in the urban fabric and their architecture, of the missionary presence on the isthmus.

49 Poulain, "Décoration de la basilique du Sacré-Cœur par M. Hulot."
50 Thomine, "Les églises en France," 81.
51 Jarrassé, *Une histoire des synagogues françaises*, 302.
52 AF: Notice on the vicariate apostolic of Port Said and the events from October 15, 1956 to July 15, 1957. Nasser nationalized the Suez Canal Company on July 26, 1956.

8.19 Ismailia's church façade: detail with beetle.
[Photo: Céline Frémaux, 2009]

A study of the use of space by the places of worship of all the religions underlines the fact that town planning and architectural decisions regarding sacred buildings resulted, on company land, in interaction among a number of participants and reflected nationalistic strategies. Each community tried to position its own nation in an area of the Egyptian territory coveted by colonial powers. Built in cosmopolitan towns where immigrants associated national attachments with religion, these places of worship were an expression of identity inspired by traditional religious architecture in the countries of origin. The cosmopolitanism of the Suez isthmus towns required the competing missions to play a subtle game through the use of space and shape in order to stand out. Although the towns of Port Said, Ismailia, and Suez were economically and culturally French-dominated (the Suez Maritime Canal Universal Company, which owned the concessions on which the towns were built, was French-administered), they were also influenced by a fine territorial meshing in which the various communities of immigrants organized themselves around their places of worship.

Through the construction of churches, the Catholic missions contributed to shaping the Suez Canal towns. However, they appear only to have played a secondary role in the majority of projects; it was the company that controlled the establishment of the churches through its monopoly of the area's management and decided on the styles of the churches whose construction it financed. Its criteria were to ensure its reputation as a company that gave religious support to its employees, to ensure the prestige of the canal towns, and to assert French predominance.

The main issue for religious architecture in the cosmopolitan towns was not so much the production of an expression of difference as the expression of an identity. The architecture of churches in the canal towns was undoubtedly missionary, but it interacted with the conditions in the cosmopolitan towns against a backdrop of imperial domination.

Cosmopolitanism is often viewed by historians as the myth of a lost "Golden Age" during which different populations lived together; however, the architectural feature of places of worship, the epicenters of communities, often reveal competition between these communities and a will to leave their mark on the towns in question.

BIBLIOGRAPHY

Archival sources

Cairo, Archives of the Sœurs du Bon Pasteur (Sisters of the Good Shepherd) (Casa Generalizia, Suore del Buon Pastore, Rome; Maison Mère: Sœurs du Bon Pasteur, 3, rue Brault 49045 Angers Cedex 01, France)

Paris/Cairo, Archives franciscaines (Archives of the Franciscans) (AF)

Rome, Archives of the Brothers of Christian Instruction of Ploërmel (ABCI) Archives des Frères de l'Instruction Chrétienne de Ploërmel

Roubaix, Archives nationales du Monde de Travail (National Archives of the World of Work) (ANMT), Collection of the Association du Souvenir de Ferdinand de Lesseps et du canal de Suez.

Vatican City, Vatican Archives, Archive of the Sacra Congregrazione della Affari Ecclesiastici Straordinari (Congregation for Extraordinary Ecclesiastical Affairs, AES)

Primary literature

Baillère, Henri. *En Égypte, 1867. Alexandrie, Port-Saïd, Suez, Le Caire, journal d'un touriste.* Paris: JB Baillère et fils, 1867.

Costantini, Celso. *L'art chrétien dans les missions.* Bruges: Desclée de Brouwer, 1949 (1st edition in Italian: 1940).

Dubois, Henri. *Le répertoire africain. Conférence des missions catholiques d'Afrique.* Rome: Sodalité de S. Pierre Claver, 1932.

Duval, Charles. "La nouvelle église d'Ismaïlia (Egypte)." *L'Architecture*, 15 October 1930.

Hakim, G. "À Port-Saïd". *Le Lien, revue mensuelle grecque-catholique*, 5 (1940) 2, 4.

Poulain, Gaston. "Décoration de la basilique du Sacré-Cœur par M. Hulot." *L'Architecture*, 44 (1931) 9, 349-354.

Secondary literature

Anastassiadou-Dumont, Méropi, ed. *Identités confessionnelles et espace urbain en terres d'islam. Special issue of Revue des mondes musulmans et de la Méditerranée*, (2005) 107-110. Aix-en-Provence: Edisud, 2005.

Bergeron, Louis. *Le Creusot, une ville industrielle, un patrimoine glorieux.* Paris: Belin-Herscher, 2001.

Cassis, Violette. *Pages d'histoire.* Cairo: Religieuses du Bon Pasteur, 1998.

Ciranna, Simonetta. "Italian Architects: The Builders of Churches in the Capitals of the Mediterranean." *Journal of the Islamic Environmental Design Research Center*, 1-2 (1997-1999), 96-103.

Ciranna, Simonetta. "Italian Architects and Holy Space in Egypt," in: Volait, Mercedes, ed. *Le Caire-Alexandrie. Architectures européennes 1850-1950.* Cairo: Cedej-IFAO, 2001, 49-53.

Colonas, Vassilis. "Présence grecque et héritage architectural à Alexandrie," in: Volait, Mercedes, ed. *Le Caire-Alexandrie. Architectures européennes 1850-1950.* Cairo: Cedej-IFAO, 2001, 77-83.

Décobert, Christian, ed. *Valeurs et distance. Identités et sociétés en Égypte.* Paris: Maisonneuve et Larose, 2000.

Frémaux, Céline. *Construire des églises en France dans la seconde moitié du XXe siècle: de la commande à la réalisation. L'exemple du Nord-Pas-de-Calais.* Thesis (D. Art History). Rennes 2, 2005.

Frémaux, Céline. "La chapelle d'Hem, un chantier exemplaire de la synthèse des arts?" in: Frémaux, Céline, ed. *Architecture religieuse du XXe siècle en France: quel patrimoine?* Rennes: PUR, 2007, 95-103.

Frémaux, Céline. *La Reconstruction dans l'Est de la Somme. L'architecture religieuse et son décor.* Amiens: Service régional de l'inventaire/Ministère de la Culture, 2007.

Frémaux, Céline. "Histoires, architectures," in: Piaton, Claudine, ed. *Ismaïlia. Architectures XIX-XXe siècles.* Cairo: IFAO, 2009, 2-72.

Frémaux, Céline. "Ismaïlia: L'invention d'un paysage urbain au cœur de l'isthme de Suez (Égypte)." *Histoire de l'art*, 65 (2009), 81-92.

Frémaux, Céline and Volait, Mercedes. "Inventing Space in the Age of Empire: Planning Experiments and Achievements along Suez Canal in Egypt (1859-1956)." *Planning Perspectives*, 2 (2009), 255-262.

Frémaux, Céline. "Town Planning, Architecture, and Migration in Suez Canal Port Cities: Exchanges and Resistances," in: Hein, Carola, ed. *Port Cities: Dynamic Landscapes and Global Networks.* London-New York: Routledge, 2011, 156-173.

Frémaux, Céline. "Port-Tawfiq, l'entrée du canal par la mer Rouge" in: Piaton, Claudine, ed. *Suez, histoire et architecture.* Cairo: IFAO, 2011, 83-119.

Frémaux Céline, "La Compagnie du Canal de Suez et la construction des lieux de culte. Enjeux spirituels et enjeux politiques de l'architecture religieuse dans l'isthme," in: Piaton, Claudine, ed. *L'isthme et l'Égypte au temps de la Compagnie universelle du canal maritime de Suez (1858-1956).* Cairo: IFAO, 2016, 15-46.

Godoli, Ezio and Giacomelli, Milva, eds. *Architetti e Ingegneri dal Levante al Magreb 1848-1945.* Florence: Maschietto editore, 2005.

Ilbert, Robert. *Alexandrie, 1830-1930: histoire d'une communauté citadine.* Cairo: Institut français d'archéologie orientale, 1996, 2 vols.

Ilbert, Robert and Yannakakis, Ilios, eds. *Alexandrie 1860-1960: un modèle éphémère de convivialité: communautés et identité cosmopolite.* Paris: Autrement, 1992.

Jarrassé, Dominique. *Une histoire des synagogues françaises: entre Occident et Orient: essai.* Arles: Actes Sud, 1997.

Le Bas, Antoine. *Des sanctuaires hors les murs. Églises de la proche banlieue parisienne 1801-1965.* Paris: Monum, 2002.

Mayeur, Catherine. "Un collège jésuite face à la société multiconfessionnelle égyptienne: la Sainte-Famille au Caire (1879-1919)." *Revue d'histoire de l'Église de France*, 78 (1992) 201, 265-286.

Montel, Nathalie. *Le chantier du canal de Suez (1859-1869). Une histoire des pratiques techniques.* Paris: Éditions In Forma/Presses des Ponts et Chaussées, 1998.

Piaton, Claudine, ed. *L'isthme et l'Égypte au temps de la Compagnie universelle du canal maritime de Suez (1858-1956).* Cairo: Institut français d'archéologie orientale, 2016.

Piaton, Claudine. "Architecture patronale dans l'isthme de Suez (1859-1956)." *Annales islamologiques*, 50 (2016), 11-53. <https://doi.org/10.4000/anisl.2112>.

Piquet, Caroline. "Port-Fouad: New-Harmony dans l'isthme de Suez," in: Barjot, Dominique, ed. *Le travail à l'époque contemporaine.* Paris: Éditions du CTHS, 2005, 163-179.

Thomine, Alice. "Les églises en France de la loi de Séparation de l'Église et de l'État à la Première Guerre mondiale: chocs et traditions," in: Frémaux, Céline, ed. *Architecture religieuse du XXe siècle en France: quel patrimoine?* Rennes: PUR, 2007, 81-86.

9
Civilizing Space in West China
Re-examining the Place of the Christian University in Chengdu, 1909-1933

Lawrence Braschi

On a rainy afternoon in February 1909, a Canadian couple and their seven month old daughter moved into their new home, surrounded by green fields and with the scent of flowers coming through the open windows. They were representatives of the Canadian Methodist Mission to West China, and in their imagination the surrounding fields and waterways were already transformed into the thirteenth Protestant mission university in China: the West China Union University. For the Carscallens and their successors the university was intended to be one more haven of Christian learning, a civilized and civilizing influence on the surrounding country, an institution at which future Chinese Christian leaders would be taught and trained. To the more antagonistic editors of local newspapers, however, the university would become another 'imperial fortress', home to 'foreign dogs' and their slaves – Chinese students who debased themselves and their nation by seeking education at the hands of proselytising foreigners.[1] Educational missionaries in West China during the first half of the twentieth century lived in a contested space. The prominence of mission universities in Chinese higher education during the 1920s led them to play a symbolic role in the "emotionalized nationalism and anti-imperialism" which was rapidly forming in urban China in the wake of the May Fourth movement.[2]

However, there is also a less well studied contestation which involved the mission universities: the dynamics of resistance and adaptation which played out at a more humble level, the quotidian implications of the changes they wrought on urban and personal spaces. Missionary colleges and universities were a constituent part of much wider educational changes in Republican China, which affected urban land use, the public visibility and place inhabited by students, the clothes they wore, and the new spatial disciplines by which they were regulated. These implications are the focus of this chapter. By placing the West China Union University (Huaxi Xiehe Daxue, 華西協合大學) in the context of broader educational change, while also fixing it in its local, semi-urban space in the city of Chengdu 成都 (Sichuan province), a different perspective is uncovered on the 'long conversation' between Sichuanese Chinese and Protestant educational missionaries.

The implications of Protestant missionary education in Western China[3]

The Protestant missionaries who first moved into West China during the 1880s and 1890s had the resource of a considerable personal and 'institutional memory' gained in other parts of China since the Protestant mission to China began in 1807, and of educational missions around the world. This experience had increasingly come to emphasize the central place of mission schooling. Missionaries like Virgil Chittenden Hart (1840-1904) had worked for several years in Fuzhou, Jiujiang and central China before being allowed to settle in West China under the 'unequal' Yantai (Chefoo) convention of 1876. As one of the pioneering Canadian missionaries, he immediately set about establishing a school at Jiading 嘉定 (Shanghai). Mission schools were started in West China, therefore, almost as soon as a settled mission presence was established. In the treaty port

9.1 Civilizing and modernizing space and time: the Coles Memorial clock tower in the campus of West China Union University, Chengdu. [Maredsous Abbey Archive, Father Gresnigt papers]

1. For the arrival of Crawford R. Carscallen and his family, see Zhang Liping, *Jiaohui Daxue zai Zhongguo* [Mission Universities in China], 16. For some Chinese opinions, see Ibid., 91.
2. Lutz, *Chinese Politics and Christian Missions*, 6.
3. The first Catholic schools in West China were established much earlier. An 'underground' Catholic seminary was created at Luoranggou in 1767, and a number of catechetical schools had already been functioning. These were designed for children and their converts and served by Chinese lay staff. See Charbonnier, "La Catéchèse du prêtre Chinois André Li." However the number of students in Catholic schools in Sichuan remained small and relatively isolated, their spatial implications on the city were on quite a different order from the prominent place of the Protestant University.

of Chongqing (Chungking), the British and Irish Friends Foreign Missionary Association (FFMA) and the American Methodist Episcopal Church (MEC) established local primary schools. In 1891, the first foreign school in Chengdu, the capital of Sichuan province, was opened by the MEC under Henry Olin Cady (1857-1916). In 1893 the Canadian Methodist George E. Hartwell (1865-1943) and his wife established a second mission school in Chengdu with twenty-three students. The social and spatial implications of these schools were initially much more attuned to local Sichuanese sentiment than were other mission institutions and buildings, for example, churches and hospitals.

For the next ten years, the mission schools remained small institutions, with between twenty and fifty pupils. Most of the pupils came from poor families of Christian converts, some of whom were sent from hundreds of *li* away to gain a 'Christian' education. The high esteem placed by Chinese culture on education and literacy also meant that some families who could not afford to tutor their young children privately, sent them to the mission schools in much the same way as they might have sent them to Buddhist charitable schools (*yixue*, 義學) to gain basic literacy. In 1898, Cady's school held an enrolment of 46 students, though only 28 were able to attend on a regular basis.[4] The school was located in the Methodist mission, a large house inside the city walls, rented by Cady from a local Chinese landlord. Fees were kept to a bare minimum. The teaching was conducted in Chinese, concentrating on Chinese classics and commentaries in the morning with instruction in the Bible, mathematics and geography in the afternoon. Chinese history and literature were taught by Chinese tutors. Christian and 'foreign' subjects were taught by missionaries in Chinese or through translators.

In some of the surrounding rural missions even smaller church schools were run by local Chinese pastors out of homes, and education focussed almost entirely on Biblical subjects and basic literacy. The West China Christian Educational Union, begun in 1905, was formed to integrate all these schools into a structured, pedagogic ladder.

Spatially and culturally these early mission schools caused fewer affronts to local sensibilities then did other contemporary missionary institutions. Missionaries and Chinese Christian converts had been won special protection from Chinese law under the rules of extraterritoriality. Consequently any disputes involving converts and missionaries had to be passed upward to the imperial *Zongli Yamen* for foreign affairs, where a resolution could be negotiated with the foreign powers. As a consequence, records of disputes with missionaries and Christian converts were carefully recorded by provincial and national officials in what came to be known as 'religious cases' (*jiao'an*, 教案). The records in Sichuan indicate that schools were rarely the cause for local dissension in the period 1875-1900.[5] More of these 'religious cases' occurred in late-nineteenth-century Sichuan than in any other province of the Chinese empire, perhaps reflecting the worried conservatism of many Sichuanese officials and gentry and the resentment of large sections of the local population toward the behaviour of Chinese Christian converts. The locating of Catholic churches on prominent sites in urban centres sparked resentment in towns and cities across eastern Sichuan. 'Religious cases' in these localities were contests over church land and buildings. Their connection with Catholic orphanages at which many young children died reinvigorated old legends of foreign alchemy requiring Chinese body parts. Protestant churches, although usually less prominently situated, also created local unrest by providing novel and officially unregulated spaces where the sexes might mingle and where heterodox teachings were preached. In one case, the governor of Sichuan had to intervene to request the relocation of a Methodist church near Chongqing after it had initially been built on a pre-existing sacred site. As a result of these growing contestations, missionaries, converts and their associates became the primary suspects for kidnapping, organ-snatching and foetus theft in late-nineteenth-century Sichuan.[6]

---

4   *Annual report of the Missionary Society of the Methodist Episcopal Church 1891*.

5   *Jiaowu jiao'an dang* [A Record of Religious Affairs and Missionary Cases].

6   ter Haar, *Telling Stories*, 154; Wyman, "The Ambiguities of Chinese Antiforeignism."

The other most visible missionary establishment in West China, the hospital, also often became the focus of local dispute as part of wider local concerns and fears about Western medicine. The largest anti-Christian protest in Chengdu followed the death of a patient from peritonitis in 1895. Following a dispute between the patient's husband and the Canadian doctor, the dead woman's body was displayed in public for several days, exacerbating fears. During the next public festival, placards appeared around the hospital purportedly from a Chinese servant there, claiming that he had witnessed foreign doctors extracting oil from the children they had kidnapped and held there. A Chinese crowd stormed the hospital, before looting and burning all missionary buildings in the city. It must also be noted that the Methodist hospital was among the first large, foreign buildings in the city, standing two storeys high, and with a Western-style roof. Its prominent location next to a parade ground and public square made it highly visible in the urban context. Early 1895 was also unusually dry sparking rumours that new missionary buildings, including the hospital, were disrupting the natural ecology of the region.[7]

On the other hand, several reasons can be adduced to the schools' relatively nonconfrontational status. Mission schools transferred easily into the conventional terrain of Chinese religious involvement in local society. Charitable schools had long been supported by urban Buddhist foundations. These were frequently designated for students from poor families, and provided a similar mixture of foundational literary, practical and religious learning as did Christian mission schools. Furthermore, Protestant schools hired respected Chinese figures to do much of their teaching. Hybrid Sino-Western schooling allowed some students to gain significant recognition from the Chinese imperial examination system. One of Olin Cady's students was made passed the provincial civil service examinations in 1902, gaining the rank of *juren* 舉人 and the right to official appointment.[8]

Recurring difficulties in buying land meant that schools were usually located in rented premises, keeping their profile within the comfortable norms of local architecture. Consequently the spatial implications of these schools on local society were relatively minor: their size was limited and they conformed to existing social expectation. Crudely speaking, schools were also the most successful mission institutions in West China for the conversion of Chinese to Christianity.[9]

The growth and development of 'New Schooling'

The place and scope of mission education in China changed radically during the first decade of the twentieth century, dramatically altering the status and place of the Christian missions as a whole. These changes paved the way for a mission university to be constructed in Chengdu. Chinese imperial defeat at the hands of the Japanese in 1895 and a savage foreign invasion following the Boxer Uprising in 1900 led to a deepening crisis at the Chinese court and a crisis of confidence among leading governors. Under extreme internal and external pressure, the Chinese imperial court began implementing 'new

9.2 Hart College under construction, with intact grave mounds in the foreground.
[Private collection]

7 A selection of *jiao'an* records on the incident are reproduced in Sichuan Provincial Archives, ed., *Sichuan jiao'an yu yihequan dang'an* [Records of Sichuanese religious cases and the Boxers], vol. 2; for a contemporary Canadian missionary reaction, see Rev. James Endicott in *The Chinese Recorder*, 26 (1895), 341-343 and 391-399. The incident is well covered in articles by Paulsen, "The Szechwan Riots of 1895" and Hyatt, "The Chengtu Riots (1895)," but they omit the spatial configuration of the protests.
8 *Annual report of the Missionary Society of the Methodist Episcopal Church 1902*.
9 Hart, ed., *Our West China Mission*, 186-187.

policies' (*xinzheng*, 新政), which included a radical abolition of the traditional civil service examinations in 1903 and a wholesale reform of the education system.[10] New curricula required students throughout the Chinese empire to study 'Western learning' (*xixue*, 西學): European languages, mathematics, international geography and economics. This sudden change caught traditional Chinese academies in Chengdu off-guard, and they were ill-equipped to meet the sudden demand for the new subjects. Many of their buildings were torn down and replaced with temporary classrooms. The new provincial college was rebuilt three times in seven years as its size and functions changed. Other government schools were placed in requisitioned temple buildings.

The new schools required the addition of several novel features to Chinese pedagogic architecture – a playing field, large forward-centred classrooms with blackboards and desks, opening glassed windows designed to allow in air and light. Local materials entailed certain modifications, but essentially these were buildings following foreign designs, exacting foreign disciplines on students and teachers alike. The new schools abandoned the ritual religious and community functions of the old Confucian academies, and were disconnected from the traditional locus of educational aspiration, the Confucian temple. Though they expanded rapidly, they caused considerable controversy. There are several instances where new government schools, designed along these novel lines, and the teachers associated with them, were targeted by local gangs during the anarchic period of the 1911 Xinhai Revolution. Together with police stations and *lijin* 釐金 tax agencies, they were symbolic of a contested national intrusion into local affairs.[11]

Wealthier students travelled to the Chinese east coast, or sailed abroad to study in Japan, beginning an era of international student networks from Sichuan. Remaining students faced restricted options: a small number of new government schools, one Japanese school in Chengdu, a French railway school, and the schools of Protestant or Catholic missions. By 1905 the Chengdu Methodist School, run by the Carscallens, held an enrolment of 150, with much larger fees being charged. A further thirty-three students were attending the pioneering Canadian Methodist school for girls. In just over a decade (1905-1918) the West China Christian Educational Union expanded rapidly to include over 330 schools and 14,604 pupils. Education "occupied the foremost place" in the Sichuan mission and mission schools were "overflowing" with students.[12]

For the Protestant missionaries in Western China this sudden demand for Western-style learning coincided with a highpoint in confidence and aspiration. Their support base at home was at its widest point including networks formed of businessmen, laymen and women, and counted leading political, ecclesiastical and business leaders among its number.[13] The transference of the social gospel from the metropolitan churches of the West to mission work in China meant that cultural transformation was increasingly the expectation of a younger generation of missionaries. However, this rapid transformation of the scale and scope of mission endeavour placed missionary educators into conflicts with local Chinese, a position not ameliorated by the missionaries' intention of providing education only on their own terms.

For Protestant missionaries in Chengdu seeking to extend their school system in size and scope, the degree of local opposition also increased. Far greater cooperation with civilian authorities was required than hitherto, and missionaries were slow to understand the implications of their new institutions for local communities. The much greater size of the new institutions and the scale of the long term investment required the various mission societies to buy the required land; no longer could the schools be housed in rented Chinese or mission properties. The largest of these investments, and the one with the greatest impact on local Sichuanese society, was the new mission university in Chengdu, the educational centre of Southwest China and the apex of the missionaries' efforts.

---

10 The literature on the *xinzheng* period is already extensive and constantly growing, see Reynolds, *China 1898-1912*. For the educational changes during the period, see Borthwick, *Education and Social Change in China*; and for an important urban case study, Buck, "Educational Modernisation in Tsinan, 1899-1937."

11 For one example see the biography of Hu Yujie 胡御階 in Ren Yimin, ed., *Sichuan Jinxiandai Renwuzhuan* [Biographies of Modern Sichuan], vol. 5, 78-83.

12 "Missionary Activity in the Capital," *West China Missionary News* (hereafter *WCMN*), 7 (1905) 2, 31; E.W. Wallace, "West China Christian Educational Union. Reports to the Board of Education," 28 October – 3 November 1918, repr. *WCMN*, 20 (1918) 10, 11-17; LSP, "Missionaries as Specialists," *WCMN*, 8 (1906) 1, 1-2.

13 See Rabe, *The Home Base of American China Missions*. Among the British missions, the FFMA also reached its apogee in the first decade of the twentieth century, see Tyzack, *Friends to China*.

9.3 *One of the university buildings.* [Maredsous Abbey Archive, Father Gresnigt papers]

Situating West China Union University

The proposed site of the new West China Union University changed several times. Negotiations with local government and landholders soon showed that there was insufficient room within the city walls to build a major new campus. Much of the western part of the city until 1910 contained the Manchu garrison, to which foreigners had severely limited access. By contrast with the eastern cities, where missionaries could frequently site their schools prominently within foreign concessions, in West China they were required to negotiate for land outside city centres.

Surrounding Chengdu's city walls were a mixture of farmlands, temple properties and gravelands. Sites east of the city wall around the Thunder-God Temple 雷公庙 were examined and found impracticable. Eventually a southern site was chosen, close to the main bridge into the city, proximate to two relatively small temples – the Southern Platform Temple 南台寺 and the Ox King Temple 牛王寺. The initial forty acre site was composed mostly of farmland, but also held some gravelands (*yizhong*, 義冢) and communal land belonging to the temples.

Crossing the site were several small canals and irrigation dikes which were used by farmers to convey water to their fields and to bring their produce to the city markets. The new university would be the first major structure to the southeast of the old city, situated along one of the canals which came to be known by the university's name: the West China embankment 華西坝.

As a consequence of these negotiations, the eventual site of the university proved difficult on several fronts. It was located far away from other missionary institutions, particularly the mission hospitals in the north of the city. As the university came to increasingly specialize in medicine so the distance from the urban teaching hospitals meant that students and staff had to travel long distances daily. More importantly, funds and land were not allocated to provide houses and accommodation for Chinese staff, most of which continued to live in the city until the 1930s. This exacerbated the divisions between Chinese and foreign faculty.

On the other hand, the largely undeveloped site allowed the university planners to conceive a bold, impressive campus, filling the space with sculptured grounds and striking buildings. As in the case of the American University of Beirut they were building for

9.4 Layout Plan of West China Union University, Chengdu.
[The Builder: A Journal for the Architect and Constructor; special supplement of drawings exhibited at the Royal Academy, 1924]

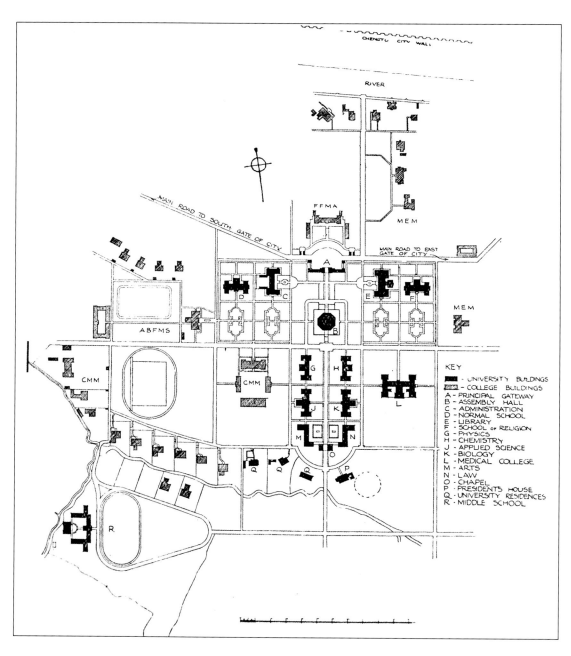

14 London, Friends House, Friends Service Council Archive (hereafter FSC), CH/14 1906: "Statement in Reference to the Founding of a College by the FFMA in Connection with the Proposed Union University at Chentu," n.d. (c. 1906).

15 Ibid.: "Statement Presented to Drs Burton and Chamberlain on their visit to Chentu," n.d. (c. 1906).

effect and for the future; to establish a permanent civilizing presence in the (politically) unsettled region of West China. The campus site outside the walls, meant that missionary planners thought that they would have to make few concessions to the nearby Chinese city of around 400,000 people. Maps of the campus barely sketch any relation with the city, noting only the river and outlining only the city wall beyond [Fig. 9.4]. For one mission agency, the university was to be a self-contained, independent Christian base of operations, allowing an "attack [to] be made upon 'official China' and through them upon the whole people."[14] It would enable Chinese connected with the mission "to take their place among the educated classes" of the city without having to enter the "imperial city" with its increasingly atheist education.[15] Such attitudes of isolation and impact were forcibly changed as missionaries had to begin negotiation with local landholders.

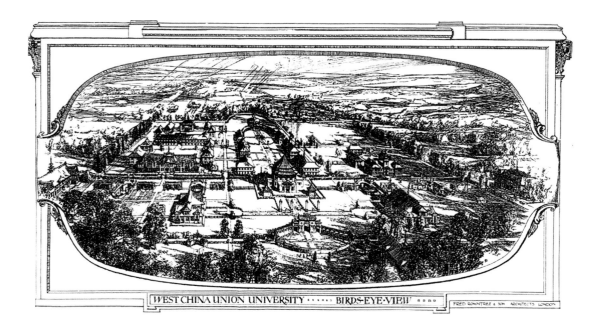

9.5 Bird's-eye view of West China Union University from the south, designed by Fred Rowntree & son, architects, London 1920.

[Wikimedia Commons, Rowntree07.Jpg]

Securing ownership of university land would continue to exercise university, civic and military leaders for several years to come. Farmlands in the west of China were owned by single family units, unlike the much more complicated ownership patterns in southeast China. This meant that farmland could be purchased outright from farmers willing to sell, often for a good price. Such sales in 1908, 1911 and 1917 were relatively uncontroversial. Even so, some of the adjacent farmland belonged to urban institutions, in one case to the county school. Many such schools held endowments of farmland. Revenues furnished part of the school's income and provided scholarships and stipends. These two small fields were never sold to the missionaries, and continued to be farmed into the 1930s.

Negotiations with the temples and over the gravelands could be more complicated. For some in Chengdu these communal gravelands were inalienable. Most were overseen by a proprietor (*yezhu*, 業主) who maintained the grave structures and handled the interment of new bodies. However the right to sell the land under their jurisdiction was a bone of contention. In some cases the land was owned by one or more families. In others cases the land was conventionally deemed to belong to the city and had not been developed owing to traditions and taboos concerning disturbing the dead. In 1911, just after the declaration of the pro-Chinese republic, an unnamed proprietor not only refused to sell adjacent gravelands to the university, but also took the unusual step of publishing a public promissory declaration with the local magistrate to guarantee the future inalienability of the contentious land. Others, such as the Luo 羅 family, were content to sell gravelands they were no longer using. In 1917 they sold part of the Yulin embankment 玉林壩 which provided space for the university's new administrative building.[16]

During periods of relative calm, such as the early 1920s, the university succeeded in buying substantial gravelands used by the Qi family for Mexican 2,025$. The family agreed to remove the graves to another location, and the university subsequently took down the grave houses. In other cases, families agreed for the university to own the land so long as the graves were left intact, and access granted for ritual commemorations. In 1922 there were still three such clusters of graves on the university site, including 8 or 9 *mu* (acres) of gravelands which remained on the Yulin embankment [Fig. 9.2].[17]

16 Zhang Xianfang and Hou Yun, "Chengdu renmin fandui 'Huada zhucheng' de douzheng" [Chengdu residents' struggle against the establishment of Huaxi University], 164.
17 FSC CH/14 1921-1925: Joseph Beech, "Annual Report of the Board of Governors," 1922.

9.6 Pagoda Building on the campus of West China Union University. Color slide of a photo taken by Sydney D. Gamble in 1917.
[Duke University Libraries, Sidney Gamble Photographs Collection, RL_10074_LS_0223]

In 1925, when the issue of Christian education was becoming a national issue of contestation, sales of land to the university had to be ratified by increasingly senior members of Chengdu's government. In April of that year a proprietor had begun negotiations to sell a plot of land containing several hundred graves. Senior figures in the city's cultural establishment (the 'five elders and seven sages' 五老七賢) sought to prevent the sale by consecrating the land to the Buddhist bodhi-sattva Guanyin. When the university authorities pressed ahead with the sale, the elders and sages petitioned the Chengdu magistrate for a construction of a temple instead. It was only when the university gained the sanction of the self-consciously modernizing military governor Yang Sen 楊森 (1884-1977) that the sale of land was confirmed. Yang even suggested that he would come down and remove the graves in person.[18] In a similar case another military general Liu Chengxun 劉成勳 (1884-1944) forced a proprietor to sell two *mu* of land to the university against the wishes of the family.[19] However in 1925, the prohibitive price of adjacent land to the main university site prevent the Church Missionary Society from buying it, and military pressure on the landlord could force him to back down.

Reliance on the volatile strength of local military figures was a precarious existence. General Yang Sen was forced out of Chengdu later in 1925 and many succeeding generals were much less willing to aid the missionaries in local disputes. Purchase of land had also to be legally approved and ratified by the civil governor's office, which charged a ten percent levy on the sale price. As the governors were always short of cash, such regulations proved a valuable revenue stream, perhaps indicating why several incumbents put pressure on local landholders to sell. On the other hand, governors frequently attempted to add fees above and beyond the ten percent.[20] Access and payment for land could therefore become a way in which parts of the local community sought to control or restrict missionary activity, or turn it to their best advantage. For a few landholders, it seems that there was a greater principle at stake – the inalienability of land to foreigners. Unfortunately we do not have the detail in their reasoning to understand whether such opposition was to foreigners' extraterritorial rights, their proclamation of a foreign religion, or antagonism to the way in which foreigners had behaved in Chengdu or other parts of China. Nevertheless, this opposition preceded the more explicit nationalism of the 'educational rights recovery movement', which only became a feature of Chengdu's public life from the mid-1920s.

18 Ibid.: Joseph Beech, "President's Report to the Board of Governors," April 9, 1924.
19 Zhang Xianfang and Hou Yun, "Chengdu renmin fandui," 164.
20 FSC CH/14 1921-1925: Joseph Beech, "Annual Report of the Board of Governors," 1922.

Architectural adaptation

The mission societies united at West China Union University (WCUU) also gave much attention to an architectural appearance which matched their own civilizing aspirations yet which would also be identifiable as 'Chinese'. Missionary architects in Chengdu had already begun attempting to assimilate traditional Chinese architectural forms, especially temple roofs, door arches and gateways, into buildings designed with an essentially Western functionality as for the Canadian hospital buildings built in 1902. The university buildings, represent the most ambitious attempts at such architectural fusion and were frequently cited by (Western) visitors as a particularly successful example. The resulting stone, brick and wood structures embody both the universal Protestant missionary aims of Christianizing, civilizing and educating, and attempts to reflect and refract local architectural styles.

After gaining tenders from several Western architects in 1911, the Board of Governors at WCUU selected the architectural firm Rowntree & Sons to prepare detailed plans. Fred Rowntree (1860-1927), a London-based Quaker, had already designed a number of public buildings in England and Scotland, and would go on to make his name by designing penitentiaries and asylums. He travelled to China in 1912, visiting several cities on the way to reaching Chengdu in late summer. His designs were particularly inspired by Chinese temple architecture, featuring pagoda style towers integrated into some of the larger academic buildings while each would be fitted with the large curving roofs and protruding eaves of Chinese temples and official residences [Figs. 9.3, 9.5 and 9.6]. As one missionary reviewer later argued, the architect was

> able to adapt the best features of Chinese Temple Architecture together with a western interior. This has been done by covering an up-to-date educational building with a Chinese roof in such a way as to blend the two in a very pleas-

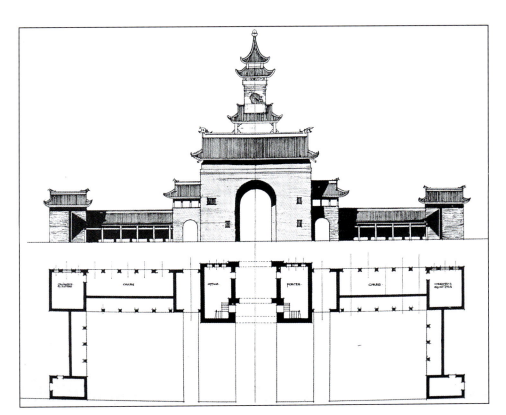

9.7 Plan of the Main Entrance Way to the University, never built.
[The Builder: A Journal for the Architect and Constructor; *special supplement of drawings exhibited at the Royal Academy, 1924*]

9.8 Interior Gate leading to teachers' accommodation.
[The Builder: A Journal for the Architect and Constructor; *special supplement of drawings exhibited at the Royal Academy, 1924*]

9.9 Sketch of the interior of the Lamont Library Building.
[The Builder: A Journal for the Architect and Constructor; *special supplement of drawings exhibited at the Royal Academy, 1924*]

21 WCMN, April 1927, 13; that several of the Rowntree-designed buildings still remain as part of what is now Sichuan University's highly rated School of Medicine indicates that perhaps the anonymous missionary was correct to ascribe their long-term acceptance by the Sichuanese.

ing whole. While other architects have adopted the Chinese temple or palace style, Mr. Rowntree has succeeded in adapting the best features of the native architecture and so produced a new style which there is little doubt will be accepted by the Chinese.[21]

As the buildings were built, and increasingly modified from the original Rowntree designs, they also incorporated local building techniques. This was partly down to necessity. Dr. Will Adams, who had given up medical practice to supervise the construction of the Canadian missionary work, had been driven to breakdown by attempts to introduce foreign construction methods as well as having to 'count every plank and nail twice'. His successor, Walter Small, made frequent adjustments to Rowntree's designs to make use of local resources and skills, and to avoid pitfalls which Rowntree had not anticipated. For example, Chinese-style tiles were used to roof all the academic buildings. However their extra weight had not been calculated into Rowntree's designs, and they caused the roof trusses to spread outwards and require substantial reinforcement.[22]

The most prominent results of Rowntree's architectural fusion included the entrance gates to the administration building, which reflected the architecture of the entrance way to provincial examination halls [Fig. 9.7]. Other gateways in the campus were built entirely in the Chinese style, portals belonging to one world transfigured into another [Fig. 9.8]. Similarly the designs for the interior of the spectacular (and increasingly over-budget) Lamont Library building utilized local Chinese craftsmanship to replicate the roof trusses and decorative elements more commonly found in Buddhist temples and official Chinese architecture. Nevertheless, the wide interior was ordered in spacious ideas of a Western library, with neat rows of bookshelves at the far end [Fig. 9.9]. Its capacious hall could hold up to 500 students and faculty and was regularly used for university ceremonies. Under the carved, brightly painted beams, graduating students were given gilt-edged copies of the Bible, and instructed on their need to serve the church and the nation. This reorientation of internal space, redeploying local designs and patterns in the new purposes of a Western-style Christian education, graphically illustrated the civilizing mission. A new aesthetic, combining Eastern and Western design, functioned to mould a unique institutional identity in Western China.

Foreign visitors continued to compliment the university throughout the following decades. Most focussed on the architecture's combination of 'peace, progress and order'. A sense of peace was enhanced by sculptured gardens and walkways throughout the campus, with the temple-like roofs emerging above lawns, bushes and small waterways. One visiting bishop remarked: "It is hard to exaggerate the impression which the magnificent buildings of the University and its beautiful grounds make when seen for the first time. The high spiritual tone [is] most refreshing."[23] This 'refreshing' tone for a visiting European may be attributed to the missionaries' refusal to apply accepted norms of Chinese architectural groups. Ever since the *Rites of Zhou* 周禮, Chinese design had grouped buildings in quadrangles, with the most important buildings surrounded by symmetrical outbuildings, divided by screens and walls to create small, linked courtyards and gardens. The missionaries instead chose a largely open campus, with little symmetry and an emphasis on individual buildings. To Chinese visitors, the campus resembled more an open garden. Many residents of the southern part of the city took to strolling through the grounds in times of peace or seeking sanctuary there during times of urban warfare, took to calling it the 'Western Heaven'.[24]

The social implications of walls

As China became increasingly lawless during the first decades of the Republican period (1912-1949), so security came to dominate many concerns at the university. Threats to personal and material security came from a number of sources, but were seldom differentiated in missionary accounts. Threats included those inspired by Chinese religious sectarian groups, heirs to the Boxers and Red Lanterns, as well as the temperamental bands of military deserters which thronged the province. Individuals claiming to speak for the Red Lanterns (*hongdeng she*, 紅燈社) continued to publish periodic pamphlets detailing the coming retribution against missionaries and converts. In 1925 a female Canadian missionary, the daughter of a Toronto mayor, was killed on the streets of Chengdu, while one of the WCUU medical professors was shot and injured whilst travelling. Nationalist elements in the city were also angry over the continued protection offered to missionaries by the 'unequal treaties' and their vanguard role in cultural imperialism. Some formed a Sichuan branch of the Anti-Imperial Alliance, and looked for ways to undermine the missionary presence. In 1932, the Communists of the Hubei-Hunan-Anhui Soviet arrived in Sichuan and added their threat to the missionary enterprise.

However it was the more daily security concerns which were a constant anxiety, as instability in the province led to desperation amongst its inhabitants. The university and its foreign residents were highly visible targets for thieves, while the campus grounds often attracted vagrants and refugees. Female Chinese students were frequently the subject of harassment and intrusive curiosity. The surrounding gravelands and fields were uninhabited and allowed easy access into the university property. Many missionary residences were burgled several times during the 1920s.[25] In 1930 another robbery on the campus ended in great tragedy, when a well-respected Chemistry professor, Clifford Stubbs (1889-1930), was killed over his bicycle. The response of much of the faculty, foreign and Chinese, was to demand that a security wall be erected. With the ratification of the military authorities, the university constructed a wall around its 3000 *mu* (200 hectare) of land. This action curtailed access to the canals and streams which flowed through the campus. These restrictions adversely affected the several hundred farmers who worked the fields adjacent to the university, who could no longer use the canals to take their produce to markets in the city. Restricted access also angered the hundreds of workers at three adjacent brick kilns, many of whom used the university as a convenient thoroughfare to their work. The wall extended their daily journey by several kilometres.

Rumours spread quickly that the university was intending to train its own police force,

22 Austin, *Saving China*, 114-115.
23 *Proceedings of the Church Missionary Society*, 1921-1922.
24 "Editorial," *WCMN*, March 1928, 3.
25 See e.g. London, University of London, School of Oriental and African Studies (hereafter SOAS), PP MS 16 Papers of William Gawan Sewell: William and Hilda Sewell, Journal Letter, January 1, 1925, 1.

26 Quoted in Zhang Xianfang and Hou Yun, "Chengdu renmin fandui," 166.
27 FSC CH/15 1929-1932: "Report of the West China Union University for the Year Ending June 30th, 1931."

creating a *de facto* foreign concession within the new wall. The Sichuan Provincial Press Association 四川省報界聯合會 joined the emerging protest with a manifesto statement:

1. Chinese and foreigners must equally be protected by law.
2. Countermand WCUU leaders' business [dealings] and all foreigners' commercial and financial activities in China.
3. Oppose Westerner's reckless use of religion and education, under whatever description, to fraudulently expropriate Chinese lands.
4. Oppose to the death attempts by Chengdu's foreign Huaxi [WCUU] University to build a foreign concession and train a concession police force.[26]

Despite attempts at mediation by various sides, anger continued to grow. The Sichuan Anti-Imperial Alliance 四川各界反帝大同盟 also began protesting about the loss of Chinese rights, while farmers presented petitions to the municipal and provincial government offices. The protests culminated after the Alliance organized a rally on August 4. Hundreds of flag-waving, slogan-shouting Chinese encircled the university and began tearing down the new wall. No further damage was done to the university, indicating that the proximate cause of the anger had been largely removed. Military forces stationed at the university refused to intervene until frantic calls from the missionaries secured reinforcements from the city.

In subsequent reports the missionaries linked the conflict over the security wall to the wider conflict between Nationalists and Communists. They alleged local military generals were sympathetic to the Communist cause, and had helped foment the crisis. Actually, Nationalist forces in the Sichuan provincial government were more sympathetic to mission education and later ordered a cessation to the campaign against the 'foreign concession'. Notices were sent to the Chengdu newspapers instructing them to refrain from any further incitement.[27] Missionaries seemed less inclined to see opposition to the wall in local terms, precipitated by the spatial transformations they had initiated, the disruptions that their buildings had on local life. On the other hand, although it has been tempting for nationalist critics of the missionaries to ascribe all such confrontations to the anti-colonial struggle, similar events occurred in the history of Chengdu's national university.

Spatial configuration and institutional identity

The new architectural settings of the University provided new ways of inculcating discipline, identity and loyalty among students. The campus, divided as it was from the rest of the city, remained under missionary disciplines until the late 1920s when student protests and Nationalist government regulations began to impinge on their authority. Thus the way in which these architectural spaces were used changed markedly during this period [Fig. 9.10]. Student routines were inextricably linked with the growing architecture of the campus. The first few students lived highly regimented lives in the few dor-

9.10 Chemistry building and Western Style garden with Chinese pavillion at West China Union University, c.1945. [Los Angeles, USC Libraries]

9.11 West China Union University houses and community in the enclosed playgrounds, c.1915.
[Toronto, University of Toronto, Victoria University Library, credit Johns Family]

mitory buildings and classrooms, with daily obligations to attend religious services. Later students were surrounded by rules governing playing fields, new laboratories, access to their female peers, as well as an array of spiritual, physical and mental exercises designed to train them for future leadership. The move from a primarily Christian civilizing space to a nationalist one can be seen in some of the following elements.

In 1925, the construction of a clock tower [Fig. 9.1] inaugurated a new civilizing and modernizing regimen on university life. Up until that point, the various small household and classroom clocks were apt to show different times and students were prone to blame them for turning up to classes late. The Chinese post office attempted to solve the problem by periodically sending round a clock to all the houses and classrooms on campus so that staff could adjust the clocks. When the new tower was completed in the summer of 1926, its bell was first used to summon all on campus for a commencement service. Afterwards it chimed the hours for the campus, ensuring a new punctuality for students. Indeed its chimes could be heard across the southern half of the city, replacing the drum tower as the principle means of public timekeeping. The new regimen was by no means universally popular, and was reflected in criticisms of the tower: "not at all pretty and out of harmony with the other buildings."[28] Its utility, however, was manifold. A water tank in the roof, pumped full every morning by a 'coolie', provided running water for the university laboratories. Its upper storey room, meanwhile, provided a bird's eye view of the campus and was used for faculty prayer meetings. In another measure of the tower's central importance, it was named after one of the university's principle donors, the New York surgeon and philanthropist Jonathan Ackerman Coles (1843-1925), who had also donated the bell. Atop the clock tower was an electric globe, a symbol of progress long before the rest of the university buildings were electrified in 1930.

Another new discipline was exercised by the university playing fields [Fig. 9.11]. Traditionally Chinese students had had little involvement in physical activities, preferring cultivating the mind and spirit. With the Chengdu YMCA as an important agent of change, physical education became an important component of all mission schools and the university. Students competed against other schools, under the flags and banners of their various institutions. Revealingly, one missionary teacher concluded that "perhaps our greatest asset in the matter of discipline [is] the fact that we play football and swim with the boys and become as much as possible one with them."[29] Tennis courts, football fields and an athletics track were all used to develop a 'muscular Christianity'

28 SOAS PP MS/16/Sewell/File 1: William and Hilda Sewell, Journal Letter no. 24, October 1, 1926.
29 R.L. Stewart, "The Union Middle School, Chengtu," *WCMN*, June 1913, 10.

9.12 Graduating students procession. [Toronto, University of Toronto, Victoria University Library, © Walmsley Family]

among the students as well as a loyalty to the identity of the mission schools. In 1933 the Christian mission schools sponsored the first marathon to be held in West China.[30]

It was on the playing fields that annual athletics meetings began to take place. The first ever public sports 'Field Day' in Chengdu was held on the northern parade ground in 1906, attended by students from forty of the new-style government and mission schools. The advantage of better acquain-tance with such sports and better facilities meant that mission students frequently took all the prizes. In 1924, such an occasion provoked anger, and foreign teachers had to be protected from the crowd by police. The following year, government school students refused to run against the mission students and separate races had to be held. The mission students were accused of being "foreign slaves, fed out of a foreign rice bowl and believing in a false religion."[31] Two government school students were arrested for spreading pamphlets inciting violence against the foreigners.

Playing fields were also the site of increasingly heated disputes with the garrison of Chinese soldiers stationed at the university. The soldiers used the athletic grounds for drills and parades, as well as less formal jollities and entertainments. The missionaries were exasperated at the degradation to the spiritual tone and uplift of the campus, and sought regularly to have the garrison removed. In 1928, the Church Missionary Society even postponed the completion of their playing field in a bid to prevent its use in this way. In 1933, the pacific Friends Mission entirely dug up their playing fields and turned them into vegetable patches to prevent the military from drilling students on them. The missionaries who were used to exacting out athletic disciplines on Chinese students could no longer dictate how their sports fields were to be used.

Missionaries had already lost their ability to dictate the internal spaces of the university. This can perhaps be seen most clearly in the changing nature of the 'University Day' celebrations, held annually in April in the Lamont Library. While the university was securely in missionary hands, the celebrations consisted of Biblical readings, Christian lessons and hymns. It was usually addressed by a leading missionary figure. Internal and external pressure against religious education mounted during the 1920s and the ceremony began to change. In 1926, the congregated students and faculty were addressed instead

30 For a broader discussion of the role of missionaries in introducing sports into China, see Morris, *Marrow of the Nation*.
31 SOAS PP MS/16/Sewell/File 1: William and Hilda Sewell, Journal Letter, April 10, 1925.

by the president of the (secular) government university in Chengdu, Zhang Lan 張瀾 (1872-1955). Two years later the guests of honour were Chengdu's leading generals. The Chinese national anthem was played and the whole gathering bowed three times to a portrait of the founder of the Chinese Republic, Sun Yat-sen (1866-1925). His will and testament were read out, and three minutes of silent prayer were offered. No mention of Christianity was made until one of the founders gave a speech on the history of the university.[32]

A contested public space for women

One further aspect which affected West China Union University from 1926 was the admission of female students. Young women were rarely formally educated in imperial West China, and when they were it was done in isolation from their male counterparts. Female teachers were equally unprecedented. One early example in the difference in attitudes was played out when a young female CIM missionary was invited to give English lessons at the government middle school. The story also illustrates the potentially hazardous construction of the new-style classrooms that were built for the schools:

> I was the first lady foreigner allowed to teach within those wall, and naturally I was a tremendous curiosity … one day when the classroom was rather more crowded than usual, about half the floor caved in. It was very weird to see the students disappearing to the foundations! Fortunately no one was hurt … The President of the school apologised to me for the students crowding around so, and asked me to deal gently with them, as it was so contrary to all their notions that a woman could teach.[33]

When female students were finally admitted to the university, they were of great curiosity to their male counterparts. High walls were constructed around the girls' dormitories to prevent curious students from trying to get a glimpse of this rare breed of emancipated female. Frustrated male students quipped that the female dormitory was more inaccessible than the nunnery on a nearby hill.[34] From the outset female students at WCUU dressed differently from their counterparts in the urban community [Fig. 9.12]. Students admitted to mission schools had to have unbound feet, a policy which had preceded the widespread campaigns to abolish footbinding in Sichuan.[35] Female students also increasingly adopted a new dress style, the *qipao* 旗袍, derived perhaps from the long-sleeved, full-length *changyi* 長衣 (gown) worn by Manchu women, but also resembling the scholarly male robes *changpao* 長袍. First associated with this new generation of young educated women in the 1920s, "its popularisation was also directly due to the importance of education in facilitating women's entrance into public spaces."[36] Female students at WCUU also partook in athletic events, gymnastics and archery, where they wore Western-style shirts and shorts.

Such revolutions in the aesthetics and practicalities of female clothing drew attention and occasional protests from outside the university. Particularly troublesome for the female students were boys from the neighbouring government school for sericulture. Many of these students came from rural counties around the city, and the school had a poor reputation for discipline. Their school also lacked facilities for sport and recreation, which meant that its students regularly used the grounds and fields at WCUU. While on the campus, they were known for following and harassing the female students. When one WCUU student confiscated a camera that sericulture students had been using to photograph her, the incident rapidly escalated. After a day of preparing slogans, writing pamphlets and 'big character posters', sericulture students encircled the university. They shouted their "slogans against foreign slaves, Christianity and [WCUU's Chinese vice-president] Lincoln Chang."[37]

32 Ibid., File 3: William and Hilda Sewell, Journal Letter no. 49, April 7, 1929.
33 Hampson, "Work Among Chinese Students in Chengtu," *WCMN*, Aug. 1913, 24-25.
34 Zhang Liping, *Jiaohui daxue zai Zhongguo*, 64.
35 Killam, "Annual Report of the 天理足會"[Anti-footbinding Society], *WCMN*, 6 (1904) 3, 60-61.
36 Edwards, "Dressing for power," *WCMN*, 6 (1904) 3, 61; Clark, "The Cheung Sam."
37 SOAS PP MS/16/Sewell/File 3: William Sewell, Copy of Journal no. 52, December 15, 1929.

However, during the increasingly militarized 1930s, female student uniforms increasingly came to resemble military uniforms. In part this was a practical element, as all Chinese universities were instructed to include military drilling in the curriculum in 1928. Many Christian missionaries, particularly those with the pacifist Quakers, found this unacceptable and an undermining of the Christian ethos of the university. Initial compromises meant that students were trained away from the campus, but the militarization of the curriculum steadily increased into the war years of the 1930s, a change reflected in the prominence of the military-style uniforms.

Mission schools, extraterritoriality and local integration

As this chapter has attempted to show, foreign missionaries' rights to build and run educational institutions in China were contested at the local level by a variety of individuals and collective movements, whose composition and intentions varied considerably. The spatial development of the West China Union University was shaped by negotiation and confrontation with such Chinese actors.

In some cases similar processes dictated the development of government institutions in Chengdu, in which the authority of central government collided with local sentiments. Both national (*guoli*, 國立) and mission schools introduced 'foreign' teaching to West China: they changed, distorted or replaced existing social and physical spaces with ones derived from outside the West Chinese cultural experience. However, the mission institutions were twice foreign in that they were protected by the controversial rights of extraterritoriality, exempting them and their occupants from local and national Chinese jurisdiction. Hence the conflicts that they engendered were almost entirely with 'private' citizens: landowners, farmers and students. Local government figures could obstruct the development of the university but did not ultimately have the authority to force it to compromise.

Mission universities in China were created and maintained under the penumbra of imperial power. They were reliant on 'unequal treaties' for juridical and military protection. In Chengdu WCUU was not especially part of the 'informal empire': most university graduates continued to work with the missions or in the medical profession rather than entering government service or foreign companies.[38] However, the missionary institutions provided room for the blurring of the 'objective facts' of Great Power imperialism which infuriated nationalist opponents. For an educator, nationalist and social activist like Yun Daiying 惲代英 (1895-1931), the problem was that as the number of missionary graduates increased, so the number of Chinese doctors, chemists or educationalists willing to contest imperialism declined.[39] Nevertheless, through the local agencies of farmers, militarists, students and journalists, and as the balance of power in China shifted toward the Nationalists, so the mission universities moved increasingly into the orbit of Chinese control.

So it was that in 1933 West China Union University was finally registered with the National Board of Education, an event which was marked by two days of celebrations. Plays and musicals were hosted during the day, while films were projected in the evenings. All the university buildings were opened to Chinese public view for the first time, including the new teaching buildings, the Lamont Library and the girls' dormitory. The first Chinese president of the University, Zhang Linggao 張凌高 (1890-1955) promised "I will try to make things we do inside open to [local people], if possible, and so to cast away all misunderstandings and suspicions."[40] Registration gave the Chinese Nationalist government for the first time authority over the University, requiring greater Chinese participation at all levels of administration and modifications to the university curricula. Now it was the Chinese who would increasingly determine the civilizing mission of the university.

38 See Minden, *Bamboo Stone*.
39 Yun Daiying, "Fandui Diguo Zhuyi de Wenhua Qinlüe" [Oppose Imperialist Cultural Invasion].
40 FSC CH/14 1932-1935: Letter Zhang Linggao to Board of Governors, May 17, 1934.

BIBLIOGRAPHY

Archives

London, Friends House, Friends Service Council Archive (FSC).

London, University of London, School of Oriental and African Studies Archives (SOAS), PP MS 16: Papers of William Gawan Sewell, 1917-1980.

Primary Literature

Annual report of the Missionary Society of the Methodist Episcopal Church, 1891 and 1902. New York: Missionary Society of the Methodist Episcopal Church, 1892; 1903.

Hart, Virgil. ed. *Our West China Mission*. Toronto: n.p., 1920.

Proceedings of the Church Missionary Society. London: Jaques and Co. and C. Whittingham, 1921-1922.

Sewell, William G. *China Through a College Window*. London: Cargate Press, 1939.

Sichuan Provincial Archives, ed. 四川省档案馆, *Sichuan jiaoan yu yihequan dang'an* 四川教案与义和拳档案 [Records of Sichuanese religious cases and the Boxers]. Chengdu: Sichuan Renmin Chubanshe, 1985, 2 vols.

The Builder: A Journal for the Architect and the Constructor. Special supplement of drawings exhibited at the Royal Academy. London, 1924.

West China Missionary News (*WCMN*). Chengdu, monthly from 1899 until 1943.

Secondary Literature

Austin, Alvyn. *Saving China: Canadian Missionaries in the Middle Kingdom, 1888-1959*. Toronto: University of Toronto Press, 1986.

Borthwick, Sally. *Education and Social Change in China: The Beginnings of the Modern Era*. Stanford: Stanford University Press, 1983.

Buck, David D. "Educational Modernisation in Tsinan, 1899-1937," in: Elvin, Mark and Skinner, William, eds. *The Chinese City Between Two Worlds*. Stanford: Stanford University Press, 1974.

Charbonnier, Jean. "La catéchèse du prêtre chinois André Li (1692-1775) dans la Province du Sichuan". Paper presented at an international symposium on the History of the Catholic Church in China, Taibei, September 7-10, 2001. *Bulletin EDA n° 337* [*Églises d'Asie*], Agence d'Information des missions étrangères de Paris September 16, 2001. <http://eglasie.mepasie.org/asie-du-nord-est/chine/2001-09-16-la-catechese-du-pretre-chinois-andre-li-1692-1775>.

Clark, Hazel. "The Cheung Sam: Issues of Fashion and Cultural Identity," in: Steele, Valerie and Major, John S., eds. *China Chic: East Meets West*. New Haven: Yale University Press, 1999, 155-165.

Cody, Jeffrey W. "American Geometries and the Architecture of Christian Campuses in China," in: Bays, Daniel H. and Widmer, Ellen, eds. *China's Christian Colleges. Cross-Cultural Connections, 1900-1950*. Stanford: Stanford University Press, 2009, 27-56.

Cody, Jeffrey W. *Building in China: Henry K. Murphy's "Adaptive Architecture", 1914-1935*. Hong Kong: Chinese University Press, 2001.

Hyatt, Irwin. "The Chengtu Riots (1895): Myths and Politics." *Papers on China*, 18 (1964), 26-54.

Jiaowu jiao'an dang 教務教案檔 [A Record of Religious Affairs and Missionary Cases]. Taibei: Institute for Modern History, Academica Sinica, 1974-1981, 21 vols.

Kapp, Robert. *Szechwan and the Chinese Republic: Provincial Militarism and Central Power, 1911-1938*. New Haven: Yale University Press, 1973.

Li Danke. "Popular Culture in the Making of Anti-Imperialist and Nationalist Sentiments in Sichuan." *Modern China*, 30 (2004) 4, 470-505.

Lutz, Jessie G. *China and the Christian Colleges 1850-1950*. Ithaca-London: Cornell University Press, 1971.

Lutz, Jessie G. *Chinese Politics and Christian Missions: The Anti-Christian Movements of 1920-1928*. Indiana: Cross Cultural Publications Inc., 1988.

Minden, Karen. *Bamboo Stone: The Evolution of a Chinese Medical Elite*. Toronto: Toronto University Press, 1994.

Morris, Andrew D. *Marrow of the Nation: A History of Sport and Physical Culture in Republican China*. Berkeley: Berkeley University Press, 2004.

Paulsen, George E. "The Szechwan Riots of 1895 and American "Missionary Diplomacy"". *Journal of Asian Studies*, 28 (1969) 2, 285-298.

Rabe, Valentin H. *The Home Base of American China Missions, 1880-1920*. Harvard East Asian Monographs, 75. Cambridge: Harvard University Press, 1978.

Ren Yimin 任一民, ed. *Sichuan jinxiandai renwuzhua*, 四川近现代人物传 [Biographies of Modern Sichuanese]. Chengdu: Sichuan Daxue Chubanshe, 1989, 6 vols.

Reynolds, Douglas R. *China 1898-1912: The Xinzheng Revolution and Japan*. Cambridge: Harvard University Press, 1993.

Rowe, Peter G. and Seng Kuan. *Architectural Encounters with Essence and Form in Modern China*. Cambridge: MIT Press, 2002.

Stapleton, Kristin. *Civilizing Chengdu: Chinese Urban Reform, 1895-1939*. Cambridge: Harvard University Press, 2000.

ter Haar, Barend. *Telling Stories: Witchcraft and Scapegoating in Chinese History*. Leiden: Brill, 2006.

Tyzack, Charles. *Friends to China: The Davidson Brothers and the Friends' Mission to China, 1886-1939*. York: William Sessions Limited, 1988.

Wang Di. *Street Culture in Chengdu: Public Space, Urban Commoners and Local Politics, 1870-1930*. Stanford: Stanford University Press, 2003.

Wu Yu 吳虞, *Wu Yu riji* 吳虞日記 [The Diary of Wu Yu]. Chengdu: Sichuan Renmin Chubanshe, 1984.

Wyman, Judith. "The Ambiguities of Chinese Antiforeignism: Chongqing 1870-1900." *Late Imperial China*, 18 (1997) 2, 86-122.

Yun Daiying 惲代英. "Fandui diguo zhuyi de wenhua qinlüe", 反對帝國主義的文化侵略 [Oppose Imperialist Cultural Invasion], in: *Yun Daiying xuanji*, 惲代英選集 [Selected works of Yun Daiying]. Beijing: Renmin Chubanshe, 1984, vol. 2, 820-824.

Zhang Liping 張麗萍. *Jiaohui Daxue zai Zhongguo – Huaxi Xiehe Daxue*, 教會大學在中國 – 華西協和大學 [Mission Universities in China – the West China Union University]. Shijiazhuang: Hebei Jiaoyu Chubanshe, 2004.

Zhang Xianfang 張先坊 and Hou Yun 後雲. "Chengdu renmin fandui 'Huaxi zhucheng' de douzheng", 成都人民反對「華大築城」的斗爭 [Chengdu residents' struggle against the establishment of Huaxi University] in: *Sichuan wenshi ziliao xuanji*, 17 (1965), 164-179.

10
A Highly "Mediated Monument" of Tropical Modernism in Central Africa

Unpacking the Complex Agendas behind the Design and Construction of the Collège du Saint-Esprit in Bujumbura, Burundi

Johan Lagae

From the Protestant mission where Oswald was employed as an orderly, a road carved out of the slope of the hill led to the new Catholic high school. To build this impressive complex of glass and concrete which dominated the capital city and Lake Tanganyika, it had been necessary to flatten a complete hilltop. From his verandah, Oswald could admire the construction that was not yet completely finished. Proud embodiment of the Church, it also formed a parting gift from the Belgian authorities. Its sports ground included a football pitch as well as an Olympic-sized swimming pool. In the near future, pupils could be seen exercising there, shortly after dawn, under the watchful eye of the Fathers, dressed in their impeccable white cassocks.[1]

A "mediated monument" of Tropical Modernism

In his 1994 novel Éclipse *sur le lac Tanganyika*, the Belgian author Albert Russo provides the reader with a compelling image of the Collège du Saint-Esprit [Holy Spirit High School],[2] a late colonial educational complex in Bujumbura. It had been built between 1952 and 1961 at a time when the city was still the capital of the Trust Territory of Ruanda-Urundi, then under Belgian rule.

Russo's description of the edifice as an impressive piece of architecture, built from glass and concrete and situated in a dominant position on a hill top overlooking the city and the lake [Fig. 10.1], resonates with the impact had by the complex on Maurice Lavanoux (1894-1974) in the late 1950s, while he was editor-in-chief of the American journal *Liturgical Arts*. Lavanoux introduced the complex with a double page spread in one of the two issues he devoted to the theme of contemporary religious architecture in Africa in 1958.[3] He also mentioned it explicitly in his "Editor's Diary," writing that "I had first seen this group of buildings from the plane and I *knew* I would see it later. From the air the main building reminded me of Wah Yan College, Kowloon (Hong Kong), also conducted by the Jesuit fathers."[4] The Hong Kong complex forms a good example of what in architectural historiography has been termed "tropical modernism," a particular idiom of climate-responsive post-war architecture in the Tropics, most often composed as configurations of slender, elongated, and well-oriented volumes with flat roofs raised on *pilotis* and with façades largely defined by architectonic devices such as *brise-soleils* and claustras.[5] The Collège du Saint-Esprit, designed by the prominent Belgian architect Roger Bastin (1913-1986), can easily be included in this category. In its overall layout and with its Corbusian formal language and architectonic features, which speak of a climate-responsive design approach, it is reminiscent of the university campus of Ibadan, arguably the most iconic and best-known example of "tropical modernism," built between 1948 and 1958

10.1 A bird's eye view on the Collège du Saint-Esprit, shortly after completion (c. 1962) and showing the complex situated in the hilly landscape at the outskirts of the city of Bujumbura, Burundi. [Leuven, KADOC-KU Leuven, Picture archive of the South Belgian Jesuit Province: 4485/1]

1. Russo, *Éclipse sur le lac Tanganyika*, 7 (author's translation).
2. Belgium acquired the territory of the former German colony of Ruanda-Urundi in 1919, first as a Mandate Territory and, in 1946, as a Trust Territory of the United Nations. See Weinstein, *Historical Dictionary of Burundi*, 5-11 (chronology).
3. *Liturgical Arts*, 26 (1958) 4, 122-123.
4. *Liturgical Arts*, 26 (1958) 4, 137-138 ("Editor's Diary," original emphasis). Lavanoux also mentions the project in later issues: *Liturgical Arts*, 27 (1958) 1, 11; 29 (1960) 1, 11. The Wan Yan College in Kowloon was mentioned several times in *Liturgical Arts* (21 (1953) 4 & 27 (1959) 4), and also in, among others, the journal *Architectural Review*, 1956, 713, 322, & 1960, 761, 73.
5. Fry and Drew, *Tropical Architecture*, counts as the seminal reference for what is described as Tropical Modernism in contemporary scholarship. Scholars such as Hannah le Roux, Iain Jackson, and many others have conducted important research on this topic.

10.2 The Collège du Saint-Esprit from the east with the city of Bujumbura and Lake Tanganyika in the background. Photograph taken by Christine Bastin in the early 1990s.
[© Christine Bastin - Archives UCLouvain, Faculté LOCI / Fonds Roger Bastin]

6   Ibadan University features prominently in Fry and Drew, *Tropical Architecture*, but was also widely published in the architectural press of the time (e.g., in *Architectural Record*, (1957) August, 158-161; Zodiac, (1958) 2, 127-135). Livsey, *Nigeria's University Age*, situates this project in the historical context of decolonization.
7   Kultermann, *Neues Bauen in Afrika*, 26.
8   *La Maison*, 22 (1966) 8, 1966, 8, 242-244; Flouquet, "Roger Bastin," 232; Bontridder, *Hedendaagse bouwkunst in België*, 60; Bekaert and Strauven, *Bouwen in België*, 262-265; Lanotte, *Roger Bastin*.

according to a design by British architects Maxwell Fry (1899-1987) and Jane Drew (1911-1996) [Fig. 10.2].[6]

It was not by chance that the architectural critic Udo Kultermann (1927-2013) should have mentioned the college, albeit briefly, in his seminal 1963 survey of modernist architecture in Africa, identifying it as, in his opinion, the only noteworthy architectural project in Rwanda-Burundi.[7] Yet, coverage of the Collège du Saint-Esprit in regular architectural publications, both contemporary and more recent, remains conspicuously rare. Although several Belgian authors, such as Pierre-Louis Flouquet (1900-1967), Canon André Lanotte (1914-2010), and Geert Bekaert (1928-2016), all pointed out its importance within Bastin's work, it only featured prominently in the 1966 issue of the Belgian architectural journal *La Maison* devoted to Roger Bastin [Fig. 10.3].[8]

Discussion of "overseas" architectural projects, in Africa in particular, remained scarce in the Belgian professional press at that time. Moreover, the Collège du Saint-Esprit was the first large-scale project by the architect, who initially made his reputation through single-family houses and some church designs, later followed by public buildings such as the Mariemont Museum in 1962-1967, the Great Seminary in Namur in 1958-1967, and the controversial and only partly executed project for the Museum of Modern Art in Brussels in 1967-1984.

The absence of the Collège du Saint-Esprit in the architectural press of the 1950-1960s stands in strong contrast to the remarkable attention it received in other sources during this period. Photographs of the complex appeared time and again in illustrated books and travelogues on Central Africa, in colonial magazines and missionary periodicals as well as in newspapers, while it also featured, often prominently, in several documentary and propaganda films. To use a notion coined by architectural historian Lawrence Vale, the Collège du Saint-Esprit was a "mediated monument," an edifice that gained meaning as much through the widely circulating images of it as through its physical existence.[9] The spectacular setting of the complex, situated like a shining acropolis in the hills on the outskirts of the city of Bujumbura, gave it a strong visual appeal, but so did its modernist, elegant architectural design to those outside the architectural profession. How the school's architecture could easily be instrumentalized in a discursive way becomes clear, for instance, in the photographic series included in a travelogue to Central Africa, authored by the Hungarian-born Swiss journalist and photographer Paul Almasy (1906-2003) – it appeared in seventeen episodes in the Flemish weekly family and sports magazine *Zondagsvriend* under the title "Kongo zoals het is" [Congo As It Is]. The richly illustrated episode devoted to the Collège du Saint-Esprit, was headed "Non-racial education, X: the example of Usumbura" and fills three spreads on large page format.[10] It opens with a full-page photograph presenting the complex under construction as a shining piece of modernist architecture, clearly set in opposition to a series of vernacular dwellings with thatched roofs in the foreground, thus visually staging the contrast between progress and tradition, on which the entire discourse around the college's educational experiment of interracial education was constructed [Fig. 10.4].

9 Vale, "Mediated monuments and national identity."
10 Almasy, "Kongo zoals het is."

10.3 Presentation of the Collège du Saint-Esprit in the issue of the architectural journal La Maison, 22 (1966) 8, devoted to Roger Bastin, 242-243. [Leuven, KU Leuven, Libraries, Artes University Library: Z6817]

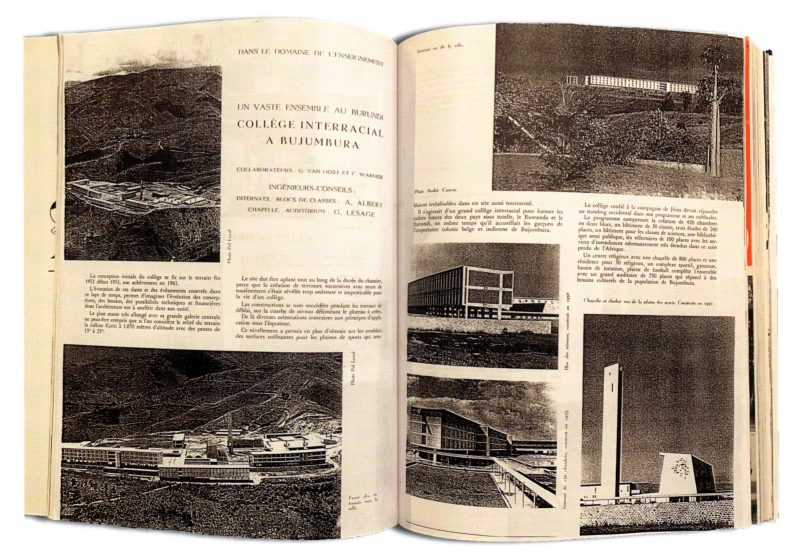

10.4 Almasy, Paul. "Kongo zoals het is. Onderwijs zonder rassenonderscheid. X. – Het voorbeeld van Usumbura". Zondagsvriend, 21 (1957), 20-21. [Leuven, KADOC-KU Leuven, Heritage Library: KYC 29]

11 Russo, Éclipse sur le lac Tanganyika, blurb (author's translation).
12 See bibliography.
13 For a substantial discussion of the design and building process, see Lagae, 'Kongo zoals het is', 357-480.

Presented on the right, beneath the title, is a view of a classroom with pupils of different origin and skin color, sitting next to one another in a "comradely" manner, as the caption has it. Photographs on the following pages depict – or, better perhaps, stage – other scenes of daily life in the playgrounds, staircases, dining hall, etc. If it was the experiment with interracial education that triggered Almasy's interest in the Collège du Saint-Esprit, its architectural appearance played a major role in conveying the narrative to a broad audience.

The images included in Almasy's piece are reminiscent of the scenery of the Collège du Saint-Esprit evoked in the above mentioned passage from Russo's novel. But, by setting the stage from the vantage point of the Protestant missionary post down the hill, Russo also hints at some of the tensions that were intrinsically bound to this particular educational institution and its construction. As such, his depiction of the Collège du Saint-Esprit is also in line with the larger scope of his novel, which engages explicitly with the "complexity of a troubled time that saw the growth of hatred and ethnic rivalries [*rivalités tribales*], which were the harbingers of the humanitarian drama of which we are now aware."[11] As it was conceived as the first interracial secondary school in Belgian-ruled Central Africa, the foundation of the Collège du Saint-Esprit was an enterprise in which many different stakeholders were involved, each with their own particular agenda: the Jesuits, who actually ran the college, saw it as a powerful instrument to train the future elite of Belgian Africa; the Belgian colonial government, which invested significantly in its construction, both financially and discursively, promoted the institute to legitimize their rule in the Trust Territory of Ruanda-Urundi *vis-à-vis* the United Nations; in local newspapers, certain communities within Bujumbura's late colonial urban society voiced outspoken opinions against the "luxury" of the edifice and the specific program of interracial education it accommodated, testifying to the ideological oppositions within late colonial society between Catholics and Liberals, which, unsurprisingly, emerged at a time when the mother country was pervaded by a vehement "Second School War" (1950-1959); the White Fathers (*Missionnaires d'Afrique*), who became involved in its building process, would use photographs of the building site in a campaign to recruit much needed missionary brothers capable of securing the logistics of their booming activities in the region. Taken together, these perspectives on (the role of) the Collège du Saint-Esprit highlight different, and at times conflicting, views of how the future of this part of the world was envisioned by the many organizations and stakeholders involved, all of whom deployed the striking architecture of the complex to articulate their position.

In this chapter we will focus mainly on this diverse mediation of the Collège du Saint-Esprit through images and words, drawing on a wide array of published and unpublished sources and giving particular attention to the visual [Fig. 10.5].[12]

The actual design and construction of this peculiar example of tropical modernist architecture is thus not at the center of the discussion which follows.[13] Rather we seek to discuss here, first and foremost, the "Politics of Design" that underscore this project, as well as to demonstrate that its specific architectural language, spatial organization, and urban location were powerful elements in the many ways this experiment in interracial education was mediated.[14]

Paving the way for a "splendid experience that might set the tone for the whole of Africa"

The origin of the Collège du Saint-Esprit goes back to 1944, the year in which Mutara III Rudahigwa (1911-1959), the *Mwami* or indigenous king of Ruanda, asked the Jesuits to establish a secondary school to educate the youth of his court.[15] The request was surprising given that the White Fathers were the acting missionary society in the wider region. After lengthy negotiations between the *Mwami* and the two Catholic societies, a project was initiated in 1949 in Gatarara, near Nyanza, which was the seat of the *Mwami*'s power at that time. Father Léon Verwilghen SJ (1915-2009), a man who combined religious zeal with great entrepreneurial and diplomatic skills, was appointed to coordinate the project. Construction work started the following year, but proved cumbersome because of the site conditions. Moreover, Verwilghen showed little enthusiasm for the design that he had been offered for the school. When he sought the advice of his uncle, the prominent architect-urbanist Raphaël Verwilghen (1885-1963), the latter advised him to approach Roger Bastin, a former student of his at the La Cambre architectural school, to at least "save the design of the school's church."[16] Probably at Verwilghen's request, Bastin drew up a new design for the whole complex. In the meantime, Verwilghen was forced to re-negotiate the entire project because Léon Pétillon (1903-1996), the acting Governor General of the Belgian Congo, had informed the Jesuits in May 1952 that constructing a secondary school in Gatagara was no longer an option, and that the institute was to be built in Bujumbura, then capital of the Trust Territory of Ruanda-Urundi.

But, more importantly, in line with the new ideas on colonial education that emerged around 1948, the institute was now also redefined as a secondary school for interracial education, the first of its kind in the wider region.[17] Pétillon later declared that the decision to relocate the school was based on pragmatic reasons, as the more central location in Bujumbura would allow for the recruitment of the best students from the three adjacent territories of Ruanda, Urundi, and Congo in order to turn it into Belgian Africa's principal elite educational facility.[18] One can safely assume that the relocation from Gatagara to Bujumbura also allowed the colonial authorities to exercise much stricter control over what was considered an important, yet rather risky, educational project, especially given the ponderous negotiations with the *Mwami,* who felt betrayed by the whole affair.

Once the decision had been taken to build the Collège du Saint-Esprit in Bujumbura as the first interracial secondary school in Central Africa, it became a prestige project for both the Jesuits and the Belgian state. In a letter to Bastin, dated June 1952, Father Verwilghen voiced the great expectations entailed by the project, stating that "it was, of course, a splendid experience that might set the tone for the whole of Africa!"[19] A more

14 We borrow the notion 'Politics of Design' from Wright, *The Politics of Design in French Colonial Urbanism.*

15 For an official account of the institute's origin, see Pilette, "Le Collège Interracial;" Pilette, "L'Université d'Usumbura."

16 Interview with Madeleine Bastin, 1996. This is confirmed in AAVV, "Un bock avec… Roger Bastin," 17.

17 On the educational policies in the region during colonial times, see De Paepe and Van Rompaey, *In het teken van de bevoogding*; Greenland, *Western Education in Burundi.*

18 Pétillon, *Témoignage et Réflexions*, 329, note 11. As a former governor of Ruanda-Urundi, Pétillon knew the territory, had authored the *Ten-Year Plan for its Social and Economic Development*, and had also visited the Gatagara site. See Papers L. Pétillon, file 3537.

19 Letter from Verwilghen to Bastin, June 8, 1952 (Fonds R. Bastin) (author's translation).

10.5 A film crew at the Collège du Saint-Esprit, still under construction, c. 1957.
[Brussels, Archives UCLouvain, Faculté LOCI / Fonds Roger Bastin]

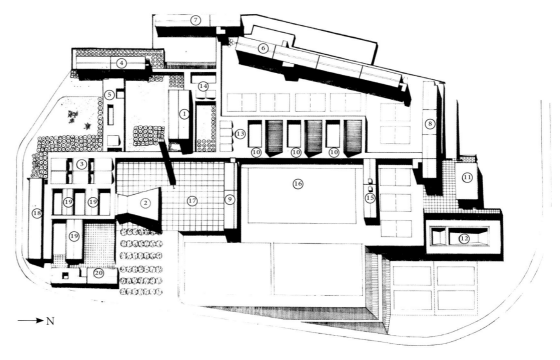

10.6 Masterplan of the finished complex of the Collège du Saint-Esprit, designed for a population of 400 students, encompassing all the educational functions as well as some public facilities: 1. chapel, 2. auditorium/festivities hall, 3. refectories, 4. priests' residence, 5. administration and reception, 6-7. dormitories, 8. classrooms, 9. science block, 10. study hall and parlors, 11. gymnasium, 12. swimming pool, 13. library for the public, 14. sacristy, 15. dispensary/sanitary block, 16. stadium, 17. entrance courtyard, 18. general service area, 19. central control area, 20. workshops. Plan published in Liturgical Arts, 26 (1958) 4, 122.
[Leuven, KU Leuven, Maurits Sabbe Library: L05: 264*LITU]

20 Rapport sur l'administration belge au Ruanda-Urundi pendant l'année 1952, 204.

than substantial subsidy of around 148 million francs was invested into the construction by the Belgian authorities, an amount that almost equaled the construction costs of the most prominent public edifice to be built in the Belgian Congo: the residence of the governor general in Léopoldville (now Kinshasa). Not surprisingly, the project provoked criticism, especially from Liberal political circles *en métropole* who were seeking to break the Catholic monopoly in colonial educational affairs. Pétillon, however, would legitimize this very substantial expense by arguing that it was more cost-effective to invest in one well-equipped facility than to build several secondary school complexes across the region. Moreover, the fact that the Jesuits would run the school implied that, according to new official guidelines approved in 1952, the Belgian state only needed to finance 80% of the total cost, while the missionary society would secure the remaining 20%.[20]

The prestigious character of the project was reflected in the vast building program, which Verwilghen communicated to Bastin: the interracial Collège du Saint-Esprit was to include dormitories with 400 individual rooms for students, each with their own shower facility, and complete with several recreation rooms, 24 classes with office spaces and academic rooms, four large auditoria, a science block with laboratories, several study halls, a large-scale dining hall with a well-equipped kitchen, a library, a residence for teachers – containing eighteen units with their own dining hall, a small chapel, a leisure room, and a small library – a large chapel able to accommodate 800 to 1,000 people, a festivities hall with 800 seats and another 400 on a balcony, a substantial service wing, and extensive sport facilities, including a well-equipped gym hall, a large swimming pool, and several sport fields [Fig. 10.6].

Teaching at the College du Saint-Esprit was modeled on that of the Jesuit colleges in Belgium, so that it could become the training ground for the future elite of Belgian Africa, while the infrastructure and comfort of the complex itself was planned to match, if not surpass, that of most elite schools in Belgium. Father Verwilghen was well aware of the potential controversy that such a level of "luxury" might trigger and asked Bastin to keep functional indications on the architectural drawings to be submitted to the authorities for approval deliberately vague. In the

10.7 First sketch of the project drawn in blue ink on an aerial photograph from the west by Roger Bastin taken early 1953 during his first trip to Bujumbura, attached to a letter sent to his wife, Madeleine Bastin.
[Namur, Personal archives, Family Bastin]

following months, he also asked the architect to keep the project confidential in order not to hamper the complex negotiations he was forced to conduct with parties on all sides.

The project and its substantial funding were finally secured by December 1952 and Bastin immediately travelled to Bujumbura for a two-month trip during which he would work out the contours of a masterplan in close collaboration with Verwilghen.

In the meantime, the latter had been investigating a potential location and proposed a site situated on a hill overlooking the city of Bujumbura. The choice was remarkable as the hill in question had to be flattened in order to create a plateau wide enough to accommodate the large-scale complex. It became a challenging enterprise that would require five years of intensive work with a powerful "payscraper" machine, the acquisition of which the Jesuit father had secured himself. Jesuit sources suggest that the site was chosen because the micro-climate in the hills was better than conditions in the city near the lake, which was situated 300 meters below. This, it was argued, would facilitate the acclimatization of the many students arriving from the high-altitude villages in the school's extensive recruitment area.[21] Bastin's first sketch, drawn on the photograph of the hilly landscape he attached to a letter to his wife, already contains the essence of the complex as eventually realized: a horizontal line composed of a series of slender, elongated volumes on *pilotis* delicately integrated into the landscape and punctuated by the vertical element of the chapel bell-tower [Fig. 10.7].

In March 1953, Bastin returned to Belgium. Throughout the entire design and building process, which lasted until 1962, Verwilghen and Bastin worked together closely, albeit mainly from a distance, communicating on an extremely regular basis via letters that often contained photographs of the building site, detailed reports of ongoing construction work, and, on many occasions, urgent issues to be solved. Verwilghen was not only deeply versed in securing the necessary funds for the prestigious project, but also took on the overall coordination, including direct engagement in the construction process. On a daily basis, he collaborated with Engelhemus Supersaxo M.Afr. (1909-2002), the skilled Swiss brother-builder the Jesuits had succeeded in "borrowing" from the White Fathers.

21 See, for instance, Derouau, "Élèves blancs et noirs fraternisent." Lavanoux reiterated this argument in his discussion of the project in "The Editor's Diary: XXV," 138.

10.8 "The tree artisans": Father Léon Verwilghen SJ, architect Roger Bastin and brother Engelhemus Supersaxo M. Afr. on the building site of the Collège du Saint-Esprit, 1954. [Leuven, KADOC-KU Leuven, Picture archive of the South Belgian Jesuit Province: 4485/1]

22 Gabin, *Espoirs d'Afrique*. Unless noted, the quotes are taken from the voice-over, the text of which was found in Gabin's archive in 1996.
23 Gabin, *Espoirs d'Afrique*.
24 Gabin, "Caméra sur les collèges africains;" Dubuisson-Brouha, Natalis and Paulus, *Le problème d'enseignement*, 1, 24-25.
25 In colonial times, *Ntore*-dances constituted a highly "mediated" form of "traditional culture." For a contemporary description, see Périer, "Danseurs du Ruanda."

That the daring architectural project for the Collège du Saint-Esprit should eventually have been built as designed was in no small degree thanks to the major and sustained effort by this trio of its commissioner, architect, and builder, as well as to the good relationships between them. Their role in securing the successful completion of this striking architectural design in no small part enabled the complex to become such a powerful "mediated monument" [Fig. 10.8].

"Espoirs d'Afrique". Guaranteeing Africa's future through emancipation and discipline

In 1961, the French Father Jacques Gabin SJ (1918-2013) directed a documentary entitled *Espoirs d'Afrique*.[22] Promoting the educational project of the five Jesuit colleges in Africa – Collège Temara (Rabat, Morocco), Collège de Fort-Archambault (Chad), Collège Libermann (Douala, Cameroun), Collège Albert Ier (Kinshasa), and Collège du Saint-Esprit (Bujumbura) – the documentary received an award at the festival for missionary films in Lille, France, the following year.

Just as Africa was going through a turbulent process of decolonization, the documentary depicted a hopeful future for the continent that would result from a "harmonious coexistence between the races." The educational model offered by the congregation, so the documentary suggests, provided a guarantee of shaping such a future. To that end, this education directly addressed a key challenge that faced students enrolled in these Jesuit colleges, which was articulated as follows in the voice-over:

> (For these students) Africa seems divided between two worlds: the ancestral civilization of their parents and the modern civilization of their own generation. Traditional village huts and the reinforced concrete of the new towns. Now, they have their own college, sports ground, and buildings that seems to wipe out the tradition of rural life (…) In this way, a confrontation between two civilizations is being played out in these colleges in Africa, with African culture at stake.[23]

Bringing tropical modernist design to the hilly landscapes of Bujumbura, dotted with vernacular dwellings, the Collège du Saint-Esprit embodied this tension in a particularly palpable way. However, according to Gabin's film and the accompanying article "Caméra sur les collèges africains," written in the same year, the school also provided the ultimate educational model for how to negotiate this tension between two worlds. In the teaching at the Collège du Saint-Esprit "two humanist traditions" were joined through an Africanization of the curriculum. The Africanization of education in Africa was a topic regularly discussed at the time: from May 23 to 28, 1960, the Semaine de l'Enseignement au Ruanda-Urundi was held in Bujumbura and the topic was high on its agenda.[24] The most explicit aspect of this Africanization was the introduction into the physical training program of so-called *Ntore*-dances, the origin of which were warlike dances performed by the sons of chiefs or eminent figures from the court of the *Mwami* of Rwanda[25]:

> At the College of Usumbura, the teachers have understood the challenge. When the dancers from Rwanda parade along beautiful terraces, the pride of a race, the joy of ancient rhythms will flourish. (…) Faithful to their African culture but open-minded to the culture of the world, these boys have already encountered other rhythms. That evening, during the fourth year secondary school, Emmanuel performed Beethoven: 'Für Elise' was already leading him far away from his ancestral mountains… In such a way, these students are discovering another language and are enriched by another culture. The history of the world starts to make sense (…) Attached to their own culture, which is more intuitive than logic-based, the students now absorb, together with European languages, the precise and conceptual thinking of a training in Latin. Their development is shaped by two humanisms.[26]

For the Jesuits, training Africa's future elite was not simply a question of offering all students, regardless of their background and origin, access to an education along the best standards available *en metropole*, but rather required an approach that simultaneously remained respectful to their roots in order to prepare them for a more harmonious coexistence.

The *Ntore*-dances formed a key feature in the Jesuits' mediation of the Collège du Saint-Esprit. They were performed whenever important guests visited the school, from King Baudouin to delegations from the United Nations [Fig. 10.9].

Yet, they also indicate that the Africanization introduced into the curriculum was highly selective, as it privileged Rwandan rather than Burundese culture. As such, this choice testifies to the congregation's ongoing allegiance to their initial "patron", the *Mwami* of Ruanda. With their focus on masculine power and elegance, and their strict

group choreography, these *Ntore*-dances fitted perfectly into the disciplining model of Jesuit education and, as such, formed the equivalent of the gymnastics exercises that were a crucial component of the curriculum.[27] At the Collège du Saint-Esprit, as well as in colonial education more broadly, *mens sana in corpore sano* formed a key *leitmotiv*. "Paramilitary rhythmic gymnastics" was not only a trope in the mediation of the college, but, as scholars Ramirez and Rolot have demonstrated, in the overall visual repertoire of Belgian colonial propaganda.[28]

Such a focus on strategies of discipline pervaded every dimension of the Collège du Saint-Esprit, from the design of the dormitories to that of the study halls. Verwilghen provided Bastin with specific guidelines as to the interior distribution of these facilities that would foster control. In this sense, the dormitories at the Collège du Saint-Esprit – conceived as a battery of identical rooms organized along a long, straight corridor with one unit reserved for a supervisor – followed the conventional typology of the nineteenth-century boarding school. In this respect, they differ substantially from Maxwell Fry and Jane Drew's design for the halls of residence of University College of Ibadan, which were planned around intimate quad-

10.9 Ntore dances as part of the curriculum at the Collège du Saint-Esprit. Photo taken by Paul Almasy. [Leuven, KADOC-KU Leuven, Picture archive of the South Belgian Jesuit Province: 4484]

Historian René Lemarchand defined the *Intore* (the chosen ones) as the Kinyarwanda term for young men recruited by the king or his chiefs to undergo military training, and has shown that in the 1950s under the regime of Mutara III Rudahigwa, the then Mwami, these dances were revitalized as a cultural expression for political means. Lemarchand, *Rwanda and Burundi*, 200 and passim.

26 Gabin, *Espoirs d'Afrique*.
27 In 1957, Jean Weynants (1926-2013), the lay gymnastics teacher at the Collège du Saint-Esprit, would give a lecture entitled "La formation du caractère par l'éducation physique" (Échos, 2 (1957), 12). We interviewed Jean Weynants in June 1996.
28 Ramirez and Rolot, *Histoire du cinéma colonial*, 170-171.

10.10 The all-seeing eye of the Jesuit fathers at the Collège du Saint-Esprit; undated photograph.
[Brussels, Archives UCLouvain, Faculté LOCI / Fonds Roger Bastin]

29 The section on "Educational Buildings" in Fry and Drew, *Tropical Architecture*, 1956, includes explicit advice to design small and more intimate family-like sleeping units for boarding schools in Africa.
30 Pilette "Le Collège Interracial," 154.
31 We can draw a parallel with the spatial strategies pursued by the Jesuits in the Kwango-region, see De Meulder, "Mavula."
32 Gabin, *Espoirs d'Afrique*; Gabin, "Caméra sur les collèges africains," 19-20; Ramirez and Rolot, *Histoire du cinéma colonial*, 385-400 (Chapter 2: "les pièges de la ville et la reconquête de la brousse").

rangles, in a reinterpretation of old Oxbridge colleges.[29] Because there were no strict architectural boundaries, it is suggested by official Jesuit historiography of the complex that the Collège du Saint-Esprit constituted "a space which is not enclosed, has no closed horizons, is not isolated," and that the school thus differed substantially from the "huis-clos" of the Collège Saint-Michel in Brussels, which was completely fenced off from the street by high, enclosing walls and entry gates.[30] One can nevertheless argue that, in its overall spatial organization, the Collège du Saint-Esprit resembled a panopticon-like prison, the typology of which was aimed at exercising complete control. With its open galleries and staircases, and its overall layout which created strong visual connections across the whole complex, students had, in fact, little room to maneuver when it came to escaping the all-seeing eye of their teachers [Fig. 10.10].

Moreover, the choice to locate the Collège du Saint-Esprit on a plateau at a distance of five kilometers from the city center, to which it was connected via a single road, with steep slopes around it on all sides, seems to testify to a clear attempt by the Jesuits to create a heterotopia that would "protect" their pupils from the lure of the colonial city.[31] Jacques Gabin's aforementioned 1961 film and article contain an explicit articulation of this fear of the presumed "degeneration" through alcohol abuse and loose mores emerging in urban Africa in the mid-1950s, triggered by the (omni) presence of bar dancing "with seductive women" and cinemas where the urban youth was exposed to violent and erotic movies without censorship.[32] The Jesuits were eager, however, to convey the message that by organizing many extra-curricular activities in the city, the Collège du Saint-Esprit was not too isolated, no doubt to ensure the school continued to appeal to Bujumbura's white community, many members of which, as we will later see, were skeptical about sending their children to a Catholic school. In 1956, rector Father Walthère Derouau SJ (1904-2000), not without a sense of irony, wrote that, "depending on one's sympathetic inclination towards the school" the Collège du Saint-Esprit could be compared either "to Mont-Cassin, to Montserrat or… to an Alcazar."[33]

While the Collège du Saint-Esprit can be read as a panopticon, its architecture of covered walkways, wide flights of steps towards playgrounds, and slender vertical staircases with large openings onto the landscape also provided a perfect setting for a staging of what historian Betty Eggermont has coined as the "choreography of schooling," that "ideal of simultaneous movements of pupils" comprised of regular and standardized bodily movements, involving "lining up when the school bell rings, filling into the classroom in silence, assuming fixed places in the classroom, raising a hand before speaking, and so on"[34] [Fig. 10.11].

In that sense, the Collège du Saint-Esprit also becomes, in the best Jesuit tradition, a theater.[35] This helps explain why the view of the complex as seen from the city was a matter of great concern to Verwilghen. At one stage, he intervened directly in the design process in order to ensure that one of the two

10.11 The 'choreography of schooling' at the Collège du Saint-Esprit, as captured in Paul Almasy's 1957 account of the school in Zondagsvriend, 21 (1957), 22-23.
[Leuven, KADOC-KU Leuven, Heritage Library: KYC 29]

dormitory buildings would be built on a level below that of the main plateau. Verwilghen was indeed keen to make sure that the effect of the chapel and bell tower would remain visible as a vertical accent when seen from the city, a design feature already present in Bastin's first sketch.

Divergent opinions on training the future elite of the "Belgian-Congolese community"

Not coincidentally, this striking view from the city, as well as scenes of activities taking place on the terraces in front of the dormitories and overlooking the city and lake, recur in the visual mediation of the Collège du Saint-Esprit. For instance, it features prominently in L'enseignement au Ruanda-Urundi, a 1960 documentary directed by J.-N. Pascal and P. Laval for the Service de l'Information du Ruanda-Urundi.[36]

The school and its educational project are presented in a lengthy sequence of about ten minutes, which provides the viewer with a rich and well-framed architectural walk through the complex. The voice-over equally stresses the daring design, describing it in terms of avant-garde architecture, characterized by a simplicity of lines and well-balanced visual perspectives, seen as "unique" on the African continent [Figs. 10.12-10.14]. As is the case in many other key sources, a direct analogy is constructed here between the modern architecture and the "progressive" model of interracial education:

> No distinction of race whatsoever, but rather one main point of convergence: friendship and comradery. A single goal: to build the Africa of tomorrow and, more particularly, the Ruanda-Urundi. Hence, in an avant-garde setting, the new generation of this country is taking its very first steps into a modern world, a world in which such pedagogical institutions are, unfortunately, rare.

As such, the documentary served the agenda of the Belgian government, which was eager to present the interracial Collège du Saint-Esprit as proof of its "progressive rule." Such

33 Derouau, "Une expérience interraciale," 1-4. Monte Cassino is the mother abbey of the Benedictine Order in the Italy; Montserrat Abbey is also a Marian pilgrimage in Catalonia; Alcazar stands for a class of fortified structures built in late medieval Spain. See Lagae, "Montcassin, Montserrat or … an Alcazar."
34 Eggermont, "The choreography of schooling as site of struggle," 130
35 There is a substantial literature on this topic, among others: Krautheimer, *The Rome of Alexander VII*; Levy, *Propaganda and the Jesuit Baroque*; Van Eck and Bussels, *Theatricality in Early Modern Art and Architecture*.
36 Pascal and Laval, *L'enseignement au Ruanda-Urundi*. The following quotes taken from the voice-over have been translated by the author.

10.12 View from the roof of the sacristy towards the class block, with the large dormitory on the left and the study halls with inclined roofs on the right. The bright polychromy, designed by artist Louis Londot, was described in contemporary sources as giving the complex an "African character". Photograph taken by Christine Bastin in the early 1990s. [© Christine Bastin - Archives UCLouvain, Faculté LOCI / Fonds Roger Bastin]

37 Weinstein, *Historical Dictionary of Burundi*.
38 *UN Nations Visiting Mission to Trust Territories in East Africa, 1951*, 82 [New York, Dag Hammerskjold Library].
39 Pétillon, *Récit. Congo*, 259. See also Stenmans and Reyntjes, *La pensée politique*, 35-54.
40 Pétillon, *Récit. Congo*, 286.
41 Levie, *Afrikaans Humanisme*, 1957.
42 *United Nations Visiting Mission to Trust Territories in East Africa, 1957*, 99 [New York, Dag Hammerskjold Library].

a message was all the more important since Ruanda-Urundi was not a colony in the strict sense of the word at that time, but a trust territory of the United Nations governed by Belgium.[37] This required Belgium to submit yearly reports to the United Nations to describe the efforts being made to gradually emancipate the region's population. It is striking that the Collège du Saint-Esprit should feature much more prominently in these documents than in the yearly reports on the Belgian Administration of Ruanda-Urundi submitted by the Minister of Colonies to the Belgian Chamber of Representatives. Having said that, the United Nations was following the whole affair with a peculiar interest, especially since it had already urged the Belgian government to establish a school for secondary education in Bujumbura in 1951, as it felt that the ambitions devised for the territory's school building program, as described in the Ten-Year Plan for the Economic and Social Development of Ruanda-Urundi, were too limited.[38]

When Governor General Léon Pétillon forced the Jesuit Fathers to relocate the planned college in Gatagara to Bujumbura, it may therefore not, as earlier discussed, have been related exclusively to the colonial authorities' desire to gain greater control over the project, but should also be understood as an effort to respond in a more visible manner to the United Nations' expectations; after all, Bujumbura was the capital city of the Trust Territory of Ruanda-Urundi. However, the building of the Collège du Saint-Esprit also made the ideal project for testing out the new political concept of a "Belgian-Congolese community," which Pétillon started to advocate for from 1952 onwards.[39] The introduction of interracial education constituted a powerful tool for realizing such a concept. While the idea of founding mixed schools in the colony had been formulated as early as 1948, Pétillon no doubt believed that the Trust Territory would lend itself more easily to the first application of such an educational experiment than the Belgian Congo, where the color bar still strongly pervaded all aspects of life.[40] In this respect, a 1957 film entitled *Afrikaans Humanisme. Opvoeding en algemeen onderwijs in Belgisch Congo en Ruanda-Urundi* [African Humanism. Parenting and general education in Belgian Congo and Ruanda-Urundi] and distributed by the Centre d'Information et de Documentation, a key instrument of official colonial propaganda, forms a crucial source given its intent as a tool to promote the concept of the "Belgian-Congolese community."[41] In fact, as the scholars Ramirez and Rolot have argued in their in-depth investigation of colonial cinema in Belgian Africa, the film even goes so far as to suggest that "racial intermingling" was already a reality, proof of which was provided, among others, by a sequence on the Collège du Saint-Esprit, which was praised in the film for its "modern, light, and airy spaces". At the time, the complex was far from complete and therefore only featured briefly. However, similar comments were made in a report by a UN mission that inspected the trust territories in Africa that same year and had visited the Collège du Saint-Esprit: "the mission was very favorably impressed by the degree to which the interracial principle was applied in the secondary schools."[42] When, during a UN plenary meeting in 1958, some member states voiced criticism of the, in their opinion, still too limited initiatives developed by Belgium to foster the political emancipation of the African population, unsurprisingly the special Belgian representative explicitly referred to the success of the educational project of the "Collège interracial du Saint-Esprit at Usumbura, where no distinction whatever was made between African and white children."[43]

As Ramirez and Rolot point out, the mediation of interracial education in Belgian Africa in 1950s propaganda films such as *Afrikaans Humanisme* was more of a "projection into the future of a political project" than a reality on the ground.[44] The numbers available as to the student population of the Collège du Saint-Esprit are telling in this respect: only one in four students was of European origin and very few of these were actually resident in the school as boarders. Moreover, the fact that the Collège du Saint-Esprit was run by Jesuit fathers raised questions from many different factions within Bujumbura's urban society, which was quite heterogeneous in terms of race, ethnicity, religion, and class. For one thing, the strong emphasis on *Ntore*-dances in Jesuit discourse on the Africanization of the curriculum did not appeal to the region's African community as a whole, many of whom considered it proof of the congregation's preference for Tutsi culture and its continuing allegiance to the court of the *Mwami* in Rwanda in particular. A 1956 document entitled the *Manifesto of the Bahutu*, which formed an annex to the 1957 UN inspection mission report discussed earlier, is revealing in this respect: "The advantages of modern civilization are, it would appear, being made available through education, predominantly to one recipient – the Mututsi."[45] The fact that "Muslim students" were allowed to enter the Collège du Saint-Esprit, seemed in tune with the prominence of the city's large Swahili community, but in reality only involved a minority group of boys who had demonstrated that they had the talent required to successfully follow the elite training program. In fact, as historian Geert Castryck has aptly noted, the Swahili community in Bujumbura was perfectly capable of organizing itself within the restrictions set out by the colonial authorities, not only in terms of work, dwellings, and leisure activities, but also in the field of education.[46] It should also not be forgotten that, in this particular African region, colonial education had long since served as a direct instrument for controlling the spread of Islam. The deep-seated fear voiced within circles of colonial policy makers during the late 1940s regarding the emergence of so-called Koranic schools and the "immoral, antinational, and xenophobic messages" they might spread, had echoes in Bujumbura's urban society throughout the 1950s.[47]

From the outset, Liberal politicians in Belgium had questioned the plan to have so-called "Muslim students" trained by Catholic teachers at the Collège du Saint-Esprit, and advocated for the principle of having them educated by members of their own religious community. Rather than testifying to an open-mindedness towards Bujumbura's Swahili community, this liberal discourse spoke more of an anticlerical conviction and deliberate attempt to break the Catholic monopoly on education in Belgian Africa. The Liberal lobby, backed by forces within the United Nations, proved strong enough

10.13 View on the covered central walkway of the complex, with playgrounds and large dormitory in the background, and the classroom-block on the right. [© Christine Bastin - Archives UCLouvain, Faculté LOCI / Fonds Roger Bastin]

43 United Nations, *Trusteeship Council*, session 21, meeting 854, points 3-4. The Collège du Saint-Esprit was also mentioned in meeting 851, points 45-46, and meeting 853, points 36-37 (<digitallibrary.un.org/>).
44 "[…] projection dans l'avenir d'un dessin politique."Cf. Ramirez and Rolot, *Histoire du cinéma colonial*, 211-212.
45 *United Nations Visiting Mission to Trust Territories in East Africa 1957. Report on Ruanda-Urundi*, 39-42 (Annex 1 "Manifesto of the Bahutu") and 42-46 (Annex 2 "Statements of Views").
46 Castryck, *Moslims in Usumbura*.
47 See, for instance, J. Vanhove, *Note pour mr. le chef de cabinet*, April 14, 1949 (Papers A. Dequae, 619/1).

10.14 View from the north on the dispensary/sanitary block, with the science block, the tower of the chapel and the study halls in the background.
[© Christine Bastin - Archives UCLouvain, Faculté LOCI / Fonds Roger Bastin]

48 The first architectural project for an Athenée Royal can be found in *Rapport sur l'administration belge du Ruanda-Urundi pendant l'année 1955*, 253 (perspective drawing) and 267.
49 Ramirez and Rolot, *Histoire du cinéma colonial*, 179 (author's translation).
50 *UN Visiting Mission to Trust Territories in East Africa 1957. Report on Ruanda-Urundi*, 2-4 (on political advancement).
51 *La Chronique Congolaise*, October 22 1952, 1 (author's translation). For a similar critique phrased in harsher tones, see *La Dépêche du Ruanda-Urundi*, October 24 1952, 5.
52 Maus, "À propos du collège interracial," 8 (author's translation).
53 *Rapport sur l'administration belge au Ruanda-Urundi pendant l'année 1952*, 204.
54 Verwilghen to Bastin, October 17 1953. See also file D31, folder "Correspondance menuiserie métallique," (Fonds R. Bastin).

to force the colonial authorities to build a second secondary school in the city center of Bujumbura, the so-called Athenée Royal, from 1955 onwards.[48] The institute also features in Pascal and Laval's aforementioned 1960 documentary *L'Enseignement au Ruanda-Urundi*, yet the focus was less on its architectural appearance, which was described in the voice-over as "new and completely stripped down," but rather on the facilities with which the school was equipped, particularly the science labs.

In that respect, the mediation of the Athenée Royal drew on a strong visual trope of colonial propaganda, namely "the image of a Congolese bent over a microscope […] as the symbol *par excellence* of the intellectual advancement of the Black."[49]

When submitting its report, the 1957 UN inspection mission stated that "it was glad to see how positive, constructive, and cooperative was the attitude of the European population as a whole" vis-à-vis the introduction of interracial education.[50] However, a survey we conducted of the leading local press published in Bujumbura at the time – the bi-weekly *La Chronique Congolaise* and *La Dépêche du Ruanda-Urundi* – suggests otherwise. The former, in particular, acted as the mouthpiece for the community of colonizers, or white colonial settlers in the city, who, from the very beginning, were extremely critical of the whole affair, which they saw as just another prestige project enforced in a top-down manner by the colonial authorities and the United Nations. In 1952, *La Chronique Congolaise* described the whole initiative as "premature" based on the argument that:

> Education, indeed, is only just beginning to bear its first fruits among Hindu children – even if we can recognize that the results obtained are very encouraging – but we very much doubt that the same is true among the natives. An old proverb teaches us that we must not hitch the plow before the oxen.[51]

Within the circles of the UCORUDI, the association for white settlers active within the Trust Territory, there were significant concerns that, in the projected future of a "Belgian-Congolese community," of which they believed the Collège du Saint-Esprit formed the perfect embodiment, they would be denied political rights and hence reduced, in the words of their president Albert Maus, to "purely tolerated foreigners" or, worse still, "possible pariahs."[52]

Constructing a new world with "God's hands"?

While this challenge speaks of an anti-Catholic resentment among the large Liberal faction within Bujumbura's white community, some corporatist considerations were also at play in their criticism. The community of locally based white traders, builders, and contractors in particular would voice their discontent, as they felt completely bypassed in the construction of the Collège du Saint-Esprit. This was, however, linked to the specific funding scheme. Given that the institute was intended to be run by Jesuit fathers, the Belgian authorities, as mentioned above, provided only 80% of the total cost of the complex, the missionary congregation being in charge of securing the other 20%.[53] While this formula was beneficial for the Belgian government, it demanded creative measures on behalf of the Jesuits, as due to the scale of the complex, this 20% amounted to a very substantial sum. By necessity, Father Verwilghen became very closely involved in procuring the necessary building materials to minimize costs as much as possible. Correspondence with architect Roger Bastin reveals that they both toured Europe in 1952 to negotiate contracts with firms capable of supplying quality building components at modest prices. The aluminum louvres that were extensively used throughout the building, for instance, were bought from the Italian firm Curtisa, rather than from the Belgian company Chamebel, which, at the time, was a major player in the colonial building industry and would have been the logical partner when it came to supplying building components of that kind, as it specialized in metal joinery.[54]

For the Jesuits, the most substantial profit when securing 20% of the total building cost was to be made by avoiding outsourcing construction work to an official building contractor and instead keeping it "in house." Given the size of the complex and the complexity of several parts of Bastin's design, this option was far from obvious. Again, Father Verwilghen provided proof of his diplomatic skills as he succeeded in convincing the missionary congregation of the White Fathers to "lend" their most talented builder for the job. As a result, the Swiss born missionary brother Engelhemus [Oswald] Supersaxo took charge of the building site, leading a large cohort of locally recruited laborers,[55] which, for particular spells during the eight-year period of construction, numbered over 300 men.

By the time the building site started, Supersaxo, who had been active in the region since 1946 but had worked for the congregation since the early 1930s, had already established quite a reputation as a skilled builder of exceptional talent.[56] In a portrait of Supersaxo that featured in a 1948 issue of *Missions*, the White Fathers' Swiss periodical, it was reported that "a coadjutor brother, especially one with the skills of Brother Engelhemus, provides such precious services that cannot be appreciated in money."[57]

All things considered, Bastin seemed to have bothered little about constraints regarding available technical equipment, building materials, and skilled labor. Many of his design propositions were indeed quite demanding in terms of execution.[58] The slender concrete shells covering the dining halls are a case in point, as are the butterfly roofs of the dormitory buildings and the Jesuit fathers' residence, the execution of which became a point of heated debate between the commissioner and the architect [Fig. 10.15].

Initially, Father Verwilghen seriously questioned the construction logic of this particular roof solution, which he deemed not climate responsive, considering the heavy tropical rains Bujumbura often faced. These butterfly roofs, which formed a signature element of 1950s modernist architecture, were crucial for Bastin, however, as they allowed him to bring what he believed was much needed elegance to the elongated volumes. That Father Verwilghen finally gave in was in large part due to the fact that the three volumes covered by these roofs constituted the complex's public façade towards the city, making their aesthet-

10.15 The butterfly roof as used for the residence of the Jesuit Fathers, c.1958. [Brussels, Archives UCLouvain, Faculté LOCI / Fonds Roger Bastin]

55 Scant information is known as to the origin and recruitment methods of the laborers involved in the construction work. In 1958, Supersaxo would be replaced for a long period by his nephew Edmund Bumann to allow him to take official leave from his missionary duties.

56 Bumann, *Das Heilig-Geist-Kolleg in Usumbura*, is a hagiographic visual account. For a historical contextualization of Supersaxo, drawing on missionary periodicals, the archives of the White Fathers in Rome, and the personal archive of Supersaxo, whom we interviewed in 1996, see Lagae, "Les mains de Dieu."

57 "Des neiges du Cervin aux rives du Tanganika" (author's translation).

58 The substantial correspondence between Verwilghen and Bastin is often illustrated with building site photographs, sketches, and lengthy passages on the ongoing work. It allows us to reconstruct the whole construction process in great detail.

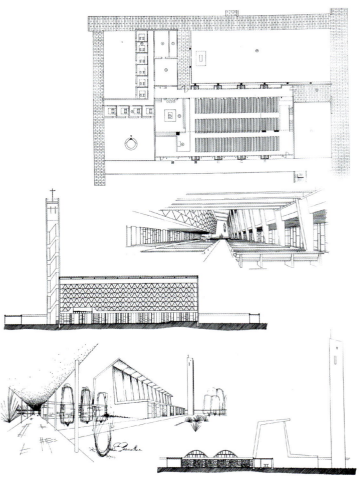

10.16 The chapel of the Collège du Saint-Esprit from the east.
[© Christine Bastin - Archives UCLouvain, Faculté LOCI / Fonds Roger Bastin]

10.17 Plan, section, facade and perspective view on the chapel and clock tower, published in Liturgical Arts, *26 (1958) 4, 123. [Leuven, KU Leuven, Maurits Sabbe Library: L05: 264*LITU]*

59   Verwilghen to Bastin, October 3, 1953 [1954] (Fonds R. Bastin).
60   *Liturgical Arts* 1958 pleaded for buildings decoration by artists "trained in an indigenous manner." Art produced by the Saint Luke School in Kinshasa was deemed promising. Lavanoux, "Prolegomena," 70; "The Editor's Diary: XXV," 133.
61   AAVV, "Un bock avec… Roger Bastin," (author's translation).

ics a matter that transcended rational and functionalist considerations.

The chapel is the part of the complex that speaks most of Verwilghen's trust in both Bastin's architectural design and Supersaxo's skills as a builder. Situated at the center of the complex, it formed the heart of the Collège du Saint-Esprit. Together with the large festivities hall, located at the entrance of the complex, the chapel, designed to accommodate 800 to 1,000 people, was a key instrument in anchoring the Collège du Saint-Esprit in the local community of Bujumbura and its immediate hinterland [Figs. 10.16-10.18].

From the very beginning, Father Verwilghen paid particular attention to its design process, as becomes clear from his correspondence with Bastin. In his first proposal, the architect came up with a daring re-interpretation of the basilica typology. While the spatial organization respected the principle of a high, central nave with two, lower aisles on each side, Bastin radically changed the typology by opting for an asymmetrical configuration in which the row of columns between the nave and left aisle was eliminated to create a continuous, uninterrupted floorspace to accommodate the large community, with a narrower passage on the right. With the height of the central nave reaching 14.20 meters, and the ceiling of the side aisles measuring 3.30 meters, this was a structurally daring proposal. Inside, the church space developed thanks to the rhythm of a series of impressive, tapered column-beam elements on the right that articulated the play of structural forces, while on the left hand side, the folded plate forming the side wall of the central nave and ceiling of the left aisle was hung on a series of tapered beam-rib structural elements that were only visible on the outside. This structural solution also enabled a very different regime of natural illumination: in contrast with the basilica typology, the central nave was kept in the dark, only interrupted by a slender, continuous strip of daylight underneath the ceiling on the left, also allowing for ventilation. The two aisles, with completely glazed facades, were bathed in daylight.

When Verwilghen received the first sketch design for the chapel, he expressed his satisfaction with the proposal – "[the design for the chapel] is very promising and I do hope it will be the College's masterpiece" – but he also articulated his concerns regarding the difficulties this proposal would entail for Supersaxo and his workers, writing that "the immense concrete beams are somewhat frightening, even if I do not see another solution."[59] Yet, it is telling that Verwilghen never fundamentally questioned the concept. No doubt, the first sketches of the interior drawn by Bastin allowed him to anticipate the strong impression this liturgical space would make on the community gathered in the chapel. It should also not be forgotten that it was precisely because of Bastin's proven expertise in creating meaningful liturgical spaces that Verwilghen had approached the architect to collaborate on the design of the Collège du Saint-Esprit in the first place. This expertise enabled Verwilghen and Bastin to engage in an intense and fruitful dialogue on the integration of religious art in the chapel's design. Bastin was involved in the revival of liturgical arts in the diocese of Namur, as stimulated by Canon André Lanotte and promoted by *Art d'Église*. It resulted in a series of commissions granted to the progressive Belgian artists Louis-Marie Londot, Maurice Rocher, Philippe Denis, and Jean Williame. Rather than opting for the integration of the work of local artists and craftsman, as was argued for in the pages of *Liturgical Arts* at the time.[60] Londot did the chapel's stained-glass window and the striking polychromy of the Collège.

All in all, the chapel was an impressive piece of architecture. According to a 1960 interview, Bastin, when confronted for the first time with the chapel in its finished form, is said to have uttered: "It's the exaltation of the Gothic chapel!" and Verwilghen also explicitly voiced his satisfaction with the end result in a letter to the architect.[61] Yet, when viewed within Bastin's portfolio of religious

10.18 *The interior of the chapel from the west during mass, providing a view on the gallery and the stained glass window designed by artist Louis Londot. Photograph by Joseph Scherschel published in* The National Geographical Magazine, *122 (1962) 5, 605.*
[Ghent, Ghent University Library: P.416]

projects of the time, most of which have an intimate feel, the chapel of the Collège du Saint-Esprit instead stands out as a building that conveys a clear image of an *Ecclesia triumphans*. But then, this chapel was, of course, also intended to anchor the Collège du Saint-Esprit's educational project firmly within the Jesuits' missionary agenda. Just like Bastin's *Civitas Dei*-project for the Brussels 1958 World's Fair, this was a prestigious project of religious architecture, designed to impress and embedded within an outspoken ambition of proselytism. In that sense, it also differed substantially from the emerging production of more modest, welcoming missionary churches that were discussed, among others, within the circles of the Swiss-based Christliche Architektengemeinschaft für die Missionen, founded in 1957, the work of which was also followed with interest in Belgium.[62]

Building site photographs of the chapel under construction provide a glimpse of the complexity of the task at hand for brother Supersaxo. Modest scaffolding and formwork in wood rose up to 15 meters, while the slender sections of both structural elements and the plates of the ceiling and walls, which gave the project its elegance, required the extremely precise positioning of the steel rebars. As the chapel was one of the final parts of the complex to be built, Supersaxo had already managed to train a number of African workers over several years to the point that they were able to deal with complex tasks and even lead parts of the construction site somewhat autonomously. Interviewed in 1958, Supersaxo explicitly pointed out the effort this had entailed for the workers involved:

> One has deciphered the [construction] drawings with my assistance. He demonstrated an eagerness to learn how to read a plan and often stayed up late at night, after a long day of work, to gain a sound understanding. This worker has now become a very valuable asset on the building site. I've tasked him with the positioning of the rebars for the reinforced concrete, a job that requires delicate handling.[63]

The trust Supersaxo placed in his workers stands in contrast with the stereotypical and blatantly paternalistic comments on the alleged limited skills of African laborers regularly encountered in contemporary sources.[64] No surprise then that the empowering effect of this training was explicitly highlighted as a positive outcome in the reports of several UN missions that visited the Collège du Saint-Esprit: "The excellent technical work being carried out in the construction of the building by African workers under the supervision of lay brothers, provides an example of the ability of Africans to acquire skills when given proper guidance."[65] As Supersaxo remembered many years later, several African workers would start their own construction businesses after the school's completion.[66]

The mediation of the Collège du Saint-Esprit by the White Fathers is largely in keeping with the praise for the interracial educational experiment also encountered in Jesuit and Belgian government sources.[67] Yet, part of it complements the narrative around the emancipatory nature of the institution in a significant way because of the attention paid to its construction work. A powerful example is provided by a spread in a 1958 issue of *Missions*, which included construction site photographs [Fig 10.19].

These images are accompanied by the following, evocative testimony, written by a certain Bernard Akakpo, suggesting that the congregation displayed a sensitivity to the emergence of African voices who claimed the right to build their own future. Building an Africa that could be proud of itself and in which everyone could live in harmony in an "African spirit", so the text argues, required taking into consideration the particular needs of the young generation of workers and responding to these through concrete actions and initiatives, such as the introduction of professional courses:

---

62 The Christliche Architektengemeinschaft für die Missionen was founded in 1957 by the Swiss sculptor Albert Wider. For a general survey and individual projects, see Dahinden, *Construire pour l'Église dans le monde*. See also two issues on missionary architecture in the journal *Art d'Église* 109 (1959), and a critical assessment of the movement by Bekaert, "Kunst en missie," 154-155.

63 Brother Engelhemus cited by Father Bernard Jobin M.Afr., themed file on the Collège du Saint-Esprit, *Missions*, 1958, 2, 28 (author's translation).

64 See, among others, Fivez, *A Concrete State*.

65 *United Nations Visiting Mission to Trust Territories in East Africa, 1954. Report on Trust Territory of Ruanda-Urundi*, 11-12 (<digitallibrary.un.org>).

66 Interview with Engelhemus Supersaxo, 1996.

67 In 1958, for instance, *D'Weiss Patren an Afrika*, the Luxembourg White Father's periodical, stated that: "Der Bau von Usumbura hat Schule gemacht, bevor er als Schule im Betrieb war. Heute sind überall in Afrika interrassiale Kollegien, und die Weißen und Schwarzen finden es heute ganz natürlich, daß ihre Kinder, die studieren wollen, ein und dieselbe Schule besuchen."

In conclusion, we would like to state that the place of young people in this Africa that is on the move should be reflected through an intense search for knowledge and training, both general and practical in nature; but also through gaining an awareness of responsibility, as well as a clear desire to act in order to change what does not work in our country.

It is telling that two of these construction site photographs should have been taken at the Collège du Saint-Esprit. Highlighting the figure of the (young) African laborer, these photographs thus seem to suggest that the empowerment of the Collège du Saint-Esprit went beyond the strict group of African students following an elite education or performing *Ntore*-dances. Yet, further research is needed to establish how active the congregation actually was in promoting progressive voices such as Akakpo's, as overall, the mediation of the (construction work of the) Collège du Saint-Esprit in the White Fathers' sources remains part of the congregation's more self-supporting agendas. First, there is a strong emphasis on the collective effort of building, which in itself forms a powerful trope in (Catholic) missionary propaganda. The emphasis in these sources remains largely on the community of anonymous builders, rather than on the individual worker. In that respect, the photographs of the building site of the Collège du Saint-Esprit are reminiscent of images that featured mainly in pre-World War II, but also some post-war, missionary publications, depicting Africans felling trees or baking bricks. This conveyed the message that through the act of erecting a church or a school together, under the supervision of a missionary father or brother, a community of converts could be shaped. An article entitled "A nation builds its own church: a film strip: churches grow out of the jungle," which featured in a 1935 issue of *Afrika Bote*, the German magazine of the White Fathers, forms a case in point.[68] Was the Collège du Saint-Esprit not similarly built by "Gods' hands"?[69]

Second, we can discern an explicit narrative of emulation in many of the photographs of the Collège du Saint-Esprit construction site presented in the media of the White Fathers: Brother Supersaxo is often depicted as the key figure, demonstrating to a number of African workers how a specific task should be executed [Fig. 10.20].

10.19 These two photographs of the building site of the Collège du Saint-Esprit were published in a 1958 issue of Missions, *the White Fathers' missionary journal and accompanied by a text authored by Bernard Akakpo which begins with the sentence* "We want to build an Africa worthy of itself" (Nous voulons bâtir une Afrique digne d'elle-même). *[Leuven, KADOC-KU Leuven, Picture archive of the South Belgian Jesuit Province: 4485/1]*

68 "Ein Volk baut sich seine Kirche." Similar (visual) discourse in the Dutch periodical *Nieuw Afrika*, (February 6, 1936), 23, and, after the war, in *Missions*, (1948) 2, 37-42, and *Nieuw Afrika*, (1955) 2, 50 and cover.

69 The notion "Les mains de Dieu" has been borrowed from Deneef, "La geste des frères-coadjuteurs."

Gedul·lig muß der gute Bruder seinen Arbeitern zuerst alles vormachen

Wir brauchen Brüder!

Pilze schießen von selbst aus dem Boden heraus. Die Mission aber wächst nicht von selbst. Es genügt nicht, daß man die Afrikaner tauft. Sie brauchen Kirchen, Schulen, Spitäler. Gott hilft schon : Aber Gott braucht Menschen. Er braucht Menschen zum Taufen, Predigen, Sakramente spenden ! Er braucht auch Menschen, um die Kirchen, Schulen und Spitäler zu bauen. Unser Herrgott braucht auch Missionsbrüder.

Unverbindliche Auskunft : Weiße Väter, Afrikamissionare, Reckenbühlstraße 14, Luzern.

10.20 "We need [missionary] brother-builders" (Wir brauchen Brüder). Page for a White Fathers recruitment campaign, showing brother Engelhemus Supersaxo and two African laborers at work on the construction site at the Collège du Saint-Esprit, published in Christi Reich, 11 (1958), back cover. [Fribourg (CH), Pères Blancs Archives and Library: collection of missionary journals of the White Fathers]

Accompanied by titles such as "Un travail de pionnier", "Pourquoi sont-ils si peu nombreux?"; "Ils sont nécessaires, les Frères"; "Wir brauchen Brüder!" or "Ci occorrono Fratelli", such images targeted a specific audience:[70] in fact, the Collège du Saint-Esprit building site photographs provided a powerful instrument in the White Fathers' recruitment campaign, which accelerated in the second half of the 1940s, as the congregation was desperately in need of more missionary brothers to secure important logistical support for their booming missionary activities in Africa.[71] This last example makes it clear that the mediation of the Collège du Saint-Esprit could thus serve the very specific, different, and at times divergent agendas of the stakeholders involved.

A highly "mediated" but failed experiment?

Construction work on the Collège du Saint-Esprit came to an end in 1962, the year in which the Trust Territory of Ruanda-Urundi morphed into two independent nations at a time of great political turmoil. The UN visiting mission that navigated the Trust Territory in 1960 had, in fact, already reported that the region was in a state of siege.[72] Given that classes had started in 1955, two cohorts of students had been able to complete the curriculum of this particular experiment with interracial education in Central Africa. The Collège du Saint-Esprit would soon become a part of the National University of Burundi. In the decades that followed, the institution went through turbulent times, with the Jesuit Fathers being evicted from the premises throughout most of the 1980s, only to be allowed to return on site in the early 1990s. Despite the intense episodes of violence and rebellion that shook both the capital city of Bujumbura and the larger Great Lakes region in the following decades, the Collège du Saint-Esprit has survived to the present day in a rather decent state and still functions as a facility for secondary education.

Seminal studies on the history of the Great Lakes region point out the importance of the Collège du Saint-Esprit in the formation of the first political elite of independent Burundi. It tellingly features as a separate lemma in the 1976 *Historical Dictionary of Burundi*.[73] A comprehensive story of the role played by the institute in the decolonization process of the region and how it contributed to producing a generation of "Students of the World," to use a phrase coined by historian Pedro Monaville, still needs to be written.[74] The several conversations we have had over many years with locals and visitors to Bujumbura have all pointed out the significance of the Collège du Saint-Esprit in both the urban and national memory, but the extent to which the school truly functions as a "place of memory" still needs to be established.[75] The reconstruction of the various agendas that underscored the foundation of the Collège du Saint-Esprit and its mediation that we have presented in this chapter forms a first and necessary step in such an assessment.

As we have demonstrated throughout this chapter, the striking modernist architecture of the Collège du Saint-Esprit was crucial to the large-scale mediation of the complex as an innovative interracial educational experiment in a wide variety of sources, produced by the myriad of parties involved. The most articulate expression of this connection between novel architecture and innovative program can be found in a text published in a 1958 issue of Missions. It was written by Father Bernard Jobin M.Afr. (1924-2020), a missionary-architect of the congregation of the White Fathers:

> Reinforced concrete buildings. Clarity in the layout of its different rooms. There is a frank articulation of materials. The structure is clear and flexible. The proportions of the building radiate nobility. The functional aspect of the whole clearly asserts the beauty of the volumes [...] Giving young Africans a complex of this kind is already showing them a noble and balanced building, and placing them in a favorable climate for their personal and social development. It is all too true that the environment has a singular influence on its inhabitants. Airy, well-lit classrooms, well-distributed buildings, an order, logic and harmony that already emanate from the physical structure, in turn shape the rhythm of the students' lives. This is the role of contemporary architecture. Its quality is to serve the vital needs of a community: air, sun, space, tranquility, which are the favorable and normal conditions for a studious life. The material conditions for setting up an interracial college in Usumbura, in the heart of Africa, could not have been better. Relationships for study and friendship between Africans and Europeans are facilitated as much as possible by the layout, organization, and management of the entire college.[76]

In light of the extremely turbulent episodes of ethnic violence that shook the Great Lakes region in the mid-1990s, as well as the longer history of conflicts and tensions that pervade the area, one cannot but be struck by the optimism of Jobin's words; it is an optimism that also appears in Father Gabin's film *Espoirs d'Afrique* and most of the mediation discussed in this chapter. But that history has proven awfully wrong. Seen from today's perspective, it is tempting to denounce this optimism as a disturbing form of naivety, and the whole project as a completely failed educational experiment, despite the genuine conviction of the those involved that they were building a better future for Africa. This chapter, however, does not seek to make such a judgement. Rather it points to something else, namely that modernist architecture, despite what has been argued for a very long time in the historiography of the Modern Movement in architecture, is not, by default, a project of social emancipation. As much as we might be seduced by the elegant lines of Bastin's design for the Collège du Saint-Esprit, its photogenic tropical modernist appearance, its sensitive insertion into the hilly landscapes on the outskirts of Bujumbura, and the stunning panoramic views it offered of its surroundings, we hope this chapter has clarified that it is essential and timely to unpack the "politics of design" behind this particular architectural project, built against a specific and geopolitically charged backdrop in Central Africa.

70 *Missions*, (1958) 5-7, and *Christi Reich*, (1958) 11-12.
71 On this recruitment campaign, see Lagae, "Les mains de Dieu."
72 *United Nations Visiting Mission to Trust Territories in East Africa 1960. Report on Ruanda-Urundi*, 9-51 (<https://digitallibrary.un.org/>).
73 Weinstein, *Historical Dictionary of Burundi*, 6. Also the lemma devoted to the Collège du Saint-Esprit (Ibid. 112): "Collège du Saint-Esprit. A state [sic] secondary school built in 1954 [sic] by the Belgians at Bujumbura. The Rwandans were very disappointed that the school was not constructed in their territory, causing some rivalry between the two parts of Ruanda-Urundi. Many of Burundi's future leaders, including President Michel Micombero are among its graduates. Father Gabriel Barakana, a Jesuit, ran the school from independence [sic] until ca. 1970, when he became Rector of the University. The Collège was Burundi's only secondary school to offer both the traditional and the modern humanities programs. It changed its curriculum like other secondary schools: Collège Notre-Dame at Gitega and the Athénée Nationale."
74 Monaville, *Students of the World*. For a recent account of the Ibadan University College, see Livsey, *Nigeria's University Age*.
75 The notion of "lieu de mémoire" was coined in 1984 by French historian Pierre Nora. Its relevance for architectural history research on (post)colonial contexts is discussed by Çelik, "Colonial/postcolonial Intersections."
76 Jobin, "Au cœur de l'Afrique". We interviewed Father Jobin in 1996.

BIBLIOGRAPHY

Our analysis draws heavily on the extensive personal archive of Roger Bastin. It is currently held by LOCI, Brussels, but was still kept at the architect's family home in Namur when we consulted it during our research in the mid-1990s. In that same period, we also conducted research in the libraries and archives of the Jesuits and White Fathers, in Leuven, Brussels, Rome, and Fribourg, although many of the specific files related to the Collège du Saint-Esprit were then not yet accessible for research. We have not yet returned to these archives to consult recently opened files. During our research in the mid-1990s, fieldwork in Bujumbura was not an option due to the political turmoil in the Great Lakes Region. As yet, we have been unable to visit the Collège du Saint-Esprit.

Contemporary sources on colonial policies and colonial education in particular were helpful in contextualizing the project, as were the personal papers we consulted of former Governor General Léon Pétillon, minister of colonies André Dequae and governor of Ruanda-Urundi J.P. Harroy. In the Dag Hammerskjold Library in New York, we tracked down reports drafted by United Nations missions that visited the Trust Territory of Ruanda-Urundi. Finally, we interviewed several of those involved in the period 1995-1996, as well as some teachers who took part in the training program at the Collège du Saint-Esprit during the 1950s and 1960s.

Archival sources

Brussels (B), Archives UCLouvain, Faculté LOCI, Faculté d'architecture, d'ingénierie architecturale, d'urbanisme
  Fonds Roger Bastin: complete set of architectural drawings related to the design and building of the Collège du Saint-Esprit, as well as the full correspondence between Léon Verwilghen and Roger Bastin on the project for the period 1951-1962.
Brussels (B), State Archives
  Papers Léon Pétillon, 3537.
Fribourg (CH), Pères Blancs
  Archives and Library: collection of missionary journals of the White Fathers.
Leuven (B), KADOC-KU Leuven
  Archives de la Province belge méridionale de la Compagnie de Jésus, 354
  Papers André Dequae

New York (USA), Dag Hammerskjold Library: reports of United Nations visiting missions to the Trust Territory of Ruanda-Urundi during the 1950s.
  UN Nations Visiting Mission to Trust Territories in East Africa, 1951. Report on Trust Territory of Ruanda-Urundi, 1951, doc. T/948.
  UN Nations Visiting Mission to Trust Territories in East Africa, 1957. Report on Trust Territory of Ruanda-Urundi, 1957, doc. T/1346.
Rome (I), White Fathers
  Archives of the Society of Missionaries of Africa: files related to the training of missionary brothers.
Tervuren (B), Africa Museum, History Department
  Papers J.P. Harroy.
Veyras (CH), Pères Blancs
  Personal archive of Engelhemus [Oswald] Supersaxo

Films

Gabin, Jacques SJ. *Espoirs d'Afrique*, 30'. [Lille, personal archive J. Gabin.]
Levie, Pierre. *Afrikaans Humanisme. Opvoeding en algemeen onderwijs in Belgisch Congo en Ruanda-Urundi*, distributed by the Centre d'Information et de Documentation, 1957, 12'. [Tervuren, Africa Museum, Film Collection: 723.]
Pascal, J.N. and Laval, Pol. *L'enseignement au Ruanda-Urundi*, 1960, 18'. [Tervuren, Africa Museum, Film Collection: 1682.]

Oral Sources

Interview with Madeleine Bastin, widow of architect Roger Bastin, by the author, Namur (B), April 1996.
Interview with Father Léon Verwilghen SJ by the author, Collège Saint-Michel, Etterbeek (B), May 1996.
Interview with Brother Engelhemus [Oswald] Supersaxo M.Afr. by the author, Veyras (CH), September 1996.
Interview with Father architect Bernard Jobin M.Afr. by the author, Veyras (CH), September 1996.
Interview with Jean Weynants by the author, Brussels (B), June 1996.

Primary literature

AAVV. "Un bock avec… Roger Bastin." *Pourquoi Pas? Congo*, 11 (1960) 20, 18.
AAVV, "Ein Volk baut sich seine Kirche: Ein Filmstreifen: aus dem Urwald wachsen Kirchen." *Afrika Bote*, 10 (1935), 253-263.
Almasy, Paul. "Kongo zoals het is. Onderwijs zonder rassenonderscheid. X: het voorbeeld van Usumbura." *Zondagsvriend*, (1957) 21, 20-25.
Bekaert, Geert. "Kunst en missie." *Nieuwe stemmen*, 6-7 (1961) [thematic issue "Gewijde kunst"], 151-155.
Bontridder, Albert. *Hedendaagse bouwkunst in België. Dialoog tussen licht en stilte / L'architecture contemporaine en Belgique. Le dialogue de la lumière et du silence*. Antwerp: Helios, 1963.
Dahinden, Justus. *Construire pour l'Église dans le monde*. Fribourg: Saint-Paul, 1971 [originally published as: *Bauen für die Kirche in der Welt*. Zürich, 1966].
Derouau, Walthère (SJ). "Une expérience interraciale en Afrique Centrale. Le Collège du Saint-Esprit à Usumbura." *Missi (édition belge)*, 6 (June-July 1960), 1-4.
Derouau, Walthère (SJ). "Élèves blancs et noirs fraternisent au Collège interracial d'Usumbura. Une lettre du R.P. Derouau s.j." *Courrier du soir*, August 30 1956, 3 [newspaper clipping in Archives de la Province belge méridionale de la Compagnie de Jésus, 354].
"Des neiges du Cervin aux rives du Tanganika." *Missions*, (1948) 6, 147.
Dubuisson-Brouha (Mrs), Natalis, E. and Paulus, J. *Le problème d'enseignement dans le Ruanda-Urundi. Rapport d'une mission d'étude constituée par la Fondation de l'Université de Liège pour les Recherches Scientifique au Congo Belge et au Ruanda-Urundi*. Brussels, 1958.
"Ein Volk baut sich seine Kirche: Ein Filmstreifen: aus dem Urwald wachsen Kirchen." *Afrika Bote*, 1935, 10, 253-263.
Flouquet, Pierre-Louis. "Roger Bastin. Architecture et poésie." *La Maison*, 22 (1966) 8, 232.
Fry, Maxwell. "A College in the Tropics: Ibadan." *Zodiac*, 2 (1958), 127-135.
Fry, Maxwell. "An African Environment Molds a Campus." *Architectural Record*, 122 (August 1957) 2, 158-161.
Fry, Maxwell and Drew, Jane. *Tropical Architecture in the Humid Zone*. London, 1956.
Gabin, Jacques (SJ). "Caméra sur les collèges africains." *Jésuites de France* (August 1961), 19-25.

Jobin, Bernard (M.Afr). "Au cœur de l'Afrique, Noirs et Blancs étudient côte à côte." *Missions*, 2 (1958), 20-25.

Kultermann, Udo. *Neues Bauen in Afrika*. Tübingen: Wasmuth Verlag, 1963.

La Chronique Congolaise, October 22, 1952.

La Dépêche du Ruanda-Urundi, October 24, 1952.

La Fay, Howard. "Freedom's Progress South of the Sahara." *The National Geographical Magazine*, 122 (1962) 5, 603-637.

Lavanoux, Maurice. "Prolegomena." *Liturgical Arts*, 26 (1958) 3, 68-70.

Lavanoux, Maurice. "The Editor's Diary: XXV." *Liturgical Arts*, , 26 (1958) 4, 132-140.

Maus, Albert. "À propos du collège interracial." *La Chronique Congolaise*, October 25 1952, 8.

Périer, Gaston-Denys. "Danseurs du Ruanda." *La Revue Nationale*, 211 (1952), 174-175.

Pétillon, Léon. *Témoignage et réflexions*. Brussels: La Renaissance du Livre, 1967.

Pétillon, Léon. *Récit. Congo 1929-1958*. Brussels: La Renaissance du Livre, 1985.

Rapport sur l'administration belge au Ruanda-Urundi pendant l'année 1952 présenté par le Ministre des Colonies. Brussels, 1953.

Rapport sur l'administration belge du Ruanda-Urundi pendant l'année 1955 présenté aux Chambres par le Ministre des Colonies, Brussels, 1956.

Russo, Albert. *Éclipse sur le lac Tanganyika*. Paris: Le Nouvel Athanor, 1994.

United Nations, Trusteeship Council 21st session official records, 851th Meeting, Tuesday February 4 1958, New York, point 46. <https://digitallibrary.un.org/record/1634815?ln=en>.

United Nations, Trusteeship Council 21st session official records, 853th Meeting, Thursday February 6 1958, New York, points 36-37. <https://digitallibrary.un.org/>.

United Nations, Trusteeship Council 21st session official records, 854th Meeting, Friday February 7 1958, New York. <https://digitallibrary.un.org/record/1634852?ln=en>.

United Nations Visiting Mission to Trust Territories in East Africa, 1954. Report on Trust Territory of Ruanda-Urundi, 1954, New York, doc. T/1141. <https://digitallibrary.un.org/record/3951104>.

United Nations Visiting Mission to Trust Territories in East Africa 1957. Report on Ruanda-Urundi. Official Records of Trusteeship Council, session 21, January 30-March 26, 1958, New York, doc. T/1402, 39-42 (Annex 1, "Manifesto of the Bahutu") and 42-46 (Annex 2: Statements of Views"). <https://digitallibrary.un.org/record/1299065?ln=en>.

United Nations Visiting Mission to Trust Territories in East Africa 1960. Report on Ruanda-Urundi, New York, June 3 1960, doc. T/1538. <https://digitallibrary.un.org/record/732686?ln=en>.

Secondary literature

Bekaert, Geert and Strauven, Francis. *Bouwen in België 1945-1970 / La Construction en Belgique 1945-1970*. Brussels: Confédération nationale de la construction, 1971.

Bumann, Edmund. *Das Heilig-Geist-Kolleg in Usumbura. Das Werk eines Wallisers in Afrika. Bruder Oswald Supersaxo*. S.l., 2005.

Castryck, Geert. *Moslims in Usumbura (1897-1962): sociale geschiedenis van de islamitische gemeenschappen van Usumbura in de koloniale tijd*. Unpublished PhD dissertation, Ghent University, 2006.

Çelik, Zeynep. "Colonial/postcolonial Intersections. Lieux de mémoire in Algiers." *Third Text*, 13 (1999) 49, 63-72.

De Meulder, Bruno. "Mavula: An African Heterotopia in Kwango, 1895-1911." *Journal of Architectural Education*, 52 (1998), 1, 20-29.

Deneef, Alain. "La geste des frères-coadjuteurs. Les mains de Dieu," in: Deneef, Alain, ed. *Les Jésuites au Congo/Zaïre. Cent ans d'épopée*, Brussels: ARAECSM, 1995, 62-69.

De Paepe, Marc and Van Rompaey, Lies. *In het teken van de bevoogding. De educatieve actie in Belgisch-Kongo (1908-1960)*. Leuven-Apeldoorn: Garant, 1995.

Eggermont, Betty. "The choreography of schooling as site of struggle: Belgian primary schools, 1880-1940." *History of Education*, 2 (2001), 129-140.

Fivez, Robby. *A Concrete State: Constructing Materials and Building Ambitions in the (Belgian) Congo*. Unpublished PhD dissertation, Ghent University / Université Libre de Bruxelles, 2023.

Greenland, Jeremy. *Western Education in Burundi 1916-1973: The Consequences of Instrumentalism* (Les Cahiers du CEDAF, 2-3). Tervuren, 1980.

Krautheimer, Richard. *The Rome of Alexander VII*. Princeton: Princeton University Press, 1986.

Lagae, Johan. *'Kongo zoals het is'. Drie architectuurverhalen uit de Belgische kolonisatiegeschiedenis (1920-1960)*. Unpublished PhD dissertation, Ghent University, 2002.

Lagae, Johan. "*Les mains de Dieu*. Quelques réflexions sur l'imaginaire littéraire et visuelle autour d'une figure missionnaire, le frère-bâtisseur de la congrégation des Pères Blancs (1935-1960)," in: Halen, Pierre, ed. *Approches du roman et du théâtre missionnaires*. Berlin: Peter Lang Verlag, 2006, 103-139.

Lagae, Johan. "Montcassin, Montserrat or … an Alcazar? Architecture, Propaganda and Everyday School Practices in the Collège du Saint-Esprit in Bujumbura (Burundi)," in: Fassil, Demissie, ed. *Colonial Architecture and Urbanism in Africa: Intertwined and Contested Histories*. Farnham: Ashgate, 2012, 277-294.

Lanotte, André. *Roger Bastin. Architecte 1913-1986*. Liège: Mardaga, 2000.

Lemarchand, René. *Rwanda and Burundi*. New York: Praeger Publishers, 1970.

Levy, Evonne Anita. *Propaganda and the Jesuit Baroque*. Berkeley, CA: University of California Press, 2004.

Livsey, Tim. *Nigeria's University Age: Reframing Decolonisation and Development*. New York: Palgrave Macmillan, 2017.

Monaville, Pedro. *Students of the World. Global 1968 and Decolonization in the Congo*. Durham: Duke University Press, 2022.

Pilette, Maurice. "Le Collège Interracial du Saint-Esprit à Usumbura, 1952," in: Deneef, Alain, ed. *De la mission du Kwango à la Province d'Afrique Centrale. Les Jésuites au Congo. Cent ans d'épopée*. Brussels: ARAECSM, 1995, 130-138.

Pilette, Maurice. "L'Université d'Usumbura, 1960" in: Deneef, Alain, ed. *De la mission du Kwango à la Province d'Afrique Centrale. Les Jésuites au Congo. Cent ans d'épopée*. Brussels: ARAECSM, 1995, 139-143.

Ramirez, Francis and Rolot, Christian. *Histoire du cinéma colonial au Zaïre, au Rwanda et au Burundi*. Tervuren: Africa Museum, 1985.

Stenmans, Alain and Reyntjes, Filip. *La pensée politique du gouverneur général Pétillon*. Brussels, 1993.

Vale, Lawrence J. "Mediated Monuments and National Identity." *The Journal of Architecture*, 4 (1999) 4, 391-408.

van Eck, Caroline and Bussels, Stijn, eds. *Theatricality in Early Modern Art and Architecture*. Chichester: Wiley-Blackwell, 2011.

Weinstein, Warren. *Historical Dictionary of Burundi*. New Jersey: Scarecrow Press, 1976.

Wright, Gwendolyn. *The Politics of Design in French Colonial Urbanism*. Chicago: University of Chicago Press, 1991.

ABBREVIATIONS

APCM =	American Presbyterian Congo Mission
CDD =	Congregation of the Disciples of the Lord
CICM =	Congregation of the Immaculate Heart of Mary (Scheut Fathers)
CIM =	China Inland Mission
CM =	Congregation of the Mission (Lazarists / Vincentians)
CMB =	Christian Mission to Buddhists in China
CMS =	Church Missionary Society
CMM =	Canadian Methodist Mission
CSSp =	Congregation of the Holy Spirit
ELML =	Evangelical Lutheran Mission of Leipzig
FdlC =	Filles de la Charité de Saint Vincent de Paul
FICP =	Brothers of Christian Instruction of Ploërmel
FSC =	Friends Service Council
HM =	Hernsbrucker Mission
IFMA =	Interdenominational Foreign mission Association
LMS =	London Missionary Society (congregational)
MAfr =	Missionaries of Africa (White Fathers)
MEM / PIME =	Milan Foreign Missions / Pontifical Institute of Foreign Missions
MEP =	Foreign Mission of Paris
MM =	Maryknoll Fathers & Brothers
OCD =	Order of Discalced Carmelites
OFM =	Order of Friars Minor (Franciscans)
OP =	Order of Preachers (Dominicans)
OPM =	Oeuvres pontificales missionnaires
OSB =	Order of Saint Benedict (Benedictines)
RGS =	Sisters of the Good Shepherd
SAM =	Society of the Auxiliaries of the Missions
SJ =	Society of Jesus (Jesuits)
SSJ =	Society of Saint Joseph of the Sacred Heart (Joséphites)
SVD =	Society of the Divine Word (Steyl Missionaries)
UFS =	United Free Church of Scotland (Presbyterian)
YMCA =	Young Men's Christian Association (interdenominational)

INDEX OF PERSONS

The Chinese names are romanized into pinyin, followed by simplified characters. The religious affiliations are mentioned with the conventional acronyms (see Abbreviations).

Abimelech (Old Testament): 22.
Abraham (Old Testament): 22.
Adam (Old Testament): 18.
Adams, Will: 220.
Akakpo, Bernard: 246–247, 247 fig.10.19.
Albrand, Étienne 白新德望 MEP (1805–1853): 156, 157 n.37.
Almasy, Paul (1906–2003): 231, 232, 232 fig.10.4, 237 fig.10.9, 239 fig.10.11.
Amsler, Nadine (°1983) 149.
Anderson, Vernon Andy APCM (1896–1999): 80.
Anthony of Padua OFM (1195–1231): 188.
Antonius, Raymond: 198.
Armstrong (Capitain): 9.
Arregui y Yparaguirre, Joseph 陈若瑟 OP (1903–1979): 90.

Baillière, Henri (1840–1905): 203 n.35.
Barakana, Gabriel SJ (1914–1999): 249 n.73.
Barsalou, Léonide MAfr: 8.
Bastin, Christine: 230 fig.10.2, 231 fig.10.3, 233.
Bastin, Madeleine: 233 n.16, 235 fig.10.7.
Bastin, Roger (1913–1986): 229–230, 231 fig.10.3, 233–234, 235, 235 fig.10.7, 236 fig.10.8, 237, 239, 243, 243 n.58, 244–246, 249.
Baudouin of Belgium, King (1930–1993): 71, 73, 80, 237.
Bax, Jacques 巴耆贤 CICM (1924–1895): 184.
Beethoven, Ludwig van (1770–1827): 237.
Bekaert, Geert (1928–2016): 230.
Bellot, Paul OSB (1876–1944): 171 n.80.
Benedict XV [Giacomo della Chiesa] (1854–1922): XV, 95, 140.
Berthemy, Jules-François-Gustave (1826–1902): 35.
Bogey, Alexis OFM: 205.
Boiteux, Lucien 何维光 MEP (1902–1944): 122 fig.6.22.
Bonnet, Edgar (1881–1967): 202 n.31, 202 fig.8.13.
Bray, Gérard 白振铎 CM (1825–1905): 173.
Bullock, Nicholas: XXIX.
Bumann, Edmund: 243 n.55.
Buxton, Thomas Fowell (1786–1845): 30.

Cady, Henry Olin MEC (1857–1916): 212, 213.
Cai Xiang-yu (°1981): 109.
Cambier, Eméry CICM (1865–1943): 75.
Capers, W.J.: 126 fig.6.29.
Castryck, Geert (°1974): 241.
Cepeck, Edouard: 201.
Cham [Ham] (Old Testament): XII, XII fig.0.6.
Champollion, Jean-François (1790–1832): 196.

Chang, Lincoln: 225.
Chen Guodi, Aloysius 陈国砥 OFM (1875–1930): 95 n.45.
Cheng Hede, Odoric Simon 成和德 OFM (1873–1928): 95 n.45.
Chollet, Jean-Marie MAfr: 8.
Ciranna, Simonetta (°1958): 198, 205.
Clare of Assisi OFM (1194–1253): 95.
Cleys, Bram: XXV, XXIX.
Coleman, Simon: 26.
Coles, Jonathan Ackerman (1843–1925): 211-212 fig.9.1, 223.
Colombel, Augustin 高龙鞶 SJ (1833–1905): 134.
Colonas, Vassilis: 198.
Comaroff, Jean (°1946): 24.
Comaroff, John (°1945): 24.
Confucius 孔子 (551–478 BC): 109, 142.
Cornelis, Sabine (°1958): XXIX.
Costantini, Celso 刚恒毅 (1876–1958): XV, XXII n.49, 56, 58, 59.
Couvreux, Alphonse (1820–1890): 202 n.29.
Crane, Charles L. APCM: 76.

Daguin, Florent 孔主教 CM (1815–1859): 170 n.73.
Dalmond Pierre CSSp (1800–1848): VIII fig.0.6.
de Benoist, Louis (1882–1957): 202, 203 n.36.
de Boer, Jorrit 姚 OFM: 94 fig.5.6.
De Clercq, Auguste CICM (1870–1939): 66, 73.
de la Hoz, Thomas 杨多默 OP (1879–1949): 88 n.11.
de Lesseps, Ferdinand (1805–1894): 195, 195 n.4, 196, 197 n.9, 199–201.
De Maeyer, Jan (°1952): XXIX.
De Meulder, Bruno (°1960): XVII, XXIX.
De Moerloose, Alphonse 和羹柏 CICM (1858–1932): 55, 121 fig.6.17, 147 n.5, 160, 162–164, 163 figs.7.23–7.24, 164 n.52, 167, 168 fig.7.29, 174, 176–178, 176 fig.7.38, 176 n.97, 177 n.98, 179 fig.7.41, 184–185, 187, 189–190, 190 n.149-150.
de Prunelé, Pierre 晋都禄 SJ (1881–1969): 112 fig.6.3,
de Reviers de Mauny, Joseph SJ (1872–1974): 107 fig.6.1.
De Smet, Leo 石德懋 CICM (1881–1951): 184.
de Vigneron, Jacques 陶开花 CICM (1900–1939): 121 fig.6.17.
de Vogüé, Louis (1868–1948): 202 n.31, 202 fig.8.13, 204.
De Wilde, Karel CICM (1908–1994): 81.
Defèbvre, André 戴福瑞 CM (1886–1967): 49 fig.3.19.
Dehergne, Joseph 容振花 SJ (1903–1990): XV.
Delaplace, Louis Gabriel 田嘉壁 CM (1820–1884): 170 n.76.
Della Corte, Agnello 谷振声 SJ (1819–1896): 55.

Denis, Philippe (1912–1978): 245.
Dequeker, Paul CICM (1930–2017): XXIV fig.0.13.
Derouau, Walthère SJ (1904–2000): 238.
Dery, Peter Poreku (1918–2008): 14 fig.1.7.
Devos, Heliodoor 德玉亮 CICM (1847–1887): 187.
Dewart, Joan Cameron: 13 fig.1.6.
Di Gang [Ti Kang], Joseph 狄刚 (1928–2022): 100 n.75.
Dierickx, Petrus 孔模范 CICM (1862–1946): 184.
Doré, Henri 禄是遒 SJ (1859–1931): 152.
Dou Baojin [Tou Paozin], Peter 杜宝晋 (1911–1986): 92.
Drew, Jane (1911–1996): XXIII, 230, 237.
Dunch, Ryan 唐日安: XX.
Durand, William / Guillaume (c.1237–1296): 150 n.13.

Eggermont, Betty: 238.
Erasme, Father OFM: 200.
Eve (Old Testament): 18.

Fahy, Eugene 费济时 SJ (1911–1996): 91, 93.
Favier, Alphonse 樊国梁 CM (1837–1905): 44–45, 170 n.76, 172.
Ferguson, George Ekem (1865–1897): 6.
Fernández, Clemente 林茏才 OP (1879–1952): 88 n.11.
Flouquet, Pierre-Louis (1900–1967): 230.
Foucault, Michel (1926–1984): XVI-XVII.
Fourchard, Laurent: 81.
Francis de Sales (1567–1622): 197, 199, 205.
Francis of Assisi OFM (1181/1182–1226): 95, 202.
Francis Xavier SJ (1506–1552): 53, 54 fig.3.26.
Freedman, Maurice (1929–1975): 109.
Frericks, Epiphanus OFM (?–1940): 152 fig.7.6.
Fry, Maxwell (1899–1987): XXIII, 230, 237.

Gabet, Joseph 秦噶哔 CM (1808–1853): X, X n.11.
Gabin, Jacques SJ (1918–2013): 236, 236 n.24, 238, 249.
Gamble, Sidney David 甘博 (1890–1968): 218 fig.9.6.
Gall, Eugène MAfr: 8.
Gérard, Auguste (1852–1922): 35.
Gerholtz ELML: 23.
Gibbon, Father OFM: 199.
Goody, Jack (1918–2015): 12.
Graul, Karl ELML (1814–1864): 19.
Gregory XVI [Bartolomeo Cappellari] (1765–1846): 183.
Gresnigt, Adelbert 葛利斯 OSB (1877–1956): 60.
Guanyin: 217.
Guilbaud, Joseph Henri 石介臣 MEP (1882–1962): 46.

Guillon, Laurent 纪隆 MEP (1854–1900): 45.
Guissart, L.: 73 n.25.
Guo Ruoshi [Kuo Joshih] 郭若石 CDD (1906–1995): 90, 96, 100.

Hamer, Ferdinand 韩默理 CICM (1840–1900): 175–176.
Han Chengliang, Gaspar 韩承良 OFM (1928–2004): 96.
Hart, Virgil Chittenden 赫斐秋 CMM (1840–1904): 211.
Hartwell, George Everson CMM (1862–1945): 212.
Hawkins, Sean: 6, 12.
Hermand, Louis 双国英 SJ (1873–1939): 36, 36 fig.3.4, 152.
Heymans, Maurice (1909–1991): 69, 69 n.16.
Heynen, Hilde (°1959): X, XXIII, 140 n.117.
Hiral, Ange-Marie OFM (1871–1952): 195 n.2, 202, 203 fig.8.14.
Hirsch, Eric: 18.
Hoffman HM: 19, 29.
Hoffmann, Friedrich Eduard (1818–1900): 177.
Howard, Allen M. (°1938): XXIX.
Hu Yujie 胡御阶: 214 n.11.
Hugelier, Gentiel 恩特里 OFM (1896–1975): 94, 98, 99, 99 fig.5.12.
Huc, Évariste 古伯察 CM (1813–1860): X, X n.11.
Hulot, Louis-Jean (1871–1959): 205–207, 207 fig.8.18.

Ignatius of Loyola SJ (1491–1556): 40.
Ilbert, Robert (°1950): 196.
Ittameier HM: 19.

Jackson, Iain (°1984): 229 n.5.
Jacob (Old Testament): 22.
Japheth (Old Testament): XII.
Japiot, Émile 毕如春 SJ (1849–1902): 119.
Jarrassé, Dominique (°1955): 207.
Jiang Jieshi [Ciang Kai-shek] 蒋介石 (1887–1975): 92.
Jobin, Bernard MAfr (1924–2020): 246 n.63, 249, 249 n.76.
John Paul II [Karol Wojtyła] (1920–2005): 53.
John XXIII [Angelo Roncalli] (1881–1963): 93, 102.

Kangxi 康熙, Emperor (1654–1722): 149.
Kanig, Gerhard ELML (1875–1958): 22, 24–26.
Kettel, Georges CICM (1897–1972): 72 n.22.
Kiema wa Umo: 29.
Kolb, George (? –1899): 21.
Koot, Basilide MAfr: 9.
Krapf, Johann Ludwig ELML (1810–1881): 17, 19, 21, 23, 30.
Kultermann, Udo (1927–2013): 230.

Kupfer, William F. 葵文兴 MM (1909–1998): 90.

Lagae, Johan (°1968): XXVII, XXIX.
Lamy, Eugène 纳密 MEP (1841–1909): 116.
Languillat, Adrien 郎樑仁 SJ (1808–1878): 112, 130 n.85.
Lanotte, André (1914–2010): 230, 245.
Lantin, Robert CICM (1906–1969): 67, 67 n.10, 73.
Larochelle MAfr: 14.
Laval, P.: 239.
Lavanoux, Maurice (1894–1974): 229, 235 n.21.
Lavigerie, Charles MAfr (1825–1892): 8.
Le Corbusier [Charles-Édouard Jeanneret] (1887–1965): XXIII n.52.
le Roux, Hannah: 229 n.5, 232.
Lebbe, Vincent 雷鸣远 CM (1877–1940): 40, 40 n.22, 58.
Lefebvre, Henri (1901–1991): XVIII.
Lemarchand, René (°1932): 25.
Lemmens, Willem 兰广济 CICM (1860–1943) 176, 177 n.98.
Leopold II of Belgium, King (1835–1909): XI, 75.
Liang Jiansen, Paul 梁建森 (°1964..): 180 n.113.
Lin Daiyuan, Petrus 林道原 (1837–1891): 186.
Lindblom, Karl Gerhard (1887–1969): 26 n.33.
Lippens, Aimé CICM (1887–1958): 66.
Liu Chengxun 刘成勋 (1884–1944): 218.
Livingstone, David LMS (1813–1873): XI, XI n.11, 30.
Londot, Louis-Marie (1924–2010): 245, 245 fig.10.18.
Loos, Adolph (1870–1933): XXIII n.52.
Lü Haiping 吕海平: 173 n.88.
Luitpolt, Prince Regent of Bavaria (1821–1912): 21, 21 n.16.
Luo Guang [Lo Kuang] 罗光 (1911–2004): 92.
Luo Wei 罗薇: 147 n.4, 190 n.152.
Luo 罗 family, Chengdu: 217.

Mao Zedong 毛泽东 (1893–1976): 142, 155 n.31, 186.
Mariot, Léon 马历耀 SJ (1830–1902): 181.
Mary, Mother of Jesus (1st c.): XI, XII fig.0.6, 53–56, 81, 196, 205.
Maubant, Pierre MEP (1803–1839): 175 n.93.
Maus, Albert CICM (1902–1961): 242.
McCoy, Remigius MAfr (1897–1993): 9–10, 13 fig.1.6.
Mels, Bernard CICM (1908–1992): 81–82.
Mencius 孟子 (c. 372–289 BC): 109.
Mercenier, Gustave CICM (1904–1982): 66.
Meyer, Birgit (°1960): 26.
Meyer, Henri (1841–1899): 39 fig.3.6.
Micombero, Michel (1940–1983): 249 n.73.
Miserez, Martin SSJ: 73 n.25.
Mohamed Sa'id Pasha (1822–1863): 195 n.4.

Monaville, Pedro: 248.
Montgomery: 29.
Morin, Oscar MAfr (1878–1952): 8.
Moritz, Benoît: 65, 69.
Mouly, Joseph-Martial 孟振生 CM (1807–1868): 168–169, 169 n.68, 170 n.73 and 76, 171, 183.
Moyne, Samuel (°1972): XX.
Muhammad Ali Pasha (1769–1849): 197, 203.
Muller Myrdahl, Tiffany: 107.
Mutara III Rudahigwa, Mwami of Ruanda (1911–1959): 233, 237, 236 n.25, 241.

Napoleon III, Emperor (1808–1873): 42.
Nasser, Gamal Abdel (1818–1970): 207 n.52.
Ndaywel è Nziem, Isidore (°1944): 75.
Nehru, Jawaharial (1889–1964), Pandit: 76 n.34.
Nicolini-Zani, Matteo (°1975): 57.
Niu Huiqing [Niu Huiching], Thomas 牛会卿 (1895–1973): 91, 93.
Nkongolo, Joseph Ngogi (1916–1999): 82.
Noah (Old Testament): XII.
Nora, Pierre (°1931): 249 n.75.
Nsanka Joseph: 66.
Nuyts, Jozef 饶启迪 CICM (1898–1986): 147 n.5, 167, 177.

Pakenham, Thomas (°1933): XIV.
Palladio, Andrea (1508–1580): 170 n.78.
Paquet, Arthur MAfr: 9.
Paris, Jules Prosper SJ (1846–1931): 55.
Parrenin, Dominique 巴多明 SJ (1665–1741): 183.
Pascal, J.-N.: 239.
Peigneux, Firmin (1904–1968): 68.
Pels, Peter (°1958): 29.
Pessers, Quintinus 孔昭明 OFM (1896–1995): 119.
Pétillon, Léon (1903–1996): 233–234, 240.
Pius XI [Achille Ratti] (1857–1939): XXVI, 36, 56, 58, 197 n.11.
Pius XII [Eugenio Pacelli] (1876–1958): 56, 92, 152 n.23.
Prip-Møller, Johannes (1889–1943): VI–VII fig.0.1, XVII.
Pugin, Augustus W.N. (1812–1852): 150–151.
Put, Dunstanus 童达德 OFM (1893–1974): 95, 95 n.48.

Qi family, Chengdu: 217.

Ramirez, Francis (1947–2006): 237, 240–241.
Reichelt, Karl Ludvig 艾香德 CMB (1877–1952): XVII.
Reilly, Ralphus 雷益励 OFM (1900–1970): 95 n.48.
Reusch MM: 180 n.113.
Riberi, Antonio (1897–1967): 14.

Ricci, Matteo 利玛窦 SJ (1552–1610): IX n.2, 40, 134.
Robert, Léon 金 MEP (1866–1956): 39.
Rocher, Maurice (1918–1995): 245.
Rolot, Christian (°1947): 237, 240–241.
Rombouts, Désiré CICM (1915–1986): 74.
Rondelez, Valère CICM (1904–1983): 169, 171.
Ross, John 罗约翰 UFS (1841–1915): 173.
Rowntree, Fred (1860–1927): 217 fig. 9.5, 219, 220, 220 n.21.
Rubbens, Edmond 刘拯灵 CICM (1859–1929): 164 n.52, 164 fig.7.25, 185.
Russo, Albert (°1943): 229.

Said, Edward W. (1935–2003): X, XXII.
Sartory, Andrew: XX.
Sauberlich, Günther HM: 21, 21 n.16.
Scarpa, Emilio (1895–1945): 198.
Scherschel, Joseph (1921–2004): 245 fig.10.18.
Segers, Arthur 司化兴 CICM (1874–1935): 186 fig.7.49.
Segers, Jozef 司化隆 CICM (1868–1900): 185.
Seguin, Pierre (1872–1958): 206.
Sépinski, Agostino OFM (1900–1978): 100.
Sem [Chem] (Old Testament): XII, XII fig.0.6.
Sewell, William Gawan FSC (1898–1984): 221 n.25, 223 n.28, 224 n.31–32, 225 n.37.
Shen Peiquan [Chen Peiqian], Thomas 申培谦 OFM (1927–2022): 95 n.48, 100.
Small, Walter: 220.
So, John: 174.
Soubirous, Bernadette (1844–1879): 81, 82 fig.4.20.
Staubli, Albert 新托利 MM (1895–1967): 180.
Steenackers, Jan-Baptist 司福音 CICM (1848–1912): 168 fig.7.29, 186.
Standaert, Nicolas 钟鸣旦 SJ (°1959): IX.
Stewart, Charles: 18.
Stubbs, Clifford (1889-1930): 221.
Sun Yat-sen [Sun Zhongshan] 孙中山 (1866–1925): 223.
Supersaxo, Engelhemus [Oswald] MAfr (1909–2002): 235, 236 fig.10.8, 243, 243 n.55, 246, 246 n.63 and 66, 247, 248 fig.10.20.
Sweeten, Alan Richard: 147 n.4, 152, 169, 173.

Tagliabue, François-Ferdinand 戴济世 CM (1822–1890): 170, 183.
Thérèse of Lisieux OCD (1873–1897): 57.
Timmer, Odoricus 翟守仁 OFM (1859–1943): 128.
Tournon, Paul (1881–1964): 206.
Troeltsch, Ernst (1865–1923): 18.

Vagnone, Alfonso 高一志 SJ (1568–1640): 119 n.58.
Vale, Lawrence J. (°1959): 230.

Van Aertselaer, Jerome 方济众 CICM (1845–1924): 162, 163 fig.7.23, 164 n.52, 174–175, 177, 177 n.98, 185, 189.
Van Assche, Auguste (1926–1907): 171 n.80.
Van Dijk, Leo 狄化淳 CICM (1878–1951): 146–147 fig.7.1, 181.
Van Dorpe, Franz 陶维新 CICM (1878–1944): 163 fig.7.24, 189, 190 fig.7.55, 190 n.149, 191 fig.7.57.
Van Haelst, Albert CICM (1903–1976): 72.
Van Hecken, Jozef 贺歌南 CICM (1905–1988): 126 fig.6.29.
Van Melckebeke, Carlo 王守礼 CICM (1898–1980): 126 fig.6.29.
Van Merris, Paul CICM (1885–1943): 67.
van Spreeken, Johannes SJ (1892–1968): XXVII fig.0.14.
Van Steenwinckel, Methodius 孟照琨 OFM (1891–1969): 95, 96.
Vatu, Emma: 30.
Verbist, Théophile 南怀义 CICM (1823–1868): 185–186, 185 n.136.
Verdier, Jean (1864–1940): 200.
Verellen, Karel 袁萬福 CICM (1859–1925): 187, 187 n.145, 188 fig.7.52.
Verhaeghen, Theotimus 德希圣 OFM (1867–1904): 48 fig.3.17.
Vérineux, André 费声远 MEP (1897–1983): 90, 93.
Verriest, Georges (1887–1979): 66 n.6, 70 n.20.
Verwilghen, Léon SJ (1915–2009): 233–235, 236 fig.10.8, 237–239, 243, 243 n.58, 244–245.
Verwilghen, Raphaël (1885–1963): 233.
Vinčić, Mgr: 201.
Voisin, François-Philippe: 200.
von Wissmann, Herman (1853–1905): 65.

Wang 王, carpenter: 187.
Washburn, H.M. APCM: 76.
Weynants, Jean (1926–2013): 237.
Whittal (Colonel): 9.
Wider, Albert (1910–1985): 246 n.62.
Wiest, Jean-Paul (°1941): 42.
Williame, Jean (1932–2014): 245.
Williams, Maynard Owen (1888–1963): 175 fig.7.37.

Xu Guangqi, Paul 徐光启 (1562–1633): 40, 134, 136 figs.6.38–6.39.

Yang Sen 杨森 (1884–1977): 218.
Yu Zhang: 112.
Yun Daiying 恽代英 (1895–1931): 226.

Zhang Dongliang, Andrew 张东亮: 173 n.87.
Zhang Lan (1872–1955): 225.
Zhang Linggao 张凌高 (1890–1955): 226, 226 n.40.
Zhao [Chao], Petrus 兆: 184.
Zheng Tianxiang [Cheng Tien-siang], Joseph 郑天祥 OP (1922–1990): 88 n.11.
Zhu Kaimin, 朱開敏 Simon SJ (1868–1960): 37.
Zhu Yongchun [Master Zhu] 朱用纯 (1627–1698): 151 n.21.

INDEX OF PLACES

The Chinese names are romanized into pinyin, followed by simplified characters. The Chinese provinces are the current ones.

Aberdeen 阿伯丁 (Hong Kong, China): 142.
Alexandria (Egypt): 198–200.
Algiers (Algeria): 8–9.
Ambodifotatra de Sainte-Marie (Analanjirofo Region, Republic of Madagascar): VIII fig.0.4.
Anguo 安国 (Hebei, China): 58.
Anqing 安庆 (Anhui, China): 36 fig.3.4, 37.
Anshun [Ganchouen] 安顺 (Guizhou, China): 115–116, 116 fig.6.10, 117 figs.6.11–6.12.
Antananarivo / Tananarive (Republic of Madagascar): XXVIII fig.0.14.
Athens (Greece): 198.

Balagai [Palakai] 巴拉盖 (Inner Mongolia, China): 51.
Banana (Congo Central Province, RD Congo): XXII fig.0.11.
Baoding 保定 (Hebei, China): 56.
Bechuanaland (Botswana): 24,
Beersheba (Israel): 22.
Beijing [Peking] 北京 (Beijing, China): XX n.44, 34–35, n.5, 41, 44, 44 figs.3.12–3.13, 57–58, 60, 60 fig.3.31, 95, 119, 127, 130 n.87, 142, 149, 162, 169–171, 173–174, 177 n.104, 183.
Beirut (Lebanon): 215.
Bengbu 蚌埠 (Anhui, China): 36 fig.3.4, 37, 59.
Bethel / Beitin (Israel): 22.
Boma (Bas Congo, RD Congo): XXIII fig.0.12.
Brasilia (Brasil): XXIII n.53.
Brussels (Belgium): 230, 238, 246.
Bujumbura / Usumbura (Burundi): XXIII, XXVII, 75 n.27, 229–251, 220 fig.10.1, 221 fig.10.2, 232 fig.10.4, 233 fig.10.5, 234 fig.10.6, 235 fig.10.7, 237 fig.10.9, 238 fig.10.10, 239 fig.10.11, 240 fig.10.12, 241 fig.10.13, 242 fig.10.14, 243 fig.10.15, 244 figs.10.16–10.17, 245 fig.10.18, 247 fig.10.19.
Bunkonde (DR Congo), former Hemptinne Saint-Benoît (Belgian Congo): 68.

Cairo (Egypt): 197, 206.
Canton: see Guangzhou (Guangdong, China).
Casablanca (Morocco): 206.
Chandigarh (India): XXIII n.53.
Changsha 长沙 (Hunan, China): 41, Changzhou 常州 (Jiangsu, China): 37.
Chartres (France): 142.
Chengdu 成都 (Sichuan, China): XXVII, 41, 211–226, fig.9.1 to fig.9.12.
Chenggong 成功 (Taiwan, China): 96, 97 fig.5.9, 99 n.66.
Chizhou 池州 (Anhui, China): 37.

Chongming 崇明岛 (Jiangsu, China): 149 fig.7.4, 158 fig.7.16.
Chongqing [Chungking] 重庆 (Chongqing, China): 57 n.79, 211, 212.
Coquilhatville (Belgian Congo): see Mbandaka (DR Congo).

Dabaogou 大保沟 (Shanxi, China): 159, 160 fig.7.20.
Dafagong 大法公 (Inner Mongolia, China): 166 n.57, 167, 167 n.58–59, 187, 188 fig.7.55.
Daffiama (Ghana): 14.
Dagaraland (Ghana): 6–14.
Damietta (Egypt): 200.
Daming [Taming] 大名 (Hebei, China): 127, 132–133, 132 fig.6.34, 133 figs.6.35–6.36, 141.
Danzishan 担子山 (Hubei, China): 49 fig.3.18.
Datong 大同 (Shanxi, China): 128 n.83–84.
Daxi [Tahsi] 大溪 (Taiwan, China): 95 n.48, 100 n.74.
Dayushan [Lantao] 大屿山 (Hong Kong, China): 57.
Demba (Luluaburg, Belgian Congo): 77.
Djebel Mariam (Egypt): 204.
Dongchuan 东川 (Yunnan, China): 46.
Dongjiadu 董家渡 (Shanghai, China): 134–135, 134 n.104, 155 fig.7.10, 177 n.104.
Donglü 东闾 (Hebei, China): 56.
Dukou 渡口 (Inner Mongolia, China): 176, 176 fig.7.38.

Élisabethville (Belgian Congo): see Lubumbashi (DR Congo).
Ershisiqingdi 二十四顷地 (Inner Mongolia, China): 176 fig.7.39, 177 n.99.

Fayed (Egypt): 206.
Fenyang 汾阳 (Shanxi, China): 95 n.45.
Fort-Archambault: see Sarh (Chad).
Fuzhou [Fuchow] 福州 (Fujian, China): 41, 88, 211.

Gaojiazhuang [Kaokiatchoang] 高家庄 / Lucheng 路程 (Shanxi, China): 112 fig.6.4, 157 fig.7.14.
Gaoxiong [Kaohsiung / Kaoshung] 高雄 (Taiwan, China): 90, 91 fig.5.4, 92–93.
Gatarara (Burundi): 233, 233 n.18, 240.
Ghent [Gent] (Belgium): 68.
Gitega / Kitega (Burundi): 249 n.73.
Gold Coast (Ghana): 6.
Gonghui 公会 (Inner Mongolia, China): 177 n.106, 178 fig.7.40.
Guangzhou [Canton] 广州 (Guangdong, China): XI fig.0.5, XXI-XXII, 38, 39 fig.3.6, 40 fig.3.7, 41–44, 43 figs.3.10–3.11, 57 n.79, 60, 108, 119, 127, 130 n.87, 177 n.104.
Guangzhouwan 广州湾 (Guangdong, China): 38.

Guiyang 贵阳 (Guizhou, China): 50 fig.3.20, 156.
Gulangyu 鼓浪屿 [Kulangsu] (Fujian, China): 38.
Gwangju 광주 (South Korea): 174 fig.7.36.

Haimen 海门 (Jiangsu, China): 36 fig.3.4, 37.
Haizhou 海州 (Jiangsu, China), 37.
Halagou 哈拉沟 (Hebei, China): 121 fig.6.17, 178 n.107.
Hangzhou 杭州 (Zhejiang, China): 114 n.48.
Hankou 汉口 (Hubei, China): 39.
Haolaishan 壕赖山 (Inner Mongolia, China): 154 fig.7.9.
Harbin [Ha'erbin] 哈尔滨 (Heilongjiang, China): 39 fig.3.6.
Heerlen (The Netherlands): 119.
Hemptinne Saint-Benoît (Belgian Congo): see Bunkonde (DR Congo).
Hengtang 横塘 [Wang-daong] / Sijing 泗泾 (Shanghai, China): cover.
Hong Kong 香港 (Hong Kong, China): VII fig.0.1, XIV n.27, XV, XVII, XXI, XXVI, 35, 38–40, 57, 57 n.79, 60, 87, 89, 89 fig.5.3, 93 fig.5.5, 95, 95 n.45, 114 n.48, 142, 177 n.104, 229; see also: Tao Fong Shan 道风山, Kowloon 九龙, Shaian 沙田.
Houban [Aupoa] 后坂 (Fujian, China): 34 fig.3.2.
Houjiazhuang 侯家庄 [Howkiachwan / Heou-kia-tchoang] (Jiangsu, China): 125, 125 fig.6.28, 127.
Huaiyin 淮阴 (Jiangsu, China): 36–37.
Hualian [Hwalien] 花莲 (Taiwan, China): 90–91, 91 fig.5.4, 92, 94 fig.5.6.
Hualiling 花梨岭 (Hubei, China): 124 fig.6.23, fig.6.25.
Huangpu [Whampoa] 黄埔 (Guangdong, China): 35.
Huhehaote [Hohhot] 呼和浩特 / Suiyuan 绥远 (Inner Mongolia, China): 58, 176, 182 n.121.

Ibadan (Nigeria): 237, 249 n.74.
Ikutha (Kenya): 19, 23, 24, 25 fig.2.8, 26 fig.2.9, 26, 27 fig.2.10.
Ismailia (Egypt): XXVI, 194 fig.8.2, 195–196, 197 fig.8.5, 198 fig.8.6, 199, 201, 201 fig.8.10, 202, 202 figs.8.11–8.12, 205, 206–208, 207 fig.8.18, 208 fig.8.20.

Jiading 嘉定 (Shanghai, China): 211.
Jiaxing 嘉兴 (Zhejiang, China): 57 n.79.
Jiayi [Kiayi / Chiayi] 嘉义 (Taiwan, China): 90–91, 91 fig.5.4, 92–93.
Jilong [Keelung / Chilung] 基隆 (Taiwan, China): 97.
Jimba (Kenya): 19.
Jinan 济南 (Shandong, China): 41, 128 n.84, 177 n.104.

Jinguashi 金瓜石 (Taiwan, China): 96–97, 97 fig.5.9, 98 n.58, 100 n.71.
Jingzhou 荆州 (Hubei, China): 48 fig.3.17.
Jirapa (Ghana): 6, 9, 10 fig.1.5, 13 fig.1.6, 15.
Jiujiang 九江 (Jiangxi, China): 211.

Kaifeng 开封 (Henan, China): 57 n.83, 60, 128 n.84, 177 n.104.
Kamilabi (Kananga, DR Congo): 76, 79.
Kananga (DR Congo), former Luluaburg (Belgian Congo): XXV, 64–84.
Kanyuka (Kananga, DR Congo): 80.
Katoka (Kananga, DR Congo): 68, 71, 71 fig.4.8, 72–74, 74 fig.4.12, 76, 78, 78 fig.4.16, 79–81, 81 fig.4.19, 83.
Kibwezi (Kenya): 24, 30.
Kinshasa (DR Congo): 75 n.28, 79, 83, 234, 236, 244 n.60.
Ko (Ghana): 14-15.
Kowloon [Jiulong] 九龙 (Hong Kong, China): XXII n.43, 40–42, 142, 229, 229 n.4.
Kraainem (Belgium): 171 n.80.
Kulitu 苦立图 (Inner Mongolia, China): 170 n.73.
Kunming 昆明 (Yunnan, China): 57 n.79.
Kwango (DR Congo): XVII.

Laohugou 老虎沟 (Hebei, China): 122 fig.6.19, 148 fig.7.2, 166, 166 n.57,167 fig.7.28, 167 n.58–59, 185–186, 186 figs.7.48–7.49, 187.
Laoxikai 老西开 (Tianjin, China): 40.
Leipzig (Germany): XXIV, 17–19, 21–30.
Léopoldville (Belgian Congo): see Kinshasa (DR Congo).
Leuven (Belgium): 94.
Liangcheng 凉城 / Xianghuodi [Siang-hoa-ti] (Inner Mongolia, China): 178, 178 n.107 and 110, 179 fig.7.41.
Lianhe 联合 (Taiwan, China): 96, 97 fig.5.9.
Lille (France): 236.
Lilunga (North Kivu, DR Congo), former Tongres-Sainte-Marie (Belgian Congo): XVII fig.0.7.
Lingjia 凌家 (Jiangxi, China): 173.
Lourdes (France): XX, 54, 81, 121.
Lu'an 潞安 / Changzhi 长治 [(Shanxi, China): 118, 127–128, 129 fig.6.30.
Lubumbashi (DR Congo): 79, 83.
Luebo (DR Congo): 82.
Lujiabang 禄葭浜 (Jiangsu, China): 181, 181 fig.7.43.
Lulong 庐龙 (Hebei, China): 178 n.107.
Luluaburg (Belgian Congo) XXV, 64–84: see Kananga (DR Congo).
Lulugare (Kananga, DR Congo): 65-66.
Lusambo (DR Congo): 66, 68.

Macao [Aomen] 澳门 (China): XIX fig.0.9, XIV n.27, XV, 34, 34 n.5, 35, 57, 57 n.79, 87, 89, 93 fig.5.5, 95.
Machakos (Kenya), former Ulu: 19, 21, 24.
Majazi 馬架子 (Inner Mongolia, China): 166 n.57, 167 n.58–59, 187, 188 fig.7.51.
Malacca (Malaysia): 53, 95.
Malandji (Luluaburg, Belgian Congo): 65 n.4.
Manhui 蛮会 (Inner Mongolia, China): 161 fig.7.21.
Maredret (Belgium): 171 n.80.
Mariemont / Morlanwelz (Belgium): 230.
Marseille (France): 40.
Mbandaka (DR Congo): 79.
Mbungu (Kenya): 19, 23.
Meiguiyingzi 玫瑰营子 (Inner Mongolia, China): 50, 56, 166 n.57, 167 n.58–59, 189–190, 190 figs.7.55–7.56, 191 fig.7.57.
Miambani (Kenya): 23.
Mikalayi Saint-Joseph (Luluaburg, Belgian Congo): 66 fig.4.3; 67, 70, 77.
Milan (Italy): 170 n.77.
Mombasa (Kenya): 19.
Monte Cassino / Montecassino (Italy): 238, 239 n.33.
Montreuil (France): 206.
Montserrat (Spain): 238, 239 n.33.
Moung-Ko-Tchenn ? (Inner Mongolia, China): 154 fig.7.8.
Mozishan 磨子山 (Inner Mongolia, China): 56, 190 n.149.
Mulango (Kenya): 23, 23 fig.2.5, 24, 25 fig.2.7, 28, 28 fig.2.11.
Mushenge-Mweka (DR Congo): 73.
Mweka (DR Congo): 73 n.25.

Namur (Belgium): 230.
Nandom (Ghana): 14, 14 fig.1.7, 15.
Nangang 南港 (Taiwan, China): 96, 97 figs.5.9–5.10, 98, 98 fig.5.11, 99 n.66, 99 figs.5.12-5.13, 100 n.71, 101, 101 fig.5.15.
Nanhaoqian 南壕堑 (Inner Mongolia, China): XVIII fig.0.8.
Nanjing 南京 (Jiangsu, China): 34 n.5, 36, 36 fig.3.4, 37, 41, 55, 135.
Nansongshan 南松山 (Taiwan, China): 96–97, 97 fig.5.9, 99 n.66, 100 n.71.
Nantou 南投 (Taiwan, China): 90, 90 n.21.
Navrongo (Ghana): 8, 9.
Ndesha (Luluaburg, Belgian Congo): 76–77, 77 fig.4.15, 78, 80, 80 fig.4.18.
Neihu 内湖 (Taiwan, China): 96, 97 fig.5.9, 98.
Ngaliema (Kinshasa, DR Congo): XXIV fig.0.13.
Nganza (Luluaburg, Belgian Congo): 79.
Ningbo (Zhejiang, China): 141 fig.6.43, 177 n.104.
Ningguo 宁国 (Anhui, China): 36.
Nioki (Mai-Nombe, DR Congo): VI-VII fig.0.2.

Ntambue Saint-Bernard (Luluaburg, Belgian Congo): 77, 78.
Nyanza (Burundi): 233.
Nzambani (Kenya): 22, 22 fig.2.4.

Ouagadougou (Burkina Faso): 81.
Oxbridge (England): 238.

Paris (France): 37, 39, 54, 199–200, 205–206.
Penghu 澎湖 (Taiwan, China): 92.
Port Fouad (Egypt): 199–200, 200 fig.8.9.
Port Said (Egypt): XXVI, 195–196, 196 figs.8.3-8.4, 198, 198 fig.8.7, 199–201, 206 fig.8.17, 207–208.
Port Tawfiq (Egypt): see Suez.
Puqi 蒲圻 (Hebei, China): 95 n.45.
Puyang [Kaizhou] 濮阳 (Henan, China): 119–120, 120 fig.6.16, 133 n.95, 141.

Qianjia [Ziéka] 钱家 (Shanghai): 122 fig.6.20.
Qilaowengeqi 其老文个气 (Inner Mongolia, China): 160.
Qingdao [Tsingtao] 青岛 (Shandong): 39 fig.3.6, 59.
Qisumu [Tsi-sou-mou] 七苏木 (Inner Mongolia, China): 162, 189 n.147.
Québec (Canada): 37.

Rabat (Morocco): 236.
Rome (Italy): 9, 34, 53, 60, 92, 93 fig.5.5, 95, 177, 243 n.56.
Ruifang 瑞芳 (Taiwan, China): 96–97, 97 fig.5.9, 99 n.66, 100 n.71.

Saint-Clément (Kananga, DR Congo): 66, 67, 67 fig.4.4, 68, 68 fig.4.5, 69, 69 fig.4.6, 70, 71, 72, 78, 83.
Sainte-Marie Island (Republic of Madagascar): VIII fig.0.4.
Sandaohe [San-tao-ho] 三道河 (Inner Mongolia, China): 163, 175.
Sanshenggong 三盛公 (Inner Mongolia, China): 175–176, 175 fig.7.37.
Sanshijiazi 三十家子 (Hebei, China): 185.
Sarh (Chad): 236.
Shabo'er 沙钵儿 [Cha-pa-eul / Sa-perh?] (Inner Mongolia, China): 162, 164, 164 fig.7.25, 164 n.52, 166 n.57, 167, 167 n.58–59, 185.
Shamian 沙面 (Guangdong, China): 38, 40 fig.3.7.
Shangchuan [Sancian] 上川岛 (Guangdong, China): 53, 54 fig.3.26.

Shanghai 上海 (Shanghai, China): 36, 36 fig.3.4, 38–39, 39 fig.3.6, 41, 41 fig.3.8, 55, 58, 60, 108, 114, 114 n.48, 114 fig.6.9, 132, 134–139, 142, 172, 177 n.104, 181, 181 fig.7.43, 181, 182 figs.7.44–7.45, 182 n.121; see also Xujiahui 徐家汇, Tushanwan 土山湾, Dongjiadu 董家渡, Jiading 嘉定.
Shanhou 山後 (Inner Mongolia, China): 113 fig.6.5.
Shatin [Shatian] 沙田 (Hong Kong, China): VII fig.0.1, XVII.
Shazidi [Chatseti] 沙子地 (Hubei, China): 124 fig.6.24.
Shebiya [Shabernoor] 舍必崖 (Inner Mongolia, China): 160, 161 fig.7.22.
Shenjiamen 沈家门 (Zhejiang, China): 47 fig.3.16.
Shenyang [Mukden] 沈阳 (Liaoning, China): 45, 45 fig.3.14, 173.
Sheshan [Zô-cè] 佘山 (Shanghai, China): 54–56, 55 fig.3.27, 158, 159 fig.7.17, 178 n.107.
Shilawushuhao 什拉乌素壕 (Inner Mongolia, China): VIII fig.0.3.
Shimonoseki [Maguan] 马关 (Japan): 88 n.10.
Shuangshuzi 双树子 (Hebei, China): 178 n.107.
Shuinandong 水南洞 (Taiwan, China): 96–97, 97 fig.5.9, 98 n.58, 99 n.66, 100 n.71.
Sijiaoting 四脚亭 (Taiwan, China): 96–97, 97 fig.5.9, 99, 100 n.71, 100 fig.5.14.
Songjiang 松江 (Shanghai, China): 54, 135.
Songpuxiang 松浦乡 (Zhejiang, China): 49 fig.3.19.
Stanley Bay 赤柱 (Hong Kong, China): 90.
Suez / Port Tawfiq (Egypt): 195, 204–205, 205 fig.8.16, 208.
Suez Canal (Egypt): XXII, XXVI, 194–209, 195 fig.8.1.
Suiyuan 绥远 (Inner Mongolia, China): see Huhehaote 呼和浩特.
Suzhou [Soochow] 苏州 (Jiangsu, China): 36–37.

Tainan 台南 (Taiwan, China): 91, 91 fig.5.4, 92–94.
Taipei [Taibei / Taipeh] 台北 (Taiwan, China): XXV, 87, 90, 91 fig.5.4, 93–98, 100–102.
Taiyuan 太原 (Shanxi, China): 128 n.84, 156, 156 fig.7.12, 182 n.122.
Taizhong [Taichung] 台中 (Taiwan, China): 90, 90 n.21, 91 fig.5.4, 92–93.
Tamale (Ghana): 14 fig.1.7.
Tanga (Tanzania): 19.
Tangmuqiao 唐墓桥 (Shanghai, China): 177 n.104.
Tanlicun 滩里村 / Taiyuan 太原 (Shanxi, China): 173, 173 fig.7.34.
Tao Fong Shan [Dao Feng Shan] 道风山 (Hong Kong, China): VII fig.01, XVII.

Tianjin [Tientsin] 天津 (Tianjin, China): 35, 38, 40–41, 52–53, 52 fig.3.23, 53 fig.3.24, 55, 142, 172, 172 fig.7.33, 177 n.104.
Tongjiayingzi 佟家营子 (Inner Mongolia, China): 166 n.57, 167, 167 n.58–59, 187–188, 188 fig.7.53.
Tongres-Sainte-Marie (Belgian Congo): see Lilunga (DR Congo).
Toronto (Canada): 220.
Tousumu 头苏木 (Inner Mongolia, China): 167, 167 n.58–59, 168 fig.7.30, 188–189, 189 fig.7.54.
Trent [Trento] (Italy): 150, 175.
Tshikaji (DR Congo): 77.
Tshimbi (Luluaburg, Belgian Congo): 76, 79, 79 fig.4.17.
Tumenzishan 土门子山 (Inner Mongolia, China): 159 fig.7.18.
Turin (Italy): 37.
Tushan 土山 / Pixian 邳县 (Jiangsu, China): 152.
Tushanwan [T'ou-Sè-Wè] 土山湾 (Shanghai, China): 40, 57, 107 fig.6.1, 134–139, 135 n.107, 136 fig.6.38–6.39, 137 fig.6.40, 138 fig.6.41, 172.

Ukamba (Kenya): 17–30, 20 fig.2.2.
Ulu (Kenya): see Machakos.
Uluguru (Kenya): 24.
Usumbura (Burundi): see Bujumbura.

Vatican (Rome, Vatican City State): XIV, XXV, 93 fig.5.5, 114, 151 n.17, 171, 177, 195.
Venice (Italy): XXII n.49, 170 n.78.
Villers / Villers-la-Ville (Belgium): 190 n.150.

Wa (Ghana): 9.
Waterloo (Belgium): 171 fig.7.32, 171 n.80.
Weiyuankou 韦源口 (Hubei, China): 122 fig.6.18.
Wiitu (Kenya): 22, 22 fig.2.3.
Wijnegem (Belgium): 187.
Wufeng 雾峰 (Taiwan, China): 90 n.21.
Wuhan 武汉 (Hubei, China): 39, 41, 60.
Wuhe 五河 (Jiangsu, China): 36.
Wuhu 芜湖 (Anhui, China): 36, 36 fig.3.4, 37, 177 n.104.
Wusungtulu ? (Jehol ?, China): 160 fig.7.19.

Xiamen [Amoy] 厦门 (Fujian, China): 38, 88.
Xianggang 香港: see Hong Kong.
Xianxian [Sien-Hsien] 献县 (Hebei, China): 127, 130–132, 130 fig.6.31, 131 figs.6.32–6.33, 141; see also Zhangjiazhuang 张家庄.
Xiaoqiaopan 小桥畔 (Shaanxi, China): 50–51, 126 fig.6.29, 127, 166, 166 n.57, 167 n.58–59, 168 fig.7.29, 186–187, 187 fig.7.50.
Ximenting [Ximending] 西门町, Taibei 台北 (Taiwan, China): 96, 96 figs.5.7–5.8, 97 fig.5.9, 99 n.66, 101.
Xindi 新地 (Guangdong, China): 54 fig.3.26.

Xinhui 新会 (Guangdong, China): 180, 180 fig.7.42.
Xinjiang 新绛 / Jiangzhou [Kiangchow] 绛州 (Shanxi, China): 118–119, 118 figs.6.13–6.15, 128 n.84, 141.
Xinzhu [Hsinchu] 新竹 (Taiwan, China): 91, 91 fig.5.4, 92–94.
Xinzhuang 新庄 (Shanxi, China): 158 fig.7.15.
Xishahe [Sichaho] 细沙河 (Badong, China): 124 fig.6.26.
Xishahe 细沙河 / Longpi 龙坯 (Hubei, China): 151 fig.7.5.
Xishan 西山 (Chongqing, China): 57 n.83.
Xitougai [Chitougai] 西頭岩 / 迟頭岩 (Guizhou, China): 46 fig.3.15.
Xiwanzi 西湾子 [Si-wantze] / Chongli 崇礼 (Hebei, China): 59, 114 fig.6.7. 162–163, 165–166, 165 fig.7.26, 166 fig.7.27, 166 n.57, 167 n.58–59, 168–170, 170 fig.7.31, 175, 177, 183–185, 184 figs.7.46–47.
Xizhi 汐止 (Taiwan, China): 96, 97 fig.5.9, 99, 99 n.66, 100 n.71, 101, 101 fig.5.16.
Xuanhua 宣化 (Hebei, China): 59 fig.3.30, 60, 177 n.104, 178 n.107.
Xujiahui [Zi-ka-wei] 徐家汇 (Shanghai, China): 40–41, 107 fig.6.1, 114 n.48, 134–139, 135 fig.6.37, 136 figs.6.38–6.39, 137 fig.6.40, 138 fig.6.41, 139 fig.6.42, 172, 181 fig.7.43.
Xuzhou [Süchow] 徐州 (Jiangsu, China): 36 fig.3.4, 37, 37 fig.3.5, 125.

Yanggu 阳谷 (Shandong, China): 91.
Yangjiaping 杨家坪 (Hebei, China): 57, 58 fig.3.29.
Yangzhou 扬州 (Jiangsu, China): 36–37, 91, 142 fig.6.44.
Yanji 延吉 (Jilin, China): 57 n.83.
Yantai [Chefoo] 烟台 (Shandong, China): 211.
Yaojiazhuang 姚嫁莊 (Shanxi, China): 122 fig.6.21.
Yibin 宜宾 / Suifu 叙州府 (Sichuan, China): 157 fig.7.13.
Yichang 宜昌 (Hubei, China): 53 fig.3.25, 87, 94, 182 n.121.
Yilan 宜兰 (Taiwan, China): 97.
Yingkou 营口 (Liaoning, China): 90.
Yiwan 宜湾 (Taiwan, China): 94 fig.5.6.
Yongchun 永春 (Taiwan, China): 96, 97 fig.5.9, 98 n.5.9.
Yongin 용인시 (South Korea): 174 fig.7.35.
Yongjiachang 永嘉场 (Zhejiang, China): 35 fig.3.3.
Yongpingfu 永平府 (Hebei, China): 178 n.107.

Zhanghua [Changhua] 彰化 (Taiwan, China): 90.

Zhangjiazhuang 张家庄 (Tchang-kia-tchouang, Hebei): 130–132, 130 fig.6.31, 131 figs.6.32–6.33; see also Xianxian 献县.

Zhangpingzi [Tchangpintze] 長坪子 (Sichuan, China): 122 fig.6.22.

Zhengding 正定 (Hebei, China): 57, 59.

Zhangjiakou 张家口 (Hebei, China): XVIII fig.0.8.

Zhenjiang 镇江 (Jiangsu, China): 36.

Zhonglun 中仑 (Taiwan, China): 96, 97 fig.5.9, 98 n.58, 100 n.71, 101.

Zhongxing 中兴 (Taiwan, China): 90 n.21.

Zhoushan 舟山岛 (Zhejiang, China): 47 fig.3.16.

Zhuizishan 锥子山 (Hebei, China): 123, 124 fig.6.27.

AUTHORS

Leon Bouwmeester (also known as Chu Bo-ning 朱柏寧) is a Taiwanese architectural history researcher who holds a MA degree in Building and Planning from National Taiwan University, a BA in Architecture from National Taipei University of Technology, and a BA in Psychology from Fu Jen Catholic University. Since 2019 he is doing a PhD at KU Leuven, Department of Architecture, with a Taiwan Government Scholarship. His research deals with Catholic architecture and space in Taiwan in the early post-war time (1949-1970s).

Lawrence Braschi is a serving Anglican minister in the Church of England. He studied Chinese history and religion at the School of Oriental and African Studies (University of London) and served as Director of the China Desk, for Churches Together in Britain and Ireland.

Bram Cleys is a historian. He works as coordinator of a provenance research project on the Congolese collection in the Museum MAS in Antwerp. He conducted research into the history of missionary work in Belgian Congo and was, among other things, co-editor of the book *Religion, Colonization and Decolonisation in Congo, 1885-1960* (2020).

Thomas Coomans (Chinese name 高曼士) holds a PhD in Archaeology and Art History from the Université Catholique de Louvain (UCLouvain) and is senior full professor at the Department of Architecture at KU Leuven where he teaches architectural history, theory and history of conservation, and building archaeology. He is also programme director of the Advanced Master in Conservation of Monuments and Sites (RLICC). Since more than thirty years his research and publications explore different aspects of Christian architecture: abbeys and monastic complexes, Gothic churches in the Low Countries, nineteenth-century reception of medieval architecture, adaptive reuse of churches. Since 2012, he is developing research on architectural transfers between Chinese and Western architecture––especially church architecture in China (1840s-1940s)––which benefits from a long term collaboration with Peking University, School of Archaeology and Museology. He has been adjunct assistant professor at the School of Architecture at the Chinese University of Hong Kong, and visiting professor at the Institute for Humanities and Social Sciences at Peking University. He is a member of the ICOMOS Scientific Committee on Places of Religion and Ritual.

Céline Frémaux defended in 2005 a PhD in architectural history and heritage at the Université de Rennes on post-World War II churches in the north of France. She has worked as a researcher at the INHA (National institute for art history) and at the CNRS (French National Scientific Research) on the project "Inventing Space in the Age of Empire: Planning Experiments and Achievements along Suez Canal in Egypt (1859-1869)". Then she has developed several projects in French Guyana concerning both material and intangible cultural heritage in French Guyana and in Guadeloupe (Carribeans).

Johan Lagae is senior full professor at Ghent University, where he teaches twentieth-century Architectural History with a global focus. He holds a PhD on colonial architecture in the Democratic Republic of Congo and has published widely on the topic, as well as on twentieth-century architectural and urban history in Central-Africa, on the notion of colonial built heritage and on photography in (post)colonial Africa. He co-authored two books on the architecture and urban landscapes of Kinshasa and most recently co-edited, together with architect Nina Berre and anthropologist Paul Wenzel Geissler, the volume *African Modernism and its Afterlives* (2022). He currently acts as co-editor-in-chief of *ABE Journal*. Johan Lagae (co-)curated several Congo-related exhibitions, and has collaborated with several artists from DR Congo, among others Patrick Mudekereza and Sammy Baloji (most recently for the latter's project *Aequare. The Future that never was*-project, presented at the Venice Architecture Biennale 2023). Johan Lagae was recipient of various grants, held a Francqui Chair at the Université Libre de Bruxelles in 2020 and was a 2019-2020 fellow at the Institute for Advanced Studies in Paris.

Maarten Onneweer studied cultural anthropology and development sociology at Leiden University, The Netherlands. For his PhD he researched the history of water development of the Kitui District in Kenya. The thesis looks at the environmental history of the Kitui district to understand current development practices. As part of this research he published on the sociality of resources encounters, describing how the development encounter led to rumours of the alienation of Kitui's riches. From 2006 to 2012, he lectured on development anthropology, the anthropology of landscape, environment and natural resources, political ecology and gender at several Dutch universities. Currently he works as consultant and programs manager for *Aidenvironment* the Netherlands on water management in developing countries.

Alexis B. Tengan is a Ghanaian independent scholar in social and cultural anthropology resident in Belgium and a former teacher of religious sciences. He studied at the University of Ghana (Accra), at Lumen Vitae Pastoral Institute (Brussels) and at the Catholic University Leuven. As a teacher, he has taught for many years, both in Ghana and in Belgium. He has also been visiting scholar to many higher institutions in Europe and Africa. He has carried out research on farming systems throughout northern Ghana, including the relationship between art, medicine and religion, and on Dagara Bagr secret society and myths. His publications in these areas include the 2006 *Mythical narratives in ritual: Dagara black bagr* and the 2018 *Of Life and Health: The Language of Art and Religion in an African Medical System*. He has established and is now curating a private museum of sacred art and objects with studios in Belgium and Ghana.

COLOPHON

Final editing
Luc Vints

Copy editing
Lieve Claes and Luc Vints

Layout
Alexis Vermeylen

KADOC
Documentation and Research Centre on
Religion, Culture and Society
KU Leuven
Vlamingenstraat 39
B - 3000 Leuven
http://kadoc.kuleuven.be

Leuven University Press
Minderbroedersstraat 4
B - 3000 Leuven
info@lup.be
www.lup.be